THE
LOVE OF
WISDOM

A CHRISTIAN INTRODUCTION
TO PHILOSOPHY

STEVEN B. COWAN

JAMES S. SPIEGEL

NASHVILLE, TENNESSEE

ISBN: 978-0-8054-4770-5

Published by B&H Publishing Group
Nashville, Tennessee

Dewey Decimal Classification: 100
Subject Heading: PHILOSOPHY\AESTHETICS\PHILOSOPHY—
POLITICAL ASPECTS

Printed in the United States of America
4 5 6 7 8 9 10 11 12 • 18 17 16 15 14
R

CONTENTS

ACKNOWLEDGMENTS

A work like this would not be possible without the help and support of many other people. We wish therefore to extend to everyone who played a part in its production our sincerest, heartfelt gratitude.

I (Steve) wish first to thank my beautiful wife, Ronda, and our extraordinary son, Oliver, for the many hours they spent away from me while I completed my part of the manuscript. Their sacrifice will not go unrewarded either in this life or the one to come. Ronda also deserves praise for reading many pages of "that philosophy stuff" so I could make sure the material is accessible to the nonspecialist. I also extend my gratitude to my colleagues and students at Southeastern Bible College who encouraged me throughout this project and allowed me the time to work on it.

I (Jim) would like to thank my wonderful wife, Amy, whose consistent support and encouragement are crucial to my livelihood as a teacher and writer. Thanks also to my children, Bailey, Samuel, Magdalene, and Andrew, whose affection blesses me in ways they will never know. I am also grateful to the good people of New Life Presbyterian Church in Yorktown, Indiana, and to my colleagues and students at Taylor University. These are special Christian communities of which I am privileged to be a part. Whatever professional success I enjoy is due in no small part to their faithfulness and good will.

We also wish to thank the editorial staff at B&H, especially Ray Clendenen and Terry Wilder, for their encouragement throughout this project and their superb editing of the manuscript. We are grateful as well to Thomas Senor and J. P. Moreland for their comments and suggestions on various parts of the manuscript. It is a much better book because of their input (though we take responsibility for any remaining flaws). Thanks also to Alyssa Lehr and Michael Glawson, who prepared the glossary—our students will no doubt be grateful, too.

We want to acknowledge the following publishers for their generous permission to use previously published material. Thanks to Crossway Books for parts of chapters three, five, and six, which were drawn from Spiegel's book *The Benefits of Providence*. Thanks to the publisher of *Science and Christian Belief* for portions of chapter three, to the publisher of *Philosophia Christi* for parts of chapter three, to the publisher of *Areopagus Journal* for some sections of chapter nine, and to Blackwell Publishing for portions of the introduction and chapter six. And, while we are on the subject of publishing, we should note here that we used the Holman Christian Standard Bible translation wherever Scripture is quoted, except where otherwise indicated.

Finally, we would like to acknowledge two individuals who have left an indelible imprint on our lives with regard to philosophical studies and Christian living. Steve and Jim dedicate this book, respectively, to Thomas Senor and Wynn Kenyon, both of whom are model professors, mentors, and lovers of wisdom.

Introduction

WHAT IS PHILOSOPHY?

Many years ago there was a popular song which posed life's most fundamental philosophical question:

> What's it all about, Alfie?
> Is it just for the moment we live?
> What's it all about
> When you sort it out, Alfie?[1]

What *is* it all about? In other words, what is the meaning of life? What makes this question so challenging is the fact that to answer it properly one must answer several other difficult questions: What are human beings? Where did we come from? Are we responsible for how we live? What happens after we die? Is there a God? If so, what is God like? Can we know the answers to such questions? Can we know anything at all?

These are sometimes called the "Big Questions" in the sense that they are the most important questions one can ask. Whatever else you might want to find out during your brief time on this planet, these are questions for which you should seek answers. Ironically, many people work hard to *avoid* dealing with such questions, either because they find them too difficult or because they fear the answers they might discover. But, of course, these are poor excuses for not looking for ultimate meaning in life.

This book is all about the Big Questions. In this sense, you might say, this book is all about what life is all about. We will explore issues about who we are, where we came from, who made us, where we are going, whether we are free, how we should live, why we suffer, the value of beauty, the nature of goodness, and the nature of God. And we will consider the wide variety of answers that have been given to all of these questions. In discussing the issues we aim to be fair, but we will not

---

[1] Burt Bacharach, "Alfie" (1966).

I

pretend to be neutral. We are Christian philosophers, and our distinctive worldview will directly impact how we deal with most issues. Of course, all authors of textbooks write from the perspective of a particular worldview. As one philosopher recently put it, there is no view from nowhere.[2] We just thought it would be wise to let you know our perspective at the outset—even to the point of communicating this in the book's subtitle.

Philosophical Method

Our aim, as the book's title suggests, is to introduce you to philosophy in the original sense of the word—*the love of wisdom* (from the Greek *philo* and *sophia*). Philosophy is properly about more than acquiring an intellectual grasp of answers to life's Big Questions. It is about gaining insights which culminate in a life well-lived. Good philosophers not only think well but live virtuously. In this sense, we share the same mission as the most famous philosopher in Western history.

The Life of Socrates

Socrates (469–399 BC) lived in a time and place in which there was social upheaval and increasing cynicism about the meaning of life. He became famous (or infamous) in ancient Greece for accosting people on the street with inquiries about truth, goodness, knowledge, and many other issues. But he did not do so for the sake of idle entertainment. Rather, these impromptu interviews were inspired by a pronouncement by the Oracle at Delphi, who supposedly spoke for the god Apollo. The oracle declared that Socrates was the wisest man in all of Athens. When news of this got back to Socrates, he scoffed, insisting that there were many Athenians much wiser than he. But when some insisted that it was so, he set out to disprove the oracle. The best way to do so, he figured, would be to find someone who could answer some of the questions about which he was ignorant—questions about the nature of truth, goodness, knowledge, and so on. And so began the random Socratic interviews on the streets of Athens.

What Socrates learned in the process surprised him. He interviewed all kinds of people, without discriminating on the basis of reputation or social standing. He discovered that those who were purported to be most wise had fewer reasons for their beliefs and were less patient than the so-called ignorant. But in every case he found that no one had any better answers to his questions than he did. All were alike ignorant about the basic philosophical issues he raised. But those he interviewed did not

[2] Thomas Nagel, *The View from Nowhere* (New York: Oxford University Press, 1989).

perceive their own ignorance, whereas Socrates knew he was ignorant. "All I know is that I know nothing," he declared. His fellow Athenians did not even know this much about themselves. Thus, he realized, the Oracle was correct after all. Socrates was indeed the wisest man in all of Athens. For it is better to know you are ignorant than to be ignorant and think otherwise.

The publicans and other esteemed Athenians began to resent Socrates' constant questioning. Not only did it reveal their own ignorance, but they feared this would undermine their political authority. Eventually, Socrates was indicted for impiety. More specifically, Socrates was charged with (1) introducing unfamiliar religious practices and failure to worship the state gods and (2) corrupting the youth at Athens. The first charge concerned Socrates' skepticism about the Greek pantheon of gods and his conviction that there was actually one God who will ultimately judge us all. The second charge pertained to the fact that Socrates developed a large following of young people, many of whom were impressed by their mentor's life and philosophical methodology. One of these was a young man by the name of Plato.

Socrates defended himself ably in court, as was recounted by Plato in the *Apology*. During his trial he not only defended himself against his formal charges but he also explained his life mission:

> It is my belief that no greater good has ever befallen you in this city than my service to my God. For I spend all my time going about trying to persuade you, young and old, to make your first and chief concern not for your bodies nor for your possessions, but for the highest welfare of your souls, proclaiming as I go [that] wealth does not bring goodness, but goodness brings wealth and every other blessing, both to the individual and to the state.[3]

Despite his defense, Socrates was convicted on both charges and given the death penalty, via the drinking of hemlock. He went to his death willingly and became a martyr for philosophy. However, not long after his death, the Athenians realized their blunder and erected a statue in Socrates' honor. To this day he remains the model philosopher for his sincere quest for truth and virtue and for his rigorous methodology.

The Socratic Method

If Socrates' mission was unique, so was his method of teaching. Today the phrase "Socratic method" is typically used to refer to the technique

---

[3] Plato, *Apology*, trans. Hugh Tredennick, in *The Collected Dialogues of Plato*, ed. Edith Hamilton and Huntington Cairns (Princeton: Princeton University Press, 1961), 16.

of question and answer to teach or discover truth, also known as *dialectic*. While this is certainly an important aspect of Socrates' approach, it is only one aspect of his overall approach, which features several helpful guidelines for an effective quest for truth. Another key element is sometimes called *Socratic ignorance*. Socrates declared, "I am quite conscious of my ignorance."[4] This confession revealed a humble recognition of the limits of his understanding. (In some of Plato's dialogues Socrates also appears to feign ignorance about an issue—sometimes called Socratic irony—in order to illustrate a point or to drive the dialogue in a particular direction.) The primary value of such humility is how it demonstrates a teachable spirit—something that is a prerequisite for a student of philosophy or any other discipline.

Socrates also played the role of philosophical *midwife*, helping others to give birth to their ideas. This he did through rational debate, a process that is sometimes painful but, when properly done, always worthwhile. This aspect of the Socratic method also underscores for us the fact that philosophy is properly a community affair. If you are reading this book for a class, then you are formally part of such a community. But even if you are not, we hope you will process the ideas you encounter here with others who share your interest in philosophy. Such interaction makes for the most fertile intellectual soil in the pursuit of wisdom.

Finally, and returning to the point of his ultimate mission, Socrates repeatedly emphasized the point that moral knowledge is not mere acquisition of information but personal change. To know the good is to do it, Socrates declared. That is, if you really know the right thing to do in a situation, then your behavior will prove it. To act immorally is to prove your ignorance.[5] Socrates' view here probably overintellectualizes moral goodness, especially given the biblical theme of moral weakness, which recognizes that people sometimes act against their better judgment. But his emphasis on the connection between belief and behavior is crucial, especially given the natural human tendency toward hypocrisy.

Other Elements of the Philosophical Method

The above themes are more or less distinctive to Socrates' philosophical approach. But he was part of a tradition that long preceded him and which continues to this day. The defining characteristics of this broader tradition are more difficult to nail down. But there are certain activities that tend to distinguish philosophical inquiry—not in the sense that only philosophers engage in them so much as philoso-

---

[4] Ibid., 8.
[5] See Plato's *Protagoras*, in *The Collected Dialogues of Plato*, 357–58.

phers place a special *emphasis* on them. Here are three key aspects of the philosophical method.

1. ***Defining Terms.*** A good philosopher always takes care to define terms. Not only does this make key concepts clear and distinct in one's mind but it also prevents merely verbal disputes. The American pragmatist philosopher William James related an experience that illustrates this.[6] While camping with friends, James went off for a short solitary hike only to return to find the others embroiled in a heated debate. The subject of the dispute was an experience most of us have had. Suppose a man tries to get a close look at a squirrel, but it hides behind a tree. And when he circles around the tree, so does the squirrel, always keeping the tree between itself and the man. As James's friends discussed this, the question arose: *"Does the man go round the squirrel or not?"* Since opinions were evenly divided, they asked James to break the tie. His response: The answer depends on what is meant by "going round" the squirrel. If this means going from the north, then to the east, then to the south, and then to the west of the squirrel, then yes the man is going around it. But if this means moving from the front, then to the left, then to the back, and then to the right of the animal, then clearly the man is *not* going around the squirrel. In this way, James showed the men that they were hung up over the definition of a term and not really debating a substantive issue. Their dispute was merely verbal.

Not only can defining terms prevent such petty squabbles, it also helps to clarify genuinely important debates, from the morality of abortion and war to questions about human freedom and the nature of God. In the chapters that follow we will see how the definition of key terms is crucial for understanding each of the issues discussed. Unless we define our terms carefully, we can hardly understand philosophical questions much less arrive at trustworthy answers.

2. ***Using Arguments.*** Philosophers place a special emphasis on supporting truth claims with evidence. Everyone has convictions of various kinds. We all hold beliefs about the existence of God, the human soul, life after death, the rightness or wrongness of capital punishment, and any number of other issues. But what distinguishes us is how rational our beliefs are in terms of how well-grounded they are in *good reasons*. Whatever you might believe about the above issues, can you offer reasonable grounds for your beliefs? To support a truth claim with good reasons is to give an argument for it. Here we are using the term *argument* in the logical sense, as opposed to the sense of the term when we refer to a quarrel or heated exchange. It is healthy to have strong feelings

---

[6] William James, *Pragmatism* (Indianapolis: Hackett, 1981), 25.

about one's belief commitments, and philosophers are as deeply passionate about their convictions as anyone. But emotions can cloud our judgment at times and interfere with careful inquiry into critical issues. This is why self-control is crucial for doing philosophy, and good philosophers are well-practiced at restraining their emotions when debating issues.

Unfortunately, many aspects of our culture do not prize careful reasoning or self-control. In fact, from Hollywood to Saks Fifth Avenue the constant message is that feelings should be the ultimate determinant for how we think and act. Even when it comes to the most important decisions in life, from our careers to whom we marry, we are often told to "do what feels right" or "follow your heart." While such platitudes have a positive ring about them, they are really quite dangerous if followed consistently. Life's biggest decisions should be grounded in good reasons. And the same is true for all of our beliefs about important issues, such as those discussed in this book.

3. *Identifying Presuppositions.* The previous two paragraphs actually contain arguments about, well, the importance of arguments. As will be discussed in depth in the next chapter, an argument reasons from premises to a main point or conclusion. While our conclusion—that one's beliefs should be grounded in good reasons—is stated explicitly, some of our premises are not. In fact, we have taken several facts and values for granted in the above paragraphs. For example, we *assumed* that it is not good to have one's judgment clouded by emotions; we *assumed* that the common platitudes in quotes are dangerous; and, we *assumed,* if only by insinuation, that it is unwise to live according to such platitudes. All truth claims which are assumed without argument are called *presuppositions.* While we could argue for each of our presuppositions above, every argument we used would itself make several presuppositions. In turn, we could provide arguments for those presuppositions, and so on. However, this process cannot go on forever. This shows that one cannot avoid having presuppositions. But what distinguishes a good thinker is her ability to *identify* presuppositions, both in her own arguments and in the arguments of others.

At the beginning of the twentieth century the mathematician Kurt Gödel (1906–1978) proved his "incompleteness theorems," which showed that all rational systems are necessarily incomplete. No matter how thorough and rigorous one is in trying to prove all of one's claims, there will always be assumptions one takes for granted. Thus, the question is not whether or not you will have presuppositions but whether you are *aware* of them and *why* you make those presuppositions rather than others. Good philosophers have a healthy self-awareness when it comes to their own presuppositions, and they can often tell you why they presuppose the things they do.

The Concept of Worldview

Having clarified some key aspects of philosophical method, let us consider now one of the main goals of philosophy, specifically to develop a reasonable *worldview*.[7] A worldview is a conceptual scheme or intellectual framework by which a person organizes and interprets experience. More specifically, a worldview is a set of beliefs, values, and presuppositions concerning life's most fundamental issues. You might say it is a *perspective* on reality. Like tinted glasses, a worldview "colors" the way we see things and shapes our interpretation of the world. And, it must be emphasized, *everyone* has a worldview.

What precisely are the fundamental issues, the Big Questions one's answers to which comprise one's worldview? Here Christian philosopher Ronald Nash is helpful.[8] He analyzes worldviews under five categories, each corresponding to a traditional branch of philosophy:

1. God (Theology)
2. Reality (Metaphysics)
3. Knowledge (Epistemology)
4. Human Beings (Anthropology)
5. Values (Ethics, Aesthetics, Political Philosophy)

1. *God.* Every worldview includes beliefs about God. Some worldviews, such as Christian *theism*, affirm the existence of a Creator who is eternal, immutable, omnipotent, omniscient, and omnibenevolent.[9] Moreover, this divine being, though distinct from His creation, is intimately involved in the course of history and the affairs of His creatures. Some people affirm that a God with these exalted attributes exists but has little or nothing to do with the world (*deism*). *Pantheism* is a worldview that affirms the divinity of all things—everything that exists is either identical with God or an aspect of God. Other worldviews claim that there are multiple gods who are more limited in nature (*polytheism*). Finally, naturalistic *atheists* deny the existence of any supernatural

---

[7] Much of the content of this section is adapted from G. Kurian, *Encyclopedia of Christian Civilization* (Oxford: Blackwell, 2009), s.v. "Christian Worldview" by Steven B. Cowan.

[8] Ronald H. Nash, *Worldviews in Conflict* (Grand Rapids: Zondervan, 1992), 26–32. In his work, Nash simply lists ethics as his fifth category. We have broadened that category in accordance with contemporary usage to include all the major aspects of value theory.

[9] More will be said about these divine attributes in chapter six.

beings, typically claiming such beliefs to be the product of ignorance and superstition. In any case, what one believes about God fundamentally affects how one interprets experience.

2. *Reality.* Every person has metaphysical beliefs about the nature of reality. The atheist will likely embrace *materialism*, the view that the ultimate reality is matter. All that exists, according to the atheist, is the physical universe. For the pantheist, in contrast, ultimate reality is spirit or mind. Many pantheists believe that the physical universe discerned by our five senses is an illusion (the Hindu word is *maya*). Reality is purely spiritual or mental. Still others (e.g., most Christians and other theists) espouse some form of metaphysical *dualism* that acknowledges the existence of both matter and spirit. Unlike the materialist, both the pantheist and the dualist admit that there are real entities that lie beyond the purview of the natural sciences.

3. *Knowledge.* Every worldview makes claims in the area of epistemology, claims about whether or not human beings can achieve knowledge and what kind of knowledge we can have. Most theists maintain that God created us with the capacity to understand the created order and to have personal knowledge of God as well. Moreover, most theists believe that God has actually spoken in history and revealed Himself through prophets and holy Scripture. The naturalistic atheist, because she believes that the physical universe is the only reality, limits what human beings can know to what is discoverable by science. The pantheist who believes that the physical world is an illusion opts for *mysticism* as her epistemology. Naturally, such a pantheist puts little credence in science or sense experience for discovering knowledge. Moreover, she believes that the individual self and its mind are illusions, too. So pantheism does not advocate the use of human reason as a valid source of knowledge any more than sense experience. For the pantheist, the only way to have anything that might be called knowledge is by subjective, mystical experience achieved through meditation or some other technique that alleges to transcend the mind and the senses. And what we come to "know" through mystical experience cannot be understood by the mind or described in words.

4. *Human Beings.* What is the nature of human beings? What are we composed of? What is our source or origin? What happens to us after we die? Many pantheists deny any ultimate reality to the individual self or soul, seeing it as part of the illusion of *maya*. Insofar as the self is considered real, pantheists tend to see human beings as a part of the divine whole, no more or less divine than everything else. After death, the self or soul simply merges with or is absorbed by God. Naturalistic

atheists are *physicalists*, seeing human beings as purely physical entities that have evolved from a common ancestor. Our conscious minds are entirely explicable in terms of biological processes, and at death the person simply ceases to exist. Christian theists hold that human beings were created by God and endowed by Him with dignity and purpose. Most Christians are *dualists*, holding that we are a duality of body and soul. That is, human beings have a material component (body) and an immaterial component (soul). This dualism provides for the possibility of free agency and life after death

5. *Values.* Every person has values pertaining to many different aspects of life. Our values determine our priorities, guide our actions, and ground our ultimate life commitments. Our values include those which are political, social, economic, and aesthetic, but our most critical values pertain to ethics. These have to do with how we ought to treat other people. Both pantheism and naturalism often lead to *moral relativism*, the view that what count as right and wrong is a matter of personal or cultural preference. One reason for this is that both pantheism and naturalism tend to regard human concerns as ultimate. Theists, however, regard God as the ultimate good and maintain that God created human beings to reflect His character. This implies a kind of *moral objectivism*, the view that moral values transcend human beings and require universal adherence.

Although there are many worldviews, only one worldview can be true. Sadly, many people never reflect critically on their fundamental beliefs in the above areas to carefully check the truth of their worldview. They hold the beliefs or values they do because they inherited them from their parents or because they are popular among their peers. But, to quote Socrates again, "the unexamined life is not worth living." The discipline of philosophy requires that one take a hard look at one's worldview and examine it by means of the philosophical method laid out in the previous section with the goal of ascertaining whether that worldview is true. By doing so one may hold one's beliefs and values more confidently or one may be led to embrace a different worldview that seems more nearly correct. This is both the benefit and danger of philosophy.

As noted earlier, we, the authors of this book, readily affirm the truth of the Christian theistic worldview. So, for us, there is a sense in which philosophy is not a *quest* for the true worldview. Nevertheless, there is still much value in the study of philosophy. We ask you to adopt with us the principle of *fides quaerens intellectum* ("faith seeking understanding"). This principle will lead you to pursue philosophical questions, first, as a way of *confirming your worldview*. We believe that the Christian worldview as revealed in Scripture will be consistent with what the best, good-faith efforts of human reason can discern. We believe that all truth is God's truth and that God will not contradict what He reveals in the natural realm with what He reveals in Scripture. So philosophy can provide, in some cases, evidence that confirms the truth of what Christians believe.

Second, this principle will lead you to pursue philosophical questions as a way of *better understanding your faith*. Explicitly asking and seeking to answer philosophical questions will clarify for you *what* it is that you believe. We say that we believe in God. But what do we *mean* by the word *God*? And we say He is omnipotent, omniscient, and so forth, but what do these attributes *mean*? We believe that human beings are morally responsible for their actions. But what makes us responsible? Is it because we have free will? What exactly is free will, and how free need one be in order to be responsible? Philosophical study can bring clarity to questions like these.

Aims and Overview

As important as it is to build a Christian worldview, the most important goal in doing philosophy is the acquisition of wisdom. Earlier we noted how the original sense of our discipline's name is the *love* of wisdom. But this actually sets too low a standard. We don't want merely to love wisdom but to *acquire* it—to actually become wiser through our inquiry into life's most pressing questions. We really want to find out, when we sort it out, what life is all about. And, more than this, we want our lives to change in a positive way from a practical standpoint.

In this sense, our approach in this book reflects the Socratic mission, which is unfortunately often neglected by philosophers these days. Like Socrates, we aim *to use reason in service of goodness*. There are two aspects to this idea that we should spell out in order to make clear our ultimate aims in writing this book. First, this means that, when done properly, philosophical inquiry should culminate in one's living a more virtuous life. As important as it is to grow in knowledge, this is wasted if it is put to poor use. Whatever philosophical insights may be gleaned by readers of this book, it is our sincere prayer that these insights will help you to live more faithfully, serving God and other people.

Second, reason must serve goodness in the sense that the latter is a prerequisite for proper use of the former. Scripture teaches that God grants understanding to the simple and wisdom to the humble (see Pss 19:7; 25:9; and Prov 1:4). And, on the negative side, we are told that sin corrupts good thinking, that a person's vice can cause her to suppress obvious truths (see Rom 1:18–32). The biblical theme here is that rational inquiry is not a morally neutral matter. Our spiritual condition directly impacts the process of belief-formation and our sensitivity to evidence and arguments. Again, this is especially so when it comes to ultimate issues, such as are dealt with in philosophy, particularly in philosophy of religion and ethics, where one's conclusions will have significant implications for how one should live. It therefore behooves us not only to be morally serious but also to be wary of how our personal biases may at any time cloud our judgment. We must constantly consider how what we *want* to be true may impact what we actually *believe* to be true. The Bible says that "the heart is more deceitful than anything else" (Jer 17:9), and keeping this in mind is essential to doing Christian philosophy.

Wherever appropriate throughout the book we have brought theological considerations to bear on the subject at hand. The degree of illumination that Scripture provides on different philosophical questions varies widely. In some cases, biblical teaching will settle a particular question, such as in the case of God's existence or the debate over the objectivity of moral values. Still, in such cases we are no less thorough in our exploration of the available philosophical arguments and positions, though we are also happy to draw a strong conclusion on the issue. In other cases, theological opinion is as varied as that among philosophers, such as regarding theories of knowledge and some metaphysical issues.

In the medieval period theology was regarded as the queen of the disciplines, in the sense that all other disciplinary studies were seen as subservient to our understanding of God. Accordingly, some dubbed philosophy as the "handmaid to theology" in the sense that, when done responsibly, philosophy is especially helpful to the study of God. We, the authors, share this conviction and have used this as our model in introducing you to philosophical studies. Toward this end we have integrated theological reflections throughout. Sometimes these show the implications of philosophical ideas for theological doctrine, and in other cases we consult Scripture to illuminate the philosophical discussion.

The organization of this book reflects the major subfields in philosophy, as all philosophical inquiry deals with knowledge, being, or value. The first chapter is devoted to an introduction to logic and the concept of truth. Since the entire book and, indeed, all of human thought depend upon logic, we begin here. We lay out what might be called the "philosopher's toolbox," a summary of the principles of sound reasoning. This discussion is foundational to the remainder of the book since the rules of logic will be utilized to assess and propose various philosophical views throughout. Also, since the philosophical quest is essentially a search for truth, it is essential that the subject of truth be discussed at the outset. This we do in the second part of the first chapter, as we explore the three major theories of truth.

The second chapter deals with another foundational concept—knowledge. In this chapter we first deal with the challenge of skepticism: How do we respond to arguments which intend to show that we don't know anything? Next we discuss the two major epistemological traditions—rationalism and empiricism. The remainder of the chapter is devoted to more recent philosophical debates about the definition of knowledge. We explore such questions as these: What distinguishes knowledge from mere opinion? Must a person be able to provide evidence for her beliefs to have knowledge? And is knowledge the same thing as certainty?

By far the most influential category of knowledge is science. Moreover, there are many controversies at the intersection of science and other subject areas, especially theology and the study of human nature. For this reason we have devoted an entire chapter to the philosophy of science. We discuss such questions as these: How is science to be defined? What are the laws of nature? Is the scientific method more reliable than other methods of acquiring knowledge? And what are the ultimate aims of science? Or is it even correct to suggest that science really has ultimate aims? We close the chapter with a discussion of the relationship between science and theology.

The next major section of the book begins with a look at metaphysics, the study of what is real. Though several of the other chapters in the book deal with metaphysical issues, here we focus primarily on the most basic metaphysical topics that sometimes go under the heading of *ontology* (the nature of being). For example, what is the underlying "stuff" of reality—material, spiritual, or both? We also take up the question of universals. Are there such things as essences that are shared by all objects of a particular sort, such as baseballs and dogs? Or are there only particular objects? And what, after all, *is* a particular object?

We continue our metaphysical inquiries in chapter five, but here the questions all have to do with human beings. Do we have souls or are we entirely material in composition? And how do we account for personal identity through time? Am I the same person I was ten years ago or even as an infant? If so, then in virtue of what factors? Also, are human beings free or are all our choices determined? Or are freedom and determinism compatible? And can human freedom and responsibility be reconciled with God's foreknowledge? The chapter ends with a discussion about the end of life. What evidence is there for life after death?

In chapter 6 we discuss what is arguably the most important philosophical issue, namely the existence and nature of God. This chapter could very well have been placed earlier in the book, but we chose to put it here as the capstone to earlier discussions of epistemology and metaphysics. Though the existence of God can inform the answers one gives to many of the earlier questions, it is also true that the answers to those questions prepare the way for discussing issues in philosophy of religion. In this chapter, we explore questions such as: What evidence is there that God exists? Do we need arguments for God in order to believe rationally? What characteristics does God have? If God exists, why is there evil?

The book's third main section is devoted to the subject of values. In chapter 7 we discuss ethics, or the study of the good life. We discuss the nature of moral values and consider the question whether moral values are entirely relative. Or are there absolute moral standards that apply to everyone? If so, then where do they come from? Are they dictated by something in the physical world or do they have a transcendent source, namely God? If moral values originate from God, then what role do divine commands and the Golden Rule play in ethics?

Chapter 8 applies value inquiry to the state, asking what a just society would look like. We begin by providing some clarity about such basic political concepts as justice, rights, and laws. Then we look at several major theories of the state, including anarchy, monarchy, and social contract theory. Next we take up the question of distributive justice. How much, if at all, should resources be redistributed by the state? We consider a variety of responses to this question then close the chapter with a discussion of some difficult issues at the interface of politics and religion. What is the proper role of religion in public discourse? And when, if ever, are we justified in engaging in civil disobedience?

In the book's final chapter, we take up issues in the philosophy of art. This subject is placed under the heading of "values" because it pertains to beauty, which is the primary aesthetic *value*. In this chapter we discuss a variety of views regarding the essence of art. We also discuss the question whether there are standards for art. If so, then are they all local and relative? Or are there absolute aesthetic standards? Is beauty a real quality of things or is it in the eye of the beholder? We close the chapter with a discussion of the relationship between art and ethics. How should we approach instances of art that are morally problematic? We offer several guidelines for navigating cases where aesthetic and moral values seem to clash.

In each chapter we list important technical terms pertinent to that chapter. These terms are fully defined in the glossary at the end of the book. We also include questions for reflection at the end of every major section. These may be used to facilitate classroom discussion or simply to enhance the reader's interaction with the material. Throughout the book we have strived for balance in covering the issues and have tried to present each viewpoint as fairly as possible. We only defend firm positions on those topics that are most central to the Christian worldview. Where Christian philosophers differ significantly, we have left the discussions more open-ended. We think this approach will make the text more user-friendly for instructors who may not agree with the authors at certain points, and hopefully it will encourage students to dig deeper.

As you read this book and explore the Big Questions, we hope that you find the discussion helpful in clarifying and assessing your own worldview. And whether or not you happen to be a Christian, we hope that you gain a deeper appreciation for philosophical studies and that you grow in the love and acquisition of wisdom.

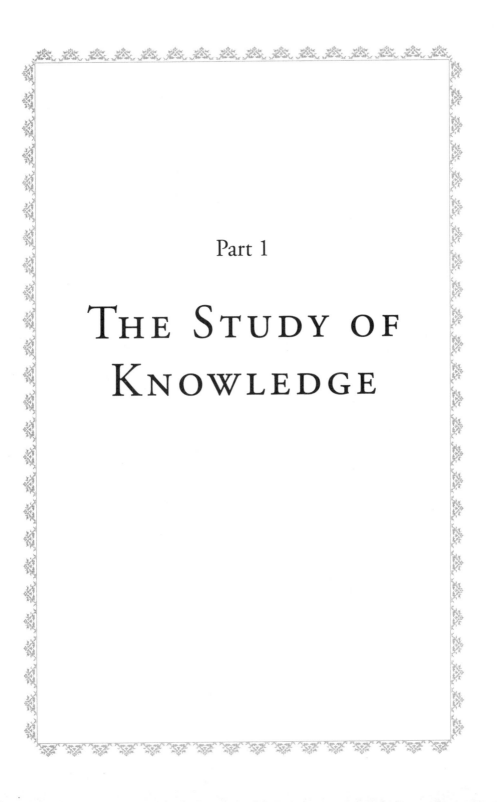

Part 1

THE STUDY OF KNOWLEDGE

Chapter One

LOGIC AND TRUTH: WHAT IS TRUTH?

*"The first and last thing required of
genius is the love of truth."*

—Goethe

1.1 The Science of Reasoning

1.1.1 The Laws of Thought

1.1.2 Arguments

1.1.3 Major Fallacies

1.2 Is Anything True?

1.2.1 Is It True That There Is No Truth?

1.2.2 What Is Truth

Glossary Terms

Argument

Coherence theory of truth

Correspondence theory of truth

Deduction

Fallacy

Induction

Law of excluded middle

Law of identity

Law of noncontradiction

Logic

Objectivism (about truth)

Pragmatic theory of truth

Relativism (about truth)

Syllogism

Truth

At one point in Lewis Carroll's *Alice's Adventures in Wonderland*, Alice attends a tea party where she meets some strange characters: the March Hare, the Mad Hatter, and the Dormouse. During the tea party the following conversation takes place:

> "You should say what you mean," [said the March Hare to Alice].
>
> "I do," Alice hastily replied; "at least—at least I mean what I say—that's the same thing you know."
>
> "Not the same thing a bit!" said the Hatter. "Why, you might just as well say that 'I see what I eat' is the same thing as 'I eat what I see'!"
>
> "You might just as well say," added the March Hare, "that 'I like what I get' is the same thing as 'I get what I like'!"
>
> "You might just as well say," added the Dormouse, which seemed to be talking in its sleep, "that 'I breathe when I sleep' is the same thing as 'I sleep when I breathe'!"
>
> "It *is* the same thing with you," said the Hatter, and here the conversation dropped.[1]

Carroll has given us here a humorous, though poignant, example of the importance of logic and the pursuit of truth. Indeed, this story illustrates the connection between truth and logic. If the philosopher is to pursue truth and discover the true worldview (as we discussed in the introduction), then logic is an essential tool. In this chapter, we will explain the basic principles of logic—the science of sound reasoning. Then we will examine the nature of truth itself, a question of special importance in our culture today.

§ 1.1 The Science of Reasoning

Logic is the primary tool of philosophers. In logic, the philosopher has a set of basic rules and principles for governing his thinking, for dictating when and how to draw conclusions from other things believed, and for evaluating the views of others. Logic, in other words, constitutes a science of reasoning. We will begin our discussion with the most fundamental logical principles.

---

[1] Lewis Carroll, *Alice's Adventures in Wonderland* (New York: Peebles Press, n.d.), 75–76.

1.1.1 The Laws of Thought

Basic to all logic are the three *laws of thought* (sometimes called the laws of logic).[2] All the other principles of logic flow from and presuppose these three principles. One of these is the *law of noncontradiction*. This law simply states that *no proposition can be both true and false at the same time and in the same sense*. Each part of this law is crucial for avoiding misunderstanding. The law of noncontradiction does not assert that a proposition (i.e., a statement) cannot be true and false at different times. Obviously, the following statements can both be true so long as they are asserted at different points in time:

> "Barack Obama is the current president of the United States."
> "Barack Obama is not the current president of the United States."

If the first proposition were uttered in 2009, then it would be true. And if the second one were uttered in 2005, it would be true. All that the law of noncontradiction rules out is both statements being true *at the same time*. Likewise, the law of noncontradiction can allow that two statements can be both true and false even at the same time if the statements *have different meanings*. Consider these two statements:

> "Al Gore is cold."
> "Al Gore is not cold."

Both of these statements can be true even at the same time as long as the word "cold" means something different in each case. Suppose that, in the first statement, "cold" means *emotionally cold* (i.e., distant, aloof), while in the second statement, "cold" means *physically cold* (i.e, cold in temperature). In this case, obviously, both statements can be true simultaneously. All that the law of noncontradiction rules out is both statements being simultaneously true in the same sense.

Another law of logic is the *law of excluded middle*. According to this law, *every proposition must be either true or false*. The law excludes a third alternative. So, the proposition, "Barack Obama is the current U.S. president" is either true or false. It must be one or the other. There is no "middle ground" between truth and falsehood.

The *law of identity* is the third and most fundamental law of thought.[3] This law states that every proposition is identical to itself. Or,

---

[2] Much of the material in this section and the next is adapted from Steven B. Cowan, "Minding Your P's and Q's: A Primer on Logic for Christians," *Areopagus Journal* 6:2 (March-April 2006): 16–22.

[3] It is interesting to note that when God names himself for Moses in the Old Testament he does so in terms of this law: "I am who I am" (Exod 3:14).

put another way, *if a proposition is true, then it is true.* So, if it is true that Barack Obama is the U.S. president, then it is true that he is the president. At first blush, this law may seem so simple and obvious as to be hardly worth stating. However, some very interesting and important philosophical problems turn on the truth of this law. And the other two laws of thought are actually derived from this one. This is why it is the most basic of the logical laws.

Such are the basic laws of logic on which all other logical principles depend. Though some have challenged the necessary truth of these laws, they are indispensable for clear thinking.[4]

1.1.2 Arguments

Logic is primarily about the construction and evaluation of arguments. An *argument* is a set of propositions or statements that purports to prove something. As such, an argument has two parts: (1) the conclusion of the argument is that proposition which one is trying to prove, and (2) the premises of the argument are those propositions that provide reasons for accepting the conclusion. Let's look more closely at the nature of arguments and see how they are supposed to work.

Deduction and Induction

Arguments may be either deductive or inductive. *Deduction* is a kind of reasoning by which we draw inferences (i.e., conclusions) that are guaranteed by a set of premises. In a good *deductive argument*, the premises (if true) provide conclusive grounds for the conclusion. That is, the conclusion of a deductive argument follows from the premises with absolute certainty. Consider the following deductive argument:

> All men are mortal.
> Socrates is a man.
> Therefore, Socrates is mortal.

A moment's reflection on this argument reveals that the conclusion follows from the premises of this argument. If the premises are true, then the conclusion cannot fail to be true.

Induction is a type of reasoning by which we infer conclusions that are likely, but not guaranteed, based on the premises. *Inductive arguments* establish their conclusions with only a degree of probability. The premises, that is, only imply that the conclusion is probable, not certain. Here is an example of an inductive argument:

---

[4] For a defense of the rational inescapability and necessary truth of the principles of logic, see Cowan, "Minding Your P's and Q's," 16–18.

Out of 1,000 people surveyed in Birmingham, Alabama,
    70 percent agree that capital punishment is morally permissible.
Therefore, it is likely that approximately 70 percent of the
    citizens of Birmingham, Alabama, agree that capital
    punishment is morally permissible.

Again, only a little reflection makes clear, even if the premise of this argument is true, that the conclusion is not certain. The premise makes the conclusion probable, but does not guarantee its truth. We all use inductive reasoning in many aspects of our daily lives, and we will examine inductive arguments at various points in this book. However, in the remainder of our discussion of logic, we will confine ourselves mostly to a discussion of deductive arguments.

Validity and Soundness

In evaluating deductive arguments, the first thing to consider is whether the argument is valid. The concept of *validity* applies to an argument when its conclusion follows logically from its premises. More precisely, a valid argument is one in which, if the premises are true, the conclusion must also be true. It is very important that the student of logic understand what validity does and does not imply. To say that an argument is valid is not to say that its conclusion *is* true. Nor is it to claim that any of its premises are true. In fact, an argument can be valid even if every proposition in the argument is false. Consider the following argument:

All people have brown hair.
All brown-haired things have four arms.
Therefore, all people have four arms.

Every statement in this argument is obviously false. Yet this argument is valid! You can see this if you pretend for a moment that the premises of this argument are true. *If* the premises were true, then the conclusion would have to be true as well. To say that an argument is valid is to make no claim about the truth or falsity of any statement in the argument. It is only to make a claim about the structure or form of the argument. A valid argument has a structure which is such that, *if the premises are true*, then the conclusion has to be true. Another way of putting this is that a valid argument preserves truth. True premises preserve truth through to the conclusion.

Claiming that an argument is sound makes a stronger claim than validity. *Soundness* is a property of arguments that are both valid *and* have all true premises. In other words

validity + true premises = soundness

If an argument is sound, then its conclusion is true and (assuming that you know the argument is sound) you must believe the conclusion. Knowing whether an argument is sound is much more difficult than knowing if it is valid. To test an argument for validity, one need only inspect the form of the argument. To test an argument for soundness, one must evaluate whether the premises are true. Sometimes that is not too difficult, but often it is very difficult. As a discipline, logic is mostly concerned with validity, and that is what we will focus on in what follows.

Some Valid Argument Forms

Let us distinguish between an argument and an argument form. An argument has some definite content as in the examples we used in the previous section. An *argument form*, however, is like a skeleton or blueprint; it is a basic pattern of argument. There are some common deductive argument forms that are known to be valid. If one can memorize these forms, then one can often easily discern whether an argument is valid. Most of the arguments that we will examine are called *syllogisms*. A syllogism is an argument (or argument form) that contains exactly three propositions (two premises and a conclusion). There are three types of syllogisms that we will discuss.

1. *Categorical Syllogisms.* This type of syllogism is so called because it contains only categorical propositions, statements that assert or deny inclusion in a given class or category. There are many possible categorical syllogisms (256 to be exact), but only a handful are valid. Here are three such argument forms:[5]

    I. All M are P.
       All S are M.
       Therefore, all S are P.

    II. No M are P.
       All S are M
       Therefore, no S are P.

    III. All M are P.
       Some S are M.
       Therefore, some S are P.

---

[5] In categorical syllogisms, the symbol "S" stands for the term that appears as the subject of the conclusion, the letter "P" for the term that appears as the predicate of the conclusion, and "M" for the "middle term," the term that does not appear in the conclusion but only in the premises.

Any arguments that correspond to these forms are valid. Here are some concrete examples that correspond to the above argument forms respectively:

> All dogs are animals.
> All collies are dogs.
> Therefore, all collies are animals.

> No dogs are cats.
> All collies are dogs.
> Therefore, no collies are cats.

> All Christians are heaven-bound.
> Some Baptists are Christians.
> Therefore, some Baptists are heaven-bound.

2. Hypothetical Syllogisms. These are syllogisms that have at least one hypothetical or conditional premise. A conditional is a statement that has the form, "If P then Q." The first part of a conditional statement (the part corresponding to P) is called the *antecedent*, and the second part (corresponding to Q) is called the *consequent*. There are three valid hypothetical syllogisms:

IV. Pure Hypothetical Syllogism

> If P then Q.
> If Q then R.
> Therefore, if P then R.

Example:

> If God exists, then we have a reason to be moral.
> If we have a reason to be moral, then we have a reason to
>   refrain from murder.
> Therefore, if God exists, then we have a reason to
>   refrain from murder.

V. *Modus Ponens*

> If P then Q.
> P.
> Therefore, Q.

Example:

If God exists, then we have a reason to be moral.
God exists.
Therefore, we have a reason to be moral.

VI. *Modus Tollens*

If P then Q.
Not-Q.
Therefore, not-P.

Example:

If there are no objective moral principles, then murder is
    morally permissible.
Murder is not morally permissible.
Therefore, there are objective moral principles.

3. Disjunctive Syllogism. This kind of syllogism has a *disjunction* as its major premise. A disjunction is a statement that has the form "Either P or Q." The two parts of the disjunction (P and Q) are called *disjuncts*. Thus, the disjunctive syllogism has this form:

VII. Either P or Q.
Not-P.
Therefore, Q.

A disjunction claims that at least one of its disjuncts is true. Since the second premise tells us that one of the disjuncts, namely P, is false, we know that Q has to be true. Consider this example:

Either Miami or Birmingham is in Alabama.
Miami is not in Alabama.
Therefore, Birmingham is in Alabama.

As noted above, the argument forms that we have so far discussed are syllogisms (arguments with two premises and a conclusion). The remaining argument forms that we will introduce are of different types.

4. Constructive Dilemma. This form of argument is often used when one wants to force his opponent to choose between two unpleasant options (thus the title "dilemma"). The constructive dilemma has this form:

VIII. If P then Q; and if R then S.
  P or R.
  Therefore, Q or S.

Notice that the first premise conjoins two conditional statements. The second premise and the conclusion are disjunctive statements related to the terms in the conditionals. Here is an example:

> If the Democrats win the next presidential election, then taxes will be raised; and if the Republicans win the next presidential election, then the poor will continue to suffer needlessly.
> Either the Democrats win the next presidential election or the Republicans do.
> Therefore, either taxes will be raised or the poor will continue to suffer needlessly.

Though the premises of this argument are questionable, it is relatively easy to see that the conclusion would be true if the premises are true.

5. *Reductio ad Absurdum.* This is a form of argument that appears often in philosophical literature and sometimes in everyday discourse. The Latin phrase *reductio ad absurdum* means "reduction to the absurd" and aptly describes the strategy behind this argument form. The basic idea behind the *reductio* argument is to show an opponent's view to be false by arguing that it leads to a contradiction or an otherwise obvious falsehood. Since any proposition that implies a falsehood must also be false, one way to prove a statement to be false is to show that if it were true it would lead to a falsehood. We may express the basic pattern as follows:

IX. Assume P (the claim to be proven false).
  ⋮
  Q.
  Not-Q.
  Therefore, not-P.

The first premise of the *reductio* form (P) assumes, for the sake of argument, the truth of the proposition that one wants to prove false. In this example, the argument proceeds by making valid deductions from P until one deduces a contradiction (e.g., Q and not-Q). P is thus shown to be false since contradictions cannot be true. Here is a formal sketch of a *reductio ad absurdum* used by Jesus in Matthew 12:25–27:[6]

---

[6] Though we have formulated the structure of this argument quite differently, we are nevertheless indebted to Douglas Groothuis for this example (see his *On Jesus* [Belmont, CA: Wadsworth, 2003], 34–35).

(1) Jesus exorcises demons by the power of Satan. (Assumption to be proved false)

(2) If Jesus exorcises demons by the power of Satan, then Satan is destroying his own kingdom.

(3) Satan is destroying his own kingdom. (Deduced from 1 & 2 by modus ponens)

(4) Satan would not destroy his own kingdom. (A common-sense truth)

(5) Therefore, Jesus does not exorcise demons by the power of Satan. (Since 3 & 4 are contradictory, 1 must be false)

There are many more forms of deductive argument, some much more complex than those we have outlined here. If the student can master these simple argument forms, though, it will go a long way in equipping him to evaluate the arguments he encounters in everyday life.

1.1.3 Major Fallacies

As you may have already guessed, not every argument form is valid. An argument is invalid when the conclusion does not follow from the premises even if the premises are true. In other words, in an invalid argument, the premises do not guarantee the truth of the conclusion—it's possible for the premises to be true while the conclusion is false. Every invalid argument is guilty of some *fallacy*. A fallacy is a mistake in reasoning. More specifically, a fallacy involves drawing a conclusion from reasons that do not adequately support it.

There are two major kinds of fallacies. First, there are *formal fallacies*. These are fallacies that relate to the form or structure of a deductive argument and can always be discovered by inspecting the form of an argument. Second, there are *informal fallacies*, which can only be detected by inspecting the content of an argument, not just its structure. In what follows, we will discuss some common examples of both types of fallacies.

Formal Fallacies

Below are four formal fallacies. These are not the only ones, but they are the most common and easily discerned.

1. *The Undistributed Middle.* Most of the 256 possible categorical syllogisms are invalid. We don't have space here to discuss all of them, but there is one invalid form that occurs often and is easy to detect.

All P is M.
All S is M.
Therefore, All S is P.

Without getting too technical, the basic problem here is that the middle term (M) is "undistributed"—which means that nowhere in the argument is reference made to the entire class of things that are M. A valid categorical syllogism must always refer at some point to the whole of the M-class, but that does not happen in this argument form. Consider this example:

All dogs are animals.
All cats are animals.
Therefore, all cats are dogs.

Clearly, this conclusion does not follow from the premises, even though both premises are true. The term *dog* in the first premise picks out only a segment of the class of animals. Likewise, the term *cat* only picks out a segment of the class of animals. And the problem is that there is no reason to think, given only these two premises, that the two segments picked out by "dog" and "cat" overlap in any way. Hence, neither occurrence of the term *animal* makes reference to the entirety of the animal class, and thus the premises give us no reason to think that the cat class is contained within the dog class, which the conclusion would require to be the case.

2. *Affirming the Consequent.* This fallacy bears some resemblance to *modus ponens*, one of the valid argument forms discussed above. But whereas modus ponens affirms the antecedent in the second premise, this fallacious form affirms the consequent.

If P then Q.
Q.
Therefore P.

To see the fallacious nature of this argument form, consider this argument:

If George Washington was assassinated, then he is dead.
George Washington is dead.
Therefore, George Washington was assassinated.

Both premises of this argument are true, but the conclusion is known to be false. Obviously, the fact that George Washington is dead does not give us reason to believe that he was assassinated because he could have died for any number of other reasons. (In fact, he died from pneumonia.)

3. Denying the Antecedent. This fallacy looks similar to *modus tollens*, but the second premise denies the antecedent instead of the consequent.

> If P then Q.
> Not-P.
> Therefore, not-Q.

Here is an example:

> If George Washington was assassinated, then he is dead.
> George Washington was not assassinated.
> Therefore, George Washington is not dead.

We know that George Washington *is* dead, but the premises of this argument are true. So, there must be a fallacy here. The fact that Washington was not assassinated does not imply the conclusion that he isn't dead because, again, he could have died by another cause.

4. Affirming a Disjunct. Recall that a disjunction claims only that *at least* one of the disjuncts is true. This leaves open the possibility that both disjuncts could be true. Thus, the following argument form is invalid:

> Either P or Q.
> P.
> Therefore, not-Q.

Since both disjuncts *could* be true, knowing (via the second premise) that one of them is true does not allow us to say that the other disjunct is false. The following example illustrates the point:

> Either Montgomery or Birmingham is in Alabama.
> Montgomery is in Alabama.
> Therefore, Birmingham is not in Alabama.

Informal Fallacies

There are many informal fallacies (by some counts, well over one hundred!). Fortunately, some are more common than others. Here we mention twelve common types. The last three are unique to inductive arguments.

1. *False Dilemma.* This fallacy is committed when someone argues that one must choose between two options when there is actually another alternative. Of course, sometimes there are only two options, but often there are more. Suppose someone makes this claim: "Either we allow abortion on demand to be legal or we force children to be raised in homes where they are not wanted." This is a false dilemma. Obviously, there are other alternatives such as putting the "unwanted" children up for adoption.

2. *Begging the Question.* This fallacy is committed when someone's argument assumes the truth of what he is trying to prove. In other words, he uses the conclusion as a premise in the argument. Someone who commits this fallacy is arguing in a circle. Some Christians have been guilty of this, for example, when they argue: "The Bible is the Word of God because the Bible says that it is the Word of God, and we know that whatever the Bible says is true because it's the Word of God." Notice that the Bible's being the Word of God is what the argument is designed to prove, but one of the reasons for believing that claim is that the Bible is the Word of God!

3. *Argument from Ignorance.* Someone might argue that a proposition is true simply because it has not been proven false. Conversely, someone could claim that a proposition is false just because it has not been proven true. But the fact that our evidence doesn't show that a proposition is false usually is no evidence that it is true (and vice-versa). It may be the case that we haven't yet uncovered evidence for its falsehood or it is the kind of thing that simply cannot be proven either way. Consider this example: "God must not exist because no one has ever proven that He exists." As the saying goes, "Absence of evidence isn't evidence of absence." Of course it is equally fallacious to argue thus: "God must exist because no one has ever proven that He doesn't." We need some caution at this point, however. In some cases, there may be good reason to think that we would have found evidence for the truth or falsity of a particular proposition if it existed. For example, since Mormonism claims that a huge, relatively advanced civilization existed in North America 2,000 years ago, the fact that no archaeological artifacts from that civilization have been found seems to be significant counterevidence.

4. *Equivocation.* This fallacy is committed when a word or phrase is used in different senses in different places in the argument. Such shifts in meaning can lead one to draw inferences that are unwarranted. Consider these two examples:

Pigs are filthy animals.
All men are pigs.
Therefore, all men are filthy animals.

Brad Pitt is really something!
Something is fishy.
Therefore, Brad Pitt is fishy.

5. Straw Man. It is very common for someone to argue against a particular viewpoint by attacking a weak argument for that view while ignoring stronger arguments that might be offered. This is the Straw Man fallacy. For example: "We should not ban hardcore pornographic magazines just because some people find nudity distasteful." Here the arguer is trying to make you think that the only reason people oppose pornography is because it offends their personal sensibilities. He ignores the fact that many oppose it for better reasons such as the claim that it demeans or exploits women or leads to bad moral character.

6. Attacking the Person. This fallacy occurs when someone attacks the character or circumstances of the person giving an argument rather than attacking the argument itself. For example: "Oscar Wilde's position on art theory should be rejected because he was a homosexual." It may be true that Wilde was a homosexual, but that fact has no bearing on whether or not his views on art theory are acceptable. Here is another example: "We should not listen to Al Gore's view on global warming. After all, he is influenced by the Democratic party." Perhaps Gore's views are influenced by his ties to the Democratic party, but that association is irrelevant to the acceptability of his arguments for his view.

7. Appeal to Popularity. This is one of the most frequently committed fallacies in our consumeristic culture. It is sometimes called the "bandwagon fallacy." It is committed when the reason given for adopting some viewpoint is that it is what the majority does or what is currently in fashion. Consider: "More Americans get their news from ABC than from any other network." The fact that most Americans watch ABC News, by itself, is irrelevant to the question of whether or not ABC is the best news source (which, of course, is the implied conclusion). Celebrity endorsements of products are a frequent way in which this fallacy is committed. We are told by advertisers that we should wear Nike shoes because that is the shoe LeBron James wears; or we ought to support a particular political candidate because Oprah Winfrey endorses him.

8. Composition. This fallacy occurs when someone argues that because the parts of a thing have a certain characteristic, the whole must have that characteristic also. No doubt, there are cases in which the whole must have the same quality that the parts have. For example, if all the parts of an object are red, we know that the whole object must also be red. But this is not always the case. If someone tells you that all the parts of an automobile weigh less than 100 pounds, and therefore the whole automobile weighs less than 100 pounds, we can be sure that he is mistaken. Here is another example: "Chinese households have fewer Bibles on average than American households. Therefore, there are fewer Bibles in China than America."

9. Division. This fallacy is the opposite of composition. Just as it is a mistake to automatically assume that the whole must have the same characteristics as the parts, it can be equally fallacious to assume that the parts must have the same characteristics as the whole. Just because the automobile as a whole weighs over a ton, it doesn't follow that the parts each weigh over a ton. Here is another example: "Ten percent of Americans are atheists. Michael Shermer is an American. So, Michael Shermer is ten percent atheist."

10. False Cause. This fallacy is committed when someone presumes without good evidence that there is a causal connection between two events. The most common form of this fallacy is assuming that some event x is the cause of y simply because x occurs before y. For example, "Every time the Sun comes up, the rooster crows just a moment before. So the rooster's crowing must cause the Sun to rise." Here is a more serious example: "The moral decline in our nation began just about the time the Supreme Court outlawed prayer and Bible-reading in public schools. You see what happens when God is removed from public education?"

11. Hasty Generalization. Many inductive arguments draw general conclusions such as "Most college students are young" and "20 percent of Americans like jazz." Such generalizations are usually made on the basis of empirical observations and surveys. This is perfectly appropriate *per se*. Sometimes, however, the samples selected for observation are too small to generate reliable results. When this happens, the researcher commits the fallacy of hasty generalization. Suppose we want to know the opinions of students at the State University on the issue of capital punishment. We interview ten students and six of them say that they support capital punishment. It would clearly be inappropriate to conclude that 60 percent of the student body favors the death penalty. Such a generalization is not acceptable because the sample was too small.

12. Biased Generalization. Inductive generalizations can go wrong another way. Even when the sample selected for scientific study is large enough, a generalization can still be unjustified if the sample is not selected randomly. Suppose that we interview 1,000 students at the State University about capital punishment (usually a large enough sample for most population groups). But suppose that all of the students interviewed are members of sororities and fraternities. Can we trust the results of a generalization about all the university's students? No, because there may be some characteristic unique to campus Greeks not shared by the larger student body that biases them in a particular direction on the issue. To be unbiased the sample needs to be randomly selected from the broad scope of the population with which the study is concerned.

The fallacies discussed above are very common not only in philosophy but in everyday life. If you gain an understanding of these fallacies, you will be able to identify many invalid arguments when you encounter them.

Questions for Reflection

1. We have claimed that the three laws of thought are necessarily true and are indispensable for clear thinking. Do you agree? Is it possible for them to be false? Why or why not?

2. Following are some deductive arguments. Are they valid or invalid? Justify your answers by identifying the valid argument form or the formal fallacy committed in each case. If you think the argument is valid, try also to determine whether the argument is sound or unsound.

   A. If God existed, there would be no evil.
      There is evil.
      Therefore, God does not exist.

   B. If God existed, there would be no evil.
      God exists.
      Therefore, there is no evil.

   C. If Jesus rose from the dead, then he is a trustworthy teacher.
      Jesus is a trustworthy teacher.
      Therefore, Jesus rose from the dead.

   D. All Christians are evangelists.
      All Presbyterians are Christians.
      Therefore, all Presbyterians are evangelists.

    E. All philosophers are smart.
       Some Republicans are smart.
       Therefore, some Republicans are philosophers.

    F. Either Peter or Judas betrayed Jesus.
       Peter did not betray Jesus.
       Therefore, Judas betrayed Jesus.

    G. Either Thomas or Peter had doubts.
       Thomas had doubts.
       Therefore, Peter did not have doubts.

    H. If Socrates was an atheist, then he broke the laws of
       Athens.
       If he broke the laws of Athens, then he deserved to be
       punished.
       Therefore, if Socrates was an atheist, then he deserved to be
       punished.

3. Following are some arguments that commit informal fallacies.
   Identify which fallacy is committed in each case.

    A. "We cannot believe Jesus' claim to be the Messiah because
       He is a friend of tax-collectors and sinners!"

    B. "Creationism must be false since creationists believe the
       unlikely hypothesis that the universe was created in 4004
       BC."

    C. "Jack, you really ought to come to the party with us
       tonight! All of the most important people on campus will
       be there, and you will want to meet them."

    D. The Pharisees say to Jesus, "Either you support the nation
       of Israel or you pay taxes to Caesar. Your choice."

    E. "Contrary to intelligent design theory (which proposes
       supernatural causes), science can only explain things by
       appeals to natural causes. The reason is that science is
       committed to finding natural explanations."

    F. "The witch of Endor called for Samuel's spirit to appear.
       Samuel appeared soon after. Therefore, the witch of Endor
       made Samuel appear."

G. "Each member of the Chicago Bulls basketball team is an excellent player. Therefore, the Bulls are an excellent team."

H. "No one has been able to conclusively link violent video games to juvenile delinquency. The only reasonable conclusion is that there is no connection."

§ 1.2 Is Anything True?

So far in this chapter we have discussed the nature of logic. The principles of logic enable us to evaluate arguments to determine whether a particular proposition may be inferred from others that are accepted as true. I can know that "Socrates is mortal" if I know that two other statements are true, namely, "All men are mortal" and "Socrates is a man." A key notion in logic, then, is the concept of *truth*. But, someone might ask, *Is anything true?* This is perhaps the central philosophical question of our postmodern culture. Today, the pervasive mantra is that truth is relative. There is no such thing as real, absolute truth. What counts as true is simply a matter of personal or cultural preference.

As suggested in the previous sentence, this relativism about truth comes in two forms. One form is called *subjectivism*. This view may be explained by use of an analogy. Some people today say that truth is like flavors of ice cream. One person, let's call her Sally, thinks that vanilla ice cream tastes best. Her friend Bill thinks that chocolate is best. Who is right, Sally or Bill? Well, in a sense, they are *both* right! The best flavor of ice cream is a subjective matter. It depends upon a person's individual tastes or preferences. Likewise, the theory goes, with all other "truth" claims. One person believes that God exists, another doesn't. One person believes that cheating on exams is wrong, another doesn't. One person believes that 2+2=4, while another believes that 2+2=5. Who is right? Those who claim that truth is relative say that they are *all* right. Truth is simply whatever a person prefers it to be.

The other form of relativism about truth is called *conventionalism*. According to this view, truth is defined not by individuals but by cultures. "Truth" is merely a social construct. It is what people within a certain group or culture have agreed to believe for pragmatic reasons. Some cultures believe in God because that belief "works for them." Some Eastern cultures reject mathematical "truths" as absolute because such truths do not fit with their conviction that logic and mathematics are human inventions and not aspects of ultimate reality.

It may be helpful in understanding relativism to contrast it with its opposite, absolutism or *objectivism*. The objectivist about truth believes that truth is *not* a matter of subjective or cultural preference. Rather, truth is a real feature of the world that is independent of what a person or group thinks about it. Thus, for the objectivist, if a proposition is true, then it is so whether or not any person believes it. Further, it is true for everyone at all times and places. Relativism, however, denies that truth is objective. There is no single truth that is true for everyone at all times and places. Thus, one postmodern writer, John Caputo, asserts, "The truth is that there is no truth."[7]

If such relativism about truth is correct, then the other questions that concern philosophers are probably irrelevant. After all, philosophy is usually conceived as aiming to discover what is really true.

1.2.1 Is It True That There Is No Truth?

So, is it true that nothing is true? Think carefully about that question. If you do, you will see that it is simply not possible for truth to be relative. The relativist makes something like the following assertion:

> "There are no absolute truths."

Now we can ask a simple question regarding this statement: *Is it true?* That is, is it truly the case that there are no absolute truths? Notice that this is a self-defeating claim. For, by saying that it is true that there are no truths, one asserts that there is in fact one truth after all, namely, the *truth that there is no truth*! In other words, if the statement "There are no absolute truths" is true, then it is false!

Perhaps the relativist has a way out of this conundrum. He may appeal to his own relativistic theory to justify his claim. Perhaps he can say, "The statement 'There are no absolute truths' is true for me, though it may not be true for you." Of course, if he makes this move, then he provides no reason whatever for anyone else to adopt his view and he can have no objection to another person who claims that there are absolute truths. For him there are no absolute truths. However, for you and me there are, and we need not care much about what he thinks anymore than Bill needs to care that Sally thinks that vanilla ice cream is best—for Bill, chocolate is best and that's all there is to it.

On further reflection, though, even this move does not rescue the relativist from self-refutation. It only pushes his problem back a step. Now we can ask, "Is it true that the statement 'There are no absolute

---

[7] John D. Caputo, *Radical Hermeneutics* (Bloomington: Indiana University Press, 1987), 156.

truths' is true for you, but not for me?" Again, if he says yes, then he contradicts himself.

Some relativists (in particular, the conventionalists) attempt to avoid the problems that we have raised by offering more sophisticated theses. Rather than making the simple and obviously self-refuting claim that truth is relative, they may say something like this:

"All truth-claims are socially conditioned."

By this they mean that everything a person believes is the result of his social up-bringing. If a person believes some proposition, then it is because his society has conditioned him to believe it. This view supposes, again, that no one knows (or could know) the absolute truth about anything. Beliefs that are the result of social conditioning can make no legitimate claim to being objectively true.

Yet, even this more sophisticated relativism is self-defeating. Notice that the statement "All truth-claims are socially conditioned" purports to be a truth-claim. If so, then anyone who believes it is socially conditioned to believe it and thus it turns out to be unjustified. As William Lane Craig puts it,

> If postmodernist claims are objectively true, then those claims are themselves the mere products of social forces and so are not objectively true. Of course, if postmodernist claims are not objectively true, then they are just the arbitrary opinions of certain people that we are free to ignore.[8]

So it is false that there is no truth. In fact, since the denial of absolute truth is self-defeating, the idea that truth is relative is logically impossible. There must be objective truth.

1.2.2 What Is Truth?

We have seen that there is objective truth. But what do we mean by the word *truth*? We have been using the term as if it were perfectly clear what truth is, but the nature of truth is actually a subject of considerable debate. Historically, there have been three major theories of truth among philosophers: the correspondence theory, the coherence theory, and the pragmatic theory.

---

[8] William Lane Craig, "A Classical Apologist's Response to Cumulative Case Apologetics," in *Five Views on Apologetics*, ed. Steven B. Cowan (Grand Rapids: Zondervan, 2000), 182–83.

The Correspondence Theory of Truth

The correspondence theory of truth might be said to be the ordinary or "common sense" view of truth that most people assume in everyday usage. One of the earliest statements of this theory was made by the ancient Greek philosopher Aristotle, who said, "To say that what is, is not, or that what is not is, is false; but to say that what is, is, and what is not is not, is true."[9] Perhaps more precisely, we can say that according to the correspondence theory of truth,

> *A proposition is true if and only if it corresponds to the way things actually are.*

So, for example, the proposition, "George Washington was the first president of the United States," is true if and only if, in fact, George Washington was the first president of the United States. Likewise, "The Earth revolves around the Sun" is true just in case the Earth actually does revolve around the Sun. To use a negative example, the proposition, "Sherlock Holmes is a real person," is true if and only if Sherlock Holmes is a real person. Of course, we know that the latter proposition is false because Sherlock Holmes is a fictional character. In any case, the idea behind the correspondence theory of truth is that true statements are true in virtue of their matching up with or corresponding to the way things actually are in reality.

It is very important at this point to avoid a possible confusion. People often misunderstand the correspondence theory by failing to distinguish between (1) *knowing* that a proposition is true and (2) a proposition's *being* true. The correspondence theory of truth is all about (2) and not at all about (1). In other words, the correspondence theory aims to explain what makes a proposition true, not how or whether we can *know* that it is true. A statement can *be* true (or false) even if we do not or even cannot know that it is true (or false). For example, the following statement is either true or false:

> "There is a purple grain of sand on the far side of the Moon."

It may be quite impossible for me or anyone else ever to find out whether this statement is true. Nevertheless, the correspondence theory of truth tells me the conditions under which it would be true: *if there is a purple grain of sand on the far side of the Moon.*

The correspondence theory of truth seems to capture what we mean by "truth" in ordinary discourse. It is not without its critics, however. The

[9] Aristotle, *Metaphysics* IV:7, 1011b.

most significant objection raised against it has to do with the idea of correspondence. What exactly do we mean when we say that a proposition *corresponds* to reality? Opponents of the correspondence theory sometimes claim that the concept of correspondence is vague or mysterious and thus the theory is useless in helping us understand what truth is.

Correspondence is supposed to be a relation that exists between facts about reality and propositions. Take again the proposition, "George Washington was the first president of the United States." What precisely is the relation between this statement and the real world that we are calling "correspondence"? Is the statement supposed to somehow "picture" reality the way a photograph might resemble what it is a photograph of? Surely not. The statement "George Washington was the first president of the United States" does not look or smell like the man George Washington, nor does it live in Virginia. Well, is correspondence a *causal* relation? That is, does the proposition "George Washington was the first president of the United States" *make* it the case that George Washington was the first president? Of course not. This difficulty in specifying the precise nature of correspondence has led many philosophers to reject the correspondence theory.

There are two ways a correspondence theorist might respond to this objection. First, he can argue that too much is being made of the term *correspondence* in the definition of the correspondence theory. The use of the term *correspondence* may be seen as simply idiomatic and can be dispensed with in such a way as to leave no mysterious, unexplained relation.[10] For example, instead of saying that a proposition is true if and only if it corresponds to reality, the correspondence theorist can simply say,

A proposition is true if and only if it is the case.

Notice that the word *correspondence* does not occur in this definition. Truth is defined simply in terms of a proposition's accurately expressing or describing a fact about the world.

On the other hand, the defender of the correspondence theory may argue that the correspondence relation is a fundamental relation that is not analyzable in terms of other kinds of relations. In other words, the objection assumes that the correspondence relation must be reducible to some other relational concept like "picturing" or "causing." But why can we not understand correspondence the same way we understand resemblance or causation? People seldom charge a theory with being mysterious if it uses the term *resembles* or the term *causes*. And it just

---

[10] See Richard L. Kirkham, *Theories of Truth: A Critical Introduction* (Cambridge, MA: MIT Press, 1992), 134–36.

so happens that people in ordinary discourse do not usually think that correspondence is a particularly strange idea either.

Another related objection to the correspondence theory is that it seems to be committed to the existence of very strange entities. For example, it seems to be committed to the existence of "facts." (Remember that we have said that truth has to do with a statement's correspondence to "facts.") But what exactly are facts? They are not physical objects. One cannot get into a car and drive over to the "fact warehouse" and look at them. We may understand what a statement is. We may understand what is meant by the entities referred to in a given sentence such as "George Washington" and "president." But what are these things called "facts"?

It may be possible to give an account of "facts" that removes the apparent mystery associated with them. However, it should be noted that the objection is based on a suspicion that anything that is not physical and/or accessible to our five senses is at best mysterious and, at worst, unreal. In other words, in this objection there seems to be an implicit commitment to *naturalism*—the view that only physical things exist. The naturalist is typically skeptical about the existence of abstract objects like facts, numbers, properties, and the like. In chapter four we will examine the question of whether or not abstract entities exist. Suffice it to say here that the correspondence theorist may be able to defend the existence of abstract objects like facts and thus rebut the objection.

The opponent of the correspondence theory may grant, however, that facts exist but argue that the correspondence theory would also seem to commit us to the existence not just of facts *per se*, but of peculiar kinds of facts. For instance, consider these statements:

(1) Either my wife loves me or I will be miserable.
(2) If this book doesn't sell a lot of copies, then Cowan and Spiegel have wasted their time writing it.

Statement (1) is a disjunctive (either-or) statement, and statement (2) is a conditional (if-then) statement. Although it seems to make sense to think that these statements can be true or false, some philosophers find it puzzling to think that there are such things as disjunctive and conditional facts. That is, maybe it makes sense to say that "it is a fact that my wife loves me" or that "Spiegel and Cowan have wasted their time writing this book"—what philosophers call "atomic facts." Yet, isn't it bizarre to think that there are nonatomic facts like (1) and (2)? On the other hand, other philosophers do not find such facts puzzling at all. As Richard Kirkham has put it, "Surely it is not incorrect English . . . for an ordinary person to say 'It is a fact that either the train gets here on time or I shall be late' or 'It is a fact that if the price of corn does not rise, then I shall go broke.'"[11] The reason some philosophers balk at such "funny facts" may be, again, an aversion to the existence of nonnatural abstract entities.

The Coherence Theory of Truth

The most widely held alternative to the correspondence theory is the coherence theory of truth. According to this view,

> *A proposition is true if and only if it coheres with the set of beliefs that a person holds.*

The first thing to note about the coherence theory of truth is that it analyzes the notion of truth without any reference to the real, external world. One does not need, on this theory, to look out into the world to determine whether a belief one holds is true. Rather, one need only look inward at her set of beliefs. Imagine a person named Pam who has the following beliefs (and imagine, if you can, that these are the *only* beliefs she has):

> The Earth revolves around the Sun.
> The Moon revolves around the Sun.
> The Moon sometimes blocks an earthling's view of the
>   Sun.

Suppose now that Pam is entertaining whether or not to accept as true the proposition that "The Moon revolves around the Earth." On the correspondence theory, Pam would have to do some scientific research (e.g., read an astronomy text, look through a telescope, etc.) in order to ascertain the truth or falsity of this proposition. However, on the coherence theory, Pam simply needs to compare this new statement with what she already believes and figure out whether or not it coheres with those other statements.

At this point, similar to concerns raised with the correspondence theory above, one may wonder exactly what is meant by the term *coherence*. There have been many attempts to specify the concept of coherence as it relates to the coherence theory of truth. The details of the various theories need not concern us here. Let us simply note that every version of the coherence theory holds that coherence means, first of all, *logical consistency*. Two or more propositions are logically consistent just in case they do not contradict each other. Secondly, coherence involves some kind of *inferential or explanatory relationship* between beliefs in the

---

[11] Ibid., 139.

system. That is, each belief in a coherent system of beliefs may be logically inferred from the others or helps to explain (or is explained by) the others. Thus understood, Pam should have no problem in affirming as true the statement that "The Moon revolves around the Earth" because it does not contradict any of her other beliefs and may provide an explanation for her belief that the Moon sometimes blocks the Sun.

However, suppose now that Pam is confronted with the claims that "The Earth moves in a straight line" and "George Washington was the first U.S. president." Pam could admit neither of these statements into her belief system. The first ("The Earth moves in a straight line") contradicts Pam's belief that the Earth revolves around the Sun. The second statement ("George Washington was the first U.S. president") does not contradict any of Pam's beliefs, but it is hard to see how it could play any kind of explanatory or inferential role with her other beliefs.

The coherence theory of truth is subject to a number of serious objections. First, it appears to entail that contradictory propositions can both be true. The reason is that it is possible for different people to have contradictory coherent systems of belief. Consider Pam's friend Sam. Sam has the following set of beliefs:

> The Sun revolves around the Earth.
> The Moon does not revolve around the Sun.
> The Moon never blocks an earthling's view of the Sun.

On the coherence theory of truth, Sam's beliefs are true because they comprise a coherent set. Notice, however, that his beliefs are logically contradictory to Pam's. So, it appears that the coherence theory of truth entails that contradictions can be true—which is absurd.

Second, for the same reasons, the coherence theory implies that truth is relative. Notice that according to the coherence theory of truth what counts as true is relative to different people's belief systems. For Pam, it is true that the Earth revolves around the Sun; but for Sam, that proposition is false. Instead, for him, it is true that the Sun revolves around the Earth. Thus, the coherence theory seems to imply relativism about truth. However, we saw in the last section that such relativism is false. This implies that the coherence theory must be rejected.

Third, the coherence theory of truth cuts the knower off from the world. As we saw in describing the coherence theory, it defines "truth" simply in terms of coherence within a set of beliefs, with no reference whatever to the world outside a person's mind. That is, whether or not "George Washington was the first U.S. president" is true has nothing to do with the way the world is (or was). Its truth is merely a matter of coherence with a person's set of beliefs. This is a problem because it seems clear to most people that truth does have something to do with the way the world is. For example, when thinking about Sam's set of beliefs above, most of the readers of this book no doubt thought, "He's mistaken. His beliefs are totally false." But why did you think that? Is it not because you know that scientific research about the *world* has shown that the Earth revolves around the Sun and because *reality* is such that the Moon does revolve around the Sun (because it revolves around the Earth) and because your *experience* tells you that there are solar eclipses? Hence, coherent or not, Sam's beliefs are simply false because they do not match up with the way the world is.

To escape this problem and the previous one, many advocates of the coherence theory of truth adopt a radical form of *antirealism* which says that there is no way the world really is. There is no world outside of the individual's mind. The world, or reality, is a mental construct and there can be as many "realities" as there are minds. This kind of antirealism, though popular in postmodern culture, also suffers from serious objections. For one thing, if there is no one way that the world really is apart from my mental construction of it, then what about *other* minds? The existence of other minds and other people would turn out to be simply the mental constructs of my own mind! This means, presumably, that other minds are actually fictitious. Therefore, antirealism seems to imply a radical *solipsism* (the view that only I exist).

Worse still, antirealism (like its cousin, relativism) is self-defeating. To see this, consider the fact that, according to antirealism, reality (all of it!) is a construct of my own mind. But, this means that my own mind is a construct of my own mind because, presumably, my mind is part of "reality." Yet, this is clearly absurd. For my own mind to be the construct of my own mind, it would have to be both objectively real (i.e., not a fictitious mental construct) and not objectively real at the same time.

Because of problems like these, most philosophers reject the coherence theory of truth and adopt some version of the correspondence theory despite whatever difficulties it may have. Before we conclude in favor of the correspondence theory, however, we must examine one other theory of truth.

The Pragmatic Theory of Truth

In the nineteenth century, philosophers Charles S. Peirce, William James, and others founded a school of philosophy known as *pragmatism*. Central to this school of thought was a pragmatic theory of truth. According to the pragmatic theory, *truth is what works*. Various members of the pragmatic school developed the details of their theory of truth differently. For example, Peirce defined truth in accordance with the consensus of opinion reached on a particular matter by truth-seekers. He said, "The opinion which is fated to be ultimately agreed to by all who investigate is what we mean by truth."[12] James claimed that those statements "are true which guide us to beneficial interaction with sensible particulars,"[13] and that "the possession of true thoughts means everywhere the possession of invaluable instruments of action."[14] For him, truth was a matter of having beliefs that effectively guided one's actions. The contemporary pragmatist, Richard Rorty, claims that "truth is what our peers will . . . let us get away with saying."[15]

Laying aside these variations, what all pragmatic theories of truth have in common is the idea that truth is to be defined in terms of usefulness in achieving one's goals. That is, the pragmatic theory of truth asserts that

> *A proposition is true if and only if it is useful to the believer in achieving desirable results.*

It is important to point out that most pragmatists understand "usefulness" as *long-term* usefulness. A belief that is useful for accomplishing short-term projects but leads ultimately to undesirable consequences would not be considered true by most pragmatists.

To illustrate the pragmatic theory, suppose that Babe Ruth believed that he was the best baseball player who ever lived. And let us suppose that it was his believing this that caused him to be such a great hitter over the course of his career. That is, if he had not believed that he was the best baseball player, he would not have done so well overall. According to pragmatism, Babe Ruth's belief was true because it worked for him; it resulted in his success as a baseball player. On the other hand, suppose an individual, Jeff, has had the belief for some time that the Oakland Raiders are the best professional football team. This belief, however, has not proven very useful for Jeff. For one thing, since he doesn't really watch a lot of football anyway, this belief has almost no impact on his daily life—it contributes to none of his life goals. Moreover, on the few occasions each year when he actually watches the Raiders play, it causes him frustration and disappointment. So, since his belief that the Raid-

---

[12] See Charles S. Peirce, *Collected Papers of Charles Sanders Peirce* (Cambridge, MA: Harvard University Press, 1931–1958), 5:407 (cf. also 5:565).

[13] William James, *The Meaning of Truth* (Cambridge, MA: Harvard University Press, 1909), 51.

[14] William James, *Pragmatism* (Cambridge, MA: Harvard University Press, 1907), 97.

[15] Richard Rorty, *Philosophy and the Mirror of Nature* (Princeton, NJ: Princeton University Press, 1979), 176.

ers are the best pro football team is not useful, it is false according to pragmatism.

Pragmatism certainly has a valuable insight into the nature of truth. Experience tells us that true beliefs do tend to be useful in various ways and false beliefs are often harmful. This partly explains why we value the pursuit of truth. However, there are serious problems with defining truth in terms of usefulness. First, it seems counterintuitive to think that truth is defined simply as what works or is useful. The reason is that on some occasions true beliefs might not turn out to be useful, and false beliefs sometimes can be useful. For example, we think that the Ptolemaic view of the solar system—that the Sun and stars revolve around the Earth—is false. However, that view proved very useful for hundreds of years in helping sailors navigate the seas and allowing astronomers to predict eclipses, and so forth. We also happen to think that it is true that penguins live in Antarctica, yet for the vast majority of people this belief is of no practical benefit.

More serious is the charge that the pragmatic theory of truth is self-defeating. The question before us is whether or not the pragmatic theory of truth is true. If it is true, then it must be useful to believe it. But apparently, most philosophers and scientists have not found the pragmatic theory of truth to be useful. Instead, they have held to the correspondence theory of truth, apparently finding it more useful to the practice of philosophy and science to reject the pragmatic theory. And even those who adopt the pragmatic theory could conceivably find that it is not useful to do so in the long run. What if adopting the pragmatic theory of truth prevented scientists from exploring scientific theories that, in the short-term, offered no practical benefits but would have done so in the long-term if they had been pursued? Though speculative, this possibility is certainly plausible. So, on its own criterion, there is reason to think that the pragmatic theory of truth is not practical and therefore refutes itself.

Thirdly, the pragmatic theory of truth implies relativism.[16] Again, suppose that Babe Ruth believes that he is the best-ever baseball player and that this belief proves very useful to him. Thus, according to the pragmatic theory, Ruth's belief is true. But, suppose as well that Lou Gehrig believes that *he* is the best baseball player ever and his belief also results in his having an outstanding baseball career. This would mean, according to the pragmatic theory, that Gehrig's belief is as true as Ruth's! And Gehrig's belief about himself, of course, entails that Ruth is *not* the best baseball player. So, depending upon which person's belief we are considering, Babe Ruth both is and is not the best baseball player

[16] The following example is a variant of one offered by L. Kirkham, *Theories of Truth*, 96–97.

ever. The pragmatic theory commits us, then, to the view that truth is relative because truth depends simply upon what beliefs an individual finds personally useful. But we have seen that relativism is false. Therefore, the pragmatic theory of truth must be false.

Conclusion

We have examined the three most prominent theories of truth in the history of philosophy: the correspondence theory, the coherence theory, and the pragmatic theory. We have seen that the latter two suffer from significant problems, most notably that they imply that truth is relative—something that we showed to be logically impossible. Despite whatever problems it may have, the correspondence theory is far more plausible than its alternatives. Throughout the rest of this book, therefore, we will assume that the correspondence theory is the correct account of truth.

This conclusion has important implications for the Christian faith. In our introduction, we made the claim that philosophy is the handmaid of theology. In the present context, this means that philosophy assists theology in clarifying the nature of theological truth-claims. Christians believe that Christianity is *true*. Likewise, we believe that the teachings of the Bible are true. But what do we mean by such assertions? Our defense of the correspondence theory of truth suggests a clear answer. To say that Christianity is true is to say that the Christian worldview corresponds to reality. To say that what the Bible teaches is true means that the propositions asserted by the biblical authors match the way things really are.[17]

---

[17] This is not to deny that there are other aspects or dimensions of truth besides correspondence with reality. It is simply to say that the primary meaning of the concept of truth has to do with the correspondence of a proposition to reality—what is sometimes called *propositional truth*. Many postmodern writers, who deny a correspondence view of truth, often claim that truth is not about propositions and facts. Rather, truth is *personal*. They attempt to explain what they mean by quoting Jesus' statement in John 14:6: "I am the way, the *truth*, and the life." In this text, Jesus claims to be "the truth." So, according to this view, truth is personal; it is not about correspondence to reality, but about relationships. However, it is highly unlikely that this postmodern interpretation of Jesus' statement is correct, and just as unlikely that Jesus undermines the correspondence theory of truth. In the same chapter, just a few verses later (v. 17), Jesus speaks about sending "the Spirit of truth." Now if truth is Jesus, who is this Spirit of truth? And notice that the job of this Spirit of truth is to teach the disciples what Jesus had earlier taught (v. 26) and to reveal to them yet further spiritual truths (16:12–13). Obviously, Jesus is speaking here of *propositional* truth. So, when Jesus calls Himself "the truth," this is simply a figure of speech meaning that He embodies truth; or He is the perfect example of the truth; that one may find the truth if one follows Him. For more on this, read the article by Greg Koukl, "Jesus, Propositions, and the True Message of the Gospel" (http://www.str.org/site/News2?page=NewsArticle&id=6869).

This provides both confidence and a potential challenge to Christian faith. On the one hand, our belief that Christianity (and the Bible) is true should give us confidence that what we believe will be consistent with everything else we discover about the world. As some Christian writers have put it, "All truth is God's truth." So whatever truth the scientist discovers by looking through his telescope, or whatever truth the historian uncovers in his research, will fit comfortably with the truths revealed in Scripture.

On the other hand, the correspondence theory of truth (with its concomitant rejection of relativism) challenges us to be prepared to defend what we believe (cp. 1 Pet 3:15). Sometimes scientists and historians (and others) make claims based on their research that seem to conflict with the Christian worldview. When this happens, there are two possibilities that the Christian faces. One possibility is that the scientist or historian who contradicts Christian belief is right and the Christian has got it wrong. A commitment to truth as correspondence requires that Christians not retreat into blind faith but seriously consider the possibility that we may need to adjust at least some of our beliefs. Of course, the other possibility is that the scientist or historian has made a mistake and that the Christian has got it right. This possibility challenges the Christian to work hard to point out the other's errors and to vindicate Christian truth-claims. Throughout the rest of this book, where appropriate, we will help the reader to do just that.

Questions for Reflection

1. Many people embrace relativism about truth because they believe that those who claim to have the absolute truth are arrogant and/or intolerant of those who hold different views. Is it necessarily true that claiming to have the truth is arrogant or intolerant? Why or why not?

2. Does rejecting relativism about truth mean that we can always know what the truth is on a given topic? Why or why not? If not, what attitude should we have toward those who disagree with us on difficult questions?

3. Consider the three theories of truth discussed above. What implications might each theory have for defending the truth of the Christian faith and the authority of the Bible?

4. We have argued that the coherence and pragmatic theories of truth lead to relativism. Can you think of any way that these theories can escape this objection?

For Further Reading

On Logic

Geisler, Norman L., and Ronald M. Brooks. *Come Let Us Reason: An Introduction to Logical Thinking.* Grand Rapids: Baker, 1990.

Hurley, Patrick. *A Concise Introduction to Logic.* 9th ed. Belmont, CA: Wadsworth, 2006.

Lee, Steven P. *What Is the Argument? Critical Thinking in the Real World.* New York: McGraw-Hill, 2002.

On Truth

Blanshard, Brand, *The Nature of Thought.* Vol. 2. New York: MacMillan, 1941.

Copan, Paul. *Is Everything Really Relative? Examining the Assumptions of Relativism and the Culture of Truth Decay.* Norcross, GA: Ravi Zacharias International Ministries, 1999.

Groothuis, Douglas. *Truth Decay: Defending Christianity Against the Challenges of Postmodernism.* Downers Grove, IL: InterVarsity, 2000.

James, William. *The Meaning of Truth.* Harvard University Press, 1909.

Kirkham, Richard. *Theories of Truth: A Critical Introduction.* MIT Press, 2001.

Tarski, Alfred. "The Semantic Conception of Truth," *Philosophy and Phenomenological Research* 4 (1944): 341–76.

Chapter Two

EPISTEMOLOGY: HOW DO WE KNOW?

*"It requires a very unusual mind to
make an analysis of the obvious."*

—Alfred North Whitehead

Glossary Terms

A posteriori knowledge	*Foundationalism*
A priori knowledge	*Internalism*
Basic belief	*Justification*
Belief	*Knowledge*
Coherentism	*Nonbasic belief*
Contextualism	*Rationalism*
Doxastic voluntarism	*Reliabilism*
Empiricism	*Skepticism*
Epistemology	*Solipsism*
Externalism	*Virtue epistemology*

The movie *The Matrix* tells the science fiction story of a future time in which most human beings are slaves to an intelligent supercomputer. The interesting thing is that none of them know it. The computer and its mechanized civilization use humans as a power source, making them live in vats of chemicals "plugged in" to a power grid. To control them the computer connects their minds to "the matrix," a sophisticated virtual reality in which people interact with one another in what appears to be the normal way. Essentially, they are trapped in a vivid, computer-generated dream world. No one in the matrix knows that the colors, smells, sounds, tastes, and tactile sensations they experience are illusions.

No one knows, that is, until someone from the outside—someone who is not trapped in the matrix—breaks in and reveals the truth. Morpheus is such an "outsider." When he meets Neo, the movie's main protagonist, he asks, "Have you ever had a dream, Neo, that you were so sure was real? What if you were unable to wake from that dream? How would you know the difference between the dream world and the real world?" Morpheus eventually reveals to Neo that he is in fact in a "dream world" and helps him to escape the clutches of the supercomputer. Once freed, he is able to see reality as it actually is. He is able to know the truth.

The writers of *The Matrix* have obviously reflected on some of the most interesting and timeless philosophical issues. The questions that Morpheus asks Neo are questions that we could ask ourselves, and many people in history have posed them. How do I know that I am not in a dream world right now? How do I know whether or not all of my experience is simply an illusion? Is there a way to know? Do I have any knowledge at all? If I do have knowledge, how much can I have? What kinds of things can I know? How do I know them? And are there some things I can *never* know?

Epistemology is a branch of philosophy that is concerned with the nature and scope of knowledge and the justification of beliefs. It seeks to answer the kinds of questions we just raised. Yet these questions are not simply a foil for fun adventure stories. They have real, practical significance. For example, suppose that your physician has diagnosed you with a deadly form of cancer, and he tells you that you can be cured if you adopt a strict regimen of diet and exercise. In such a situation, you hope that your doctor knows what he is talking about. What he knows *matters*. Likewise, consider the following scenario envisioned by philosopher W. K. Clifford:

> A shipowner was about to send to sea an emigrant-ship. He knew that she was old, and not over-well built at the first; that she had seen many seas and climes, and often had needed repairs. Doubts had been suggested to him that possibly she was not seaworthy. These doubts preyed upon his mind, and made him unhappy; he thought that perhaps he ought to have her thoroughly overhauled and refitted, even though this should put him to great expense. Before the ship sailed, however, he succeeded in overcoming these melancholy reflections. He said to himself that she had gone safely through so many voyages and weathered so many storms that it was idle to suppose that she would not come safely home from this trip also. . . . In such ways he acquired a sincere and comfortable conviction that his vessel was thoroughly safe and seaworthy; he watched her departure with a light heart . . . and he got his insurance-money when she went down in mid-ocean and told no tales.[1]

This story shows us that what we believe has ethical implications. We use or misuse our knowledge in such a way that other people are affected. So what we believe is profoundly important, as is the issue as to whether or not we have knowledge. In this chapter, then, we will explore the topic of epistemology and specifically consider the following questions:

- Can we know?
- What is knowledge?
- How are our beliefs justified?

[1] W. K. Clifford, "The Ethics of Belief," in *Lectures and Essays* (London: MacMillan, 1879).

§ 2.1 Can We Know?

In the previous chapter, we saw that there is such a thing as objective truth. Yet, this fact does not tell us whether we can discover any or much of that truth. It is one thing to know that the truth "is out there," but another thing entirely to know what the truth is. Of course, we often take it for granted that we know certain things. In this section, however, we will consider a challenge that may be raised to our claim to know.

2.1.1 The Skeptical Challenge

Consider the following list of beliefs that I ordinarily think that I know:

> There is an oak tree outside my study window.
> I had pancakes for breakfast this morning.
> I own a TV set.
> LeBron James is a professional basketball player.

Most people in the world believe similar things and never entertain any serious doubts about them. Yet, some philosophers challenge our claims to know these things. These philosophers are called skeptics. *Skepticism* is the view that we have no knowledge or (less radically) that our knowledge is very limited. Someone inclined toward skepticism could raise challenges to every one of my beliefs listed above. For example, he might ask me how I know that there is an oak tree outside my study window. Suppose I reply that I know it because I saw it when I peeked through the blinds yesterday. The skeptic will not be satisfied. He may ask something like, "How do you know that someone did not come along and chop the tree down last night while you were sleeping?" Or, he might say, "How do you even know that the tree you saw yesterday was a real tree? Maybe it was a papier-mâché replica of a tree that you saw."

The skeptic may challenge my belief that I had pancakes for breakfast as well. He can remind me, for instance, that my memory has proven faulty in the past. "How do you know that it is reliable now? In fact, how can you ever be sure that your memory is accurate? Perhaps you popped into existence five minutes ago with a store of false memories already 'hardwired' into your brain."

None of my other beliefs listed above will fare any better in the hands of the skeptic. In each case, he can simply ask me once again, "How do you know?" And he can always come up with some scenario that raises a possibility that I cannot rule out and that calls the belief into doubt. Actually, though, the skeptic need not tackle all of my beliefs in a piecemeal fashion. He could challenge all of the beliefs I have listed in one fell swoop. French philosopher and mathematician René Descartes (1596–1650) cast doubt on almost all of his prior beliefs when he entertained the possibility that he was being systematically deceived by an evil genius. Descartes surmised that all of the things that he saw, heard, smelled, tasted, and felt could be fed directly into his mind by this evil genius so that nothing in his experience would be real. Descartes' "evil genius" scenario is very much like the scenario described in *The Matrix*. Indeed, the idea of the computer matrix is simply a contemporary twist on Descartes' story. How do we know that we are not in the matrix right now? How do we know if any of the ordinary beliefs that we have are actually true rather than illusions created by the supercomputer? If I *am* in the matrix, then all of the beliefs that I listed above are dubious.

Take any scenario like Descartes' evil genius story or the matrix scenario that calls into doubt all or most of the ordinary beliefs that we typically take for granted and that we cannot seem to rule out. Let us call any such story a *skeptical hypothesis*. The skeptic puts forward such skeptical hypotheses as genuine possibilities that I cannot rule out. It is *possible* that I am being systematically deceived by an evil genius, and it is *possible* that I am in the matrix, and I apparently have no way to show that these possibilities are false. From here Descartes argues that we cannot claim to know any of the beliefs that are called into question by the skeptical hypothesis. This is what we will call the "skeptical challenge." Let us express this challenge as a formal argument (where the letter p stands for any proposition that the skeptical hypothesis calls into question such as those listed above):

(1) If there is a skeptical hypothesis for some belief p of mine, then I do not know p.
(2) There is a skeptical hypothesis for p.
(3) Therefore, I do not know p.

Is there a good response to the skeptical challenge? If there is, it will involve showing that at least one of the premises of this argument is false (or at least questionable). Historically, there have been two broad approaches to meeting the skeptical challenge, both of which attempt, in different ways, to call premise (2) of the argument into question. We will look at each of these in what follows.

Before we do that, however, we should mention that the Christian ought to have a particular interest in this question. Christianity is a *knowledge tradition*—meaning that Christians have historically claimed that our faith is objectively true and that its major doctrines can be known. Moreover, in the Bible the term *know* appears more than 1,300 times. Some of these uses are figurative as when we are told that "Adam knew his wife and she conceived" (Gen 4:1). But many times the word *know* is used to refer to our intellectual grasp of factual truths—truths about the world, about ourselves, and about God. Consider, for example, that the book of Proverbs was given to us by God so that we could "*know* wisdom" (Prov 1:2), and Paul insists that no human being has an excuse for not worshipping God because "what can be *known* about God is plain to them, because God has shown it to them" (Rom 1:19). So the Bible teaches us that knowledge is possible, even knowledge of important religious matters. The skeptical challenge calls into question this vital Christian belief. Therefore, it merits our attention all the more. And this is one specific place where philosophy can prove its worth as the handmaid to theology. As we will see, the skeptical challenge can be met.

2.1.2 The Rationalist Response

One response to the skeptical challenge is *rationalism*, the view that all knowledge ultimately comes through reason. Rationalists typically distrust our senses and believe that gaining knowledge is a matter of logically deducing true propositions from absolutely certain starting axioms. The foundational axioms are said to be known immediately or intuitively without the need of sensory experience or deductive inference. Such knowledge is called *a priori* knowledge (as opposed to *a posteriori* knowledge which is known on the basis of experience). Early rationalists often referred to such *a priori* knowledge as "innate ideas"—ideas that are somehow ingrained in the minds of all people regardless of their individual experiences.

The paradigm example of a rationalist is Descartes. He is well-known for his procedure of *methodological doubt* by which he doubted everything that could be doubted. He did this in order to discover some truth that could *not* be doubted and upon which he could build a system of knowledge. And this is where his "evil genius" hypothesis came in. Descartes thought that it was possible that everything he currently experienced—all that he saw, heard, smelled, touched, and tasted—as well as everything that he had previously experienced, could be the result of the deceptive activity of an evil genius. So Descartes concluded that he could not (at least initially) trust the deliverances of his senses. And since his senses could not be relied upon to give him accurate information about the world, sensory experience cannot be the ultimate source of human knowledge.

Despite this conclusion, Descartes thought that we can have real knowledge. He was not a skeptic. In fact, he thought that we can even know the things we learn from sensory experience—we just cannot know those things *because* we experience them. How can we know, then? Descartes believed that we gain knowledge through the use of reason or intellect. To show this, he had to prove that there are some beliefs that cannot be doubted under any circumstances.

The first indubitable truth that Descartes discovered was the truth of his own existence. Here is how he described this discovery:

> I have persuaded myself that there is nothing at all in the world: no heaven, no earth, no minds, no bodies. Is it not then true that I do not exist? But certainly I should exist, if I were to persuade myself of something. But there is a deceiver (I know not who he is) powerful and sly in the highest degree, who is always purposely deceiving me. Then there is no doubt that I exist, if he deceives me. And deceive me as he will, he can never bring it about that I am nothing so long as I shall think that I am something. Thus it must be granted that, after weighing carefully and sufficiently everything, one must come to the considered judgment that the statement "I am, I exist" is necessarily true every time it is uttered by me or conceived in my mind.[2]

Descartes is the one who coined the famous phrase, *cogito ergo sum*—"I think; therefore I am." The idea is that I cannot be deceived unless I exist. The evil genius, if he exists, cannot deceive me if I do not exist to be deceived. Therefore, I must exist.

From this point, Descartes argues that we can rule out the skeptical hypothesis of the evil genius and have knowledge of the world of external, material objects. In order to reach this conclusion, however, he believes that we first must establish some other propositions, which in turn give us grounds for believing in the existence of material objects:

(1) I have an idea of an absolutely perfect being (i.e., God).
(2) Only an absolutely perfect being could be the cause of my idea of it.
(3) Therefore, God exists.
(4) God, by definition, is not a deceiver.
(5) God is the cause of all my cognitive faculties (e.g., my abilities to reason and sense things).
(6) Since God is not a deceiver, He would not give me cognitive faculties that are unreliable.
(7) My senses give me ideas of (alleged) material objects.
(8) Therefore, material objects exist.

[2] René Descartes, *Meditations on First Philosophy*, trans. Donald A. Cress (Indianapolis: Hackett, 1979), 17.

Descartes' argument has been challenged at numerous points. We will not survey all of the possible problems that have been raised. We will simply focus on the one that seems most decisive to the majority of critics, namely, the fact that *his argument seems to be circular*. Notice that for Descartes to reach the conclusion that material objects exist, he has to ward off the possibility that he is being systematically deceived by the evil genius. In order to do this, he first has to prove that his cognitive faculties are reliable (step 6). But before he does that he has to prove that God exists (steps 1–3) and that He is not a deceiver (step 4). But Descartes' argument for God's existence and goodness makes great use of his cognitive faculties *before* he establishes that they are trustworthy. In other words, steps 1–4 of the argument seem to already assume what Descartes is trying to prove in step 6. This means that Descartes' argument is circular. This problem of circularity, which generally tends to plague rationalist responses to skepticism, is called the "Cartesian circle."

2.1.3 The Empiricist Response

Whereas the rationalist says that knowledge is gained primarily via reason rather than experience, *empiricism* takes the opposite approach and says that all knowledge arises from experience. The empiricist rejects the rationalist belief that some ideas are innate or knowable apart from experience.

John Locke (1632–1704) was an early modern empiricist. He believed that experience came in two varieties: sensation and reflection. *Sensation* is that aspect of experience in which we have immediate sensory encounters with physical objects by seeing, hearing, touching, smelling, or tasting. In the process of sensation, the mind (which at birth is a *tabula rasa*—blank slate) acquires ideas of various kinds—ideas of colors, shapes, sounds, textures, and the like. According to Locke and other empiricists, all of our ideas are ultimately derived from sensation.

Of course, someone may point out that we have ideas of many things that we have never experienced. For example, I have an idea of a golden mountain. Yet, I have never seen a golden mountain. How, then, does Locke account for this idea? This is where reflection comes in. *Reflection* is what we do with ideas after we acquire them through sensation. By reflection we are able to combine ideas acquired from sensation and come up with ideas of things that we have never actually experienced— like golden mountains. Reflection never gives us any ideas except those which trace back to experience, such as our sensations of gold and sensations of mountains. But via reflection we may combine these ideas in unique and interesting ways.

Another important aspect of Locke's empiricism is his *representational theory of perception* (see figure 2.1). Most philosophers of Locke's day, including Descartes, believed that we do not directly perceive the external world (i.e., the world external to our minds that contains tables, chairs, cats, dogs, other people, etc.). What we actually perceive are mental images or ideas that are presumably caused by external objects. For example, when I see a tree, I am not seeing something that exists outside my mind. What I am "seeing" is a mental representation of a tree which is caused by the real, external tree. But, I have no direct perceptual access to the real tree.

Figure 2.1

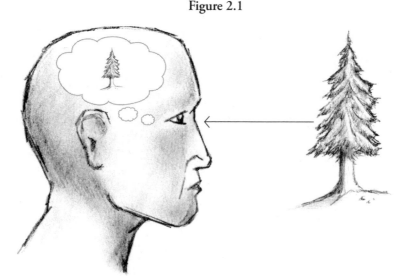

One reason that Locke and others were led to this view is the commonsense distinction we make between appearance and reality. Have you ever made one of those cute vacation photos where a person standing in the foreground puts his hands on either side of a tall building in the background to make it look like he is a giant trying to squash the building? Or better, have you ever held your hand up beside a tall building that is far away so that your hand appears to be the same size as the building? You know in both cases that the building is really very large. Yet, if you think about it, you will have to admit that what you actually *see* when you observe the building in these cases is relatively small. One explanation for this phenomenon is that what you actually see is small because what you see is not the building at all, but a mental image of the building. Another way of putting this is that, according to Locke's representational theory of perception, all of the things that we perceive actually exist only in our minds. They are ideas *caused* by things in the external world. This view may seem more plausible if you consider again the movie *The Matrix*. The characters in the movie had exactly the same experiences whether they were in the virtual reality matrix or not. But while in the matrix everything they perceived was in their minds. Locke's view is that our perceptual experiences are just like being in the matrix, except that the things we perceive in this matrix are being caused by similar, material things outside our minds.[3]

Needless to say, Locke had to admit that sensation—from which we get our ideas of particular things external to our minds such as tables and chairs and cats and dogs—can never provide us with absolute certainty, but only various degrees of probability. Reflection, which has to do only with the contents of our minds, can give us quite a bit of certainty (after all, it doesn't seem that I can be mistaken that my idea of red is different than my idea of white or that 2+2=4). But our senses sometimes err. Moreover, Locke had read Descartes and he knew that it was at least possible that one could be dreaming at any time one seems to perceive external objects. So since all we ever directly perceive are mental representations, there is no way to be absolutely certain that our sensory experiences are reliable indicators of the truth about the world.

Yet Locke did not think that this lack of certainty was cause for great concern. He wrote,

> [I]f after all this any one will be so skeptical, as to distrust his senses, and to affirm that all we see and hear, feel and taste, think and do, during our whole being, is but the series and deluding appearances of a long dream . . . and therefore will question the existence of all things . . . I make him this answer, that the certainty of things existing in *rerum natura* [the nature of things], when we have the testimony of our senses for it, is not only as great as our frame can attain to, but as our condition needs.[4]

We may not have certainty that our senses give us knowledge of an external world, says Locke, but we do not need certainty for our practical purposes in this world. The probability our senses give us is sufficient for everyday life.

Like rationalism, Locke's empiricism has been subjected to serious criticism. Whatever merits his view may have in explaining how humans

---

[3] We owe this helpful point to Thomas Senor.
[4] John Locke, *An Essay Concerning Human Understanding*, IV.11.8.

acquire knowledge, there are several potential problems when considering his view as a solution to the challenge of skepticism. Keep in mind that empiricism (at least as it was presented by Locke and other early empiricists) seeks to refute the skeptic, just as the rationalist does, by showing *how* we know what we claim to know. But this immediately opens the door to a strong skeptical challenge. As we have noted, Locke believed that the ideas that we directly perceive are representations of external objects. So, for example, the mental image of a tree that I "see" is supposedly caused by a real, physical tree that I *don't* actually see. But, why should we think that? How do we know that my visual sensation of a tree is caused by a tree?

Locke thought that one reason to think that tree ideas are caused by trees is the fact that I am passive during sensation. I open my eyes and I see things like trees whether I want to or not. But this reason is unlikely to convince the skeptic. He can reply to Locke by admitting that the passivity of sensation gives some reason to think that ideas of trees come from a source outside my mind. However, why must that source resemble the idea? Why must tree ideas be caused by trees rather than, say, Descartes' evil genius?

Another famous empiricist, David Hume (1711–1776), actually *used* empiricism to support skepticism.[5] Like Locke, Hume thought that all of our ideas are ultimately traceable to what he called sensory impressions. An impression is what we immediately experience in sensation—the experience one has when he is presently seeing, hearing, and so forth. Also, like Locke, Hume thought that we could have a high degree of certainty about truths of reason (which Hume called "relations of ideas"). However, truths of reason do not get us out of our minds to the "real" world.

Taking the empiricist principle (that knowledge arises only from what we experience) very strictly, Hume concluded that we really have no significant knowledge of the extra-mental world at all. For Hume, nothing is knowable unless one can have an impression of it. Locke believed that our ideas of trees were caused by trees, for example. Hume pointed out that (on empiricist principles) we really have no experience of trees. All we experience are mental impressions that we take to be representations of trees. But, again, how can we know that tree ideas are caused by trees? How can I even know if there are such things as trees outside of my mind?

More radical still, Hume questioned Locke's belief in causality itself. Not only did Locke believe that there are external material objects that lie behind our perceptual experience; he also believed, as we have noted, that those external objects *cause* our perceptions. Hume, however,

[5] See David Hume, *Enquiry Concerning Human Understanding*, II–V.

pointed out that we have never actually observed causation—that is, a "necessary connection" between events in our experience. Take the game of billiards for example. Suppose you strike the cue ball with the cue and it rolls across the table to impact the eight ball. Immediately upon impact, the eight-ball also moves. Naturally, we are inclined to say that the cue ball *caused* the eight ball to move. But how can we know this? Consider that in this example, all we actually observe are two distinct events: (A) the cue ball's collision with the eight ball and (B) the eight-ball's subsequent motion (see figure 2.2). According to Hume, we cannot know that (A) caused (B) unless we can also observe or otherwise discover a "necessary connection" between these events. We certainly don't *observe* a necessary connection. As we have seen, all we observe are events (A) and (B).

Figure 2.2

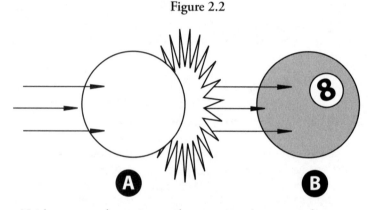

Neither can we know it somehow *a priori* (i.e., apart from experience). To prove this, Hume asks us to imagine that we have just come into the world and have never seen solid objects colliding before. If we were asked what would happen if the cue ball were to collide with the eight ball, could we know with certainty that the eight-ball motion would be the consequence? Hume says no. From the standpoint of reason alone, we could just as well conceive the eight ball remaining motionless and the cue ball bouncing off, or the eight ball going up instead of horizontally, or changing into a bouquet of flowers, or an infinite number of other possibilities.

But, of course, we have not just come into the world, and we have seen events like (A) followed immediately by events like (B) many times. Why can't we say that we know that (A) caused (B) based on past experience? Well, says Hume, past experience is all well and good, but it cannot establish a *necessary* causal connection between events like (A) and (B). Why not? Because we have no reason to think that the future will be like the past. Up to this point the world has seemed to work in a certain way such that (A)-type events are always followed by (B)-type events. But, tomorrow all that could change. Maybe God will fiddle with the laws of nature while we sleep tonight and when we wake up (A)-type events will no longer cause (B)-type events.

The upshot of Hume's critique is that we can know nothing beyond what we have had direct impressions of and the logical relations between ideas produced by those impressions. This means that we can have no *metaphysical* knowledge, no knowledge of reality beyond our immediate, personal experience. The implications of Hume's empiricism are profound. It is not just the existence of material objects and causal relations that are called into question. Since we have no sensory impressions of God, and neither can we infer God's existence through causal reasoning based on things we have experienced, God is unknowable. Since we have no impressions of things like "wrongness" or "rightness," but only subjective feelings about actions that people perform, we cannot know absolute moral truths. Since I have no impression of other minds, I cannot know that other people exist. Since I have no impression of a "self" or "soul," but only impressions of internal feelings and images, I cannot even know that *I* exist.

Hume is widely regarded by philosophers as having taken empiricism to its logical conclusion—a radical form of skepticism. Not everyone agrees with this conclusion, of course, but it is not easy to see where Hume goes wrong if one starts with empiricist premises.

Where does this leave us? We have seen that the two major historical strategies for meeting the skeptical challenge have significant flaws. The Cartesian rationalist seems caught in a circle unable to prove that one's cognitive faculties are reliable without assuming that they are reliable. The empiricist, relying entirely on sense experience, appears to be limited in his knowledge claims to reports about what he directly and immediately perceives. For these reasons, it seems that neither approach is able to rule out the skeptical hypothesis.

Does this mean that the skeptic wins? Have we no significant knowledge after all? Not necessarily. The rationalist and empiricist responses that we have surveyed were aimed at undermining the second premise of the skeptical challenge—that there is a skeptical hypothesis for *p*. Recall, however, the first premise in the skeptical argument:

> *If there is a skeptical hypothesis for some belief* p *of mine, then I do not know* p.

The skeptic thinks that by simply raising the possibility of a skeptical hypothesis that cannot be definitively ruled out, he can undermine our knowledge of the things we ordinarily believe. The rationalists and empiricists that we have discussed seek to overcome this challenge by *refuting* the skeptic, showing that the skeptical hypotheses are *false* (or at least highly unlikely)—that we are, in fact, *not* in the matrix or being deceived by an evil genius. Unfortunately, we have seen that it is unclear whether this task can be accomplished.

Perhaps, however, what we should say is that the task of meeting the skeptical challenge cannot be accomplished *with certainty*. Why is it that the empiricist and rationalist cannot seem to refute the skeptic? It is because we cannot rule out as false or highly improbable the skeptical hypotheses. Put another way, we cannot be absolutely certain that our cognitive faculties are reliable or that we are not in the matrix, and so forth. The fact that we cannot rule out the possibility that we are in the matrix makes it less than completely certain that our cognitive faculties are trustworthy indicators of truth. And because of this apparent lack of certainty, the skeptic thinks we cannot know most of the things we ordinarily believe.

Here is where the first premise of the skeptical argument comes into play. That premise presupposes that knowledge requires absolute certainty. But does it? This is the question we turn to next.

2.1.4 Do We Need Certainty?

The skeptic believes that knowledge requires certainty. The skeptic also believes, of course, that this demand for certainty cannot be met. For this reason, the skeptic denies us the right to claim knowledge. As we have seen, refuting the skeptic by showing that skeptical hypotheses can be ruled out is very difficult, if not impossible.

However, we may not have to refute the skeptic in order to make a legitimate claim to knowledge. Perhaps all we have to do is *rebut* the skeptic. A rebuttal is different than a refutation. In a philosophical debate, one *refutes* his opponent when he proves his opponent's view to be false. Refutations can sometimes be hard to accomplish as in the present case. Alternatively, one *rebuts* his opponent when he shows that his opponent has not proven *his* view to be true. So, perhaps all that is necessary to overcome the skeptical challenge is to show that the skeptic has not proven his skepticism to be warranted—that is, that he has not proven that we do not know the things we ordinarily think we know. Such a rebuttal may be accomplished by showing that knowledge does not require certainty.

We should begin by noting that the skeptic has not given us any reason to believe that the skeptical hypotheses are true. Of course, it is *possible* that I am in the matrix, and it is probably the case that I cannot prove that I'm *not* in the matrix. But, has the skeptic given us any reason to think that we actually *are* in the matrix? Not at all. The skeptic doesn't even claim that we are in the matrix or are deceived by an evil genius. He only claims that we cannot rule it out. But why should this fact (if it is a fact) call into doubt our strongly held commonsense beliefs? The skeptic assumes that all of our beliefs are guilty until proven innocent. But why not assume, rather, that our beliefs (or at least some of them) are innocent until proven guilty? Perhaps the skeptic, rather than those who claim knowledge, should bear the burden of proof.

More directly, we can say that it is not clear that knowledge requires having absolute certainty. It is only because the skeptic assumes that certainty is necessary for knowledge that he thinks that posing his "How do you know?" question is enough to prove we have no knowledge. But it may be that the skeptic is wrong in assuming that knowledge requires certainty. If so, then we may reject premise (1) of the skeptical challenge. Just because there is a skeptical hypothesis for my belief *p* that I cannot rule out, it does not necessarily provide a reason to think I do not know *p*.

The idea that knowledge does not require certainty, for what it's worth, does happen to comport with our everyday use of the word "know." Consider the following statements:

"I know that my name is Steve Cowan."
"I know that my wife does not like liver and onions."
"I know that Barack Obama is the current U.S. president."
"I know that the South lost the American Civil War."

In everyday life, we all presume to have knowledge of such things. We claim to know our own names and would find it strange if, after stating our names to someone, he asked us, "Are you sure?" We make frequent knowledge-claims about the character traits of others, about their likes and dislikes, and even make reliable predictions of their behavior on the basis of such claims. So I claim to know that if I cooked liver and onions for my wife for dinner tonight, she would refuse to eat it (there's more for me that way, see?). No one thinks twice about using the word *know* in such a case.

Though many postmodernists would question it today, we still make many claims about the past and use the word *know* when doing so. Southerners certainly think they *know* that the South lost the Civil War! And when Jay Leno does his man-on-the-street interviews and finds far too many Americans who *don't* know who the president is, those of us with even a modicum of education cringe.

The point of all this is that we ordinarily use the word *know* in these and many similar situations. Yet, if pressed, we would have to admit that we do not have the absolute certainty that the skeptic wants about any of these things. One of two things follows from this observation. Either we do *not* know these propositions and our use of the word *know* in these cases is illegitimate, or our use of *know* is perfectly appropriate and the skeptic is using a highly technical sense of the word *know*—a sense that requires a certainty that our ordinary use of the term does not. If ordinary language is a fair guide to the appropriate use of our words, then the latter possibility is more likely correct.

This brings us back to something that John Locke said. You may recall that in his response to skepticism, he remarked that our certainty is "as great . . . as our condition needs." Even though we might like to have the absolute certainty that would satisfy the skeptic's technical sense of "know," it does not seem that the needs and requirements of everyday life demand it. Nor would the lack of that certainty appear to threaten our use of the word *know*. Here it is important to recognize that saying that a given proposition is not absolutely certain need not commit us to saying that it is totally uncertain. Certitude comes in degrees. And one degree of certainty may be adequate for some of our purposes while another degree is required for other purposes. For the sake of illustration, let us distinguish four levels of certainty that a proposition p could have and rank them with the numerals 0, 1, 2, and 3 as follows:

> 3 – Beyond all doubt
> 2 – Beyond a reasonable doubt
> 1 – More probable than not
> 0 – Equally probable and improbable

If p is as certain as level 3 (beyond all doubt), then it is *absolutely* certain. At this level, doubt about p is not possible. This level of certainty, however, is very hard to come by. Indeed, most philosophers would say that very few, if any, propositions rise to this level of certainty. Perhaps this would include the truths of mathematics, the laws of logic, and statements such as "I exist," but not much else. If one insists that certainty is required for knowledge, then only these rare propositions that reach level 3 can be said to be known.

On the other hand, if certainty is not required for knowledge (and our ordinary use of the word would indicate that it is not), then we can say we know a proposition even at some of the lower levels of certainty. For example, if a proposition rises to level 2—beyond a reasonable doubt— could we not say that we know it? Even though level 2 propositions can be doubted, those doubts would be, by definition, *unreasonable*. It is helpful to note that *this* level of certainty is used in the criminal court system, not level 3. If level 3 was required before a jury could convict an accused criminal, then no one would ever be convicted! But, juries send criminals to the gas chamber on no more than level 2 certainty. In fact, this level of certainty is often called "moral certainty" because we tend to think, at least in everyday discourse, that a person who does not believe a proposition that reaches level 2 is morally irresponsible.

Level 1 certainty is more fuzzy and itself admits of varying degrees. At this level, a proposition is more probably true than false. That is, even though there is significant evidence against a proposition's being true, the preponderance of evidence is in its favor. We should probably be reluctant to say that we *know* the proposition is true at this level. Yet, at the same time, it would seem that we have an obligation to believe it in this case. Usually it would be odd at best to say that a person is acting responsibly in refusing to believe what the greatest evidence suggests is true.[6]

What about the case in which the evidence for and against a proposition is equally weighted? This is level 0 certainty, the level at which a proposition is as probably false as true. Anyone who believes that a proposition is no more certain than this surely cannot claim to know it. All things being equal, the correct stance to take toward a proposition in this situation is to *withhold* belief about it—to neither believe nor disbelieve the proposition.[7]

The main point here, again, is that certainty comes in degrees. And though not being absolutely certain may sometimes prevent us from having knowledge, it need not always do so as long as we do not insist that knowledge requires absolute certainty.

Questions for Reflection

1. With the use of a concordance, survey the Bible and make a list of the different kinds of propositions that it says we can know. Would any of these propositions escape the skeptical challenge? Why or why not?

---

[6] This point needs to be qualified somewhat. Suppose, for example, that the proposition not-*p* has been a cherished and long-held belief, one which, if given up, would call into question many other important beliefs one has. In this case, one would not necessarily be irresponsible if he rejected *p*, at least initially. The preponderance of evidence for *p*, however, should perhaps elicit a serious investigation to try to refute or rebut the evidence for *p*. Failing that, it might *then* be correct to say that the person who rejects *p* is acting irresponsibly.

[7] Qualifications are needed here as well. The reason is that things are usually not equal. Suppose, for example, that one has a *pragmatic* reason to believe *p* such as the fact, say, that rejecting or withholding *p* would bring one great psychological discomfort or would cause one to believe contrary to the tradition of one's community, and membership in that community is very important to one. In cases like these, it may be permissible to believe *p*, though it would still be inappropriate to say that one knows *p*.

2. Besides the charge of circularity, what other objections might be made to Descartes' argument for material things? Can his argument be modified to escape any of these objections?

3. Both modern rationalists and modern empiricists believed that we do not directly perceive objects in the external world, but only mental representations. This belief was due primarily to the distinction between appearance and reality. What are some other examples of this distinction that might support their belief? What objections might be made to the representational theory of perception?

4. What response can be made to Hume's critique of causation? How, if at all, can we know causal connections between things?

5. What degree of certainty do you think is required for knowledge? Why do you think so?

§ 2.2 What Is Knowledge?

So far in this chapter we have used the term *knowledge* as if we had a pretty good grasp of what we meant by it. It turns out, however, that this word is used in more than one way in ordinary discourse. In fact, we can distinguish three specific types of knowledge picked out by our ordinary uses of the term *knowledge*. First of all, we sometimes use the term *knowledge* to refer to a skill or ability that a person has—so called "how-to" knowledge. We might say, for instance, "Derek Jeter knows baseball" or "Sally knows how to ride a bike." So used, the term *knowledge* refers to what we may call *procedural knowledge*. Another type of knowledge can be seen in statements like "Steven Spielberg knows George Lucas" and "Prince William knows what it's like to lose a loved one." The kind of knowledge mentioned in these statements is "knowledge by acquaintance" or *experiential knowledge*, whereby a person is directly acquainted with some person or object.

Epistemology is not usually concerned with procedural and experiential knowledge, however. The kind of knowledge that occupies (and has occupied) our attention in this chapter is *propositional knowledge*. Sometimes called "knowledge-that," propositional knowledge has to do with a person's knowledge that a particular proposition is true. A proposition can be defined here as the content of a statement that can be either true or false. So, for example, the following statements are about claims to propositional knowledge:

> "I know that bachelors are unmarried."
> "I know that the Earth revolves around the Sun."
> "I know that courage is a virtue."

It may still be asked, however, what exactly it means to have propositional knowledge. Though the focus of epistemologists is propositional knowledge, the precise definition of propositional knowledge is a matter of considerable debate. People believe many things. We have beliefs about ourselves, about others, about the world. We have empirical, religious, and political beliefs. But, surely, not all of our beliefs constitute knowledge. For example, I as a Christian believe that Jesus is God in the flesh, whereas my Muslim acquaintance Sammy believes that Jesus was merely a prophet and certainly not God. At most, one of us has knowledge, while the other has a false opinion. When can we say that a person actually has propositional *knowledge* and not mere opinion? This is the question we will pursue in this section.

2.2.1 The Justified True Belief Account

Going back at least as far as the ancient Greek philosopher Plato, the traditional definition of propositional knowledge is that it is *justified true belief*. Sometimes called the "traditional tripartite analysis" of knowledge, we will simply call it the *JTB Account* of knowledge (where JTB stands for "justified true belief"). Stated more formally, the JTB Account goes as follows:

> *S knows p if and only if:*
>
> *(1) S believes p,*
> *(2) p is true, and*
> *(3) S is justified in believing p.*

According to the JTB Account, in order to know *p*, all three of these conditions must be met. That is, each condition is individually necessary. Surely, in order to know something, a person must believe it. Consider, for example, someone who says, "I know that the Earth revolves around the Sun, but I don't believe it." Such a claim is nonsensical.

Likewise, it is a necessary condition for knowledge that what a person believes is true.[8] Someone cannot know a false proposition. He may *believe* something that is false, but he can't *know* it. Recall that many people in the past sincerely believed that the Earth is flat. We now know that their belief was false. Would it be correct, then, to say that the "flat-Earth believers" *knew* that the Earth was flat? Of course not. They had a sincere belief, but a false belief—and the falsehood of their belief prevented them from having genuine knowledge. (Keep in mind that

---

[8] The concept of truth employed here is the correspondence view of truth defended in chapter one.

we should distinguish between *thinking* that you know something and really knowing it.)

Having a true belief, however, is not sufficient for having knowledge. Consider the following case. John gets a fortune cookie at his neighborhood Chinese restaurant which reads: "You will soon receive a great reward." On the basis of this fortune cookie, John comes to believe that he will win the state lottery. As it happens, the next day John does indeed win the lottery. He believed he would win and his belief was true. But, did he *know* he would win the lottery? No way. A person might come to have a true belief as a result of luck or on the basis of a source known to be unreliable. In such cases, as with John, we would not say he has knowledge. Whatever knowledge is, it cannot simply be a matter of luck. Besides true belief, then, what else is required for knowledge? The answer is that a person also needs *some reason or justification for holding the belief;* some reason, that is, for thinking that the belief in question is true.

So, according to the JTB Account, a person S must have a justified true belief in order to have knowledge. Moreover, if S meets all three conditions, the JTB Account asserts that this is sufficient for S to know *p*. Nothing further is required for propositional knowledge.

However, the traditional JTB Account has been powerfully challenged in recent decades. In a now-famous three-page article published in 1963, epistemologist Edmund Gettier argued that, while justified true belief may be necessary for knowledge, it is not sufficient.[9] He provided some counterexamples involving people who apparently had a justified true belief but did not seem to have knowledge.

Here is an example similar to the ones Gettier presented. Suppose that J. Jonah Jameson, editor of the *Daily Bugle*, attends a formal ball in downtown New York. In the middle of the festivities, someone in a Spider-Man costume leaps from the balcony of the ballroom, grabs hold of the chandelier, and swings across the room to grab some draperies, and then slides to the floor to dart in and out among the guests as policemen are in hot pursuit. Jameson witnesses the whole affair and forms the belief, "Spider-Man is in the ballroom." The man in the costume is not really Spider-Man, though. He is an imposter, someone pretending to be Spider-Man for cheap thrills. Yet, as it turns out, Spider-Man's alter-ego, Peter Parker, *is* in the ballroom taking photos for the *Daily Bugle*. Now it seems clear that Jameson has a justified true belief. He believes that Spider-Man is in the ballroom. He is justified in believing this because he sees what looks like Spider-Man in the ballroom and the person he thinks is Spider-Man is behaving in an irresponsible,

---

[9] Edmund L. Gettier, "Is Justified True Belief Knowledge?" *Analysis* 23 (1963): 121–123.

menacing way as Jameson has always thought Spider-Man to behave. Moreover, since Peter Parker—alias Spider-Man—is actually present at the ball, Jameson's belief is true. Spider-Man *is* in the ballroom! So, Jameson has a justified true belief. Does he have knowledge? It would seem not. For it is mere luck or coincidence that makes Jameson's belief true—specifically the coincidence (unbeknownst to Jameson) that Peter Parker is Spider-Man.

This and similar counterexamples to the JTB Account pose what is called the *Gettier Problem*. If such "Gettier counterexamples" are correct, then knowledge cannot be mere justified true belief. In the next section we will look at some attempts to solve this problem.

2.2.2 Proposed Solutions to the Gettier Problem

The Gettier Problem threatens to undermine the traditional view that knowledge is justified true belief. And, in so doing, it opens up the whole question as to just what propositional knowledge really is. Several different ways of responding to the Gettier Problem have been proposed. We do not have space to consider all of them, but we will look at some representative accounts.

Strengthening the Justification Condition

Despite the Gettier counterexamples, some philosophers are convinced that the traditional JTB Account is correct. They believe that the alleged counterexamples are ill-conceived in that the persons in the counterexamples do not really have a justified true belief. Specifically, they lack justification. In the example given above, we said that J. Jonah Jameson was justified in believing that Spider-Man was in the ballroom. According to these defenders of the JTB Account, Jameson was not justified in so believing. Why not? Because one's justifying reasons for holding a belief, on this view, must actually entail the belief in question. In other words, an adequate justification for a belief must provide certainty. Since Jameson's seeing a man in a Spider-Man costume at the ball doesn't by itself guarantee that Spider-Man was at the ball, Jameson was not justified in believing that Spider-Man was at the ball.

There are problems with this response to the Gettier Problem, however. For one thing, it would imply that many things we think we know are not in fact known, including our memory beliefs, our belief in a mind-independent external world, our belief in other minds, and our ethical and religious beliefs. The reason is that no belief derived from these sources is absolutely certain. As we saw earlier, there are reasons to think that knowledge does not require absolute certainty. If that is right, then the solution that strengthens the justification condition so as to require absolute certainty is misguided.

Another problem for this solution is that it would imply that there is no such thing as a justified *false* belief. Yet this seems counterintuitive. For example, though there really is no Santa Claus (sorry if you're just learning this for the first time!), would we not say that young children who believe in Santa Claus on the testimony of their parents are justified in their belief? In the past, many people believed that the Earth was at the center of the universe and all of the celestial bodies revolved around the Earth. We know now that they were mistaken, but at the time they had good reasons to believe as they did. Most of us would agree that they were justified in their belief. But on the solution we are considering, you would *not* be justified in believing the Earth is round. For reasons like these, few philosophers have adopted this solution to the Gettier problem.

Adding a Fourth Condition

By far, the most popular method of attempting to solve the Gettier Problem is to add a fourth condition to the JTB Account. Several proposals have been made concerning what the fourth condition should be, none of which have received wide acceptance among philosophers. Nonetheless, we will discuss two of the most prominent of these proposals.

One proposed fourth condition for knowledge is that *a person's justification for a belief not be derived from a false belief.* Recall again the Spider-Man case. We said that Jameson was justified in believing that Spider-Man was in the ballroom. But, why? Obviously because he believed that the man in the Spider-Man costume was really Spider-Man. But that belief was false. So, although Jameson had a justified belief, that belief was obtained via a false belief. According to advocates of this solution, then, if we simply add the requirement that to have knowledge one's justified belief cannot be derived from a false belief, we will have an adequate account of propositional knowledge.

The "no-false-belief condition" does seem adequate to address the original Gettier counterexamples like the Spider-Man story sketched above. Unfortunately, there are other Gettier-type counterexamples that undermine this solution as well. Consider this counterexample:[10] Suppose that General "Thunderbolt" Ross has just witnessed Bruce Banner being bombarded by gamma rays in an underground military laboratory. Banner is transformed into the Incredible Hulk for the first time.

---

[10] The following counterexample is a variation on one presented by John Pollock, "The Gettier Problem," in *Human Knowledge: Classical and Contemporary Approaches*, 2nd ed., ed. Paul K. Moser and Arnold vander Nat (Oxford: Oxford University Press, 1995), 276–277.

Ross notices that the Hulk's skin color is green and comes to believe the proposition, "That hulking monster is green!" Of course, as all comic book fans know, the Hulk's skin *is* green. So, General Ross has a justified true belief about the Hulk's color. Moreover, his belief is not derived from any false beliefs. However, unbeknownst to Ross, the emergency lighting in the lab is also green. This means that the Hulk's skin would have appeared green to Ross even if it were not green. Therefore, it would be a mistake for us to say that General Ross *knows* that the Hulk is green. He has a justified true belief that is not acquired via any false beliefs and yet he still lacks knowledge.

The previous example provides the impetus for another proposed "fourth-condition" solution to the Gettier Problem. This proposal adds what is called a "defeasibility condition" to justified true belief. The proposal is that for *S* to know a justified true proposition P, *there must also be no true proposition Q which, if S were to come to justifiably believe Q, he would no longer be justified in believing P.* In other words, there must not be another *true* proposition which the person does not currently believe, but which, if he did believe it, would nullify his justification. For example, in the Spider-Man case, the reason Jameson fails to have knowledge (according to this solution) is that there is another *true* proposition ("The man in the costume is not really Spider-Man") which, if he came to believe it, would defeat Jameson's justification for believing that Spider-Man was in the ballroom. Likewise, if General Ross came to know that the lights in the lab were green, his justification for believing that the Hulk is green would be defeated.

Problems have been raised regarding this solution, too. It may be the case that a person can have knowledge without satisfying the defeasibility condition. If so, this would show that the defeasibility condition is not a necessary condition for knowledge. Consider the following case:[11] Suppose that Neo, the character in *The Matrix*, witnesses from a distance Mr. Smith torturing Morpheus to obtain information from him. Neo understandably forms the justified belief, "Mr. Smith tortured Morpheus today." And let us suppose that Neo's justified belief is true. However, unbeknownst to Neo, Cypher reported to Trinity that he saw Mr. Smith somewhere else at precisely the same time that Neo saw Mr. Smith and, what's more, he has learned that there is another agent who looks just like Mr. Smith who was seen in the vicinity of Morpheus today. Additionally, let's suppose that both Trinity and Neo have always believed Cypher to be a trustworthy and reliable source. Of course,

---

[11] The following counterexample is a variation on one presented by Keith Lehrer and Thomas Paxson Jr., "Knowledge: Undefeated Justified True Belief," *Journal of Philosophy* 66 (1966): 225–37.

as all *Matrix* fans know, Cypher is actually in league with Mr. Smith and we may surmise that he lied to Trinity to cover his own tracks. In this example, as stipulated by the defeasibility condition, there is a true proposition that, had Neo known it, would have undermined his justification—namely, that "Cypher reported to Trinity that he saw Mr. Smith somewhere else and Mr. Smith has a double who was seen in the vicinity of Morpheus." According to this proposed solution to the Gettier problem, the existence of this true proposition would prevent Neo from knowing that Mr. Smith tortured Morpheus. However, we have additional information that, if Neo was privy to it, would undermine his confidence in Cypher's testimony and restore his initial justification. All of this means that we are inclined to say that Neo *knows* that Mr. Smith tortured Morpheus in spite of the presence of the defeater.[12]

Of course, the defender of the defeasibility condition may point out that the reason why Neo knows that Mr. Smith tortured Morpheus despite the presence of the defeater is only because of the presence of a defeater-defeater: the true proposition that Cypher is in league with Mr. Smith. To repair this kind of problem, the defender of the defeasibility condition would simply add another condition to rule out defeater-defeaters. But, then, wouldn't he also have to add yet another condition to rule out defeater-defeater-defeaters—and so on? This kind of worry has made some philosophers think that the defeasibility condition is actually a requirement of omniscience—a requirement that no human could meet.

Replacing the Justification Condition

Some epistemologists have argued that the solution to the Gettier problem lies not in the addition of a fourth condition, but rather in the replacement of the justification condition with something else. On this approach, knowledge would not be justified true belief, but true belief plus some other factor that is truth-conducive. We will discuss the most popular version of this solution, a view called *reliabilism*.

According to reliabilism, for S to know a true belief *p*, *his true belief p must be produced by a reliable belief-forming process.* By a "reliable" process, the reliabilist usually means a process that generally (or mostly) produces true beliefs. For the reliabilist, it does not matter so much whether a person can give an adequate account of his reasons for a belief. What matters is that his beliefs be produced in a reliable way. Examples of putative reliable belief-forming processes could include vision, hear-

---

[12] For those who are unfamiliar with *The Matrix* films, Neo is the main protagonist in the story. He, Morpheus, Trinity, and Cypher are part of a team seeking to free human beings from enslavement to the matrix, though the latter turns traitor. Mr. Smith is an enemy agent.

ing, memory, testimony from trustworthy people, the scientific method, and such. Of course, these processes *per se* are not always reliable. Take vision, for example. If a person is near-sighted and tries to see at a distance, any beliefs he forms on the basis of vision will be less likely to be true. Moreover, even when a person's faculty of vision is perfectly normal, the environment he occupies can render his vision-acquired beliefs less likely to be true. Thus, if a person with normal vision is in a dark room, his vision in that circumstance is unreliable. For reasons like these, when a reliabilist speaks of a "reliable process," he usually refers to more than certain cognitive faculties and processes like vision, hearing, testimony, and so forth. The description of a reliable process will include the assumption that such faculties are being used in an appropriate environment or circumstance.

Armed with this basic conception of a reliable belief-forming process, the reliabilist has a potential solution to the Gettier Problem. In all the Gettier counterexamples, the person in question formed his belief by an unreliable process. Consider the Hulk case. Though we may assume that General Ross's eyesight was fine, his visual environment was not. Recall that the lighting in the lab was green and would have made the Hulk look green no matter what. Likewise in both the Spider-Man case and the Neo/Mr. Smith case—there were deceptive and misleading elements in the cognitive environments (i.e., the Spider-Man pretender and the lying Cypher) which rendered Jameson's and Neo's belief-forming processes unreliable.

Like all the views we have surveyed in this section, reliabilism, too, has been subject to criticism. One initial problem has to do with how to specify precisely the range or scope of a reliable belief-forming process. Known as the *generality problem*, it has to do with just how broadly or narrowly to construe a reliable process. On the one hand, we can construe a reliable process too broadly. If, for example, we simply say that vision *per se* is a reliable belief-forming process, then (as noted above) we can think of innumerable circumstances (such as the Hulk example) in which vision is clearly unreliable. Indeed, we can probably think of far more circumstances in which vision is unreliable than those in which it is reliable. One wonders, then, if vision really is reliable in the reliabilist's sense.

On the other hand, we can construe a reliable belief-forming process too narrowly as in this example: *Steve Cowan's vision at 12:00 noon on Friday, January 1, 2009, in his backyard observing a bluebird on his fence ten feet away.* We may surmise that this belief-forming process is highly reliable. We should also note that it is a process that will happen only once. As such it will not be of much help to reliabilism. The reliabilist needs a noncircular way of specifying a reliable belief-forming process that falls between these extremes. However, it is not easy to see how this can be done.

Even if the reliabilist can overcome the generality problem, another problem is that *it seems not to provide a sufficient condition for knowledge*. One may have a true belief formed by a reliable process, but still fail to have knowledge. Consider this well-known example from Laurence BonJour:

> Norman, under certain conditions which usually obtain, is a completely reliable clairvoyant with respect to certain kinds of subject matter. He possesses no evidence or reasons of any kind for or against the general possibility of such a cognitive power or for or against the thesis that he possesses it. One day Norman comes to believe that the President is in New York City, though he has no evidence either for or against this belief. In fact the belief is true and results from his clairvoyant power under circumstances in which it is completely reliable.[13]

Norman's true belief that the president is in New York City is reliably formed by his clairvoyant power (though he has no idea that he has this power—from his perspective the belief that the president is in New York City simply popped into his head). Norman meets the conditions that reliabilism sets down for knowledge, but surely Norman does *not* know that the president is in New York City. The problem, of course, is that it does not seem that Norman is *justified* in believing that the president is in New York City. This would appear to indicate that justification is, as noted earlier, a necessary condition of knowledge and that this condition cannot simply be replaced by the notion of a reliable belief-forming process.

There have been several other suggestions for solving the Gettier Problem. As the reader can no doubt see, it is a very difficult problem. Suffice it to say that there is at present no general consensus among philosophers, Christian and non-Christian alike, as to how to solve this puzzle. There is perhaps one note of reassurance. If you were able to follow the various Gettier counterexamples that have been discussed and were able to confidently say in each case, "Yes, that person has knowledge" or "No, that person does not have knowledge," then that is a pretty good indication that you and the rest of us really do have some good idea of what knowledge is even if it is difficult to define knowledge in precise terms.

---

[13] Laurence BonJour, *The Structure of Empirical Knowledge* (Cambridge, MA: Harvard University Press, 1985), 41.

2.2.3 Internalism vs. Externalism

Before we leave the question of the definition of knowledge, though, there is another important issue that must be addressed. Most of the proposed solutions to the Gettier Problem that we discussed above are versions of a broader view called *internalism*. According to the internalist, the grounds or basis for a person's justification for a belief must be internal to his mind. In other words, justification requires that a person have *cognitive access* to his justifying grounds. That is, he must be able upon mere introspection to cite why he is justified in holding the belief in question. For example, if I see a tree outside my office window and come to believe the proposition, "There is a tree outside my office window," I can refer to my perceptual experience of the tree to justify my belief. I have introspective cognitive access to my perceptual experiences, and therefore I can cite them in accordance with the internalist requirement.

The alternative to internalism is called *externalism*. For the externalist, who either dismisses the need for justification or redefines it, a person does not need cognitive access to the grounds of his belief. All that matters for a true belief to count as knowledge is that the belief be caused or formed in an appropriate way. It is irrelevant whether or not the person knows or is even able to know that his belief was formed appropriately. The justifying grounds of his belief are *external* to his mind. For example, recall the view known as reliabilism that we surveyed in the previous section. As we saw, the reliabilist contends that a person has knowledge so long as he has a true belief that is produced by a reliable process. Reliabilism is a version of externalism. Notice that nothing is stated here about the person knowing or justifiably believing that his belief-forming process actually is reliable. What matters is simply that his belief is, as a matter of fact, reliably produced—whether he knows it or not.

The debate between internalism and externalism is one of the most challenging and intense debates in contemporary philosophy, and Christians are divided on the issue themselves. We will not resolve the debate here, but we will briefly lay out some of the most significant arguments on each side.

For and Against Internalism

One argument in favor of internalism takes us back to the ethics of belief brought up in the introduction to this chapter. Recall W. K. Clifford's story of the ship owner who believed that his ship was seaworthy though he had no good reason to believe it. We said that the ship owner acted irresponsibly in believing as he did. He had a duty to refrain from believing his ship was seaworthy. Our intuitions about this and similar cases have given rise to what is called the *deontological view* of epistemic justification. According to this view, I have epistemic duties just as I have moral duties. I *ought* to believe (or at least it is permissible for me to believe) what I have good reason to believe and I *ought not* to believe something unless I have good reasons for believing it. More exactly, "A subject *S* is justified in believing that *p* provided *S* does not violate any epistemic duties."[14] The deontological view of justification entails internalism. If I ought to believe only what I have good reason to believe, then I must, if I am to fulfill my epistemic responsibilities, have cognitive access to the justifying grounds of my beliefs.

Not everyone is convinced that the deontological view is correct. For one thing, there is significant disagreement over what our epistemic obligations are. More seriously, it is argued that the deontological view requires *doxastic voluntarism*, the idea that the acquisition of beliefs is under one's control. However, as William Alston has pointed out, many of my beliefs are not under my control, but are acquired involuntarily.[15] For example, if I look out the window and see a tree, I immediately and involuntarily form the belief that there is a tree outside the window. I cannot help but form this belief. Since doxastic voluntarism seems false, there is reason to question the deontological view.

Though the deontological view of justification provides a powerful motivation toward internalism, the internalist need not base his position on that view. Another reason to favor internalism has to do with the human quest for truth. It is natural for human beings to pursue knowledge. We have a strong and incurable desire to discover the truth about a wide range of things. Moreover, having true beliefs as opposed to false beliefs serves our interests in many ways. For example, knowing the laws of physics can aid us in space exploration perhaps to discover new materials to replace diminishing resources on earth. So it is to our advantage to have true beliefs and avoid having false beliefs. But to do this we have to be able to distinguish true beliefs from false beliefs. And the only way for us to make this distinction is to have internal cognitive access to those features of a proposition that are indicative of truth and/or falsity. This fact requires that we adopt internalism because the externalist believes that the features that are conducive to the truth of a belief are external to the believer—which means that we *cannot* know if our beliefs are true or not.

---

[14] Robert Audi, *The Cambridge Dictionary of Philosophy*, 2nd ed. (Cambridge: Cambridge University Press, 1999), s.v. "epistemic deontologism," by Matthias Steup.

[15] William P. Alston, "Concepts of Epistemic Justification," in *Empirical Knowledge: Readings in Contemporary Epistemology* (Savage, MD: Rowman and Littlefield, 1986), 30–34.

The externalist will be quick to remind us, however, that a justified belief can be *false*. People in earlier ages, for instance, were justified in believing that the Sun revolved around the Earth—all their empirical observations confirmed this hypothesis. Yet, they were wrong. So, having an (internally) justified belief is not sufficient for distinguishing truth from falsehood and thus not sufficient for knowledge.

It may not be necessary either. Some philosophers raise the problem of "forgotten evidence." Suppose there is a mathematician who works out a very difficult and lengthy proof and uses his conclusion to solve other problems. Years later, he remembers his conclusion and continues to use it to solve other problems, but he has forgotten most of the steps in the proof that led to the conclusion. As Louis Pojman asks, "Isn't he still justified in his belief, even though he has forgotten how he arrived at it?"[16]—even though, that is, he has no cognitive access to the justifying grounds of his conclusion?

For and Against Externalism

A significant consideration in favor of externalism is the apparent inability of internalism to explain how children and higher animals have knowledge. Consider a young child of two years of age who sees her favorite doll on a shelf out of her reach. Upon seeing the toy she points and says, "Dolly," requesting her mother to retrieve it for her. Surely, says the externalist, the child knows the doll is on the shelf. But does she have the kind of cognitive accessibility required by internalism? Can she cite reasons for her belief? The externalist thinks not.

Of course, it is open to the internalist to respond in one of two ways. First, he can argue that the child does not in fact have knowledge (since she has no cognitive access to justifying reasons). Alternatively, the internalist can agree that the child has knowledge and argue that she does indeed have cognitive access to justifying reasons. Although she may not have the mental development to articulate her reasons, she does after all *see* the doll and it is her seeing the doll that justifies her in believing the doll is on the shelf.

Another consideration in support of externalism is the apparent failure of internalism (the traditional view for most of history) to provide solutions to the major problems of epistemology. For instance, the challenge of skepticism seems to be a predominantly internalist challenge. The skeptic asks that troubling question, "How do you know?" It is the internalist who feels constrained to give him a direct answer. The externalist, on the other hand, can skirt the challenge of skepticism by saying

---

[16] Louis P. Pojman, *What Can We Know? An Introduction to the Theory of Knowledge*, 2nd ed. (Belmont, CA: Wadsworth, 2001), 142–43.

that we have knowledge when our true beliefs are appropriately formed whether or not we know they are appropriately formed. In other words, the externalist claims that we never have to answer the skeptics "how-do-you-know" question. We may simply ignore it.

There are serious objections to externalism, though. First of all, there is the generality problem, the difficulty mentioned earlier in connection with reliabilism of specifying a reliable process either too broadly or too narrowly. Secondly, counterexamples have been offered by internalists to show that the externalist requirement for justified belief is neither sufficient nor necessary. For example, recall the case discussed earlier of "clairvoyant Norman," who always reliably knows the location of the president. Because Norman is unaware that he even has a clairvoyant faculty, has no explanation for why he finds himself with beliefs about the president's location, and never knows whether these beliefs are true or not, it is at least questionable that Norman *knows* the president's location.[17] The upshot of this example seems to be that having a reliably produced belief (i.e., satisfying the externalist requirement for justification) may not be sufficient for knowledge.

Other counterexamples have been offered to show that externalism does not provide a necessary condition for justification, either.[18] Imagine a group of people who live in a world very much like our own and whose cognitive experience is precisely the same as ours. They see, hear, and feel precisely as we do. They reason, conduct scientific experiments, and theorize as we do. There is just one difference. Whereas our beliefs are produced in the normal (and presumably reliable) way and are largely true, the experiences of this group and their resultant beliefs are entirely due to their being in the "matrix" and are largely false (i.e., unknown to them, all of their conscious experiences take place in a computer-generated virtual reality while their bodies lie sleeping in chemical vats). Their beliefs would result from an *un*reliable process. Yet would not their beliefs be justified? Their cognitive experience is indistinguishable from ours. We think our beliefs are justified. So there is no ground for saying that this unfortunate group's beliefs are unjustified—even though their beliefs are not reliably produced. Hence, it appears that one can have a justified belief without satisfying any externalist criterion.

The internalist thinks that these counterexamples to externalism support the traditional intuition that knowledge and justification require having internal cognitive access to one's justifying evidence. One

---

[17] For other similar counterexamples, see Keith Lehrer, *Theory of Knowledge* (Boulder, CO: Westview, 1990), 163–164.

[18] See, e.g., Laurence BonJour, *Epistemology: Classic Problems and Contemporary Responses* (Lanham, MD: Rowman and Littlefield, 2002), 228–29.

way that the externalist can reply to these objections is simply to "bite the bullet" and say, our intuitions notwithstanding, that Norman is justified and does have knowledge because his true belief is reliably produced, and that the group deceived by the matrix is not justified because their belief is not reliably produced. Our intuitions to the contrary, he may say, are simply mistaken.

There are other possible responses and counterresponses on both sides of this debate, but we will not explore them here. Suffice it to say that the division between internalism and externalism is sharp and the debate rages on.

2.2.4 Virtue Epistemology

In looking at the nature of knowledge and justification, so far we have seen how two major debates in epistemology seem to be unresolvable. (In any case, they are currently unresolved.) Many have attempted to solve the Gettier problem, but no satisfactory solution seems within reach. And the internalism-externalism debate shows no sign of reaching a consensus. For this reason, some people despair that the fundamental project of epistemology—to define knowledge—is destined for failure. In recent years an innovative approach to epistemology has been developed that many believe promises to rescue epistemology by transcending these debates. This approach, known as *virtue epistemology*, proposes that to understand the nature of knowledge it is crucial that personal character traits be taken into account.

Virtue and Knowledge

Notice how both internalism and externalism are *belief-based* theories. That is, they proceed on the assumption that the proper focus in epistemology is beliefs. Virtue epistemologists, in contrast, propose that the study of knowledge should be *person-based*.[19] According to the virtue approach, since knowledge is achieved by persons, it is only reasonable that we should take into account personal characteristics. And the sorts of traits that are most relevant to the acquisition of knowledge are, of

---

[19] We noted how the internalist's approach to knowledge is deontological (duty-oriented). In contrast, the externalist's approach is *consequentialist*. That is, the externalist's main concern is desirable consequences. As it turns out, both internalism and externalism are patterned after the two dominant ethical traditions of the modern period—Kantian ethics and utilitarianism, which are deontolotical and consequentialist, respectively (see chapter seven for a full discussion of both theories). Both of these traditions are *act-based*, while virtue ethics, in contrast, is *person-based*. The reemergence of virtue theory in the last two decades revitalized the field of ethics at a time when it had grown stagnant. Virtue epistemology seems to be doing the same for the study of knowledge.

course, intellectual in nature. Thus, says the virtue epistemologist, the key to knowledge is intellectual *virtue.*

So what *is* virtue? This concept goes all the way back to—you guessed it—the ancient Greek philosophers, namely Socrates, Plato and, especially, Aristotle. They understood a virtue as any specific excellence. And Aristotle observed that in human beings virtue comes in two forms—moral and intellectual. Moral virtues include such qualities as courage, generosity, temperance, justice, and wisdom. These are traits that enable a person to flourish as an individual and positively contribute to a flourishing society. Moral virtues cannot be taught, however. They are skills that can only be acquired through training—repeatedly performing good actions until one finally develops a sincere desire to act virtuously for its own sake.

Aristotle maintained that, unlike moral virtues, intellectual virtues *can* be taught. Aristotle's list of intellectual virtues was relatively short, including such qualities as the ability to perform logical operations and make correct calculations, as well as practical wisdom or sagacity. Contemporary virtue epistemologists include such traits as attentiveness, open-mindedness, good memory, diligence in inquiry, inventiveness, intellectual courage, insight into persons, fairness in assessing evidence and arguments, and the ability to recognize trustworthy authorities. Virtue epistemologist Ernest Sosa describes such characteristics as "stable dispositions for belief acquisition."[20] Many virtue epistemologists emphasize that the intellectual virtues cannot simply be taught but must be developed through intentional practice, much like the moral virtues. Still others regard intellectual virtue as a particular *kind* of moral virtue.

Linda Zagzebski, another leading virtue epistemologist, notes that an important component in any virtue is one's motivation. Virtuous people have specific aims, and their particular virtues reflect these aims. For example, a courageous person manifests a desire to protect others, and a generous person is motivated to help people. Similarly, intellectual virtues reflect particular motivations, though they happen to be cognitive in nature. Zagzebski observes that the intellectually virtuous person is motivated toward truth. Intellectual virtues, she says, all derive from "the motivation to have cognitive contact with reality."[21]

---

[20] Ernest Sosa, "The Raft and the Pyramid: Coherence Versus Foundations in the Theory of Knowledge," *Midwest Studies in Philosophy, Volume 5: Studies in Epistemology,* ed. Peter French (Minneapolis: University of Minnesota Press, 1980): 236.

[21] Linda T. Zagzebski, *Virtues of the Mind: An Inquiry into the Nature of Virtue and the Ethical Foundations of Knowledge* (Cambridge: Cambridge University Press, 1996), 167.

So how do virtue epistemologists define knowledge? Knowledge, they say, is grounded in intellectual virtue. Some, such as Sosa, would say that a person's intellectual virtues *justify* his beliefs, while others, such as Zagzebski, prefer to avoid talk of justification. Zagzebski defines knowledge as "a state of true belief arising out of acts of intellectual virtue."[22] But all virtue epistemologists would affirm the truth and belief components of the traditional JTB Account. And, likewise, they would all affirm the centrality of intellectual virtue as a truth-conducive personal trait.

Advantages and Shortcomings of Virtue Epistemology

There are many advantages of virtue epistemology. One of the biggest advantages touted by proponents of this approach is how it appears to circumvent the Gettier problem, at least in many cases. Because Gettier-type cases usually arise when there is an element of luck involved when the subject acquires a true belief, virtue epistemology is immune to this problem because belief acquisition must be intentional and purposeful. Thus, consider the cases of General Ross, J. Jonah Jameson, Norman the clairvoyant, and John the lottery winner, discussed earlier. In none of these cases did intellectual virtues play a role in bringing about their true beliefs. So, according to virtue epistemology, these individuals don't have knowledge for this reason. The Gettier problem arises in the first place because the JTB Account fails to mandate that one's true beliefs be considered in connection with one's character.

Another advantage of virtue epistemology worth noting is how this approach accounts for children's knowledge. Even a little child can know many things, despite the fact that they might not be able to articulate the reasons for their beliefs. Zagzebski explains that "even young children can perform acts of intellectual virtue before they are old enough to acquire intellectual virtues." They can do so, she says, by simply imitating "the behavior of intellectually virtuous persons in their belief-forming processes."[23]

Earlier we noted how the capacity to account for children's knowledge was a strength of externalism. So, is virtue epistemology a particular kind of externalism and, in particular, reliabilism? While some versions of the theory fall into this category, others do not. Virtue epistemologists such as Sosa who are inclined to think of intellectual virtues as truth-conductive cognitive faculties, dispositions or powers, are often called *virtue reliabilists*. Others, like Zagzebski, see intellectual virtues as essentially moral in nature and as traits over which we have significant

[22] Ibid., 271.
[23] Ibid., 280.

control and responsibility. Those who take this perspective are *virtue responsibilists*.

For virtue responsibilists, the acquisition of knowledge is essentially a moral enterprise. For this reason, this particular brand of virtue epistemology is attractive from a Christian perspective. As noted above, Scripture often speaks of the importance of knowledge. Moreover, the Bible teaches that God will hold us accountable for our beliefs as well as our behavior and that the way we behave impacts how we think and believe (see Rom 1:18–32). The morality of our behavior influences what we know. Because of this close connection between conduct and knowledge, we cannot do epistemology in isolation from ethics, and this is precisely the mistake that many epistemologists have made, according to virtue responsibilists.

For all its strengths, virtue epistemology is not without its shortcomings. One of these regards the lack of attention that this theory gives to considerations of justification. While the justification component in the JTB Account surely needs to be supplemented, as the Gettier problem shows, it cannot be ignored. Virtue epistemology does not adequately account for the demand for justification of beliefs in ordinary discourse. The role of evidence in providing grounds for beliefs is significant, even if it is not the whole story in epistemology. So perhaps the best approach would be to affirm the insights of virtue epistemology without scuttling the traditional interest in epistemic justification.

Another problem concerns a potential abuse of the virtue responsibilist brand of virtue epistemology. Although we are morally accountable for how we inquire into issues and form beliefs, not all of us have the same opportunities to advance ourselves intellectually and develop the virtues of the mind. Some people are privileged to receive educations that endow them with significant intellectual traits, including the ability to do rigorous inquiry and belief assessment. Many people have not been so privileged. And even those of us who have been blessed with advanced educations differ in our natural aptitudes and intellectual endowments. So those sympathetic with virtue responsibilism must be careful not to judge others with false or questionable beliefs as necessarily irresponsible or immoral. All of us hold false beliefs of some kind or other, even the most circumspect virtue epistemologist.

Questions for Reflection

1. Some people have defined knowledge as simply sincerely held belief. Is this view defensible? What problems do you see with it?

2. Do you think that the objections to the "no false belief" and "defeasibility" solutions to the Gettier problem are decisive? Why or why not? Can either of these solutions be modified to avoid the objections?

3. Do you think it is possible to specify the scope of a reliable process so as to avoid the generality problem? If so, how?

4. One response that the reliabilist might give to the "clairvoyant Norman" counterexample is to "bite the bullet" and insist that Norman *does* have knowledge. Is this response adequate? Why or why not?

5. Consider the various objections to internalism and externalism. How might the internalist respond? How might the externalist respond? In the end, which view do you think is more satisfactory?

6. Suppose we view reliabilism as a version of the "fourth condition" solution to the Gettier Problem, analyzing knowledge as *justified true belief that is produced by a reliable belief-forming process* (thus combining internalism and externalism). Would this be an adequate definition? Why or why not?

7. All things considered, is virtue epistemology a better approach to the study of knowledge than internalism and externalism? Why or why not?

§ 2.3 What Is the Structure of Justification?

One last topic to be considered in our discussion of epistemology concerns the structure of epistemic justification. In order to understand the issues involved we need to introduce the concept of a *noetic structure*.[24] The word *noetic* comes from the Greek word *nous* ("mind"). So a person's noetic structure consists of his entire set of beliefs together with the logical and explanatory relations among those beliefs. People do not simply have a collection of beliefs. Rather, their beliefs are related in various ways. For example, as I write this sentence, I believe that today is Thursday. I believe this because I also believe, and remember having believed, that yesterday was Wednesday, and I believe that Thursday always follows Wednesday. Likewise, since I believe that the Earth revolves around the Sun and that the Moon revolves around the Earth, I also believe that the moon revolves around the Sun. Many things we believe, in other words, depend upon other things we believe. We often

---

[24] The term *noetic structure* and other terms in this section such as *properly basic* (see below) are terms first introduced by Alvin Plantinga. See his "Reason and Belief in God," in *Faith and Rationality: Reason and Belief in God*, ed. Alvin Plantinga and Nicholas Wolterstorff (Notre Dame: University of Notre Dame Press, 1983).

infer one belief from another, or one belief is used to explain another, and so on. A person's noetic structure includes more than simply a set of beliefs, then. It also includes the relationships that exist among those beliefs. So the question we will address in this section is: how should a person's noetic structure be arranged in order to optimize his rationality? Or, put another way, what is the proper way that a person's system of beliefs should be structured so that his beliefs are justified? There are three major competing theories about how best to answer these questions—foundationalism, coherentism, and contextualism.

2.3.1 Foundationalism

When construction workers make a building, the first thing they do is lay a foundation. The foundation is stable, solid, immovable (at least they hope it is!). On top of the foundation they erect the building itself, what is called the superstructure. The superstructure rests on the foundation, upon which it depends for its own stability and integrity. If the foundation is weak, if it is not stable, then the security of the superstructure is threatened. Regarding the justification of belief, most philosophers down through history have held the view known as *foundationalism*. The foundationalist believes that a good noetic structure is very much like a building that rests on a solid foundation. He believes that a person's belief-system, if it is to be justified, must be grounded in foundational beliefs that are immune, or at least resistant, to doubt.

The foundationalist distinguishes two kinds of beliefs. First, there are *nonbasic beliefs*, beliefs that are based on and justified by other beliefs. Recall my belief that the Moon revolves around the Sun. That belief was deduced from—and thus based on—my belief that the Earth revolves around the Sun and my belief that the Moon revolves around the Earth. A simpler example would be my belief that my wife has just arrived home from shopping. This belief is based on (let's say) my belief that I just saw her car pull into the driveway of our home. Beliefs that get their justification from other beliefs in this way are nonbasic beliefs.

Second, there are *basic beliefs*. A basic belief is a belief that is not based on or justified by another belief; it is a belief that a person holds independently of other beliefs. Basic beliefs, if they are justified, are justified immediately or directly (in ways to be discussed below) rather than mediately through inference from other beliefs. When a basic belief *is* justified, it is called a *properly* basic belief. As we will see, foundationalists differ over what counts as a properly basic belief. In any case, foundationalism may be described as the view that justification (and knowledge) rests on the foundation of properly basic beliefs, beliefs that are justified apart from other beliefs. So we may more formally characterize foundationalism as the view that

> *A belief* p *is justified for a person* S *if and only if: (1)* p *is a properly basic belief for* S *or (2)* p *is ultimately based on a properly basic belief for* S.

With the foregoing concepts and definition in mind, we can see that foundationalism imagines that a good noetic structure is like a tree (see figure 2.3). At the bottom, at the tips of the "roots," are properly basic beliefs that provide support (i.e., justification) for the nonbasic beliefs built on the foundation.

Figure 2.3

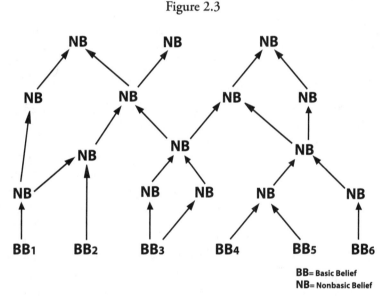

BB= Basic Belief
NB= Nonbasic Belief

Classical vs. Modest Foundationalism

Two issues play a role in demarcating various versions of foundationalism. One of these is the question of what counts as a properly basic belief. The earliest foundationalists in modern philosophy (e.g., Descartes and Locke) believed that the only beliefs that could be justified independently of other beliefs—that is, the only beliefs that could be properly basic—were beliefs that were absolutely certain or at least nearly so. Typically, this meant that properly basic beliefs were limited to beliefs concerning propositions that were either (1) self-evident, (2) incorrigible, or (3) evident to the senses. A *self-evident* proposition is one whose truth is immediately clear as soon as one grasps its meaning.

For example, the proposition "All bachelors are unmarried" is said to be self-evident in this way because it is true by definition. Some simple mathematical propositions such as 2+2=4 could also be considered self-evident. An *incorrigible* proposition is one which it is psychologically impossible for a person to be mistaken about. Take the proposition, "I am in pain." Can you be mistaken concerning whether you are in pain or not? It is difficult to think so. Lastly, a proposition is *evident to the senses* if its content is the object of an immediate sensory experience. Suppose I peer out my window again and see what appears to be a tree. Whether or not what I see really is a tree is something I can be mistaken about, but it is clear to me that I see what *seems* to be a tree. To use some philosophical jargon, it is evident to me that I am *being appeared to treely.* So for this version of foundationalism, beliefs that are self-evidently true, beliefs that I cannot be mistaken about, and beliefs about my immediate sensory experience are the only beliefs that can be properly basic. Any other beliefs, if they are to be justified, must be based on other beliefs. This strong version of foundationalism is known today as *classical foundationalism.*

Few foundationalists today are classical foundationalists. Most adopt a stance called *modest foundationalism,* which allows for more kinds of belief to count as properly basic. They agree that self-evident, incorrigible, and immediate sensory beliefs are properly basic, but they see serious problems with limiting proper basicality to these types alone. For one thing, as we have already seen, very few of our beliefs, if any, are absolutely certain. The skeptical challenge shows us that almost everything that we believe can be doubted in one way or another. Indeed, even beliefs that seem incorrigible may be called into question, such as the proposition, "I am in pain." Louis Pojman provides this example:

> A gullible woman who is having shoulder pains sees her physician, who, believing the woman to be a hypochondriac, informs her that she is mistaken about these pains. "They are really acute tickles," he avers. "Acute tickles sometimes resemble pains, but they are really more pleasurable." The gullible woman believes the physician and the next day tells her husband that she is having tickling sensations in her left shoulder.[25]

Moreover, if we limit properly basic beliefs to those allowed by classical foundationalism, then many commonsense beliefs that we believe to be justified will likely turn out to be unjustified. For example, we believe that we are justified in believing that there is a mind-independent external world. That is, we believe that we are not trapped in the "matrix"

---

[25] Pojman, *What Can We Know?*, 103.

or being systematically deceived by Descartes' evil genius—we believe that our senses give us accurate information about a world outside our minds. Yet, these beliefs could not be justified if classical foundationalism is true. Our belief in a mind-independent external world is neither self-evident, incorrigible, nor evident to the senses. Neither does there seem to be any good argument to prove our belief true (unless one is able to provide a decisive refutation to the skeptical challenge). Likewise, our belief in other minds and our memory beliefs would be unjustified if classical foundationalism were true. I believe for example that there are other minds besides my own (e.g., my wife's mind). And I believe that I had a pastry for breakfast this morning. But neither of these beliefs can be proven by argument (again, unless there is a decisive refutation of skepticism), nor do they meet the criteria stipulated by classical foundationalism.

The most serious problem with classical foundationalism, however, is that it is self-defeating. Classical foundationalism claims that

> *A belief* B *is properly basic for a person* S *if and only if* B *is (1) self-evident to* S, *(2) incorrigible for* S, *or (3) evident to the senses of* S.

Alvin Plantinga, however, has shown that classical foundationalism fails to meet its own criteria.[26] The belief that the above definition is true is neither self-evident, incorrigible, nor evident to the senses. This means that belief in classical foundationalism, by its own criteria, *cannot* be properly basic. The only way that classical foundationalism could be justified, then, is if we had an argument leading to classical foundationalism from premises that are properly basic. But no one has offered any convincing argument in defense of classical foundationalism. So classical foundationalism is untenable.

For these reasons, the modest foundationalist does not restrict what can be properly basic to the self-evident, incorrigible, and evident to the senses. He will also count as properly basic belief in other minds, belief in an external world, memory beliefs, and other beliefs that are less than absolutely certain. In general, modest foundationalists will grant that any belief that is held in a basic way (i.e., not based on other beliefs) and that seems evidently true to a person can count as properly basic. Of course, such properly basic beliefs are defeasible. That is, they are subject to possible defeaters that undermine their proper basicality. When a person encounters a defeater for one of his properly basic beliefs, he must either produce a defeater-defeater or else no longer consider that belief

---

[26] See Alvin Plantinga, "Reason and Belief in God," 59–63.

properly basic—which means if he wants to be justified in continuing to hold that belief, he must have reasons in the form of other beliefs.

Another issue that demarcates different versions of foundationalism has to do with the nature of the justifying relationship between basic and nonbasic beliefs. The classical foundationalists held that the relationship was one of deductive inference. On this view, the only justified beliefs are those that are properly basic (in the classical foundationalist sense) and those nonbasic beliefs that could be logically deduced from properly basic beliefs. As you might guess, this meant that there would be precious few justified beliefs. What's more, there are many nonbasic beliefs that we think are justified which are clearly not logically deduced from basic beliefs. Take my belief that my wife has arrived home from shopping. The basic belief from which that belief is derived is my belief that I just saw her car pull into the driveway. Most of us would agree that my belief that she has arrived home is justified. But that belief is not the result of a logical deduction. Why not? Because my seeing her car pull into the driveway does not necessarily entail that my wife has arrived home. For instance, the car I saw pull into the driveway could be an hallucination planted in my mind by Descartes' evil genius. Or less fancifully, it could be another car that looks very similar to my wife's car. Or it could be my wife's car alright, but my wife might not be in it—perhaps she loaned it to her father (whom she met at the market) and sent him to our home to retrieve her checkbook, which she forgot to take with her. In any case, the point is that I cannot logically deduce from the visual experience I have of the car in the driveway that my wife has arrived home. At best, my belief that she has arrived home may be inferred as probable.

The modest foundationalist, then, not only allows for more kinds of belief to count as properly basic, but he also allows for other types of connection between basic and nonbasic beliefs. He allows for inductive inference, as in the case discussed in the last paragraph. He also allows for *explanatory* relationships in which a nonbasic belief is justified in virtue of providing an adequate explanation for one's experience.

An Argument for Foundationalism

Regardless of what version of foundationalism one adopts, all foundationalists are motivated strongly by an argument known as *the regress argument*. The argument goes like this: Suppose I tell you that I believe a certain proposition p. You then ask me why I am justified in believing p. I reply that my belief p is justified by another belief q (and let's suppose it is). Of course, you could ask me what justifies q, and suppose I reply that q is justified by r. This could go on for quite a while.

This process of justification involves, of course, a chain or *regress* of justifications. There seem to be four possible ways that the rest of the story could go:

1. *The regress could come to an end with a justifying belief x that is itself unjustified.* This option is untenable because if *x* is unjustified, it is very difficult to see how *x* could provide justification for the belief next to it in the chain. And then that belief would not justify the one next to it, and so on up the chain to *p*. In other words, if the regress ends in an unjustified belief—a mere assumption or item of blind faith—then no belief in the chain will be justified. As an old adage goes, you can't give what you don't have! And if *x* does not have justification, it cannot give justification.

2. *The regress could continue infinitely.* But this will not work either. If I attempt to justify *p* by appealing to *q*, and justify *q* by appealing to *r*, and so on *ad infinitum*, then all I am doing is infinitely *postponing* the justification of *p* and all the rest. As Laurence BonJour explains, "In such a justificatory chain, the justification conferred at each step is only *provisional*, dependent on whether the beliefs further along in the chain are justified. But then if the regress continues infinitely, *all* of the alleged justification remains merely provisional."[27]

3. *The regress could be circular.* That is, perhaps the regress doubles back upon itself such that a belief earlier in the chain is repeated. For example, after appealing to *p* as justified by *q*, and *q* as justified by *r*, you ask me what justifies *r*, and I say that *p* justifies *r*. Of course, *p* is the belief that I started with. This answer begs the question. What it says in effect is that *p* justifies *p*! But this provides no real answer to the question why *p* is justified. It leaves us precisely where we began. Circular justification would result in spinning our wheels from a logical standpoint.

4. *The regress could come to an end with a justifying belief x that is itself justified immediately apart from other beliefs.* This is the solution that the foundationalist favors. He believes that there are beliefs which can be justified in some way independent of other beliefs. He believes, that is, that there are properly basic beliefs, and that these basic beliefs serve as the foundation for all of our justified nonbasic beliefs.

Problems with Foundationalism

The most significant objection to foundationalism has to do with how properly basic beliefs are justified. As we have stipulated, a properly basic belief is a belief that is in fact justified, but it does not get its justification from other beliefs. Where then does its justification come from? The

---

[27] BonJour, *Epistemology*, 196 (italics his).

answer, in a word, is *experience*. For example, let's consider again that tree outside my window. According to the foundationalist, what justifies my apparent basic belief that there is a tree outside my window is not another belief, but simply my immediate perceptual experience of the tree. Put in other terms, my basic beliefs receive their justification from my direct introspective awareness of the contents of my experience. Experience here, of course, is not limited to perceptual experience. My properly basic belief that "All bachelors are unmarried" is also justified by experience but not of course an experience of a perception of a physical object. Rather, it is justified by my awareness of the meaning of the proposition.

This account of the justification of basic beliefs presupposes that something is *given* to us in experience in an unconceptualized form. The idea is that our experience is provided with "raw" data of some kind, data which is initially uninterpreted and uncategorized by our minds. To focus on visual perception, by way of example, we can say that the foundationalist is committed to the possibility of "simple seeing." He believes it is possible to see something (i.e., have a visual perception) without necessarily "seeing as" or "seeing that." In other words, it is possible, on this view, to open my eyes and see something without consciously seeing it "as a tree" or seeing "that it is a tree."

Critics of foundationalism believe that this idea of "the given" in experience is unsustainable—thus they speak of the *myth of the given*.[28] In our postmodern era it is common to hear that all observation is "theory-laden."[29] That is, there is no such thing as simple seeing, only "seeing as" and "seeing that." A simple way of illustrating the point is the well-worn duck-rabbit illustration (see figure 2.4).

Figure 2.4

[28] See, e.g., Wilfrid Sellars, "Empiricism and the Philosophy of Mind," in *Science, Perception, and Reality*, ed. Wilfrid Sellars (London: Routledge & Kegan Paul, 1963).

[29] This idea has been ably propounded by Thomas L. Kuhn, *The Structure of Scientific Revolutions*, 2nd ed. (Chicago: University of Chicago Press, 1970). See chapter three for a fuller discussion of his ideas.

When you look at this figure, what do you see? A duck or a rabbit? Well, it depends upon what conceptual "grid" you come to it with; *what* it is is determined by your background assumptions. Again, the idea is that observation and perception appear to be theory-laden—what we observe is dependent on our prior conceptions and beliefs. Apparently, this poses a problem for foundationalism since the foundationalist believes that we can (and do) have preconceptual perceptions.

The foundationalist is likely to respond, first, by claiming that it is not at all clear that there is only "seeing as" and "seeing that." Indeed, it is arguable that both of these types of seeing presuppose simple seeing and would be impossible without it. Moreover, he could point out that the duck-rabbit illustration is misleading. To be sure, when I *interpret* the drawing, I must interpret it according to concepts that I bring with me. So we might admit the theory-ladenness of interpretation. Yet it does not follow from this fact that I do not and cannot have a preconceptual awareness of the drawing *per se*. After all, if I am to interpret the image, I must first have an awareness of it.

The foundationalist may support his point here by citing a common experience that people have. Suppose during an outdoor conversation with you about the merits of foundationalism, a flock of geese fly overhead within my visual field, but I take no conscious notice of it and form no beliefs about it. Later you ask me, "Did you see that flock of geese?" I think for a moment and remember the flock and say, "Now that you mention it, yeah, I saw it." This kind of common experience is easily explainable on foundationalist terms. The explanation is that when the geese flew by I was "given" a nonconceptual and nonpropositional experience which I later conceptualized and propositionalized when your question jogged my memory.

Additionally, the foundationalist could argue that to insist strongly on the theory-ladenness of observation is self-defeating. The postmodern advocate of theory-ladenness says, "All observation is theory-laden." This statement presumably is an observation itself. But if all observation is theory-laden, then *this* observation is theory-laden. That is, the belief that all observation is theory-laden would simply be the belief of a person who has imposed his own conceptual grid on his observations. If that is so, then no one else need adopt his view of observation.

Despite what may be said in defense of foundationalism, many philosophers today have rejected it and have sought a different account of the structure of justification. We look next at the primary contender.

2.3.2 Coherentism

The major alternative to foundationalism is *coherentism* (not to be confused with the coherence theory of truth[30]). The coherentist rejects the idea of basic beliefs. For him, all beliefs are nonbasic, as all justified beliefs get their justification from other beliefs.

One may wonder at the outset how coherentism handles the regress problem discussed above. That problem suggested that if all justification is via other beliefs, then a chain of justification either (1) ends in an unjustified belief, (2) leads to an infinite regress, or (3) turns out to be circular. Contemporary coherentists, however, point out that the regress problem assumes that epistemic justification is linear. The coherentist rejects this assumption and sees justification as *holistic*. No belief, on this view, is justified simply by one or a few other beliefs in a linear chain. Rather, every justified belief in a person's noetic structure is justified by the person's *whole system* of beliefs. The coherentist views justification not on the metaphor of a building with a foundation or a tree with its branches, but on the metaphor of a web (see figure 2.5). In a web, every strand is dependent on every other strand. All the strands provide mu-

Figure 2.5

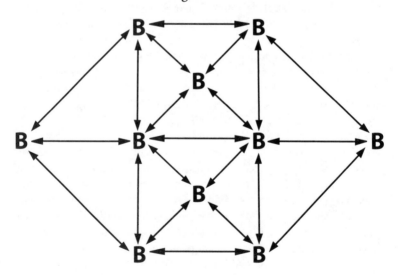

---

[30] A coherence theory of justification is consistent with either a coherence or correspondence theory of truth. Keep in mind that the coherence theory of truth is about what it means for a proposition to *be true*. A coherence theory of justification is about what it means for a person to be *justified in believing* a proposition.

tual support for one another. Likewise, in a good noetic structure, every belief depends for its justification on every other belief and plays a role in the justification of every other belief.

The Nature of Coherence

An important issue that coherentists have to face is defining the precise nature of coherence. It might be thought initially that "coherence" can be defined simply as logical consistency. A coherent noetic structure, on this view, would be one in which all the beliefs contained in that structure are logically consistent (i.e., not contradictory). A moment's reflection will show that this account of coherence will not do. Imagine a person who has a noetic structure containing the following three beliefs:

> Superman loves Lois Lane.
> The Yankees are a good baseball team.
> Bill Gates is very wealthy.

These beliefs are logically consistent. There is no contradiction in holding all three simultaneously. But they are completely unrelated. There seems to be no reason to think that these beliefs do or even could provide mutual support for one another in the way that the coherentist's holistic approach suggests. As BonJour puts it, "[I]t would be odd and misleading . . . to suggest that this mere lack of conflict provides any real *justification* for these beliefs, any positive reason for thinking that they are true."[31]

The coherentist needs something stronger than mere logical consistency. Probably the most common position is to define coherence in terms of *inference*. There are three types of inference that the coherentist can use, and most coherentists think that all three types are relevant. There is *deductive* inference in which a conclusion follows with certainty from its premises. There is also *inductive* inference in which a conclusion follows from its premises with a degree of probability. Last, there is what is called *inference to the best explanation,* according to which a conclusion is derived as preferable to competing hypotheses because it best explains the data. A system of beliefs is coherent, on this account, if the various beliefs stand in inferential relations with one another in one or more of these three types of inference. In other words, each belief in the system can be logically inferred (either by deduction, induction, or inference to the best explanation) from the other beliefs in the system.

---

[31] BonJour, *Epistemology*, 203 (italics his).

Problems for Coherentism

There are two standard objections to coherentism. The first is called the *isolation problem*. If, as the coherentist asserts, epistemic justification is simply a matter of coherence as defined above, then it would seem that justification need have nothing to do with experience or the way the external world is. In other words, a person could have a completely coherent system of beliefs and yet his noetic structure be completely isolated from the world. The problem here is that we can easily imagine perfectly coherent systems of belief that are completely fictitious. Any well-written novel could qualify as a coherent system. So, imagine, for example, a person (let's call him Dave) who has read J.R.R. Tolkien's *The Lord of the Rings* trilogy and finds the life of a person in Middle Earth far more interesting than and preferable to life in the real world. Somehow, perhaps through some mental illness, he convinces himself that all the propositions in the trilogy are true and even imagines himself living in Middle Earth as one of the characters in the story. Dave's beliefs are coherent. Are they justified? It's very doubtful that they are. Why? Because Dave's beliefs are isolated from experience of the real world. The objects of his beliefs are totally fictitious and are apparently impervious to input from experience.

A second objection to coherentism is the *alternative coherent systems problem*. Simply put, two different people could have equally coherent but completely contradictory systems of belief. And the problem is that coherentism appears to offer no criterion by which to adjudicate which person's system of beliefs is more likely to be true. Indeed, on coherentist grounds, it would seem that one system is just as likely as the other to be true since justification is defined simply in terms of coherence.

A coherentist could respond to these problems by adopting a coherence theory of truth. In that case, the isolation problem would no longer be a problem because it assumes a correspondence notion of truth. On a coherence theory of truth, we need not assume that there is an external "reality" to which our coherent system of beliefs must correspond. The alternative coherent systems objection would also evaporate if the coherentist is willing to embrace relativism. The relativist, of course, believes that two contradictory systems can both be true. Given the numerous problems that we saw with relativism and the coherence theory of truth, however, the price of this solution is much too costly.

A more promising approach to solving these problems is to try to find a way consistent with coherentist principles to allow experience and observation to play a role in justification. Following a suggestion by Laurence BonJour,[32] the coherentist could insist (contra foundational-

---

[32] See ibid., 206–209.

ism) that beliefs acquired from experience are not justified by experience, but nevertheless grant the obvious point that many of our beliefs are *caused* by experience. These beliefs so caused are then justified by the further *belief* that experience-caused beliefs are in general justified. And this latter belief is justified by an inductive inference from many cases of true beliefs acquired from experience.

If it works, this solution solves the isolation problem because it allows (and perhaps requires) that beliefs caused by experience of the real world be part of a person's noetic structure. It also potentially solves the alternative coherent systems problem because, as BonJour explains, it requires of any coherent system that it "(i) must include such an observational ingredient and (ii) must *remain* coherent as new observational beliefs are added."[33] It is not universally agreed, even among coherentists, that BonJour's suggested solution to the isolation and alternative systems problems succeeds. But we will not pursue the matter further here. Suffice it to say that many coherentists think that something *like* BonJour's proposal is needed to make coherentism a viable alternative to foundationalism.

A more serious problem for coherentism remains. It would seem that even the holistic coherentism we have outlined in this section is subject to a *regress problem*. According to coherentism, a belief p is justified for a person S just in case p coheres with his system of beliefs. Now consider the fact that before p can be admitted entrance into S's noetic structure, S must determine whether or not p does in fact cohere with his system of beliefs. This would seem to require that S form the belief "P coheres with my system of beliefs." Let us call this latter belief (the one that judges p to cohere) q. The question to ask now is: *what justifies S in believing q?* It would seem that S must form an additional belief r, namely, "q coheres with my system of beliefs." But, again, this would require S to believe yet another belief t, "r coheres with my system of beliefs," *ad infinitum*. It is unclear whether coherentism has the resources to respond to this objection.

2.3.3 Contextualism

Foundationalism and coherentism have been the major competitors in the debate regarding the structure of justification. In recent times, however, another theory has been developed called *contextualism*.[34]

---

[33] Ibid., 208–9.

[34] For defenses of contextualist theories of justification, see Stewart Cohen, "Contextualism, Skepticism, and the Structure of Reasons," *Philosophical Perspectives* 13 (1999): 57–89; Fred Dretske, "The Pragmatic Dimension of Knowledge," *Philosophical Studies* 40 (1981): 363–78; and Richard Rorty, *Philosophy and the Mirror of Nature* (Princeton: Princeton University Press,

According to this view, epistemic justification is relative to a specific context. Contextualists rightly point out that in ordinary situations in which people ask whether or not a particular belief is justified, they do so while taking the vast majority of their beliefs for granted and raising questions only within a limited sphere of inquiry. Given this insight into the ordinary way in which people tend to justify most of their beliefs, the contextualist argues that epistemic justification is just a matter of asking the right questions within a limited context. The idea is that beliefs can be justified in one context that might not be justified in other contexts.

The Relevant Alternatives View

As with the other theories of justification we have examined, there are several versions of contextualism. One prominent version is the *relevant alternatives view*. According to this view, a person is justified in believing a particular proposition just in case he can rule out all the relevant alternatives. A *relevant* alternative is one that is significant in the actual context in which a question of justification is raised. For example, suppose that Henry and his son make a visit to the local zoo.[35] In one particular exhibit, they see what appears to be a zebra and Henry comes to believe that what he sees *is* a zebra. His son, however, asks him if the animal could be a mule painted with stripes. In such a context, in order to justify his belief that he sees a zebra, Henry would ordinarily limit his inquiry to the specific question at hand—whether or not the animal could be a painted mule. And he would likely examine the animal for evidence that it was a painted mule (e.g., mules are typically larger than zebras and paint would likely be detectable on the animal's fur). Henry, in seeking to justify his belief that he sees a zebra, would not concern himself with more global questions such as whether or not he was in the matrix or deceived by Descartes' evil genius. So, Henry is justified in believing that he sees a zebra just in case he can rule out the possibility that the animal in question is a painted mule. He need not rule out the possibility that he is being deceived by the evil genius because—in Henry's context—this latter possibility is not relevant. His son did not ask him about evil geniuses; he only asked about painted mules!

1979). It should be pointed out that contextualism is not always seen as an alternative to foundationalism and coherentism. It might rather be seen as a *supplement* to either. So, for example, one might adopt a foundationalist view of justification but add that what counts as a properly basic belief will vary from context to context. Similarly, a coherentist contextualist will add that certain kinds of inferential relations justify beliefs in some contexts but not others.

[35] This example was first provided by Dretske in "The Pragmatic Dimension of Knowledge."

Problems for Contextualism

There are problems with the relevant alternatives view, however, and for contextualism generally. For one thing, it must be recognized that contextualists insist that questions of justification are relative to a given person's local context because they believe that the more global questions (e.g., "Are we in the matrix?") do not have satisfactory answers. To see the potential problem with this, consider an altered version of the example concerning Henry and his son. Suppose, instead of asking if the animal could be a painted mule, his son asked, "Dad, could that apparent zebra really be just a perceptual illusion caused by a Cartesian evil genius?" In *this* context, Henry, in order to be justified and have knowledge, would have to rule out the evil genius hypothesis, something (presumably) he cannot do. So, in the altered context (though it is perceptually identical to the original context), Henry is not justified in his belief (and thus does not know) that he sees a zebra.

But if Henry is not justified in his belief in the broader context of the "evil genius" question, why should we consider him justified in the narrower "painted mule" context? After all, the possibility that the animal is a painted mule logically *presupposes* that what Henry sees is *not* an illusion generated by an evil genius. So wouldn't Henry, if he is justified in ruling out the painted mule hypothesis, also have to be justified in ruling out the evil genius hypothesis? Conversely, if he is *not* justified in ruling out the evil genius hypothesis, wouldn't he also *not* be justified in ruling out the painted mule hypothesis?[36]

Another way to make the same point is to note that the relevant alternatives view would seem to require us to believe that the broader epistemic questions are irrelevant to most ordinary contexts simply because those questions are not specifically asked in those contexts. But, why would the fact that a question is not asked (but which *could* be asked in the same perceptual circumstances) make that question irrelevant to a person's *being* justified?

To avoid this difficulty the contextualist may argue that epistemic terms like *justified* and *know* have different meanings in different contexts. An analogy might help to make the point. Suppose that Henry and his son continue on their zoo expedition.[37] Henry sees a baby elephant that is standing next to a monkey and says, "Look at that baby elephant. He is so big!" But later Henry sees the same baby elephant

---

[36] These questions point out that the contextualist is committed to denying what is called the epistemic closure principle, which states: *If S is justified in believing that p, and p entails q, then S is justified in believing that q.* Many philosophers believe that denying the epistemic closure principle is highly counterintuitive.

[37] This example is borrowed from Richard Feldman, *Epistemology* (Upper Saddle River, NJ: Prentice-Hall, 2003), 152–53.

standing next to its mother and says, "Look how small that baby elephant is!" Has Henry contradicted himself? Not at all. Words like "big"
and "small" are relative to the classes in which we compare things. Relative to monkeys, baby elephants are big, but relative to adult elephants,
baby elephants are small. In the same way, says the contextualist, words
like "justified" and "know" are relative to the contexts in which we use
them. For example, relative to the broader context of concern about
evil geniuses, the word *know* means one thing (and we lack knowledge
in that context), and relative to more ordinary contexts, *know* means
something else—something less stringent—which allows us to say that
we have knowledge in those contexts.

In response, one might question the idea that epistemic terms really
are analogous to words like *big* and *small*. As Richard Feldman points
out,[38] the reason we don't think that Henry contradicted himself is that
we all understand that what Henry meant in his two statements was "big
for an animal" and "not big for an elephant" respectively. However, when
the skeptic poses the possibility of the evil genius and asks us whether we
are really justified in believing that we see a zebra, it doesn't seem quite
as obvious that we may reply, "Well, what I meant was 'I am justified
in believing that I see a zebra in the ordinary, narrow context,' and not
'I am justified in believing that I see a zebra in the broader, skeptical
context.'" If, like most noncontextualists, you believe that the skeptical
arguments actually pose a challenge to our ordinary beliefs that deserve
some kind of serious reply, then you will not find such a response to the
skeptic satisfactory.

A second objection that arises from considerations raised in the previous paragraphs is that contextualism, seen as an alternative to foundationalism and coherentism, seems committed to the first response to
the epistemic regress problem, namely, that the epistemic regress comes
to an end with justifying beliefs that are themselves *unjustified*. And it
is questionable that unjustified beliefs really can confer justification on
other beliefs. Let's go back once more to the zoo with Henry and his
son as they stand in front of the zebra exhibit. Henry has formed the
belief that what he sees is a zebra, but his son has called that belief into
question by asking about the possibility of a painted mule. Suppose
now that Henry examines the animal up close and is unable to see any
evidence of paint on the animal's fur and thus forms the belief that there
is no paint on the animal's fur. This latter belief (let's say) justifies his
belief that he sees a zebra and not a painted mule. But what justifies his
belief that there is no paint on the animal's fur? Well, presumably, it is
his belief that if there were paint on the animal's fur, he would be able

[38] Ibid., 154–55.

to see it. But what justifies *this* belief? He would have to believe that his eyesight is reliable. However, that would be the case only if he is not being deceived by a Cartesian evil genius, something he cannot know on contextualist grounds. So his belief that he would see paint if it were there is not justified.

The regress of justification comes to an end with an unjustified belief. Why, then, should we think that his belief that there is no paint on the fur is justified? If it's not, then his belief that he sees a zebra would seem unjustified too. It appears that the contextualist avoids this difficulty only by ignoring it. He refuses to follow the regress past the second link in the chain by declaring subsequent links irrelevant to Henry's immediate context. But the problem is that *every* link in the chain *seems* relevant to Henry's immediate context. Henry's belief that the animal is a zebra is dependent for its present justification on his belief that there is no paint on the animal's fur. But the latter belief does not stand in isolation from other things that Henry believes. Unless the latter belief is itself justified, it is difficult to imagine that his initial belief is truly justified.

Another problem for contextualism is that it seems to set the standard for knowledge too high. By admitting that we lack knowledge in the broad, skeptical context, the contextualist accepts the skeptic's view that knowledge requires absolute certainty. As we saw earlier, however, there is reason to believe that knowledge does not require absolute certainty. If that is right, then contextualism constitutes an unnecessary concession to skepticism.

Conclusion

In this chapter, we have discussed some of the central questions of epistemology. For the Christian, these questions are of paramount importance since Christianity claims to be a knowledge tradition. Of the issues surveyed, perhaps the one most relevant to defending Christianity's claim to be a knowledge tradition is the challenge of skepticism. If Christians know such propositions as "God exists," "Jesus rose from the dead," and "The Bible is divine revelation," then any strong form of skepticism that would rule out such religious knowledge must be false. Moreover, assuming the falsity of skepticism, it would seem incumbent upon the Christian to make a serious attempt to respond to the challenge posed by the skeptic.

One promising way of meeting this challenge, as we have seen, is to question the skeptical assumption that knowledge requires absolute certainty. Questioning this assumption commits us, of course, to the idea that there are some things that we know and are justified in believing which we may not be able to *prove* (with absolute certainty) that we know. Taking this stance, however, does not put the Christian in an unusual and lonely position philosophically. In fact, most nonskeptical philosophers respond to skepticism in precisely the same way.

The other questions addressed in this chapter ("What is knowledge?" and "How are beliefs justified?") are questions that allow the Christian a greater amount of flexibility philosophically. There is no single *Christian* solution to the Gettier Problem, and Christian philosophers are free to disagree over the internalism/externalism debate and the viability of virtue epistemology. Christian philosophers also divide over the question of the structure of justification. Both coherentism and foundationalism have able defenders among Christian scholars. We believe that contextualism, however, is more problematic from a Christian point of view because it appears to concede too much to the skeptic.

Questions for Reflection

1. Is it really the case, as Pojman suggests, that a person's belief that he is in pain is not incorrigible (recall the example of the gullible woman on p. 85)?
2. Do you see any problems with the modest foundationalist allowing a larger set of beliefs than those which are certain to count as properly basic? Why or why not?
3. What do you think of the idea of "the given"? Is it a myth after all? If you think it is, how would you reply to the foundationalist's arguments to the contrary?
4. What do you think of the coherentist's response to the isolation and alternative coherent systems objections? Does his attempt to allow a role for experience in justification work? Why or why not?
5. Is there a way for the coherentist to respond to the revised regress problem mentioned at the end of that section? If so, how?
6. A version of contextualism favored by some postmodern thinkers says that *a belief p is justified for a person S if and only if p is a belief shared by S's community or inferable from beliefs shared by S's community*. What problems might this theory have?
7. Consider some important Christian beliefs such as (a) the existence of God, (b) the deity of Christ, (c) the authority of Scripture, and (d) the universality of sin. How would a foundationalist justify these beliefs? How would a coherentist justify them? How would a contextualist?

For Further Reading

On Epistemology Generally

Audi, Robert. *Belief, Justification, and Knowledge*. Belmont, CA: Wadsworth, 1988.

BonJour, Laurence. *Epistemology: Classic Problems and Contemporary Responses*. Lanham, MD: Rowman and Littlefield, 2002.

Chisholm, Roderick. *Theory of Knowledge*. 3rd ed. Englewood Cliffs, NJ: Prentice-Hall, 1989.

Feldman, Richard. *Epistemology*. Englewood Cliffs, NJ: Prentice-Hall, 2003.

Pojman, Louis P. *What Can We Know? An Introduction to the Theory of Knowledge*. 2nd ed. Belmont, CA: Wadsworth, 2001.

Wood, W. Jay. *Epistemology: Becoming Intellectually Virtuous*. Downers Grove, IL: InterVarsity, 1998.

On Skepticism

Moreland, J. P., and William Lane Craig. *Philosophical Foundations for a Christian Worldview*. Downers Grove, IL: InterVarsity, 2003, chap. 4.

Stroud, Barry. "The Problem of the External World." In *Epistemology: An Anthology*, ed. Ernest Sosa and Jaegwon Kim. Malden, MA: Blackwell, 2000.

On Rationalism and Empiricism

Aune, Bruce. *Rationalism, Empiricism, and Pragmatism: An Introduction*. New York: McGraw-Hill, 1970.

Descartes, René. *Meditations on First Philosophy*, II-VI.

Locke, John. *An Essay Concerning Human Understanding*, 2.I-VII, 3.I-III, XI.

Miller, Ed L. *Questions That Matter: An Invitation to Philosophy*. 4th ed. New York: McGraw-Hill, 1996, chaps. 9–10.

On the Gettier Problem

Gettier, Edmund. "Is Justified True Belief Knowledge?" *Analysis* 23 (1963): 121–23.

Harmon, Gilbert. *Thought*. Princeton: Princeton University Press, 1973, 120–41.

Pollock, John, *Contemporary Theories of Knowledge*. Lanham, MD: Rowman and Littlefield, 1986, 180–93.

Moser, Paul K.. *Knowledge and Evidence*. Cambridge: Cambridge University Press, 1989, chap. 6.

On Internalism, Externalism, and Virtue Epistemology

Goldman, Alvin I. "What Is Justified Belief?" In *Justification and Knowledge*, ed.
    G.S. Pappas. Dordrecht: D. Reidel, 1979, 1–23.
Moser, Paul K. *Knowledge and Evidence*. Cambridge: Cambridge University
    Press, 1989, chap. 2.
Pollock, John. "Reliability and Justified Belief." *Canadian Journal of Philosophy*
    14 (1984): 103–14.
Zagzebski, Linda. *Virtues of the Mind: An Inquiry into the Nature of Virtue and
    the Ethical Foundations of Knowledge*. Cambridge: Cambridge University
    Press, 2002.

On the Structure of Justification

BonJour, Laurence. *The Structure of Empirical Knowledge*. Cambridge, MA:
    Harvard University Press, 1985.
Dretske, Fred. "The Pragmatic Dimension of Knowledge." *Philosophical Studies*
    40 (1981): 363–78.
Moser, Paul K.. *Knowledge and Evidence*. Cambridge: Cambridge University
    Press, 1989, chap. 4.
Swinburne, Richard. *Epistemic Justification*. Oxford: Oxford University Press,
    2001.

Chapter 3

PHILOSOPHY OF SCIENCE: WHAT CAN SCIENCE TELL US?

*"I do not feel obliged to believe that the same
God who has endowed us with sense, reason, and
intellect has intended us to forego their use."*

—Galileo Galilei

3.5 Science and Theology

3.5.1 Two Kinds of Naturalism

3.5.2 Critical Reflections on Methodological Naturalism

3.5.3 Theistic Science

Glossary Terms

Falsificationism	*Paradigm*
Functional integrity	*Problem of induction*
Inductivism	*Regularity theory*
Instrumentalism	*of natural laws*
Intelligent design theory	*Scientific nonrealism*
Metaphysical naturalism	*Scientific realism*
Methodological naturalism	*Scientism*
Necessitarian theory	*Theistic science*
of natural laws	*Uniformity of nature*

I n Robert Pirsig's novel *Zen and the Art of Motorcycle Maintenance*, the narrator and main character describes a 17-day motorcycle tour with his son and some friends, John and Sylvia. Along the way, they discuss philosophy, art, culture and, of course, motorcycle maintenance. Early in their adventure the conversation turns to science, and the narrator says to his friend, John:

> "It's completely natural . . . to think of Europeans who believed in ghosts or Indians who believed in ghosts as ignorant. The scientific point of view has wiped out every other view to a point where they all seem primitive, so that if a person today talks about ghosts or spirits he is considered ignorant or maybe nutty. It's just all but completely impossible to imagine a world where ghosts can actually exist."

John nods affirmatively and I continue:

> "My own opinion is that the intellect of modern man isn't that superior. IQs aren't that much different. Those Indians and medieval men were just as intelligent as we are, but the context in which they thought was completely different. Within that *context* of thought, ghosts and spirits are quite as real as atoms,

particles, photons and quants are to a modern man. In *that* sense I believe in ghosts. Modern man has his ghosts and spirits . . ."[1]

The narrator goes on to suggest that scientific ideas are mere human inventions, no more objectively real than cultural traditions about spirits that cause thunder, lightning, wind, and rain.

Many people would find it ridiculous or even offensive to suggest that scientific theories are no more rational than primitive mythologies. Most of us would recognize that science affords us knowledge and many would view it as an especially trustworthy form of knowledge. This is evident in popular phrases like "This isn't rocket science" and the common reverence for institutions of science, from NASA to modern medicine. We are impressed by the practical achievements of science, from antibiotics to landing men on the Moon. And it is a short psychological step from such impressions to the conviction that science is the ultimate *model* for knowledge and epistemic methodology.

Some even go so far as to insist that the scientific method is the *only* trustworthy methodology for acquiring knowledge. This is the perspective taken by a character in the film adaptation of another significant work of twentieth-century fiction—Dr. Seuss's *Horton Hears a Who*. In the book the kangaroo protests Horton's insistence that there is life in a tiny speck of dust. In the film adaptation of Seuss's book the kangaroo declares with exasperation, "If you can't see, hear, or feel something, it doesn't exist!"[2] From this perspective, when it comes to informing us about the nature of reality, science is king.

Pirsig's narrator and Seuss's kangaroo represent two extreme views, but both of these perspectives have been earnestly defended by philosophers of science. In this chapter we will discuss each of these views as well as some moderate positions on the nature and authority of science. We will also look at some specific issues related to the nature of scientific laws, the presuppositions of science, and the relationship between science and theology.

§ 3.1 The Nature and Limits of Science

One of the major problems in philosophy of science is a boundary issue. How should science be defined and what are its limits? In this section we will address both of these questions.

---

[1] Robert M. Pirsig, *Zen and the Art of Motorcycle Maintenance: An Inquiry into Values* (New York: Bantam, 1984), 29. Emphases are the author's.

[2] *Horton Hears a Who!* (G; 88 mins.; 2008), directed by Jimmy Hayward and Steve Martino.

3.1.1 Defining Science

What *is* science? Dictionary definitions of the term typically make reference to the systematic organization of data and the prediction and explanation of natural phenomena. As a rough definition, then, we might say that science involves systematic inquiry into the natural world which aims to organize, predict, and explain empirical data. While this definition is helpful to a degree, we run into problems when we inquire about its key terms. For example, what does it mean to say that data is "empirical"? Direct sensory observation? If so, then this is much too narrow as a condition for scientific inquiry, as much data used by scientists is obtained indirectly through analytical tools such as meters, gauges, litmus paper, and microscopes. But if we allow for "empirical" to include data obtained indirectly, then this makes it difficult to distinguish science from some other disciplines, such as history and journalism, where data is obtained indirectly through eyewitness testimony and other means.

Suppose we look to the concepts of "prediction" and "explanation" to distinguish science. Setting aside the matter of defining these terms, a moment's reflection reveals that neither of these is a *necessary* condition for scientific research. Many scientific studies focus on past events about which no predictions can be made, such as astrophysical research on the Big Bang and paleontological and archaeological inquiry about ancient fossils and people groups, respectively. And much scientific research, such as classifying organisms, is not concerned with explanation of data. Nor are prediction or explanation *sufficient* conditions for science. Predictions are made in many nonscientific contexts, from horse-racing to astrology. And many nonscientific academic disciplines explain empirical data, such as when historians explain the collapse of the Roman Empire or when biblical scholars explain the apostle John's use of apocalyptic language in the book of Revelation.

Some prefer to define science in other terms such as the repeatability of experiments and the testability and falsifiability of hypotheses. But such criteria run aground the same way as the above proposals do. Repeatable experimentation is not possible in scientific fields dealing with past events, such as paleontology, archaeology, and astrophysical research on the Big Bang. And to the extent that studies can be repeated in these areas, the same is possible in many other academic disciplines, where data can be checked or tested by other scholars in order to verify a researcher's claims. Similarly, the testing and falsification of hypotheses is a standard aspect of every academic discipline, not just science.

We could consider more proposals for necessary or sufficient conditions for science, but the point should be clear by now. Defining *science* is problematic, to say the least, and the attempt to do so is itself a philosophical undertaking.[3] One obvious lesson here is that it is naïve to speak dogmatically about the essence of science or about its superiority or inferiority to other fields of inquiry. This lesson will be reinforced when we examine some philosophies of science below.

3.1.2 Presuppositions of Science

Earlier we mentioned the extreme view expressed by the kangaroo in *Horton Hears a Who*. She asserted that only what can be empirically verified can be known. This claim is known as *scientism*. It is rarely defended by scholars because it is so obviously flawed. The main problem with scientism is that it is self-defeating, for this view itself cannot be empirically verified. How could one demonstrate scientifically that all nonempirical truth-claims are unknowable? The idea is, of course, absurd. Thus, it turns out that by its own standard scientism must be rejected as an object of knowledge. Even if scientism were true, it could never be known to be true!

As if its self-defeating nature was not a serious enough problem with scientism, there is another difficulty with the theory. Science, like all empirical disciplines, rests on numerous assumptions that cannot be proven empirically. That is, there are many nonscientific, philosophical assumptions that scientists must make when doing their research.

1. *The laws of thought* – As we saw in chapter 1, we all must follow the basic principles of rationality in the search for truth in any discipline. These are: (1) the law of identity, (2) the law of excluded middle, and (3) the law of noncontradiction. The laws of thought cannot be proven scientifically because all scientific inquiry, indeed all thinking and acting, presupposes them. In fact, they cannot be proven in the usual sense of the term, since any argument would in turn rely upon them. So foundational are the laws of thought that the only real proof of which they are susceptible is the impossibility of denying them. (See chapter 1 for an elaboration of this point.)

2. *The general reliability of sense perception* – One thing we can safely assert about science is that it crucially involves empirical data and requires use of the senses. But how does one know that one's senses are reliable? This is yet another assumption that the scientist must make. You might be tempted to suggest that one can have, say, one's eyes and ears checked by a physiologist to confirm their reliability, but notice the

---

[3] For an extensive discussion of the problem of defining science, see J. P. Moreland's *Christianity and the Nature of Science* (Grand Rapids: Baker, 1989), chapter 1. Our short discussion of the issue here takes its cue from Moreland's excellent analysis.

problem with this suggestion. It *assumes* that one's senses are already generally reliable. For how else could you know that the physiologist (or anything else, for that matter) exists? Thus, as with the laws of thought, the general reliability of sense perception is something that we must presuppose not only in doing science but in everyday experience.

3. *The law of causality* – Scientists often make causal claims about the world, for example, that HIV causes AIDS, that the tides are caus-ally impacted by the moon, and so forth. In all of their research scien-tists make a very basic assumption: that every effect must have a cause. Events do not simply happen without a reason. Every state of affairs has a sufficient explanation. This universal claim about the world cannot be proven, as this would require an exhaustive knowledge of all phenomena in the history of the cosmos. So it must be taken for granted and thus constitutes another presupposition of both science and common sense.

4. *The uniformity of nature* – Have you ever considered the pos-sibility that gravitational forces will suddenly cease? Or that water will suddenly become flammable? Or that the Sun will spontaneously turn into ice? If not, this is because you assume that the laws of nature will re-main constant and that the future will resemble the past when it comes to such regularities. Scientists, too, must presuppose the uniformity of natural laws. Although science has given us rigorous *statements* of the laws of nature, it cannot explain them, much less provide evidence that they will continue to hold in the future. This is yet another presupposi-tion of science.

5. *Values* – Empirical science is entirely descriptive in nature. That is, it can only tell us how the world is; science cannot tell us how it *ought* to be. Yet there are many values that scientists assume and apply when doing their research. Some of these are moral (e.g., the value of honesty in conducting research and reporting data and the value of compassion when doing research on animals). Some values are social and political (e.g., value judgments regarding which topics deserve special attention and corporate or government funding, such as cancer or AIDS research). And some values are aesthetic, such as when scientists demonstrate a preference for particular theories based on their elegance or parsimony (e.g., Copernican astronomy, natural selection, or $E=MC^2$).

These are just five major assumptions of science. They demonstrate the foolishness of advocates of scientism when they claim that all knowl-edge comes through science. Moreover, since these presuppositions are all philosophical in nature, it follows that science is ultimately depen-dent upon the discipline of philosophy.

Questions for Reflection

1. Do you believe that the term *science* can be precisely defined? If so, how would you propose to define it (in such a way as to overcome the problems discussed above)?
2. Scientism is plainly an irrational view, yet many people in our culture affirm it. Can you think of some factors—cultural, psychological, etc.—which might motivate people to take this perspective?
3. Can you think of some other presuppositions of science besides those discussed above?

§ 3.2 Scientific Realism

Having noted the limits of science and the difficulty of even defining it, we need to keep in mind just how much science has changed the world. All of the technologies of modern life, from cars and computers to toasters and air conditioners, are the result of scientific research. And medical science has significantly improved the quality of our lives in countless ways. Indeed, the achievements of science are formidable. It is easy to see why many people conclude from this that scientists are special in their capacity to discover truth about the world. But is this so? Is science, in fact, even concerned with truth at all? With regard to the relationship between science and truth, there are two fundamental perspectives. *Scientific realism* is the view that scientific theories properly aim to give us a true account of the physical world. In other words, the realist says that science is successful precisely because its descriptions of the world tend to correspond to the way the world really is. On the other hand, *scientific nonrealism* denies this claim, insisting that science is not ultimately about truth. For all of its practical achievements, science does not aim at accurate descriptions of reality. Its ultimate concerns lie elsewhere.

In the next two sections we will look at the debate between realism and nonrealism in some detail. We will see how versions of each perspective represent a broad spectrum of views on the aims of science and the purpose of scientific theories.

3.2.1 Inductivism

One popular view of science is known as *inductivism*. According to this view, a scientist begins by simply observing the world and gathering data. As her data base grows she begins to make generalizations about her observations, and eventually she formulates an hypothesis or theory which explains the data. Next the scientist tests her theory by running experiments, and she gathers more data. This additional data, in turn, either confirms or falsifies her theory. This process continues until the theory is either proven false or satisfactorily confirmed. Thus, with adequate testing, the scientist may conclude with confidence that her theory is either true or false.

The Process of Confirmation

The nineteenth-century inductivist William Whewell (1794–1866) observed that a scientific theory is not built through simple enumeration of observable phenomena but is only indirectly suggested by them. Through a special inferential process he calls "colligation," a scientist arrives at a theoretical account that unites and clarifies all of the observations. Whewell compares particular facts to individual pearls. A theory must unite the facts as a string unites pearls. This creates a "true bond of unity by which the phenomena are held together."[4] Further empirical data then serve to confirm the theory, though not to prove it, and from this general theory specific propositions about matters of fact may be explored.

To highlight the main features of inductivism, let us consider an example. In San Francisco in the early 1980s there arose numerous cases of uncommon diseases, such as Kaposi's sarcoma and pneumocystis pneumonia, each of which was associated with generally depressed immune system function. Soon cases of the same symptoms occurred elsewhere in California and in New York. After studying dozens of these patients, researchers discovered that a previously unknown virus was present in each instance. Scientists therefore posited that this virus was a causal agent in compromising immune system function. As new cases of the disease complex were discovered, the virus was also found in these patients, thus confirming the hypothesis. Eventually, researchers concluded that the disease, now called AIDS, is indeed caused by the virus, now known as the human immunodeficiency virus, or HIV. This form of inductive reasoning can be represented as follows:

> X preceded (or was present with) Y in case A.
> X preceded (or was present with) Y in case B.
> X preceded (or was present with) Y in case C.
> . . . . etc.
> Therefore, it is likely that X causes Y.

This example illustrates the central claims of inductivism. First, scientific observation precedes theory. That is, it is possible for scientists to observe the world in a fairly objective way, to do theory-neutral experimentation and data gathering. And when it comes to formulating

---

[4] William Whewell, *The Philosophy of the Inductive Sciences* (London: John W. Parker, 1847), 2:46.

theories, scientists can do so strictly in terms of the experimental data. Early AIDS researchers did just this as they looked at multiple cases of the disease and searched for microorganisms, culminating in the discovery of HIV. Second, as a discipline, science advances through a simple accumulation of experimental data and construction of theories built strictly upon the data. The discovery of HIV-AIDS added to the body of knowledge in medicine and epidemiology, and our understanding in these fields continues to expand. And, third, science is, or at any rate can be, a completely rational enterprise. While human bias may sometimes interfere with particular applications of the scientific method, the method itself is thoroughly rational and it is possible to make firm conclusions about the truth or falsity of theories when the method is carefully applied. AIDS researchers inquired into the various dimensions of this disease in a systematic and dispassionate way, making well-justified inferences as to the underlying causes.

The Problem of Induction (and Other Difficulties with Inductivism)

Inductivism has a lot of intuitive appeal, as it offers a simple and straightforward account of scientific inquiry. It also reinforces the common sense notion that science is a rigorous discipline, in fact the most rational among the disciplines. However, for all of its strengths, inductivism suffers from two serious shortcomings. First, it naïvely assumes the possibility of theory-neutral observation. For a variety of reasons this is a dubious notion. For one thing, psychological studies have shown that people tend to observe the world and interpret data in light of preconceptions, however fair-minded they strive to be. History seems to bear out this point in every subfield of science, as defenders of theories from Ptolemaic astronomy to the phlogiston theory of combustion to Newtonian concepts of absolute time and space held tenaciously to their views, even against overwhelming evidence. This issue will be discussed in more detail when we look at Kuhn's philosophy of science.

Another problem with inductivism is that it is not clear just how much confirming experimental data is necessary to demonstrate the truth of a particular theory. Exactly when is a scientist justified in moving from the claim that her theory is *confirmed* by the data to the much stronger claim that her theory is *true*? In reference to our example, at what point are researchers justified in moving from the observation that HIV is correlated with AIDS in cases A, B, C, D . . . X to the conclusion that HIV is the *cause* of *all* cases of AIDS? Inductivism gives us no clear criteria for this important logical step.

This difficulty with inductive reasoning reveals a problem that is fundamental to the practice of science, as scientific inquiry routinely involves reasoning from particular observations to universal conclusions and making assumptions about the future based on past experiences. For instance, based on past sunrises one concludes that the sun will rise tomorrow. As noted above, scientists must assume that the laws of nature are constant. Without this assumption no experimental procedures are possible. Of course, it is not only scientists who make this assumption. While inductive inference happens to be especially crucial to science, we all reason in this way every day. Everyone reasons from observed events to the unobserved, inferring from what we have experienced to what lies beyond experience, such as future events. But most people do not recognize that this inference is problematic.

David Hume (1711–1776) was the first to identify the problem formally. In his *Treatise of Human Nature* he makes this shockingly bold claim:

> there is nothing in any object considered in itself which can afford us a reason for drawing a conclusion beyond it; and, even after the observation of the frequent or constant conjunction of objects, we have no reason to draw any inference concerning any object beyond those of which we have had experience.[5]

Hume's argument for this thesis is set in the context of his discussion of causality, which we examined in the previous chapter. According to Hume, we cannot justify our belief in a necessary connection between a cause and its effect. We cannot justify it by experience, because we never sense a necessary connection between a cause and effect. And we cannot justify it by reason, since we can always conceive the occurrence of any cause without its being accompanied by its usual effect.

Hume also pointed out the circularity of attempts to prove causal laws. In appealing to experience to justify belief in causal laws one can only appeal to past and present experiences. However, in doing so we inevitably beg the question, for such reasoning is based on the premise that the future will resemble the past. But *it is our belief that the future will resemble the past* that we are trying to justify. Hume concludes, "It is impossible, therefore, that any arguments from experience can prove this resemblance of the past to the future; since all these arguments are founded on the supposition of that resemblance."[6]

Hume's argument undermines belief in the uniformity of nature and may be rephrased as follows. In order to justify our belief that nature is uniform, our only possible recourse is to appeal to the fact that in the

---

[5] David Hume, *A Treatise of Human Nature*, 2nd ed., ed. L. A. Selby-Bigge (Oxford: Oxford University Press, 1978), 139.

[6] Ibid., 71.

past nature has been uniform. Obviously, in arguing this way we presuppose that nature is uniform, the very belief we are attempting to justify. So we are arguing in a circle. The upshot, in Hume's view, is that our belief in the uniformity of nature is unjustified.

This is the *problem of induction*. And since science depends on nature being uniform, it is a *very* serious problem. Is a solution possible? Hume's own response was to take a pragmatic approach. Despite his argument that there are no rational grounds for believing that the future will resemble the past, he grants that this belief is irresistible, and although entirely a product of human psychology, it is in fact very practical. If we are to get along in life, we must assume, if not in word at least in deed, that nature is uniform. It is a sort of "animal faith" that abides with us for our own good. This approach, however, is widely regarded as deficient, as it is basically a concession to skepticism. (Indeed, Hume himself was a strong skeptic.) Consequently, philosophers have developed a variety of strategies to solve the problem, which we will discuss throughout this chapter.

3.2.2 Falsificationism

The problem of induction suggested to many philosophers that the business of science does not have to do with proving theories true so much as proving theories *false*. Accordingly, Karl Popper (1902–1994) developed a philosophy of science that fastened on this point.

Popper's Demarcation Project

Popper was disturbed by the many thinkers who dubiously advanced their theories as "scientific." He was especially bothered by the Marxist theory of history and Freudian psychology, neither of which seemed capable of refutation even in principle. For example, when a Marxist claims that history is determined by economic factors, there is no way to empirically test this claim. And when a Freudian interprets a person's behavior as manifesting repressed anger, this claim cannot be tested empirically. Such theories are really no more scientific than astrology, says Popper. For just as in the case of astrological predictions, our observations about history and personal behavior can always be reinterpreted to fit the claims of the Marxist and Freudian, respectively. For example, no matter what factors really gave rise to, say, the stagnation of the American auto industry, the Marxist can point to specific cases of labor strife as signs of the alienating effects of capitalism. And if a person denies being angry with her Freudian analyst, the Freudian can retort that this very denial is itself a sign of her repressed anger.

So the pressing concern for Popper became the problem of demarcation. That is, how do we draw the line between science and pseudoscience? Popper suggested that the failure to make this demarcation clearly has caused all sorts of confusion among scholars and ordinary folk alike. In response, he proposed the *criterion of falsifiability* as a solution, insisting that "statements or systems of statements, in order to be ranked as scientific, must be capable of conflicting with possible, or conceivable, observations."[7] The claims of Marxists, Freudians, and astrologists are always so vague that they do not generate truly testable predictions. Einstein's relativity theory, by contrast, generated many specific predictions which could be tested and which thereby presented opportunities for falsifying the theory. One such prediction was that light from distant stars would bend as it passed by the sun. In August 1919 this claim was put to the test during a solar eclipse, and Einstein's theory survived the test. Concomitantly, the classical Newtonians' claim was falsified. Thus, because they were falsifiable, both theories proved genuinely scientific, though only one of them survived for further testing.

So, according to Popper, science is essentially about trial and error or, to use his terminology, "conjectures" and "refutations." Scientific theories are not proven or inferred but rather are speculative conjectures dreamed up by researchers to overcome problems encountered by previous theories in accounting for empirical data. Though theories are never proven, some can be deemed superior because of their ability to resist refutation through rigorous testing. When it comes to scientific research, says Popper, the fittest theories survive. And a sign of theoretical fitness is the capacity of a theory to generate *risky* predictions. The more bold and novel a conjecture, the more impressive it is when the theory resists falsification. Einstein's prediction that light would bend was certainly bold in this respect. Many of his contemporaries found the idea absurd prior to testing. This is what made the results of the 1919 experiment so stunning and why this single event was virtually decisive in favor of relativity theory.

Popper is careful to note that despite the impressiveness of such fulfilled predictions, scientific theories are never positively proven. In terms of final proof, theories can only be demonstrated to be false. Thus, the logic of science is about *modus tollens*:

> If P then Q.
> Not-Q.
> Therefore, not-P.

---

[7] Karl Popper, "Science: Conjectures and Refutations" in *The Theory of Knowledge: Classical and Contemporary Readings*, 3rd ed., ed. Louis P. Pojman (Belmont, CA: Wadsworth, 2003), 488.

Or to use a concrete example:

1. If classical Newtonian physics is true, then light will travel in a straight line as it passes by a large body such as the sun.
2. Light bends when it passes by the sun, as observed in August 1919.
3. Therefore, classical Newtonian physics is false.

And scientists must resist the temptation to *affirm the consequent*:

If P then Q.
Q.
Therefore, P.

As was noted in chapter 1, this is a logical fallacy, which is committed in the following argument:

1. If Einstein's theory of relativity is true, then light will bend as it passes the sun.
2. Light does bend when it passes by the sun.
3. Therefore, Einstein's theory is true.

Although the reasoning here is invalid, this is a tempting inference in the case of a conjecture as bold as Einstein's. But good scientists resist this temptation to infer the truth of their theories. Here we see how Popper's falsificationism offers a solution to the problem of induction. According to Popper, inductive reasoning, strictly speaking, has no use in science. "There is," he says, "no need even to mention induction."[8] An hypothesis is never verified or confirmed, though it does achieve what Popper calls "corroboration" through successful testing. A well-corroborated theory is one that is a bold conjecture that has endured numerous tests without falsification.

Sometimes a theory need only be modified in order to overcome certain difficulties presented by experimental data. However, falsificationists warn, not just any alterations to a theory are appropriate. In Popper's words, the modifications themselves must be "independently testable." This point may be illustrated by a chapter from the history of astronomy. For centuries most people were Ptolemaic geocentrists, believing that the Earth is at the center of the universe and that the Sun and other planets orbit our planet. In the sixteenth century Copernicus became famous for his defense of heliocentrism, the view that Earth and the other planets in our solar system orbit the Sun. Later, with the advent of the telescope, many astronomers began to side with

[8] Karl Popper, *The Logic of Scientific Discovery* (New York: Harper and Row, 1959), 315.

Copernicus, especially as they observed that the other planets moved in irregular patterns as they moved around the Earth. In fact, some planets appeared to stop, restart, and even go backwards in their orbits. With the advance of telescope technology these irregularities became more pronounced. Copernicus's theory was later defended by Galileo, as more experimental data were provided by increasingly powerful telescopes.

Geocentrists and heliocentrists agreed that planetary motion should be expected to be smooth. Thus, Galileo argued that the apparent stopping and restarting of planets in their orbits essentially falsified geocentrism. That Copernicanism could easily account for smooth, regular planetary orbits further corroborated the theory (to use Popper's terminology). However, the geocentrists had a retort. The planets only *appeared* to stop and restart in their orbits. In fact, they proposed, the planets occasionally do loops within their orbits—a phenomenon they referred to as "epicycles." And in some cases the movements of the planets even called for loops within the loops (epi-epicycles?). Needless to say, Galileo and the other Copernicans were not impressed. But how could such a modification to geocentrism be refuted?

This is precisely Popper's point when he insists that modifications to a theory must be "independently testable." A modification to a theory which fails to be independently testable is known as an *ad hoc* modification. Another classic example of an *ad hoc* theory from the history of science regards a theory of combustion from the nineteenth century. At that time many scientists maintained that when objects burn they release a substance known as "phlogiston." However, it was eventually discovered that some objects gain weight after burning, which appeared to falsify the phlogiston theory. Defenders of the view, however, explained this by proposing that phlogiston has "negative weight," a claim which is *ad hoc* because it cannot be tested. Critics of Darwinism have proposed the following as yet another example. As he developed his theory of evolution, Darwin noted that the fossil evidence would be key to the success of his theory, which predicted both intermediate fossil forms (paleontological evidence for many extinct organisms which bridge biological gaps between known organisms) and gradualism (the emergence of increasingly complex organisms over long periods of time). When it became clear that paleontology had not borne out Darwin's prediction, Stephen Jay Gould proposed a theory known as "punctuated equilibrium"—the notion that evolutionary history is marked by long phases of stasis, or lack of biological change, punctuated by sudden dramatic changes of increased complexity. While this modification appears to resolve the lack of paleontological evidence for Darwinism, it is also independently untestable and is thus an *ad hoc* modification.

Problems with Falsificationism

Popper's approach has been very influential, but critics have pointed out many serious problems with the view. First, falsificationists assume, much like inductivists, that scientists' observations of phenomena can be theory-independent. There are good reasons to doubt this is so, as was already noted and will be discussed further below. A second problem with falsificationism concerns the fact that it is difficult to distinguish Popper's notion of corroboration from the role of confirmation in inductivism. Moreover, his claim that science does not involve theory verification seems to fly in the face of the plain facts of the scientific enterprise. Most scientists, it seems, *are* interested in showing not only that some hypotheses are false but also that others are at least likely to be true. Thus, Popper's suggestion that scientists need not use induction appears inaccurate.

A more serious problem concerns the difficulty in actually falsifying theories. When an experiment is conducted critical assumptions are always made, so it is not only the theory that is evaluated but also these "auxiliary assumptions." And when falsifying data results, one cannot be absolutely certain that it is the theory rather than the auxiliary assumptions which have been falsified. Consider another example from early modern astronomy. Some critics of Copernican theory objected because it implied that the Earth is spinning very fast (approximately 1,000 miles per hour) and that this would have absurd consequences. First, if our planet is spinning so incredibly fast, then why aren't objects flying off? Moreover, if the Earth is spinning, then one would expect objects dropped from the top of a tall tower to land some distance away from the base of the tower, a phenomenon which is in fact never observed.

What such critics overlooked was the fact that not only the Earth but everything on its surface was spinning at the same rate. They did not appreciate the concept of the Earth's atmosphere, which helps to make the rate of the spinning of our planet and everything on it imperceptible to us. Effectively, then, the geocentrists made a dubious assumption about the Earth's atmosphere. Thus, when testing Copernicanism in light of these observations about stationary and dropped objects, the experimental results did not falsify the Copernican theory but rather showed the auxiliary assumption to be false, as follows (where C=Copernicanism, A=Auxiliary assumption and E=Expected observations):

If (C & A), then E.
Not-E.
Therefore, not-(C & A).

Thus, the experimental data contradicting the expectations demonstrate the falsehood of either the theory or the auxiliary assumption (or both). But which is it? Without a clear answer, one cannot claim to have falsified the Copernican theory. In any scientific experiment similar auxiliary assumptions are made. And when falsifying data are gathered, one cannot be sure when it is the theory or an assumption that is proven false. Scientists are, of course, aware of this problem, and many researchers run further experiments to test a questionable assumption. However, not all assumptions can be identified, and even when an auxiliary assumption is tested, the test involves yet more auxiliary assumptions. So, it seems, scientific theories cannot be conclusively falsified after all. It is noteworthy that Popper recognized this problem with his theory and for this reason he compared the construction of scientific theory to building on a swamp. This is not an encouraging metaphor for those looking for a solid foundation for science!

Questions for Reflection

1. Which general perspective on science, realism or nonrealism, do you think most children are taught in schools in our culture? What accounts for this?
2. It appears that most people are unaware that there is a problem of induction, though this is a serious problem for the rationality of science. Why do you suppose this problem is relatively unrecognized?
3. If falsifiability of theories is not a satisfactory way to distinguish science from nonscience, then how do you propose this distinction be made?
4. Can you think of an original example of an *ad hoc* hypothesis, whether from science or some other context such as theology?

§ 3.3 Scientific Nonrealism

Given the problems with various aspects of scientific realism, it is no wonder that many scientists and philosophers of science have turned to nonrealist philosophies of science. Recall that scientific realists claim that scientific theories aim to provide a true account of natural phenomena, while scientific nonrealists maintain that science is not really about truth. In this section we will take a look at some nonrealist perspectives on science.

3.3.1 Instrumentalism

The most impressive thing about science is its practical achievements. Scientists have been able to construct amazing technologies, from automobiles to computers, and create medicines, vaccines, and surgical procedures to overcome health problems that for most of human history were fatal, from small pox to appendicitis. Thus, notwithstanding the problems with scientific realism, science deserves special recognition. Some philosophers of science have preferred to surrender the effort to justify belief in the *truth* of scientific theories and to focus on their practicality. This approach is known as scientific *instrumentalism*.

Instrumentalists assert that scientific theories do not describe the world but rather function as tools for solving problems by predicting and explaining observable phenomena. On this view, theoretical entities such as protons, quarks, and electromagnetic fields, are merely useful fictions. The instrumentalist approach, then, focuses on the practical value of science. Not surprisingly, some of the American pragmatists, such as John Dewey, were sympathetic with this approach. Dewey writes, "'Water' in ordinary experience designates an essence of something which has familiar bearings and uses in human life, drink and cleansing and the extinguishing of fire. But H_2O gets away from these connections and embodies in its essence only instrumental efficiency in respect of things independent of human affairs."[9] A more recent instrumentalist philosopher of science, Larry Laudan, expresses the view succinctly when he declares that "science is an inquiry system for the solution of problems" and that "the adequacy of individual theories is a function of how many significant empirical problems they solve."[10]

Instrumentalists recognize that we often find irresistible the impulse to declare very successful theories to be "true" while we will call "false" others that fail. But such assertions should be understood in the pragmatic sense of truth, where the term is not meant to denote anything beyond practicality. The atomic theory of the atom and the theory of relativity in physics have been very useful, while Ptolemaic geocentrism and the phlogiston theory of combustion have not. To call the former theories "true" and the latter ones "false" is merely a shorthand way of referring to this fact.

One of the assets of scientific instrumentalism is how it manages to skirt the problem of induction, which, as we have seen, is the Achilles heel of scientific realism. Since instrumentalists stop short of claiming the truth or falsity of theories, they assume no burden of justifying the

[9] John Dewey, *Experience and Nature* (New York: Dover, 1958), 193.
[10] Larry Laudan, *Progress and Its Problems: Toward a Theory of Scientific Growth* (Berkeley: University of California Press, 1977), 126 and 119.

inductive method. The most well-known pragmatic treatment of the problem is that of Hans Reichenbach.[11] He acknowledges the force of Hume's arguments and concedes the impossibility of giving a rational justification of induction. Still, he counsels against casting away the method entirely, for vindication of induction is possible on the grounds that it will succeed if anything succeeds. If there is uniformity in nature, then induction is a viable method, for so long as some method of predicting the future works, induction will also succeed. And if nature is not uniform, induction will fail along with every alternative method.

Suppose, for instance, that the practice of crystal gazing has been effective for predicting the future. If this were so, then an inductive argument for the continued success of crystal gazing could be made from its prior efficacy. Therefore, as long as crystal gazing or any other method enjoyed success, so would the method of induction. Reichenbach's conclusion, then, is that there is nothing to lose and much to gain by employing the inductive method. The problem with Reichenbach's pragmatic approach to induction is that it is less a solution than a wager, a variation of Hume's response to his own arguments, largely conceding to them. Reichenbach provides us only with practical recommendations for assuming the uniformity of nature, as opposed to *rational grounds for believing* in the uniformity of nature.

Returning to scientific instrumentalism as a general philosophy of science, this perspective has some significant strengths. Not the least of these is its insight into the importance of the usefulness of scientific theories in solving problems. Science as a discipline is inspired by practical concerns, and instrumentalism takes this seriously. But where instrumentalism goes wrong is in emphasizing practicality to the exclusion of concerns about truth. Indeed, the fact that a particular theory is practical itself needs an explanation. *Why* is the atomic theory of combustion so useful? And *why* does the theory of relativity solve so many problems in physics that the old Newtonian model could not? That these theories enable us to make novel predictions and create new technologies suggests that there is something about the world that corresponds with these theoretical models. In other words, the practicality of successful scientific theories seems best explained by scientific realism (and the correspondence theory of truth affirmed by realism).

Scientific instrumentalism is also undermined by certain technological advances that confirm the correspondence of particular theories to the world. For example, some former theoretical entities are now observable. Microorganisms and large molecules that once could only

---

[11] See Reichenbach's *Experience and Prediction* (Chicago: University of Chicago Press, 1938), chapter 5.

be theorized can now be observed through powerful microscopes. And planets that once could only be hypothesized to exist are now visible through telescopes. These observations now confirm that key aspects of germ theory, atomic theory, and heliocentrism are *true* in the sense that they correspond to the way the world actually is.

3.3.2 Kuhn's Paradigms

As we have seen, instrumentalists reject the realist thesis that scientific theories properly aim to describe the world. But it is noteworthy that instrumentalists agree with realists in affirming that science is ultimately a rational discipline. In other words, realists and instrumentalists alike maintain that scientific inference and theory selection are properly based on evidence and objective reasoning and that careful scientific inquiry often achieves such objectivity. However, some recent philosophers of science have challenged even this supposition, maintaining that science is not fundamentally a rational enterprise. The most influential critic of the rationality of science has been Thomas Kuhn (1922–1996). In his landmark work, *The Structure of Scientific Revolutions,* Kuhn argued that the history of science demonstrates that, despite the ideals of the scientific community, actual practice in the discipline is far from rational in any objective sense of the term.

Scientific Revolutions

One of Kuhn's pivotal claims is that *observation of the world is theory-laden.* That is, our perceptions are always impacted by our presuppositions, whether these are simple concepts regarding race and gender or full-blown theories. The world we see is always interpreted through these constructs so we never have direct, objective access to it. Scientists, argues Kuhn, are not exempt from this fact of human psychology. Even the most fair-minded scientist observes in light of the model or "paradigm" she embraces. Thus, says Kuhn, a Ptolemaic astronomer literally "sees" the Sun move across the sky, while the Copernican "sees" the Earth rotating on its axis. And when a creationist and a Darwinist visit the zoo, the former "sees" intelligent design in every aspect of each creature, while the latter "sees" the results of millions of years of natural selection and random mutation.

A critical implication here is that neutral observation is impossible. Scientists always labor under the influence of some paradigm or other. Interpretation of the data is unavoidable. This is often illustrated with the "duck-rabbit" drawing that we introduced in chapter 2 (see figure 3.1). While the same drawing can be variously perceived as either a duck or a rabbit, it cannot be simultaneously seen as both. And once one is able to see the drawing as a duck and/or a rabbit, it is impossible to see it as merely formless lines.

Figure 3.1

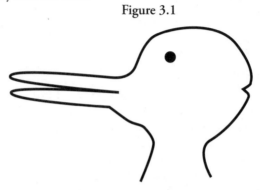

The term *paradigm* is somewhat vague, but Kuhn distinguished between two distinct aspects of the concept. One of these he calls the "disciplinary matrix," which refers to "the entire constellation of beliefs, values, techniques, and so on shared by members of a given community."[12] Another, more specific, sense of the term refers to "exemplars," which are the accepted problem-solving techniques within a discipline. In physics, chemistry, and biology, as well as the social sciences, there are disciplinary matrices and exemplars according to which practitioners abide. And in both senses of the term, a paradigm consistently colors a scientist's observations of the world and interpretations of experimental data. There is no such thing as neutral or objective research. Scientists always labor under the influence of their paradigm, including the very means by which the problems in their field are identified and solved.

Kuhn challenged the notion that scientific progress occurs by simple accumulation of data. Instead, he maintained, *the history of science proceeds through paradigm shifts*. By this he means that after a paradigm has been developed for a while, another paradigm comes along and displaces it. After this shift has taken place, the new paradigm is developed until yet another paradigm replaces it. The process follows a basic pattern (see figure 3.2). In the earliest years of a fledgling science there is a brief period of *pre-science* in which research is done without a guiding paradigm. Eventually, a theoretical account is given for the empirical data, and the first paradigm in the field is born. Scientists then do research in service of this paradigm, a stage Kuhn calls *normal science*. But as more research is done there inevitably emerge data that do not fit into the reigning paradigm. Such anomalies, which take the form of

---

[12] Thomas S. Kuhn, *The Structure of Scientific Revolutions*, 2nd ed. (Chicago: University of Chicago Press, 1970), 175.

inexplicable phenomena or theoretical puzzles, introduce a period of *crisis* for the paradigm and generate further research aimed at explaining the anomalies and resolving the crisis. If this research succeeds, then normal science resumes. But if this research fails and a new paradigm is proposed that incorporates the anomalous data, then there is a shift to the new paradigm. Kuhn calls this a scientific *revolution*. This term, he suggests, is appropriate because paradigm shifts in science are like political revolutions in that they are human-made, relatively sudden, and highly disruptive.

Figure 3.2

Pre-science→ Normal Science → Crisis → Revolution → New Normal Science → New Crisis, etc.

A natural question to ask at this point is how rival paradigms are assessed. In terms of what standards are theories evaluated? Kuhn's answer is that if one is asking for objective, rational standards by which paradigms are evaluated, there are none. As he puts it, *scientific paradigms are incommensurable*. That is, paradigms cannot be compared or assessed by any single standard or set of criteria. Rather, each paradigm contains its own standards of rationality. In fact, such standards or criteria for scientific rationality are part of what constitutes a paradigm. What counts as rational for a geocentrist is different than what counts as rational for a heliocentrist. The criteria for scientific inference are different for a quantum physicist than for a classical Newtonian. According to Kuhn, this accounts for the stalemates among proponents of competing paradigms. He explains:

> To the extent . . . that two scientific schools disagree about what is a problem and what a solution, they will inevitably talk through each other when debating the relative merits of their respective paradigms. In the partially circular arguments that regularly result, each paradigm will be shown to satisfy more or less the criteria it dictates for itself and to fall short of a few of those dictated by its opponent.[13]

That no debate across paradigm boundaries is possible is one of the major reasons why the Kuhnian must conclude that science is not a rational enterprise. But, of course, something must explain scientific revolutions. If it is not objective evidence and rational inference, then what does cause them? Kuhn is not altogether clear on this point, but he does note that it comes down to the "needs" of the scientific community and thus

[13] Ibid., 109–10.

boils down to sociological factors. He also notes that aesthetic consider-ations, personal tenacity, and even faith come into play in causing one paradigm to prevail over another. But what are not relevant are evidence and rational arguments. "The competition between paradigms," insists Kuhn, "is not the sort of battle that can be resolved by proofs."[14]

Objections to Kuhn's View

In the last half century Kuhn's philosophy of science has generated as much discussion and debate as anything else in the field of philosophy. As the decades have passed since the publication of *The Structure of Scientific Revolutions*, Kuhn's ideas have become more widely accepted. But there are still many fierce critics. We will briefly discuss four of the more common objections to Kuhn's theory.

First, some object that Kuhn's theory simply does not fit the com-mon-sense view that science is a rational enterprise. Not only does the progress of science—at least in the form of practical success—suggest that our theories are more and more closely approximating the truth about the natural world, but much about the field of science, from the use of the scientific method to scientific conferences and publications suggests that there are shared rational standards for inquiry and that evidence does carry the day in science. Of course, to this Kuhn would say that if this is the common-sense view, then so much the worse for common sense. Appearances to the contrary notwithstanding, he insists, ultimately science does not give us objective truth, nor is it ultimately rational.

Other critics have fastened on the implication of Kuhn's view that it provides no way of making a public, objective defense or critique of a theory. That is, if we adopt a Kuhnian perspective, then there is no way we can say one theory is better than another, which seems absurd. In response, again, Kuhn is happy to bite this bullet and heartily agree that no scientific theory is really objectively better than another. Paradigms are only superior to other paradigms relative to their own internal ratio-nal standards.

Two other criticisms of Kuhn are more powerful. First, Kuhn's theory cannot adequately account for why scientific revolutions take place. If all theory selection is relative to community "needs" and is therefore always primarily a matter of sociology and psychology, then why should so painful and disruptive an event as a scientific revolu-tion ever occur? Also, Kuhn's theory cannot explain why a crucial test could so decisively settle a scientific dispute. For example, consider the solar eclipse experiment that refuted classical Newtonian physics and

---

[14] Ibid., 148.

confirmed relativity theory in 1919. Essentially overnight this experiment ended the debate and constituted a victory for Einstein and his advocates. This case, like many others, seems to qualify as a *rational* refutation of a reigning paradigm.

Finally, many have argued that Kuhn's theory is self-defeating. His claims about the paradigm-relativity of scientific truth claims can easily be extended to all other disciplines, including philosophy. So if all truth claims are simply relative to theoretical perspectives and cannot be regarded as objectively true, then this applies to Kuhn's philosophy of science itself. Given his claims, he cannot say that his view is objectively *true*. His is only one paradigm that happens to meet some community's needs, presumably that of the philosophical community. But, then, if he is not offering us a true account of science, then why should we bother listening to him?

3.3.3 Feyerabend's Anarchism

Kuhn's philosophy of science is highly relativistic and is viewed by many as a skeptical extreme. But an even more extreme skepticism about science was developed by Paul Feyerabend (1924–1994). According to Feyerabend, science is not constrained by any clear-cut methodological rules when it comes to theory assessment and selection. That is to say, in science "anything goes." For this reason, Feyerabend describes his approach as an anarchist philosophy of science.

Science as Mythology

Feyerabend is sympathetic with Kuhn's claim that scientific theories are incommensurable. They cannot be compared by a single rational standard. And since there is no way to compare and assess scientific theories objectively, it is impossible to show that any scientific theory offers a better explanation of data than any nonscientific theory. For this reason Feyerabend sees theory incommensurability as leading to a subjectivist view of science. He writes, "[W]hat remains . . . are aesthetic judgments, judgments of taste, metaphysical prejudices, religious desires, in short, *what remains are our subjective wishes.*"[15]

Such a view contradicts the traditional conception of science, which Feyerabend calls a "fairy tale":

> According to the fairy tale the success of science is the result of
> a subtle, but carefully balanced combination of inventiveness
> and control. Scientists have *ideas*. And they have special *methods*

---

[15] Paul Feyerabend, *Against Method: Outline of an Anarchist Theory of Knowledge* (London: New Left, 1975), 285. Emphasis is the author's.

for improving ideas. The theories of science have passed the test of method. They give a better account of the world than ideas which have not passed the test.

The fairy tale explains why modern society treats science in a special way and why it grants it privileges not enjoyed by other institutions.[16]

In fact, Feyerabend claims, science is much more like mythology than philosophers of science want to admit. "Rational reconstructions," he says, "take 'basic scientific wisdom' *for granted*. They do not *show* that it is better than the 'basic wisdom' of witches and warlocks."[17]

Notice how Feyerabend's thesis is essentially the same as that of the narrator of Pirsig's book, who suggested that Western science appeals to its own system of ghosts and spirits. There is some merit to this comparison. Consider the law of gravity, for instance. No one has ever had a sense experience of gravity itself. Rather it is a concept that is used to explain events that we do experience with our senses. Early modern philosophers used to call such explanations "occult" in the sense that they appeal to something that is known only by its effects. This is no different than appeals to ghosts in popular thought—they are known only by their effects. This similarity helps to explain why Feyerabend and Pirsig's narrator would characterize science as mythological.

It is tempting here to suggest that we simply compare scientific methods with other methodologies to demonstrate the superiority of science. But this is not an option, because such a comparison would itself necessarily involve either a scientific or nonscientific method. So the inquiry would be unfairly biased. For this reason, again, all that is left is subjective preference, which according to Feyerabend is expressed in raw, intolerant coercion: "[Science] reigns supreme because its practitioners are *unable to understand*, and *unwilling to condone*, different ideologies, because they have the *power* to enforce their wishes."[18]

Feyerabend's philosophy of science is actually driven by a more fundamental concern about human freedom. He believes that the ideal society is one in which citizens are completely self-determining. In Western societies, however, science has become the standard for knowledge and its method is dogmatically enforced at all academic levels. Science is essentially an institutionalized ideology that is forced upon people so that they are not really free to pursue all avenues of understanding. Thus, Feyerabend complains that "while an American can now choose

---

[16] Ibid., 300. Emphases are the author's.
[17] Ibid., 205. Emphases are the author's.
[18] Ibid., 299. Emphases are the author's.

the religion he likes, he is still not permitted to demand that his children learn magic rather than science at school. There is a separation between state and Church, there is no separation between state and science."[19] In an ideal state, says Feyerabend, there is methodological neutrality when it comes to knowledge. But in teaching the scientific method and a particular set of theories, public schools are biased and limit our freedom. Today our society needs to be free from the tyranny of science just as much as we need freedom from a state religion. Science is but one knowledge tradition, and our public schools should reflect this.

Objections to Feyerabend's View

Feyerabend's anarchist approach continues to raise eyebrows, but even those who firmly oppose his ideas tend to recognize the merit of many of his concerns. In standardizing any beliefs or methodology a society runs a great risk. If the beliefs are mistaken or the method is faulty, then the entire population is deceived. And Feyerabend makes a good point about freedom of inquiry in our country. As the recent documentary *Expelled* powerfully illustrates, dogmatic insistence on a particular scientific paradigm not only violates the spirit of academic freedom but is professionally and personally oppressive.[20]

However, most critics believe that Feyerabend goes too far in advocating epistemological anarchy and denying that science is in any sense superior to other methodologies. As we have already noted in discussing other philosophies of science, the practical achievements of science suggest a correspondence to reality of many of its theories, and this is clearly something that can hardly be claimed for witches, warlocks, and practitioners of magic. If, as Feyerabend insists, no methodology is really superior to any other, then how do we explain the remarkable technological advances of science that other methodologies cannot even begin to approach? While it is true that many of these technologies, such as internal combustion engines and nuclear power, have been abused and caused much suffering, the fact that science has generated such technologies is in itself impressive and seems explicable only by a realist perspective.

Secondly, Feyerabend insightfully extends many of Kuhn's arguments, but he goes too far in opting for a subjectivist theory of scientific theory selection. The difficulty of finding objective standards for assessing paradigms does not entail a wholesale rejection of objectivity in science. Indeed, to conclude from his failure to identify objective rational standards that there are none is not only an unjustified inference

[19] Ibid.
[20] *Expelled: No Intelligence Allowed* (Premise, 2008; 90 mins; PG), directed by Nathan Frankowski.

but a kind of arrogance. And to insist on this basis that "anything goes" in science is probably every bit as dangerous as the scientific dogmatism he so strongly opposes.

3.3.4 Final Thoughts on Realism and Nonrealism

We have examined different versions of scientific realism and non-realism and noted the strengths and difficulties with each perspective. So where does this leave us? We would like to close this part of our discussion with several summary observations. First, the problem of induction presents a serious limitation for all realist theories. Since inductive reasoning cannot be justified without *assuming* the reliability of inductive reasoning, this shows that it must be presupposed from the outset. In other words, it appears that Hume was right: induction is a sort of faith that is essential to the practice of science. However, as we will show below, this does not mean that this faith cannot be reasonable and well-grounded.

Second, nonrealist views cannot adequately account for the practical success of science. While instrumentalists focus on the practicality of science, they do not explain it, nor do they even attempt to do so. And Kuhn and Feyerabend are loathe even to admit the practical success of science. But the accomplishments of science should not be ignored or downplayed. While there have been, and will likely continue to be, many abuses of science and its technologies, this does not negate the fact that through scientific research human beings have accomplished wondrous things. It is hard to imagine how these achievements could be accounted for without acknowledging that successful theories more or less describe or correspond to the physical world.

This brings us to our third point. Whatever philosophy of science one opts for, one must keep in mind that one's view needs to accord with a commitment to the correspondence theory of truth. As we saw in chapter 1, we must accept the correspondence theory for both philosophical and theological reasons. Some would claim that this creates a presumption in favor of scientific realism. However, the nonrealist could agree that all truth is correspondence to reality, while holding that scientific theories are just not the sorts of things that are true—they serve some other function (e.g., solving problems, meeting community needs, etc.). In this way one may affirm scientific nonrealism while maintaining one's commitment to the correspondence theory of truth.

We would recommend some form of humble realism that acknowledges that scientific theories do have truth values, even though they typically serve other functions as well and despite the fact that the scientific community is as fallen as the rest of society. Yes, science is often abused. And it is true that personal hubris, professional ambition, quirks of history and sociology, and all sorts of random factors impact scientific inquiry. Still, many researchers apply the scientific method rigorously and responsibly, and when they do so, genuine insights into the natural world, as well as significant practical achievements, are possible.

Lastly, we must keep in mind that, however well executed, scientific inquiry can never enable us to discover the ultimate truths about reality. As Christians, we believe that God is the ultimate reality, and He is a transcendent spirit (cp. Jn. 4:24). Thus, for all of its usefulness, science can inform us about God only indirectly—through our study of the physical world. This point will keep us grounded in the truth that science pertains to a limited domain. We will return to this important point shortly when we consider the issue of science and theology.

Questions for Reflection

1. Are you a scientific realist or nonrealist? What are the main reasons that you take the view you do? What theological considerations, if any, inform your position on this issue?
2. Do you think the practical achievements of science make the realist position about science more compelling? Why or why not?
3. As was noted, Kuhn's philosophy of science did not win many adherents in the years immediately following the publication of *The Structure of Scientific Revolutions*. But as the decades have passed, a large number of philosophers, and nonphilosophers, have adopted a Kuhnian perspective. Why might this be so?
4. To what extent, if at all, does Feyerabend's anarchism have genuine insights? Is his perspective dangerous or healthy for science? For intellectual inquiry generally?

§ 3.4 Laws of Nature

We have seen how scientific realism suffers from serious problems when it comes to justifying scientific truth claims. Some would suggest that this is not really a problem for realism because of the tenuous nature of theories of all kinds. Perhaps, then, we should look to more secure territory when it comes to scientific truth claims, and many would claim that there is nothing more secure in science than the laws of nature. In this section we will look at a variety of perspectives on natural laws.

3.4.1 Philosophical Perspectives on the Laws of Nature

What is a law of nature? All philosophers of science would agree that natural laws are, at the least, regularities. Consider the inverse square law of gravitation, which says that every object is attracted to other objects proportional to their size and inversely proportional to the square of the distance between them. In other words, gravitational attraction increases with objects' size and decreases with the distance. This is a regularity in nature. Many other law-like constants are observable in the world, including the laws of thermodynamics, Boyle's law, the Meissner effect, Faraday's law, Avagadro's constant, Ampere's law, the ideal gas law, and scores of others. That nature displays an astonishing consistency in its operations is empirically obvious. What is a matter of dispute is just how we are to understand these regularities. Three basic perspectives have been taken on this issue—the regularity view, instrumentalism, and the necessitarian approach.

The Regularity and Instrumentalist Views

Proponents of the *regularity view* regard laws as summary descriptions of how things have happened and will continue to happen. On this view, the laws of nature are simply generalized statements about nature's workings and the question *why* these regularities occur is either ignored or seen as illegitimate. Thus, regularity theorists are concerned only with the fact of nature's regularity and refuse to propose causal explanations for this fact. Regularity theorists' hesitance to offer such accounts traces back to David Hume's critique of causality.

As we saw above, *instrumentalists* take a pragmatic tack when it comes to the scientific enterprise generally, and this includes their view of the laws of nature. They say that the apparent universality of certain phenomena is not what is of first importance in science. Rather, it is the practical value of the general statements that matters. Thus, for the instrumentalist, the laws of nature are useful fictions. They do not have a truth-value but are essentially conceptual tools that scientists use to make inferences and solve problems.

Note that regularity theorists and instrumentalists refrain from making metaphysical claims about the laws of nature. That is, they do not offer deep explanations about the cause(s) of the laws of nature. Proponents of the third approach, however, do venture to make metaphysical claims.

The Necessitarian View

Necessitarians maintain that nature's regularities reflect not just how the world in fact behaves but how it *must* behave. An especially strong brand of necessitarianism sees the laws of nature as logically necessary. Proponents of this view often describe the laws of nature as instances of universal truths, exceptions to which are logically impossible. This view is commonly rejected because it is possible to conceive of a world in which our current physical laws do not hold (which should be impossible, given the logical necessitarian position). Moreover, if the laws of nature were logically necessary truths, then we would not need to rely upon empirical inquiry to discover them but could arrive at the laws of nature through simple reflection. Thus, since most such laws are not discoverable in such an *a priori* manner, this shows that they are not logically necessary.

More typically, necessitarians ground their conception of natural laws in what they regard as active powers inherent in physical systems. Thus, A. F. Chalmers writes, "The inverse square law of gravitation describes quantitatively the power to attract possessed by massive bodies, and the laws of classical electromagnetic theory describe, among other things, the capacity of charged bodies to attract and radiate. It is the active powers at work in nature that makes laws true when they are true."[21] This analysis accounts for law-like behavior by appealing to efficient causation, which in turn is explained by the natural dispositions of material objects. Chalmers takes this view to be implicit in the intuition that "the material world is active. Things happen in the world of their own accord, and they happen because entities in the world possess the capacity or power or disposition or tendency to act or behave in the way that they do."[22] One advantage of such a view is that the laws of nature may accordingly be seen as so many expressions of the more fundamental law of causality. And appeals to the laws of nature hold the promise of providing genuine causal explanations for phenomena.

But causal necessitarianism has some serious problems. Again, Hume's analysis of causality is the main difficulty. As a thoroughgoing empiricist, Hume asked what empirical evidence we have for the idea. To be precise, what we experience when observing a causal relation (such as in a game of billiards) is one event (the moving of the cue ball) occurring just prior to another (the moving of the eight ball). We also observe contiguity (the two balls touching), and we observe the same sorts of events occurring repeatedly, what Hume calls a "constant conjunction" of similar events. However, says Hume, "we are never able, in a single instance, to discover any power or necessary connection; any quality, which binds the effect to the cause, and renders the one an

---

[21] A. F. Chalmers, *What Is This Thing Called Science?* 3rd ed. (Indianapolis: Hackett, 1999), 219.

[22] Ibid., 218.

infallible consequence of the other. We only find that the one does actually, in fact, follow from the other."[23] Moreover, according to Hume, the temporal priority, contiguity, and constant conjunction do not justify our inferring a power or necessary connection between a cause and its effect. Hume's critique thus undermines the causal necessitarian view of the laws of nature, founded as it is upon the notion that there are active powers inherent in material objects.

Still, philosophers like Chalmers persist in their commitment to the notion that the laws of nature are causally necessary. This is understandable, given the naturalism of such philosophers. For the theist, this alternative is not necessary. To affirm that God sustains the universe appears to render necessitarianism (in any form) unnecessary, perhaps even foolish. If God sustains the universe from moment to moment (as is affirmed in such biblical passages as Heb 1:3 and Acts 17:28), then what other explanation for nature's regularities is possible? As Christian philosopher Richard Swinburne notes, "[T]he theist holds that any natural laws only operate because God brings it about that they do. That things have the effects in accord with natural laws which they do is, for the theist, itself an act of God."[24] If Swinburne is correct, then such things as "dispositions," "powers," and "forces" in nature are themselves divine handiwork. The universe does not run on its own. Rather, God upholds and directs it from moment to moment. When looking for an active agent to explain nature's regularities we need only look to God.

3.4.2 The Laws of Nature, the Problem of Induction, and Divine Providence

If the theist is correct in seeing the laws of nature as aspects of God's governance of the physical order, then something interesting follows as regards the biggest challenge to a realist philosophy of science. Specifically, herein lies a potential solution to the problem of induction. First, note that the regularities in nature make life possible in this world. We could not survive without being able to depend on gravity, the laws of thermodynamics, and other laws that make possible everything from our ability to make fire and grow crops to our capacity to make countless technologies. In short, regularities in nature are useful for human welfare and, thus, indirectly testify to the existence of a purposeful, intelligent, and powerful mind at work behind the cosmic scene who seeks to benefit his creatures. That is, the laws of nature evidence the existence of a benevolent God.

---

[23] David Hume, *The Essential Works of Hume*, ed. Ralph Cohen (New York: Bantam, 1965), 90.
[24] Richard Swinburne, *The Coherence of Theism* (Oxford: Oxford University Press, 1993), 143.

Now since God is benevolent, we can trust that the regularities in nature will indeed remain constant as they have in the past, that they are in fact lawful. That is, we can trust that the future will resemble the past. Why? Because if, after observing the constancy of nature and employing this knowledge for our own benefit, this regularity ceased, the results would be catastrophic for us. We might cite as a simple example the chemistry of water. If the freezing point of water suddenly rose a few degrees, the consequences for the human race, as well as for the rest of the animal kingdom, would be devastating. Ice would sink instead of floating, so oceans and lakes would freeze from top to bottom thus killing all marine life and making human life impossible. In short, humankind would be devastated if there occurred deviations from the normal course of nature's basic operations, and this would be inconsistent with the goodness of God and His love for His creatures. Therefore, we can and should believe that the future will resemble the past, since a loving God rules the world. Providence assures us that there are indeed "laws" of nature, so our belief that nature is uniform is not mere instinct or custom but is justified and hence rational.[25] (Figure 3.3 represents the justification of induction according to the theistic doctrine of providence. The arrows in the diagram indicate inferences and may be interpreted as meaning "strongly suggests" or "provides good reasons for believing." From the regularities of nature and the benefits derived from exploiting them we conclude that an almighty and benevolent God exists. And given our knowledge of these attributes of God we are justified in believing that nature is uniform.)

Figure 3.3

Regularities in Nature	$\rightarrow$	The Existence of an Almighty and Benevolent God	$\rightarrow$	The Uniformity of Nature

Now I want to draw attention to a significant implication of this view for the general practice of science. Since the laws of nature are some of the most basic tools of empirical science, it follows from this model that the scientific enterprise as a whole is girded on the foundation of trust in divine providence. Rational scientific investigation critically presupposes reliance upon God to continue governing the cosmos as He has in the past. And every scientist who embarks on gaining insight about the natural world at least implicitly demonstrates this faith. Faith may be defined as an active trust in something or someone. So when it comes to the basic principle

---

[25] This general approach is an adaptation of that implicit in the philosophy of George Berkeley. See James S. Spiegel, "A Berkeleyan Approach to the Problem of Induction," *Science and Christian Belief* 10:1 (April 1998): 73–84.

that nature is uniform, the scientist exercises faith, whether or not she believes in the supernatural, precisely because no empirical evidence sufficient to justify this belief can be provided. So the question is not *whether* the scientist exhibits faith, but *what kind* of faith she exhibits.[26]

We believe that this theistic justification of induction is the only solution to this problem which has vexed science for generations. Naturally, those who are not sympathetic to theism will not find this approach appealing. But, of course, this would not be the first instance in which a theistic solution to a scientific problem has been rejected because of a naturalistic bias. Next we will take a closer look at naturalism and scientific methodology.

Questions for Reflection

1. Why do you suppose most people do not question the law of causality? Is Hume's critique of causality a threat to science?
2. With which view on the laws of nature are you most sympathetic and why? Are there biblical considerations, aside from those discussed above, that should inform a Christian's perspective on this issue?
3. Do you believe it is accurate to say that all scientific research is conducted on the basis of faith? Why or why not?

§ 3.5 Science and Theology

A current debate among Christians concerns how science is to be practiced in light of one's religious worldview. In doing scientific research, may we take theological considerations into account? How one answers this question will determine one's perspective on the origins debate, among other things.

3.5.1 Two Kinds of Naturalism

Those who object to bringing theological convictions to bear on the practice of science may do so for one of two reasons. They may do so because they are *metaphysical naturalists*, believing that only the physical world exists. Thus, on this view, there are no supernatural beings, in-

---

[26] Here we see the sense in Dallas Willard's claim that "faith is not restricted to religious people" (from "The Three-Stage Argument for the Existence of God," *Contemporary Perspectives on Religious Epistemology*, ed. R. Douglas Geivett and Brendan Sweetman [Oxford: Oxford University Press, 1992], 222). William James brilliantly argues for this point in "The Sentiment of Rationality," in *The Will to Believe and Other Essays* (New York: Dover, 1956). There he concludes, "The only escape from faith is mental nullity" (p. 93).

cluding God, angels, and human souls. For the metaphysical naturalist to appeal to supernatural entities in explaining natural phenomena is a waste of time because such things do not exist. Still others, including many Christian philosophers and scientists, object to involving theology with science for methodological reasons. They maintain that although the supernatural realm exists, science should be practiced without any reference to this realm. This view is known as *methodological naturalism,* and its proponents base their perspective on what they conceive to be the goal of science, namely to explain natural phenomena in terms of other natural phenomena. Methodological naturalists see no reasonable exceptions to this rule, so they reject all references to supernatural agents in the context of science.

Methodological naturalists are careful to insist that methodological naturalism does not imply metaphysical naturalism. That is, one may practice science *as if* only the physical world exists without affirming, even implicitly, that *in fact* only the physical world exists. This approach, they maintain, is simply a matter of respecting proper disciplinary boundaries. Science, by definition, pertains to the natural world, while other fields, such as metaphysics and theology, delve into issues about the supernatural. Some methodological naturalists offer a different kind of argument that appeals to the concept of the *functional integrity* of the physical world. Physicist Howard J. Van Till explains that this is the assumption that the cosmos "has been equipped by the Creator to do whatever the Creator calls upon it to do. It suffers no gaps or deficiencies in its economy that need to be bridged either by words of magic or by the Creator's direct manipulation."[27] Thus, functional integrity implies that we need not look beyond the physical world itself for the causes of natural phenomena, whether we are inquiring about the motion of bodies, the nature of living species, or human consciousness. Functional integrity rules out supernatural causes for physical events. Philosopher of science Ernan McMullin agrees, noting that "from the theological and philosophical standpoints, [supernatural] intervention is, if anything, antecedently *improbable.*"[28] Diogenes Allen gives yet another affirmation of this approach and connects it to methodological naturalism:

> God can never properly be used in scientific accounts, which are formulated in terms of the relations between the members of the

[27] Howard J. Van Till, "Is Special Creationism a Heresy?" *Christian Scholar's Review* 22:4 (June 1993): 385. See also John Stek, "What Says the Scriptures?" in *Portraits of Creation: Biblical and Scientific Perspectives on the World's Formation,* ed. H. J. Van Till, R. E. Snow, J. H. Stek, and D. A. Young (Grand Rapids: Eerdmans, 1990).

[28] Ernan McMullin, "Plantinga's Defense of Special Creation," *Christian Scholar's Review* 21:1 (September 1991): 74. Author's emphasis.

universe, because that would reduce God to the status of a creature. According to a Christian conception of God as a creator
of a universe that is rational through and through, there are no
missing relations between the members of nature. If in our study
of nature we run into what seems to be an instance of a connection missing between members of nature, the Christian doctrine
of creation implies that we should keep looking for one.[29]

The prominent issue at stake here, of course, is biological origins.
And when methodological naturalists assert that there are "no gaps" or
"missing relations between members of nature" they mean to include
those apparent gaps between organisms that evolutionists claim to have
evolved from one another. They maintain that to appeal to God in order to account for biological phenomena is unscientific. It is essentially
being lazy, giving up. As Allen says, when good scientists fail to find a
natural explanation for some phenomenon, they keep looking.

3.5.2 Critical Reflections on Methodological Naturalism

So what should we make of the claims of methodological naturalism? One of the merits of this approach is its concern to ward off the
"God-of-the-gaps" mentality which has long been a pitfall for theistic
scientists. Those who take this approach see God or other supernatural
beings as causal explanations for those "gaps" in our knowledge that
cannot be explained naturally. Whether it is fire, lightning, or the rising
of the sun, there have always been theists who have appealed to God to
explain such things when natural causes seemed unavailable. Then when
natural causes were eventually discovered, those theists looked foolish, as
did all theological musings about the physical world. The lesson, then,
is that we should always avoid appealing to God to account for gaps in
our knowledge about the physical world. Otherwise, as the capacity of
science to explain physical events increases, the need for God appears
proportionately smaller. Methodological naturalists therefore aim to
guard against this psychological effect by insisting that we never appeal
to supernatural causes when doing science. If nothing else, the Christian
theist must affirm their motives.

However, critics respond that the fallacies of past inferences to the
supernatural need not bind those today who might have much stronger
grounds to conclude that God directly caused a particular phenomenon.
In other words, *abuses* of the inference to God does not imply that there
are no *proper uses* of this inference. Perhaps a rigorous account of infer-

---

[29] Diogenes Allen, *Christian Belief in a Postmodern World* (Louisville: Westminster/John
Knox, 1989), 45.

ences to divine intervention in the world can be developed. This is precisely what proponents of the Intelligent Design (ID) movement claim. We will look at ID theory more closely below.

What of the methodological naturalist's argument appealing to functional integrity? Does it have merit? There appear to be two problems with this argument. First, it is interesting to note that the doctrine of functional integrity is essentially a *theological* doctrine. That is, it is directly grounded in a particular view about God and His relation to the world (specifically, that God never intervenes in the world to cause natural phenomena). Now it is odd, to say the least, that methodological naturalism—which bars all appeals to theological explanations for natural events—should depend upon a theological doctrine. On the one hand, they claim that one must do scientific inquiry *as if* only the physical world exists and, on the other hand, they justify this methodological mandate by appealing to a theological doctrine. This raises the question: If theology can legitimately inform choice of scientific methodology, then why can't it also inform scientific theory selection?

Secondly, we may ask why we should accept the doctrine of functional integrity. It is not a thesis that can be supported scientifically, so what sort of justification can be given for the doctrine? Looking to Scripture for support is problematic because, if anything, Scripture strongly supports the idea that God causally acts in the physical world and directly affects natural phenomena of various kinds, which is especially obvious in the case of miracles—including the virgin birth and resurrection of Jesus. But if functional integrity is true and there are no events that need be explained by divine activity, then such miracles are impossible. Indeed, if we are to take functional integrity seriously, this doctrine seems more akin to deism than theism.

Here the methodological naturalist may reply that no reliance upon functional integrity is necessary to justify this approach to science. She may appeal instead to a more practical tack. Some argue that the practice of science is much like a game, where the challenge is to explain natural phenomena in terms of natural causes. Those who appeal to God and other supernatural entities essentially opt out of the game, like a football player running out of bounds and then back in again, proclaiming "I scored!" as he steps into the end zone. This is simply breaking the rules. Thus, when ID theorists appeal to the supernatural, they are not playing the game of science correctly. In reply, we may ask, who says the "game" of science must be played this way? Who says that *all* appeals to supernatural causes must be considered "out of bounds"? Here we see that the analogy begs the question because it assumes from the outset that inferring the existence of supernatural entities is always illegitimate.

The methodological naturalist insists that dealing with the supernatural *is* always illegitimate in the context of science. Some argue that it is a simple matter of defining the academic disciplines and maintaining research objectivity in science.[30] In such fields as theology and metaphysics it is perfectly appropriate to consider the supernatural but not in science. However, even here the methodological naturalist is mistaken. Such reasoning forgets that scientists traffic in the supernatural on a regular basis, such as when they appeal to principles of logic and even mathematical concepts. Logical rules (e.g., *modus ponens*, the law of noncontradiction, etc.) and numbers (e.g., "7," "3.14," etc.) are not physical things or in any way part of nature.[31] They are supernatural. Yet scientists use such concepts constantly. Indeed, it would be impossible to do biology, chemistry, or physics without logic or numbers. So, in this sense, science fundamentally involves and depends upon the supernatural. Furthermore, as we saw above, belief in the uniformity of nature presupposes a sort of faith, which all theists would acknowledge to be grounded in divine providence. But if this assumption upon which all of science rests regards a supernatural cause, then why should it be "against the rules" of science to infer supernatural causes when it is dictated by the evidence? The pressing question for theistic methodological naturalists amounts to this: If theistic scientists legitimately make *assumptions* about the supernatural, then why can't they make *inferences* about the supernatural? Assumptions and inferences are alike essential aspects to any method of inquiry, whatever the discipline. What distinguishes them, of course, is that the former occur at the "front end" of inquiry, while the latter occur at the "back end" of inquiry. So when it comes to scientific inquiry, why disallow the supernatural at the back end when it has already been present throughout the inquiry in the form of assumptions about the supernatural?

3.5.3 Theistic Science

We have found some serious problems with methodological naturalism and the leading arguments used to defend it.[32] But if this approach to science is flawed, what is a better alternative? Many have proposed

[30] See, for example, Robert O'Connor, "Science on Trial: Exploring the Rationality of Methodological Naturalism," *Perspectives on Science and Christian Faith* 49:1 (March 1997): 15–30.

[31] See chapter 4 for a detailed discussion of why such things are not physical.

[32] For some good critiques of methodological naturalism, see Robert A. Larmer, "Is Methodological Naturalism Question-Begging?" *Philosophia Christi* 5:1 (2003): 113–30; Stephen Meyer, "The Methodological Equivalence of Design and Descent" in *The Creation Hypothesis*, ed. J. P. Moreland (Downers Grove, IL: InterVarsity, 1994); J. P. Moreland, "Theistic Science and Methodological Naturalism," in *The Creation Hypothesis*; and Alvin Plantinga, "Method-

what is called *theistic science*, which takes into account theological considerations when doing science. Alvin Plantinga, for example, defends this position by arguing from the principle that "the rational thing is to use all that you know in trying to understand a given phenomenon."[33] Plantinga reminds Christians that we really do know many things about God and the natural world from Scripture and theological inquiry, and Christian natural scientists should not pretend not to know these things when they do science.

Proponents of theistic science point out that while the primary aim of science is to search out natural causes, some dead ends may properly lead us to infer supernatural causes. For example, physicists may conclude from the "fine-tuning" of the cosmos in terms of the laws of physics that the universe must have been designed.[34] And biologists may infer intelligent design from the complexity of biological structures and processes. Because the origins issue is at the center of the dispute over scientific methodology, it will be worthwhile to examine the intelligent design theory in some detail.

ID theorists, who practice a form of theistic science, distinguish between two kinds of biological complexity that justify the inference to intelligent design. These are *irreducible complexity* and *specified complexity* in living organisms. An irreducibly complex system is *complex* in the sense that it is composed of many interactive parts that combine to serve a particular function. Its complexity is *irreducible* in the sense that removal of any one of its components would render the overall system completely nonfunctional. For example, consider a mousetrap, which without the spring, catch, holding bar, or hammer is useless. Thus, Michael Behe notes, "an irreducibly complex system cannot be produced directly (that is, by continuously improving the initial function, which continues to work by the same mechanism) by slight, successive modifications of a precursor system, because any precursor to an irreducibly complex system that is missing a part is by definition nonfunctional."[35] Behe describes numerous biochemical systems, from structures such as bacterial flagella to processes such as blood coagulation, noting how their irreducible complexity cannot be accounted for naturalistically.

What ID theorists call "specified complexity" refers to the match between an event and a pattern that are both complex and independent of

ological Naturalism," *Origins and Design* 18:1 (Winter 1997): 18–27; and *idem*, "Methodological Naturalism, Part 2," *Origins and Design* 18:2 (Fall 1997): 22–33.

[33] Alvin Plantinga, "Methodological Naturalism?" *Perspectives on Science and Christian Faith* 49:3 (September 1997): 144.

[34] See chapter 6 for a discussion of the "fine-tuning" argument for God's existence.

[35] Michael J. Behe, *Darwin's Black Box: The Biochemical Challenge to Evolution* (New York: The Free Press, 1996), 39.

one another. Thus, the event of an arrow hitting a bull's-eye is a case of such specification in ordinary experience, as the event (the arrow shot) and the pattern (the bull's-eye) are independently given. If the bull's-eye is drawn around an already shot arrow, then there is no such independence, hence no specificity. Examples of biological specificity include the amino acids sequencing in complex proteins and nucleotide base sequencing in DNA molecules.[36]

The prevalence of specified complexity and irreducible complexity in living organisms strongly suggests special theistic design, according to ID theorists. William Dembski, a leading light of ID theory, summarizes the essence of this paradigm as affirming the following propositions:

ID1: Specified complexity and irreducible complexity are reliable indicators or hallmarks of design.

ID2: Biological systems exhibit specified complexity and employ irreducibly complex subsystems.

ID3: Naturalistic mechanisms or undirected causes do not suffice to explain the origin of specified complexity or irreducible complexity.

ID4: Therefore, intelligent design constitutes the best explanation for the origin of specified complexity and irreducible complexity in biological systems.[37]

For the ID theorist, then, there is an openness to inferring intelligent agents as causes of natural phenomena. But in rigorously formulating their methodology, they seek to avoid the God-of-the-gaps mentality. Only when a scientist can conclude that it is impossible for a given phenomenon to have a natural cause is it appropriate to infer an intelligent cause. However, the question arises, how can a scientist know for sure when a given instance of biological complexity is such that it cannot possibly have been caused naturally? Herein lies the challenge to ID theory and the mandate to be exceedingly careful when making inferences and pronouncements about supernatural causes.

It is important to keep in mind that to practice theistic science need not commit one to creationism, the view that God specially created the various kinds of organisms. One could practice theistic science and potentially conclude with Darwinists that all living forms descended from

---

[36] For a full explication of the concept of specified complexity, see William A. Dembski, *Intelligent Design: The Bridge Between Science and Theology* (Downers Grove, IL: InterVarsity, 1999), chapter 5. And for biological examples, see Stephen C. Meyer, "Evidence for Design in Physics and Biology: From the Origin of the Universe to the Origin of Life," in *Science and Evidence for Design in the Universe* (San Francisco: Ignatius, 2000), esp. 68–71.

[37] William A. Dembski, *The Design Revolution* (Downers Grove, IL: InterVarsity, 2004), 42.

a common ancestor through random mutations and natural selection. In contrast, the methodological naturalist is open to only one theoretical option, namely the evolutionary explanation. The methodological naturalist essentially insists that we conclude *in advance* of inquiry that there is a naturalistic explanation for the complexity and diversity of living organisms, while the ID theorist contends that we should only make such conclusions *on the basis* of inquiry. Did speciation occur as a part of the original divine creative activity or afterwards? This question is the crux of the controversy over biological origins. The methodological naturalist is by definition foreclosed in favor of the latter option, while the ID theorist is properly open to either possibility. Of course, the methodological naturalist will defend her foreclosure in view of the integrity of *scientific* inquiry. In contrast, the ID theorist will defend her approach in terms of the integrity of inquiry *generally*.

Questions for Reflection

1. Some writers, such as Phillip Johnson, have argued that methodological naturalism tends to lead to metaphysical naturalism. Do you agree with this claim? Why or why not?
2. What, if anything, can ID theorists do to avoid slipping into the God-of-the-gaps mentality?
3. With which approach are you most sympathetic, methodological naturalism or theistic science? Why?
4. For Christians, how important is the issue of the relationship between science and theology?

Conclusion

These days it is natural for people to have a deep respect for science because of its impressive accomplishments over the last century. This is why it can be jarring to bring a critical eye to the scientific method and scientific theory. In this chapter we have discussed many philosophical questions that arise as we consider the nature and purposes of science. We began by noting that even the term *science* defies easy definition, and we noted several philosophical presuppositions that must be made in order to engage in scientific research, many of which cannot be proven by any method, let alone scientifically.

The bulk of this chapter was devoted to what must be considered the central question in philosophy of science: Is the purpose of science to discover truth? We noted that scientific realists answer this question affirmatively, while nonrealists answer negatively, and we examined some highly influential versions of each of these perspectives. In light of our analysis, we suggested that a "humble realism" might best account for the arguments and problems on either side, most notably such matters as the problem of induction, the theory-ladenness of observation, and the tremendous practical achievements of science.

It is noteworthy that when we turned our attention to the subject of science and theology, the problems we discussed there regarding scientific methodology assumed the truth of scientific realism. Methodological naturalists and ID theorists alike are convinced that the causes they infer regarding such phenomena as speciation and the Big Bang are real and that Darwinism and creationism are more or less *true*. If scientific nonrealism is the correct view, however, much of the debate between these paradigms just might be moot. We say it "might" be moot, because an instrumentalist may insist that even though truth is not the ultimate issue in this debate, practicality remains an objective reality and these theories may be assessed according to this end. Kuhnians and anarchists like Feyerabend, on the other hand, would regard this whole debate as ultimately nonrational and more about such things as community needs, subjective fancies, and brute power plays.

Wherever one lands about these issues, it is instructive to see how even the most practically successful method of acquiring knowledge is riddled with problems. Thus, it turns out that scientific theorizing is as subject to criticism as the technologies science produces. And among the questions raised by science, many are unanswerable by the method of this discipline itself. Some of these are questions in metaphysics, the subfield of philosophy to which we turn next.

For Further Reading

On Philosophy of Science in General

Chalmers, A. F. *What Is This Thing Called Science?* 3rd ed. Indianapolis: Hackett, 1999.

Godfrey-Smith, Peter. *Theory and Reality: An Introduction to the Philosophy of Science.* Chicago: University of Chicago Press, 2003.

Okasha, Samir. *Philosophy of Science: A Very Short Introduction.* New York: Oxford University Press, 2002.

Rosenberg, Alex. *Philosophy of Science: A Contemporary Introduction.* 2nd ed. New York: Routledge, 2005.

On the Scientific Realism/Nonrealism Debate

Cohen, R. S., R. Hilpinen, and Ren-Zong Qiu, eds. *Realism and Anti-Realism in the Philosophy of Science*. New York: Springer, 1996.

Niiniluoto, Ilkka. *Critical Scientific Realism*. New York: Oxford University Press, 2002.

Psillos, Stathis. *Scientific Realism: How Science Tracks Truth*. New York: Routledge, 1999.

Van Frassen, Bas. *The Scientific Image*. New York: Oxford University Press, 1980.

On Scientific Laws

Hanzel, Igor. *The Concept of Scientific Law in the Philosophy of Science and Epistemology: A Study of Theoretical Reason*. New York: Springer, 1999.

Murphy, Nancey C., Robert J. Russell, and C. J. Isham, eds. *Quantum Cosmology and the Laws of Nature: Scientific Perspectives on Divine Action*. Notre Dame: University of Notre Dame Press, 1997.

On Science and Theology

McGrath, Alister E. *Science and Religion: An Introduction*. Oxford: Wiley-Blackwell, 1998.

Moreland, J. P. *Christianity and the Nature of Science*. Grand Rapids: Baker, 1989.

Morris, Tim, and Don Pletcher. *Science and Grace: God's Reign in the Natural Sciences*. Wheaton, IL: Crossway, 2006.

Polkinghorne, John C. *Science and Theology: An Introduction*. Minneapolis: Fortress, 1998.

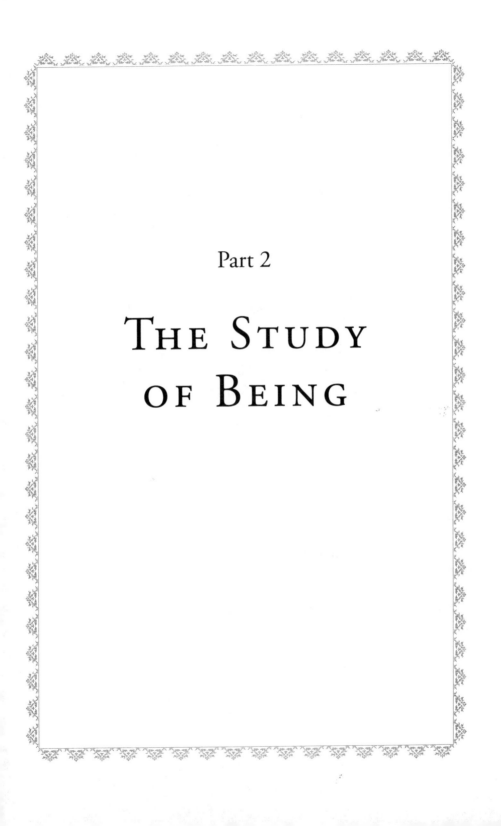

Part 2

THE STUDY
OF BEING

Chapter 4

METAPHYSICS: WHAT IS REAL?

"It's all in Plato, all in Plato."

—C. S. Lewis
(Lord Digory in *The Last Battle*)

Glossary Terms

Bundle theory	*Ontology*
Conceptualism	*Phenomena*
Dualism (metaphysical)	*Platonism*
Idealism	*Properties*
Logical positivism	*Propositions*
Materialism	*Relations*
Mereological essentialism	*Substance view*
Metaphysics	*Substratum view*
Nominalism	*Universals*
Noumena	*Verification principle*

A t the end of C. S. Lewis's *The Last Battle* (the final volume in The Chronicles of Narnia), Lord Digory, Edmund, Lucy, Peter, and others have just witnessed the destruction of Narnia, the land where they had experienced many adventures. Now they find themselves in a new but strangely familiar place.

> "If you ask me," said Edmund, "it's like somewhere in the Narnian world. Look at those mountains ahead—and the big ice-mountains beyond them. Surely they're rather like the mountains we used to see from Narnia, the ones up Westward beyond the Waterfall?"
>
> "Yes, so they are," said Peter. "Only these are bigger."
>
> . . . .
>
> "Those hills," said Lucy, "the nice woody ones and the blue ones behind—aren't they very like the Southern border of Narnia?"
>
> "Like!" cried Edmund after a moment's silence. "Why, they're exactly like. Look, there's Mount Pire with his forked head, and there's the pass into Archenland and everything!"
>
> "And yet they're not like," said Lucy. "They're different. They have more colors on them and they look further away than I remembered and they're more . . . more . . . oh, I don't know . . . "
>
> "More like the real thing," said the Lord Digory softly.[1]

---

[1] C. S. Lewis, *The Last Battle* (New York: HarperCollins, 1984), 193.

The characters in The Chronicles of Narnia discover that the Narnia they once knew and loved was not the *real* Narnia. In fact, their home in England where they were born and lived was not the real England, either. Rather, these lands of their earlier experiences were what C. S. Lewis called "shadowlands." They were shadows or faint replicas of the real things, the real Narnia and the real England, that they would experience and enjoy forever now that their lives in those shadowlands had come to an end.

What is real? Is the world that you see, hear, and touch the *real* world? Or is it only a shadow of something far more real and significant? Is the world we experience now like the world of the movie *The Matrix*, simply an illusion or hoax foisted on us by malevolent powers? Perhaps someone will offer us a "blue pill" as Morpheus did to Neo, and we will awaken in a very different reality.

Or suppose that this world we experience every day *is* the real world. We might still wonder what the nature of the world is. What is it *made of*? Most scientists today tell us that the physical objects that we observe (like this book or your body) are composed of very tiny particles of matter called atoms. Yet, we don't see atoms. We don't hear them or smell them or taste them. What we see and touch are hands and books and tables and chairs and rocks and trees, and so forth. If the scientists are right, the real nature of the world is very different than it appears to us. Perhaps that conclusion should not be so startling to us. But, there are more questions. Supposing that the scientists are right about atoms, we might wonder still whether the material world composed of atoms and physical energy exhausts the nature of reality. Is there a reality beyond the physical universe? Is there a God? Do angels and demons exist? Do human beings have souls, a nonphysical part of them that is not subject to death and decay as our bodies are?

Questions like these (and many more) are the subject matter of *metaphysics*, a branch of philosophy concerned with the nature of reality. It seeks to answer the question: *what is real?* Metaphysical issues arise in different chapters of this book. In the next chapter, we will look at philosophical questions related to the nature of human beings—questions such as whether or not human beings have an immaterial component (i.e., a soul), and whether or not we have free will. Back in chapter 1, we discussed the existence and nature of truth. Chapter 6 will consider the existence and nature of God. All of these are metaphysical questions. However, in the present chapter, we will focus on the most basic and general metaphysical issues, what philosophers sometimes call *ontology* (the study of being as being). Put simply, ontologists ask: *what is there?*

- What is the underlying nature of the world?
- Are there universals?
- What is a particular thing?

Before we look at these questions, though, it is important that we examine some potential obstacles to the very possibility of metaphysics.

§ 4.1 Obstacles to Metaphysics

For much of the nineteenth and twentieth centuries the discipline of metaphysics was treated with suspicion, even scorn. Though a lot of metaphysical work had been done in previous ages, most philosophers in the modern era had come to believe that genuine metaphysical knowledge is impossible. The basis for this metaphysical skepticism is found in two places: the epistemology of Immanuel Kant and the semantics of logical positivism. In this section, we will briefly discuss these potential obstacles to metaphysics and show that they can be overcome.

4.1.1 Kantian Epistemology

The Enlightenment philosopher Immanuel Kant (1724–1804) spent his early philosophical career as a rationalist in the vein of René Descartes until he read the work of the British philosopher David Hume. As Kant himself put it, Hume awakened him from his "dogmatic slumbers."[2] To Kant, Hume's skepticism posed a serious challenge to human knowledge including that derived from science, a discipline with which Kant was fascinated. In order to salvage scientific knowledge from the threat of Hume, Kant developed a revolutionary new approach to knowledge.

Kant's "Copernican Revolution"

As Kant conceived it, his theory of knowledge constituted a "Copernican Revolution" in epistemology. Just as Copernicus turned astronomy on its head by shifting the center of the universe from the Earth to the Sun, Kant reversed the way philosophers previously thought about knowledge. Prior to Kant, philosophers believed that there is a mind-independent world which is at the "center" of our knowledge. On this view, our minds acquire knowledge of the world by conforming to the world. In other words, in order to have knowledge of the tree outside my office window, my mind must make an adjustment—specifically, my thoughts about the tree must conform to the tree itself. Only when

---

[2] Immanuel Kant, *Prolegomena to Any Future Metaphysics* (Oxford: Oxford University Press, 2004), 67.

my thoughts about the tree must conform to the tree itself. Only when I am thinking correctly about the tree external to my mind can I be said to have knowledge of the tree.

Kant believed that this "world-centered" approach to knowledge is what led to the thoroughgoing skepticism of David Hume. How can we ever know if our thoughts and beliefs actually do conform to the world? Hume argued that we can never have knowledge about these matters. In order to overcome this problem, Kant argued that the mind, not the world, is the center of our knowledge. Our perceptions are shaped by the innate structures of the mind in order to produce knowledge. For Kant, my mind does not conform to the tree in order for me to know it. On the contrary, my very experience of the tree is the result of my perceptions of the world conforming to a conceptual scheme imposed on them by my mind.

As Kant explains it, the mind is structured by what he calls two forms of intuition (space and time) and twelve categories of the understanding (substance, plurality, causality, etc.) (see figure 4.1). These forms and categories provide the necessary conditions for thought and experience—we cannot have experience except in terms of these categories. For example, we cannot experience any object except in space and time. (Try to imagine anything that you might experience that is not in space and time.) And we cannot experience anything unless it has a definite quantity (e.g., one, two, ten, etc.). Kant explains that things in the external world (he called them the "things-in-themselves") provide input or data that go into the mind. The mind then organizes and structures that data in accordance with the forms of intuition and categories of the understanding. The "output" of this process is what we see, hear, touch, taste, and feel—that is, what we experience through the senses. This output is what Kant calls empirical knowledge.

This "revolution" in epistemology allows Kant to respond to Hume's skepticism. Hume, for example, argued that we cannot know causal connections between the objects of our experience. However, Kant's epistemology suggests that we do in fact know that objects in our experience are causally connected. We know this because the mind structures our experience in terms of cause and effect. In other words, we know cause and effect relationships between objects because the mind *imposes* cause and effect relationships on the objects of our experience. In this way, Kant believed that he was able to salvage scientific knowledge from the threat of Hume.

An important implication of Kant's epistemology is his distinction between what he called the *noumenal* and *phenomenal* worlds. Kant's Copernican Revolution implies that the world as it appears to us (the

Figure 4.1

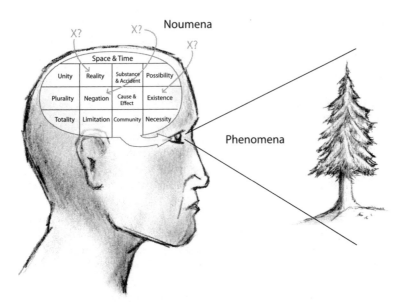

phenomenal world) and the "real" world outside of our minds (the noumenal world) are distinct. And, further, we cannot know the real world, the noumenal world. All we can know is the world of appearances, the world as it has been organized by the categories of the mind. Practically speaking, this means that the only things we can know are those things accessible to the five senses, the phenomena. Anything beyond the five senses is strictly unknowable. But those things knowable through the senses are not the things-in-themselves, the noumena. We have no access to the noumena prior to their being organized and structured by our minds. Though Kant thought that the noumena provided the data for our phenomenal experiences, they are strictly unknowable. So we cannot know if the things we meet in our experience (e.g., a horse or a car) are anything like the noumena. As far as we know, there are no horses or cars in the noumenal realm—these things may exist only in the phenomenal realm. Also unknowable are the self, God, and anything else that traditionally goes under the rubric of metaphysics. All such things are part of the unknowable noumenal realm. Kant's view, then, would imply that we cannot have any metaphysical knowledge, knowledge of what is ultimately real.

A Response to Kant's Metaphysical Skepticism

As Alvin Plantinga has pointed out, Kant's "way of thinking displays a deep incoherence."[3] Consider this. Kant refers to and talks a lot about the noumena. He even claims that they stand in causal relations with the phenomena (i.e., the phenomena exist in part because the noumena exist and are acted upon by the categories of the mind). Not only that, but Kant attributes properties to the noumena such as being atemporal and nonspatial. But, if Kant's view were true, these properties would not apply. Rather, Plantinga shows that, on Kant's view, "the noumena would have to drop out altogether, so that all that there is is what has been structured or made by us. The idea that there might be reality beyond what we ourselves have constructed out of experience would not be so much as thinkable."[4] The point is that Kant's distinction between the noumenal and the phenomenal is self-defeating.

Moreover, if the noumena "drop out altogether" as Plantinga says they must, Kant's view would lead to a radical relativism and antirealism. If the world of experience is nothing more than a product of our minds, then it could very well be that our different minds create different "realities"—realities that are possibly contradictory. So, on Kant's epistemology, it could be true for me that unicorns exist yet false for you—and we would both be right! Worse, there might be no reality at all other than what *my* mind constructs for itself—*you* might not exist at all because, as far as I can tell, you are just a phenomenon created by the categories of my mind. We have already responded in some detail to this kind of postmodern relativism (see chap. 1), so we will not belabor the point here. For reasons like these, we need not see Kant's epistemology as an obstacle to metaphysics.

4.1.2 Logical Positivism

Another attempt to undermine the possibility of metaphysics came from the Vienna Circle of the early twentieth century led by philosopher Moritz Schlick (1882–1936). Their viewpoint came to be known as *logical positivism*. In order to elevate science as a unique and privileged way of knowing and eradicate speculative metaphysics (which they saw as confused and subjective), the logical positivists developed the *verification principle of meaning*, according to which only propositions that could be empirically verified would count as meaningful. The verification principle went through several versions over the years, but A.J.

---

[3] Alvin Plantinga, *Warranted Christian Belief* (Oxford: Oxford University Press, 2000), 20.

[4] Ibid.

Ayer (1910–1989), one of the premier defenders of logical positivism, defined it this way:[5]

> *A proposition is meaningful if and only if it is empirically verifiable in principle.*

The qualifying phrase "in principle" is important here. Ayer did not want to rule out as meaningless propositions that are unverifiable merely because of practical difficulties. So his version of the verification principle does not require that we be able in actual practice to verify a proposition. It is enough that we can conceive of physically possible circumstances that would allow us to make the requisite empirical observations. For example, given our current technology and the great distances involved, we cannot at present empirically verify this proposition: *There is a Mercury-sized planet orbiting the star Deneb.* However, we can conceive that one day we might be able to send a starship to Deneb and see whether or not there is a Mercury-sized planet orbiting that star. So this proposition is at least verifiable *in principle.*

The problem for metaphysics, though, is that statements like the following do not seem empirically verifiable even in principle:

> God exists.
>
> Lassie exemplifies the property *being a dog.*
>
> Human beings have free will.

God is not a physical being, but an immaterial Spirit. You cannot go out into the world and "see" God. The property *being a dog* (as we will see later) does not exist in space and time; if it exists, it is an abstract entity. And whether or not human beings have free will is arguably something we could never verify through observation. According to the logical positivist, these metaphysical propositions are worse than false—they are literally meaningless. Saying "God exists" or "Humans have free will" is no more meaningful than saying "blikkety-blik-blak." Therefore, if the verification principle is true, metaphysical knowledge is impossible.

Fortunately for the metaphysician, the verification principle is not true. Indeed, it is quite obviously false. The reason is that it is self-defeating. Notice that the verification principle lays out a criterion for what it means for *any* statement to be meaningful. That criterion stipulates that meaningfulness depends upon the possibility of empirical verification. But consider the statement of the verification principle itself. Is

---

[5] A.J. Ayer, "Language, Truth and Logic," in *Classics of Philosophy*, 2nd ed., ed. Louis P. Pojman (Oxford: Oxford University Press, 2003), 1226–33.

it possible, even in principle, to empirically verify the proposition that *"a proposition is meaningful if and only if it is empirically verifiable in principle"*? No, it is not. There are no conceivable physical circumstances that would allow us to verify that statement. So the verification principle fails its own criterion. If the principle is true, then it is meaningless! Since it is self-defeating (and thus false), it can pose no obstacle to the possibility of metaphysics.

Questions for Reflection

1. What, if anything, do you find helpful or plausible in Kant's epistemology? How might these features be incorporated into an overall theory of knowledge without running into the problems mentioned here?
2. Can you think of any refinements to the verification principle that would allow it to avoid self-defeat? If we reject any and all versions of the verification principle, does this mean that any sentence whatsoever would count as meaningful? Why or why not?
3. Even supposing that Kant and the logical positivists failed to provide obstacles to doing metaphysics, are there any lessons to be learned from them concerning metaphysics?

§ 4.2 What Is the Nature of the World?

Perhaps the most basic metaphysical question has to do with the underlying nature of reality. The question can be approached from different angles. We might ask, what is the world (or the things in the world) made of? Of what are things composed? Or, we may ask (what might amount to the same thing), what kinds of things are there? The earliest philosophers in Western history were preoccupied with these very questions. Thales (c. 585 BC), the first Western philosopher, answered the questions quite simply. He said that everything that exists is made of water. Water is the most basic element of reality. Water, of course, is made of water. But so are rocks, trees, dogs, air, fire, and people. Before you conclude that Thales was crazy, consider the fact that water is capable of taking on all three states of matter—solid, liquid, and gas—and that these three states are distinguished in part by their relative density. And consider that the human body is composed of about 75 percent water. So, given Thales's position in history, it was not all that radical to think that rocks are just very dense water; that air is very rarefied (thin) water; and that human beings are moderately dense water.

Other early philosophers gave different answers than Thales, though. Empedocles (484–424 BC) claimed that there are four equally basic elements: earth, air, fire, and water. Heraclitus (535–475 BC) identified ultimate reality with fire, and Parmenides (515–450 BC) claimed that reality consisted of one, simple, immutable thing (all the diversity we experience being simply an illusion). A bit later Democritus (460–370 BC) argued that everything was composed of tiny, invisible, and indivisible particles of matter called "atoms." Thus, his view was called *atomism.*

In each of these attempts to explain the underlying nature of the world, these philosophers were wrestling with *the problem of the one and the many.* This problem has to do with giving an account of both the apparent diversity and unity of the world. To illustrate, consider two dogs, Fido and Rover. Fido is a dachshund. Rover is a St. Bernard. Fido and Rover are very different. One is small; one is large. One has short hair and a long snout, while the other has shaggy hair and a short snout. Fido is rambunctious and often jittery, while Rover is always calm and relaxed. They are quite different in these and many other ways, but they are both dogs. Why? No one would think that our classification of Fido and Rover into the dog class is arbitrary. But what accounts for their unity? What makes them both dogs? This question exhibits the problem of the one and the many. In this example, it is the problem of explaining the basis for both the diversity and unity of Fido and Rover.

We could illustrate the problem in any number of other ways. For example, what makes you and the person who lives next door both human beings? Or what makes a pair of qualitatively identical marbles *two* marbles and not just one? In the former case, philosophers usually seek to specify what diverse things have in common—to cite some factor or factors that unify the diverse things. In the latter case (the marbles), they try to specify how they differ. Thales sought to ground the unity of all the diverse things that we observe in the world by going beyond appearances and claiming that diversity and unity can be explained by different densities of water. The atomists solved the problem of the one and the many by locating diversity and unity in different configurations and densities of atoms. Of course, this did not solve but merely postponed a solution, for we can ask the same unity-and-diversity questions about the atoms and their configuration. Parmenides "resolved" the problem by denying the existence of diversity.

We will not discuss the specifics of these early theories in this section. What we will do is discuss the three broad approaches to the question of the nature of the world that have been proposed in the history of philosophy: dualism, materialism, and idealism. To these we now turn.

4.2.1 Dualism

Prominent in the history of philosophy, and especially in the history of Christian thought, has been some form of metaphysical *dualism*. Basically, dualism is the view that the nature of reality cannot be exhausted by appeal to only one kind of underlying stuff. Rather, there are two fundamental types of things, substances, or realms. There is, first, the physical or material realm of reality populated by the familiar objects of our sensory experience—dogs, cats, tables, chairs, and such. Second, there is an immaterial or spiritual realm where exist God, angels, human souls, and other nonphysical things that we do not experience through our senses, but perhaps we can know and experience by other means.

A very influential dualist theory was formulated by the ancient philosopher Plato (427–347 BC). For Plato there were two worlds or levels of reality. There is the imperfect, changing, temporal world of particular things (dogs, cats, tables, chairs, rocks, human bodies, etc). This world, for Plato, could not be ultimately real nor could it provide any basis for the unity of things. All we see in the physical world is diversity and change. We know that Fido and Rover are both dogs, but there is nothing in Fido and Rover, nothing in the physical world, that *makes* them both dogs. The physical world is the realm of the many, not the one. This led Plato to conclude that there must be another realm, a nonphysical or spiritual reality that grounded the unity of things in the material world. Things in this spiritual realm are perfect, immutable, and eternal.

How does this distinction between the physical and spiritual realms solve the problem of the one and the many? What makes Fido and Rover both dogs? Plato's answer lies in his view of the relation between the two worlds. In brief, they are related much the same way that shadows are related to the things that cast them, or the way mirror images are related to the things they reflect. More specifically, the spiritual realm is the world of the "Forms." A Form is, for Plato, an eternal, immutable exemplar of the particular things in the material world. So, for example, the spiritual world contains the Form of the Dog (or "dogness"). Fido and Rover are both dogs because they are imperfect copies or instances of the Dog Form that exists in the spiritual realm.

Plato's solution, of course, implies that the spiritual world is *more real* than the material world of particular things. This means that there are levels of being, that things can exist that are more or less real than other things. Like the land of Narnia in Lewis's tales, which was only a shadow of the real Narnia that his characters entered in the final story, the physical world is a shadowy, less real replica of the real, ideal, spiritual world of the Forms. Plato also believed, for this reason, that the material world (and material stuff) was inherently evil. Some early Christian philosophers (e.g., Augustine, Boethius, Anselm) essentially adopted Plato's metaphysical views, though conceiving of the Forms as ideas in God's mind and rejecting the notion that matter is evil.

Another prominent dualist in the history of philosophy is René Descartes. His dualism was primarily motivated by a desire to understand the nature of the human self. With his famous *cogito ergo sum* ("I think, therefore I am"), he identified the essential nature of the self as a *mind*, an immaterial substance. Thus, he made a sharp distinction between the mind and the body. Human beings, for Descartes, are composed of two very different kinds of substances—a physical substance (body) and a spiritual or immaterial substance (mind). Of course, there are things that are purely physical on Descartes' view such as rocks, planets, trees, and (interestingly) animals. There are also purely immaterial things such as God and angels. Like Plato, Descartes envisioned a reality that was dualistic. Unlike Plato, he did not devalue the material world nor adopt the view that there were levels of being. For Descartes, the material and immaterial aspects of reality were equally real. Moreover, these two realms causally interact with each other. God interacts with the created (physical) order in creating and sustaining it. The human mind interacts with the body, causing it to move, and is itself affected by things in the world through sensation.

Reasons for Dualism

Philosophical reasons offered in support of dualism are typically *descriptive-factual* and *explanatory reasons*. That is, dualism is said to capture the most accurate description of and is the best explanation for the full range of human experience and knowledge. For example, as we saw with Plato, dualism is offered as the best solution to the problem of the one and the many. The physical world is full of diversity and constant change, and there seems no basis in that realm for affirming the unity of classes of things like dogs, chairs, human beings, and such. Yet, we seem to *know* that there is unity among things. We know that Fido and Rover are both dogs despite their differences. Dualism offers us a ready solution. Diverse things in the material world are unified by their being instances or replicas of abstract properties or Forms that exist in another dimension of reality.

Likewise (as we will show in more detail in chap. 5), there are great difficulties in attempting accurately to describe or explain consciousness in materialist terms. Many philosophers are drawn to dualism because it seems difficult at best to describe or explain our beliefs, desires, and sensory experiences (e.g., pains, sensations of colors and sounds) as simply physical events occurring in the human brain—which would have to be the case if dualism were false and materialism true.

Additionally, evidence for the existence of God is taken as evidence for dualism. If God exists and is not a physical being, then it cannot be the case that the material universe exhausts the nature of reality. Assuming, contrary to idealism (see below), that the universe is indeed material in nature, God's existence would mean that reality is at least minimally dualistic—that is, there would be two kinds of substances, material and immaterial, even if God were the only immaterial thing.

Dualism also offers a plausible account of the belief of most people throughout history that there is life after death. Our bodies die and decay. If I am to survive the death of my body, it makes sense to think that there is a part of me that is not physical, my spirit or soul, that lives on in a nonphysical realm.

There have been some biblical reasons given in support of dualism as well. For example, the Bible begins with the assertion, "In the beginning God created the heavens and the earth" (Gen 1:1). Since God is not a physical object, but an immaterial being (cp. John 4:24, etc.), this text supports the existence of an immaterial realm. That God creates the "heavens" and presumably angels also provides reason to embrace a spiritual dimension of reality. But God also created the Earth and the plants, animals, and human bodies that populate it. Many take this text, then, to support the belief that God created a material universe in addition to an immaterial realm.

Jesus appears to affirm a body/soul dualism when He warns, "Do not fear those who kill the body but are unable to kill the soul; but rather fear Him who is able to destroy both soul and body in hell" (Matt 10:28). And the apostle Paul does likewise when he says that Christians "are satisfied . . . to be out of the body and at home with the Lord" (2 Cor 5:8). Further, the book of Hebrews seems to lend support to a Platonic dualism when the author says that the tabernacle that accompanied the Israelites in the desert was but a shadow and copy patterned after the true tabernacle in heaven where Christ entered and "offered one sacrifice for sins for all time" (Heb 10:12; cp. 8:1–6; 9:1–14,23–24). These and other biblical passages are used to defend metaphysical dualism.

Arguments Against Dualism

There are two major avenues of attack against dualism. First, there is what is known as *the interaction problem*. If there are two fundamentally different kinds of substances, physical and spiritual (or material and immaterial), how do they interact with each other? Consider that material substances have certain properties. For example, they are spatial (i.e., located in space), extended (taking up space), mutable, and temporal (in time). Immaterial substances are not spatial or extended. At least some of them (God and Forms) are immutable and timeless. Yet dualists tend to believe that there is causal interaction between the two realms. For example, not only does God create the material world, according to dualists, He also causally interacts with it by sustaining its existence and performing the occasional miracle. The human soul causes the physical body to move, and the body can have causal affects on the soul (such as when a person stubs his toe and has a sensation of pain). But seeing that immaterial things and material things are so radically different, how is such interaction possible? Many philosophers have concluded that interaction is not possible and have rejected dualism as a result.[6]

Another objection to dualism is an appeal to *Ockham's Razor.* This is what is otherwise known as the "principle of parsimony." Ockham's Razor says that out of a set of plausible explanations that are otherwise equal in explanatory power the simplest explanation is to be preferred. Since most of the positive arguments for dualism are explanatory arguments—that is, arguments that claim that dualism is the best explanation for certain phenomena—their plausibility is dependent upon the inadequacy of simpler, nondualist explanations. However, both of the alternatives to dualism—materialism and idealism—purport to offer adequate and simpler explanations for the things that dualism attempts to explain. Such a claim may or may not be true. To know which side is correct we will need to examine these alternative views.

4.2.2 Materialism

Materialism is the view that all that exists is matter and the physical laws that govern its behavior. No immaterial substances (e.g., God, angels, souls) exist. This means that human beings are simply physical organisms. What we call the "soul" or "mind" is simply the brain and its functions. An example of an early modern materialist is the philosopher Thomas Hobbes. He wrote,

> The World, (I mean not the Earth onely . . . but the *Universe,* that is, the whole masse of all things that are) is Corporeall, that is to say, Body; and hath the dimensions of Magnitude, namely, Length, Bredth, and Depth: also every part of Body, is likewise Body, and hath the like dimensions; and consequently every part of the Universe, is Body; and that which is not Body,

---

[6] The interaction problem will be discussed in more detail in connection with the mind-body problem in the next chapter.

is no part of the Universe: And because the Universe is All, that which is no part of it, is *Nothing*; and consequently *no where*.[7]

The contemporary philosopher J. J. C. Smart concurs. He writes, "[T]here is nothing in the world over and above those entities which are postulated by physics."[8] For Smart and other materialists, the only thing that exists is matter.

Many materialists liken the universe to a gigantic, complex machine in which all the various parts of the universe interact according to fixed natural laws. For this reason, materialism is often associated with the doctrine of *hard determinism*, the view that everything that occurs in the physical world (which is all of reality) is necessitated by the laws of physics.[9] Given that human beings are material things, they too must be part of this mechanistic reality. Hard determinism thus implies that we are not free and not morally responsible for our actions. Moreover, materialism in general would seem to imply that there is no life after death. If I am a purely physical organism, then when my body dies, *I* die.

There are different versions of materialism, but the most common form is called *atomism*. We were introduced to atomism above when we discussed the views of the ancient philosopher Democritus. Atomists believe that material objects are composed of tiny, invisible particles of matter that are configured in diverse ways. Not every atomist is a materialist. Many dualists believe that physical things are composed of atoms. But atomists who are also materialists believe that *everything* that exists is made of atoms.

Reasons for Materialism

As indicated in the last section, one reason offered for adopting materialism is Ockham's Razor. By reducing everything that exists to matter, the materialist purports to give a more simple account of reality than the dualist. There is no need, he thinks, to postulate the existence of immaterial substances that we cannot directly experience. Everything that we experience can be explained in terms of material substance. For example, concerning the problem of the one and the many, we can say that Fido and Rover are both dogs, despite their differences, because the

---

[7] Thomas Hobbes, *Leviathan* (New York: Penguin, 1988), 689. Interestingly, Hobbes did not deny the existence of God or angels, but thought of them as translucent bodies rather than immaterial spirits. Not surprisingly, most subsequent materialists did not follow him in this opinion but simply denied their existence.

[8] J. J. C. Smart, "Materialism," *Journal of Philosophy* 22 (October 1963): 651.

[9] Of course, modern quantum physics claims that the behavior of some subatomic particles at the "quantum level" are not determined but are undetermined. Even so, most quantum physicists still claim that what happens at the "macro" level (the level of medium-sized objects like rocks, trees, and planets) is determined.

atoms that compose their bodies are arranged in similar (though not completely identical) ways. Or, to appeal to biological factors, we can say that they have almost identical DNA.

Regarding the nature of the human mind, the materialist believes that he can account for consciousness without appeal to ephemeral "spirits." The materialist takes notice of the fact that there is a strong correlation between mental events (beliefs, desires, sensations) and what is going on in the human brain. When a person sees the color red, for example, the neuroscientist can observe a particular pattern of activity in a certain region of his brain. Conversely, the neuroscientist can stimulate certain regions of a person's brain, causing him to "see" a particular color or feel a certain emotion. And, as we all know, damage to a person's brain always results in a corresponding adverse effect on the person's mind. Brain damage means *mind* damage. Many philosophers take this mind-brain correlation as evidence that mental events are nothing but physical events in the brain, and thus the "mind" is nothing but the brain—a purely physical thing. Moreover, it may be possible to account for human behavior in terms of matter. If Darwinism is true (and contemporary materialists think it is), then the origin of human beings can be accounted for solely in biological terms and all of our capacities and behaviors explained in terms of random mutation and natural selection. According to Daniel Dennett, a materialist and evolutionist philosopher,

> The more we learn about how we have evolved, and how our brains work, the more certain we are becoming that there is no [supernatural] extra ingredient. We are each *made of* mindless robots [i.e., cells] and nothing else, no non-physical, non-robotic ingredients at all. The differences among people are all due to the way their particular robotic teams are put together, over a lifetime of growth and experience.[10]

Hence, the materialist believes that he can account for the nature of human beings in terms of matter alone. Likewise, he believes that there is no need to believe in God. The existence of God is often invoked to explain the origin of the physical universe. Where did it all come from? Since something cannot come from nothing, something outside the universe (something not part of it or subject to its physical laws) must have created it. However, the materialist believes that a materialistic account of the universe as a whole is available, too. Some materialists argue that the physical universe is eternal. It did not come into existence at some time in the past, but has always existed. Others attempt to explain how

[10] Daniel C. Dennett, *Freedom Evolves* (New York: Viking, 2003), 2–3.

the universe may have come into existence (and is therefore not eternal) as a result of some natural mechanism. For example, according to some quantum physicists, subatomic particles may come into existence without a cause from fluctuations in a quantum vacuum. Why couldn't the entire universe result from the same kind of process?

Another argument for materialism, suggested by some of the previous points, is the *progress of science*. It seems that science has increasingly been able to explain the nature and operation of the physical universe. Moreover, there is the fact that phenomena once explained by appeal to supernatural forces can now be explained by purely natural phenomena. For example, people who suffer from epilepsy were once thought to be possessed by demons. Now, of course, we know that their seizures are due to defects in the brain. The motion of the planets at one time was thought to be caused by supernatural forces, but now we can explain it by appeal to gravity, Newton's laws of motion, and so forth. Hence, the materialist asserts that science will likely one day yield a "theory of everything" that gives a completely naturalistic account of the whole of reality without recourse to any supernatural, nonmaterial entities.

Arguments Against Materialism

From a Christian perspective, materialism as a complete worldview is wholly unacceptable. The Christian's commitment to theism entails a rejection of materialism because theism by definition requires the existence of at least one immaterial entity, namely God. So the Christian must reject materialism.

However, there are other philosophical reasons to consider materialism suspect. For one thing, it is not clear that materialism really satisfies the demands of Ockham's Razor. That principle requires us to accept a simpler theory over a more complex one, all things being equal. But the dualist denies that all things *are* equal. He claims that when one accurately describes sensations, desires, beliefs, and thoughts, one does not use physical language at all. Materialism fails to comport with these facts. Additionally, Ockhams' Razor applies only on the condition that the simpler theory actually provides an adequate explanation for the phenomena that both theories aim to explain. Though materialism is simpler than dualism, it is questionable whether it provides plausible explanations for what it claims to explain. First of all, take the materialist account of the origin of the universe. As we will see in chapter 6, it is most probable that the intricate complexity and fine-tuning of the physical universe is due to the activity of an intelligent designer. What's more, it is arguable that a universe that has no beginning is logically impossible. We will have to defer the case for God's existence until later, but suffice it to say for now that there is reason to believe that a "theory of everything" that excludes God is implausible.

Secondly, the fact that there is a correlation—even a strong causal connection—between mental events and brain events does not prove that mind and brain are identical or that the mind is ultimately material. There are many things in our experience that are correlated and even causally related, but are not identical. For example, there is a strong correlation between smoking and lung cancer. It is likely that the former is the cause of the latter, but smoking and lung cancer are obviously not the same thing. Moreover, as we will see later, the mind appears to have properties that the brain does not have (and vice-versa), a strong indication that mind and brain are distinct.

Additionally, if materialism implies that human beings do not have the freedom requisite for moral responsibility (as Dennett's evolutionary account of human behavior suggests), then we may have a *prima facie* reason to reject materialism. The reason is that most of us are strongly inclined to think that we are morally responsible for what we do. This is a deeply ingrained belief that we do not readily question and which we might expect an adequate metaphysical theory to explain. Rather than explaining how and why we are responsible, materialism denies that we have moral responsibility. Our behavior is due simply to the way our "robot cells" are arranged. Similar considerations may apply to the materialist denial of life after death. If we have evidence for life after death (another question we will explore in chap. 5), then materialism would be shown to be inadequate.

Lastly, it is not clear that materialism really offers an adequate solution to the problem of the one and the many. Recall that the atomist accounts for the similarity between Fido and Rover by appealing to the idea that they are both composed of atoms arranged in a similar way. There is nothing deeper than this that unites them. There is not, for example, any Platonic Form or essence like "dogness" that they exemplify. Such Forms or universals, if they exist, are not physical things. Materialism seems to require some form of *nominalism*, the view that there are no universals or essences like dogness, tableness, or human nature. Nominalism says that universal terms like these are simply names that we adopt by convention for things that appear similar to us. We will see later in this chapter that nominalism is problematic. If so, then so is materialism.

Well, what about the progress of science? Doesn't that support materialism? There are at least two reasons to say no. First, even assuming that science has made progress in giving us an increasingly accurate picture of the physical universe, it would not prove materialism. If dualism

were true, for example, we might still expect that science could discover
the nature of the physical aspect of reality, but such knowledge would
not exhaust the whole of reality. Unless we have a materialistic "theory
of everything" that adequately handles the problems noted above, then
the progress of science would provide little support for materialism. Second, we saw in the last chapter that there is considerable debate about
the nature of science and what exactly it can and cannot show us about
the world. For example, many philosophers of science are nonrealists
about scientific theories. That is, they believe that scientific theories do
not really describe the underlying nature of reality but are merely "useful
fictions." Any appeal to the alleged progress of science in support of materialism will depend upon a defense of scientific realism. Such scientific
realism may, of course, be true, but any argument for materialism based
on it will be no stronger than the case for scientific realism itself.

Most of the points made so far are merely suggestive and require
the reader to look to other chapters for elaboration. We would like to
offer a more developed argument here to show that materialism must
be rejected. Christian philosopher Alvin Plantinga has given a strong
argument to show that materialism is actually self-defeating.[11] We may
formulate Plantinga's argument as follows:

> (1) If materialism is true, then our cognitive faculties aim
> at survival not truth (because materialism assumes
> Darwinism).
> (2) If our cognitive faculties aim at survival not truth, then
> we have good reason to doubt that our beliefs are true
> (because false beliefs can ensure survival as well as true
> ones).
> (3) If we have good reason to doubt that our beliefs are true,
> then the materialist has good reason to doubt that
> materialism is true.
> (4) Therefore, if materialism is true, then the materialist has
> good reason to doubt that materialism is true.

The idea here is that materialism, if true, would prevent us from
having any justified beliefs (and any knowledge), including any justified
belief in materialism. Thus any belief in materialism defeats itself.

To understand Plantinga's argument, it is vital to keep in mind the
contemporary connection of materialism with Darwinian evolution.
The materialistic evolutionist believes that human beings, and thus all

---

[11] See Alvin Plantinga, *Warrant and Proper Function* (Oxford: Oxford University Press,
1993), 216–37. Plantinga's argument was actually aimed at naturalism (see introduction to
this book, pp. 7–9).

of their natural abilities and faculties, are the result of natural selection and random mutations. This means that our cognitive faculties (e.g., our senses and intellect—those faculties that provide us with beliefs) are also the result of natural selection and random mutations. But according to Darwinism, natural selection only guarantees the survival of the fittest organisms. So human beings developed belief-forming faculties, according to materialistic evolution, just because those faculties contributed to the survival of the human species. We did not develop such faculties for the purpose of discovering and knowing the truth about the world. Evolution is indifferent to truth and falsehood *per se*. What evolution "cares" about is survival. These facts tell us that premise (1) of the argument is true.

Premise (2) is supported by the fact that false beliefs can contribute to an organism's survival just as well as true beliefs. To demonstrate this point, Plantinga paints this hypothetical scenario:

> Paul is a prehistoric hominid; the exigencies of survival call for him to display tiger-avoidance behavior. There will be many behaviors that are appropriate: fleeing, for example, or climbing a steep rock face, or crawling into a hole too small to admit the tiger, or leaping into a handy lake. Pick any such appropriate specific behavior B. Paul engages in B, we think, because, sensible fellow that he is, he has an aversion to being eaten and believes that B is a good means of thwarting the tiger's intensions.
>
> But clearly this avoidance behavior could be the result of a thousand other belief-desire combinations. . . . Perhaps Paul very much *likes* the idea of being eaten, but whenever he sees a tiger, always runs off looking for a better prospect because he thinks it unlikely that the tiger he sees will eat him. This will get his body parts in the right place so far as survival is concerned, without involving much by way of true belief.[12]

If false beliefs can be as useful to survival as true ones, then it would seem to follow that we have no good reason to believe *any* of our beliefs. This is because, for all we know, we are like Paul—holding all or mostly false beliefs generated by cognitive faculties whose only function is to enable us to survive in dangerous environments. This doesn't mean, given materialism, that all of our beliefs *are* false, but just that we have good reason to doubt them.

---

[12] Ibid., 225.

Of course, the materialistic evolutionist believes that materialism is true. But, if materialism *is* true, then the materialist's belief in materialism is the result of natural selection, which aims, not at truth, but at survival. And this means that, for all the materialist knows, his belief in materialism is nothing more than a survival mechanism—a belief that enables him to survive but does not necessarily give him accurate information about the world. So premise (3) is true. It follows, then, that if materialism is true, the materialist has good reason to doubt that materialism is true. Hence, materialism is self-defeating. And any self-defeating proposition is unworthy of belief.

4.2.3 Idealism

The final perspective on the nature of the world is *idealism*. This view may be construed as the polar opposite of materialism. Whereas materialism asserts that all reality is matter and denies that there are any nonmaterial things, the idealist denies the existence of matter and believes that all reality is mental. There are several forms of idealism, but the most well-known and influential version in the history of Western philosophy is the idealism espoused by Bishop George Berkeley (1685–1753). It is his version that we will discuss in this section.

For Berkeley, the only things that exist are minds and their ideas. His view of reality is often expressed in the Latin phrase *esse est percipi* ("to be is to be perceived") which seems to indicate that being perceived is a necessary condition for anything at all to exist—but this would not be quite right. Berkeley believed that for a thing to exist meant for it to be *either* a perceiver (a mind) or a thing perceived by a mind (an idea). So, the phrase "to be is to be perceived" applied directly only to non-thinking things. But, in any case, Berkeley denied that there was any such thing as mind-independent matter.

Did this mean that Berkeley believed that the world we experience through our five senses is unreal—an illusion?[13] By no means. Berkeley insisted that on his view the world filled with tables and chairs and cats and dogs is just as real as it is on the dualist and materialist views. Anticipating this objection, he wrote, "Well say you according to this new Doctrine all is but mere Idea. . . . I answer things are as real and exist *in rerum natura* [in the nature of things] as much as ever."[14] By saying that the world of sensory experience is ideal or mental, Berkeley did not mean that it is an illusion or a figment of one's subjective imagination.

---

[13] Some types of idealism, such as classical Hinduism, do claim that the material world is an illusion.

[14] George Berkeley, *Philosophical Commentaries*, sect. 535, in *The Works of George Berkeley*, ed. A. A. Luce and T. E. Jessop (InteLex database: www.nlx.com).

The world does not necessarily depend upon human beings or one human being for its existence. It exists just as independently of you and me on his view as it does on the materialist or dualist view. He simply denied that this world exists outside of all minds.

To get a handle on Berkeley's meaning, perhaps the following analogy may help. Suppose that you—that is, your mind—dwelt in the Matrix (from the movie *The Matrix*). In that condition you can see things, hear things, touch, smell, and taste things. You might even believe (wrongly) that the things you sense are made of matter. In fact, your experience would be indistinguishable from the experience of a person who *did* dwell in a material world. Of course, in the movie, the Matrix was a "virtual reality" created by a computer for malevolent purposes and there was a real world outside the Matrix where the physical bodies of those minds trapped in the Matrix actually existed. But suppose that there was no reality outside the Matrix. Suppose that all that existed "outside" the Matrix were disembodied minds, all of which experienced and interacted within the same Matrix. If you can grasp this possibility, then you have a pretty good handle on Berkeley's idealistic metaphysic. For Berkeley, the world is like the Matrix (minus the material world outside the Matrix)—it is a systematic collection of colors, sounds, textures, smells, and tastes—and it is real. *It's just not made of matter!* Instead, it's made of ideas.

To many people, Berkeley's view seems counterintuitive. For one thing, his view seems to imply that physical objects do not exist when no one is present to perceive them. Consider the desk in my office. Does it vanish when I leave my office only magically to reappear when I walk back in? Such a view seems to violate common sense. But if the essence of physical objects is to be perceived, wouldn't this odd view be the logical result? Berkeley did not think so. He believed that there is one mind who always perceives my desk and all other objects in the world, even when no one else perceives them. The potential objection to Berkeley that we are considering was put in the form of a limerick many years ago:

> There once was a man who said, "God
> Must think it exceedingly odd
> If he finds that this tree
> Continues to be
> When there's no one about in the Quad."[15]

---

[15] Attributed to Msgr. Ronald Knox.

To which a follower of Berkeley cleverly responded:

> Dear Sir,
>
> Your astonishment's odd:
> I am always about in the Quad.
> And that's why the tree
> Will continue to be,
> Since observed by
>   Yours Faithfully,
>   God.[16]

Berkeley was a devout Christian. Like all Christians, he believed that God is the creator and sustainer of the world. But, for Berkeley, God did not create a world of mind-independent matter. Rather, He made a world of minds and ideas. The "matrix" that we call the created physical world is constantly sustained by God, and God ties every finite mind into it so that they might have meaningful interactions and fulfill His redemptive purposes. So it is because God is actively involved that my experiences of the world are regular and orderly and intersect with yours.

Arguments for Idealism

Like materialism, the Berkeleyan idealist appeals to Ockham's Razor to support his view. He believes that he can account for our experience without recourse to dualism. Unlike materialism, however, idealism arguably offers a more satisfactory nondualist account. For one thing, there is nothing in idealism that is obviously inconsistent with the Christian worldview.[17] Berkeley can acknowledge that there is a supernatural, immaterial reality. For him, God is a great Spirit or Mind and other spiritual beings exist too, namely angelic and human minds. Conversely, he can acknowledge the reality of the world (though, of course, it is not material in the sense most dualists and materialists believe). For another thing, just like the dualist (and unlike the materialist), the idealist believes that God's existence is required to explain the existence of the world and of other finite minds. Berkeley was happy to endorse many of the traditional proofs for God's existence that many Christian dualists affirm.

Concerning the mind-body problem, the idealist can avoid the question of interaction between mind and body because on his view physical bodies are not distinct substances with properties very different from the mind. Just as the materialist reduces the mental to matter (unsuccess-

---

[16] Anonymous.

[17] For a detailed defense of the Christian orthodoxy of Berkeley's idealism, see James S. Spiegel, "The Theological Orthodoxy of Berkeley's Immaterialism," *Faith and Philosophy* 13:2 (April 1996): 216–35.

fully we think), the idealist reduces the physical to the mental. The latter reduction may have problems (as we will explore below), but there is nothing strange or implausible about minds and ideas interacting with each other. On the contrary, minds and ideas normally go together.

Additionally, idealism would not create any significant problems for human moral responsibility—at least none that would not also plague the dualist. Nor is there a problem with accounting for life after death. It is perfectly consistent with idealism that human minds go on living when their bodies die. Death would be tantamount to God's "unplugging" a human being's mind from the earthly "matrix" and plugging it in to a different "matrix," but would not imply or require that the mind ceased to exist or ceased to have conscious experiences.

Concerning the problem of universals, an idealist need not embrace nominalism. He can affirm the real existence of properties and universals like "dogness" and "humanity" (see section 4.3 below), though he may understand them to exist as ideas in God's mind.

But what positive reason is there to adopt Berkeleyan idealism? To be sure, it does seem (despite the above advantages) to defy common sense.[18] The answer, for Berkeley and his followers, is that idealism *must* be true because *the idea of matter is unnecessary and absurd.* To understand why the idealist thinks this is so, we need to revisit something we discussed in chapter 2. Recall John Locke's representational theory of perception. Locke, along with Descartes and Hume, thought that we do not have direct perceptual experiences of external physical objects. When I perceive a tree, for example, I am not directly aware of a tree that is "out there"— outside my mind. Rather, I directly perceive a mental image, an idea. The tree that I actually "see" is in my mind—it is a collection of qualities or properties like greenness, ovalness, and such.

The most common argument in favor of this representational theory of perception is *the argument from illusion*, which we alluded to briefly in chapter 2. Recall the example of seeing a tall building from a great distance and how it looks small to the eyes. What I see, what I directly experience in my visual field, is a small object (even though, because I know that the building is far away, I believe it to be "really" quite large). Consider also the phenomenon of seeing a stick submerged in water. The stick appears bent. What I am immediately aware of *is* bent (though I believe it is "really" straight). Again, think of the common coffee table. Viewed directly from above, the coffee table appears rectangular (the shape I take the table "really" to have). However, if you view it from an angle from across the

---

[18] However, Berkeley was adamant that his idealism was consistent with common sense— more so even than dualism or materialism. The reason for this will become evident in the following discussion.

room, what you see is a trapezoid. Moreover, the color of the table (supposing the room is lighted) will change depending on the lighting and where you are standing in relation to it.

In each of these cases, what I am immediately aware of, what I directly experience in my visual field, is, respectively, small, bent, trapezoidal, and, say, the color brown. What are we to make of this? Those advocating representationalism take these facts as evidence that we do not directly perceive external, material objects, but ideas. That is, what we perceive are subjective, mental entities. The tree, the bent stick, the trapezoidal brown shape, the small building exist in my mind not in the external world.

Now for Locke and Descartes (who were Berkeley's immediate predecessors) my perceptual ideas are *caused* by and *represent* external, material objects. I have the idea of a tree, building, or table because there is a tree, building, or table *outside* my mind that causally interacts with my senses to produce that idea in my mind. Berkeley agreed with them on one aspect of the representationalist theory—he agreed, that is, that the immediate objects of perception are ideas. But he believed that it was a serious mistake to conclude that there were unperceivable material objects that lie behind our ideas. One reason was that such a view apparently leads to skepticism. After all, how does one know that the ideas he experiences in perception are caused by external material objects? Even if we could know they are caused by external objects, how does one know that the ideas are anything like the objects that cause them? As we saw in our discussion of Descartes' epistemology, my ideas and perceptions may be caused by an evil genius rather than material objects. Berkeley therefore saw the specter of skepticism lurking behind the representational theory of perception. But what if our ideas did not represent anything beyond themselves? What if my mental, subjective idea of the tree *is* the tree? That is, what if the objects in the world—dogs, cats, trees, and such— were simply bundles of ideas? If so, then the dualism between appearance and reality that threatens skepticism would vanish.

Another more serious reason was that, given representationalism, belief in matter was absurd or meaningless. Consider, first, the suggestion that matter serves no useful function or purpose. On this theory one never sees, hears, smells, tastes, or touches matter. We never have any contact with matter. All we have perceptual contact with are our ideas that, *supposedly*, are caused by matter. Locke, the representationalist, understood matter or material substance as a theoretical substratum underpinning all the properties we actually perceive, but since we do not actually perceive matter, he conceded that it was a mysterious "something I know not what."[19] But, then, what real need is there for this concept? Berkeley

---

[19] John Locke, *An Essay Concerning Human Understanding*, II.23.

contended that if we removed the idea of matter from our conception of reality, the world we experience would remain unchanged. Matter is not necessary to explain our ideas or our experience and, as noted above, *keeping* the idea of matter threatens to lead us into skepticism.

Consider, secondly, that the concept of matter is itself problematic (at least if representationalism is true). If matter is simply the substratum for properties (like greenness, ovalness, etc.), then it would appear that matter *per se* has no properties. But how can there be something that has no properties? How would it differ from nothing at all? Moreover, Berkeley offers his so-called "Master Argument" against matter: He contends that we simply cannot have a conception of matter in any case. He asks us to try to formulate an idea of matter in Locke's sense of the term. It cannot be done because, by definition, any idea one has will be a mind-dependent, nonmaterial object. To conceive of a Lockean material substance, one has to conceive of something that is not perceived by any mind, something existing independently of a mind. But any idea of a "material" substance is an *idea*—a subjective, mental entity! We simply cannot conceive of mind-independent objects, but we would have to be able to do so in order to have a coherent idea of matter. So the idea of matter is absurd.

Against Idealism

The reader should readily observe that many of the positive arguments for idealism given above are directed at the representational theory of perception. One strategy for avoiding the idealist's conclusions, then, is to opt for a different view of perception. Though it is safe to say that representationalism is the prevalent view among contemporary philosophers, there are a considerable number who espouse a contrary view called *direct realism*. According to this view, we directly experience external, material objects. External objects are not, contrary to representationalism, mediated to our minds by ideas. Rather, in perception, material objects are immediately present to us. If so, then idealism is shown to be false.

In response to the argument from illusion, the direct realist can say, for example, that the stick submerged in water may look bent in such circumstances, but he need not concede that what he perceives *is* bent. A perceived object may have different appearances in different situations, but it does not follow that what is perceived is other than an external object. Here, of course, the representationalist and idealist counter-reply that the direct realist grants that in such cases things are not as they appear. But, then, how can he say that our experience of material objects is *direct?*

Direct realism may also founder on the consideration of the causal processes involved in perception if we allow that there are external material objects. For example, the unreflective person may think of his eyes as being something like windows through which he is looking. His mind stands "behind" his eyes like a person standing at a window and looks out at the objects in his front yard. But, of course, our eyes are nothing like windows. There is a very complicated causal process involved in visual perception. Light bounces off the material objects, enters the retina of the eye, and sets off a lengthy series of molecular and physiological changes in the brain that eventually produce a particular perception in the mind. This being the case, in what sense do we *directly* perceive external objects?

Most direct realists respond by conceding that there are indeed *causal* intermediaries involved in perception. Perception is thus causally indirect. However, perception is direct in the sense that a person need not be aware of these causal intermediaries when perceiving an external object. All that one need be aware of is the external object thus perceived in virtue of these complicated causal processes. In other words, the direct realist claims that perception is causally indirect, but *intentionally direct*. My perceptions are *about* external objects, not ideas or any other causal intermediary.[20]

However, Laurence BonJour counters that if intentional directness is all that direct realism amounts to, then "the view that results is still fundamentally a version of representationalism."[21] It would still be the case, that is, that "[m]aterial objects, understood in a realist [nonidealist] way, are outside the mind, metaphysically distinct from any sort of experience or awareness of them, and related to conscious experience only via a highly complicated causal chain."[22]

So appealing to direct realism as a way to avoid the idealist's conclusions is problematic. There are, however, some other possible responses. For one thing, as will be seen in the next section, there may be ways to defend the existence of matter without committing oneself to the absurd view that matter has no properties. Additionally, it is not clear that Berkeley's "Master Argument" succeeds in showing the inconceivability of matter. Critics point out that Berkeley fails to distinguish between a representation of something and the something a representation represents. But if we make such a distinction, then

> we realize that although we must have some conception or
> representation in order to conceive of something, and *that*

[20] For further discussion and defenses of direct realism see, Michael Huemer, *Skepticism and the Veil of Perception* (Lanham, MD: Rowman and Littlefield, 2001); and J. P. Moreland and Garrett Deweese, "A Premature Report of Foundationalism's Demise," in *Reclaiming the Center: Confronting Evangelical Accommodation in Postmodern Times*, ed. Millard J. Erickson, Paul Kjoss Helseth, and Justin Taylor (Wheaton, IL: Crossway, 2004), 81–107.

[21] Laurence BonJour, *Epistemology: Classic Problems and Contemporary Responses* (Lanham, MD: Rowman and Littlefield, 2002), 156.

[22] Laurence BonJour, "Epistemological Problems of Perception," in *Stanford Encyclopedia of Philosophy* (http://plato.stanford.edu/entries/perception-episprob/).

representation is in some sense thought of, it does not follow (contra Berkeley) that what we conceive *of* must be a thought-of object. That is, when we imagine a tree standing alone in a forest, we (arguably) conceive of an unthought-of object, though of course we must employ a thought in order to accomplish this feat.[23]

Still, even if these last points are correct, they do not refute idealism. They only show that dualism and the representational theory of perception are tenable. But, given what we have said so far, so is idealism. Christians have adopted either view, though most have embraced dualism. The reason, apparently, is that dualism (which acknowledges the existence of both material and immaterial substances) seems to comport quite well with the common sense of ordinary people. Idealism, on the other hand, has at least the virtue of being a simpler theory. Later in this chapter, we will consider another metaphysical topic that may have implications for the discussion of the present section. We will consider the nature of individual things. What conclusions we reach on that topic may dispose us in one direction or the other concerning the choice between dualism and Berkeleyan idealism. Before we do that, however, we must consider the question of universals.

Questions for Reflection

1. What do you think of Ockham's Razor, the principle that, other things being equal, the simplest theory should be preferred? Is this principle true? Why do you think philosophers and scientists tend to hold this principle?
2. Dualism faces the problem of explaining how God, an immaterial being, can causally interact with a material universe. Can you think of how the dualist might respond to this problem?
3. Suppose a materialist responded to Plantinga's argument that materialism is self-defeating by claiming that the same problem plagues the theist. Given that the theist admits that his cognitive faculties are fallible (i.e., he sometimes has false beliefs even though his faculties are supposedly created by God), how do we know that God hasn't created us to get our beliefs wrong *most* of the time? Would this possibility give us a reason to doubt the reliability of our cognitive faculties on theism? How would you respond to this problem?

---

[23] Lisa Downing, "George Berkeley," in the *Stanford Encyclopedia of Philosophy* (http://plato.standford.edu/entries/berkeley/).

4. An old story has it that philosopher Samuel Johnson was walking along with a friend discussing Berkeley's idealism when he kicked a rock and exclaimed, "I refute it thus!" Do you think Johnson has refuted Berkeley? Why or why not?
5. An idealist might appeal to Acts 17:28, Colossians 1:17, and Hebrews 2:10 to support his view biblically. How might these texts do so? How would (or could) the idealist deal with the texts used to support dualism? Are you convinced? Why or why not?
6. We suggested above that direct realism is problematic. Can you think of any way to defend it?
7. Here is a simple argument for idealism: The physical world depends upon God and God is a mind. Therefore, the physical world is mind-dependent. What do you think of this argument?

§ 4.3 Are There Universals?

In the introduction to this chapter, we brought up the problem of the one and the many. This is the problem of giving an account of the diversity and unity of the things in our experience. Put another way, the problem involves seeking to understand both the similarities and differences that things have. Recall our two dogs, Fido (the dachshund) and Rover (the St. Bernard). What explains the fact that they are both dogs though they are in many ways different? Philosophers have offered three different theories for solving this problem that we explore in this section.

4.3.1 Platonism

In the history of philosophy, the answer with the longest pedigree is called *Platonism* (named after the Greek philosopher Plato). This view is also known today as *realism*, but since that term is used in several other ways in different areas of philosophy (see its use in chap. 3 for instance), we will stick with the more distinctive term *Platonism*.[24] In this section we will describe the main features of Platonism and outline the major reasons why many philosophers hold this view.

The Nature of Universals

At face value, Platonism's answer to the problem of the one and the many is simple and straightforward. Plato, as noted earlier, believed in something called "Forms" that provided the unity for all the diverse things

---

[24] Strictly speaking, Platonism is only one version of realism. Another version is Aristotelianism. The two versions differ primarily over the question of whether or not there are any unexemplified universals—the latter denying and the former affirming that there are. For the sake of simplicity and space, we will not consider the Aristotelian view of universals here.

in the physical realm. What makes Fido and Rover both dogs is that they each partake of (resemble or imitate) the eternal Form of "dogness."

What Plato called "Forms" have been replaced by contemporary philosophers with a more refined notion called *universals*. A universal is an abstract entity. This means that it does not exist in space and time. It is neither a concrete object (where "concrete" is the opposite of "abstract"), nor is it physical. Universals are also "multiply instantiable." This means that they can be had by more than one thing at the same time. Fido cannot exist in more than one place at a time because Fido is a concrete particular. Nevertheless, Fido being, say, brown in color has the property "brownness." But so do many pieces of furniture. So do the Cleveland Browns' jerseys. Universals like the property *being brown*, unlike particulars, can exist in more than one place at a time. Moreover, universals are eternal; they do not come into being at some point in time. For this reason they are thought by philosophers to necessarily exist—that is, each universal exists in every possible world. The Platonist is committed to the real existence of universals. And he appeals to their existence, in part, as the solution to the problem of the one and the many.

It is important to recognize that there are different kinds of universals. Perhaps the most obvious kind is *properties*. A property is a characteristic or quality of a thing. Or, you might say that a property is a way that something can be. For example, as we noted above, Fido has the property of "brownness" or *being brown*. He also has the properties of *being small* and *being a dachshund*. In contrast, Rover has the properties of *being large* and *being a St. Bernard*. Both dogs obviously have many more properties, some of which they have in common and some not.

Relations are another kind of universal. Unlike properties, which apply to individual things, relations are universals that link multiple things together in various ways. More specifically, relations mark how one thing stands relative to other things. For example, Fido stands in the relation *smaller than* to Rover. Conversely, Rover stands in the relation *bigger than* to Fido. There are many other relations that these dogs and other things could have such as *to the left of, older than, the son of, sharper teeth than, loved by*, and so on. We should add that, according to some philosophers, although relations are distinct from properties, things that have relations also exemplify *relational properties*. These are properties that things have in virtue of standing in relations. So, since Rover stands in the relation *bigger than* to Fido, Rover has the relational property *being bigger than Fido*. Likewise Fido has the relational property *being smaller than Rover*.

Yet another kind of universal is *propositions*. We have used the term *proposition* rather loosely in other parts of this book, often as a synonym for *statement*. Technically speaking, however, propositions and statements are not the same thing, at least not for the Platonist. A statement is simply a particular utterance (or written sentence) by a person at a particular time. A proposition, on the other hand, is the content or meaning of a statement. To illustrate the difference, suppose that a boy named Timmy, the owner of our St. Bernard, Rover, gets stuck in a snow bank during the winter. Rover comes to his rescue, pulling him out of the snow bank and dragging him safely home. Later Timmy makes the statement to his friends, "Rover saved my life." But suppose that you make the very same statement to your friends. Have you said the same thing that Timmy has said? Absolutely not. For one thing, even if you had a dog named Rover when you were a child, it was not the same dog as Timmy's (probably not even the same *kind* of dog). Moreover, unless your dog saved your life too, your statement, unlike Timmy's, is a lie. So, what's the difference between your statement and Timmy's? According to the Platonists, though you both make the same statement or utterance, your statements express different propositions. Timmy's statement expresses the proposition that *his* dog Rover—the St. Bernard owned by him—saved his life at a particular place at a particular time. Your statement does not express *that* proposition but a very different one. Moreover, it is clear that Timmy could have expressed the same proposition he did express by means of a different statement. For example, he could have expressed that proposition by saying, "My life was saved by Rover" or "Rover *rettete mein Leben*" (German for "Rover saved my life"). But this seems to imply that the propositions expressed by our statements cannot be identical to any concrete statement or sentence that exists in space and time. For this reason, the Platonist claims that propositions are universals.

The last thing to note in understanding Platonism is the relationship between universals and particular concrete objects. We have said that things like Fido and Rover "have" properties, that they "stand in" certain relations, and they "express" propositions. The more precise way of stating the connection between universals and particulars is to say that things *instantiate* or *exemplify* universals. So, for example, Fido exemplifies *being brown* and *being smaller than Rover*. This means that exemplification is a special sort of relation that exists between universals and the things that exemplify them. Put in commonsense language, the exemplification relation is just the "having" relation.

We can put all that we have said about Platonism into a diagram (figure 4.2) that we hope will make it clearer. In the diagram are four particulars: the dogs Rover and Fido, Timmy the boy owner of Rover, and Timmy's statement, "Rover saved my life." The line above these particulars represents the division between the concrete and abstract

Figure 4.2

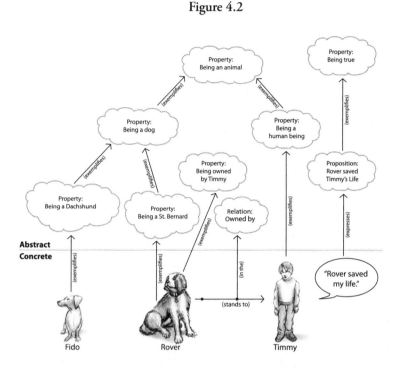

"realms." The "clouds" above the line are abstract entities, various universals that are exemplified in these particulars. As you can see, Fido exemplifies the property *being a dachshund*. Rover exemplifies the property *being a St. Bernard*. In virtue of exemplifying these properties, they also both exemplify the property *being a dog*. Notice that Rover also stands to Timmy in the relation *owned by*. For this reason, he also exemplifies the relational property *being owned by Timmy*. Timmy exemplifies the property *being a human being*. And he and the two dogs all exemplify the property *being an animal*.[25] Timmy's statement, "Rover saved my life" expresses the proposition *Rover saved Timmy's life*. What is more, since that proposition corresponds to the way the world is (see chap. 1), it exemplifies the property *being true*.

Reasons for Platonism

Why adopt Platonism? One reason has already been given, namely that it provides a straightforward solution to the problem of the one and

---

[25] Here the term *animal* is to be understood in its ancient sense of referring to an animate biological organism (human bodies at least are animals in *this* sense) and not in the contemporary colloquial sense in which it is a contrast term with *human beings*.

the many. It explains the similarity between things like Rover and Fido by appealing to abstract entities. But there are other reasons. A second is that *it provides a ready account of predication*. A common use of human language is to predicate. What this means is that we often use subject-predicate sentences to describe things, to point out characteristics that they have. Consider the following statements:

> George Washington had wooden teeth.
> The *Mona Lisa* is beautiful.
> Fido is brown.

What exactly is going on when we make these statements and others like them? The Platonist has a ready answer: In the predicates of these sentences, we are ascribing properties to their subjects. For example, when we say that George Washington had wooden teeth, we are asserting that George Washington had the property of *having wooden teeth*. Likewise, we are saying that the *Mona Lisa* has the property of *being beautiful* and that Fido has the property of *being brown*. Of course, this account implies that there are such things as properties (a kind of universal).

So, there are at least two phenomena that the Platonist believes he can readily explain. There is the phenomenon of resemblance or shared characteristics, and there is the phenomenon of predication. There are other important phenomena that Platonism helps us understand as well, but we need not mention them here. The point is that Platonism would seem to have much to recommend it unless alternative views can do the same work better or more simply.

4.3.2 Nominalism

Basically, *nominalism* is the view that there are no universals. The nominalist admits the existence only of particulars. The primary motivation for this view is concern for simplicity. Just as the materialist and the idealist object to metaphysical dualism on the grounds that they can provide a simpler explanation for certain phenomena, the nominalist believes that he can account for all the phenomena that Platonism seeks to explain but without appeal to "exotic entities" such as universals. Thus, the nominalist wields Ockham's Razor against Platonism to support his own view, attempting to give an account of the two phenomena noted above that Platonism seeks to explain, and doing so while only assuming the existence of particulars. (It's worth noting that William of Ockham [c. 1287–1347], after whom Ockham's Razor is named, first employed this principle in one of the earliest defenses of nominalism.)An additional motivation for many is to preserve a naturalist worldview—that everything that exists is a part of the space-time physical cosmos. Since universals defy this stipulation, they have to go. In this section we will describe and evaluate two versions of nominalism, one extreme and one moderate.

Extreme Nominalism

Extreme versions of nominalism simply deny the existence of properties and relations altogether, irrespective of whether they are taken as universals or as some sort of particular. They believe that language that seems to suggest the existence of universals can be recast in such a way as to affirm only the existence of particulars (e.g., individual dogs, humans, rocks, etc.). In other words, the extreme nominalist believes that statements which appear to refer to universals can be reduced to statements equivalent in meaning but which refer only to concrete objects. Moreover, they believe that we can explain the resemblances between things only by appealing to particulars.

There are several varieties of extreme nominalism, but perhaps the most prominent one seeks to reduce universal language to membership in sets. Take the sentence

(1) Fido is brown.

According to this version of extreme nominalism, (1) simply means

(1′) Fido is a member of the set of brown things.

Notice that what appears to be a reference to a property (brown) has been replaced with a particular (the set of brown things). So despite appearances, (1) does not refer to some exotic abstract entity, but simply to a particular. This allows the nominalist to give straightforward accounts of predication and resemblance. The extreme nominalist holds that predication is simply assertion of set membership, as in the translation of (1) into (1′) above. Similarly, resemblance can be characterized as set membership. Suppose that, in addition to (1), the following sentence is true:

(2) Rover is brown.

This statement, according to extreme nominalism, would be equivalent to

(2′) Rover is a member of the set of brown things.

What the extreme nominalist claims is that both (1) and (2) are true (and the resemblance of Fido and Rover is explained) in virtue of the fact that Rover and Fido are members of the same set, namely the set of brown things.

Of course, this nominalist strategy works only if reductive sentences like (1′) and (2′) are equivalent in meaning to sentences like (1) and (2) respectively. It is doubtful that they are. For we may ask the question: *why* are Fido and Rover members of the set of brown things? It will not do for the extreme nominalist to say, "Because Fido and Rover are brown." It will not do because this reply makes reference to properties! The extreme nominalist says that sentence (1) *just means* "Fido is a member of the set of brown things" and (2) *just means* "Rover is a member of the set of brown things." But, if that is what (1) and (2) mean, then we cannot talk about brownness independently of the set of brown things. Which means that we cannot appeal to the brownness of Fido and Rover to answer the question of why Fido and Rover are members of the set of brown things. So, it does not seem that (1′) is equivalent in meaning to (1) or (2′) to (2) after all.

Another related difficulty for this version of extreme nominalism is known as the *companionship problem*. Consider a possible world that contains exactly three items. And suppose that each of these items has exactly two characteristics: they are each red and round. In this world, all the red things are round and all the round things are red. In other words, the set of red things and the set of round things completely overlap—they have identical members. Now it seems clear that redness and roundness are two distinct properties. Yet the extreme nominalist has to say that they are *not* two distinct properties. Since the set of round things and the set of red things share all their members, the extreme nominalist has to say that redness and roundness are identical. He has no way on his theory to distinguish them. But this is absurd.

For reasons like these, extreme nominalism does not give us an adequate account of predication and resemblance. We turn now to discuss a less extreme form of nominalism.

Moderate Nominalism (Trope Theory)

There are versions of nominalism that admit the existence of properties but hold that properties are themselves particulars of a sort. They are not fully abstract entities in the sense claimed by Platonists; rather, they are *abstract particulars*. Here the word *abstract* does not refer to something outside of space and time (as the Platonist uses it), but simply to something that we can think about or concentrate on in isolation from other things.[26] Consider two red apples. Now focus your

---

[26] The Platonist uses the word *abstract* in an *ontological* sense to refer to the nature of certain kinds of entities. The moderate nominalist uses the term *abstract* in a merely *epistemological*

attention on the redness of each apple and ignore any and all other features the apple has. The redness of each apple is, according to moderate nominalism, an abstract particular. What is most important for this view is that *each* "redness" is a particular—an individual thing in its own right. The redness of the first apple, we may call redness$_1$ and the redness of the second apple we may call redness$_2$. Thus, redness$_1$ is a particular and redness$_2$ is a particular. Such abstract particulars are often called "tropes," and this version of nominalism is usually known as *trope theory*.

Where trope theory differs from extreme nominalism is that, whereas the latter identifies "redness" with the set of red things (like red apples, red cars, etc.), the trope theorist identifies redness with the set of red abstract particulars. That is, for the trope theorist, "redness" is simply the set {redness$_1$, redness$_2$, redness$_3$, . . .}. Moreover, trope theory accepts the existence of irreducible properties, even though it treats them as particulars, while extreme nominalism reduces properties to sets. Trope theory departs from Platonism, however, by stipulating that these various red tropes are not one and the same redness, but are different individual things. The Platonist sees these various "rednesses" as simply different instances of the single property redness, a universal. That is, for the Platonist, redness$_1$ and redness$_2$ are numerically the same redness, just instanced at two different locations simultaneously. Not so for the trope theorist.

It should be clear, then, how trope theory handles the phenomena of resemblance and predication. Regarding the latter, consider again the statement

    (1) Fido is brown.

The extreme nominalist understands this to mean that Fido, the particular dog, belongs to the set of brown things. The trope theorist, however, translates (1) as

    (1″) Fido has brown$_1$, and brown$_1$ is a member of the set of
        brown abstract particulars.

A similar translation would be made of (2) concerning the dog Rover, and this suggests that the trope theorist accounts for the resemblance in color between Fido and Rover by simply saying that they have similar tropes.

---

sense to refer to a mental process of isolating or abstracting certain features of concrete things for the purpose of analysis.

Trope theory has the advantage of being able to avoid at least some of the problems that plague extreme nominalism. For example, they can avoid the companionship problem because, in the example given above, redness and roundness are different tropes and can be distinguished as such. The roundness of each of the three items is a distinct set of tropes from the set of redness tropes.[27] Furthermore, the trope theorist's account of predication seems plausible as far as it goes.

But there is a serious problem with trope theory nonetheless. As we just saw, the trope theorist seeks to explain the resemblances between things like the color of Fido and Rover by appealing to the similarities and differences of their color tropes. Fido and Rover are both brown because Fido's brown trope resembles Rover's brown trope. It is not clear, however, that this view of resemblance is adequate. It merely relocates the problem to a different level. Now we may ask: *why* does Rover's brown trope resemble Fido's brown trope? Most trope theorists answer this question by saying that the resemblances between tropes are simply brute, primitive facts that cannot be explained. This answer seems unsatisfactory because the Platonist has a theory that apparently *does* explain the phenomenon of resemblance. Why opt for a theory that leaves a fundamental question unanswered over a theory that has an answer in hand? Moreover, the view that resemblance is a brute fact can easily degenerate (and often does for many nominalists) into the view that our beliefs about resemblances between things are not objective truths at all but are conventions that human beings adopt more or less arbitrarily. We explore this problem in more detail in the next section.

Nominalism and Ethics

One more criticism of nominalism ought to be especially pertinent to Christians (and anyone who takes morality seriously). Above we said that nominalism, because it considers the phenomenon of resemblance a brute fact, tends to promote the attitude that our attributions of resemblance are mere conventions. What lies behind this tendency is the

---

[27] It is often charged that trope theory does suffer from its own version of the companionship difficulty. This version turns on classes of possible but nonexistent beings. For example, consider the class of hobbits and the class of orcs (fictional beings in Tolkien's *Lord of the Rings* stories). Clearly, the property *being a hobbit* is distinct from the property of *being an orc*. But, since neither hobbits nor orcs actually exist, the set consisting of all things that are hobbits is empty and so is the set of things that are orcs. Now there can be two different sets only where there is some difference in set membership. But these two sets have exactly the same members—none! This means that the two sets are identical. And according to trope theory, this would mean that hobbits are identical to orcs—which is clearly false. It is open to the trope theorist to respond to this problem, however, by simply denying that there are tropes corresponding to possible but nonexistent beings (see Michael J. Loux, *Metaphysics: A Contemporary Introduction*, 2nd ed. [New York: Routledge, 2002], 91–92).

fact that nominalism rejects the existence of universal *essences*. An essence is the set of properties without which a thing would not exist. For example, we would say that Socrates has the essential property of *being human*. There are lots of nonessential properties that Socrates has such as *being snub-nosed* or *being a citizen of Athens*. He could fail to have those properties and still exist. But if he failed to have *being human*, he would fail to exist as well. By rejecting universals, both the extreme nominalist and the trope nominalist reject essences.[28]

The relevance of this is found in the fact that these essences are universals. They are things like *being human, being a dog, being a philosopher*, and so on. Nominalism rejects the existence of universals, so it must likewise reject the existence of essences. The problem is that this has devastating implications for ethics. For example, most of us believe in human rights—that people ought to be treated with dignity, that they ought not be killed unjustly or exploited for the benefit of a few. But, if there are no essences that objectively define what it means to be human, then to whom shall we attribute human rights? The nominalist leaves it open for us to decide who does and does not count as a human being based on our personal or collective interests. And if it is not in our interest to count certain minority groups as human (e.g., Jews, blacks, or unborn children), then we may exclude them from the definition of what counts as a human—and still maintain that we believe in human rights!

We see the ethical consequences of nominalism in our culture today. Unborn children may be aborted in our society because they have in fact been redefined as not being human persons. Those who see unborn children this way must reject the idea that there is an essence of human personhood that a fetus has from the moment of its existence. Rather, "personhood" is a contingent characteristic that the fetus develops (or fails to develop) based on certain physical or social conditions. Likewise, the current debate over same-sex marriage is closely tied to the question of universal essences. Those who defend traditional marriage claim that there is an essence to the concept of marriage that defines it as a covenant between one man and one woman. Those who want to allow same-sex marriage, on the other hand, claim that marriage is a social convention that may be defined (or redefined) as we wish. Similar remarks could be made of many other ethical issues in our

---

[28] It is important to note that the trope theorist must only reject *universal* essences—essences shared by multiple things. He could, however, accept *individual* essences like *being Socrates* or *being this redness*. The problem raised here concerning ethics affects trope theory nonetheless.

culture including such topics as embryonic stem cell research, genetic engineering, and cloning.

The redefinitions of human nature and institutions like marriage that are occurring in our society and that allow such troubling developments could not occur on a Platonist understanding of properties and universals. This is why Richard Weaver lays the blame for the moral and social decline of Western civilization at the doorstep of nominalism. He writes,

> The denial of universals carries with it the denial of everything transcending experience. The denial of everything transcending experience means inevitably . . . the denial of truth. With the denial of objective truth there is no escape from the relativism of "man is the measure of all things."[29]

Since nominalism suffers from the metaphysical problems we have discussed, and since it appears to lead to moral relativism,[30] it is best not to see it as a viable alternative to Platonism.

4.3.3 Conceptualism

A view that attempts to steer a middle course between Platonism and nominalism is *conceptualism*. This is the view that properties and other universals are mental concepts. A concept is a mental entity that we use to think about things. When I see a dog, for example, I usually recognize it *as* a dog. When I do this, I am classifying the thing I see (the dog) under a concept that I have in my mind, the concept of a dog.

Similarly, when I simply think about dogs in general, I am thinking about a concept. My concepts, like those of dogs, houses, colors, and such, can and do apply to many things. My concept of a dog applies to Fido and Rover as does my concept of the color brown. This makes my concepts general in a way similar to Platonism. But notice, my concepts are in my mind. They are not things external to me. There is not some extra-mental entity (an exotic Platonic universal) in addition to my concept of a dog that is shared by Fido, Rover, and other dogs.

Unfortunately, while promising, conceptualism is problematic. For one thing, it implies that if there were no mental concepts, there would be no properties. Yet suppose that no human beings or any other being with a mind ever existed, but that the physical universe did. In such a case, since no minds exist, there would be no concepts.[31] Yet, surely

---

[29] Richard M. Weaver, *Ideas Have Consequences* (Chicago: University of Chicago Press, 1948), 4.

[30] For a more detailed discussion of moral relativism and its problems, see chapter 7.

[31] Of course, a theist will view this scenario as being impossible since there can be no physical universe without a Creator. We include it here because not all conceptualists are theists and to set up the "theistic solution" to these difficulties below.

properties *would* exist. There would be lots of things in the universe such as stars, planets, asteroids, rocks, trees, and such. Wouldn't there have to be, then, properties like *being a star, being a tree, being larger than a rock*, and so forth? We can state the same problem even in a world that contains minds. Suppose that there is in our universe (which contains minds) a being which no person has ever conceived of. Imagine, for example, that quarks exist, but we never discovered or even imagined them. But surely quarks would have properties even though there was no concept of a quark.

For another thing, conceptualism seems to fall short in the same way as nominalism when it comes to accounting for resemblances among things. Conceptualism cannot explain why we group things together under the same concept. For example, we say that Fido and Rover are both brown. But why? Obviously it is because Fido and Rover resemble one another in their brownness. But then we cannot explain the resemblance between Fido and Rover by appealing to the concept of brownness. Instead, the existence of the concept of brownness is explained by their (and other brown things') resemblance. The best the conceptualist can do is say that the resemblances between things are brute facts. This answer, of course, is exactly the same as that of the nominalist and suffers from the same problems.

One way out of these difficulties for the conceptualist is to adopt theism, the belief that God exists. On this assumption, there would never be a time or place in which some mind, namely God's, did not exist to observe and think about the physical world. And since God is omniscient, He could never be ignorant of any existing thing like quarks. Moreover, like Augustine, a theist could say (in the vein of conceptualism) that properties and other universals are simply divine ideas. That is, universals are eternal, immutable ideas in God's mind. The reason Fido and Rover resemble each other in color, the theistic conceptualist could say, is that their colors are both copies or instances of the eternal idea of brownness in God's mind.

Though perhaps salvaging conceptualism from the aforementioned difficulties, this solution actually seems to make conceptualism into a form of realism (Platonism). On this view, the divine ideas serve as universals or exemplars that are exemplified by particular things outside of God's mind. This being the case, conceptualism should not be seen as an alternative to Platonism but simply as a modified Platonism. Our conclusion in this section, therefore, is that some form of Platonism seems not only best from a philosophical perspective but also seems to comport well with Christian theism. Universals exist and may be construed as divine ideas.

Questions for Reflection

1. Read Hebrews 8:1–6; 9:11–12,23–25; 10:1–4; and 11:8–16. Do these texts support Platonism? Why or why not?
2. Draw a diagram like that in figure 4.2 to portray the following event: The serpent hangs from a tree branch over Eve and says to her, "You shall not surely die."
3. Theists believe that God has many essential characteristics such as *being omnipotent, being omniscient, being immaterial,* and so on. If God exemplifies such properties, then would it not have to be the case that God *depends* on those properties, and that they are in some sense *prior* to Him? Is this a problem for Platonism? If so, how might it be solved?
4. How would the extreme nominalist and the trope theorist translate the statement, "Red is a color"? Would these translations be adequate? Why or why not?
5. Can you think of any ways to rescue nominalism or conceptualism from the problems raised about them in this section?

§ 4.4 What Is a Particular Thing?

The world we experience seems filled with particular, individual things. There are natural things like mountains, lakes, geysers, and planets. There are living organisms such as flowers, trees, dogs, cats, and human beings. And there are artifacts—things made by human beings—such as houses, cars, books, and bridges. Moreover, if one is a Christian, we believe that there are individual things that exist beyond our ordinary sensory experiences, things like angels, human souls, and God. Whether any such individual thing is some kind of natural body, or a living organism, or an artifact, or a supernatural being, let us simply call it, as we have earlier, a *particular*. The question we wish to ask in this section concerns how to characterize particulars. What exactly *are* they? What makes Everest the particular mountain it is? What makes Seabiscuit the horse he is? And what makes you the particular human you are?

Some might be tempted to answer, along with the ancient atomist Democritus, that particulars are simply collections of atoms (tiny invisible particles of matter) that are arranged in various configurations. There are several reasons why this answer just won't do. For one thing, atoms are themselves particulars. Perhaps it is the case that the particular things in our ordinary experience—macro-entities like mountains, horses, and human beings—are composed of atoms, but what are we to say about the atoms, the individual particulars that compose everything else? We cannot say that atoms are made of atoms. And if atoms are made out of something else, then appealing to atoms would not give us the ultimate answer to our question of what particulars are. Moreover, if we believe (as Christians do) that there are some particulars that are not material at all (e.g., God and angels), then the atomic answer would at best characterize *some* particulars but not all. It would seem then that we need a more general theory for characterizing particulars, one that is more metaphysically neutral regarding the existence of material and/or immaterial particulars.

Before we discuss a few possible views on the nature of particulars, though, we need to explain a couple of metaphysical principles that are often utilized in theorizing about this and several other metaphysical topics. The first principle is called the *principle of the indiscernability of identicals*. According to this principle, any "two" objects that are numerically identical—that is, they are really only one thing—will have all their properties in common. In other words, numerically identical things will not differ in any way. Stated more formally, the principle says

> *For any particulars* a *and* b, *if* a *is identical to* b, *then for any property* P *that* a *has,* b *also has* P.

So, if someone says, for example, that "Cassius Clay is Muhammad Ali," that statement is true only if Cassius Clay and Muhammad Ali have exactly the same properties. We happen to know that Clay and Ali are the same person. Hence, they must have all their properties in common. The principle of the indiscernability of identicals is virtually undisputed by philosophers. It is widely accepted as a necessary truth (one that cannot possibly be false). We will consider it as such in this book.

The other principle is the *principle of the identity of indiscernibles*. You may see this principle as the converse of the previous one. Whereas the principle of the indiscernability of identicals says that identical things have all the same properties, this principle states that things that have all the same properties are identical. More formally stated, it asserts

> *For any particulars* a *and* b, *if* a *and* b *share all the same properties, then* a *and* b *are identical.*

For example, since we know that Cassius Clay has certain properties and that Muhammad Ali has all the same properties, this principle entails that Cassius Clay and Muhammad Ali must be the same thing. The principle of the identity of indiscernibles is more controversial than the previous principle. Indeed, most contemporary philosophers reject it due to what appear to be obvious counterexamples. We will discuss this matter in the subsequent section.

It is very important to understand that both of these principles concern *numerical* identity. Students often confuse this with mere *qualitative* identity. The latter kind of identity involves the similarities between distinct objects of the same kind. For example, suppose that you have agreed to meet a friend at the local coffee shop one morning. You ride to the shop on your new Harley Davidson motorcycle, arriving a bit early. A few minutes later, your friend pulls up beside you riding the very same model Harley that you rode. Surprised, you exclaim, "You've got the same bike that I have!" In what way are you using the word *same* here? Clearly you do not mean that your friend has the very same individual bike that you rode to the coffee shop. Instead, you are speaking about what we call *qualitative* sameness. You are saying that your friend is riding another bike of the same kind. In this regard, philosophers distinguish between *types* and *tokens*. While you and your friend both have the same *type* motorcycle, each of you has a different *token* of that type.

Numerical identity is different from qualitative identity. Suppose that your Harley Davidson has been stolen. So you have to drive your car to the coffee shop instead. While you and your friend are sipping coffee and mourning the fact that you can't both go on a bike ride, someone else pulls up on a Harley. Peering out the window, you shout, "That's my bike!" Your friend says, "Are you sure? Maybe it just looks like your bike." You look more closely and notice that the bike has the license plate number that your bike has, and it even has the small scratch on the gas tank that yours has. It even has your name printed on the saddle bags. "No," you reply. "That's the same bike as mine!" Here you are using the word *same* in a very different way. You are not claiming that this newly arrived bike is another token of the same type as your bike, you are claiming that it is the very same token—the *numerically* identical bike. You immediately call the police.

The principles we have been elaborating are concerned with numerical identity, not merely qualitative identity. With this in mind, we turn to the more general views on the nature of particulars.

4.4.1 The Bundle Theory

One of the more general views regarding particulars is called the *bundle theory*. According to this view, particulars are collections of properties. There is nothing more or less to them than the sum of the properties they exemplify. To illustrate, consider a basketball. On the bundle theory, a particular basketball is simply the collection or "bundle" of its properties. It is the sum of the attributes *being spherical, being orange, being 30 inches in circumference, being filled with air,* and so on. That is what the basketball *is.* It is constituted by these properties and is nothing over and above the sum of them.

At first blush this view may seem a bit odd. We ordinarily speak of particulars as *having* their properties. That is, we tend to distinguish between the particular thing and its properties. The particular is one thing, its properties another. So, for example, we might say that the basketball *has* an orange color or *has* a 30-inch circumference. The bundle theory, however, suggests that this way of speaking is not quite accurate. Since the basketball is not something distinct from its properties but simply *is* the bundle of its properties, we must say, more literally, that the basketball is *constituted* by orangeness, a 30-inch circumference, and so forth. Despite its oddness some very influential philosophers have held this view, including Berkeley, Hume, Bertrand Russell, and A. J. Ayer.

Problems for the Bundle Theory

The bundle theory has been subjected to numerous criticisms. Bundle theorists have been quite resourceful, however, in responding to most of them.[32] Nevertheless, there are two objections to the bundle theory that pose serious difficulties for the view. First, the bundle theory entails that every attribute of a particular is essential to it—a view known as *mereological essentialism.*[33] Ordinarily, we tend to distinguish the essential and the accidental properties of things. An *essential* property is one that a thing cannot lack and be the thing it is. For example, we would say that the property *being human* is essential to Socrates. If Socrates lacked this property, Socrates would not exist. However, we think that Socrates possesses some properties that are not essential to him. He has properties that are *accidental,* properties that he could either have or lack and still exist. For example, Socrates has the property *being snub-nosed.* It seems that we can conceive of Socrates existing even if his nose was long and straight. If so, then *being snub-nosed* is an accidental property of Socrates.

However, the bundle theory cannot support the distinction between essential and accidental properties. If objects just are collections of properties, then any variation in properties means a variation in the thing itself. For example, imagine a particular thing S that is constituted by the set of properties $\{P_1, P_2, P_3\}$ so that S is nothing more than that set of properties. Now imagine that S loses property P_3 and gains property

---

[32] For detailed discussions of all the objections to bundle theory and possible responses see Michael J. Loux, *Metaphysics,* 105–16; and Cynthia MacDonald, *Varieties of Things: Foundations of Contemporary Metaphysics* (Malden, MA: Blackwell, 2005), 81–110.

[33] Mereology is the branch of metaphysics that studies the relationship between parts and wholes.

P_4, so that now we have a set of properties $\{P_1, P_2, P_4\}$. What results? Simply a minor change in the characteristics of S? No. Rather, what we have now is an altogether different particular—S^*. So it appears that the bundle theory is committed to mereological essentialism—the idea that particulars have all their properties or parts essentially. Of course, it is open to the bundle theorist to claim that things *do* have all their properties essentially despite our ordinary way of speaking. The problem is that this view seems counterintuitive.

Another objection, one that most metaphysicians take as decisive, is that the bundle theory depends upon a false version of the principle of the identity of indiscernibles. Recall that this principle states that any objects that have exactly the same properties must be numerically identical. Keeping in mind the point made in the last paragraph—that the bundle theory holds that particulars have all their properties essentially—it would follow that no two particulars could be qualitatively identical. If it is the case (as the bundle theory says) that any variation in properties entails a different particular thing, then it must also be true that sameness of properties entails sameness of thing—and this is just what the principle of the identity of indiscernibles says.

The problem, according to the objection, is that the principle of the identity of indiscernibles is most likely false, at least in the form needed by the bundle theory. Consider a factory that produces Barbie dolls. The assembly line of this factory churns out several hundred dolls each day, each one qualitatively identical. Each Barbie doll is exactly 11.5 inches tall, has the very same length of golden blonde hair, has the very same skin tone, and the very same insanely implausible feminine characteristics. Each doll is qualitatively the same, yet they are numerically distinct. Do we not have here a counterexample to the principle of the identity of indiscernibles?

The bundle theorist is likely to respond (as many readers are no doubt thinking themselves) that the Barbie dolls are not *completely* qualitatively identical. After all, each doll occupies a different region of space. So their spatial properties are not the same. Which means that the dolls are not really counterexamples to the principle of the identity of indiscernibles.

However, the objector to the bundle theory is not finished. He will acknowledge that the Barbie dolls differ with respect to their spatial properties, but will claim that this point is irrelevant. To see why, we must distinguish what are called pure and impure properties. A *pure property* is one that a thing may have that does not depend upon or require the existence of any other particular—properties like *having blonde hair, being 11.5 inches tall, being tanned, being a doll,* and so on.

An *impure property*, however, is a property that a particular can have only if some other particulars exist, a property that we earlier called a relational property—such as *being to the left of, being taller than, being older than*, and so on. It should be easy to see that an object may have a pure property even if no other particular existed. However, nothing can have an impure property unless at least one other particular existed. Barbie doll #1 cannot be to the left of nothing! It must be to the left of some other thing, say, Barbie doll #2. And, says the critic of the bundle theory, spatial properties are impure properties—which means that the Barbie dolls differ only with respect to impure properties.[34]

To see the importance of this point, let us also distinguish two versions of the principle of the identity of indiscernibles, a weak version and a strong version. According to the *weak version*

> *For any particulars* a *and* b, *if* a *and* b *share all the same pure and impure properties, then* a *and* b *are identical.*

This version of the principle is unassailable. Things that are absolutely identical with respect to every kind of property they have cannot be distinct but must be numerically identical. However, the *strong version* of the principle states that

> *For any particulars* a *and* b, *if* a *and* b *share all the same pure properties, then* a *and* b *are identical.*

While the weak version is necessarily true, the strong version is certainly false. The Barbie dolls mentioned above are obvious counterexamples. They have all the same pure properties, but they are *not* numerically identical. The significance of this point is that the bundle theory would seem to have to depend on the strong version of the principle in order to escape circularity. The bundle theory is designed to give us an account of what it means to be a particular thing. But if impure properties are allowed to be part of the account, then the bundle theory's analysis will be circular. It will, that is, include in its account of what it means to be a particular thing *other particular things* (since impure properties presuppose the existence of other particulars). So, the only noncircular way for the bundle theory to define particulars is to appeal to the strong version of the principle of the identity of indiscernibles. But that version is false. So, the bundle theory would appear to be false as well.

---

[34] Of course, the Barbie dolls might differ with regard to other than spatial properties (e.g., temporal properties), but it is arguable that all such properties are impure ones.

Prospects for the Bundle Theory

Is there any salvaging the bundle theory? Well, first, it is worth pointing out that our discussion of the bundle theory has presupposed throughout a realist or Platonist view of properties, a view that sees properties as real abstract entities (see § 4.2.1 above). It is possible that a bundle theory might adopt a nominalist view of properties and escape these objections.[35] This might be too high a price to pay if it turns out that nominalism is less plausible than its alternatives, a conclusion we defended above.

It is also plausible that a Berkeleyan idealist can escape the force of these objections. While the Berkeleyan must embrace something like the bundle theory in his account of the ordinary objects of sense perception, he need not (indeed cannot) adopt a bundle theory as a general account of particulars. The reason is that the Berkeleyan idealist does not believe that minds or souls are simply bundles of properties. Hence, he must embrace an alternative theory of particulars with regard to minds. This would allow him to escape the force of the above objections to the bundle theory by restricting its scope to sensible objects alone. With regard to the first objection, the Berkeleyan would have to say that *sensible* objects do have all of their properties essentially, but this may not be as counterintuitive as it first seems. Mereological essentialism is often seen as true (or at least plausible) with regard to artifacts (e.g., cars, bridges, tables) and even inanimate objects like rocks and lakes. But, on the Berkeleyan view, everything we experience through the senses (including the bodies of living things) is literally an artifact made by God as part of the cosmic "matrix." Mereological essentialism has seemed less plausible (and counterintuitive) with regard to such living things, says the Berkeleyan, because we associate substantial souls or minds with them and these bodies are *not* essentially related to these minds. That is, the bodies of living things may change (and thus not literally be the same body anymore), but there is something underlying that change that remains the same, namely the mind associated with the bodies that exist before and after the change.

As for the second objection—the claim that the bundle theory depends upon the false strong version of the principle of the identity of indiscernibles—the Berkeleyan idealist could grant that it refutes the

---

[35] The reason is that, for the nominalist, to say that two things have the "same properties" is just a manner of speaking. The nominalist believes that only particulars exist, so each property had by any given thing is itself a particular, not a universal. Which means that if a particular *S* has the property *being red* and another particular *S** has the property *being red*, *S* and *S** do not literally share the same property. Rather, the redness of *S* and the redness of *S** are seen as distinct particulars in themselves. For more on this nominalist strategy for defending the bundle theory, see Michael Loux, *Metaphysics*, 113–14.

bundle theory as a general account of particulars, but again deny that it counts against a more restrictive bundle theory regarding sensible objects. The point is that a Berkeleyan may insist that *his* bundle theory only requires the weak version of the principle of the identity of indiscernibles, which everyone acknowledges to be true. It is obvious that sensible objects have both pure and impure properties and that it is not possible for any two of them to be distinct and yet have all their pure and impure properties in common. The appeal to the weak version of the principle is not circular for the Berkeleyan because he is not giving a general account of all particulars but only certain kinds of particulars, namely the objects of sense perception.

So the bundle theory may not be completely disparaged by the above objections. However, those who are not sympathetic to either nominalism or Berkeleyan idealism will not be impressed. Moreover, even the Berkeleyan will need another account of particulars than the bundle theory because he restricts that view to sensible objects only. Therefore, we turn to the next general view of particulars.

4.4.2 The Substratum View

In the previous section, we mentioned that we ordinarily speak of particulars *possessing* their properties. This means that we usually think of properties being the properties *of something*—something that is not itself a property. Our ordinary way of speaking is aptly captured by the *substratum view* of particulars. On this view, particulars are not simply bundles of properties. In addition to a thing's properties, there is a distinct entity that underlies the properties, that "supports" or "bears" the properties. This additional entity is called the "substratum." The substratum is not a property but a very different kind of thing. In fact, according to this view, the substratum of a particular is completely bare. Considered in itself it has no properties whatsoever. This view seems to capture our ordinary language concerning properties being the properties of something. Properties are possessed by a bare substratum.

To illustrate the view, consider again a typical basketball. The basketball has certain properties as we noted earlier such as *being spherical, being orange*, and *being 30 inches in circumference*. On the bundle theory this collection of properties is all the basketball amounts to. On the substratum view, however, there is something else that bears these properties—the substratum—which in itself has none of these properties. The substratum is neither spherical, orange, nor 30 inches in circumference. Yet, the properties are unified and held together by their attachment to the substratum. The basketball, then, is not a bundle of properties, but is a composite made up of a bare substratum and a certain set of properties attached to it. Many eminent philosophers have held this view, among them John Locke, Gustav Bergman (1906–1987), and Bertrand Russell (early in his career).

One initial objection to the substratum view is to claim that it is contradictory. It might seem that adherents of the substratum view are committed to holding that substrata both have and do not have properties. On the one hand, when they claim that properties are the properties of the substrata, they seem to affirm that substrata have properties. On the other hand, when they describe a substratum as being bare, they claim that it has no properties. Thus, substrata have properties and they do not have properties. But this is absurd.

In response, the substratum theorist will claim that the objection is confused. The theory claims only that the substratum *in itself* is bare. When one considers a concrete particular such as a basketball, then, to be sure, the substratum has properties. The substratum of a basketball bears the properties of *being spherical, being orange,* and *being 30 inches in circumference*. But, the substratum, considered by itself as a distinct constituent part of the basketball, does not have properties; it is bare. Another way of putting this is that a substratum has no essential properties. Whatever properties it has are the accidental properties that, combined with the bare substratum, constitute a particular thing.

This response to the objection sounds right as far as it goes. However, it raises other more devastating objections. The substratum theorist says that substrata have no essential properties, but would they not by definition be necessarily bare? That is, wouldn't substrata have the *essential* property of *having no essential properties*? It would seem so. They would also have the essential property of *being the bearer of properties*. This means that substrata both do and do not have essential properties. So the substratum theory seems to be contradictory after all.

Perhaps the substratum theorist can adjust his theory and admit that substrata do have at least some essential properties, namely the ones we mentioned in the last paragraph and perhaps others that are necessary for something to be the kind of thing a substratum is. Nevertheless, they would be otherwise bare and serve as the possessors of all other kinds of properties. Unfortunately, this raises another difficulty. Recall that the motivation for the substratum view was the belief that the bearer of a property and the property itself are distinct. This would seem to be as true of essential properties as much as accidental ones. Yet, as Michael Loux puts it, this "forces us to conclude that a substratum cannot be the literal possessor of any attribute essential to it."[36] So what would be the bearer of a substratum's essential properties? We would seem to require

[36] Michael Loux, *Metaphysics*, 122.

another distinct and independent substratum to be their bearer. But, then, the essential properties of that new substratum also have essential properties that require as their bearer yet another substratum. And now we are off on a vicious infinite regress of substrata for each and every particular. So it seems that the substratum view has great difficulty providing us with an ultimate subject for properties.

4.4.3 The Substance View

A third perspective on the nature of particulars is the *substance view* (also called the "substance-kind" view and the "essentialist" view). Philosophers who have held this view include Aristotle (384–322 BC), Thomas Aquinas (AD 1224–1274), P. F. Strawson (1919-), and the contemporary Christian philosopher J. P. Moreland. Substance theorists note that both of the previous views are reductionist views. That is, they attempt to define particulars by reducing them to their constituent parts. Put another way, both of the other views think of particulars as being "built up" out of other things. In the case of the bundle theory, particulars are built up out of properties. On the substratum view, they are constructed out of properties together with a bare substratum. But according to the substance view, concrete particulars themselves should be taken as the most fundamental entities. They cannot be reduced to constituent entities that are more basic than they. This is not to say that particulars do not have parts. A dog, for example, has many parts. It has a nose, two ears, two eyes, a stomach, and so on. And it also has atoms and molecules that compose its body. Nevertheless, the substance view claims that a dog cannot be reduced without remainder to those parts. As an old adage says, the whole is greater than the sum of its parts. Hence, for purposes of metaphysical analysis, the *dog*—the concrete particular—is an irreducibly basic thing. Such a basic entity the substance theorist calls a *substance*.

We need to qualify the above remarks, however. Most substance theorists do not think that everything we might ordinarily think of as a particular counts as a substance in the sense defined above. Usually it is only living things (plants, animals, and persons) that count as substances, the things that philosophers and scientists sometimes call "natural kinds." Other things such as mountains, lakes, automobiles, and such, are not substances on this view because they are not (or at least do not seem to be) things of which it can be said that the wholes are greater than their parts. Such things seem to be simply aggregates of their parts. But not so for natural kinds.

It would be helpful to see the substance view as a middle position between the bundle theory and the substratum view. Like the latter view, the substance view holds that properties are the properties *of* something; properties are possessed or had by something else. Unlike that other view, however, the thing that has the properties is not a bare substratum. Take, for example, the dog Rover we discussed earlier. According to the substance view, the possessor of Rover's properties is *Rover himself!* There is no *part* of Rover (a characterless substratum) that bears his properties. Rover, the substance, is the bearer of his properties.

Like the bundle theory, the substance view insists that what characterizes a particular is its properties. If you want to know what a particular thing is, you must have some knowledge of the properties it has. But unlike the bundle theory, the substance view does not and need not consider all of a thing's properties to be essential. They can allow for a distinction between the essential and accidental properties of a substance. The reason is that the substance view recognizes a special kind of property called a "substance-kind property" (sometimes a "natural-kind property"). As noted above, a substance is a member of a natural kind. Rover, for instance, is a member of the natural kind "dog." What makes Rover a member of that natural kind? It is simply that Rover has the *essence* of a dog. To have the essence of a dog is to have all of the essential properties of a dog. The essential properties that make a substance the kind of thing it is may be understood as a sort of complex property comprised of whatever simple properties are necessary to distinguish one natural kind from another. So the substance theorist would say that Rover exemplifies the complex natural-kind property *being a dog*. Exemplifying that property is what makes Rover the kind of thing he is, a dog. So rather than being identical with a bundle of properties all of which are essential to it (as on the bundle theory), the substance view claims that "a substance just is, in the sense of being identical with, an exemplification of a substance-kind property."[37] Substances will likely have other properties, of course. Rover, for instance, may have the property of *being brown-haired* or *being adventurous*. But these properties will be accidental to him and will serve (among other things) to distinguish him from other dogs.

The substance view appears to have the resources to avoid the problems associated with the other two views of particulars. It avoids the problems of the substratum theory because, though it requires that properties have a subject, that subject is not bare. Individual substances have many properties both essential and accidental, and those substances are not additional, bare entities over and above their properties; rather, they *just are* exemplifications of their substance-kind properties. Further, as we saw above, the substance view avoids the problem that the bundle theory has

[37] Cynthia MacDonald, *Varieties of Things*, 116.

in having to claim that all properties are essential. Moreover, the substance view is consistent with a denial of the strong version of the principle of the identity of indiscernibles. Because the advocate of the substance view does not believe that particulars are simply the bundle of their properties, but are exemplifications of their substance-kind properties, he need not be committed to the idea that things that share their pure properties are numerically identical. For while substance-kind properties are pure properties (a substance can exemplify a substance-kind property even if no other particulars exist), there can be two distinct substances that have exactly the same pure properties simply in virtue of their being two instances of a particular substance-kind property.

While the substance view does seem to avoid the problems associated with the other views, it needs to be noted that this view clearly presupposes realism about properties. Moreover, it presupposes a view called *essentialism*, which holds that concrete things have essential properties, properties that they cannot lack and continue to exist. Both realism and essentialism are controversial and often form the basis for objections to the substance view. However, our discussion of Platonism and its alternatives in section 4.2 should allow the reader to see that Platonic realism and essentialism are defensible.

Conclusion

Most of the material in this chapter has probably seemed very abstract and impractical to many readers. It may have seemed to be just a lot of "ivory tower" speculation with no real relevance to everyday life and Christian ministry. We hope that readers will be careful not to jump to this conclusion. If you have paid attention, you should be able to discern the importance of the metaphysical questions we have discussed. Obviously, as we pointed out, the question of universals has important ramifications for ethics. But so do most of the other topics we discussed. With regard to the nature of the world, we suggested that materialism implies not only moral relativism but the impossibility of moral responsibility. A pure (i.e., non-Berkeleyan) version of the bundle theory must embrace the view that every particular has its properties essentially. But this means that every time a particular loses or gains a new property, that particular ceases to exist and is replaced by a new thing. In other words, the bundle theory does not appear to allow for the notion of accidental change. When a leaf, for example, changes color from green to yellow, we do not have the same leaf with a different color, we have an entirely new leaf. The ethical implications of this are significant because it may entail that a person who commits a crime but then loses a few strands of hair is not the same person as the one who is later arrested and put on trial!

Moreover, metaphysics has ramifications for how we understand and explain several important Christian doctrines. The question of universals impacts our understanding of the nature of God and His relationship to His creation. Does God have properties? If so, does He depend upon them or vice versa? When God created the world, what did He create—a world composed of material things or an ideal "matrix"? Which view is more consistent with Scripture? Is the doctrine of the Trinity coherent? The principles of identity defined in this chapter could play a role in answering that question. These and many other doctrinal questions may be illuminated by the tools of metaphysics. This is what led John Wesley, the great Methodist minister, to ask his fellow clergymen the rhetorical question, "Is not some acquaintance with what has been termed the second part of logic, (metaphysics), if not so necessary as [logic itself], yet highly expedient?"[38] Wesley understood that metaphysics in particular (and philosophy in general) is a handmaid to theology.

Questions for Reflection

1. What do you think of the principle of the indiscernability of identicals? Is it as unproblematic as the authors suggest? Why or why not? What about the weak version of the principle of the identity of indiscernibles?

2. What is your assessment of the bundle theory? Does it make Berkeleyan idealism more attractive? Why or why not?

3. Can the substratum view be defended against the objection raised in this section? If so, how?

4. Does the substance view really deal adequately with the problems raised by the alternative views? Why or why not? Can you think of any other problems the substance view might have?

5. Can you think of any other way of characterizing particulars than those covered in this section?

---

[38] John Wesley, "An Address to the Clergy," in *The Works of John Wesley*, vol. 10 (Grand Rapids: Baker, 1979), 483.

For Further Reading

On Metaphysics in General

Conee, Earl, and Theodore Sider. *Riddles of Existence: A Guided Tour of Metaphysics.* Oxford: Oxford University Press, 2005.

Jubien, Michael. *Contemporary Metaphysics.* Malden, MA: Blackwell, 1997.

Loux, Michael J. *Metaphysics: A Contemporary Introduction.* 2nd ed. New York: Routledge, 2002.

MacDonald, Cynthia. *Varieties of Things: Foundations of Contemporary Metaphysics.* Malden, MA: Blackwell, 2005.

Taylor, Richard. *Metaphysics.* 4th ed. Englewood Cliffs, NJ: Prentice Hall, 1991.

On the Nature of the World

Armstrong, David M. "Naturalism, Materialism, and First Philosophy." In *Contemporary Materialism: A Reader*, ed. Paul K. Moser and J. D. Trout. New York: Routledge, 1995.

Russell, Bertrand. *The Problems of Philosophy*, chaps. 1–3. London: Oxford University Press, 1912.

van Inwagen, Peter. *Metaphysics*, chap. 3. Boulder, CO: Westview, 1993.

On Universals

Campbell, Keith. *Abstract Particulars.* Oxford: Basil Blackwell, 1990.

Moreland, J. P. *Universals.* London: McGill-Queen's, 2001.

Quine, W. V. O. *From a Logical Point of View*, chap. 1. Cambridge, MA: Harvard University Press, 1954.

On Particulars

Loux, Michael J. *Substance and Attribute*, chap. 9. Dordrecht: Reidel, 1978.

Moreland, J. P. "Theories of Individuation: A Reconsideration of Bare Particulars." In *Pacific Philosophical Quarterly* 79 (1998): 251–63.

Van Cleve, J. "Three Versions of the Bundle Theory." In *Philosophical Studies* 47 (1985): 95–108.

Chapter Five

HUMAN NATURE: WHAT AM I?

"Every man's life is a fairy tale,
written by God's fingers."

—Hans Christian Andersen

Glossary Terms

Agent causation	Near-death experiences
Behaviorism (philosophical)	Occasionalism
Compatibilism	Personal identity
Eliminative materialism	Physical view of
(eliminativism)	personal identity
Functionalism	Physicalism
Hard determinism	Property dualism
Incompatibilism	Reincarnation
Interactionism	Soul view of personal identity
Libertarianism	Strict-identity theory
Memory view of personal identity	(reductive materialism)
Mind-body dualism	
(substance dualism)	

A t the beginning of the film *Regarding Henry*, the title character (played by Harrison Ford) is a hard-nosed lawyer—self-
absorbed, ambitious, and cut-throat. One night after work
Henry goes out for a pack of cigarettes and the convenience store he
goes into is held up by an armed robber. Henry takes too long to hand
over his wallet, so the gunman shoots him in the head. Fortunately, it
was a low-caliber gun, so Henry survives the shooting. Yet, when Henry
regains consciousness he is completely changed. Rather than being a
hard-nosed jerk, he is gentle, sweet, and loving. What can we make of
this? How do we explain the changes in Henry? What could this story
(and the real-life cases like it) tell us about human nature?

Regarding Henry actually raises several important philosophical questions related to human nature. Most obvious is the question of personal
identity. Does *Henry* really survive the shooting at all? The post-shooting
Henry is very different than the previous Henry. Perhaps the new Henry
is a completely different person and the old Henry is now "dead." But
this raises the question of just what it means for a person to maintain
personal identity over time. What makes you the same person that you
were yesterday?

A related question has to do with *what* a human person ultimately is. Henry was shot in the head. The changes he experienced were

apparently related to damage to his brain. This prompts the question: Are we simply our brains and their functions? Or is there some part of us (say, a soul) that is not physical? Questions of life after death immediately arise in connection with these. If we are just physical beings, then it would seem that physical death means the end of us. However, if there is more to human nature than the physical, life after death is a real possibility.

Another question pertains to human agency. Could Henry have done anything besides go to that convenience store the night he was shot? Did he have the freedom to stay home or was he determined to go there? After he was shot, were his new personality and all of his subsequent choices simply the dictates of new brain chemistry? If so, could he be morally responsible for what he did?

Answers to all of these questions are central to what it means to be a human being—a topic of great importance to Christians. Christians believe that humans are created in the image of God (Gen 1:26–27). Because of this we believe that human life is sacred and that human actions have real moral significance. Moreover, we believe that there is life after death. This belief is grounded in God's promise of the resurrection of the dead. What light can philosophy shed on these convictions? In this chapter we will discuss the above questions and seek to show how philosophical study can support and illumine Christian beliefs about human nature.

§ 5.1 Do We Have Souls?

As noted above, some of the most perplexing philosophical questions concern ourselves. Chief among these is the problem of consciousness. What *is* consciousness? What are minds? Where did consciousness come from originally, and how does it develop within us individually? When it comes to the nature of the mind, philosophers tend to fall into one of two camps: mind-body dualism and physicalism. *Mind-body dualists* affirm that human beings are composed of both a material body and a supernatural aspect—the soul. Historically, Christians have favored this perspective, and it was the dominant view in the West until the mid-twentieth century. The last few decades, however, have seen the rise of *physicalism*, the view that everything in the universe, including human consciousness, can be fully described in terms of physics. In this section we will examine these two perspectives, noting the major arguments for and against each.

5.1.1 Mind-Body Dualism

Mind-body dualism is distinguished by the claim that there is something more to mind than matter, namely an immaterial soul. (In the following discussion, we will use the terms *mind* and *soul* interchangeably.) Mind-body dualists maintain that body and soul are two distinct entities or substances. Hence, the view is also called *substance dualism*. The chief modern progenitor of substance dualism was Descartes (1596–1650), but the history of substance dualism is ancient, tracing back to Socrates and, in theological history, to the Old Testament. Substance dualists agree that the basic facts of consciousness cannot be fully accounted for in physical terms. So, they insist, human nature must be supernatural as well as material.

Arguments for Mind-Body Dualism

Dozens of arguments have been offered by philosophers in defense of mind-body dualism, but a few of these have been especially influential. In the early modern period, Descartes proposed a multipronged argument for dualism in his *Meditations*. He argued that the mind and body must be separate substances because of their very distinct properties. For one thing, he noted, the mind is invisible, while the body is visible. And the essential activity of the mind—thinking—is a wholly private act, while the body's doings are always publicly observable. Secondly, the mind is unified in a way that the body is not. As Descartes puts it, "There is a great difference between the mind and the body, in that the body, from its nature, is always divisible and the mind is completely indivisible."[1] Thus, we talk about body "parts" but not parts of the mind, which Descartes takes to be a sign that they are distinct entities.

Both aspects of Descartes' argument may be challenged. First, even though the mind's operations are invisible, it does not follow from this that the mind is a separate substance from the body. Perhaps the mind is simply a feature or consequence of the brain's operations. One might affirm this while still admitting the privacy of mind. As for Descartes' indivisibility claim, many findings in the fields of psychology and neurophysiology would challenge this idea. For example, multiple personality disorders appear to provide direct support for the mind's divisibility, as do split-brain experiments on epileptics, which show that distinct domains of awareness can be distinguished within the same person. Even in the psychologically healthy, many argue, the multiple functions of mind suggest mental compartmentalization.

[1] René Descartes, *Philosophical Essays*, trans. Laurence J. Lafleur (New York: Macmillan, 1964), 139.

Although Descartes' defense of mind-body dualism has proven to be flimsy, several other arguments have been proposed that are not so easily dismissed.

1. *The Argument from Subjectivity.* Several years ago the philosopher Thomas Nagel wrote an influential essay titled "What Is It Like to Be a Bat?"[2] Nagel pointed out that what essentially characterizes consciousness is first-person subjectivity. In other words, regarding any mind we can reasonably say, *There is something that it is like to be that thing.* We can say this about people and even an animal such as a bat, whereas it does not make sense to ask what it is like to be a rock or a shoe. In other words, we recognize that animals like bats have subjective experiences even if we do not happen to know what those experiences are like. We also know that no physiological description of a bat's inner life could capture what that is like. Subjectivity necessarily eludes even the most rigorous description of brain processes. So the most exhaustive account of, say, a bat's neurological sonar mechanisms would not bring us any closer to understanding what it is like to be a bat. This is because such descriptions are necessarily third-person in nature. To ask "what is it like to be X?" is to inquire about a particular *first-person* experience. And no third-person (or "objective") description could ever provide that. This means that when it comes to minds there is something about them over and above the physical.

2. *The Argument from Qualia.* When you look at an apple, hear a siren, or feel a tickle, what you experience are certain phenomenal qualities, or "qualia" as philosophers have come to call them. All of our perceptual experiences are laden with qualia, including colors, tastes, smells, sounds, and feelings. Since qualia are such a constant part of our conscious lives, we might overlook the fact that these, too, cannot be accounted for on a physicalist view of human nature. As philosopher Frank Jackson pointed out in another landmark article, no description of the brain could possibly capture this aspect of perceptual experience.[3] Jackson offers an intriguing thought experiment to drive home his point:

> Mary is a brilliant scientist who is, for whatever reason, forced to investigate the world from a black and white room via a black and white television monitor. She specializes in the neurophysiology of vision and acquires, let us suppose, all the physical information there is to obtain about what goes on when we see ripe

---

[2] Thomas Nagel, "What Is It Like to Be a Bat?" *The Philosophical Review* 83 (1974): 435–50.

[3] See Frank Jackson's "Epiphenomenal Qualia," *Philosophical Quarterly* 32 (1982): 127–36.

tomatoes, or the sky, and use terms like 'red', 'blue', and so on. She discovers, for example, just which wavelength combinations from the sky stimulate the retina, and exactly how this produces via the central nervous system the contraction of the vocal cords and expulsion of air from the lungs that results in the uttering of the sentence 'The sky is blue'. . . . What will happen when Mary is released from her black and white room or is given a color television monitor? Will she learn anything or not?[4]

The obvious answer to Jackson's concluding question is "yes"—Mary will learn what it is like to see color! So the point here is that even a complete comprehension of the facts of the physical world, most pertinently the brain, cannot capture what it is like to have a perceptual experience of qualia such as color. This, again, shows that there is something more to mind than physical realities.

3. *The Argument from Intentionality.* Take a moment and think of your mother. Are you doing so right now? Good. Now notice something about that thought. It has a quality that philosophers call "intentionality." That is, your mental state is about something, or in this case *someone*—your mom. Although this is another feature of the mind that is easy to overlook (because it is such a routine part of our lives), it is noteworthy that mental states refer to things outside themselves. Thoughts of your mother, LeBron James, or the White House transcend themselves and even your own mind, as they refer to particular men, women, or objects. This quality of "aboutness" is yet another crucial feature of mind that distinguishes it from physical objects, as physical objects do not refer outside themselves in this way. Physical objects can have many different relations to one another. They can be "on top of," "next to," "underneath," and so forth. But they cannot refer to or be "about" one another. Another way of putting this is to say that mental states have semantic content. They carry meaning, while mere physical objects do not, no matter how complex in composition or function they might be. This, of course, includes the brain. Therefore, mental states, and the mind itself, must be distinct from the brain.

Criticisms of Dualism

The arguments from subjectivity, qualia, and intentionality are compelling to many critics of physicalism. Nonetheless, physicalism remains the dominant view among philosophers of mind today. Why? One reason is that mind-body dualism suffers from two significant problems that many believe have yet to be solved. One is the problem of making

---

[4] Ibid., 130.

sense of the causal interaction between mind and body, and the other regards the dualist's apparent violation of Ockham's Razor. We will discuss the second of these first.

1. *The Problem of Causal Overdetermination.* Brain events can always be traced back to prior physical causes. When I look at an elephant an image forms on my retina, triggering other events within my eye that result in a neural transmission to the visual center of my cerebral cortex resulting in my experience of seeing a large, gray mammal. Now if mind-body dualism is correct, then at what point does the soul get involved in such a mental event? It appears that wherever the soul's activity enters the causal nexus there will be redundant causal activity, for there will be two causal streams (one mental and the other physical) culminating in one and the same physical event. Thus we are left with one unnecessary causal explanation and a violation of Ockham's Razor (i.e., other things equal, the simplest explanation is to be preferred). Theoretical parsimony would dictate that one of these causal powers be eliminated from our account of perception (and our account of consciousness generally). And since we know that the brain is involved in human thought and action, it appears that it is the concept of the soul which should be eliminated.

2. *The Interaction Problem.* Another problem pertains to an apparent contradiction between traditional mind-body dualism and one of the laws of physics. The first law of thermodynamics (the law of energy conservation) says that energy is neither created nor destroyed. But how can the soul causally affect the body without creating energy? The dualist could simply insist that souls do create energy. But there is no empirical support for this claim, and there is a strong presumption against it, since the law of energy conservation is one of the most fundamental laws of physics. Anyway, whatever solution the dualist might propose leads back to an even more fundamental difficulty: How can material and nonmaterial substances causally interact at all? In the three and one-half centuries since Descartes' demise, mind-body dualists have had a difficult time in narrowing, much less closing, this ontological gap. Yet this is crucial if any sense is to be made of the notion of causal interaction as it applies to mind and body.

The majority opinion among dualists is that mind and body are indeed causally interactive. That is, mental operations are caused by the body (brain), and bodily movements are caused by mental operations. This version of mind-body dualism is known as *interactionism.* Interactionists tolerate the above problems because their view accommodates what to them seems an obvious truth, namely that body stimuli, such as tickling or pricking the skin, *cause* mental states, such as pleasure or pain. But, again, how can material and nonmaterial substances causally interact? To circumvent this problem, some dualists prefer to *deny* that body and soul causally interact. They embrace the view known as *occasionalism*, which maintains that the body and soul are causally independent. Mental operations are the activity of soul alone, though they are (typically) associated with brain and other bodily activity.

So how does the occasionalist account for the apparent interaction between mind and body? According to the early modern occasionalist Gottfried Leibniz (1646–1716) this appearance is due to the fact that God has coordinated mental and physical events such that body (brain) activities occur on the "occasion" of certain mental states (such as thoughts or choices) and mental states (such as sensations) occur on the "occasion" of certain bodily states (such as hand or eye movement).[5] Although occasionalism seems counterintuitive, it is noteworthy that it is immune to both of the above criticisms. By denying any causal interaction between mind and body, not only does occasionalism avoid the interaction problem but it also avoids the problem of causal overdetermination and any violation of the law of energy conservation. Despite these merits, occasionalism remains a minority view among mind-body dualists.

5.1.2 Physicalism

Given the problems with mind-body dualism as well as the advances of science in providing explanations for natural phenomena, it is not surprising that physicalism has become the dominant theoretical position in consciousness studies. However, physicalist theories of mind come in many different forms. In this section we will survey the major brands of physicalism, and we will do so in a historical format in order to display the logical progression of physicalism over the past half century or so.

Philosophical Behaviorism

The "physicalist project" in consciousness studies began in earnest with the publication of Gilbert Ryle's *The Concept of Mind* in the middle of the twentieth century.[6] This monumental work not only mercilessly critiqued the "Cartesian myth" of substance dualism but also offered a

---

[5] In addition to Leibniz, this view was held by Mohammed al Ghazali, Nicolas Malebranche, George Berkeley, and, perhaps, Jonathan Edwards—all took a strong view of divine sovereignty and affirmed some form of metaphysical idealism which affirms that the physical world is mind-dependent.

[6] Gilbert Ryle, *The Concept of Mind* (New York: Barnes and Noble, 1949).

defense of his own view, known as *philosophical behaviorism*. Ryle proposed that the Cartesian view of the mind as essentially inner, private, and distinct from the body is fundamentally flawed. It is a "category mistake," he suggested, to regard certain features of our physical lives as belonging to an altogether different ontological category, the "mental." In fact, he argued, we are purely and simply physical beings, and those qualities normally regarded as belonging to the realm of the mind (viz. beliefs, desires, emotions, pains, etc.) may be analyzed entirely in terms of behavior and dispositions to behave. To have a desire to eat is just to act in a certain way—for example, to go to the kitchen and prepare a sandwich or to say things like "I would like to have lunch now." To have a pain is just to wince, cry aloud, contort, or to be disposed to act in such ways. In any case, for Ryle, one's behavior is not a sign of a private mental event. Rather, the mental just *is* the behavior or tendencies to behave in certain ways.

The advantages of such a view are plain. Like all forms of physicalism, Ryle's account is parsimonious, uniting all of the data of human experience into a single ontological category. Moreover, behaviorism dissolves two persistent problems in the Cartesian tradition, the problem of interaction and the problem of other minds. The problem of interaction, as noted above, regards the difficulty of accounting for how two substances as different as a material body and an immaterial mind could causally interact. The problem of other minds is the difficulty of justifying one's belief that there are minds other than one's own. If I only directly experience my own thoughts and feelings, then how can I justify my belief that *every other human being* has similar thoughts and feelings? As an inductive inference, this amounts to reasoning from one case (mine) to billions of others (everyone else), which provides obviously weak grounds. Ryle's behaviorism avoids the problem of interaction by denying that humans are composed of two distinct substances. And as for the problem of other minds, the behaviorist account makes mind a public matter. One can directly experience another's mental life by simply observing her behavior. So no skeptical problem of other minds remains.

Philosophical behaviorism, therefore, has strengths as a theory of mind. It is metaphysically simple, and it eliminates in one stroke two nagging problems in philosophy. These considerations and its promise as a scientifically respectable account of human nature are why behaviorism enjoyed such popularity, albeit briefly, in philosophical circles. But the problems with this approach proved too great. For one thing, the behaviorist model cannot account for the fact that some thoughts, feelings, desires, and such are never manifested in behavior. In fact, one may act directly contrary to one's private thoughts or feelings. Moreover, there are some beliefs, such as those concerning high-level mathematics, which seem to have no possible behavioral expressions. On top of these formal problems, there is the intuitive implausibility of philosophical behaviorism. It does not account for the essential subjective nature of experience. It ignores the first-person quality of human experience that *is* private and, in a sense, inner and hidden. The root problem with behaviorism is that it confuses the *epistemological criterion* for mind with the *metaphysical reality* of the mental. Mental states are indeed expressed behaviorally, and there is much that we learn about a person's mind by observing her actions. But this is far from admitting that there is nothing more to mind than these publicly observable facts.

Strict Identity Theory and Eliminative Materialism

The next chapter in the history of physicalist theories of mind was *strict identity theory* (also known as reductive materialism). Its two leading proponents, U. T. Place and J. J. C. Smart, recognized the problems with the behaviorist approach and sought adequately to account for the inner, hidden nature of mind while at the same time salvaging scientific plausibility. Their compromise was to identify mental states with brain states. Sensations, beliefs, and general awareness are nothing more than processes in the brain. To say "I have a pain in my elbow" is just another way of saying "Nerve bundle CL-468 is firing." Like behaviorism, the identity theory is simple. Moreover, it accounts for the observed correlation between mental states and brain states. States of mind are directly and predictably alterable by neurological manipulation, through such means as manual stimulation and blood chemistry alteration.

Early critics of the identity thesis claimed that the theory was logically absurd. They pointed out that where two entities are claimed to be identical, anything that is true of one must also be true of the other (as was discussed in the previous chapter). But this is manifestly not the case as regards mental states and brain states. Consider a mental state X and the brain state Y, with which X is supposed to be identical. One may be introspectively aware of X but not Y. That is, for example, I may be immediately aware of my elbow pain and yet know absolutely nothing about my brain states. Hence, the two cannot be strictly identical. Furthermore, all brain states have physical characteristics, but mental states do not. Brain states occur in specific places and the neurological structures that constitute them have determinate shapes and sizes. But none of these predicates can be meaningfully applied to mental states, such as hunger, love, fear, or belief. For example, it does not make sense to say that one's fear has a location or that one's belief has a shape. Thus, critics argued, the notion that mental states are identical with brain processes is absurd.

With regard to this objection, however, some strict-identity theorists were quick to point out that it seems to beg the question. That is, it *assumes* that mental states cannot have size, weight, location, and the like, when this is precisely what strict-identity theory is claiming. Despite the identity theorists' ability to ward off this criticism, there emerged other problems. In addition to the failure of the theory to account for the aforementioned facts about subjectivity, qualia and intentionality, developments in neuroscience pointed in a very different direction as well. Through advances in brain scanning techniques, researchers discovered that in diverse mental activities, ranging from problem-solving to perception and emotional responses, mental activities are not localized to specific parts of the brain. Rather, many regions of the brain are involved when there are mental events. So to say that a particular belief or feeling is identical with a specific brain event proved to be far too simplistic to fit with scientists' growing understanding of the brain's complex networking.

In response to these problems, some physicalists proposed that the spirit of strict-identity theory can be preserved while withholding bold proclamations about the identity of mental events and brain events. Thus, *eliminative materialists*, such as Richard Rorty and Paul and Patricia Churchland, have emphasized that traditional mind talk—which they call "folk psychology"—can be eliminated without necessarily insisting that all such talk be substituted by references to brain physiology or any other particular physical facts. For example, phrases such as "I am in pain" might one day be replaced by phrases such as "My C-fibers are stimulated," but they might also be replaced by references to behavior or some other physical facts. The point, eliminativists tell us, is that physicalists need not commit themselves to a specific positive explanation of what mental events *are*. They need only affirm that mind is ultimately based in matter and science will one day show us how. Thus, eliminativists are open to a broad range of ways in which the folk psychology of mind-body dualism may be replaced by naturalistic expressions.

While eliminative materialism avoids the specific criticisms that devastated behaviorism and strict identity theory, the fact that the theory refuses to offer a specific account of mind is a weakness. When it comes to offering a positive account of mind, eliminativists are essentially eclectic, incorporating claims by behaviorism and strict identity theory. Unfortunately, whatever advantages such an approach provides, in terms of variety of options, these are offset by the fact that eliminativism inherits all of the problems with those theories as well. Furthermore, whatever naturalistic substitutes for mind-talk the eliminativists might embrace, these will always be subject to the problems that must plague any physicalist theory of mind, specifically their failure to account for subjectivity, qualia, and intentionality.

Functionalism

In more recent years, a view known as *functionalism* has risen to prominence among philosophers of mind, due in large part to the tremendous success and influence of computer technology. The basic proposal of the functionalists is that mental states are reducible to the functional operations of the brain and the causal roles these play in the larger human system, such as their relations to the body's behavior and environment. Early functionalists, such as Jerry Fodor and Hilary Putnam, rejected the strict identity thesis because it asked the wrong question when analyzing the brain for its capacity to explain mental states, namely "What does it *consist* of?" Such an approach is wrongheaded, they insisted. Rather, the proper question to be asked of the brain is: "What does it *do*?" The former question is that of microanalysis and is hopelessly local in its focus. Consciousness, the functionalists tell us, is not a localized feature of the brain such that particular thoughts can be linked or reduced to particular neural processes. Rather, consciousness is a broader feature of the brain, systemic in nature. Thus, a functional analysis that asks what causal roles various neurological mechanisms play in the overall brain system, as well as in the rest of the body, is necessary for getting at the essence of mind. So, for example, a functionalist would say that my "belief" that there is a computer before me is just a shorthand way of referring to some of the causal events in my brain and elsewhere in my body, as signals are sent from my retinas to the visual center of my cerebral cortex, which in turn plays a causal role in my behaving in certain ways.

In focusing on the causal roles that brain processes play in a living system, functionalists note that there is nothing special about the particular form these take in human beings, that is, our carbon-based biological brain. Such mental attributes as beliefs, intentions, and intelligence may potentially be realized in any number of systems involving anything from silicon chips to aluminum cans, so long as the right causal roles are realized. All that is necessary is functional equivalence. This thesis provides the premise of strong Artificial Intelligence (AI), the notion that the mind is essentially like a computer program. (Strong AI is distinguished from Weak AI, which merely affirms that computers are useful in understanding mind.) Of course, the implications of this claim are vast, as it holds out the promise of producing thinking, feeling, creative, and even moral and loving AIs. It is the fond hope of some theorists, such as Daniel Dennett, that this research program will one day provide the key to personal immortality. Dennett writes,

> If what you are is that organization of information that has structured your body's control system (or, to put it in its more usual provocative form, if what you are is the program that runs on your brain's computer), then you could in principle survive the death of your body as intact as a program can survive the destruction of the computer on which it was created and first run.[7]

All this would require (as if this were a small task) would be to reproduce all of the functional operations of your brain in, say, a high-powered computer, and the result would be you, or at least a replica of your mind.

One of the besetting problems with functionalism takes us back to the matter of qualia. Critics have argued that the functionalist account of mental states as reducible to causal operations within our brain/body system does not sufficiently account for the qualitative facts of mental life, such as colors, flavors, smells, and so on. The force of this objection is made plain with a famous thought experiment known as the "inverted spectrum" argument.[8] It is conceivable that the color sensations you and I experience are totally reversed, such that what you see as red, I would see as green, and vice versa—though we would call them by the same name. Now since we have no way of comparing our private visual sensations, there occur no practical, observable signs of our inverted spectra. When I say, for example, "Hand me that green book," you respond by meeting my request, and no discrepancies are ever suspected. So we are *functionally* identical. Now, if the functionalist is correct, we would have to say that there is no difference whatsoever between our mental lives, for mind is entirely analyzable in functional terms. And yet, if our spectra are inverted, there *is* indeed a difference between our mental lives, as our visual experiences are not the same. Therefore, functionalism cannot provide a complete physicalist reduction of mind to matter.

Functionalists typically respond to this objection in one of two ways. Some deny the reality of qualia, at least as essentially first-person facts about the mental life. Daniel Dennett takes such an approach, but he does so at the expense of theoretical plausibility.[9] The more reasonable

---

[7] Daniel Dennett, *Consciousness Explained* (Boston: Little, Brown, 1991), 430.

[8] This argument actually originated with John Locke in *An Essay Concerning Human Understanding* (1690), II.32.15.

[9] Daniel Dennett, *Consciousness Explained*, chap. 12.

alternative taken by functionalists is to admit qualia but insist that the identity of two intelligent systems does not require a perfect match between them when it comes to such private experiences. The problem with this approach, however, is that it grants the reality of the inner and subjective characteristics of mind that the physicalist project has been so concerned to eliminate. Realizing the unavoidability of this conclusion, some physicalists have turned to the metaphysical halfway house of property dualism.

Property Dualism

One of the leading philosophers of mind today is John Searle. He is a proponent of *property dualism*, which regards mental states as properties of the brain. A militant critic of functionalism, Searle has focused on the inability of this model to account for the mind's intentionality. He devised the now famous Chinese room argument to demonstrate this and, more specifically, to show that Strong AI is false. Imagine that you are locked in a room with a supply of Chinese language symbols and that it is your job to implement a sort of program for answering questions in Chinese. Various Chinese symbols are passed into the room, and your task is to "respond" by passing symbols back out of the room in a certain order, as stipulated by a rulebook that you diligently consult. The rules state things like "When these symbols appear in such and such order, then pass out those symbols in this order." Now although you neither understand a word of Chinese nor have any idea what any of the symbols represent, you are able to give answers to the questions which are meaningful to the Chinese speakers outside of the room.

Now the task you perform in this thought experiment is essentially that of a computer program, which is made to manipulate symbols in a way that is meaningful to a computer user but which is neither meaningful to nor in any way understood by the computer itself. Like the person in the Chinese room, computers and their programs deal only in syntax, not semantics. That is, they do not have intentionality, the capacity to grasp meanings. Therefore, no computer could ever really "think," because, as Searle notes, "thinking is more than just a matter of manipulating meaningless symbols."[10] Computers merely simulate thinking, but this is far from being conscious and having mental states such as beliefs, feelings, desires, and sensations.

[10] John Searle, *Minds, Brains and Science* (Cambridge, MA: Harvard University Press, 1984), 36.

So Searle's conclusion is that subjectivity is fundamental, a "rock-bottom element" in a proper picture of the world.[11] He maintains that consciousness is ontologically irreducible, but he guards his physicalism by affirming that consciousness is *causally reducible* to neurological brain processes. Mind is a causally emergent feature of the brain. However, contra functionalism, it is not the brain's functional operations that give rise to mind. Rather, it is the microbiological structures themselves. Thoughts, beliefs, and sensations are every bit as essentially biological as photosynthesis, mitosis, and digestion. Thus, notwithstanding his own adamant claims to the contrary, John Searle is a property dualist, as he affirms the irreducibility of consciousness *and* that "there is really nothing in the universe but physical particles and fields of forces acting on physical particles."[12] He prefers to label his view "biological naturalism."

Searle's view is strong where other physicalist theories of mind are weak. He takes subjectivity seriously, even to the point of admitting it is irreducible. But he refuses to follow this point to its obvious conclusion, namely that a thoroughgoing physicalism necessarily leaves something—the most important something—out of the picture. To affirm physicalism is to commit oneself to the notion that every fact in the world is a physical fact or else reducible to physical facts. But by Searle's own admission neither is true of the fact of first-person subjectivity, which he claims is a fundamental feature of reality. On this latter point, we believe Searle to be correct, but this claim simply cannot be squared with physicalism. Thus, Searle, like all property dualists, must choose between taking consciousness seriously enough to regard it as something ultimately nonphysical in nature or opting for a thoroughgoing physicalism. He cannot simply insist that the material body (brain) gives rise to nonmaterial (mental) properties, because this only returns us to the interaction problem (and perhaps the causal overdetermination problem) which prompted physicalists to reject substance dualism in the first place.

5.1.3 Theological Reflections on the Nature of Mind

Given the problems with physicalist theories of mind, it might seem surprising that physicalism is the dominant view in consciousness studies today. Earlier we noted that the standard criticisms of mind-body dualism (i.e., the problems of interaction and causal overdetermination) were just part of the reason that physicalism is so popular. The other major reason is the prevalence of methodological natural-

[11] John Searle, *The Rediscovery of Mind* (Cambridge, MA: MIT Press, 1992), 95.
[12] Ibid., 30.

ism, which tends to reign in consciousness studies just as it does in the biological sciences. Whatever research program one subscribes to, it seems agreed in most circles that the task of solving the riddle of human consciousness is an essentially scientific one. Those who take such a view are, of course, foreclosed to the possibility of mind-body dualism. This is a sad state of affairs because of all people philosophers should be most open to a variety of possible explanations for the phenomena they study. Since it is possible that mind is ultimately a nonphysical reality, philosophers should be open to exploring this possibility. But, as we have seen, many features of mind, such as its subjectivity, intentionality, and phenomenal qualia, suggest that it is not just possibly supernatural but *probably* so.

Still, because of the influence of methodological naturalism, several Christian philosophers of mind have recently defended their own physicalist theories of mind. Prominent among these are the views of Lynn Rudder Baker, Kevin Corcoran, and Nancey Murphy. Some, such as Murphy and Corcoran, espouse a "constitution view" of persons, according to which "persons are constituted by bodies but are not identical with the bodies that constitute them."[13] Others have opted for versions of property dualism. William Hasker, for example, has defended what he calls "emergent dualism," which sees the mind as generated by the brain but possessing qualitative differences from the neurological properties from which it arises.[14]

In the end, these theories suffer from the same sorts of problems that plague the other accounts just reviewed. This is no surprise since such theorists subject themselves to the same methodological constraints that restrict the metaphysical naturalists. If Christian devotees of methodological naturalism are constrained to appeal to physical causes in explaining consciousness, then their theories of consciousness will look no different than those of metaphysical naturalists. Nor will the problems with their accounts be any different. But the true dilemma for Christian versions of physicalism is this: If they are pure physicalists, then they are vulnerable to the arguments from subjectivity, qualia, and intentionality discussed above. But if they are essentially property dualists, then they inherit the basic problems with this view, especially the problem of accounting for how a physical system can give rise to so many nonmaterial qualities.

Although physicalism is the most popular view among philosophers of mind today, there remain many proponents of mind-body dualism. And in theological circles dualism has much strong support. It is easy to see why when one considers the strong biblical grounds for dualism. For

---

[13] Kevin J. Corcoran, "Persons and Bodies," *Faith and Philosophy* 15.3 (July 1998): 330.
[14] William Hasker, *The Emergent Self* (Ithaca, NY: Cornell University Press, 2001).

example, Paul writes, "If I am to go on living in the body, this will mean fruitful labor for me. Yet what shall I choose? I do not know! I am torn between the two: I desire to depart and be with Christ, which is better by far; but it is more necessary for you that I remain in the body" (Phil 1:22–24 NIV). In this passage the apostle speaks of departing from the body. If mind is simply an aspect of our material selves, then we could never "depart" from the body. Also, Jesus says, "Don't fear those who kill the body but are not able to kill the soul; rather, fear Him who is able to destroy both soul and body in hell" (Matt 10:28). If soul were simply an aspect of the material, then to destroy the body would necessarily be destruction of the soul as well, in which case Jesus' reference to "those who kill the body but cannot kill the soul" would be unintelligible. These are just a few of the many cases in which scriptural references to the soul cannot be squared with a physicalist perspective.[15] Thus, it appears that mind-body dualism fits best with the Christian worldview.

All things considered—given the facts of subjectivity, intentionality and phenomenal qualia, the besetting problems with physicalist theories, as well as biblical considerations—we believe that mind-body dualism is the most reasonable position regarding the nature of the mind. There remain problems with dualism, of course. But we don't believe these are nearly significant enough to warrant abandonment of this view. If anything, they should motivate further philosophical exploration into dualist theories of mind, including careful continuation of the debate between interactionist and occasionalist versions of the theory.

Questions for Reflection

1. Which view, physicalism or mind-body dualism, do you favor? Why? Which argument do you find most persuasive in support of your view?

2. Historically, most substance dualists have been interactionists rather than occasionalists, despite the fact that the latter avoids the problems of interaction and causal overdetermination. Why do you suppose this is the case?

3. Among the different brands of physicalism, which do you believe to be the strongest? Why?

---

[15] Other relevant texts include Ps 139:8; Luke 23:43; 2 Cor 5:8; Heb 12:23. For a detailed exposition of the biblical evidence for mind-body dualism, see John W. Cooper, *Body, Soul, and Life Everlasting: Biblical Anthropology and the Monism-Dualism Debate* (Grand Rapids, Mich.: Eerdmans, 2000).

4. What is your assessment of John Searle's "Chinese Room" argument? Does it succeed in refuting functionalism and perhaps other forms of physicalism?
5. Besides those discussed here, what are some other biblical texts that are relevant to the mind-body problem?

§ 5.2 What Is Personal Identity?

At the beginning of this chapter, we brought up the case of Henry from the film *Regarding Henry*. Recall that Henry's personal character traits drastically changed after he was shot. Before he was cruel and self-absorbed, but afterwards he became gentle and loving. The change is so dramatic that you might say that the new Henry is *a different person*. Now there is at least one sense in which Henry really is a different person. Recall from the previous chapter our distinction between numerical and qualitative identity. Two different things can be qualitatively identical such as two motorcycles of the same make and model. And (it seems) one thing can be qualitatively different at different times such as a particular leaf on a tree changing from green to yellow in the autumn. However, two things cannot be numerically identical. Things that are numerically identical (like Cassius Clay and Muhammad Ali) are really only one thing. With this in mind, it is obvious that Henry, after being shot, is a *qualitatively* different person. He has new personality traits that have replaced his old ones. But is the change in Henry any deeper than this? Could it be that he is not only qualitatively different but also *numerically* different? Is he in fact a different individual person than the old Henry whom we may presume is now "dead"?

Thinking about Henry raises the question of what constitutes *personal identity*. What makes someone numerically the same person from moment to moment? What kinds of characteristics does a person have that identify him (or disqualify him) as one and the same individual across time? Unless we can answer this question, then we may not be able to say for sure whether or not Henry is the same person after his shooting.

Of course, since Henry is a fictional character, it really does not matter if we cannot answer this question regarding him. But there are real-life cases very similar to Henry's, and it may matter very much indeed if we can or cannot know what constitutes personal identity. Suppose, for example, that people who undergo radical personality changes like Henry's are *not* numerically the same persons. And let us suppose, for the sake of discussion, that Henry had committed some terrible crime before he was shot. Well, since the post-shooting Henry is literally a different person than the one who committed the crime, it would be morally wrong to prosecute him for the crime committed by the previous Henry. After all, the new Henry did not do it!

The question of personal identity has important ramifications for Christian doctrine as well. For instance, Christians believe in the resurrection of the body. That is, we believe that at the end of history all of the dead will be raised from the grave. But on what grounds can we say that the person who is raised is the same person who died? In some cases, the time between a person's death and his resurrection will be many years, perhaps hundreds or thousands of years. All of the atoms that composed such a person's body will have dispersed and some of them may even have come to be parts of other people's bodies. So what makes the resurrected person the same person who died? Unless we can give a good answer to this question, the specter of incoherence may loom over the doctrine of bodily resurrection. In this section, we will survey a few answers to the question of personal identity that philosophers have proposed.

5.2.1 The Memory View

One obvious possibility—suggested by the *Regarding Henry* example—is that personal identity is tied in some way to a person's psychological characteristics. John Locke (1632–1704), for example, proposed that a person is the same person from one moment to the next as long as he maintains the continuity of his memory. Call this the *memory view* of personal identity. On this view, we can say that *a person at a certain time is the numerically identical person at a later time just in case he has memories of that earlier time.* Applied to the case of Henry, this means that the post-shooting Henry is the same person as the pre-shooting Henry only if the former remembers his life as the latter. Of course, since Henry initially suffered from amnesia, the memory view would seem to be committed to the position that the later Henry was not the same person as the earlier Henry.

The memory view is subject to several criticisms, however. First, think about the Henry case again. In the story, Henry does lose his memory of his earlier life, but he later regains his memory. So not only would the proponent of the memory view have to say that the person Henry fails to persist after the shooting and thus becomes a different person, she would also have to say that when Henry regains his lost memories, the earlier Henry is recreated! What is more, since the recreated Henry remembers being not only the pre-shooting Henry but also the post-shooting Henry, the recreated Henry is identical to the post-shooting Henry! But since the recreated Henry is identical to the pre-shooting

Henry, this entails that the pre-shooting Henry is also identical to the post-shooting Henry. In other words, the memory view commits us to saying that Henry both does and does not maintain his personal identity through time. This is contradictory and so cannot be correct.

The above problem is an instance of what is called the "transitivity problem." The problem turns on the conviction that identity is a transitive relation—that is, if A is identical to B and B is identical to C, then A is identical to C. But the memory criterion requires us to deny that A is identical to C. Imagine a soldier in middle age who remembers being a boy scout at age twelve. According to the memory view, the middle-aged soldier is the same person as the boy scout. Now imagine the soldier many years later as an old man. And suppose that the old man remembers being a soldier. So the old man is the same person as the middle-age soldier. But here is the catch: the old man does not remember being twelve years old and thus does not remember being a boy scout. Hence, according to the memory view, even though the boy scout is identical to the soldier and the soldier is identical to the old man, the boy scout is *not* identical to the old man. Yet this seems clearly wrong because it violates the principle of transitivity.

A third problem for the memory view is that it turns out to be circular. Its circularity is apparent in the phenomenon of false memories that occasionally affects most of us. Suppose the Joker wants to infiltrate Gotham's city hall and blow it up. In order to do so, he has managed to hypnotize an unsuspecting person into thinking that he (the unsuspecting person) is Batman. The man is to be dressed in a Batman costume and sent to city hall with (unbeknownst to him) a bomb inside his utility belt. As part of the ploy, the Joker has hypnotically planted false memories into the man's head, false memories of various adventures of the Caped Crusader. Now suppose that the real Batman shows up to prevent the imposter from getting into city hall with the bomb. When they meet, Batman orders the imposter to surrender. The imposter replies, sincerely, "What do you mean? I'm Batman. Take off that costume, you imposter!" Then Batman says, "No, you are not Batman. *I'm* Batman." And the imposter replies, "No, *I'm* Batman!"

Now we happen to know that the man the Joker hypnotized is not really Batman. How do we know this? It is because we know that he has false memories. But why is it that his memories of being Batman are false and the real Batman's memories of being Batman are not? It is because the hypnotized man's memories are not memories of actual experiences that he had. True memories are of experiences that are actually had by the same person who later remembers the experience. In the words of philosopher Timothy Cleveland, "The only way to know if the memory is a true one is to know if the person who had the memory is the same person who had the actual experience. But now the memory theory is chasing its own tail in a tight circle."[16] The memory criterion proposes that memory constitutes a person's personal identity, but it turns out that in order to distinguish true from false memories, the memory criterion actually presupposes personal identity. It is circular.

5.2.2 The Physical View

A view of personal identity prominent among contemporary philosophers ties personal identity to a human being's physical properties. On *the physical view*, what makes a person the same person from one time to another is that she maintains certain relevant physical characteristics. Though not necessarily connected to metaphysical materialism (see chap. 4), the physical view is often motivated by the materialist worldview. According to materialism, all that exists is matter. Materialism entails a physicalist view of human beings. It would make sense, then, for a materialist to define personal identity in physical terms.

Though a Christian theist might have reasons to hold the physical view of personal identity, it would appear to be an awkward fit. As we saw in the first section of this chapter, Scripture seems to support a dualist view of human nature. Moreover, even if some version of Christian materialism is defensible, the Christian is committed to the existence of nonhuman, nonphysical persons, namely *angels*. For a Christian, then, the physical view of personal identity could be only an account of *human* personal identity, not personal identity *per se*. Be that as it may, the physical view is widely held today and deserves our attention.

The Body and Brain Criteria

The simplest and least plausible version of the physical view utilizes the body criterion according to which a person is identical to his body. That is, *a person at a certain time is the numerically identical person at a later time just in case she is the same body at both times*. This criterion has a commonsense appeal. In ordinary life, we usually identify people by noticing features of their bodies. If asked to pick my wife out of a crowd, I would look for her by looking for her body. And it would be various physical characteristics that would allow me to distinguish her from others (e.g., size, shape, facial features, etc.).

Despite its initial appeal, the body criterion is not very plausible. Our bodies are constantly changing. They grow fatter or skinnier. They

---

[16] Timothy Cleveland, "Different Worlds, Different Bodies: Personal Identity in Narnia," in *The Chronicles of Narnia and Philosophy*, ed. Gregory Bassham and Jerry L. Walls (Peru, IL: Carus, 2005), 189.

lose hair and grow new hair. Indeed, if it is true that our bodies are composed of atoms (as most people believe), then our bodies change drastically every few years as they slough off and gain new atoms at each moment. Approximately every seven years, our bodies are comprised of a different set of atoms than they were before. So, on the body criterion, we would have to say that every seven years what we think of as your body is not really your body, but a new one that constitutes a numerically different person. But since common sense tells us that you *are* the same person as you were seven years ago, you cannot be identical to your body.

If personal identity is not grounded in the body as a whole, perhaps some specific and pertinent part of the body can do the job. The brain might be a good candidate. Our consciousness and mental life, including our memories, are correlated with brain function, so why not personal identity? The brain criterion stipulates that *a person at a certain time is the numerically identical person at a later time if and only if she has the same brain at both times.* This criterion is often supported by thought experiments involving brain transplants. Suppose that two people, Sam and Joe, are terribly injured in an automobile accident. Sam's body is badly mangled and cannot be saved, but his brain is perfectly intact, being kept alive by medical technology. Most of Joe's body, on the other hand, is free from serious injury, but a small puncture in his skull caused irreversible damage to his brain and killed him. Wanting to save life when possible, the doctors get permission from the families of Sam and Joe to transplant Sam's brain into Joe's body. After the surgery, when this person with the transplanted brain awakes, which person will he be— Sam or Joe? It seems almost certain that it will be Sam. Though waking up in Joe's body, the person will think and believe that he is Sam. He will have all the personality traits and memories of Sam. And for these reasons Sam's family will no doubt believe him to be Sam as well. Our intuitions about cases like this lend credibility to the brain criterion.

Nevertheless, there are problems. For one thing, the problem of the body criterion plagues this view as well. Though the brain loses and gains cells more slowly than other parts of the body, it too completely exchanges its atoms over time. So if personal identity requires sameness of brain, then it would seem that personal identity changes whenever the brain changes.

The strongest objection to the brain criterion, however, is called the "fission problem." We can illustrate the problem by describing a variation on the case of Sam and Joe. This time suppose that Sam's body is not damaged beyond repair and that his whole brain is perfectly healthy. Joe's brain, however, is dead as in the earlier cases. And suppose also that neither Joe's family nor Sam's can stand the thought of losing their loved one. The doctors, wanting to prevent either family from suffering, engage in a reckless experiment by surgically dividing the two hemispheres of Sam's brain. They leave one half in Sam's body and place the other half in Joe's body. When they are both nursed back to health, Sam's family is overjoyed that their loved one is alive and well. Joe's family is greatly distressed because Joe thinks that he is Sam!

In this example, we have a case of "fission." The person who is (or was) Sam has now been split into two different people both of whom have precisely the same personality traits and memories. Each of them could (and let us say *does*) make a case for really being Sam. How are we to decide? Which one *is* Sam? If the advocate of the brain criterion chooses one or the other, it would seem that her choice is arbitrary. If she says that both are Sam, this would entail that one person (the initial Sam) is numerically identical to two persons (the split Sams), which is absurd.

The Causal Continuity Criterion

It may seem that there is a fairly simple way for those who want to tie personal identity to our physical bodies to avoid some of the above problems. Recall that one of the problems with both the body criterion and brain criterion was that the body and brain undergo constant change, sloughing off atoms and getting new atoms. This means that the body and brain do not remain the same body and brain throughout the change. This in turn implies, on the body and brain criteria, that a person cannot maintain personal identity through change—a conclusion we cannot accept. However, there is an implicit assumption in these responses to the body and brain criteria. The assumption is that sameness of body (or brain) requires sameness of parts. But this assumption may be challenged.

Consider a part of your body—your brain for example. Yesterday you had a brain and at that time it was composed of certain parts, a certain set of atoms, say. Today, your brain is composed of a different set of atoms (since yesterday, your brain lost hundreds of cells and grew new ones). Nevertheless, you would say that you have the *same* brain you had yesterday. It is possible, of course, that this is just a manner of speaking and that you really do not have the numerically same brain you had yesterday. Yet it may be the case instead that you do have the same brain and that sameness of brain is not dependent on its having the same atoms from one time to the next.

How might this alternative be made plausible? One suggestion is that what makes your body or brain the same body or brain is not the sameness of parts, but the causal process in which those parts are involved. More specifically, we could say that *a body (or brain) is the same body (or brain) from one time to a later time just in case the parts that compose the body at the later time are causally continuous with those parts that composed the body at the earlier time.* The idea is that whatever parts the body has at one time are dependent on certain states or conditions of the body at an earlier time. Let us call this view the *causal continuity criterion*.

To understand this view better, it may prove helpful to relate the famous story of the Ship of Theseus. The legendary king of Athens, Theseus, sailed far and wide in a wooden ship. As individual planks of the ship began to wear out, the crew replaced them in transit one-by-one. By the time the ship returned home to Athens, every part of the ship had been replaced. Was the ship that returned home the same ship that left port many years earlier? It is certainly plausible to think so and the causal continuity view helps us see why. As each old plank is removed and the new planks added, there is one, continuous causal process. Earlier states of the ship are in causal continuity with later states of the ship. Thus, we may say that the later parts of the ship are parts of the very same ship that the old parts were. Likewise, we may say that your brain today is the same brain you had yesterday, despite changing parts, because the later parts are the result of a causal process extending back to a state of your brain yesterday. And this allows those who hold the physical view to say that you are the same person today that you were yesterday as long as you have the same brain—with "same brain" understood in terms of the causal continuity criterion.

As promising as the causal continuity view seems, it faces at least one major difficulty: the fission problem. Just as above with the brain criterion, the causal continuity criterion allows for the splitting of one person into two. Before we give an example of how that might happen, let us look again at the Ship of Theseus. As we told the story in the last paragraph, it seems plausible to think that the ship that returned home is the same one that left port earlier. Suppose, however, that as the crew removed the old planks, rather than discard them, they nailed and glued them together to construct a second ship that sailed right alongside the ship from which the planks were removed. Years later, then, when Theseus returned home, he sailed two ships into the harbor! Which ship is the ship that sailed out of the harbor earlier? Was it the ship that was constructed out of the new planks that replaced the old ones, or the ship that was reconstructed out of the old planks? The answer does not seem obvious.

We may apply the same reasoning to the causal continuity criterion for personal identity by returning to the case of Sam and Joe. Suppose, again, that the doctors perform their fission experiment and place one hemisphere of Sam's brain back in Sam's body and keep the other in Joe's body. Again, both persons wake up with Sam's memories and personality. Notice that, in this case, the two hemispheres of Sam's brain stand in causal continuity with Sam's brain before the split. So, the requirements of the causal continuity criterion are met. But this means that Sam—one person—is now identical to two people. But that is absurd.

Resurrection and the Physical View

Whether or not the physical view can be delivered from the problems we have raised, there is another consideration that makes any version of the physical view problematic from a Christian point of view. At the beginning of our discussion of personal identity, we raised the question of how the issue of personal identity relates to the Christian belief in the resurrection of the dead. What is it that makes the person resurrected at the general resurrection the same person who died in the distant past? Imagine, for instance, the apostle Paul. Tradition has it that Paul died about AD 64, a martyr during the reign of the Roman emperor Nero. Now fast forward a couple of millennia or more to the great day of Christ's return. On that day, it is God's promise that the dead will be raised to life. But is it possible for God to fulfill His promise if the physical view of personal identity is true? Many philosophers have their doubts.

Let us consider the resurrection in terms of the body criterion. We will ignore the problem raised for this view above and simply pretend that Paul's body can somehow maintain all its parts during his lifetime. On this view, for God to resurrect Paul, He has to reconstruct Paul's body in precisely the state it was in at the point of his death—which means that He has to gather all the atoms that earlier comprised Paul's body and put them back together in the same configuration. But this may be an impossible task even for God. Consider the possibility, even the likelihood, that some of the atoms that make up Paul's body are now parts of other people's bodies. Paul's original body decayed in the grave. Worms very likely ate some of his body. And let us suppose (as is entirely possible) that one of these worms was later eaten by a fish. And this fish was caught by a fisherman who ate it for dinner. In this case, some of the atoms that composed Paul's body became parts of another person's body. Now on resurrection day what is God to do? If He resurrects Paul, He cannot resurrect the other fellow because some of the other fellow's atoms will have to go to Paul. If He resurrects the other fellow, He cannot resurrect Paul. Yet God promises to resurrect *all* human beings. This is a major problem for both the body and brain versions of the physical view.

Another worry for all three versions of the physical view, including the causal continuity view, is that they entail gaps in a person's existence. Those who hold the physical view have to say that, between a person's death and her resurrection, she simply does not exist. She exists at one time. She dies and ceases to exist. Then she comes back into existence at the resurrection. Besides running up against biblical texts that seem to teach that human beings will enjoy a conscious existence (and personal identity) in the interval between death and resurrection,[17] there is a further problem: it seems unlikely that the resurrected person really is the same person as the one who died rather than a duplicate—another person who just happens to look and act like the person who died. Peter van Inwagen illustrates the difficulty:

> Suppose a certain monastery claims to have in its possession a manuscript written in St. Augustine's own hand. And suppose the monks of this monastery further claim that this manuscript was burned by Arians in the year 457. It would immediately occur to me to ask how *this* manuscript, the one I touch, could be the very manuscript that was burned in 457. Suppose their answer to this question is that God miraculously recreated Augustine's manuscript in 458. I should respond to this answer as follows: the deed it describes seems quite impossible, even as an accomplishment of omnipotence. God certainly might have created a perfect duplicate of the original manuscript, but it would not be *that* one; its earliest moment of existence would have been after Augustine's death; it would never have known the impress of his hand; it would not have been a part of the furniture of the world when he was alive; and so on.[18]

Just as it seems clear that the manuscript the monastery possesses is not the same manuscript as the one burned but merely a duplicate, it would seem clear that, on the physical view, the person resurrected is merely a duplicate of the person who died. The problem is most acute for the causal continuity view which stipulates that there must be a continuous causal chain to transfer a person's identity from one time to another. With the temporal gap between death and resurrection, there does not seem to be any such causal continuity between the person who died and

---

[17] See, e.g., Luke 23:43; 2 Cor 5:8; Phil 1:21–23.

[18] Peter van Inwagen, "The Possibility of Resurrection," *International Journal for the Philosophy of Religion* 9 (1978): 114–21.

the person who is resurrected.[19] Given these difficulties in handling the resurrection on the physical view, it might be worthwhile to consider another possibility.

5.2.3 The Soul View

In the first section of this chapter, we noted that most Christians historically have believed that human beings are a duality of body and soul. We also showed that there are reasons to think that this dualism is true and that it helps make sense of many biblical texts. It also turns out that body-soul dualism can provide a plausible solution to the problem of personal identity. On this view, a person and his identity are not tied to anything physical, or to the continuity of his memory. Personal identity across time, rather, is constituted by sameness of soul, where a soul is understood as an immaterial substance. Thus, *a person at a certain time is the numerically identical person at a later time if and only if he is (or has) the same soul at both times.* The plausibility of *the soul view* lies in the idea that a soul would remain stable and unchanging throughout all the changes that happen to a person's body and psychology. So, on the soul view, we can say that Henry is the same person both before and after being shot because he has the same soul throughout. Moreover, because the soul presumably survives the death of the body, the soul view provides a clear basis for the continuation of conscious life during the interval between death and resurrection and for our being able to say confidently that the resurrected person is the same person who died. He is the same person who died (regardless of what atoms compose his body) because he has the same soul.

A possible objection to the soul view is to claim that it is subject to the same fission problem as the physical view. Again, suppose that Sam's brain is split and placed in the bodies of both Sam and Joe, and both men awake having all of Sam's memories and characteristics and thinking they are Sam. The soul view would have to say that not only has Sam's brain split, but so has his soul. Where there was once one soul, now there are two. Which one is Sam? How can we nonarbitrarily decide? Is this not the same problem as that facing the physical view? Is it not another absurd case of one person now being identical to two? If so, the soul view would have no advantage over the physical view.

It is not clear, however, that the fission problem truly affects the soul view as suggested above. To see why, we need to clarify that the fission problem is a metaphysical problem, not an epistemological one. That is,

---

[19] For a discussion of how a physical view might allow for causal continuity across the temporal gap after all, see Kevin Corcoran, *Rethinking Human Nature: A Christian Materialist Alternative to the Soul* (Grand Rapids: Baker, 2006), 127–33.

when we discussed the physical view above, the problem was not simply our inability to *know* which person was Sam (with the possible implication that one of them really was, and the other was not, Sam). Rather, the problem was that there was no metaphysical ground for one of them, and not the other, to *be* Sam. In other words, since personal identity was supposedly constituted by the brain, there was no reason why one half of Sam's brain was Sam and the other was not. It is not simply a lack of knowledge that prevents us from choosing one half of Sam's brain rather than another; it is the lack of a basis in reality for doing so.

Those who hold the soul view, however, can say that their alleged "fission problem" is merely epistemological and not metaphysical. It is open to the soul view to say, that is, that one half of Sam's brain has Sam's soul and the other half has a different soul, even though we (and Sam) may not be able to know which. So the soul view seems able to maintain personal identity through fission. The fission of souls is not a case of one person now being identical to two, but of one person/soul splitting off from another so that there are now two different persons/souls, one identical to the previous single person and the other not.[20]

But now there may be a different problem. It could be said that there is no metaphysical ground for saying that the soul goes with one half of Sam's brain rather than the other. Why, for example, would Sam's soul go to the left half of his brain rather than the right half? Advocates of the soul view will probably have to concede that this question admits of no definite answer. Perhaps all they can say is that God simply decides to which half Sam's soul goes. In any case, the soul view proponent can maintain that there is some aspect of Sam's being (his soul) that grounds his personal identity and that survives the fission of his brain. That there is no metaphysical necessity for why Sam's soul would attach to the left half of his brain does not undermine the point that the soul view avoids the fission problem. So, even though there is a difficult question here, it is not clear that it poses an insuperable objection.

We have examined three major views on personal identity. All three views have had able defenders in history, and Christians have held all three. Obviously, the authors favor the soul view because it is consistent with other aspects of the human person that we have favored and seems to have fewer philosophical and biblical difficulties. That said, it is fair to say that there is not one view of personal identity that is *the* Christian view.

---

[20] Alternatively, the soul view could say that in the process of brain fission Sam dies (i.e., his soul is completely "severed" from his body) and that neither of the two souls that awake in the hemispheres of his brain is identical to Sam, but are both new souls. Still, the fission problem would not pose an objection to the soul view.

Questions for Reflection

1. What if Henry never regained his old memories? Would our intuitions about whether or not he maintains his personal identity be the same? Why or why not?

2. One response that an advocate of the physical view can make regarding problems with her view is to deny that personal identity is absolute. She can say, for example, that all the fission problem shows is that, in some cases, personal identity is not maintained across time—that is, after the brain fission, Sam does not survive but is replaced by two new people. Is this an adequate solution? Why or why not?

3. Can you think of a way that the physical view can make sense of personal identity across temporal gaps like that between death and resurrection? Alternatively, can you think of a way that the physical view can avoid there being a temporal gap between death and resurrection?

4. Read Luke 23:43; 2 Cor 5:8; and Phil 1:21–23. Can these texts be interpreted in a way that does not imply a disembodied intermediate state? If so, how?

5. The soul view seems to imply that psychological continuity is irrelevant to personal identity—that a person can survive even if her memories and all of her psychological characteristics are permanently lost and replaced with other psychological traits. Is this plausible? Does the soul view really have this implication?

§ 5.3 Do We Have Free Will?

One of our most firmly held convictions is that human beings are free. Free to make choices that affect our lives for better or worse; free to do good or bad; free to act or refrain from acting as we please. This is usually taken to mean that we could do otherwise than we actually do. If I happen to choose some action A, then freedom means that I could have chosen to do other than A. Probably the most significant reason for this conviction is our belief that people are generally morally responsible for their actions. We praise and reward those who do good and blame and punish those who do bad. The idea is that without significant human freedom we would simply be "robots," and robots are not morally responsible. They are not even people.

On the other hand, we believe that the world is not chaotic or random. It operates according to strict rules of cause and effect. Unsupported objects fall to the ground, sugar dissolves in water, and fire burns. In fact, we tend to believe that physical events in the universe are determined. They are not chaotic or random. If no free and rational agents existed in the universe, it is apparent that every event that happens would have been determined by an unbroken chain of causes and effects stretching all the way back to the Big Bang.

Now when we reflect upon these two sets of convictions, many people are tempted to think that human actions, being free, are exceptions to the causal determinism we see in the physical world. And yet we also have a strong tendency to *explain* human behavior. For example, suppose we hear about a young person making a choice to drop out of school. Her friends naturally ask the question, *"Why?"* And they also naturally expect there to be an answer, an answer that explains their friend's choice in terms of motives or desires that in some sense caused her action. This tendency to expect causal explanations for human behavior makes it seem that we do not really think that human actions are entirely removed from the causal nexus of the physical universe.

So are we free or not? Are we morally responsible for our actions? Or are our actions determined? Could it somehow be that we are both determined and free? The question of human freedom, or free will, and its relation to the law of causality presents one of the most difficult and perplexing philosophical problems in history. In this section, we will explore the ways that philosophers have tried to resolve the problem.

5.3.1 Incompatibilism

There are two primary ways that philosophers have understood the relationship between freedom and determinism. *Compatibilism*, which we will examine in the next section, is the view that human freedom and determinism are logically consistent. For the compatibilist, the fact that our actions are causally determined does not necessarily threaten our freedom or our moral responsibility. *Incompatibilism*, obviously, is the view that freedom and responsibility are logically inconsistent with determinism. For the incompatibilist, if our actions are causally determined then we simply are not free and, therefore, not morally responsible for the things we do.

A major argument that has been offered in defense of incompatibilism is called the *consequence argument*. Philosopher Peter van Inwagen states the argument like this:

> If determinism is true, then our acts are the consequences of the laws of nature and events in the remote past. But it is not up to us what went on before we were born; and neither is it up

to us what the laws of nature are. Therefore the consequences of theses things (including our own acts) are not up to us.[21]

We can state the argument a bit more formally and thoroughly as follows:

(1) If determinism is true, then our actions are the consequences of the laws of nature and events in the remote past.
(2) It is not in our power to change the laws of nature.
(3) It is not in our power to change events in the remote past.
(4) If our actions are the consequences of the laws of nature and events in the remote past, and it is not in our power to change these things, then we cannot do otherwise than what we do.
(5) If we cannot do otherwise than what we do, then we are not free.
(6) Therefore, if determinism is true, then we are not free.

And, of course, it is understood that if we are not free, then we are not morally responsible for our actions. The consequence argument, then, seems to provide a powerful case for incompatibilism. But, as you can probably tell, incompatibilism comes in two varieties, depending upon whether or not one thinks that determinism is true.

Hard Determinism

If an incompatibilist thinks that determinism is true, then she embraces what is called *hard determinism*. Those in this camp resolve the problem of freedom and determinism by accepting the fact that everything that exists and everything that happens, including human actions, is subject to the law of causality. On this view, human freedom and moral responsibility are illusions. Since every human choice and action are the results of causal forces outside our control, we cannot do otherwise than we do. We are not free. And this means that we are not morally responsible for what we do. Moral responsibility does not exist for human beings any more than it does for lions, trees, or rocks.

Not many philosophers in history have embraced hard determinism, but a few well-known figures have, including Baruch Spinoza (1632–1677), Baron d'Holbach (1723–1789), and B. F. Skinner (1904–1990). Among contemporary thinkers, Galen Strawson, Derk Pereboom, and Ted Honderich top the list of hard determinists.[22]

---

[21] Peter van Inwagen, *An Essay on Free Will* (Oxford: Oxford University Press, 1983), 16.
[22] See Galen Strawson, *Freedom and Belief* (Oxford: Oxford University Press, 1986); Derk Pereboom, *Living without Free Will* (Cambridge: Cambridge University, 2001); and Ted Honderich, *How Free Are You?* (Oxford: Oxford University Press, 1993).

Hard determinists get their motivation from our strong conviction that events in the physical world are causally determined, along with our tendency to give causal explanations for human behavior. It is not a big leap from these convictions to the conclusion that human actions are causally determined just like the behavior of molecules and planets. Human beings are part of the natural world, and why should we not expect that they are subject to the same causal determinants as everything else?

Of course, the hard determinist knows that people appear to make conscious choices, often as the result of deliberation. These choices are the result of a person's character—all of the desires, values, and dispositions she has—and, for the hard determinist, a person's character is the result of forces ultimately outside of her control. A person has the desires and values she has because of human biology, her specific genes inherited from her parents, her upbringing, and so forth. So a person's character is fixed largely by external factors. And once a person has a certain character, all of her actions flow from that character inevitably.

An obvious objection to hard determinism is that it would appear to make it impossible to hold people accountable for their actions. We praise and reward people for good behavior and punish people for bad behavior. However, this presupposes that people *deserve* to be rewarded and punished. But, if people are not morally responsible for their actions because those actions are not done freely, then they do not deserve anything. Human actions are no different than the actions of animals in this regard. If a cat tracks and kills a mouse, we do not think it has done something wrong—it is just doing what comes naturally. We do not punish animals for following their instincts. Hard determinism, then, would make it impossible to hold people accountable. It would call into question our system of justice as well as our practice of rewarding workers on the basis of merit.

The hard determinist can respond to this objection, though. She can agree that hard determinism eliminates our belief that people are morally accountable but insist that this does not make our practices of reward and punishment meaningless. The objection presupposes that these practices can only be justified on a *retributive* view of justice. On that theory, we reward people because they have earned some honor, and we punish people because they deserve it. And this makes sense only if people are morally responsible for their actions. But some other considerations might justify rewards and punishments. For example, we may both reward and punish people for their actions in order to promote *deterrence*. By promising pleasant consequences for good behavior and threatening unpleasant consequences for bad behavior, we may prevent people from doing things we would prefer they not do. Another potential reason for punishment is *rehabilitation*. We may subject people to criminal penalties in order to change their behavior for the better. The point, for the hard determinist, is that neither deterrence nor rehabilitation requires that people have free will or moral responsibility. In fact, determinism makes it more likely that deterrence and rehabilitation would work. If people are hardwired by nature to avoid pain and seek pleasure, as a determinist might suppose, then the threat of punishment (or promise of reward) can be both a deterrent to bad behavior and a motivation to change.

This response to the objection, as plausible as it is, may not actually succeed, however. To see why, imagine that everyone in society actually comes to believe that hard determinism is true and that no one is free and morally responsible. In such a world, most, if not all, people would naturally excuse any of their bad behavior and would resist any feelings of guilt. This could very well lead people to throw off all the constraints of morality and become thoroughly self-seeking. And in such a world, where there were no internal constraints on behavior provided by moral feelings, we might wonder how effective the external constraints provided by law would be. As America's second president, John Adams, expressed it, "We have no government armed with the power capable of contending with human passions, unbridled by morality and true religion."[23] For this reason, one hard determinist, Saul Smilansky, suggests that society ought to foster the illusion that people do have free will in order to prevent this disastrous social outcome of determinism. He writes, "People as a rule ought not to be fully aware of the ultimate inevitability of what they have done, for this will affect the way in which they hold themselves responsible."[24] This point does not prove hard determinism false, but it does perhaps point out a significant consequence of it, one which many people may find unacceptable.

Hard determinism also runs afoul of the clear teaching of Scripture. That human beings are morally responsible for their actions is assumed throughout the Bible and taught in many specific texts. When God cursed Adam and Eve and expelled them from the garden of Eden because of their disobedience (Gen 3:14–19), it is assumed that they were accountable for their sin. When Jesus said that it will be more tolerable for Sodom on the day of judgment than for Capernaum, this presup-

---

[23] John Adams, "To the Officers of the First Brigade, Third Division, Massachusetts Militia, October 11, 1798," in *The Works of John Adams, Second President of the United States* (Boston: Little Brown, 1854), IX: 229.

[24] Saul Smilansky, "Free Will, Fundamental Dualism, and the Centrality of Illusion," in *The Oxford Handbook of Free Will*, ed. Robert Kane (Oxford: Oxford University Press, 2002), 498.

poses that the people of Capernaum were morally responsible for their actions (Matt 11:23–24). Likewise, when the people who conspired to put Jesus to death are called "wicked men" this too presupposes that they were morally responsible (Acts 2:23). Moreover, the "eye-for-an-eye" principle in the Old Testament Law (Gen 9:6; Exod 21:24), as well as the Christian doctrine of hell (Matt 25:46; Rev 20:15), presupposes a retributive theory of punishment that assumes the reality of moral responsibility. Since the Bible so obviously underlines human moral responsibility, the Christian has a compelling reason to reject hard determinism.

Even apart from biblical considerations, though, we should note that the conviction that we are morally responsible for our actions is a very strong one. It would seem to most of us that this conviction should be given up only if there is no reasonable alternative. There are, however, other alternatives.

Libertarianism

Hard determinism is not the only version of incompatibilism. Like hard determinists, the adherents of *libertarianism* believe that human freedom is incompatible with determinism. Unlike hard determinists, though, libertarians reject determinism. They believe that at least some human actions are free from the nexus of cause and effect within the physical universe. Thus, the libertarian believes that human beings have (at least sometimes) the ability to do other than what they do. That is, when a person makes a free choice to do some action, she could have performed another action instead. Libertarians call this the *power of contrary choice* or *the ability to do otherwise*, and they see it as necessary for moral responsibility.

Many philosophers, past and present, have espoused libertarianism. These would include the early Augustine (354–430), Thomas Reid (1710–1796), Immanuel Kant (1724–1804), Roderick Chisholm (1916–1999), Peter van Inwagen, Robert Kane, Timothy O'Conner, Stewart Goetz, and J. P. Moreland.[25] Though probably not the majority opinion today among philosophers generally, it is safe to say that most contemporary Christian philosophers embrace libertarianism.

It is the consequence argument for incompatibilism, together with our strong intuitive sense that we are morally responsible for our actions,

---

[25] For contemporary works on libertarianism, see Peter van Inwagen, *An Essay on Free Will*; Robert Kane, *The Significance of Free Will* (Oxford: Oxford University Press, 1996); Timothy O'Conner, *Persons and Causes: The Metaphysics of Free Will* (Oxford: Oxford University Press, 2000); Stewart Goetz, "A Non-Causal Theory of Agency," *Philosophy and Phenomenological Research* 49 (1988): 303–16; and J. P. Moreland and William Lane Craig, *Philosophical Foundations for a Christian Worldview*, 267–84.

that provides the main impetus for libertarianism among many philosophers. It seems clear to us that we are accountable for what we freely do; and it seems equally clear that to be accountable we must have the power of contrary choice. But if determinism is true, then we cannot do otherwise and we, therefore, cannot be morally responsible. It is this line of thought that stands behind the libertarian view.

However, there is another reason that the libertarian thinks her view is correct. Call it the *Introspection Argument*. Robert Kane describes it this way:

> We believe we have free will when we view ourselves as agents capable of influencing the world in various ways. Open alternatives seem to lie before us. We reason and deliberate among them and choose. We feel (1) it is "up to us" what we choose and how we act; and this means we could have chosen or acted otherwise. . . . This "up-to-us-ness" also suggests that (2) the ultimate sources of our actions lie in us and not outside us in factors beyond our control.[26]

The idea is that we see ourselves as engaging in rational deliberation and choosing among a set of alternatives. We introspect, that is, that we have a kind of control over our actions, that we *ourselves* choose what we do. And if we in fact have such control as we seem to have, then we must have the ability to do otherwise. And this means that libertarianism is the correct view of human freedom.

Christian philosophers also appeal to Scripture to defend libertarianism. William Lane Craig, for example, has argued that the Scriptures "breathe libertarian human freedom."[27] To support his assertion, he cites 1 Corinthians 10:13 where Paul says, "No temptation has overtaken you except what is common to humanity. God is faithful and He will not allow you to be tempted beyond what you are able, but with the temptation He will also provide a way of escape, so that you are able to bear it." If the Christian can avoid temptation as Paul seems to indicate, then does it not follow that she has libertarian freedom?

As you might surmise, however, libertarianism has its critics. First, in response to the Introspection Argument, the compatibilist is likely to argue that its seeming that our actions are "up to us" is not the whole story about what we observe in introspection. The compatibilist will suggest that in introspection we also see ourselves acting for reasons and these reasons providing us with a sufficient condition for making the

---

[26] Robert Kane, "Libertarianism", in John Martin Fischer, Robert Kane, Derk Pereboom, and Manuel Vargas, *Four Views on Free Will* (Malden, MA: Blackwell, 2007), 5.

[27] William Lane Craig, "Ducking Friendly Fire: Davison on the Grounding Objection," *Philosophia Christi* 8:1 (2006): 161–66; cp. 163n4.

choices that we do. In other words, the compatibilist may claim that we do not see a causal gap between our reasons and our actions. When I go to the grocery store and choose the Snickers bar over the Hershey bar, it is because I wanted the Snickers bar more and that fact made it certain that I would chose the Snickers. In other words, given the state of my desires when I entered the store, I could not have done otherwise than choose the Snickers. Moreover, even if it *did* seem to us in introspection that there was a causal gap between our reasons and our actions, that would not prove that there really was such a gap. It may just be that introspection cannot perceive all of the causes of our actions that are actually present.

What about Scripture? Can the libertarian appeal to the Bible to support her view? If the Bible teaches libertarianism, then, of course, the Christian will see that as a reason to hold to libertarianism despite whatever difficulties it has. However, it is controversial that the biblical texts cited in support of libertarianism actually teach a libertarian conception of freedom. What they *do* clearly teach is that human beings are *morally responsible* for their actions. But a compatibilist will surely contend that to claim that these texts teach libertarianism is to beg the question against her view. The compatibilist also believes that we are morally responsible, but that our moral responsibility does not require the libertarian power of contrary choice. Craig and other Christian libertarians simply assume that these texts "breathe libertarian human freedom." They *do* "breathe" moral responsibility, but they breathe libertarianism if and only if the power of contrary choice is a necessary condition for moral responsibility. But that is precisely the question at issue between libertarians and compatibilists. So it is arguable, at least, that Scripture is neutral between the libertarian and compatibilist views.[28] If the Christian is to decide the issue, then, she will likely have to do so on philosophical grounds.

The most significant philosophical challenge to libertarianism is that it would seem to imply that human actions are the result of chance or are arbitrary in such a way as to undermine moral responsibility. This criticism was voiced many years ago by David Hume, who wrote that "liberty [freedom], when opposed to necessity [determinism] . . . is the same thing with chance, which is universally allowed to have no existence."[29] He went on to argue, "Actions . . . where they proceed not from some cause in the character and disposition of the person who

---

[28] It should be mentioned that the compatibilist can cite biblical texts that seem to support her view. See, e.g., Exod 4:21; 7:3; 11:9–10; Jer 13:23; Acts 2:23; Rom 8:7–8; 9:10–24.

[29] David Hume, *An Inquiry Concerning Human Understanding* (Indianapolis: Bobbs-Merrill, 1955), 105 [8.1].

performed them, they can neither redound to his honor if good, nor infamy if evil."[30]

Put another way, if freedom is incompatible with determinism (as the libertarian alleges), "it does not seem to be compatible with *indeterminism* either."[31] To see why this might be so, consider a person named Smith who is currently unemployed but has just received two job offers—let us call them Job_A and Job_B. And let us suppose that Smith freely accepts the offer for Job_A. Now the question is, *why* did Smith choose to accept the job offer? More particularly, why did she accept that offer and not the offer for Job_B? The libertarian, of course, has to say that there is nothing that determined that Smith would accept that job—she accepted the offer *freely*, after all. So there was nothing about Smith's character or her desires, nothing about her environment, nothing about the job offer, or anything else, that made Smith accept that job offer. Since it was a free act, she could have done otherwise in exactly the same circumstances. It might seem, then, that Smith's accepting the offer was *an uncaused event*. It was a matter of mere chance, something that "just happened." But if Smith's choice was just something that happened by chance, it is hard to see how it could have been under her control in any sense. How then can it be something that she is responsible for? Let us call the problem we are raising the *Libertarian's Dilemma* and state it formally as follows:

(1) If a person's actions are *determined*, then her actions are not under her control (because she lacks the ability to do otherwise).

(2) If a person's actions are *undetermined*, then her actions are not under her control (because they happen by chance).

(3) Hence, whether a person's actions are determined or undetermined, they are not under her control.

Of course, from the libertarian perspective, if an agent's actions are not under her control, she cannot be morally responsible for them. So this dilemma seems to challenge the libertarian view.

In response, the libertarian can say that it need not be the case that because Smith's choice is undetermined that it is uncaused. In other words, an action's being undetermined does not mean that the action is simply a chance event. Most libertarians today hold a theory called *agent causation*.[32] This is the view that personal agents are the direct causes of their

---

[30] Ibid., 107 [8.2].

[31] Robert Kane, *A Contemporary Introduction to Free Will* (Oxford: Oxford University Press, 2005), 33 (emphasis in original).

[32] For defenses of agent causation, see Roderick Chisholm, "Human Self and Freedom," in *Free Will*, 2nd ed., ed. Gary Watson (Oxford: Oxford University Press, 2003), 24–35;

actions. An agent is an individual substance (see chap. 4, section 4.4.3) whose will is the cause of her actions but is itself uncaused by any factors external to the will (including the agent's character). An agent, then, is a prime mover, the uncaused cause of her actions. So the libertarian who accepts agent causation can reject premise (2) of the Libertarian's Dilemma by saying that even though an agent's actions are undetermined, they are not uncaused; rather, they are *caused by the agent*.

Both nonlibertarians and many libertarians have challenged this response to the Libertarian's Dilemma by arguing that the concept of agent causation is mysterious or incoherent.[33] Whether or not this charge is accurate is a matter of considerable debate, a debate that we will not enter into here. More serious perhaps is the charge that agent causation, even if possible, does not really solve the Libertarian's Dilemma. We can still ask the question, *why* did Smith choose to accept the job offer? The libertarian, by definition, has to admit that there is a causal gap between the agent's past, her current desires, values, and circumstances, and the choices she makes. There is nothing about the agent Smith's current state or circumstances that dictates that she accept the job offer. This would make it seem, agent causation or not, that Smith accepts the offer *for no reason at all*. Her choice would appear completely random or arbitrary, and this in turn suggests that her action was not really under her control and therefore not something for which she is responsible.

The libertarian could reply that the Smith story as told above sets up a Straw Man. It is not really fair to accuse the libertarian of saying that Smith accepts the offer for no reason at all. Her having the ability to do otherwise is perfectly consistent with her having reasons for doing what she does. We might imagine, for example, that Smith has certain specific reasons for favoring Job_A which include the following: Job_A has a higher salary than Job_B and also has a more pleasant work environment. So when Smith chooses to accept the offer, she does so for these reasons, which means that her choice was not simply a matter of chance. She acts as she does for these specific reasons. So her action is not arbitrary.

However, nonlibertarians will reply that the libertarian has missed the point of the dilemma.[34] To be sure, Smith might very well have

J. P. Moreland and William Lane Craig, *Philosophical Foundations for a Christian Worldview*, 267–84; Timothy O'Conner, *Persons and Causes*.

[33] See, e.g., Robert Kane, *Free Will and Values* (Albany: State University of New York Press, 1985), 72; and Gary Watson, "Free Action and Free Will," *Mind* 96 (1987): 145–72.

[34] For a more detailed presentation of the following argument, see Steven B. Cowan, "God, Libertarian Agency, and Scientific Explanations: Problems for J. P. Moreland's Strategy for Avoiding the God of the Gaps," *Philosophia Christi* 4:1 (2002): 125–37. The reader might also want to consult the response by J. P. Moreland, "Miracles, Agency, and Theistic Science: A Reply to Steven B. Cowan," *Philosophia Christi* 4:1 (2002): 139–60.

positive reasons in favor of the job offer as the response indicates. But the very nature of libertarianism dictates that those reasons cannot really explain why Smith chose as she did. Why not? Because even with these reasons, Smith's choice is undetermined. The reasons she has for accepting Job_A do not determine that she accept it. There is, as we indicated above, a causal gap between her reason for the job and her choosing to accept the job. We can see the problem more clearly if we imagine, as is likely in most real-life cases, that Smith also has reasons in favor of Job_B, reasons which include the fact that Job_B is located closer to Smith's extended family and has more perks. Now, supposing again that Smith chooses Job_A, the question the libertarian must answer is not simply whether or not Smith has reasons in favor of Job_A. The question she must answer is: why did Smith choose Job_A *rather than* Job_B? It is difficult to imagine how the libertarian could explain this choice without conceding her position to the determinist. This is probably why many libertarians insist that such choices *cannot* be fully explained.

5.3.2 Compatibilism

As the name suggests, compatibilism is the view that freedom and determinism are compatible. That human actions are determined in some way does not, on this view, pose a threat to freedom and moral responsibility. Compatibilism is probably the majority view among contemporary philosophers generally. In the past it was defended by Aristotle, the later Augustine, Thomas Hobbes, John Locke, David Hume, Jonathan Edwards, and John Stuart Mill, among others. Contemporary compatibilists include Susan Wolff, Daniel Dennett, John Martin Fischer, Gary Watson, John Feinberg, and Paul Helm.[35]

The compatibilist attempts to do justice to the dual convictions we noted at the outset of this section, namely the conviction that we are free and responsible and the conviction that our actions are not exempt from causal explanations. Compatibilists seek to affirm both of these convictions, disagreeing with both the hard determinists and the libertarians who each deny one side of the equation.

The basic way that compatibilists address these issues is by seeking to clarify the meaning of the term *freedom* or *free will*. When we speak of doing an action freely or say that a person has free will, says the com-

---

[35] For contemporary presentations of compatibilism, see Susan Wolff, *Freedom within Reason* (Oxford: Oxford University Press, 1990); Daniel Dennett, *Elbow Room: The Varieties of Free Will Worth Having* (Cambridge, MA: MIT Press, 1984); John Martin Fischer, *The Metaphysics of Free Will* (Oxford: Blackwell, 1994); Gary Watson, ed., *Free Will*, 2nd ed.; John Feinberg, "God Ordains All Things," in *Predestination and Free Will*, ed. David Basinger and Randall Basinger (Downers Grove: InterVarsity, 1986), 19–43; Paul Helm, *Divine Providence* (Downers Grove: InterVarsity, 1994), esp. 161–216.

patibilist, what we really mean—all we *need* mean—is that the person has *the ability to do what she wants to do* and that the action performed was what the person wanted to do. Put another way, a person acts freely when she is (1) not coerced by external forces against her will and (2) there are no constraints that prevent her from acting as she desires. A person who breaks a window because she was pushed into it by another person breaks the window by coercion, not freely. Also, a person who wants to leave a room but is tied to a chair cannot do what she wants to do and so is not free. She is prevented from acting as she desires.

The compatibilist defines freedom, then, as the ability to act according to one's desires and intentions. And she maintains that determinism is compatible with this definition of freedom. As long as one has this ability, she is free and responsible for her actions. Compatibilists, however, have large hurdles to overcome in defending their view. First, they must respond to the consequence argument. Second, they must defend the adequacy of their definition of freedom by giving a plausible reason to believe that moral responsibility is compatible with determinism.

Compatibilism and the Consequence Argument

The consequence argument provides a strong motivation for incompatibilism because it has seemed to many philosophers to be sound. Its conclusion—that freedom is not compatible with determinism—seems to follow validly from its premises and its premises seem to be true. If compatibilism is to be defended, then some kind of response must be made to the consequence argument.

Most compatibilists have responded by rejecting premise (4) of the argument. Recall that premise (4) of the consequence argument went like this:

> (4) If our actions are the consequences of the laws of nature and events in the remote past, and it is not in our power to change these things, then we cannot do otherwise than what we do.

Compatibilists who take this route argue that, despite appearances, we *can* do otherwise than we do even if our actions are the inevitable consequences of the laws of nature and past events. But how can this be? Is it not obvious that we cannot do otherwise if our actions are simply the result of natural laws and past events? Well, says the compatibilist, it all depends on the meaning of the term *can*. What kind of power or ability does a person need in order for us to say plausibly she *can* do otherwise? The compatibilist who rejects premise (4) offers what she calls the "conditional analysis" of the power to do otherwise—an analysis suggested by her understanding of freedom and which is consistent with determinism. On this conditional analysis, to say that an agent can do otherwise means that she *would* have done otherwise *if she had chosen to do otherwise*. Suppose that you had toast for breakfast this morning. On the conditional analysis, you *could* have done otherwise than eat toast simply because you *would* have done otherwise if you had chosen not to eat toast. That is, even though determinism entails that you could not have refrained from choosing toast, you nevertheless could have done other than eat toast insofar as you would have refrained from doing so if you had chosen differently.

This conditional analysis response to the consequence argument has not proven very persuasive. We might all agree that the conditional statement, "If you had chosen not to eat toast, then you would have done other than eat toast" is true. But the fact is, because you were determined to make the choice you made, you could not have chosen to refrain from eating toast! In other words, given determinism, the truth of the antecedent of the conditional is not something that you have control over. What the conditional analysis does, in effect, is say that you could have chosen differently if the past had been different in some way (including being different with regard to your desires and values). But the past was what it was, and you cannot change it. Therefore, you cannot have chosen differently. To illustrate, consider the character Gollum in *The Lord of the Rings*. He is a creature consumed with the desire to possess the Ring of Power. Suppose that at some point in the story Gollum managed to get his hands on the ring. And suppose that Frodo Baggins asked him to voluntarily relinquish the ring and any claim he had to it. Readers of Tolkien's story know that Gollum's answer would be "no." We know this is how he would answer because we know that Gollum would find it psychologically impossible to give up the ring. But the conditional analysis of the power to do otherwise tells us that Gollum, even though he said no, did have the power to give up the ring. He had the power to give it up because he *would* have given it up *if he had wanted to*. Well and good. But the advocate of the conditional analysis fails to mention that Gollum just cannot want to! And this fact makes the conditional analysis suspect.

Well, if the conditional analysis fails to undermine the consequence argument, what other recourse does the compatibilist have? Rather than try to argue that compatibilism allows for a kind of ability to do otherwise, other compatibilists challenge the idea that lacking the ability to do otherwise rules out the kind of freedom necessary for moral responsibility. Recall the fifth premise of the consequence argument:

(5) If we cannot do otherwise than what we do, then we are not free.

Some compatibilists argue that even if we lack the ability to do otherwise we may nonetheless be free. Incompatibilists, they say, beg the question by incorporating a libertarian definition of "free" into premise (5) of the consequence argument. The incompatibilist assumes, that is, that freedom necessarily requires the ability to do otherwise. However, if we substitute the compatibilist view of freedom for the word *free*, then we must revise the premise as follows:

(5') If we cannot do otherwise than what we do, then we cannot do what we want to do.

The compatibilist will surely say that (5') is false. And this would allow her to say that the consequence argument is unsound.

This response to the consequence argument will prevail, though, only if the compatibilist can provide a reason to prefer her definition of freedom over that of the libertarian. And providing such a reason depends in large measure on what we think is required for moral responsibility.

Compatibilism and Moral Responsibility

It is a deeply ingrained belief of most people, including many philosophers, that moral responsibility requires the ability to do otherwise. That ability, in turn, requires that a person have alternative possibilities when making a choice. It is primarily this belief that motivates incompatibilism. Aware of this strong belief, those compatibilists who reject premise (5) of the consequence argument have sought to demonstrate that this assumption is not necessarily true. If they can do this, it would serve to make their view of freedom more appealing.

The way that compatibilists have tried to show that the ability to do otherwise is not a necessary condition for moral responsibility is to offer what are called *Frankfurt-type counterexamples*, named after Harry Frankfurt, the philosopher who first introduced them into debates on freedom.[36] The basic idea behind a Frankfurt-type counterexample is to describe a possible scenario in which an agent lacks the ability to do otherwise and yet it seems obvious that she is morally responsible. Here is a variation on one such example provided by Frankfurt. Suppose that Dr. Doom, as part of a diabolical plot to take over the world, has somehow managed to implant a computer chip into the brain of Reed Richards

---

[36] Harry G. Frankfurt, "Alternate Possibilities and Moral Responsibility," *Journal of Philosophy* 66 (1969): 829–39.

(a.k.a. Mr. Fantastic), leader of the superhero group the Fantastic Four. This chip allows Dr. Doom to monitor Richards' mental activity and know, among other things, when Richards is about to form an intention to perform some action. The chip also allows Doom, when it suits his purposes, to circumvent Richards' own control of his choices and actions and make him do what Doom wants him to do.

Now suppose that Reed Richards has to make a choice between Medusa and the She-Thing as a temporary replacement for Sue Richards (a.k.a. the Invisible Girl) while she is on maternity leave from the Fantastic Four. Unknown to Reed Richards, however, the She-Thing is in league with Dr. Doom. Of course, Doom wants Richards to choose the She-Thing. As long as Doom sees that Richards is going to choose the She-Thing, he simply continues to monitor Richards' mental activity and does not intervene in any way. If, on the other hand, Doom sees that Richards is about to choose Medusa, he will activate other capacities of the chip and manipulate Richards to choose the She-Thing instead. Now let us suppose that the first series of events actually ensues. Without any intervention from Doom, Richards forms the intention to choose the She-Thing and then chooses her.

In this scenario it seems evident that Richards cannot do otherwise than choose the She-Thing. If he were to begin to choose Medusa, Doom would intervene and prevent him from doing it. Richards appears to lack alternative possibilities. What is more, it is clear that Richards is morally responsible for choosing the She-Thing. He formed the intention to do so and then did so without any interference from Doom. It was Richards' own choice. So he was morally responsible even though he appears to lack the ability to do otherwise.

The moral of the story, for the compatibilist, is that the ability to do otherwise is not a necessary condition for moral responsibility. One can be morally responsible for her actions even if she could not have done anything other than what she did. And since the main reason to think that determinism is incompatible with freedom and responsibility is that it rules out the ability to do otherwise (a lá the consequence argument), the compatibilist concludes that there is no strong basis for incompatiblism after all—which means that compatibilism is a plausible and defensible view. As long as an agent's actions result from her own desires, values, and intentions, she can be morally responsible even if her actions are determined.

Libertarians respond to this case for compatibilism by trying to show that the agents in the Frankfurt-type counterexamples really do have alternative possibilities after all. Robert Kane provides what is perhaps the strongest such reply.[37] In response to the Dr. Doom/Reed Richards example, Kane would ask us to suppose that Richards' choice is undetermined right up to the point of the choice. In that case Doom cannot know beforehand which choice Richards will make. If he waits until Richards makes his choice before deciding to intervene, it will be too late. And in that case, Richards *will* be responsible for his choice, but he will also have had *alternative possibilities* since he could have chosen either way. On the other hand, if Doom wants to ensure that Richards chooses the She-Thing, he will have to intervene before Richards chooses, and in that case, Richards would not be morally responsible.

Compatiblists will likely object to Kane's response by denying the plausibility of the idea that many, or any, of our actions are undetermined right up to the point of choice. People have characters—stable dispositions to act in certain ways in accordance with their desires and values. Their characters allow us to reliably predict how they will act in various circumstances. So it might be implausible to think, in most cases anyway, that our actions can be undetermined right up to the point of choice. If this is correct, it would suggest that Kane's recasting of the Doom/Richards scenario is incoherent. Even if this concern is set aside, moreover, compatibilists could raise concerns about whether actions that are undetermined at the point of choice are simply the result of chance (as pointed out in our discussion of libertarianism above).

At present, the jury is still out in philosophical circles regarding the strength of Frankfurt-style counterexamples in showing that the ability to do otherwise is unnecessary for moral responsibility. It is also still a matter of considerable debate as to whether libertarians can defend the intelligibility of indeterministic action. Christians in the past and present have come down on both sides of the issue. What we are all agreed on is that human beings are morally responsible for their actions. The question as to whether such moral responsibility is compatible with determinism is where we differ.

Questions for Reflection

1. Do you believe that human beings can live without believing in moral responsibility as hard determinists suggest? Why or why not?

2. Do you think Scripture supports one view on the question of free will better than the others? If so, which one? What biblical texts would you cite to defend your view?

---

[37] See Robert Kane, *A Contemporary Introduction to Free Will*, 87–88.

3. Do you think that the libertarian's response to the Libertarian's Dilemma is adequate? Why or why not? Can you think of a better response?

4. Has the compatibilist adequately addressed the consequence argument? Why or why not?

5. What do the Frankfurt-type counterexamples prove, if anything? Do they make a compatiblist view of moral responsibility more plausible? Why or why not?

§ 5.4 Is There Life After Death?

One of the greatest fears that human beings face concerns death. This fear is so powerful that many people will go to the greatest lengths to forestall death or even avoid it altogether. For example, in the past, people have sought immortality through witchcraft or by searching the world for the "fountain of youth," like the sixteenth-century explorer Ponce de Leon. In recent times, some people (like the baseball star Ted Williams) have taken advantage of a new technology known as cryogenics to have their bodies frozen with the intent of someday being thawed and, by the "miracle" of future technology, cured of what killed them. The desperation to escape death will prompt some people to pursue almost any strange course that promises immortality.

Religion, of course, is another avenue that people pursue in the hope of overcoming death—specifically through life after death. Almost every religion promises its followers a happy eternal existence. The ancient Vikings looked forward to boisterous eternal fellowship in Valhallah in exchange for their faithful service to Odin and Thor. Some Eastern religions like Hinduism and Buddhism teach that when a person dies she lives on through reincarnation into another earthly life. The Muslim hopes that by her good deeds she can persuade Allah to permit her entrance into paradise. And if she dies a martyr for Islam such entrance is guaranteed. And Christians believe that sinners who trust in Jesus Christ and His redemptive work will receive the gift of eternal life. The most well-known biblical text says it plainly: "For God loved the world in this way: He gave His One and Only Son, so that everyone who believes in Him will not perish, but have eternal life" (John 3:16).

Religious beliefs like these give people hope in the face of death. The question that must be asked, however, is whether there is any good reason to believe in life after death. Is it a reasonable hope or nothing more than wishful thinking? Some of the earliest philosophical speculation on life after death comes from the philosopher Plato, who offered several arguments for the immortality of the soul. In his *Phaedo*, Plato argues that all learning is a form of recollection. When we acquire knowledge we do not discover new information but remember it. This means that our souls must have preexisted our bodies. Furthermore, it means that the soul can exist apart from the body, which suggests that our souls will live on after death.

Plato's argument from recollection has not proven very convincing. For one thing, it is not clear that learning is a form of recollection. For another, even if Plato can prove the preexistence of the soul, it does not follow that our souls are immortal. Preexistence notwithstanding, it may be that physical death spells the end of our souls as well. Of course, if our souls do preexist our incarnate lives, it is possible that they can postexist them too. But the point is that Plato's argument from recollection does not *prove* that there is life after death. None of his other arguments have proven any more persuasive.

So we return to the question: Is there life after death? Of course, the Christian needs no convincing. On the basis of divine revelation we are confident in the promise of everlasting life. Still, it would prove helpful to believer and nonbeliever alike if there were philosophical evidences for life after death. In what follows, we will explore a few lines of evidence that we believe make the prospect of life after death more probable than not.

5.4.1 Philosophical Arguments

It goes without saying that if metaphysical materialism is true, then the prospects for life after death are not good. Materialists and other atheists are committed to the idea that all that exists is the physical universe. Reality is constituted by matter and the laws and forces that regulate its behavior. Thus, human beings are simply material entities and do not have an immaterial component that can survive the death of the body. So, for the materialist, "When you're dead, your dead!"

But what if materialism is not true (as we argued in chap. 4)? What if, in fact, God exists (as we will argue in chap. 6)? What if there is concrete evidence that human beings are not simply material entities (as we saw earlier in this chapter)? What if there is empirical, scientific evidence for life after death? In such cases, the prospects for life after death are greatly improved. Let us take a look at these possibilities, beginning with some philosophical arguments. In the next section we will look at scientific evidence for life after death.

The Argument from Substance Dualism

In the first section of this chapter, we saw that the most reasonable view regarding the mind-body problem is that human beings have an immaterial soul. We are not purely physical entities, and the mind is not reducible to the brain and its functions. If this is so, then we have at least the possibility of life after death. On a dualist view of human persons the soul is not dependent upon the body for its existence or its operations. It *can* survive the death of the body. As we saw with Plato above, this point does not prove that there is life after death, but it makes belief in an afterlife plausible. But there are other considerations which many believe to provide even stronger reasons to believe in life after death.

The Argument from Theism and the Hope for Ultimate Justice

Sometimes the bad guys win. In fact, it often seems as if the bad guys win most of the time. The prophet Jeremiah noticed this troubling fact and queried God, "Why does the way of the wicked prosper?" (Jer 12:1). We believe that justice is a good thing and injustice is bad. We believe that just and good people ought to be rewarded and that the wicked ought to suffer the consequences of their evil deeds. Yet the opposite often seems to be the case. The wicked live pleasantly and the good do not. Many times the wicked even go to their graves enjoying the fruit of their crimes, and their victims close their eyes in death without getting the justice they deserve.

Is this just the way things are? Is the atheist Richard Dawkins correct when he says,

> In a universe of electrons and selfish genes, blind forces and genetic replication, some people are going to get hurt, other people are going to get lucky, and you won't find any rhyme or reason in it, nor any justice. The universe that we observe has precisely the properties we should expect if there is, at bottom, no design, no purpose, no evil, no good, nothing but pitiless indifference.[38]

If this earthly life is all there is, then Dawkins is right. Our desire for justice will be largely frustrated. On the other hand, if there is life after death then there is hope for final justice. There is, that is, a good possibility that ultimately the just will be vindicated and the unjust punished.

But how can we know which outcome is right? Can we hope for ultimate justice or not? Let us suppose, for the sake of argument, that justice is a real, objective moral value—that injustice really is wrong and that justice really is right. Let us suppose, that is, that moral values like justice are not simply societal conventions or personal preferences.[39] And let us also suppose that theism is true—that a personal and loving

---

[38] Richard Dawkins, "God's Utility Function," *Scientific American* (Nov. 1995): 85.

[39] See chapter 7 for a critique of moral relativism and a defense of the moral objectivism we are supposing here.

God exists. Then we may expect that He would ensure ultimate justice in the universe. He would make sure that evil men and women are punished and good men and women are rewarded. In the next chapter, we will see that there is strong evidence for the existence of such a God. Suffice it to say here that the existence of God coupled with our hope for ultimate justice provide us with significant grounds for believing in life after death.

We believe that the arguments surveyed above do provide significant reasons to believe in life after death. They are not conclusive, however, and are not likely to persuade an ardent skeptic. In the next section, we will look at evidence for life after death of a more scientific nature.

5.4.2 The Evidence of Near-Death Experiences

Though not widely known, there is actually *empirical* evidence for life after death—evidence that is scientifically verifiable. This evidence is provided by the phenomena known as *near-death experiences.* A near-death experience (NDE) is an experience had by a person who meets the criteria for clinical death in which she experiences phenomena that seem to be of a disembodied existence and/or other aspects of an afterlife. Clinical death is usually defined as the absence of any discernable signs of life such as consciousness, pulse, or breathing. Sometimes people who report NDEs also lack brain-wave activity as indicated by a flat EEG reading. As described by Gary Habermas and J. P. Moreland, NDEs are often characterized by

> the sense that one is dead, looking down on one's body, traveling down a tunnel or dark passageway, seeing a light, meeting other persons or supernatural beings [e.g., an angel or Jesus or Buddha], participating in a life review, seeing beautiful scenery, reentering one's body, and experiencing feelings of peace, including losing the fear of death.[40]

Occasionally, those having NDEs even report terrifying visits to hell.[41] In any case, most of those who report having NDEs claim that the experiences are very vivid, personally meaningful and even life-changing.

What, if anything, can we learn from NDEs about an afterlife? To answer this question we have to be careful to focus our attention on the right aspects of these experiences. In much of the popular discussion of this topic attention is given to what we may call the "heavenly" aspects of NDEs: seeing a bright light at the end of a tunnel, meeting some

---

[40] Gary Habermas and J. P. Moreland, *Beyond Death: Exploring the Evidence for Immortality* (Wheaton, IL: Crossway, 1998), 155.

[41] See, e.g., Maurice Rawlings, *Before Death Comes* (Nashville: Thomas Nelson, 1980).

supernatural or religious figure, conversations with long-dead family members and friends, and the like. Those who are skeptical of NDEs as providing evidence of an afterlife tend to focus almost entirely on these aspects of NDEs and argue that these phenomena may be given plausible natural explanations.

For example, seeing a light at the end of a dark tunnel may be attributed to oxygen deprivation that occurs when breathing and heartbeat stop for prolonged periods.[42] Other aspects of the experience can be explained psychologically. Researchers have found it interesting, for example, that Christians who experience NDEs often report meeting Jesus, but Hindus encounter Krishna or another Hindu deity, and people of other religious persuasions meet figures from their respective traditions. This strongly suggests that these aspects of NDEs are dictated by the person's cultural background and should not be taken at face value.[43]

Yet these points do not undermine the value of NDEs as evidence for life after death. All they prove is that a person's interpretation of his experience ("It was a light"; "It was Jesus!") is suspect in some cases. Nonetheless, it would still be the case that a person was having conscious experiences when her body was clinically dead! This detail certainly has some evidential value for the question of life after death. Moreover, there are other phenomena reported in NDEs that have even more evidential weight concerning the afterlife. Consider the case described by Habermas and Moreland of a young girl named Katie who almost drowned:

> After her emergency room resuscitation, a CAT scan showed massive brain swelling, and her doctor had an artificial lung machine attached to her to keep her breathing. He gave her a 10 percent chance of living. But three days later she totally recovered and relayed an amazing story. She accurately described the physical characteristics of the doctors involved in her resuscitation, details of the hospital rooms she was taken into, and reported particulars of the specific medical procedures used on her, even though she was "profoundly comatose," with her eyes closed during the entire time.
>
> As if all this was not enough, Katie . . . "followed" her family home during the time her body was comatose in the hospital and remembered seeing specific minutiae such as the selection for the evening meal prepared by her mother, how her father

---

[42] See G. M. Woerlee, "Darkness, Tunnels, and Light," *Skeptical Inquirer* 28:3 (May/June 2004): 28–32.

[43] See Carol Zaleski, *Otherworld Journeys: Accounts of Near-Death Experience in Medieval and Modern Times* (Oxford: Oxford University Press, 1988).

was reacting to her accident, and which toys her brother and sister were playing with at the time.[44]

These kinds of cases are surprisingly common and are well-documented and corroborated by medical and scientific researchers.[45] Some cases even involve blind persons who later recounted physical details of the medical procedures performed on them and accurately described the medical practitioners present, including the colors of their clothing! In other cases, people reported meeting loved ones who were recently deceased, though neither the NDE subject nor others present knew that the loved one had died. Habermas and Moreland describe one fascinating case:

> A woman who was near death perceived herself leaving her body and viewed the hospital room, the doctor shaking his head, and her distraught husband. Then she believed that she went to heaven and saw an angel, along with a familiar young man. She exclaimed, "Why, Tom, I didn't know you were up here!" Tom responded that he had just arrived, too. But the angel told the woman that she would be returning to earth. . . . Then she found herself back on the hospital bed with the doctor looking over her. Later that night, her husband got a call informing him that their friend Tom had died in an auto accident.[46]

What are we to make of these phenomena? There have been several attempts to debunk them by providing possible natural explanations or arguing that the research was tainted in some way.[47] Yet these aspects of NDEs have so far proven resilient in the face of such scrutiny.[48] Subjects of NDEs are able to see, experience, and know things independently of their physical bodies. This corroborates a dualist account of human beings and shows that a person can survive without her body. So with Habermas, Moreland, and others, we believe that NDE phenomena do provide empirical evidence for some kind of life after death.

---

[44] Habermas and Moreland, *Beyond Death*, 157.

[45] Numerous works document such NDE phenomena, such as Raymond L. Moody, *Life After Life* (Atlanta: Mockingbird, 1975); Michael B. Sabom, *Recollections of Death: A Medical Investigation* (New York: Harper & Row, 1982); Melvin Morse and Paul Perry, *Closer to the Light: Learning from the Near-Death Experiences of Children* (New York: Random House, 1990); Elizabeth Kubler-Ross, *On Children and Death* (New York: MacMillan, 1983); Karlis Osis and Erlendur Haraldsson, *At the Hour of Death* (New York: Avon, 1977); and Kenneth Ring, *Life at Death: A Scientific Investigation of Near-Death Experience* (New York: Coward, McCann, and Geoghegan, 1980).

[46] Habermas and Moreland, *Beyond Death*, 162.

[47] See, e.g., Susan Blackmore, *Dying to Live: Near-Death Experiences* (Buffalo: Prometheus, 1993); and Timothy Ferris, *The Mind's Sky* (New York: Bantom, 1992).

[48] See the detailed assessment by Habermas and Moreland, *Beyond Death*, 173–218.

Of course, none of this proves with absolute certainty that the Christian belief in eternal life is true. The NDE data are consistent with the hypothesis that a person survives her body for only a short time and then perishes. On the other hand, the data are also consistent with belief in a more robust and enduring afterlife such as that described in Scripture.

5.4.3 What about Reincarnation?

An alternative conception of the afterlife that is popular today is *reincarnation*. Hindus, Buddhists, and New Agers believe that when a person dies her soul or karmic energy transmigrates to another newborn human being or perhaps even an animal. Reincarnationists generally believe that human persons have experienced hundreds, perhaps thousands of such incarnations. What can we say about reincarnation? Does it really happen? Is there any evidence for it?

The first thing to note is that the idea of reincarnation is incompatible with Christian belief. The author of the biblical book of Hebrews says, "It is appointed for people to die once—and after this, judgment" (Heb 9:27). Moreover, and more significantly, reincarnation is inconsistent with the doctrine of resurrection. We believe that Jesus rose from the dead and that those who believe in Him will enjoy eternal life through bodily resurrection.[49] Reincarnation, which involves the migration of a soul to a new earthly existence, is inconsistent with this expectation of bodily resurrection. Thus, we have reason to reject reincarnation.

Nevertheless, those who believe in reincarnation often cite empirical evidence to support their belief. We will examine some of this evidence below.

Evidence for Reincarnation

The most interesting evidence for reincarnation comes from those who seem to remember past lives. Some alleged recollections of past lives occur as the result of hypnotic regression. People are hypnotized and then asked to go backwards in their minds to the time they were born, and then beyond that to a time before their births. Under such conditions, many people have claimed to recall details of a past life, sometimes multiple past lives that cover the course of many centuries.[50]

---

[49] For thorough presentations of the evidence for Jesus' resurrection see William Lane Craig, *The Son Rises: The Historical Evidence for the Resurrection of Jesus* (Eugene, OR: Wipf & Stock, 1981); Gary R. Habermas and Michael R. Licona, *The Case for the Resurrection of Jesus* (Grand Rapids: Kregel, 2004); and N. T. Wright, *The Resurrection of the Son of God* (Minneapolis: Fortress, 2003).

[50] See E. Zolik, "'Reincarnation' Phenomena in Hypnotic States," *International Journal of Parapsychology* 4:3 (1962): 66–78; and Ian Stevenson, "Hypnotic Regression to Previous Lives"

More impressively, some people appear to remember past lives without the aid of hypnosis. Habermas and Moreland describe one such case:

> A four-year-old boy named Prakesh began declaring that his actual name was Nirmal and that he really lived in another village. He provided details about his "real" family, such as the names of relatives and friends, as well as particulars about the family's business. He kept trying to run away to his "prior" home and talked incessantly about it, provoking the anger of his parents, who beat him for his behavior.
>
> Five years later, Nirmal's "real" father visited Prakesh's village, and Prakesh recognized him. It was discovered that Nirmal was actually the name of the man's son, who had died prior to Prakesh's birth.[51]

Subsequently, the other details of Prakesh's claims about his "real" family were corroborated. In many such cases, it is also observed that the living person has the same personality traits as the deceased individual.

What are we to make of this evidence? Reincarnation would certainly seem to explain it. But there are other possible explanations. Supporters as well as critics of reincarnation suggest the possibility that some cases like those of Prakesh are due to demonic possession. A demon, of course, is an evil immaterial spirit. Many religions such as Christianity, Islam, and Judaism believe in the existence of such spirits. Demonic possession occurs when a demon takes control of a human person's mind and body or, less severely, strongly influences a person's thoughts and actions. We may surmise that demonic spirits have access to information about past events and lives and that they would be able to communicate that information (even in the form of false memories) to the mind of a human being like Prakesh. This alternative hypothesis would explain the data just as well as the reincarnation hypothesis.

Do we have reason to prefer one of these hypotheses to the other? At least two reasons lead us to prefer the demonic possession theory. First, as Christians, we have at least a *prima facie* reason to reject reincarnation because of its conflict with biblical teaching. And since we believe that demons exist and are capable of possessing human beings, this supports the theory that past life "memories" are not genuine but are due to demonic possession. Second (and this is relevant to Christians

(Internet article accessed at http://www.healthsystem.virginia.edu/internet/personalitystudies/regression.cfm.)

[51] Habermas and Moreland, *Beyond Death*, 238. For more examples, see also Ian Stevenson, *Twenty Cases Suggestive of Reincarnation* (New York: American Society for Psychical Research, 1966).

and non-Christians alike), there are cases similar to Prakesh's in which the living person with the past life "memories" was born *before* the "remembered" person died![52] Reincarnation will not work to explain such cases. Here the demonic possession hypothesis is clearly preferable. But, if it's preferable in these cases, why not others like Prakesh's? At best the evidence for reincarnation is inconclusive.

Problems for Reincarnation

There are other reasons to reject reincarnation, though. For one, reincarnation raises concerns about personal identity. How do we know that the person supposedly reincarnated really is a person who lived before? Now in those cases where a person "remembers" a past life there may not be a problem with personal identity (but recall from above that memory is not a satisfactory criterion for personal identity). Yet, in the vast majority of cases, people do not remember having a past life. Yet reincarnationists insist that they have. The question must be asked, however, as to what criterion of personal identity is being presupposed by the reincarnationists. Many who believe in reincarnation (e.g., some forms of Buddhism) do not believe that a person's soul actually migrates from one body to another in reincarnation. Rather, they believe that a person's individual self is extinguished at death and only her karmic debt is transferred to another newborn person (we will say more about karma below). On this view, the "reincarnated" person is clearly *not* identical to the previous person who died. Indeed, it would be a stretch to call this reincarnation at all. A new person comes into being and inherits the karmic debt of another person. Some reincarnations may escape this problem by adopting the concept of the "transmigration of the soul." Here there is an immaterial element of a person that persists beyond death and enters the body of a newborn. This view essentially adopts the soul view of personal identity that we tentatively endorsed above. So it seems that on this view there could be a basis for maintaining the personal identity of a previous person and a later reincarnated one. We might still wonder, however, how meaningful such personal identity (without psychological continuity) would be for the purposes that reincarnation is supposed to serve.

More serious are concerns about justice raised by reincarnation. According to those who believe in it, the cause of reincarnation is karmic debt. Karma is the law of moral cause and effect affirmed by followers of several Eastern religions. If a person commits a bad deed, he accumulates "bad karma," which may be understood as a kind of moral debt. If a person dies with any karmic debt, he is reincarnated into a new life and given

---

[52] See Ian Stevenson, *Twenty Cases*, 228–29, 340–47.

the opportunity to pay off his debt. What is more, the physical and social conditions into which a person is reincarnated are determined by his past-life deeds. If a person is born into poverty or disease, that is because he was a bad person in his past life. Karma assumes, then, that "what a person sows, so shall he reap." Of course, in every life, people perform both good and bad deeds, so there is usually the accumulation of more karmic debt that must be eradicated in yet another incarnation. Reincarnationists believe that people generally must experience thousands, even millions, of incarnations in order to erase their karmic debt.

The problem is that this system seems unjust for several reasons. First, on the assumption that the reincarnated person is not numerically identical to the person whose karmic debt is transferred, reincarnation entails that a person is being held responsible for what another person did. Second, even if personal identity is maintained in reincarnation, it would seem counterproductive at best, and unjust at worse, that a reincarnated soul should come into the world with no memory of her past life. Would it not be more fair and more fruitful if the reincarnated person recalled the reasons for her present incarnation?

Third, most reincarnationists believe that the process of life-death-reincarnation has no beginning. No one had a *first* incarnation in which she was debt-free. Every incarnation of a person is the result of sins committed in a previous life. But this means that no person was ever in a state of innocence and then fell into karmic debt. Everyone has been perpetually in karmic debt. How can this be just?

Fourth, the doctrine of reincarnation motivates moral apathy both for oneself and toward others. Consider that a person who believes in reincarnation could very well rationalize immoral and unvirtuous behavior by saying that she can deal with her karmic debt in a later life. What is worse, the believer in reincarnation has a strong reason to refrain from helping those who are less fortunate than herself. After all, whatever condition a person is in (e.g., poverty) is the result of her past-life sins. Helping that person may even hinder her from working off her debt. So the doctrine of reincarnation seems to motivate a moral apathy that exacerbates the suffering in the world.

For these reasons, we conclude that reincarnation is not a viable view of life after death. The Christian view of personal resurrection is much to be preferred.

Conclusion

Throughout this book so far, we have emphasized those areas in which there is interface between philosophical issues and Christian belief.

Nowhere is that interface more significant than in the area of human nature. The most profound and personally relevant philosophical topics are those that deal with questions like "Who am I?" and even "*What* am I?" In this chapter we have delved into several of these questions about human nature. First, we considered whether or not the human mind (and thus the whole human being) is reducible to the physical. We saw that there are good reasons to reject physicalism and affirm mind-body dualism.

Second, we explored the question of personal identity, a question that seems on the surface to be rather abstract and unrelated to real life but which can have great ethical and religious significance. We argued that the soul view of personal identity has fewer problems than its rivals and fits nicely with our conclusions on the mind-body problem as well as with the Christian view of the afterlife.

The question of free will was our third topic in this chapter. Of all the issues discussed in this chapter, the reader perhaps found this discussion the most frustrating. This is no doubt because the tension between free will and determinism is one of the most intractable in philosophy. People's intuitions differ on whether or not freedom is compatible with determinism. Moreover, debate surrounds the proper interpretation of biblical texts related to human freedom and moral responsibility.

Lastly, we probed the question of life after death. As Christians we affirm the biblical teaching that human beings survive physical death. We offered, in the spirit of philosophy's role as the handmaid of theology, several lines of evidence that support belief in life after death, including the evidence for mind-body dualism, the evidence for God's existence coupled with the natural human hope for ultimate justice, and the evidence from near-death experiences. We also gave a response to the popular belief in reincarnation.

In the next chapter, we will explore issues even more fundamental to Christian faith, specifically questions concerning the existence and nature of God and the problem of evil.

Questions for Reflection

1. Do you believe it is natural to think that there must be ultimate justice? Could Dawkins be right that we should expect nothing in the end but "pitiless indifference"? Why or why not?
2. Is the explanation for NDE phenomena discussed in this section consistent with Scripture? Why or why not?
3. Can you think of any alternative explanations for NDE phenomena? In the end, which explanation seems best to you?

4. In addition to the biblical reasons discussed above, can you think of further biblical grounds for rejecting belief in reincarnation?

For Further Reading

On the Mind/Body Problem

McGinn, Colin. *The Mysterious Flame: Conscious Minds in a Material World.* New York: Basic, 1999.

Montero, Barbara. *On the Philosophy of Mind.* Belmont, CA: Wadsworth, 2009.

Searle, John R. *Mind: A Brief Introduction.* New York: Oxford University Press, 2004.

Swinburne, Richard. *The Evolution of the Soul* (rev. ed.). New York: Oxford University Press, 1997.

On Personal Identity

Martin, Raymond, and John Barresi, eds. *Personal Identity.* Malden, MA: Blackwell, 2003.

Parfit, Derek. *Reasons and Persons.* Oxford: Clarendon, 1984.

Shoemaker, Sydney, and Richard Swinburne. *Personal Identity.* Malden, MA: Blackwell, 1991.

On Free Will and Determinism

Fischer, John Martin. *The Metaphysics of Free Will.* Cambridge, MA: Blackwell, 1994.

Fischer, John Martin, Robert Kane, Derk Pereboom, and Manuel Vargas. *Four Views on Free Will.* Malden, MA: Blackwell, 2007.

Kane, Robert. *A Contemporary Introduction to Free Will.* Oxford: Oxford University Press, 2005.

Watson, Gary, ed. *Free Will.* 2nd ed. Oxford: Oxford University Press, 2003.

On Life After Death

Geisler, Norman L., and J. Yutaka Amano. *The Reincarnation Sensation.* Eugene, OR: Wipf and Stock, 2004.

Habermas, Gary R., and Michael R. Licona. *The Case for the Resurrection of Jesus.* Grand Rapids: Kregel, 2004.

Habermas, Gary, and J. P. Moreland. *Beyond Death: Exploring the Evidence for Immortality.* Wheaton, IL: Crossway, 1998.

Chapter Six

PHILOSOPHY OF RELIGION: IS THERE A GOD?

"A little philosophy inclineth men's minds to atheism;
but depth in philosophy bringeth
men's minds to religion."

—Francis Bacon

Glossary Terms

Actual infinite	*Omnitemporalism*
Atemporalism	*Ontological argument*
Cosmological argument	*Passibilism (and impassibilism)*
Evidentialism	*Potential infinite*
Middle knowledge	*Principle of sufficient reason*
Miracle	*Problem of evil*
Molinism	*Religious exclusivism*
Natural theology	*Religious pluralism*
Ockhamism	*Sempiternalism*
Omnipotence	*Teleological argument*
Omniscience	

I n the movie *The Lord of the Rings: The Fellowship of the Ring*, a small band of heroes is given the task of destroying a magic ring forged by the evil Lord Sauron. At one point in the story, the young hobbit Frodo, the ring-bearer, reaches a point of near despair as the fellowship trudges endlessly through the mines of Moria. He has little hope that he will succeed in accomplishing his mission. He tells the wizard Gandalf, "I wish the ring had never come to me. I wish none of this had ever happened."

"There are other forces at work in this world, Frodo, besides the will of evil," Gandalf replies. "Bilbo [Frodo's elderly uncle] was *meant* to find the ring. In which case you also were *meant* to have it. And that is an encouraging thought."

Gandalf, of course, is alluding to God. He is the "other forces" at work in the world who works providentially in history to accomplish His benevolent purposes. Because God exists and is at work in the world, there is reason to have hope even in the midst of difficult circumstances.

If, on the other hand, there is no God, and therefore no "other forces" at work besides the forces of evil and chaos, then Frodo and Gandalf would not have any reason to be encouraged. If there is no God, then the world exists for no reason, and everything that happens in history is ultimately without any purpose or significance. If there is no God, then the bad things that happen to us are just our unfortunate luck. We have no reason to hope that anything we do will make any difference in the long run. For, if there is no God, then the world not only came into existence for no reason, but everything in it (including humans) is destined for extinction as all the stars eventually burn out and the planets turn cold.

But, if God does exist, then there is purpose and meaning to life. What we do now has significance for eternity. And we can have hope that the "heat death" of the universe is not the last word. We have hope, that is, for life after death. Moreover, if God exists, there is someone to whom we are responsible. Our actions in this life are under the scrutiny of an all-knowing and perfectly good being who guarantees that justice will be done in the end. The idea that there is a "higher power" to whom we are responsible makes some people uncomfortable. The philosopher Thomas Nagel once remarked, "I want atheism to be true. . . . It isn't just that I don't believe in God, and, naturally, hope that I'm right about my belief. It's that I hope there is no God! I don't want there to be a God; I don't want the universe to be like that."[1] Nagel, like others, has a problem with "cosmic authority." He doesn't want there to be an omnipotent, omniscient, and wholly good deity to hold him accountable.

The point of all this is that it matters whether or not God exists. In fact, no other philosophical question could have greater practical significance. In this chapter, then, we will look at the question, "Does God exist?" After that, we will inquire into the nature of God and address the most significant obstacle to belief in God—the problem of evil. We will conclude the chapter with an examination of philosophical issues related to the claim that Christianity, among all the world's religions, is exclusively true.

§ 6.1 Does God Exist?

We have seen that it matters whether or not God exists. The key question before us now is: *Does* He exist? What evidence or arguments might there be for the existence of a supreme being? Is God's existence something we can *know*? Or must we simply take it on faith that God exists? One of the things that we have found very surprising as philosophy professors is the frequency with which students–both religious and non-religious–answer this question in the negative. They simply take it for granted that God's existence cannot be proven and find it amazing that anyone thinks differently. For many students today, the existence of God is purely a matter of faith. (Strangely enough, many of these same students think that atheism is somehow bizarre or evil.)

---

[1] Thomas Nagel, *The Last Word* (New York: Oxford University Press, 1997), 130.

This attitude toward the knowledge of God's existence has been re-inforced in our culture by the recent rise of a militant form of atheism. Spearheaded by authors such as Richard Dawkins, Sam Harris, Christopher Hitchens, and others,[2] these atheists have acquired an evangelistic zeal in defense of the thesis that God does not exist. Indeed, they allege that there is no evidence at all for God's existence and that belief in Him is wildly irrational and dangerous. For example, Harris insists that

> the biblical God is a fiction, like Zeus and the thousands of other dead gods whom most sane human beings now ignore. Can you prove that Zeus does not exist? Of course not. And yet, just imagine if we lived in a society where people spent tens of billions of dollars of their personal income each year propitiating the gods of Mount Olympus, where the government spent billions more in tax dollars to support institutions devoted to these gods, . . . where elected officials did their best to impede medical research out of deference to The Iliad and The Odyssey. . . . This would be a horrific misappropriation of our material, moral, and intellectual resources. And yet that is exactly the society we are living in. This is the woefully irratio-nal world that you and your fellow Christians are working so tirelessly to create.[3]

Such an attitude toward the knowledge of God's existence is rela-tively new. In fact, until the mid-to-late nineteenth century, most people in the West would have found it strange for someone to think that God's existence could *not* be proven. Throughout the history of the last two millennia, most philosophers were advocates of *natural theology*, a disci-pline that sought to discover what could be known about God through human experience and reason. They believed that God had created us in His image as rational beings and took to heart the words of the apostle Paul when he wrote that "since the creation of the world God's invisible qualities—his eternal power and divine nature—have been clearly seen, being understood from what has been made, so that men are without excuse" (Rom 1:19–20 NIV). And they constructed arguments to show that God exists.

Today, however, many people seem unaware of the classic theistic arguments. And those who know about them tend to believe that all of these arguments have been refuted. In this chapter we will see that this judgment is premature. First, however, we will take a look at the

---

[2] See Richard Dawkins, *The God Delusion* (New York: Houghton Mifflin, 2006); Sam Har-ris, *Letter to a Christian Nation* (New York: Knopf, 2006); and Christopher Hitchens, *God Is Not Great: How Religion Poisons Everything* (New York: Hachette, 2007).

[3] Sam Harris, *Letter to a Christian Nation*, 55–56.

historical development of theistic arguments in order to discern why people have become skeptical of proving God's existence.

6.1.1 Historical Attempts to Prove God's Existence

The earliest recorded arguments for God's existence can be found in some of the ancient Greek philosophers. For example, Plato offers a brief sketch of an argument in his *Laws*.[4] His student Aristotle developed a more detailed case for God. He argued for God's existence as the only basis for explaining how individual, changing things (e.g., cats, dogs, trees, humans) came into being and realized their inherent potentials.[5] However, it wasn't until the Middle Ages (AD 400–1500) that rigorous theistic arguments were developed. In this section, we will survey some of the better-known attempts made by Christian thinkers in the Middle Ages and beyond.

Anselm's Ontological Argument

Anselm of Canterbury (1033–1109) presented several arguments for God's existence, but the most famous one was his *ontological argument*. This ingenuous argument makes the case that the very idea of God proves His existence. Anselm begins his argument with a definition of God as that "than which nothing greater can be conceived."[6] In contemporary lingo, we would say that God is the greatest conceivable being (GCB). Now Anselm thought that everyone either has or at least is able to have an idea of the GCB. The question then arises as to whether or not the GCB actually exists in reality and not merely as an idea in our minds. Anselm was convinced that as soon as we understand the idea of the GCB, we immediately know that He exists. Why? Because it is greater for something to exist in reality than simply as an idea in our minds. So the greatest conceivable being must exist not only in our minds but in reality as well.

To see his point more clearly, Anselm asks us to conduct a thought experiment. He asks us to suppose that the GCB exists merely as an idea in our minds. Well, then, it would turn out that we could conceive of a being *greater* than the GCB, namely, one that exists in reality. But it is logically impossible that there be a being greater than the GCB. Hence, the GCB must exist in reality as well as in the mind.

---

[4] Plato, *Laws* X, in *Plato: The Collected Dialogues*, ed. Edith Hamilton and Huntington Cairns (Princeton, NJ: Princeton University Press, 1961), 1440–65.

[5] Aristotle, *Metaphysics* XII.6–9, in *A New Aristotle Reader*, ed. J. L. Ackrill (Princeton, NJ: Princeton University Press, 1987), 345–53.

[6] Anselm, *Proslogion* II–IV, in *St. Anslem: Basic Writings* (Peru, IL: Open Court, 1962), 7.

It might help you to follow Anselm's logic if we formalize his argument like this:

(1) I have an idea of the greatest conceivable being (GCB).
(2) That which exists in reality (and not only in my mind) is greater than that which exists only in my mind.
(3) If the GCB existed only in my mind, then the GCB would not be the GCB (because I can conceive of it existing in reality, not only in my mind) [see premise (2)].
(4) Therefore, the GCB exists in reality.

So Anselm is arguing that to deny the existence of the GCB is self-contradictory because, as premise (3) informs us, conceiving of the GCB as existing only in the mind leads to the absurd idea that the GCB is not the GCB. Therefore, it follows that the GCB really exists. So it seems that Anselm has constructed an airtight argument.

The argument has not been without its critics. In Anselm's own day, a monk named Gaunilo claimed that this argument, if it works at all, could be used to prove the existence of anything, such as the "greatest island." Anselm (and many of his defenders) thought that Gaunilo was mistaken: the argument could prove the existence of only one being, namely the greatest conceivable being (i.e., God). The reason, supposedly, was that denying the existence of things like the greatest island does not lead to a contradiction.

A more influential criticism came from Immanuel Kant (1724–1804). He rejected the second premise of the argument, which claims that it is greater to exist in reality than to exist merely as an idea. Kant believed that this premise made the unwarranted assumption that "existence" is a property. Only if existence is a property can it make sense to say that existence adds something to a being that makes it greater than it would be without it. But Kant did not believe that existence is a property. One is not adding an additional property to the concept of a thing when one says that the thing actually exists. Rather, to say that something exists is merely to say that a particular concept corresponds to something in reality.

Aquinas's Cosmological Argument

Thomas Aquinas (1225–1274) is undoubtedly the greatest philosopher of the medieval period. One of the things he is most famous for is his "five ways" of proving God's existence.[7] Three of the five ways (the three considered the most effective) are versions of the *cosmological argument*. Cosmological arguments attempt to prove the existence of

---

[7] Thomas Aquinas, *Summa Theologica*, Ia.2.3.

God from the existence of some dependent, finite beings in the world. Aquinas's second way is called the "Argument from Causation" and may be outlined as follows:

(1) There is an order of causes in the world.
(2) Nothing can be the cause of itself.
(3) Hence, everything that is caused is caused by something else.
(4) There cannot be an infinite regress of causes.
(5) Therefore, there must be a first, uncaused cause (i.e., God).

Premise (1) is based on the observation that some things in the world cause other things or events to happen. It is important to note, however, that when Aquinas refers to efficient causes here, he is referring to causes of a thing's present, ongoing existence, not only its coming into being. The cause of something's coming into being usually lies in the past and may cease to exist while the thing it causes can go on existing. For example, the cause of your coming into being was your parents, and the cause of their coming into being was your grandparents. If your parents and grandparents were no longer living, it would not affect your existence. Aquinas's argument is not just about these kinds of causes. It is also about causes of present, ongoing existence. Though your parents brought you into existence, they are not what is causing you to exist *now*. Your present cause is a combination of such factors such as the food you eat, the air you breathe, and the physical forces that hold your atoms together. Aquinas points out that nothing can be the cause of itself in this way. Something dependent on other factors for its existence cannot cause the existence of those very factors on which it depends. Put another way, something cannot cause its own existence because then it would have to exist before it existed, which is absurd. So premise (2) seems true.

Premise (3) is a conclusion drawn from (1) and (2). If there are causes of present existence and nothing can be its own cause, then anything that is caused must be caused by something else. But, premise (4) informs us that a chain of causes cannot proceed to infinity. Suppose you want to know what is the cause of some phenomenon A and you are told that B caused A. You then ask what caused B and are told that B is caused by C, and C by D, and so on. Aquinas argues that one cannot go on like this forever. Why not? Because such a procedure only postpones a causal explanation; it doesn't actually provide one. To illustrate, imagine a chain of railroad box cars [see figure 6.1]. And let us imagine that the box cars are moving in a particular direction.

Suppose you ask of box car A what is causing it to move. Suppose I tell you that the box car directly in front of A, box car B, is pulling A. But,

Figure 6.1

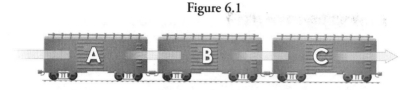

then, what is causing B to move? Well, box car C, of course! Have I really told you why box car A is moving? Not at all. And no matter how many more box cars down the line I cite as the cause for A's motion, I will never provide you with a causal explanation for the motion of A or any of the other box cars in the series. The reason is that box cars do not have the intrinsic power to make other box cars move. Each box car in the series is simply an *instrumental* cause, not a real cause. That is, each box car is an instrument through which something else that has intrinsic causal power (an engine) must channel its power if any of the box cars are to move. So in an infinite series of instrumental causes, there will be no real causation.

Aquinas argues that an infinite chain of causes in the world would contain only instrumental causes and thus no real cause. Therefore, there cannot be an infinite regress of causes. Sooner or later, we must come to the existence of something that has intrinsic causal power that is not itself caused by another. We must come, that is, to the existence of a first, uncaused cause. Aquinas believed that this uncaused cause must be God.

Numerous objections have been offered to Aquinas's argument. For example, some have said that even if the argument proves the existence of a first cause, there is no reason to believe that this first cause is God or anything much like God. Others have claimed that the argument need not lead to the existence of only one first cause. For if we start with some single, finite being A and trace its chain of causes to a first cause, what reason do we have to believe that the chain of causes for another being B will end with the very *same* first cause? For all we know, the objection goes, there could be as many first, uncaused causes as there are finite beings to be explained.

A more serious objection claims that the crucial premise (4) depends upon the *principle of sufficient reason* (PSR). The PSR states there is an explanation for every contingent fact. But, the critic asks, why should we believe that? Why can't there be some unexplainable facts—things which simply do not have rational explanations? If the PSR is false, then we may reject premise (4) and accept the possibility that there can be an infinite regress of instrumental causes or else affirm that the world is, in the words of Bertrand Russell, a "brute fact."

Paley's Teleological Argument

William Paley (1743–1805) offered an argument for God's existence that has become the most popular of them all. In his teleological or "design" argument, he likened the universe to a watch that exhibits the characteristics of intelligent design.[8] He asks us what we would think if we stumbled upon a watch lying in a meadow. Would we think that the watch, like a nearby rock, was the product of random, natural events? Surely not. We would recognize that the watch, unlike the rock, was the product of the purposeful artifice of an intelligent being. Why? Because it has many intricate and interrelated parts that work together for a purpose. Likewise with the universe. It, too, is comprised of many complex and interrelated parts that work together for various purposes. Hence, the universe, like the watch, must be the product of intelligent design.

Notice that Paley's argument takes the form of an argument from analogy. Such arguments draw conclusions about a particular entity based upon its similarities with other things. The general structure of arguments from analogy looks like this:

> Entity x has properties *a*, *b*, *c*, and *d*.
> Entity y has properties *a*, *b*, and *c*.
> Therefore, entity y probably also has property *d*.

Thus, Paley's teleological argument may be formalized as follows:

(1) A watch has many complex parts, works toward an end, is unified, and is intelligently designed.

(2) The universe has many complex parts, works toward an end, and is unified.

(3) Therefore, the universe is probably intelligently designed.

The skeptical philosopher David Hume (1711–1776) leveled numerous criticisms at the teleological argument.[9] First of all, he challenged the strength of the analogy between the universe and human artifacts like watches. Arguments from analogy derive their degree of probability from the number of ways in which the items being compared are actually similar. But, if the items are similar in only a few ways, or if there are significant *dis*similarities, then the analogy carries little weight. Hume thought that watches and universes were not very similar. Perhaps they both have intricate, interrelated parts, but in what other ways are they alike? Not many, Hume thought. Moreover, they have many differences. For example, watches are relatively small while the universe is unimagin-

---

[8] William Paley, *Natural Theology* (1802).
[9] David Hume, *Dialogues Concerning Natural Religion* (1779).

ably large; watches have a clearly discernible purpose (to tell time), but what is the universe's purpose?

Second, Hume argued that we know that things like watches are intelligently designed because we have seen them made and we have many, many examples in our experience to draw from. That is, we conclude that human artifacts are made by intelligent beings because we have observed intelligent beings making them on multiple occasions. But, there is only one universe and no human being was around to observe its origin. Hence, we cannot know if it has an intelligent designer or not.

Third, for all we know, the complex organization of the universe could have come about by chance. Hume would say it is even possible (though unlikely) that watches could come about by chance. So we cannot be certain that the universe's complexity, the cause and origin of which we have no direct experience, did not arise by chance.

Fourth, even if the universe was designed by an intelligent being, why would we suppose that it was God? Hume pointed out that we need attribute no more power and intelligence to the designer of the universe than is required to explain the universe as it is. No doubt the designer would have to be very powerful and smart to design the universe, but we need not suppose that he is all-powerful, all-knowing, or perfectly good. Indeed, the evidence might suggest that we consider the designer to be finite in power, knowledge and goodness. After all, the universe is filled with much chaos and evil.

Who Has the Last Word?

In the previous section, we surveyed three historical attempts to prove God's existence. We saw that all of the arguments—ontological, cosmological, and teleological—have been subjected to various criticisms. The criticisms of Immanuel Kant and David Hume, especially, have been considered by many subsequent thinkers to be decisive. This is one reason why today people tend to think that God's existence cannot be proven. They credit Kant, Hume, and others with having demolished the traditional theistic arguments.

However, things are not that simple. The critics of the theistic arguments need not have the last word on this subject. The fact is that many of the criticisms offered by Kant, Hume, and others, have been addressed by defenders of the arguments. In some cases, the critics have misunderstood the arguments they were critiquing. For example, Aquinas never intended his second theistic argument to establish by itself that the first cause was God. He believed that his "five ways" taken together could provide a cumulative case for the existence of God. Further, he offered additional arguments by which he attempted to infer many of the divine attributes from the nature of a first cause.

In other cases, it may be argued that the criticisms themselves fail. Perhaps, for example, the principle of sufficient reason can be defended. If so, then the cosmological argument is unscathed by that objection. Perhaps Kant is wrong in his objection to the ontological argument when he claims that existence is not a property. And perhaps Hume is wrong in suggesting that the origin of the universe needs to have been observed in order for Paley's watch analogy to work.

Most importantly, it must be noted that there are many versions of the theistic arguments. Even if Kant and Hume demolished the versions of the arguments we surveyed above, there are other versions that have been developed—many of which are designed to avoid the problems associated with the earlier arguments. Next we will look at some contemporary theistic arguments that seem to overcome many of the standard criticisms. The critics, we will see, do not have the last word on arguments for God's existence.

6.1.2 Two Contemporary Arguments for God's Existence

There are contemporary varieties of all of the traditional theistic arguments (ontological, cosmological, and teleological). Indeed there are multiple versions of each type. We cannot look at all of them here. However, we will examine the two arguments that many contemporary philosophers of religion consider to be the most compelling. These are varieties of the cosmological and teleological arguments.

The Fine-Tuning Argument

The *fine-tuning argument* is a version of the teleological argument. This version, however, has some decided advantages over Paley's famous watchmaker argument examined above. First, it is not an argument from analogy and thus does not suffer from the liabilities that such arguments tend to have, like those pointed out by Hume. Second, it appeals to the latest research in contemporary physics and cosmology.

Modern scientists have discovered that the structure of the universe as we know it was dictated by the precise values of certain "cosmic constants"–factors such as the amount of energy, the rate of expansion, the distribution of matter, the force of gravity, and such, which existed at the first instant of the so-called "Big Bang." At that precise moment, these and other cosmic constants had specific numerical values. Had the values of these constants been only slightly different than they actually were at the point of the Big Bang, then it would have been impossible for life to have arisen anywhere in the universe. Here are a few examples:[10]

1. *The rate of expansion*–if the explosion of the Big Bang had been only slightly different than it actually was (by, say, as little as one part in 10^{60}), then the universe would have either quickly collapsed or expanded far too rapidly for stars to form. In either case, life would have been impossible.

2. *The strong nuclear force*–if the force that binds protons and neutrons together had been only 5 percent weaker or stronger, then life would have been impossible.

3. *The force of gravity*–if gravity had been stronger or weaker by only 1 part in 10^{40}, then stars like our sun that are amenable to life would not have formed.

These are only a few of many such cosmic constants, and all of them are likewise "fine-tuned" for life. If any one of them had had a different value than it in fact did, then whatever universe resulted from the Big Bang would not have been life supportive. As it turns out, however, the cosmic constants had just those "settings" that would result in a life-sustaining universe. Given this cosmic "fine-tuning," we may construct an argument as follows:

(1) The fine-tuning of the universe is due either to necessity, chance, or intelligent design.

(2) The fine-tuning of the universe is not due to necessity or chance.

(3) Therefore, the fine-tuning is due to intelligent design.

The first premise of the argument exhausts the logical possibilities. Thus it has the luxury of being necessarily true. Premise (2), then, is the crucial premise. Why should we think it is true? First, it does not seem that the fine-tuning can be due to necessity, whether logical or physical. There is no law of logic or of physics that demands that the values of the cosmic constants be what they were rather than some other values. In other words, there seems to be no reason why the rate of expansion at the first instant of the Big Bang had to be what it was. Nor is there any reason why the distribution of matter had to be what it was. We can

---

[10] These examples are borrowed from Robin Collins, "A Scientific Argument for the Existence of God: The Fine-Tuning Design Argument" in *Reason for the Hope Within*, ed. Michael Murray (Grand Rapids, MI: Eerdmans, 1999), 49.

easily imagine a universe that contained more or less energy than the actual universe, or one that had more or less overall gravity. These cosmic
constants could have been different. And if they had been only slightly
different, life would be impossible.

What about chance? No doubt, the fine-tuning of the universe *could*
be due to chance. The question, though, is whether or not it would be *rational* for us to accept this possibility. The probability of the fine-tuning
happening by chance is astronomical. Robin Collins, for example, likens
the probability of the universe's fine-tuning occurring by chance to hitting an inch-wide target on a dart-board the size of the galaxy.[11] It would
be highly unlikely, to say the least.

Some have objected at this point by saying that the universe had to
have *some* configuration of cosmic constants, and we should not be surprised that the combination that came up happened to be life-support-
ive. After all, if the cosmic constants had some other combination of values, we wouldn't be around to wonder about it! But this objection will
not do. To see why, consider the following science fiction story.[12] A man
is abducted by space aliens and taken to their home planet. Once there,
he is placed in a large arena that also contains a huge pile of straw. He is
told that he must reach into the pile and pull out the shortest straw. If
he fails to do so, he will be instantly disintegrated. The man takes a deep
breath, closes his eyes, and pulls out a straw. When he opens his eyes, to
his amazement, he finds that he has drawn the shortest straw!

Now, the man (and we) can draw one of two conclusions from his
unexpected survival. Either (1) he got very lucky or (2) the game was
rigged. Both conclusions are logically possible. But which one would we
be more rational in believing? Obviously, the more rational conclusion
is that the game was rigged by an intelligent being. This is how it is with
the fine-tuning of the universe. A chance explanation is *possible*, but we
would be irrational to believe it.

The upshot of all this is that it seems that the universe was fine-tuned
by an intelligent agency for the express purpose of allowing life to exist
and thrive on this planet. This seems to be the only reasonable conclusion. Since the fine-tuning of the universe is due neither to necessity nor
chance, it must be due to intelligent design.

There is perhaps one way in which a skeptic might avoid the conclusion of this argument. He could adopt what is called the *many-universes
hypothesis*. If the Big Bang from which developed our universe is the
only Big Bang that has ever occurred, then the fine-tuning that we ob-

[11] See Collins, "A Scientific Argument for the Existence of God," 54–55, 68–70.

[12] We have borrowed this example from Peter van Inwagen, *Metaphysics* (San Francisco:
Westview, 1993), 135–36.

serve would indeed suggest the existence of an intelligent designer. But some scientists suggest that our Big Bang is not the only one. Perhaps there have been many previous Big Bangs and resultant universes, most of which were not life-supporting. If so, then the existence of a "finely-tuned" universe would not be as surprising. To illustrate, if I play one and only one game of poker, it might be surprising if the first hand I draw is a royal flush. But if I play thousands of poker games, one might surmise that sooner or later a royal flush is going to be dealt.

The many-universes hypothesis, however, has several problems. For one thing, it is an *ad hoc* hypothesis. We have no reason whatsoever to believe there have been many previous universes. There are no empirical observations or philosophical arguments that would suggest their existence. The only motive one could have for believing this hypothesis is to avoid the conclusion that the universe was intelligently designed. For another thing, we should ask what natural mechanism or law exists which could produce all these universes? It would seem that any such "universe generator" would be sufficiently complex to require an intelligent designer itself!

Another rather facile objection to the argument is what is called the "Who Designed the Designer?" objection. As atheist Richard Dawkins puts it,

> The whole argument turns on the familiar question "Who made God?", which most thinking people discover for themselves. A designer God cannot be used to explain organized complexity because any God capable of designing anything would have to be complex enough to demand the same kind of explanation in his own right.[13]

Such an objection actually misses the point of the argument. Whether the designer of the universe is complex or not, and whether or not he requires a designer, the fine-tuning argument for the intelligent design of the universe is unaffected. To see why, suppose that the rugged archaeologist Indiana Jones stumbles upon a large stone obelisk while exploring the Himalayas looking for the lost city of Shangri-la. Engraved on the obelisk is the following sequence of markings:

SHANGRI-LA WAS ONCE HERE

Indiana Jones immediately reaches the conclusion that intelligent beings, probably human, placed the obelisk there and that the markings communicate an intelligible message. However, Jones's native guide Snikwad demurs. He says, "No, Dr. Jones. Appealing to intelligent

[13] Richard Dawkins, *The God Delusion*, 109.

design is no explanation at all. If there were an intelligent designer, he would be far more complex than the markings on this obelisk and so would also require an intelligent designer. Better to chalk it up to glacier erosion or something." At this point, Indiana pulls out his whip and gives Snikwad a thrashing.

The point is this. Even if the designer is complex and in need of explanation himself, the appeal to design is nonetheless informative and plausible. Whether the designer is himself designed or not, the markings on the obelisk demand the conclusion that they were produced by an intelligent agent. Likewise—and even much more so—the evidence from the fine-tuning of the universe points to the conclusion that the universe was designed by an intelligent agency. We might like to have more information about the nature of the designer, but that is irrelevant to the conclusion we should draw regarding the nature of the universe.

Still, someone might ask, even if the teleological argument is sound, what have we really proven? At best, we have proven that the universe was designed by an intelligent being. But do we have to believe that this designer is *God*? Perhaps the intelligent designer was a very powerful, very wise, but simply finite being.

Fair enough. Strictly speaking, this argument does not *prove* the existence of God. Nevertheless, it strongly *confirms* belief in God—if God exists and designed the universe, then the fine-tuning that we observe in the universe is exactly what we would expect to see. That is, the fine-tuning of the universe is consistent with, and provides support for, the Christian worldview. But it poses a big problem for the atheistic worldview. Indeed, so impressive is the strength of this kind of design argument, that life-long atheist Antony Flew recently converted to theism as a result of examining the evidence for the universe's fine-tuning. In an interview about his conversion, Flew said, "I think that the most impressive arguments for God's existence are those that are supported by recent scientific discoveries" and that now "the argument to Intelligent Design is enormously stronger than it was when I first met it."[14]

The Kalam Cosmological Argument

There are multiple versions of the cosmological argument, many of which are very useful. We will examine one version that has gained great support in recent years and is perhaps the most compelling: the *Kalam cosmological argument*. The Kalam argument originated with Arabic philosophers in the Middle Ages but has recently been taken up by Chris-

---

[14] Antony Flew and Gary Habermas, "My Pilgrimage from Atheism to Theism: An Exclusive Interview with Former British Atheist Professor Antony Flew," *Philosophia Christi* 6:2 (Winter 2004): 197–212.

tian philosophers, especially William Lane Craig and J. P. Moreland.[15] The argument has three stages in which the following claims are successively established:

1. The universe had a beginning.
2. The beginning of the universe was caused.
3. The cause of the beginning of the universe was God.

We will discuss arguments in support of each of these claims and consider some objections as well.

1. *The universe had a beginning.* This first stage in the Kalam argument can be defended both philosophically and scientifically. The philosophical argument may be stated as follows:

(1) If the universe had no beginning, then an actually infinite number of events would have occurred prior to the present moment.
(2) It is impossible that an actually infinite number of events occurred prior to the present moment.
(3) Therefore, the universe had a beginning.

Premise (1) of this argument is uncontroversial. It is clear that if the universe literally had no beginning, then the past is infinitely long. That is, the set comprising all past events would contain an actual infinite number of members.

The crucial premise is (2). William Lane Craig and others have shown that an infinite number of concrete entities, including historical events, cannot exist because it would lead to absurdities. Before defending this assertion, let's first clarify what is and is not being claimed in this premise. First, we are not denying that a *potential* infinite series can exist. This refers to a series which can potentially increase indefinitely but which at any given point is always finite. For example, consider the process of counting all the whole numbers. Someone may start counting the whole numbers—1, 2, 3, 4, 5 . . . —and, if he could stay alive, he could continue counting them without end. Yet, no matter how long he counts, he will have only counted a finite number of numbers. Potential infinites can exist, but what our argument asserts is that no *actual, concrete* infinite series can exist. An actual infinite series is a set that already contains an infinite number of members. The set of whole numbers can be said to be comprised of an actual infinite series. So, secondly, we can

---

[15] William Lane Craig, *Reasonable Faith: Christian Truth and Apologetics* (Wheaton, IL: Crossway, 1994), 91–122; J. P. Moreland, *Scaling the Secular City: A Defense of Christianity* (Grand Rapids: Baker, 1987), 18–42.

agree that actual infinites may exist in the realm of the abstract (e.g., in mathematics). But what the Kalam argument claims is that there cannot be an actual infinite in *concrete* reality.

To see why, consider the fact that actual infinites have some very peculiar properties. For example, unlike finite sets, actually infinite sets are such that some proper subsets can be placed in one-to-one correspondence with the original set. So, again, take the set of whole numbers (1, 2, 3, 4, 5 . . .). A proper subset of this set would be the set of even numbers. Notice, however, that the members of this subset can be matched one-to-one with the whole of the original set:

1	2	3	4	5	6 . . .
2	4	6	8	10	12 . . .

Another peculiar characteristic of infinite sets is that you cannot increase or decrease their total by adding to them or subtracting from them. Infinity minus one equals infinity. Likewise, infinity plus one is infinity. In fact, infinity plus infinity is still infinity! With all this in mind, we can see why there cannot be an actual infinite in concrete reality.

Imagine a library that contains an actual infinite number of books.[16] And let us suppose that the books alternate in color such that half the books are red and half the books are blue. And let us further suppose that someone visits the library and checks out all of the red books. How many books are left in the library? As unbelievable as it sounds, according to infinite set theory, the same number of books remains in the library as before the visitor arrived! But surely there could not really be such a library—a library in which half the books are checked out and yet the number of books in the library is not diminished! In other words, to accept the reality of a library with an infinite number of books would require us to accept the logical absurdity that $X=\frac{1}{2}X$. The idea that an actual infinite series exists in concrete reality is logically absurd. And for this reason there cannot be an infinite number of past beings or events. So the universe must have had a beginning.

The second premise of our argument may be defended another way. It turns out that even if we could grant that an actual infinite might exist, it could not be "crossed" or formed one-at-a-time by successive addition. Consider once again the idea that the universe has no beginning. Then, as we have seen, the set of past events comprises an actual infinite. But, that means that in order for history to have reached the present moment, an infinite number of past events would have to have

---

[16] We owe this illustration to William Lane Craig. See William Lane Craig and Quentin Smith, *Theism, Atheism, and Big Bang Cosmology* (Oxford: Oxford University Press, 1993), 12–13.

been "crossed" or formed one-at-a-time, since history progresses linearly and is not given all at once.

The problem with this is that, by definition, an infinite cannot be formed by successive addition—which means that an infinite number of past events cannot be crossed to reach the present moment. A set with a number of members that can be traversed or completed is, by definition, a finite set. It is just not possible to cross an actual infinite. To illustrate, try to imagine someone finishing counting all of the whole numbers. You cannot imagine it, can you? Better yet, imagine a man who has been counting the negative numbers from infinity: . . . . -3, -2, -1, 0 (here 0 represents the present moment). Why didn't he finish counting yesterday? Or last year? Or a million years ago? Think about it. If the past is infinitely long, then not only is it the case that an infinite number of past events preceded the present moment, it is also the case that an infinite number of past events preceded yesterday, and last year, and a million years ago. That is, if the past is infinite, then prior to any point in the past, there was an infinite number of past events. But if an infinite *can* be crossed, then at *any* point in the past our hypothetical counter will have *already* crossed an infinite. As William Lane Craig explains,

> Thus, at no time in the infinite past could we ever find the man finishing his countdown, for by that point he should already be done! In fact, no matter how far back into the past we go, we can never find the man counting at all, for at any point we reach he will already have finished. But, if at no point in the past do we find him counting, this contradicts the hypothesis that he has been counting from eternity.[17]

As philosopher J. P. Moreland puts it, trying to cross an infinite past is like trying to jump out of a bottomless pit.[18] It simply cannot be done. So the number of past events must be finite, not infinite, and that means that the universe began to exist a finite time ago.

This conclusion is impressively confirmed by modern scientific discoveries. For example, the Big Bang theory indicates that the universe began to exist a finite time ago. According to this theory, the *space-time* universe as we know it began with a big explosion from an immeasurably minute point several billion years ago. If this theory is true (and it has sustained all attempts so far to falsify it), then it implies the conclusion that there was a beginning to the universe.

Another scientific confirmation comes from the *second law of thermodynamics,* which says that ordered systems tend toward maximum

---

[17] William Lane Craig, *Reasonable Faith*, 99.
[18] J. P. Moreland, *Scaling the Secular City*, 31.

entropy. That is, things move from order to disorder; usable energy decreases. So, according to the second law of thermodynamics, the universe is running down, moving toward maximum entropy or randomness. This suggests that the universe is only finitely old. If it had existed for an infinite time, the usable energy would have dissipated a very long time ago.

2. *The beginning of the universe was caused.* The second step of the Kalam cosmological argument is relatively easy. It is usually taken as a metaphysical truism that something cannot come from nothing. That is, whatever begins to exist must have a cause for its existence. Though some philosophers have denied this principle, the burden is clearly on them to give us a reason to believe that something could literally "pop" into existence uncaused from nothing. Indeed we have no reason to believe that this could happen and every reason to balk at such a notion.

All of us, even the most skeptical philosophers, operate every day on the assumption that whatever begins to be has a cause. Without this assumption science would be impossible. Indeed, daily experience as we know it would be impossible since so much of our experience is based on cause-and-effect reasoning. No one really believes that a tiger might pop into existence uncaused in one's living room. So why should we think things work any differently when we are talking about the beginning of the universe? There is no reason to think so. Hence, we can conclude that whatever begins to exist has a cause. Since, as we saw above, the universe began to exist, we may conclude that the beginning of the universe had a cause.

3. *The cause of the universe was God.* So far, we have shown that the universe had a beginning and that the universe had a cause. But can we know anything more specific about the nature of the cause of the universe? Some deny that we can. Once in a public debate on the existence of God an atheist made exactly this claim when critiquing the Kalam argument. He said, "Maybe the cause of the universe was a really small particle of matter." However, this individual was seriously mistaken. The cause of the universe could not have been a particle of matter or anything else that is physical. Indeed, we can show that the cause of the universe was almost certainly a *personal* being with attributes identical to the Judeo-Christian God.[19] For example, the cause of the universe must be:

---

[19] For a more detailed discussion of the following points, see William Lane Craig, *Reasonable Faith*, 116–20.

1. *Transcendent* (existing outside of time and space) because it is the creator of the space-time universe.
2. *Immutable* (changeless) since to exist outside of time implies the absence of change.
3. *Immaterial* (nonphysical) because materiality requires the potential for change.
4. *Uncaused* because if it were caused, then it would not be the ultimate cause of the universe, and the first event (beginning) of the universe would not have been the first event, which is absurd. Moreover, the fact that the cause is transcendent and immutable implies that it is uncaused and self-existent.
5. *Exceedingly powerful*, if not omnipotent, because it brought the universe into existence from nothing.
6. *Personal* because only a personal agent who can act and will for things to happen apart from prior physical conditions is adequate to explain the beginning of the universe. We have seen that the cause must be immaterial. The only immaterial things that we are familiar with that have causal power are persons. Moreover, personal beings are volitional (make choices), intentional (act for purposes), and conscious. In creating the world, the creator had to make certain conscious choices and acted for an end. Therefore, the creator is personal.
7. *Good* because he apparently designed a very complex universe with uniform laws that enable humans to live and thrive.

So we can see that the cause of the universe was a personal agent who has many of the attributes that the Bible ascribes to God. Therefore, it is reasonable for us to believe that the Kalam cosmological argument proves the existence of *God*.

There are many other arguments for God's existence than the ones we have been able to survey in this chapter. Some are better than others. We have presented enough evidence, however, for us to reasonably conclude that Gandalf's words of encouragement to Frodo are not simply fiction. Despite the wishes of Thomas Nagel and the dogmatic insistence of Dawkins and others to the contrary, Gandalf's words reflect a profound reality: the universe was created and continues to be sustained and guided by a transcendent, personal God.

6.1.3 Do We Need Arguments for Rational Belief in God?

The arguments for God's existence that we have surveyed address the suggestion that there is no evidence for God. The arguments ought to dispel this suggestion. There is considerable evidence for the existence of God. But, to address another claim often made by religious skeptics, is it the case that belief in God would be irrational without such arguments? Atheists like Nagel and Dawkins certainly think so, as do some theists. They insist that evidence for God in the form of philosophical arguments is necessary for rational theistic belief.

One primary reason for the demand for evidence is borrowed from the philosopher W. K. Clifford. Recall from chapter 2 Clifford's proposal that there is an "ethics of belief." What we believe can have consequences for other people, and this calls for us to exercise responsibility in acquiring beliefs. For this reason, Clifford insisted that "it is wrong always, everywhere, and for anyone, to believe anything upon insufficient evidence."[20] In other words, Clifford laid down a general principle that rational belief always requires evidence (usually in the form of argumentation). Clifford's principle has come to be known as *evidentialism*. In short, evidentialism is the view that no belief should be held unless one has sufficient evidence for it. It is evidentialism that motivates the claims of those who say that belief in God requires evidence.

Now it is generally agreed that evidentialism is grounded in classical foundationalism. Recall from chapter 2 that the classical foundationalist holds that a belief is properly basic if and only if it is self-evident, incorrigible, or evident to the senses (see section 2.3.1). And it should not be too hard to see that belief in God is not properly basic on this view. First of all, the proposition "God exists" does not appear to be self-evident. It seems that one can deny the existence of God without absurdity unlike statements such as "Bachelors are unmarried." The proposition "Bachelors are not unmarried" is self-contradictory because it is logically equivalent to "Unmarried men are not unmarried," which is obviously absurd. But "God does not exist" is not obviously contradictory in this way. Neither does belief in God seem incorrigible. It is logically possible that I could be mistaken in my belief in God. Many people, in fact, believe that there is powerful evidence *against* God's existence (e.g., due to the problem of evil). Finally, it is obvious that God's existence is not evident to the senses. Theists believe that God is an immaterial Spirit. He is not a physical being. It follows that we cannot directly see, hear, touch, smell, or taste God. So, if classical foundationalism is true (as

---

[20] W. K. Clifford, "The Ethics of Belief," in *Lectures and Essays* (London: Macmillan, 1879); reprinted in *Classics of Philosophy*, 2nd ed., ed. Louis P. Pojman (Oxford: Oxford University Press, 2003), 1065.

well as evidentialism), then the only way to rationally believe in God is to provide good arguments for His existence.

We also saw in chapter 2, however, that there are compelling reasons to reject classical foundationalism. It is self-defeating and, if true, it would render unjustified most of the ordinary beliefs that we think are perfectly justified. And since evidentialism is based on classical foundationalism, we have reason to reject *it*, too. Why should belief in God require evidence? Even if there are no good arguments for God's existence, as Dawkins and others suggest, why must we assume that belief in God is somehow rationally deficient?

Along with philosopher Alvin Plantinga we can ask: Why can't belief in God be properly basic? Consider one of our sensory faculties such as vision. When I peer out my window, for example, and see a tree in my front yard, I naturally and automatically form the belief, "There is a tree in my front yard." I do not infer the existence of the tree by means of any argument. I simply form the belief due to my immediate visual experience of it. My belief that there is a tree in my front yard is properly basic. Well, what if, following the Protestant Reformer John Calvin, human beings have been created by God with a *sensus divinitatis* (a sense of the divine)—a cognitive faculty analogous to vision that produces belief in God in appropriate circumstances? What if we are created such that, when we gaze upon the starry heavens or contemplate the beauty of the sunset, we naturally and inevitably come to believe that God exists? (And what if those who do not come to believe in God in such circumstances are suffering from the negative effects of sin upon their minds?) In such circumstances there would be nothing irrational about believing in God. And belief in God in such circumstances would constitute a properly basic belief. This view that belief in God can be properly basic is an aspect of what has come to be called *Reformed epistemology*, and it has gained acceptance among many contemporary philosophers. Though there are good arguments for belief in God, such arguments are not necessary for rational belief.

Some have objected to Reformed epistemology by claiming that it makes belief in God completely groundless and arbitrary. This objection is known as the "Great Pumpkin Objection." The idea of the Great Pumpkin comes from Charles Schulz's famous comic strip *Peanuts*. One character in the comic strip, Linus, looks forward each Halloween to the arrival of the Great Pumpkin. Of course, neither Linus (nor anyone else) has ever seen or heard the Great Pumpkin, and the Great Pumpkin never shows up. Nonetheless, Linus faithfully awaits his arrival each year, undaunted by past experience and the taunts of his friends. According to the Great Pumpkin objection, if we accept the idea that belief in God can be properly basic, then *any* belief—even Linus's obviously irrational belief in the Great Pumpkin—could be properly basic.

However, the objection falsely assumes that belief in God, if taken as properly basic, would be *groundless*. This need not be the case. Just as my belief that there is a tree outside my window is grounded in my visual experience of the tree, so my belief in God may be similarly grounded. A person may see (or at least think he sees) God's hand at work around him. Plantinga provides some salient examples:

> Upon reading the Bible, one may be impressed with a deep sense that God is speaking to him. Upon having done what I know is cheap, or wrong, or wicked, I may feel guilty in God's sight and form the belief *God disapproves of what I have done.* Upon confession and repentance I may feel forgiven, forming the belief *God forgives me for what I have done.*[21]

If indeed God exists and has created us to experience Him in such ways, then such grounding experiences would be veridical. In that case, then *of course* my belief in God would be properly basic. But even if God does not exist and my experiences are not veridical, then my beliefs are *still* properly basic because these experiences make it seem to me that God exists. When you believe that you had toast for breakfast because you remember it, you could be mistaken—you could have a faulty memory or it could be the case that you were created only five minutes ago with false memories implanted in your brain. Nevertheless, your belief would still be properly basic. A false belief may be properly basic just as a false belief may be justified. All that proper basicality requires is that you have some ground for your belief, not that you know that your belief is true.

A related worry that is often raised regarding Reformed epistemology is that belief in God as properly basic would make this belief immune to criticism. If I need no evidence for my belief in God, then does this mean that no amount of evidence can ever warrant my giving up that belief? Does Reformed epistemology lead to an irrational dogmatism? The answer is no. A belief can be properly basic and yet be subject to defeaters. Recall that a defeater is a proposition or set of propositions that provide counterevidence to another proposition. And since a belief can be properly basic without being self-evident or incorrigible, it is certainly possible for a properly basic belief to be challenged by counterevidence. Suppose, again, that I believe that there is a tree outside my window and I believe this because, when I look out the window, I see it. However, suppose also that one of my colleagues, whom I know to be

---

[21] Alvin Plantinga, "Reason and Belief in God," in *Faith and Rationality*, ed. Alvin Plantinga and Nicholas Wolterstorff (Norte Dame: University of Notre Dame, 1983), 80.

trustworthy, informs me that what I take to be a tree is really a papier-mâché replica of a tree placed outside my window overnight by some college pranksters and that the real tree that I remember seeing on previous occasions is being obscured by the replica. In this case, I now have a potential defeater for my original belief. And if other evidence can be brought to bear to support my colleague's assertion (e.g., I go outside and see with my own eyes and feel with my own hands that what I took to be a tree was in fact a papier-mâché replica), then my originally properly basic belief is defeated.

A defeater for a properly basic belief in God would be evidence against the existence of God. For example, the existence of evil is often cited as evidence for the nonexistence of God. If a theist is confronted with such a potential defeater, then (at least in the absence of a defeater-defeater) a properly basic belief in God may be defeated. So it is not the case that Reformed epistemology makes belief in God immune to criticism.

Does God exist? There is good evidence to think He does. And even without that evidence it can still be rational to believe in God. Of course, there are many questions that our discussion so far leaves unanswered. One of these concerns the nature of God. It is one thing to know that God (or a God) exists, but what is God like? This is the question we consider next.

Questions for Reflection

1. What do you think of the whole enterprise of trying to prove God's existence? Is it somehow irreligious or incompatible with faith? Why or why not?

2. Gaunilo's objection to Anselm's ontological argument amounted to replacing the greatest conceivable *being* in the argument with the greatest conceivable *island* and claiming that if the argument could prove the existence of former, then it could also prove the latter. Is Gaunilo right? Or is Anselm correct in claiming that his argument works only to prove the existence of the greatest conceivable *being*?

3. A common objection to Aquinas's cosmological argument is that it does not prove that there must be only one first cause. Can you think of a way that Aquinas might respond to this objection?

4. The principle of sufficient reason (PSR) has been questioned by many philosophers who ask, "Why must we believe that every contingent fact has an explanation?" What answer might be given in defense of the PSR?

5. The fine-tuning argument depends upon theories in contemporary science. Is this a problem? Why or why not?

6. Some critics of the Kalam cosmological argument say that it is true that one cannot "cross" an actual infinite number of past events *if one only has a finite time in which to do it.* But if one has an infinite amount of time, then one can traverse an infinite past. What do you think of this objection?

7. When confronted with a defeater to a properly basic belief in God, what is the believer's epistemic obligation? How strong must a defeater be to require one to give up his belief in God?

§ 6.2 What Is God Like?

One of the most important documents in the history of the Christian church is the *Westminster Confession of Faith.* Although more than three centuries old, it remains a touchstone on all matters of Christian doctrine. In that confession we find this statement:

> There is but one only, living, and true God, who is infinite in being and perfection, a most pure spirit, invisible, without body, parts, or passions; immutable, immense, eternal, incomprehensible, almighty, most wise, most holy, most free, most absolute; working all things according to the counsel of His own immutable and most righteous will, for His own glory; most loving, gracious, merciful, long-suffering, abundant in goodness and truth.... God hath all life, glory, goodness, blessedness, in and of Himself; and is alone in and unto Himself all-sufficient.... His knowledge is infinite, infallible, and independent upon the creature, so as nothing is to Him contingent, or uncertain.[22]

Most of the attributes ascribed to God in this statement are non-controversial among theists in the Judeo-Christian tradition. However, some of them have been the focus of considerable debate among both philosophers and theologians, specifically the attributes of immutability (God's being changeless), eternality (God's transcending time), impassibility (God's lacking passions), omnipotence (God's being almighty), and omniscience (God's knowing all things). And in most cases the debate has not concerned whether God has a particular attribute so much as what the attribute really *means.* In this section we will discuss most of these, and in the next section we will look at the problem of evil, which essentially centers on the attribute of divine benevolence.

[22] *The Westminster Confession of Faith,* II, 1–2.

6.2.1 Divine Omnipotence and Atemporality

Although the divine attributes of omnipotence and eternality are affirmed by all theists, there has been some disagreement over just what it means to ascribe these characteristics to God. In this section we will discuss both of these.

Divine Omnipotence

What does it mean to say that God is omnipotent? Some have defined this attribute as the power to do anything at all. But this definition raises some difficult questions. For example, can God make a square circle? Or can God make an object that is red all over and green all over at the same time? Surely we cannot answer these questions affirmatively, because such objects are self-contradictions. It seems, then, that there are things that God cannot do. This seems to imply, then, that God is *not* omnipotent, at least as we defined it above. How are we to deal with this problem? Thomas Aquinas showed that this problem can be avoided with a simple qualification to the definition.[23] Omnipotence is not the power to do anything whatsoever. Rather, it is *the power to do anything that is logically possible.* And the "logically possible" refers to anything that does not imply a contradiction. Both the notion of a square circle and that of an object that is simultaneously red all over and green all over are logically impossible, so it is not a true limitation on God's power that He is incapable of creating such things.

Contemporary philosopher of religion Richard Swinburne affirms Aquinas's approach to qualifying the concept of omnipotence. But Swinburne notes that there are actually two kinds of things that an all-powerful being cannot be reasonably expected to do.[24] One category includes the sorts of things we have already considered—things that are logically impossible. But there is another category of things God cannot do, namely anything which contradicts His own nature. Thus, while the concept of doing an evil deed is not inherently self-contradictory, this is impossible for God because He is morally perfect. Similarly, the idea of killing oneself is logically coherent, but for God to kill Himself is impossible because He is a necessary and eternal being, incapable of ceasing to exist. Therefore, God can be omnipotent while also being incapable of doing such things because they violate His nature.

Here some philosophers, such as William of Ockham (c. 1287–1347), have objected that these sorts of qualifications to the theistic doctrine of divine omnipotence nonetheless place inappropriate limits on

---

[23] Thomas Aquinas, *Summa Theologica*, Ia.25.3.
[24] Richard Swinburne, *The Coherence of Theism*, rev. ed. (Oxford: Oxford University Press, 1993), 164–65.

God. They complain that such qualifications imply that God is bound by logic. They insist that God is sovereign over logic and that He is capable of even making a truth which violates the law of noncontradiction. So, for example, God can make a square circle and He can make it true that 2+2=5.

However, two points can be made in response to this claim. First, this objection is itself unintelligible. To say that a statement could violate the law of noncontradiction and still be true is nonsense. After all, to say that a statement is "true" is to say that it is *not* false, which *assumes* the law of noncontradiction. So in proposing the objection the critic actually contradicts himself and thus self-defeats. Second, this objection mistakenly assumes that the laws of logic are entities distinct from God. In fact, a more reasonable theistic view of the logical laws is that they are themselves aspects of divine rationality. Logic, we might say, refers to the standards of thought that derive from the ground of all being, namely, God Himself. So to insist that God is bound by logic is, at bottom, just to say that God is bound by His own nature. Consequently, the above qualifications of the doctrine of omnipotence are hardly limitations at all. They only stipulate certain ways in which God must always be God! It is worth noting that Scripture affirms other things that God cannot do, such as lie (Titus 1:2) or change (Mal 3:6). It would violate God's nature to do such things. Here we are making the same point about logic and the nature of God.

Divine Atemporality

If the question of God's relationship to the laws of logic has been controversial, the question of His relationship to time has been all the more so. Historically, theists have affirmed that God transcends time, a view known as divine *atemporalism*. The standard reasons for this view appeal to the nature of God as the beginningless creator of the world, and also to the nature of time itself. With regard to the first point, if God has always existed, then it is hard to imagine how He could be limited in time. The only way to make sense of such a notion would be to affirm that time itself is co-eternal with God, but this is problematic for several reasons. For one thing, some of the most significant philosophical accounts of time, such as those of Augustine and Kant, affirm that time is relative and mind-dependent. Secondly, the relativity of time is also confirmed by science, which tells us that time is relative to such things as velocity and mass. Given the relativity of time, then, it cannot be absolute and co-eternal with God. A further argument for divine atemporalism appeals to the fact that God created the cosmos, which is a space-time continuum. As creator of the world, God must transcend it, materially, spatially, temporally, and in every other way. That God created time is also confirmed by Scripture in such passages as 1 Corinthians 2:7, 2 Timothy 1:9, and Titus 1:2, each of which affirms the fact that time had a beginning. Thus, as a beginningless being, God preexisted time and therefore transcends it.

The notion that God is an inherently temporal being is known as *sempiternalism*. In defense of their view, sempiternalists argue that if God is not essentially temporal, then He cannot be truly personal. For example, a timeless being cannot literally respond to historical events or answer the prayers of human beings. Also, many sempiternalists defend their view on the basis of scriptural accounts of God relenting and regretting some of His own actions, such as His creation of human beings (Gen 6:6) and His making Saul king (1 Sam 15:11). Still other passages indicate that God relents from plans He has made, such as His declaration through Jeremiah: "At one moment I might announce concerning a nation or a kingdom that I will uproot, tear down, and destroy it. However, if that nation I have made an announcement about, turns from its evil, I will not bring the disaster on it I had planned" (Jer 18:7–8). (See also Exod 32:14; Isa 38:1–5; Joel 2:13; Amos 7:1–6; and Jonah 3:10.) These passages seem to describe a God who is genuinely responsive to human choices and who, therefore, is essentially temporal.

In response, atemporalists insist that such biblical language really amounts to a kind of divine accommodation to our finitude. We are limited beings who dwell in space-time, so in order for God to relate to us He must speak in temporal terms. Thus, atemporalists affirm that although God appears to "respond" to historical events and even change His plans for acting in the world, these things are not literally true of Him. These are simply necessary means of communicating to temporal beings.

Atemporalists also point out that biblical descriptions of God's acting in time and His acting in space should be interpreted analogously. Spatial metaphors are used in the Bible to describe God, and certain of His activities take place in space. For instance, in 2 Samuel God declares, "From the time I brought the Israelites out of Egypt until today I have not lived in a house; instead, I have been moving around with the tabernacle tent" (7:6). In many other passages, the "hands," "arm," "mouth," "feet," and "nostrils" of God are referred to, as are His actions in space, such as dwelling in temples and cities and performing miraculous acts of parting seas, healing bodies, and impregnating a virgin. But neither spatial metaphors nor accounts of God's spatial activities should be taken to imply that God is bound by space. Rather, they communicate to us something about God's nature and show that He can and does perform actions in the spatial realm. Similarly, temporal descriptions of God and His actions should be interpreted as showing that He enters and acts in time, not that He is bound by it.[25]

Such recognition of the fact that God acts in space and time creates tension for the atemporalist view, however. How is it that God can truly be atemporal yet also act *within* time? This problem has inspired an intriguing compromise position developed by William Lane Craig, who aims to account for the insights of both atemporalism and sempiternalism. According to Craig, the atemporalists are correct in saying that God created time and transcends it. But he says that the sempiternalists' claim that God dwells in time is also correct. In fact, says Craig, God "exists at every time that ever exists."[26] Craig has dubbed his view divine *omnitemporalism*, since it affirms that

> With the creation of the universe, time began, and God entered into time at the moment of creation in virtue of his real relations with the created order. It follows that God must therefore be timeless without the universe and temporal with the universe.[27]

Because of its capacity to embrace the basic claims of atemporalism and sempiternalism, divine omnitemporalism is very attractive. Unfortunately, this view has its problems as well. For example, it appears to imply that there are two phases in the divine life, one of which is atemporal and the other temporal. And critics claim that this means God changes. However, it is not clear that this objection is a special problem for the omnitemporalist. The two "phases" of the divine life might not involve any more change in God than is implied by the fact that He created the cosmos and performs acts in the space-time realm. Since atemporalists, too, believe that God created the world and performs acts in history, then they seem to face a similar "two phases" problem.

As you can see, the issue of God's relationship to time is extremely challenging, and each view has its problems. But given its explanatory power with regard to the main insights of atemporalism and sempiternalism, the omnitemporalist theory might be the best option available.

6.2.2 Divine Omniscience

Another controversial divine attribute is omniscience. While nearly all theists readily grant that God is all-knowing, there is much debate

---

[25] On this point see Hugh J. McCann, "God Beyond Time," *Philosophy of Religion*, 2nd ed., ed. Louis P. Pojman (Belmont, CA: Wadsworth, 1994), 232.

[26] William Lane Craig, "Timelessness and Omnitemporality," in *God and Time: Four Views*, ed. Gregory E. Ganssle (Downers Grove, IL: InterVarsity, 2001), 153.

[27] Ibid., 156.

over just what this means. The sticking point regards God's knowledge of the future, specifically the future actions of human beings. Traditionally, theists have regarded this as simply an aspect of God's knowledge. However, some philosophers and theologians argue that God's foreknowledge of human actions conflicts with the notion that human beings are free.

For example, suppose that God knows today that a man named Jones will mow his lawn tomorrow. The question arises, then, as to whether or not Jones can do other than mow his lawn tomorrow. If Jones *could* do other than mow his lawn tomorrow, he would have to be able to bring it about tomorrow that God has a different belief today than He in fact has. But it is dubious that Jones has this ability. How can Jones do anything tomorrow to make it the case that God's belief today was different? A highly intuitive principle is *the principle of the fixity of the past*. This principle states that the past is irrevocably fixed and unchangeable. What's done is done. Not even God can make it the case that a past event did not happen. So how can Jones make it the case that God's believing he would mow his lawn did not happen? And since all of God's beliefs are true and therefore constitute knowledge, it would seem to follow that Jones *must* mow his lawn—he cannot do otherwise.

Several solutions have been offered for this puzzle concerning God's foreknowledge and human freedom. We will briefly survey the most prominent ones.

The Compatibilist Solution

The compatibilist solution is relatively simple and straightforward. As noted in the previous chapter, the compatibilist denies the libertarian view of freedom. He does not believe that freedom requires the power of contrary choice. On his view, Jones is free and responsible when he mows his lawn tomorrow as long as mowing his lawn is *what he wants to do*. The fact that Jones cannot do other than mow his lawn is irrelevant to the question of whether or not he is free. So the compatibilist accepts the argument about God's foreknowledge of Jones's action as a sound argument for the conclusion that Jones cannot do anything other than mow his lawn tomorrow. But, since freedom and moral responsibility are consistent with determinism, it does not follow that Jones is not free.

Though simple and straightforward, this solution to the foreknowledge-freedom problem is obviously dependent on the cogency of the compatibilist conception of freedom. One will be inclined to accept this solution only to the extent that he is willing to accept compatibilism.

The Open Theist Solution

Libertarians have offered several different solutions to the puzzle. One of these is the solution offered by the perspective known as *open theism* (sometimes called free will theism).[28] According to open theists, God does not have foreknowledge of future human actions. He knows those future events that are the direct result of physical determinism (e.g., where a particular asteroid circling Alpha Centauri will be in ten years). But God cannot know what a creature with libertarian freedom will do tomorrow. He can certainly make reasonable predictions (and be right most of the time), but He cannot have fore*knowledge* of what any free creature will do. So, according to open theism, Jones faces no threat to his freedom from God's foreknowledge when it comes to mowing or not mowing his lawn tomorrow—because God does not have foreknowledge of his free actions.

Why think that God does not have foreknowledge of free human actions? One reason comes from the argument given above about Jones mowing his lawn tomorrow. Like the compatibilist, the open theist takes that argument as being sound. God's foreknowledge of Jones's actions eliminates the ability of Jones to do otherwise. Unlike the compatibilist, however, the open theist is a libertarian who believes that freedom requires the power of contrary choice. So, for him, God's foreknowledge would eliminate Jones's freedom. But since we know that human beings like Jones are free, it must be the case that God does not have such foreknowledge.

In response, one might wonder why—if we have to make a choice between God's foreknowledge and human freedom—we have to insist on human freedom and deny divine foreknowledge. Why not rather deny human freedom (of the libertarian sort) and preserve God's foreknowledge? The open theist is likely to answer that the only way for human beings and God to have any kind of meaningful, personal relationship is for humans to have libertarian freedom.[29]

In any case, there are strong biblical reasons to believe that God has exhaustive foreknowledge even of human actions. For example, through the prophet Isaiah, God declares,

---

[28] See David Basinger, *The Case for Freewill Theism: A Philosophical Assessment* (Downers Grove, IL: InterVarsity, 1996), chap. 2; and William Hasker, "A Philosophical Perspective," in *The Openness of God*, ed. Clark Pinnock, et al. (Downers Grove, IL: InterVarsity, 1994), 126–54.

[29] See, e.g., John Sanders, *The God Who Risks: A Theology of Providence* (Downers Grove, IL: InterVarsity, 1998), 220–22. This point, however, is challenged by classical theists. See, for example, James S. Spiegel, "Does God Take Risks?" in *God Under Fire: Modern Scholarship Reinvents God*, ed. Douglas S. Huffman and Eric L. Johnson (Grand Rapids: Zondervan, 2002), 196–210.

> Remember what happened long ago,
> for I am God, and there is no other;
> [I am] God, and no one is like Me.
> I declare the end from the beginning,
> and from long ago what is not yet done,
> saying: My plan will take place,
> and I will do all My will. (Isa 46:9–10)

It is hard to make sense of God's ability to know the full scope of history and to ensure the fulfillment of His divine purpose without foreknowledge of human actions. Elsewhere, God throws down this challenge to all false gods:

> "Submit your case," says the Lord.
> "Present your arguments," says Jacob's King.
> "Let them come and tell us what will happen.
> Tell us the past events, so that we may reflect on it
>   and know the outcome.
> Or tell us the future.
> Tell us the coming events,
>   then we will know that you are gods.
> Indeed, do [something] good or bad,
>   then we will be in awe and perceive.
> Look, you are nothing
> and your work is worthless.
> Anyone who chooses you is detestable."
> (Isa 41:21–24)

Here God Himself declares that a distinguishing mark of deity is exhaustive foreknowledge. A "god" who lacks foreknowledge is a false pretender.

In Psalm 139, David expresses his faith in God's exhaustive omniscience:

> Lord, You have searched me and known me.
> You know when I sit down and when I stand up;
> You understand my thoughts from far away.
> You observe my travels and my rest;
> You are aware of all my ways.
> Before a word is on my tongue,
> You know all about it, Lord.
> You have encircled me;
> You have placed Your hand on me.

[This] extraordinary knowledge is beyond me.
It is lofty; I am unable to [reach] it. (Ps 139:1–6)

Notice that God is said to know everything about David including his every thought. More apropos, God knows David's words *before he utters them*. It is clear from Scripture that God foreknows all future events, including the future actions of His free creatures.[30]

The Ockhamist Solution

A more traditional libertarian solution was first formulated by William of Ockham. Called *Ockhamism*, this approach deals with the problem by pointing out that God's beliefs about the future are caused by the events of the future, and not vice versa. God sees what happens in the future, including the free actions of human beings, and thus acquires true beliefs about those actions and events. Put another way, if Jones were to choose to do something else tomorrow, then God would know something different about Jones today. For example, if, instead of mowing his lawn tomorrow, Jones chooses to go see a movie, then God would have foreseen *that* choice and would today believe that Jones will go to the movies tomorrow. So the fact that God knows today that Jones will mow his lawn tomorrow does not destroy Jones's freedom because it is what Jones freely chooses to do tomorrow that causes God to have today the belief about Jones that He does. It may be the case, since God *knows* what Jones *will* do, that Jones's mowing his lawn is inevitable, but it does not follow, says the Ockhamist, that his choice is determined.

Critics of Ockhamism claim that the Ockhamist misses the point of the original problem concerning God's foreknowledge and freedom. The point is not simply about how God comes to know what He knows about Jones, or about whether or not God's foreknowledge exercises some kind of causal influence on Jones. Rather, the problem is that there is a *fact about God* today—namely, that He has the (infallible) belief that Jones will mow his lawn tomorrow. When tomorrow comes, that fact about God will be a fact of the past. And past facts are fixed. The only way that Jones could do other than mow his lawn is if he could somehow alter the past, which is impossible.

Ockhamists respond to this difficulty by distinguishing between *hard facts* and *soft facts*. The former are what we might call "over-and-done-with facts," facts that are accomplished at a particular time and are completely unrelated to other times. Examples of hard facts would be *David killed Goliath* or *Jonathan Edwards preached in New England* or

---

[30] For a more detailed treatment of biblical texts supporting God's exhaustive divine foreknowledge and a response to open theists' treatment of biblical texts, see Bruce A. Ware, *God's Lesser Glory: The Diminished God of Open Theism* (Wheaton, IL: Crossway, 2000), 65–141.

My philosophy class began at 9:00 a.m. In contrast, soft facts are temporally relational facts. That is, soft facts are facts about the past that refer to and entail facts about the future. For example, *My philosophy class began at 9:00 a.m.* is a hard fact about the past, but *My philosophy class began three hours before the faculty meeting* is a soft fact about the past.

The point of this distinction is that hard facts are clearly subject to the fixity of the past. Nothing anyone can do today or at any future time can change a hard fact about the past. But soft facts do not seem to be subject to the fixity of the past. Thus, it is a hard fact about 9:00 a.m. that my class began, but it is *not* fixed at 9:00 a.m. that my class began three hours prior to the faculty meeting. The latter (soft) fact is not fixed until the time of the faculty meeting. So the Ockhamist may argue that God's belief today about Jones mowing his lawn tomorrow is a soft fact about today. Hence, Jones *can* do something tomorrow to alter what God believes today.

There is much debate, however, over whether or not the Ockhamist is right that God's beliefs can be understood as soft facts. Consider the fact that for someone, including God, to believe some proposition means that he is in a certain mental state, the state of believing that proposition. Having a certain mental state seems clearly to be a hard fact. It is unclear at best that the hardness of being in a mental state would be softened just because that mental state happens to be a belief about some future time.[31] So if Jones cannot tomorrow alter the fact that God is in a certain mental state today, then it would seem that Jones cannot alter the fact that God believes that he will mow his lawn.

The Molinist Solution

A libertarian solution that is growing in popularity among contemporary philosophers appeals to the view known as *Molinism*, named after the sixteenth-century philosopher Luis de Molina (1536–1600). The Molinist believes that God possesses something called *middle knowledge*. To say that God has middle knowledge means that God knows the truth values of *counterfactuals of freedom*, conditional statements concerning what someone with libertarian freedom would do in a hypothetical situation. A possible example of a counterfactual of freedom would be "If David had remained in Keilah, then Saul would have besieged the city." In the biblical story (1 Sam 23:1–13), God warns David to flee from the city of Keilah because King Saul is on the way to capture him. David does flee and Saul gives up his pursuit. Nevertheless, according to Molinism, God knows that *if* David had remained in Keilah, Saul *would*

---

[31] For a more detailed discussion of this point, see John Martin Fischer, *The Metaphysics of Free Will*, 117–20.

have besieged the city. For our purposes it is crucial to realize that God is supposed to know this even though Saul has libertarian freedom and could act differently from what God knows he would do.

Molinism apparently solves the foreknowledge-freedom problem by claiming that God's knowledge of the future is not direct, but indirect via middle knowledge. God knows all of the courses of action that agents could take in any given circumstance, and He then creates those circumstances that happen to bring about the outcomes He wants. So, for example, before God created Jones or anything else, He knew that Jones would freely choose to mow his lawn on a particular day if he were created and placed in a certain life situation. Since God, for His own secret reasons, wanted to create a world in which Jones mowed his lawn on that day, He created Jones and placed him in that situation, knowing that events would unfold according to His middle knowledge. So when Jones mows his lawn he does so *freely*.

A common objection to Molinism is called *the grounding objection*.[32] This objection contends that God cannot have middle knowledge because counterfactuals of freedom are ungrounded and therefore can have no truth-value. Recall that, according to libertarianism, an agent is free to do some action A only if he can do otherwise in exactly the same circumstances. There is nothing about the circumstances in which the agent is placed that determines that he do A or not-A. This being the case, it appears that there is no fact of the matter as to what a libertarian agent would do in a hypothetical situation. There is, in other words, nothing that would or could make a counterfactual of freedom true.

Ordinarily, when we think a conditional statement is true, it is because we think there is some kind of connection (e.g., a causal or logical connection) between the antecedent and the consequent. Consider, for example, the following conditional propositions:

> If a cube of sugar is placed in water, it will dissolve.
> If two lines never intersect, then they are parallel.
> If the moon is made of green cheese, then the U.S.
> president is an android.

We readily acknowledge the truth of the first of these propositions because we understand the properties of sugar and water and believe there is a causal relation between them that results in the dissolving of the sugar. The second conditional is known to be true because we know that to say that two lines never intersect logically entails that they are parallel.

---

[32] For a detailed presentation and defense of the grounding objection, see Steven B. Cowan, "The Grounding Objection to Middle Knowledge Revisited," *Religious Studies* 39 (2003): 93–102.

Regarding the third conditional, however, we reject it precisely because there is nothing to link the moon's being made of green cheese (even if that were true) to the president's being an android.

Likewise, according to the grounding objection, there is nothing to connect the antecedent of a counterfactual of freedom to its consequent. Since Saul has libertarian freedom, according to Molinism, nothing about David's remaining in Keilah guarantees that Saul will besiege the city. Thus, counterfactuals of freedom are ungrounded and lacking in truth value. This seems to suggest that God cannot know them.

Molinists have made attempts to rebut the grounding objection. The most prevalent response is to argue that counterfactuals of freedom do not need to be grounded in the way the grounding objection demands. Their truth value is claimed to be simply a brute fact that needs no further defense. This view might be supported by the claim that there are other examples of ungrounded propositions that are less controversially taken to have truth value. For example, negative existential propositions (i.e., propositions asserting that something does not exist) like "Baal does not exist" are claimed by some philosophers to be ungrounded yet true. If so, the fact that counterfactuals of freedom are ungrounded might not, by itself, be a reason to reject their truth.[33]

As the reader can tell by now, the foreknowledge-freedom problem is complex and there is no one solution on which all Christian philosophers are settled. It should be said that each of the solutions discussed has able defenders and we believe that all of them (except Open Theism) are arguably consistent with the data of Scripture.

6.2.3 Divine Emotion

Another issue pertaining to the nature of God is the question of whether God has emotions. Though seldom discussed through most of Christian history, the subject of divine emotion has received a lot of attention in recent years. This is one aspect of the broader issue of divine *passibility*. To say that God is passible is to say that He can be affected by some outside force. To affirm divine *impassibility* is to hold that God cannot be so affected. Now emotion is one major kind of affect, a particular way in which persons are sometimes moved, such as to become angry or giddy. The focus of our discussion will be just this particular kind of affect, including both pleasant and painful emotions.

Traditionally, most theologians have maintained that God is impassible and has no emotions. But this now appears to be a minority position. Apart from a few exceptions, the prevailing view among scholars

---

[33] For more on this point, see, e.g., William Lane Craig, "Middle Knowledge, Truth-Makers, and the Grounding Objection," *Faith and Philosophy* 18 (2001): 337–52.

today is that God has genuine emotions and experiences real suffering. If there is an overriding reason for this change of philosophical-theological opinion, it is that the doctrine of divine impassibility seems to contradict belief in divine relationality. Many have argued that an impassible God is cold and aloof, not personal and loving. A God void of genuine emotion, they claim, cannot be personal, which is an implication no orthodox theist can tolerate. Thus, believers have increasingly rejected divine impassibility, in favor of a picture of God that accommodates divine emotions, including joy, sorrow, affection, anger, grief, and satisfaction. In this section we will review the main arguments for each of the standard views on divine passibility.

Arguments for Divine Impassibilism

Defenders of divine impassibility have often appealed to notions of divine perfection and immutability to justify their position. This tradition traces back to Plotinus (c. AD 205–270), who argued that the very concept of eternity implies changelessness:

> One sees eternity in seeing a life that abides in the same, and always has the all present to it, not now this, and then again that, but all things at once, and not now some things, and then again others, but a partless completion, as if they were all together in a point . . .; it is something which abides in the same in itself and does not change at all but is always in the present, because nothing of it has passed away, nor again is there anything to come into being, but that which it is, it *is*.[34]

Aquinas affirmed such a conception of divine eternity, saying that "God . . . is without beginning and end, having his whole being at once."[35] And elsewhere: "God's understanding has no succession, as neither does his being. He is therefore an ever-abiding simultaneous whole."[36] Now, impassbilists argue, if this sort of changeless eternity is essential to the divine life, then it would appear that emotions are impossible for God, for emotions imply change.

Some have appealed to divine omniscience, arguing that since God knows all truths regarding all events, whether in our past, present, or future, God cannot feel genuine surprise, wonder, or disappointment about anything that happens. These and many other emotions presuppose a passage from ignorance to knowledge about aspects of the world,

---

[34] Plotinus, *Enneads*, in *Plotinus*, trans. A. H. Armstrong (London: William Heinemann, Ltd., 1967), 3:304–5.

[35] Thomas Aquinas, *The Disputed Questions on Truth*, trans. Robert W. Mulligan (Chicago: Henry Regnery, 1952), 1:98.

[36] Ibid., 218.

so they are impossible for an omniscient being. A variation of this argument from divine knowledge is offered by Paul Helm, who says "one clear reason for not ascribing . . . emotion or passion to God is that it is incompatible with his rationality and wisdom. To act upon emotion or passion is to act when the judgment is in abeyance. Emotion clouds the judgment, or functions in place of the judgment."[37] Some impassibilists have focused on the negative or painful emotions as particularly problematic, arguing that if God feels real sadness, disgust, or anger, then He is not perfectly happy.

Impassibilists also use scriptural arguments to support their view. For example, such passages as Malachi 3:6 ("I the Lord do not change," NIV) and James 1:17 (God "does not change like shifting shadows," NIV) suggest that God cannot have passions, again assuming that passions involve change. And passages such as Isaiah 46:10 ("I declare the end from the beginning, and from long ago what is not yet done, saying: My plan will take place, and I will do all My will") and Colossians 1:17 ("He is before all things, and by Him all things hold together") suggest a perfectly sovereign God for whom genuine responses to human events, emotional or otherwise, would be inappropriate.

Arguments for Divine Passibilism

The passibilists have their arguments as well. They maintain that emotion is essential to divine personhood, just as it is essential to human personhood. Theologian Jurgen Moltmann applies this point specifically to the attribute of love, noting that

> a God who cannot suffer is poorer than any man. For a God who is incapable of suffering is a being who cannot be involved. Suffering and injustice do not affect him. And because he is so completely insensitive, he cannot be affected or shaken by anything. He cannot weep, for he has no tears. But the one who cannot suffer cannot love either. So he is also a loveless being.[38]

Still others, such as Charles Taliaferro, have suggested that even the divine attribute of moral goodness presupposes passibility.[39] To make proper sense of the notion that God disapproves of human cruelty and malice, for example, we must assume that He feels real sorrow about such things. And without genuine disapproval of evil deeds (and approval of

---

[37] Paul Helm, "The Impossibility of Divine Passibility," in *The Power and Weakness of God: Impassibility and Orthodoxy*, ed. Nigel M. de S. Cameron (Edinburgh: Rutherford House, 1990), 130–31.

[38] Jürgen Moltmann, *The Crucified God* (New York: Harper and Row, 1974), 222.

[39] Charles Taliaferro, "The Passibility of God," *Religious Studies* 25:2 (1989): 220.

those who live just lives), the concept of divine goodness loses all meaning.

Some passibilists have appealed to divine omniscience in support of their view. Assume that God knows all truths and knows them fully. Not all truths can be fully known in a merely propositional way. Some can only be fully known experientially, such as knowledge of what it is like to feel pain. So God must have an experiential knowledge of such truths if He is really to know them. Now emotions are a particular kind of experience. Therefore, God knows emotions in an experiential way. And, of course, to know an emotion experientially is to have that emotion. This notion of divinely shared emotional experiences is not a merely formal point. Rather, as passibilists often point out, it has practical therapeutic value. For those who suffer it is a deep consolation to know that God suffers too and can therefore sympathize with us in our pain. In fact, many claim, sympathetic divine suffering is the key to Christian redemption, since God suffered in Christ, and this suffering brought salvation to humanity. Thus, it would appear that the central doctrine of Christian theology, the divine incarnation, provides evidence for divine passibilism.

As for the scriptural witness to this issue, passibilists maintain that we need to take seriously and at face value the numerous references to God as experiencing a range of emotions. Biblical writers attribute grief and sorrow to God such as in Genesis 6:6, which says that upon observing rampant human wickedness, "the Lord regretted that He had made man on the earth, and He was grieved in His heart." Other passages attribute further emotions to God, such as regret (1 Sam 15:11, 35), anger (Exod 4:14), love (Mal 1:2; Jer 31:3), hatred (Prov 11:2; Mal 1:3), surprise (Gen 22:12), and humor (Ps 2:4). These are only some of the more direct references to divine passions. Numerous narratives that describe or refer to the wrath, mercy, judgments, blessings, or rewards God bestows upon people may be seen as indirect evidence for the passibilist position. Christian philosopher Nicholas Wolterstorff comments on such passages: "The fact that the biblical writers speak of God as rejoicing and suffering over the state of the creation is not a superficial eliminable feature of their speech. It expresses themes deeply embedded in the biblical vision. God's love for his world is a rejoicing and suffering love."[40]

A Possible Compromise: Divine Omnipathos

Passibilists and impassibilists alike appear to have strong arguments to recommend their positions. On the one hand, it appears that God

---

[40] Nicholas Wolterstorff, "Suffering Love," in *Philosophy and the Christian Faith*, ed. Thomas Morris (Notre Dame: University of Notre Dame Press, 1988), 227.

must have emotions in order to account for His genuine personhood, relationality, and understanding of human emotions. On the other hand, God's immutability, eternality, and perfect happiness must be preserved. And biblical evidence on both sides of the debate must be accounted for. But how can this be done? One attempt at a compromise was made by St. Anselm, who offered a behavioral rendering of divine emotions. According to Anselm, God does not literally *feel* compassion, so much as God *acts* in a way that we describe as compassionate. He writes, "O Lord, . . . thou art compassionate in terms of our experience, and not compassionate in terms of thy being. . . . When thou behold-est us in our wretchedness, we experience the effect of compassion, but thou dost not experience the feeling."[41] The problem with this approach is that it is not a true compromise since it fails to affirm the heart of the passibilist's claim—that God actually *experiences* emotions, rather than merely behaving as if He does.

We believe that a true compromise position is available that affirms the basic claims made by both passibilists and impassibilists. To see what such a view amounts to we need only apply some ingenuity in combining the attributes emphasized above. Let us grant the essence of divine passibilism, that God experiences real emotions. The Lord really feels sorrow, joy, anger, humor, grief, pain, affection, and so on. But let us also concede the impassibilist's point that God is immutable and time-lessly eternal, keeping in mind that this claim implies that the divine life is lived, as it were, all at once. Taking these two points together, then, we arrive at the notion that God experiences all of His emotions at once, that is, eternally. If God is immutable and the inner life of God is one of absolute simultaneity—everything "all at once"—then if God has any feelings whatsoever, they must be eternal. So, on this view, like God's knowledge, divine feelings are ever constant and unchanging. He experiences all emotions and does so for all eternity. Thus understood, we might say that God is *omnipathic*.

What we are suggesting, then, is the possibility that both sides of this debate are correct, at least as regards their *positive* claims about God's nature, namely that God is immutable and timelessly eternal, on the one hand, and that God is personal and fully relational, on the other. We are, of course, implying that both sides have been mistaken as well, specifically in their *negative* claims or implications that God's immuta-bility and timeless eternality and God's personality and relationality are mutually exclusive.

---

[41] St. Anselm, *Basic Writings*, 2nd ed., trans. S. N. Deane (La Salle, IL: Open Court, 1962), 59.

Concerning this proposal of divine omnipathos, one matter remains to be addressed, and that is divine happiness. If God eternally experiences such emotions as anger and sorrow, then how can He be happy? In response, the defender of divine omnipathos could point out that this view is not committed to the notion that all divine emotions are experienced equally. Rather, one may affirm that God's joy and contentment prevail over all other divine emotions and that within this emotional context even emotions such as anger and sorrow are not unpleasant for God as they are for us. As finite mortals, our emotions come in succession, much like our thoughts, and we are prone to being "overcome" by anger and sorrow, which is precisely when they are unpleasant. But as an infinite being, God can never be so dominated by any of His emotions. In this way, one may say that God is perfectly content and joyful while experiencing every emotion. His being omnipathic is not inconsistent with His being eternally joyful.

We offer this model of divine omnipathos as a way of steering between the horns of the dilemma of divine passibilism and impassibilism. While this view no doubt faces difficulties of its own, we believe such an approach holds out promise for resolving a long-standing theological debate. And even if this approach proves unacceptable for some reason, perhaps another compromise position can be developed that accounts for the insights on either side of the issue.

Questions for Reflection

1. Do you think there are limits to what God can do? Why or why not?
2. Which view of God's relation to time do you think is best? Why?
3. How does your view on God's relationship to time affect the way you pray, especially when you submit requests to Him? If God transcends time, then is it reasonable to pray about past events?
4. Which solution to the foreknowledge-freedom problem do you prefer? Can you respond to the difficulties this solution faces?
5. Do you believe human emotions reflect divine emotions? If not, why not? If so, then in what ways are our emotions different from God's?
6. What do you think of the omnipathos view recommended by the authors? What problems, if any, does it have?

§ 6.3 How Can God Allow Evil?

On August 30, 2005, Americans watched in horror as the storm surge of hurricane Katrina broke several levies that kept water out of New Orleans and 80 percent of the city was flooded. Many people there lost their lives and tens of thousands were left homeless.

In the early morning of February 24, 2005, John Evander Couey, a convicted sex-offender, sneaked into the home of nine-year-old Jessica Lunsford of Homosassa, Florida, and kidnapped her. Taking her back to his residence, he raped her. When he had finished, he took her outside and buried her alive. Police later found her body.

If God—a being who is all-powerful and all-knowing—exists, then He could have prevented all of these terrible events. And since He is supposedly all-good, we might well think that He *would* prevent these things. So how could an all-powerful, all-knowing, all-good being stand idly by and allow such evils? Yet these events happened.

Such facts constitute what is known as the *problem of evil*. The problem has to do with the apparent incompatibility between the existence of God and the existence of evil. Even religious believers find it troubling that evil exists in the world—and so much evil! How and why could God allow the untold suffering that human beings have experienced? Some have found the paradox of evil to be unsolvable. For example, the ancient Greek philosopher Epicurus threw up his hands in despair of solving it, asking his famous series of questions: "Is he [i.e., God] willing to prevent evil, but not able? Then he is impotent. Is he able, but not willing? Then he is malevolent. Is he both able and willing? Whence then is evil?"[42]

In the history of philosophy, the problem of evil has sometimes been used as the basis for arguments against God's existence. Such arguments have taken several distinct forms, focusing on different aspects of the problem of evil. In this section, we will examine two such arguments to see if they provide a reason to deny the existence of God.

6.3.1 The Logical Problem of Evil

In the earliest discussions of the problem of evil, the primary focus lay in what appeared to be a logical inconsistency between the existence of God and the existence of any and all evil. Like Epicurus (noted above), other philosophers argued that the existence of *any* evil whatsoever ruled out the possibility of God's existence. In other words, the claim was made that the propositions "God exists," and "evil exists" are

---

[42] Epicurus as quoted in David Hume, *Dialogues Concerning Natural Religion*, Part X.

logically contradictory. They could not both be true. And since we all know that evil exists, we must conclude that God does not exist.

The atheist philosopher J. L. Mackie (1917–1981) formally presented the *logical problem of evil* as follows (with some modifications for clarity and precision):[43]

(1) If God exists, he is omnipotent, omniscient, and omnibenevolent.
(2) An omnipotent being has the ability to prevent evil.
(3) An omniscient being has the knowledge to prevent evil.
(4) An omnibenevolent being has the desire to prevent evil.
(5) Therefore, if God exists, there is no evil.
(6) There is evil.
(7) Therefore, God does not exist.

Are the premises of this argument true? Every theist will readily accept the truth of premise (1). God certainly has these attributes, though He has many others, too. And, of course, no theist will deny premise (6)—there is no doubt that there is much evil in the world. If these and all the other premises of the argument are true, then the conclusion follows logically—there is no God.

But, what about those other premises, premises (2) through (4)? Though some have done so, most theists would find it very difficult to deny (2).[44] After all, could not God have prevented evil simply by refusing to create anything? Or by creating a world that contains only plants and rocks and not morally significant creatures like humans? Likewise, a traditional theist will not deny (3). If God is omniscient, then He knows the truth of all propositions, past, present, and future. Nothing can take Him by surprise, not even the evil choices of His creatures. Hence, God would have complete knowledge of any and all evil.

Premise (4) of Mackie's argument asserts that God *desires* to prevent evil. Is this true? Many theists have argued that there is no need to accept this claim. If this is the case, then the theist can claim that premise (4) is false, or at least not known to be true. And if this is so, then the subconclusion (5) is unwarranted, and so is the final conclusion (7).

But how can the theist justifiably reject premise (4)? After all, no one would want to deny that God hates evil (cp. Pss 5:4; 34:16; Hab 1:13; Jas 1:13). So the theist is very likely to admit that, *all things being equal,*

---

[43] See J. L. Mackie, "Evil and Omnipotence," in *Philosophy of Religion: An Anthology*, 4th ed., ed. Louis P. Pojman (Belmont, CA: Wadsworth, 2003), 160–67.

[44] Rabbi Harold Kushner has attempted to solve the problem of evil by denying God's omnipotence. See his book *When Bad Things Happen to Good People* (New York: Schocken, 1981).

God would prefer that evil not exist in His creation. This is why theists tend to believe, as the Bible teaches, that God will one day eradicate evil from His creation. So must the theist accept premise (4)? Not necessarily. As stated, it is ambiguous. What the Christian theist can agree to is

> (4′) An omnibenevolent being has a *prima facie* desire to prevent evil.

That is, leaving all other possible considerations aside, God has *some* reason to prevent evil. But, this is consistent with God having some reason to *permit* evil as well. It is at least possible that God has a good reason—a morally sufficient reason—not to prevent some evils. If so, it is clear that premise (4′) will not allow the atheist to draw the conclusion that God's existence is incompatible with evil.

Now what might constitute a morally sufficient reason for God to allow evil? There are a number of possibilities.[45] However, the simplest suggestion is that God allows evil in order *to bring about some greater good*—a good which could not be brought about unless evil existed as its precondition. This suggestion has the luxury of being open to at least some empirical verification. For example, consider the experience of John Walsh, the producer of the famous TV program *America's Most Wanted*. Walsh's six-year-old son Adam was kidnapped and murdered, an unmistakable moral evil. Yet this tragedy led Walsh to start his TV program, which has proven decisive in saving the lives of many other kidnapped children and bringing the perpetrators to justice. On a grander scale, consider the Japanese attack on Pearl Harbor on December 7, 1941. Though obviously an atrocity, the attack precipitated the entrance of the United States into World War II, an event instrumental in the defeat of Nazi Germany and other Axis powers—which most of us consider to be a great good.

It is evident, then, that evil can often lead to considerable goods. So perhaps God is morally justified in allowing evil because He intends to use that evil to bring about greater goods. Indeed, the Bible itself indicates that such is the case. For example, consider the biblical account in which the patriarch Joseph is sold into slavery by his brothers (Gen 37:25–28). Though Joseph suffered terribly from the evil done him by his brothers, at the end of the story, after his family and many others had been saved

[45] It is important to note here that most philosophers of religion credit Alvin Plantinga with providing the decisive refutation of the logical problem of evil in general and of Mackie's version in particular with his famous "Free Will Defense" (see his *God, Freedom and Evil* [Grand Rapids: Eerdmans, 1974], 7–64). Plantinga persuasively argues that it is logically possible that the only way that God could create a world containing free creatures is by creating a world in which at least some of His creatures go morally wrong. Given this logical possibility, there simply cannot be any logical contradiction between the existence of God and the existence of evil.

from famine by his rise to prominence in Egypt, he was able to declare, "You planned evil against me; God planned it for good to bring about the present result—the survival of many people" (Gen 50:20).

Now it probably cannot be proven that all the evil that God has permitted in His creation will ultimately result in the production of goods that far outweigh the evils themselves. Nevertheless, it seems that the theist can claim that it is *possible* that they will (indeed, it is part of the Christian faith that they will—cp. Rom 8:18,28). As long as this is a logical possibility, then the theist can say that it is at least possible that

> (4″) God has a morally sufficient reason to permit evil, and thus an *ultima facie* desire not to prevent evil (i.e., a desire that overrides his *prima facie* desire to prevent it).

Given even the mere possibility of (4″), there is no reason to believe that if God exists there would be no evil. In fact, if (4″) *were* true, then we would have reason to believe that God's creation *would* contain at least some evil. Therefore, the existence of evil does not seem to provide reason to disbelieve in God.

6.3.2 The Evidential Problem of Evil

Most atheists today would grant the conclusion of the last section—that God's existence is *not* incompatible with the existence of evil per se. However, perhaps God's existence is incompatible with a certain *kind* of evil that exists. For example, the atheist William Rowe has argued that God's existence is inconsistent with *pointless* or *gratuitous* evil. By "pointless evil," Rowe means evil that cannot serve a greater good. And Rowe believes that there is such pointless evil in the world.[46] He thus concludes that God does not exist. Rowe's argument may be stated as follows:

> (1) If God existed, there would be no pointless evil.
> (2) There is pointless evil.
> (3) Therefore, God does not exist.[47]

Not every theist will grant the truth of premise (1). Some may argue that God's existence is compatible with gratuitous evil.[48] Most theists,

---

[46] See William Rowe, "The Inductive Argument from Evil Against the Existence of God," in *Philosophy of Religion: An Anthology*, 186–93.

[47] Our discussion of Rowe's argument is much indebted to Daniel Howard-Snyder, "God, Evil, and Suffering," in *Reason for the Hope Within*, ed. Michael J. Murray (Grand Rapids: Eerdmans, 1999), 101–14.

[48] See, e.g., Peter van Inwagen, "The Magnitude, Duration, and Distribution of Evil: A Theodicy," in *God, Knowledge and Mystery* (Ithaca, NY: Cornell University Press, 1995), 96–122.

however, are inclined to accept premise (1). Indeed, if you agree with the point made above that God has a morally sufficient reason (such as to bring about a greater good) for allowing any evil into His creation in the first place, then you will be inclined to grant premise (1).[49] God allows evil, but He always has a good reason for doing so, namely, to bring about some greater good that could not be achieved without evil. So, if there is pointless evil in the world, God's existence would be unlikely.

The Question of Pointless Evil

But *is* there pointless evil in the world? Rowe thinks there is. To show that there is pointless evil, Rowe introduces what he calls the "noseeum inference." Like the pesky little bugs that some readers may be familiar with, a "noseeum" is something that you cannot see. And a *noseeum inference* is a conclusion drawn on the basis of what one does not see. The basic structure of all noseeum inferences looks like this:

(1) I cannot see an *X*.
(2) Therefore, there probably is no *X*.

We all make noseeum inferences every day of our lives. Every time I go to cross a street, I look both ways and I step onto the street only after I see no car coming. Daniel Howard-Snyder gives a couple of more examples:

> Suppose that, after rummaging around carefully in my fridge, I can't find a carton of milk. Naturally enough, I infer that there isn't one there. Or suppose that, on viewing a chess match between two novices, Kasparov says to himself, "So far as I can tell, there is no way for John to get out of check," and then infers that there is no way. These are what we might call no-see-um inferences: we don't see 'um, so they ain't there![50]

Rowe applies this kind of noseeum reasoning to God and evil. Rowe suggests that if we cannot see a reason for a particular instance of evil, then there probably is not a reason. Recall the example of nine-year-old

[49] It may be helpful to note that even those theists like van Inwagen who think that God could allow pointless evils will still argue that there is at least some overarching reason that God has which morally justifies His permitting such evils. For example, it might be argued that God allows some evil things to happen that He does not specifically ordain because that is the "price" He has to pay for having a world that contains free creatures. We would suggest, however, that if this is true, then these evils are not really pointless after all. There may not be a specific reason unique to any given instance of evil for why *that* evil happened, but there is a reason that God has (a general, overarching reason) for why it happened nonetheless. This means that almost all theists, including van Inwagen, really do believe that God's existence is incompatible with truly pointless evil.

[50] Daniel Howard-Snyder, "God, Evil, and Suffering," 103.

Jessica Lunsford mentioned above. Rowe considers this event and examines all the circumstances surrounding it, and he invites us to do the
same. No matter how hard we try, we cannot see any good reason why
this child had to suffer the way she did. Since we cannot see a reason
why God would allow this child to suffer, Rowe concludes that there
probably is not a good reason—the child's suffering was pointless.

Is Rowe correct in his conclusion? Do such examples prove that
there is pointless evil in the world? It is not clear that they do. To see
why, we must recognize that noseeum inferences are not all equal. Some
noseeum inferences, as we have seen, are reasonable and appropriate.
But many are not. Suppose I look up at the night sky at the star Deneb
and I do not see a planet orbiting that star. Would it be reasonable for
me to conclude that there is no planet orbiting Deneb? Of course not.
Suppose that using the best telescopes and other imaging equipment
presently available, I still cannot see a planet around Deneb. I would still
be unjustified in concluding that there was no such planet.

What makes the difference between this latter case and, say, the case
of the milk carton in the fridge? Why is the noseeum inference regarding
the milk carton reasonable, and the one concerning the planet around
Deneb is not? Howard-Snyder explains why by outlining what we may
call the *Noseeum Rationality Principle*:

> *A noseeum inference is reasonable only if it is reasonable to*
> *believe that we would very likely see (grasp, comprehend,*
> *understand) the item in question if it existed.*[51]

The milk carton inference is reasonable because it would be reasonable for us to believe that, if there were a milk carton in the fridge, we
would see it. The inference about the planet orbiting Deneb is not reasonable because, even if there were a planet orbiting Deneb, it would not
be reasonable for me to expect to see it. The crucial question before us,
then, is whether or not Rowe's noseeum inference regarding God's reasons for evil is justified or not—whether, that is, it is more like the milk
carton example or the planet example. Or we might put the question like
this: If God has a reason for allowing an instance of evil such as the child
being tortured to death, is it reasonable for us always to expect to see it?

In his noseeum inference, Rowe *assumes* that it would be reasonable
for us to expect to see God's reasons. But should we assume this? Not if
we take account of other things that theists believe about God. On the
Christian worldview, we believe that we are finite, while God is unlimited in knowledge and power. At the very least, we should understand

[51] Ibid., 105.

our relation to God on the analogy of young children in relation to their parents. As Stephen Wykstra has pointed out, parents often have good reasons for doing things to and for their young children that their children cannot begin to fathom—things which the children may think are unjustifiably bad.[52] Consider a small child's vaccination shots. The child suffers pain and cannot comprehend the reasons for it. Yet there *are* good reasons to give those shots which justify such infliction of pain. So, clearly, the fact that the child cannot see a reason for the pain is not reason for him to believe that his parents had no good reason.

Moreover, the Bible itself tells us that God is incomparable (Isa 40–45), that His ways are past finding out (Rom 11:33), and that His ways are not our ways (Isa 55:8). God is transcendent and very different from us. We are limited, finite. God is not. God has infinite wisdom. Moreover, the sin in our hearts clouds our minds and limits our understanding even further. So, given what we know about God (that He is transcendent and infinitely wiser than we are) and given what we know about ourselves (that we are limited and sinful), what should be our *reasonable expectation* with regard to God's reasons for permitting evil? Would we expect in every case to see them? Or might we expect, in at least some cases, to be mystified? The theist is justified in believing the latter.

Therefore, Rowe's noseeum inference regarding God's reasons for permitting evil is probably not reasonable. It seems to fail the test of the Noseeum Rationality Principle. If so, then one cannot affirm premise (2) of Rowe's argument from evil. That is, we have no justification for believing that there are in fact pointless evils in the world.

Christ and the Christian Hope

There are two further considerations that Christian theists can draw upon in response to the problem of evil in all its forms. First, the Christian has the hope of eternal life and the heavenly rewards that accompany it. The Christian is promised that in heaven there will be no more pain, no more tears (Rev 21:4). Disease, suffering, and death will be eradicated forever (1 Cor 15:54–55). Believers will enjoy a blissful, abundant life in the presence of our heavenly Father for all eternity (John 10:10). So happy will be the final outcome of our lives that the apostle Paul declared, "For I consider that the sufferings of this present time are not worth comparing with the glory that is going to be revealed to us" (Rom

---

[52] Stephen J. Wykstra, "The Human Obstacle to Evidential Arguments from Suffering: On Avoiding the Evils of 'Appearance,'" *International Journal for Philosophy of Religion* 16 (1984): 73–94; and "Rowe's Noseeum Arguments from Evil," in *The Evidential Argument from Evil*, ed. Daniel Howard-Snyder (Bloomington: Indiana University Press, 1996), 126–50.

8:18). In accordance with the greater good defense discussed above, the Christian faith, in its view of the afterlife, has the resources to show that the existence of evil and suffering in the world is no obstacle to belief in God. Whatever suffering we experience, as bad as it is, will be outweighed by the heavenly goods we will enjoy later.

The redemptive work of Christ provides another resource for coping with the problem of evil. Paul also wrote these encouraging words: "If God is for us, who is against us? He did not even spare His own Son, but offered Him up for us all; how will He not also with Him grant us everything?" (Rom 8:31–32). The most horrendous evil that the world has ever known was the brutal execution of God's Son Jesus Christ. The Bible tells us that God the Father ordained this event Himself, allowing wicked men to nail Jesus to a cross (Acts 2:23). And yet, from this incomprehensibly evil event, God accomplished the awe-inspiring good of the redemption of the world. So, as Paul asked, what can we expect in the wake of the suffering that we endure in this life? If God was willing to sacrifice His own Son for us in order to bring about God's glory and our eternal good, we can be confident that the lesser evils that we face will also redound to God's glory and our good in the end. This point actually gives Christianity a major advantage over other forms of theism. Followers of religions like Islam and Judaism cannot have the same confidence that all of their sufferings will result in good. They lack any belief comparable to the atonement of Christ and thus lack any reason to believe that God would go to such lengths to turn our sufferings into blessings.

Questions for Reflection

1. Can the theist know that there are *no* pointless evils in the world? What if, as was argued in the last section, we have good, positive reasons to believe that God does in fact exist? How would this affect our assessment of the question of whether or not there are pointless evils?

2. Atheist B. C. Johnson presents the problem of evil in a dramatic and interesting way.[53] He asks us to imagine a house that catches fire with a child trapped inside. Outside, a bystander, who could easily rescue the child with little risk to himself, chooses to stand idly by and do nothing. We would all think that this bystander is morally reprehensible. Johnson argues that God is like this bystander. He is able to intervene and prevent most evils in the world

---

[53] B. C. Johnson, "Why Doesn't God Intervene to Prevent Evil?" in *Philosophy: The Quest for Truth*, 5th ed., ed. Louis P. Pojman (Oxford: Oxford University Press, 2002), 90–95.

but doesn't. Why should we not conclude, then, that God (like the human bystander at the fire) is morally reprehensible?

3. Philosophers sometimes discuss a particular type of evil called *horrendous* evil. This is a subspecies of pointless evil and refers to suffering that is so bad and so intense that the person who experiences that suffering can be said to have a life that is not worth living. Imagine for example a newborn child that is kidnapped and tortured to death, who experiences in this life almost nothing but pain. Some of the children (and others) killed in Nazi concentration camps are often said to have experienced such horrendous evil. Can the theist adequately respond to the apparent problem of horrendous evil? If so, how?

4. Open theists handle the problem of evil, in part, by denying that God has infallible knowledge of the future actions of free creatures. In other words, God does not know about many of the evils that occur in the world until they happen. What problems, if any, do you see with this solution?

5. Can you think of some more specific purposes for which God might allow evil? Why might these purposes be important to God?

§ 6.4 Is Christianity Exclusively True?

Thus far in this chapter we have discussed various aspects of the rationality of theistic belief. And we have found that, despite the formidable problem of evil, theistic belief is well-justified and may even be rational without the use of arguments. But now the question must be raised: Which form of theism is most rational? Are there good reasons to believe that Christianity is the true or most adequate form of theism? In this final section we will address this question, but first we must address a more fundamental issue, specifically whether it is even appropriate to think that there is but one way to find favor with God. Is it reasonable to believe that one theistic religion is exclusively true?

6.4.1 The Problem of Religious Pluralism

The twentieth century saw an unprecedented emergence of globalism in the West—a shift of perspective from an exclusive focus on one's own culture to a perspective that recognizes and respects diverse cultures and traditions worldwide. Globalism has impacted every academic discipline and has prompted debates in philosophy about the nature of religious truth. Our newfound appreciation for the vast diversity of religious beliefs and traditions has made it more difficult to continue to affirm the absolute truth of one's own religious beliefs. In this section, therefore, we will discuss the major views on the nature of religious truth.

Arguments for Religious Pluralism

It is now quite common to hear people say things like "All religions lead to the same place" or "People of different faiths really worship the same God." In many quarters such an attitude is considered a basic public courtesy, a way of showing respect to others in a pluralistic society. But are such claims true? Do all, or many, religions really lead to the same ultimate reality? Those who affirm this thesis are known as *religious pluralists.* They maintain that many different religions are indeed adequate to bring salvation to their followers. This view contrasts with *religious exclusivism,* which says that only one religion can be true and lead its followers to salvation. Let us look at some of the pluralist's principal arguments.

1. *The Argument from Religious Diversity.* Perhaps the most popular argument employed by religious pluralists is the argument from religious diversity. The variety and numbers of adherents to the major world religions is impressive. (See Table 6.1 for data on ten of the most significant world religions.)[54] To many, this fact alone is sufficient to persuade them that no religion is exclusively true. If just one religion is adequate for salvation, then billions of religious devotees will be excluded. Surely God will not allow this to happen.

Table 6.1

Religion	Primary Region	Number of Adherents
Baha'i	200 countries	60,000,000
Buddhism	Southeast Asia	360,000,000
Christianity	250 countries	2,000,000,000
Confucianism	Japan and Korea	250,000,000
Daoism	China	250,000,000
Hinduism	India	900,000,000
Islam	Asia, Middle East	1,300,000,000
Jainism	India	4,000,000
Judaism	Israel, United States	14,000,000
Sikhism	India, Pakistan	23,000,000

[54] This data is drawn from Winfried Corduan's *Pocket Guide to World Religions* (Downers Grove: InterVarsity, 2006).

While for some people this argument might have considerable psychological force, from a logical standpoint it is very weak. The sheer diversity of views on a matter is not relevant to the question as to how many, if any, of them are true. Also, it might make us sad to think, as exclusivism suggests, that billions might never find their way to God because their religion teaches a false doctrine of salvation. But it doesn't follow from this that God will save adherents to all or most world religions.

2. *The Argument from Unity of Teaching.* Some religious pluralists prefer to emphasize the *unity* of world religions. They argue that, despite their differences, all of the major world religions essentially teach the same thing, specifically to love others and be a good person and thus gain God's favor. Pluralist John Hick proposes that we can sum up the general function of religion as follows: "to bring us to a right relationship with the ultimate divine reality, to awareness of our true nature and our place in the Whole, into the presence of God."[55] So why can't we affirm that many religions actually succeed in fulfilling this function?

This approach certainly hits upon an important fact with regard to the major religions—each promotes an ethic of personal conduct and there is significant overlap among their moral ideals. They all tend to advocate such things as loving-kindness, generosity, and peace. The problem, however, is that there are some religions that actually deny that salvation is achieved through good moral living. Examples would include Christianity and various forms of Buddhism and Hinduism. And just what is meant by the term *God* varies among religions. For Jews, Muslims, and Christians, God is personal and distinct from us. Hindus deny that God is personal and distinct from ourselves. And Buddhists do not necessarily even believe in God. Also, Jews and Muslims maintain that God is one person, while Christians believe God to be tri-personal. These are just some of the many doctrinal contradictions between religious perspectives which preclude the possibility that all or many world religions are essentially unified in teaching.

3. *The Argument from Divine Transcendence.* A common pluralist approach is to defend their position by emphasizing our ignorance about God. God, or the ultimate reality, is far beyond our ability to comprehend; therefore it is arrogantly presumptuous to insist that one's own religion has the corner on religious truth. John Hick writes, "[O]ur systems of human concepts cannot encompass the ultimately real. It is only as humanly thought and experienced that the Real fits

[55] John Hick, "Religious Pluralism and Ultimate Reality," *Philosophy of Religion*, 2nd ed, ed. Louis Pojman (Belmont, CA: Wadsworth, 1994), 528.

into our human categories."[56] The claim here, then, is that we just don't
know enough about God or the ultimate reality to make pronouncements about the truth or falsity of different religions.

This is one of those arguments that can be very intimidating in certain hands because it makes the exclusivist appear arrogant and narrow-
minded. However, the irony is that it is the person who makes this argument who is actually being arrogant, not to mention hypocritical. On
the one hand, he insists that it is presumptuous to think that one's own
religion is exclusively true, but at the same time the pluralist insists that
we have enough knowledge to be confident that God cannot be known!
Thus, the pluralist here is making a very strong knowledge claim about
the ultimate reality. Just because their claim is dogmatically negative
(that the ultimate reality cannot be known in itself) does not change
the fact that it is a strong knowledge claim. So, if the exclusivist really
is presumptuous in claiming knowledge of God, then the pluralist who
argues this way is being no less so.

4. *The Argument from the Relativity of Truth and Logic.* Some religious pluralists argue that the mistake of exclusivism is its reliance on
Aristotelian logic and such principles as the law of noncontradiction
(which denies that contradictory propositions can be true) and the law
of excluded middle (which denies that there is a middle ground between
truth and falsity). Pluralists often appeal to a rejection of such laws of
logic in order to justify their view. As Paul Knitter writes, "all religious
experience . . . must be two-eyed, dipolar, a union of opposites."[57] And
Wilfred Cantwell Smith says: "in all ultimate matters, truth lies not in
an either-or but in a both-and."[58] Exclusivists fail to recognize this fact
and proceed in their unyielding commitment to the laws of logic.

This argument is actually self-defeating. While it challenges the laws
of logic in order to pave the way for the pluralist's thesis, it relies on these
very logical principles in order to do so. Note how both Knitter and
Smith above make a strong *absolute* truth claim, specifically that contradictory truth claims in religion must be affirmed. In making this claim
they are *opposing* the exclusivist view as false. In other words, they refuse
to follow their own counsel (which would be to affirm the truth of both
religious pluralism and religious exclusivism). Of course, the reason they
do not do this is that it cannot be done, since these two views are mutu-

---

[56] John Hick, "A Pluralist View," in *More Than One Way? Four Views on Salvation in a
Pluralistic World*, ed. Dennis L. Okholm and Timothy R. Phillips (Grand Rapids: Zondervan,
1995), 50.

[57] Paul Knitter, *No Other Name? A Critical Survey of Christian Attitudes Toward the World
Religions* (Maryknoll, NY: Orbis, 1985), 221.

[58] Wilfred Cantwell Smith, *The Faith of Other Men* (New York: New American Library,
1963), 17.

ally exclusive. Try as the pluralist might to challenge the laws of logic, he must abide by these principles like everyone else. Unfortunately, they do not respect them enough to acknowledge that these laws apply just as much when it comes to religious doctrine as they do when discussing the subject of religious pluralism.

5. *The Argument from the Relativity of Religious Perception.* A final tactic used by religious pluralists is to appeal to the limits of human religious perceptions. John Hick writes,

> Each tradition functions as a kind of mental "lens"—consisting of concepts, stories (both historical and mythical), religious practices, artistic styles, forms of life—through which we perceive the divine. And because there is a plurality of such "lenses" there is a plurality of ways in which God is concretely thought and experienced.[59]

Hick is employing a Kantian gambit here, and it actually has an important insight. It is no doubt true that religious believers interpret all of their experiences through the lens of their worldview. As we noted in the introduction to this book, though, this is true for all of us, not just the religiously inclined. The real problem with this argument, however, is how it insinuates that the "theory-ladenness" of our religious perceptions implies that there is no such thing as truth in religion. This, of course, does not follow. That all our religious experience is interpreted is perfectly consistent with the idea that there is one true religion. In fact, Hick's point helps to explain why there are so many religious beliefs despite there being just one true religion. Also, Hick ignores the possibility that religious truth might be discovered in spite of the theory-ladenness of religious perception. If scientists and other scholars can discover truth in their fields despite their research biases, then why would it not be possible to discover religious truth as well?

We can see, then, that religious pluralism poses no obstacle to Christian exclusivism. Now we turn to a problem related to the question of justifying or verifying which religion (if any) is actually true.

6.4.2 The Problem of Miracles

We have seen that it is reasonable to believe that there is only one way to find favor with God. The question we must address now is: Is Christianity true? What reason is there to believe that the Christian religion is the true religion? Put another way, do we have any reason to believe that

[59] John Hick, *Disputed Questions in Theology and the Philosophy of Religion* (New Haven: Yale University Press, 1993),159

God has uniquely revealed Himself and His will in the person and work of Jesus Christ? The most important grounds for affirmative answers to these questions are to be found in the resurrection of Jesus Christ. Given the biblical and historical evidence, it is highly probable that God did indeed raise Him from the dead.[60] Now since it is unlikely in the extreme that God would perform such a spectacular miracle for someone who made significantly false religious claims, we have reason to believe that Jesus' teachings on religious matters are true. And what Jesus taught included the claim that He is God incarnate, that He died for the sins of the world, that whoever believes in Him will have everlasting life, and that He will someday return to judge the living and the dead—in other words, the central teachings of Christianity. The conclusion to be drawn is that God has indeed spoken in history through Jesus and His apostles; Christianity is true.

Of course, Jesus' resurrection is a miracle, and the New Testament recounts how He performed many miracles as well. The truth of Christianity, therefore, entails that miracles are possible. Moreover, it requires that we be able to identify a miracle when it occurs. As you might expect, some philosophers have argued that miracles are philosophically problematic. They are either impossible or, if possible, they cannot be rationally believed. In this section, we will examine these challenges to miracle-claims and the truth of Christianity.[61]

What Is a Miracle?

Regardless of one's religious tradition, miracles are events that inspire awe and amazement (see Matt 8:27; 9:33; Mark 2:12; 5:42; Acts 5:11). They are not the kinds of things that one ordinarily expects to happen. Rather, they are extraordinary occurrences that do not follow the normal course of nature. They seem to defy the laws of nature and thus are not natural, but are supernatural events which find their source in the causal activity of the One who controls nature. Accordingly, Norman Geisler defines a miracle thusly:

> From the human vantage point a miracle, then, is an unusual event ("wonder") that conveys and confirms an unusual mes-

---

[60] For thorough presentations of the evidence for Jesus' resurrection, see William Lane Craig, *The Son Rises: The Historical Evidence for the Resurrection of Jesus* (Eugene, OR: Wipf & Stock, 1981); Gary R. Habermas and Michael R. Licona, *The Case of the Resurrection of Jesus* (Grand Rapids: Kregel, 2004); Richard Swinburne, *The Resurrection of God Incarnate* (Oxford: Oxford University Press, 2003); and N. T. Wright, *The Resurrection of the Son of God* (Minneapolis: Fortress, 2003).

[61] Much of the material that follows is adapted from George Kurian, ed., *The Encyclopedia of Christian Civilization* (Oxford: Blackwell, 2009), s.v. "Miracles," by Steven B. Cowan. Used by permission.

sage ("sign") by means of unusual power. . . . From the divine vantage point a miracle is an act of God . . . that attracts the attention of the people of God ("wonder") to the Word of God (by a "sign").[62]

Perhaps a bit more concisely, *a miracle is an event occurring in the context of legitimate religious expectation that is so contrary to the ordinary course of nature that the causal activity of God is the best explanation for its occurrence.* Let us briefly clarify this definition.

First, notice that miracles are defined as acts of God. So they presuppose the existence of God. If the naturalistic worldview were true and God did not exist, then miracles would be impossible. However, we showed earlier in this chapter that there are good reasons to believe that God does exist. So miracles cannot be said to be strictly impossible. A God who created the universe and its laws *ex nihilo* can certainly suspend those laws temporarily to do something extraordinary. So, apart from an appeal to naturalism, few have been willing to claim that miracles are impossible.

Second, our definition says that a miracle is an event that is contrary to the ordinary course of nature. No event that could be explainable by current scientific laws can count as a miracle. A miracle is an event that defies natural explanation, which is why it inspires awe and amazement.

Third, a genuine miracle will take place in the context of legitimate religious expectation. Here our attention is focused on the theological significance of miracles as signs of God's activity. It is plausible to think that if God is truly intervening miraculously in history, He is doing so (at least in part) to get our attention. If a strange event occurs in a context that gives the observer no reason to expect or anticipate God's intervention, or that does not draw our attention to God in some way, then it is unlikely that the event is actually a miracle no matter how out of the ordinary it may seem. On the other hand, if the event occurs in the context, say, of someone claiming to be a spokesperson for God speaking to people who might want or need a word from God, then the event is a candidate for a *bona fide* miracle.

Of course, we must be sensitive to the possibility of counterfeit miracles (e.g., demonic activity, fakery, etc.). Such a possibility leads us to insist on a *legitimate* religious expectation. The beliefs, desires, and expectations of those looking for a miracle as well as that of the prophet promising a miracle must be consistent with what we already know

[62] Norman L. Geisler, *Miracles and the Modern Mind: A Defense of Biblical Miracles* (Grand Rapids: Baker, 1992), 98–99.

about God.[63] This is why the Israelites were warned early in their history to be on guard against false prophets and their counterfeit miracles:

> If a prophet or a dreamer of dreams arises among you and gives you a sign or a wonder, and the sign or the wonder comes true, concerning which he spoke to you, saying, "Let us go after other gods (whom you have not known) and let us serve them," you shall not listen to the words of that prophet or that dreamer of dreams; for the Lord your God is testing you to find out if you love the Lord your God with all your heart and with all your soul. (Deut 13:1–3)

The content of previous revelation or the knowledge of God gleaned from natural theology can expose a religious expectation as illegitimate and any accompanying "miracle" as counterfeit. Suppose for example, that an alleged prophet who seems able to do some amazing things claims that God is the impersonal Hindu Brahman. Since that claim is contrary to what we already know about God via Scripture and natural theology, we have reason to doubt that he is a true prophet and to reject his "miracles" as counterfeit. Alternatively, when the religious context conforms to what we should legitimately expect from God, we may consider any purported miracle as meeting the criterion of being a divine "sign."

With our definition of a miracle in hand, let us examine some objections to miracles.

Objections to Miracles

It was noted above that those who argue that miracles are impossible typically presuppose a naturalistic worldview. One exception to this rule was the philosopher Baruch Spinoza (1632–1677). He argued that miracles are impossible because they constitute violations of the laws of nature. For him, the laws of nature are by definition immutable. So there simply cannot be any miracles because miracles would require that immutable laws be mutable.

It is now considered wrong-headed to think of the laws of nature as immutable (see chap. 3). Even most naturalists understand the laws of nature as at most contingent facts about the world that could have been different. The so-called "laws" of nature are perhaps best characterized as observed regularities—the way things are seen ordinarily to work in nature—but are not such that they could not be otherwise or be suspended by an omnipotent being.

---

[63] See the discussion by R. Douglas Geivett, "The Evidential Value of Miracles," in R. Douglas Geivett and Gary R. Habermas, eds., *In Defense of Miracles: A Comprehensive Case for God's Action in History* (Downers Grove, IL: InterVarsity, 1997), 178–95 (esp. 189–94).

More influential in raising skepticism toward miracles was the Scottish philosopher David Hume. He did not argue that miracles were impossible but rather that one could never have enough evidence to justify believing that one had occurred. His argument begins with the principle that a wise person always believes what is most probable. Hume goes on to say,

> A miracle is a violation of the laws of nature; and as a firm and unalterable experience has established these laws, the proof against a miracle, from the very nature of the fact, is as entire as any argument from experience can possibly be imagined. . . . Nothing is esteemed a miracle, if it ever happened in the common course of nature. . . . There must, therefore, be a uniform experience against every miraculous event, otherwise the event would not merit that appellation. And as a uniform experience amounts to a proof, there is here a direct and full *proof*, from the nature of the fact, against the existence of any miracle.[64]

Hume here asserts that miracles are at best rare events that are inconsistent with our common, everyday experience. Natural laws, on the other hand, describe our common experience. Natural events, then, are by definition more probable than miraculous events. So when confronted with testimony regarding the occurrence of a miracle, what is more probable—that a miracle occurred or that the person making the claim is somehow mistaken or lying? Obviously, it is more probable that a miracle has not occurred. And since the wise person always believes what is more probable, he will always refuse to believe that a miracle has occurred. Hume's point is that no amount of testimony to a supposed miraculous event can overturn a wise person's evidence for the higher probability in every case, namely the operation of natural laws. Therefore, no wise person should ever believe miracle claims.

There are several flaws in Hume's argument, however. First, his argument is circular. In claiming that there is a uniform experience against miracles, he has already concluded that miracles have not been experienced by anyone. As C. S. Lewis observed, "We know the experience against [miracles] to be uniform only if we know that all the reports of them are false. And we know all the reports to be false only if we know already that miracles have never occurred. In fact, we are arguing in a circle."[65] So Hume is actually begging the question against the credibility of miracle claims.

---

[64] David Hume, *An Enquiry Concerning Human Understanding* (Indianapolis: Bobbs-Merrill, 1955), 122–23.

[65] C. S. Lewis, *Miracles* (New York: Macmillan, 1969), 105.

Second, when Hume speaks here of probability, he seems to have in mind *statistical* or *frequency* probability. Miracles are less probable than natural events because the former are less frequent than the latter. This claim is undisputed. But a statistical improbability would not alone make miracles incredible since many statistically improbable events do happen (e.g., a royal flush in Poker). A wise person does proportion his belief to what is most probable, but here "probable" cannot just mean "the most frequent." Rather, the wise person believes what is probable given the *total evidence*, which may include the testimony of a trustworthy person or even that of his own eyes. Consequently, statistical probabilities can be overridden by other kinds of evidence that make a rare event more probable, all things considered, than a more frequent natural event. So, for example, if a friend (whom you know to be generally trustworthy) tells you that he got a royal flush in his Poker game last night and shows you the money he won to prove it, and all of his gambling buddies corroborate the story, then what is the greatest probability all things considered? What would the wise person believe? He would undoubtedly believe his friend's story, the rarity of royal flushes notwithstanding.

Another kind of objection to believing in miracles is the more contemporary argument that no matter how strange and extraordinary an event is, we should not believe it to be a miracle because science may someday be able to give a natural explanation for it.[66] The idea is that we should presume that any alleged miracle is simply a natural event that our current scientific understanding is inadequate to explain but which will be explainable by a more mature science. This argument gains some ground from the fact that many strange events that once were attributed to supernatural causes are now explainable by science (e.g., epilepsy, bumblebee flight, movements of the planets, etc.). This argument suggests that to conclude that an unusual event is a miracle is to give up on scientific study prematurely; it is to commit the familiar fallacy of the "God-of-the-gaps" that we discussed in chapter 3, only this time within the realm of history instead of science.

In response, we should first acknowledge that this argument should encourage us to avoid gullibility when confronted with a miracle claim. Not every strange and unexplained event is a miracle, and it is possible that events that we cannot explain naturally now may one day be so explained. Indeed, even from the perspective of a Christian worldview, what we call natural laws are *God's* ordinary way of acting. Miracles are exceptions to the way God normally governs His creation and therefore

---

[66] For an example of an argument of this type, see Paul Edwards, ed., *Encyclopedia of Philosophy* (New York: MacMillan, 1966), s.v. "Miracles," by Antony Flew. See also Antony Flew, "Neo-Humean Arguments about the Miraculous," in *In Defense of Miracles*, 45–57.

are to be expected only occasionally. Nevertheless, this argument does not make it irrational ever to believe that a miracle has occurred.

For one thing, the insistence that we always postpone belief in a miracle in anticipation of a future natural explanation smacks of methodological naturalism. As in the discipline of science, historians sometimes suggest that it is illegitimate to appeal to supernatural agents in historical explanations. But as we saw in chapter 3, methodological naturalism is problematic. There is no good reason to think that God cannot intervene in history and no good reason, therefore, to restrict historical research to the quest for natural explanations.

For another thing, our definition of a miracle that we outlined above enables us to identify a miracle when it occurs without falling victim to the God-of-the-gaps mentality. A miracle is not simply a strange and rare event, but one which is so extraordinary that it defies everything we currently know about scientific laws. Moreover, it is an event that takes place within a legitimate religious context; it does not just happen "out of the blue" but is consistent with what we might expect God to do in that religious context. When theists have good reason to believe that such an event has occurred in such a context, we can reasonably conclude that God did it. In such cases, God's causal activity is the *best explanation* available for the event. Of course, further scientific study might overturn such a conclusion. However, the question concerns what is most rational to believe given what we currently know, *not* what would be most rational to believe given what we might know at some later time.[67]

One more objection to miracles also comes from David Hume. He argued that miracle claims tend to cancel each other out when they are used to authenticate religious beliefs. Many religions cite miracles to support their systems of belief. This being the case, Hume said, "All the prodigies [i.e., miracles] of different religions are to be regarded as contrary facts, and the evidences of these prodigies, whether strong or weak, as opposite to each other."[68] The idea is that if miracles support every religion, then they support no religion. They cancel each other out as evidence.

This argument, though, assumes that all miracle claims are equally well-evidenced. But there is no reason to believe this is the case. While we don't have the space here to investigate miracle claims of the world's religions, suffice it to say that the historical support for the miracle claims that appear in nonChristian religions is either weak or non-existent.[69]

---

[67] For more on these points, see Stephen T. Davis, "The Question of Miracles, Ascension, and Anti-Semitism," in *Jesus' Resurrection: Fact or Figment*, 71–76.

[68] David Hume, *An Enquiry Concerning Human Understanding*, 130.

[69] For evidence for this assertion, see David K. Clark, "Miracles in the World Religions," in *In Defense of Miracles*, 199–213.

On the other hand, the evidence for the central miracle claim of Christianity—the resurrection of Jesus—is very strong. So it is not at all obvious that miracle claims from different religions cancel each other out.

The conclusion we can reach in this section is that we have every reason to believe that Christianity is exclusively true. There are no compelling reasons to think that Christian exclusivism is irrational. Further, the Scriptures teach that Christianity is the one true religion. Lastly, since there is no philosophical reason to dismiss the evidence for the miraculous resurrection of Jesus, we have good grounds for believing that God has uniquely spoken in the person and work of Jesus Christ.

Questions for Reflection

1. In our response to one of Hick's arguments for pluralism we compared the theory-ladenness of religious perception to the same phenomenon in scientific research. Do you believe this is a fair comparison? Why or why not?
2. Do you think it would be fair for God to provide salvation through only one religion? Why or why not?
3. Are you satisfied with the definition of a miracle presented in this section? Why or why not?
4. Examine some of the miracle-claims in one or two non-Christian religions (e.g., Islam, Hinduism, etc.). Are these claims credible? Why or why not?

Conclusion

In this chapter we have explored several issues in philosophy of religion that also pertain to some of the central tenets of the Christian faith. We saw that theistic belief is well-justified by evidence and that even in the absence of supporting arguments one's belief in God may be perfectly rational. We also discussed major debates regarding some of the attributes of God. We saw that good reasons can be given in defense of the traditional, orthodox accounts of divine omnipotence and omniscience. And in examining the debates over God's relationship to time and whether God has emotions we found that there are compelling arguments on both sides of these issues, suggesting that perhaps compromise positions, divine omnitemporalism and omnipathos, respectively, might be the most reasonable positions.

The biggest challenge to theistic belief is the problem of evil. In looking at this problem, we showed why belief in God is compatible with the reality of even horrendous evils. And we noted that among theistic religions, Christianity is uniquely equipped to deal with the problem of evil, as we recognize that the God-man Himself, Jesus Christ, suffered horrendously, and that this very evil—by far the worst in history—was the critical means by which the Lord brought salvation to the human race. If ever there was an example of evil being used to bring about greater good, this was it. If God can redeem the worst of evils, then why not all lesser evils?

Finally, we considered the question whether Christianity is exclusively true. We rebutted the arguments of religious pluralists, thus showing that religious exclusivism is reasonable. Next, we considered one of the major evidences for the claim that Christianity is the one true religion—miracles. We saw that, notwithstanding the skeptical claims of David Hume, one may rationally believe in the occurrence of miracles, such as the central miracle of the Christian worldview—the resurrection of Jesus Christ.

The Bible says that "the fear of the Lord is the beginning of wisdom" (Prov 9:10). This is just one reason why philosophical exploration of faith issues is so critical. To show that belief in God is rational provides assurance for believers and prods unbelievers to reconsider their skepticism. But notice that the proverb just quoted says that fear of God is only the *beginning* of wisdom. True wisdom involves much more than proper belief. It also involves righteous living—consistently behaving rightly from a moral standpoint. This is the subject of ethics, which we will explore in the next chapter.

For Further Reading

On God's Existence

Collins, Robin. "A Scientific Argument for the Existence of God: The Fine-Tuning Design Argument," in *Reason for the Hope Within*, ed. Michael Murray. Grand Rapids, MI: Eerdmans, 1999.

Craig, William Lane, and Walter Armstrong-Sinnott. *God? A Christian and Atheist Debate*. Oxford: Oxford University Press, 2004.

Davis, Stephen T. *Reason and Theistic Proofs*. Grand Rapids, MI: Eerdmans, 1997.

Moreland, J. P. *Scaling the Secular City: A Defense of Christianity*. Grand Rapids: Baker, 1987.

Moreland, J. P., and Kai Nielsen. *Does God Exist? The Great Debate*. Nashville: Thomas Nelson, 1990.

Moser, Paul K., and Paul Copan, eds. *The Rationality of Theism*. London: Routledge, 2003.

On God's Attributes

Beilby, James K., and Paul R. Eddy, eds. *Divine Foreknowledge: Four Views*. Downers Grove, IL: InterVarsity, 2001.

Erickson, Millard J. *God the Father Almighty: A Contemporary Exploration of the Divine Attributes*. Grand Rapids: Baker, 2003.

Morris, Thomas V., ed. *Divine and Human Action: Essays in the Metaphysics of Theism*. Ithaca, NY: Cornell University Press, 1988.

Swinburne, Richard. *The Coherence of Theism*. Rev. ed. Oxford: Oxford University Press, 1993.

On the Problem of Evil

Feinberg, John S. *The Many Faces of Evil: Theological Systems and the Problem of Evil*. Grand Rapids: Zondervan, 1994.

Geisler, Norman L., and Winfried Corduan. *Philosophy of Religion*. 2nd ed. Grand Rapids: Baker, 1988.

Howard-Snyder, Daniel, ed. *The Evidential Argument from Evil*. Bloomington: Indiana University Press, 1996.

Plantinga, Alvin. *God, Freedom and Evil*. Grand Rapids: Eerdmans, 1974.

van Inwagen, Peter, ed. *Christian Faith and the Problem of Evil*. Grand Rapids: Eerdmans, 2004.

On Religious Pluralism and Exclusivism

Nash, Ronald H. *Is Jesus the Only Savior?* Grand Rapids: Zondervan, 1994.

Okholm, Dennis L., and Timothy R. Phillips, eds. *More Than One Way? Four Views on Salvation in a Pluralistic World*. Grand Rapids: Zondervan, 1995.

On Miracles

Beckwith, Francis J. "Theism, Miracles, and the Modern Mind." In *The Rationality of Theism*, ed. Paul Copan and Paul K. Moser. New York: Routledge, 2003. Pp. 221–236.

Geisler, Norman L. *Miracles and the Modern Mind: A Defense of Biblical Miracles*. Grand Rapids: Baker, 1992.

Geivett, R. Douglas, and Gary R. Habermas, eds. *In Defense of Miracles: A Comprehensive Case for God's Action in History*. Downers Grove, IL: InterVarsity, 1997.

Lewis, C. S. *Miracles*. New York: Macmillan, 1969.

Part 3

THE STUDY
OF VALUE

Chapter 7

ETHICS: HOW
SHOULD WE LIVE?

*"A man without ethics is a wild beast
loosed upon this world."*

—Manly P. Hall

Glossary Terms

Act utilitarianism	*Justice*
Categorical imperative	*Metaethics*
Consequentialism	*Moral objectivism*
Cultural relativism	*Moral subjectivism*
Deontology	*Natural law*
Divine command theory	*Nihilism*
Emotivism	*Normative ethics*
Ethical egoism	*Principle of utility*
Ethical hedonism	*Psychological egoism*
Ethical naturalism	*Psychological hedonism*
Ethical nonnaturalism	*Qualitative hedonism*
Ethical relativism	*Quantitative hedonism*
Existentialism	*Rule utilitarianism*
Hypothetical imperative	*Virtue*

The Woody Allen film *Crimes and Misdemeanors* presents an excruciating moral challenge. Judah Rosenthal is a successful ophthalmologist, who has had an affair with a neurotic airline attendant, Dolores Paley. Realizing that he doesn't want to lose his devoted wife, Judah decides to end the extramarital affair. However, Dolores is desperate to continue their relationship. When Judah insists on ending it, Dolores becomes irate and threatens to tell Judah's wife about their relationship. Moreover, she threatens to accuse him of embezzlement, which would ruin his career. Desperate for help, Judah confides in his brother, Jack, who has connections to organized crime. Jack offers to solve the problem by having Dolores killed. A hit man can "take care of her" and no one could possibly trace it to Judah. Initially appalled at the suggestion, Judah comes to see that this might be the only way to save his marriage and his career. So will he resort to murder?

If you haven't done so already, you'll need to see the film for yourself to find out what Judah decides. But this plot illustrates a couple of important points about ethics. First, Judah's situation is a dilemma. Whatever choice he makes is guaranteed to bring unpleasant consequences. But the right choice in this case appears to be the one with the most devastating consequences as far as Judah is concerned. This is what makes his decision so difficult. Second, Judah finds himself in a situation in which he can do the *wrong* thing with impunity. If he has Dolores killed, no one will find out. Judah's career and marriage will be spared, the stress of Dolores' blackmailing will disappear, and Judah's life can continue as before. Or can it?

The moral question posed by *Crimes and Misdemeanors* is actually a very old one, dating back to Plato: If you knew you could get away with a very profitable crime, would you do it? This is the question posed by a character named Glaucon in Plato's *Republic*. Glaucon tells the story of a shepherd, Gyges of Lydia, who discovers a ring that can make him invisible. Using its power Gyges goes on to seduce the queen, kill the king, and establish himself as ruler of Lydia. If you had this ring, could you resist such temptation? Or would you be corrupted by the power it represents (as was Gollum in Tolkien's later use of this same ring mythology)?

This is a penetrating question, as it reveals our true motives for acting morally and perhaps also the extent of our moral commitment. How willing are you to do what is right, even if it will be unpleasant? Socrates, the founder of Western philosophical ethics, was faced with this question. While awaiting his execution after his unjust conviction for impiety, Socrates was offered the opportunity of escape. His disciple, Crito, planned to bribe the jailers and usher his mentor off to a different city where he could live out the rest of his days in peace. But Socrates refused the plan, instead preferring to submit to the state's laws and judgment. He did what he considered to be the right thing, though the consequences were perilous. Shortly afterwards Socrates was given the deadly hemlock, which he drank to his demise.

Socrates' stated mission to his fellow Athenians was to inspire them to live virtuous lives. Socrates was convinced that moral living is paramount because one day God will judge our conduct here on earth. Christians and other theists believe the same thing. For this reason, ethics is arguably the most important field in philosophy and the ultimate purpose of all our philosophizing. Philosophy, after all, is the "love of wisdom" and wisdom has to do with knowing how to conduct oneself. If all of our understanding regarding logic, epistemology, metaphysics, human nature, and God Himself doesn't translate into better living, then what good is it?

The problem is that often it is difficult to discern what course of action is best. How do we discern moral truth? What principles are there to guide us in moral decision-making? Or is there even such a thing as moral truth? Is morality rather just a matter of opinion and emotions?

And what role does religious belief properly play in ethics? These are some of the questions that we will address in this chapter.

§ 7.1 Theory and Practice

In ethics, as in many fields, there is an important distinction to be made between theoretical issues and practical matters. In this section we will discuss the relationship between moral theory and practice.

7.1.1 Some Contemporary Moral Issues

Most moral questions are easily answered and not controversial. For instance, it is clear that Judah should not kill his mistress. He should end the relationship and confess his affair to his wife. Nor should Gyges use the ring to usurp power and seduce women. In these cases, as in most of life, the values involved are simple and straightforward. But some moral situations are not so easily analyzed. Here are a few examples.

1. *Lying to the Nazis.* Suppose you are a member of the French resistance in Paris during World War II. You have learned that the Nazis have been rounding up Jews in your community and taking them to a concentration camp in Drancy, just outside of Paris. Out of sympathy for their plight, you have decided to harbor a family of Jews in your cellar. However, word has leaked to the Gestapo and they now suspect that you are keeping Jews in hiding. So one day there is a knock at the door, and you open it to see two Nazi officers before you, and one of them immediately asks you whether you are harboring Jews. What do you say? Do you tell them the truth and lead them down to your cellar to expose your terrified friends? Or do you lie? Telling the truth will almost certainly result in the death of the entire family. On the other hand, you believe that lying is wrong. So what do you do?

2. *Physician-Assisted Suicide.* Suffering from the crippling effects of amyotrophic lateral sclerosis (also known as Lou Gehrig's disease), Thomas Youk was desperate for relief. He contacted Jack Kevorkian (so-called "Dr. Death") to assist him in committing suicide. After confirming that this was indeed Youk's will, Kevorkian complied, hooking Youk up to an IV and injecting him with euthanasia solution. Is this morally justifiable? If so, then consider the assisted suicide of Kevorkian's first client, Janet Adkins. After being diagnosed with Alzheimer's Disease, she enlisted Kevorkian to end her life, though her symptoms were still mild. Just a few days earlier Adkins was well enough to play tennis. Is

there a moral difference between the cases of Youk and Adkins? When, if ever, is suicide a legitimate choice?

3. *Cruelty to Animals.* In 2007 NFL football star Michael Vick was sentenced to 23 months in prison for his involvement in a dog fighting conspiracy. The judge who sentenced Vick declared that dog fighting is "cruel and inhumane" and told Vick that he owed an apology to millions of American kids who looked up to him. While dog fighting is widely condemned by most people in our culture, bullfighting is a highly valued tradition in Spain, Portugal, and many Latin American countries. The animals used in most bullfights probably suffer as much as the animals used in dogfights. Yet matadors are revered, while someone like Michael Vick is regarded as cruel and irresponsible. Is this coherent? Is either dog fighting or bullfighting morally defensible?

Each of these scenarios presents a moral dilemma, a conflict between values that morally serious people affirm and strive to live by. Each case forces us to affirm one cherished value at the expense of another, which is why they are so agonizing. To take a clear stand on one side or the other commits one to rejecting a value one holds dear. In the first case, there is a tension between the values of truth-telling and the sanctity of life. The second pits the sanctity of life against the alleviation of suffering. The third case pits the prevention of suffering against human autonomy and pleasure.

The problem is that all (or nearly all) of us value truth-telling, pleasure, the sanctity of human life, the prevention of suffering (for humans and animals), and human autonomy (self-determination). We also find conflicts among basic moral values in other perennial moral dilemmas, including abortion (human autonomy vs. the sanctity of human life), capital punishment (sanctity of human life vs. justice), and war (justice vs. the sanctity of human life and the prevention of suffering).

7.1.2 The Role of Moral Theory

How does one go about responding to such moral dilemmas as those posed above? Must we rely on our feelings or go with what just "seems right" to us in each case? Or are there actual standards to which we may appeal when addressing such matters? If there are standards for assessing moral issues, then where do they come from? Do they derive from human nature, culture, God, or some other source? Or is it some combination of these?

Answering ethical questions is not like answering empirical questions about, say, the color or weight of a physical object. The latter are factual inquiries that can be answered through sense experience alone.

Ethical questions are more complex, involving values as well as facts. Here we may distinguish between *descriptive* and *prescriptive* fields of study. Descriptive disciplines (e.g., biology, chemistry, physics, history, psychology and sociology) aim to describe aspects of the world, such as the chemical configuration of a euthanasia solution, the geopolitical factors leading to World War II, or whether watching violent films tends to result in violent behavior. In contrast, prescriptive disciplines (e.g., ethics, politics, aesthetics, and criminal justice) aim as well to make value judgments and prescribe certain kinds of behavior, policies, or institutions. Thus, an ethicist aims to discover when, if ever, euthanasia should be practiced, or when a nation is morally justified in going to war, or how much violence in art is morally justifiable. Likewise, political philosophers and aestheticians ask normative questions about government and art, respectively (which we will deal with in the next two chapters).

The difference, then, between descriptive and prescriptive disciplines boils down to whether the focus of inquiry concerns what *is* the case or what *ought* to be the case. Descriptive studies inquire into what *is*, while prescriptive studies aim to discover what *ought* to be. Ethics aims to tell us, specifically, how a person ought to conduct herself, both generally and in specific contexts.

So what guidelines are there for moral conduct? One approach is simply to refer to situational rules taking the form "*when in situation X, do Y.*" There are well-worn platitudes for most contexts, such as "Lend a hand to a friend in need," "Be kind to strangers," "Honesty is the best policy," and "Don't put off until tomorrow what you can do today." But these are obviously insufficient for guiding our lives, because many life situations are too complex for such simple rules. Also, we may ask *why* these are good rules. What makes it right to act generously or to be kind to others?

This suggests that there are more general *principles* in virtue of which situational rules are either good or bad. Some such rules have already been mentioned above and include the following:

- The principle of autonomy—all humans should be allowed to be self-determining
- The principle of utility—maximize pleasure and minimize pain
- The principle of justice – treat like cases alike
- The principle of the sanctity of human life—respect all human life as sacred

But as we also just noted, sometimes situations arise in which these principles contradict one another. How do we resolve conflicts between basic moral principles? Which principle is supreme and trumps the rest when they point us in different directions? Here is where we discover the need for an ethical *theory*—a general framework for orienting us regarding principles and other considerations in moral decision-making.

Ethical theories not only aim to prioritize moral principles; they aim to tell us the *meaning* of moral terms, concepts, and principles. Every ethical theory asks what it means to make a moral judgment such as "Honesty is good" or "Bin Laden is bad." And moral theories aim to tell us the real meaning of such terms as *duty, right, obligation, justice,* and *virtue*. All of these theoretical concepts pertain to the branch of ethics known as *metaethics*. However, once we settle these matters, there remain many practical implications of our moral theory, and this is the concern of *normative* ethics. Normative ethics pertains to the rightness or wrongness of particular actions, policies, or laws.

So questions such as "What is justice?" and "Is autonomy more fundamental than the sanctity of life?" are metaethical matters, while the questions "Is capital punishment just?" and "Is physician-assisted suicide morally permissible?" are questions for normative ethics. Notice that one's answers to questions of the latter sort are contingent upon one's answers to the former. This shows that metaethics is more fundamental than normative ethics. In ethics, as everywhere else, theory determines practice. We cannot make reliable moral judgments unless we first have an ethical theory in place. This is why it is so important to wrestle with theoretical ethics.

Now here is one of the most basic metaethical questions we can pose: Is there absolute moral truth? That is, are there moral values that are true for everyone, regardless of their culture or personal preferences? Those who believe in a universal moral standard are known as moral *objectivists*, while those who deny it are called moral *relativists*. Each of these theoretical standpoints comes in a variety of forms, and the remainder of this chapter will be devoted to discussing versions of each.

Questions for Reflection

1. What are your initial moral opinions about the three moral cases discussed above? Why do you think your opinions are correct?
2. Do you agree that each of the moral cases forces us to choose one cherished value at the expense of another? Why or why not?
3. As you consider each of these cases, what moral values or principles tend to guide your thinking and steer you to the answers you give? Why do you consider these values or principles to be so important?

§ 7.2 Ethical Relativism

One of the most outrageous shows on daytime television is the *Jerry Springer Show*. Most episodes feature people who are involved in scandalous behavior, usually of a sexual nature. Typically, the show commences by introducing the audience to someone who admits to, say, having an affair with his sister-in-law. After Springer interviews the subject for a few minutes, the wife comes on stage, followed by the sister-in-law and some other family members—who may need to be "escorted" by the stagehands so a fight doesn't ensue. The "discussion" that follows is profane and chaotic, which is just what the audience is hoping for. The proceedings are anything but a model of serious ethical inquiry, much less moral behavior. But along the way something happens that is very telling when it comes to moral theory. Some of the guests, such as the wife and some family members, accuse the husband of wrong-doing, calling his adultery "terrible," "cruel," and "immoral," while the man and his sister-in-law deny this, saying things like "Who is to say this is wrong?" or "It can't be wrong, because we love each other." Audience members chime in on either side as well, either denouncing or defending the couple. The divide, it turns out, is between moral objectivists and relativists—the question whether adultery is objectively wrong or just a matter of personal or cultural preference.

So is adultery objectively wrong or is it just a matter of preference? Naturally, this basic issue is never addressed on the Springer show. Guests and audience members may shout at and even assault one another, but they won't debate the moral foundations supporting their judgments. This is no surprise, of course, because serious debate is not as exciting to view as lunacy and violence. Still, for all its chaos, the show clearly displays the objectivist and relativist moral perspectives. It is also instructive in confirming the fact that emotions run high when arguments run out.

7.2.1 Cultural Relativism

Ethical relativism is the view that there are no universally true moral values. But if the relativist is correct, one may ask, what is the meaning of moral judgments, such as "Honesty is good" or "Adultery is wrong"? The answer, according to the relativist, is that such statements merely reflect people's preferences. But *whose* preferences? One major form of relativism says that the key to understanding moral convictions is culture. On this view, judgments about the goodness of honesty or the sinfulness of adultery simply reflect the attitudes dominant within the society in which one lives. This view is known as *cultural relativism*.

Cultural relativism has an ancient history, tracing as far back as Herodotus (484–430 BC), who famously declared that "custom is the king over all." But this perspective did not emerge as a popular metaethical perspective until fairly recently. As the field of anthropology advanced significantly in the nineteenth century, many scholars began to conclude that the differences between cultures are vast, including the moral values affirmed among people groups. Ruth Benedict (1887–1948) was an influential twentieth-century anthropologist and popularizer of cultural relativism. She observed a wide variety of practices accepted in other cultures that were condemned in the civilized West, including homosexuality and the switching of gender roles among certain native North American groups, the practice of random revenge killing by the Kwakiutl people, and the exaltation of megalomania among people on the Northwest Coast. Benedict concluded that since these practices were "normal" within those cultures, they were considered good. In fact, she maintained, to say of a behavior "it is habitual" or to call it "morally good" are just two ways of saying the same thing. According to Benedict, "the two phrases are synonymous."[1]

William Sumner (1840–1910) was another anthropologist who concluded that moral beliefs are entirely relative to cultures. He maintained that moral convictions evolve in two stages. First, as a people group struggles to survive, they discover that certain patterns of thought and behavior are advantageous. These customs, which he calls "folkways," become entrenched and are passed on by tradition and imitation. Then, as the folkways are practiced over time, a society begins to see them as norms of behavior, essential to right living. Sumner calls these "mores"; they function as standards of right and wrong in a culture. Mores are not fixed and final but evolve in a culture as life conditions alter the folkways. And, most importantly, they are always good. As Sumner puts it, "For the people of a time and place, their own mores are always good, or rather . . . for them there can be no question of the goodness or badness of their mores. The reason is because the standards of good and right are in the mores."[2]

Benedict and Sumner well represent the cultural relativist position. Now let's apply this theory to our case studies to get a better fix on this view. How would the cultural relativist advise us regarding the Nazi inquest? Presumably in 1940s France there was a strong belief in the sanctity of human life and this was believed to take priority over truth-telling. Furthermore, Nazi anti-Semitic values were far from dominant

---

[1] Ruth Benedict, "Anthropology and the Abnormal," in *The Journal of General Psychology* 10 (1934): 73.

[2] William G. Sumner, *Folkways* (Boston: Ginn and Co., 1913), 58.

within French culture. So lying to the Nazis would be the proper response in this case, according to the cultural relativist. But, of course, if the predominant cultural value was strongly anti-Semitic, then the cultural relativist would favor telling the Nazis the truth.

As for physician-assisted suicide, the cultural relativist would say that, again, the right course of action depends upon what the mores in our culture dictate. But, at this time in our nation's history, this is not easy to ascertain, at least when it comes to those who are suffering terribly and want to die. The cultural relativist would likely say that the reason this issue is so controversial in the U.S. today is that we are in the midst of a cultural shift, where the folkway of preserving life at all costs is being displaced by the folkway of terminating life in the interest of autonomy and reduction of suffering. So to make a decision now is very difficult.

Finally, the cultural relativist would say that the case of cruelty to animals illustrates this theory's main claim. The moral rightness or wrongness of dog fighting and bullfighting can only be judged in light of the broader culture in which these amusements are practiced. Given the mores of their respective cultures, Americans are right to condemn Michael Vick and his fellow dog-fighting conspirators. But Spaniards, Portuguese, and Latin Americans are also right to approve of bullfighting. Neither form of animal torture is inherently right or wrong. It all depends upon social norms.

The Plurality Argument for Cultural Relativism

The cultural relativist's assessment of each of these cases comes down to the basic claim that there are no universal moral standards; all moral values are local. It is clear that the likes of Benedict and Sumner base this thesis on anthropological data—the variety and contradictory nature of values affirmed in different cultures around the world. But just what is the essence of their argument? It appears the cultural relativist inference could be summarized as follows:

(1) Moral values differ from culture to culture.
(2) Therefore, there is no objective moral standard.

Let us call this the *Plurality Argument* for cultural relativism. The premise is obviously true, but is the inference valid? Clearly it is not, since the plurality of views on any issue does not prove that there is no objective truth to be found. Consider the situation in astronomy 500 years ago. Some affirmed heliocentrism, the view that Earth and the other planets revolve around the Sun. Others, perhaps most, still affirmed geocentrism, the view that the Earth is at the center and the Sun along with the other planets revolve around the Earth. Still others maintained that the Earth is flat, and there were other more exotic theories as well. Now during this period there was one objective truth in the matter, although it was not clear to everyone what that truth was. Heliocentrism was true all along, despite the diversity of opinions. So why should we see things any differently when it comes to morality? That there are many conflicting opinions about proper conduct does not rule out the possibility that there is objective truth in ethics, an absolute standard to which everyone is subject.

Here cultural relativists object that the situations are very different when it comes to science and ethics, for in science there is a reliable method of inquiry by which we can discover truth. In ethics, however, there is no such method. The question of the Earth's place in the cosmos was eventually settled through empirical investigation. In moral matters no such agreement can be achieved because it is not a strictly empirical issue. Thus, the above argument may be embellished as follows:

(1) Moral values differ from culture to culture.
(2) There is no reliable method of inquiry by which to discover an objective moral standard.
(3) Therefore, there is no objective moral standard.

As common as this line of thinking is, it is poor reasoning. First, the argument is still invalid. Even if we grant the second premise along with the first, the conclusion does not follow. In fact, the possibility of *discovering* objective truth is altogether irrelevant to the question as to whether there *is* objective truth. Again, the astronomy example is instructive. For most of human history there was no reliable method for ascertaining the Earth's place in the cosmos. Until modern science developed, you might say, human beings were epistemologically barred from knowing this truth. Yet heliocentrism *was true* all along in spite of this. The revised version of the plurality argument makes a simple confusion between truth and knowledge. Just because a fact is not or cannot be known, this does not imply that it is not true. Truth, in this sense, is independent of knowledge. Our epistemological limits have no bearing on the nature of reality.

In addition to the argument being invalid, the second premise is false. It is true that the methodologies of science and ethics differ in important ways. But there *is* a reliable method of inquiry when it comes to moral truth, specifically the careful use of reason, experience, and divine revelation. Also, as we saw in chapter 3, the scientific method is not infallible, and even when used properly there are often disagreements among scientific researchers. Today there is much debate in every branch of science over a number of theoretical issues, but we know this doesn't negate the fact that there is much we do know about the world through scientific inquiry. Similarly, just because there is much disagreement about certain moral issues, this does not undermine the knowledge we do have in ethics.

Criticisms of Cultural Relativism

So the plurality argument for cultural relativism fails. That this is the best argument the cultural relativist has is testament to how irrational the view is. It is no wonder that cultural relativists are rare in the philosophical community. But the lack of good arguments on behalf of this view is only part of the problem. Probably, cultural relativism's lack of appeal owes more to its problematic implications. Moral philosopher James Rachels has noted some of these.[3] First, if cultural relativism were true, then we could not criticize the practices of another culture, no matter how heinous they seem to us. We could not condemn slavery as practiced in certain cultures where it is approved. Nor could we insist that it is wrong for other societies to practice female genital mutilation or other forms of oppression of women. We could not even condemn the Nazi holocaust or other cases of genocide, so long as these acts were approved by the broader culture in which they were performed.

Second, if cultural relativism were true, then moral progress in a society would be impossible. The notion of progress only makes sense in light of a fixed standard to which one is conforming more and more closely. But according to cultural relativism, there are no fixed moral standards, only cultural practices that shift over time. All moral change is equal, neither objectively good nor bad. So when slavery was abolished in America, this was not moral progress. Nor did we morally progress when women were granted the right to vote.

Third, cultural relativism implies that all moral reformers are corrupt. People, such as Mahatma Gandhi or Martin Luther King, who challenge a culture's accepted practices must be judged immoral, for they oppose the only standard the cultural relativist recognizes. However, once a reformer's own values are adopted by a culture, then he or she may be judged positively. So Ghandi, King, and the values they championed were not good all along but bad for a while and, once their societies changed in accordance with their views, they became good.

Clearly all of these implications of cultural relativism are absurd. Common sense tells us that some cultural practices, such as genocide and genital mutilation, are immoral, that whole cultures may progress

---

[3] James Rachels, *The Elements of Moral Philosophy*, 4th ed. (New York: McGraw Hill, 2003), 21–23.

morally, and that the values of moral reformers are good or bad independently of whether they succeed in changing cultural practice. So it appears that cultural relativism not only lacks rational grounds but also defies common-sense thinking about morality.

7.2.2 Moral Subjectivism

Another problem with cultural relativism regards the ambiguity of the notion of "culture." Just what constitutes a culture? Cultures are not synonymous with nations, since a country can be composed of multiple cultures. Even a city, such as New York or Los Angeles, can have many subcultures. In fact, we often talk of subcultures within subcultures, so where does it stop? A different brand of relativism, known as moral *subjectivism*, avoids this problem by insisting that moral values are relative to individual persons, rather than people groups. The pre-Socratic philosopher Protagoras (490–420 BC) was an early exponent of this view, as is evident in his famous dictum, "Man is the measure of all things." In the seventeenth century, Thomas Hobbes (1588–1679) espoused a version of subjectivism, declaring that "whatsoever is the object of any man's appetite or desire, that is it which he for his part call[s] *good*; and the object of his hate and aversion, *evil*."[4]

Hume's Moral Subjectivism

A century after Hobbes, David Hume (1711–1776) offered a vigorous defense of subjectivism, which to this day might remain the strongest argument for the view. According to Hume, there are two kinds of truths, those which can be known by reason alone, which he calls *relations of ideas*, and those which are known through experience, which he calls *matters of fact*. Relations of ideas include such propositions as "Triangles are three-sided" and "Bachelors are unmarried." They cannot be doubted, because they are true by definition and to deny them is self-contradictory. Matters of fact include such propositions as "Stop signs are red" and "Obama is President." They are not true by definition but are discovered through the senses.

Now according to Hume, all truths must fall into one of these two categories of relations of ideas or matters of fact. So, then, to which category do moral claims such as "Generosity is good" and "War is bad" belong? They cannot be relations of ideas, because they are not true by definition, nor does denying them imply a contradiction. But neither can they be matters of fact, since values are not perceived by the senses. So then what is the source of our moral judgments? Hume says they derive from human passions:

[4] Thomas Hobbes, *Leviathan* (New York: Macmillan, 1962), 48.

Take any action allowed to be vicious: Wilful murder, for instance. Examine it in all lights, and see if you can find that matter of fact, or real existence, which you call *vice*. In whatever way you take it, you find only certain passions, motives, volitions and thoughts. There is no other matter of fact in the case. The vice entirely escapes you, as long as you consider the object. You never can find it, till you turn your reflection into your own breast, and find a sentiment of disapprobation, which arises in you, towards this action. Here is a matter of fact; but it is the object of feeling, not reason. It lies in yourself, not in the object.[5]

Like cultural relativists, moral subjectivists deny that there is universal moral truth. But the subjectivist relativizes moral judgments more radically than the cultural relativist—down to the individual. In addition to overcoming the ambiguity problem regarding culture, subjectivism also accounts for a significant fact of human experience: our moral convictions coincide with our likes and dislikes. That is, we tend to like what we think is good and dislike what we think is wrong. It is easy to see, then, why Hobbes and Hume would equate our moral values with feelings. Another strength of the theory is its simplicity, both in terms of definition and application. With regard to our case studies, the subjectivist's construal of each is plain. The right thing to do is whatever you prefer. Would you rather save the Jewish family and risk your own life?—then go for it. If not, then telling the truth is the right option. Physician-assisted suicide? Dog fighting and bullfighting? In each case, the correct answer comes down to how you feel about it. Whatever you prefer is best.

But now back to Hume's defense of the view. Is his argument valid? Yes, it appears so. If we can only know relations of ideas and matters of fact, then this does seem to rule out moral judgments as an object of knowledge. But who says that these two categories of truth are exhaustive? Why should we trust Hume on this? Might not metaphysical truths be a third category? And moral truths still another? And what about the possibility of truths that come to us through special divine revelation? Even more possibilities might be considered. It is noteworthy that Hume offers no argument for his restriction of truth to his two categories. Thus, he commits the fallacy of false dilemma.

---

[5] David Hume, *A Treatise of Human Nature*, 2nd ed. (Oxford: Oxford University Press, 1978), 468–69.

Criticisms of Subjectivism

As for the reasonableness of moral subjectivism itself, unfortunately it inherits most of the practical problems that plague cultural relativism and even suffers from more besides these.[6] Each of the following implications contradicts common sense. First, if moral subjectivism is true, then no one can be mistaken in their moral judgments. So long as my judgments reflect my actual feelings about the person or act that I am judging, then I cannot be mistaken. But, of course, this is absurd. We take it to be an obvious fact that everyone has been mistaken in their moral judgments at one time or another.

Second, subjectivism implies that people don't really disagree about moral issues and, as a consequence, debate about ethical issues is pointless. If moral opinions are just matters of preference, then disagreement is impossible. Two people can disagree only if they make contradictory truth claims. But according to subjectivism one's moral judgments are really only statements about oneself, not an external object or state of affairs. So if the subjectivist is correct, then debating issues like euthanasia and animal rights would be as ridiculous as debating whether the taste of broccoli is pleasant or unpleasant. It follows that debate about ethical issues is pointless. You can only debate where there is possibility for disagreement about objective moral truth.

Finally, and most frighteningly, moral subjectivism has the consequence that no behavior or policy can be praised or condemned in any absolute sense. No matter what the conduct, from the most heroic acts to genocidal atrocities, when one declares them good or evil, all one is really saying is "I like it" or "I don't like it." Moreover, nobody's preferences are any more or less valid than anyone else's. If the subjectivist is correct, then the judgments of the most revered saint are no more true than those of Adolf Hitler or Saddam Hussein. Clearly, subjectivism suffers from at least as many problems as cultural relativism and is just as untenable as a moral theory.

7.2.3 Beyond Relativism

While the rise of ethical relativism in the twentieth century was a striking movement in ethics, reactions against moral objectivism would only turn more radical. For all of its problems, ethical relativism at least acknowledged that moral judgments are meaningful and have a truth value. Eventually, even these basic notions were challenged.

---

[6] Again, we are indebted to James Rachels' analysis for these criticisms. See *The Elements of Moral Philosophy*, 35–36.

Emotivism

In chapter 4 we discussed the influential twentieth-century movement known as *logical positivism*. We noted how A. J. Ayer (1910–1989) proposed the *verification principle*, which says that only those propositions which are (at least in principle) empirically verifiable are meaningful. We saw how such a standard would rule out the possibility of metaphysics and that statements such as "God exists" or "humans have souls" must be rejected as meaningless. Ayer applied this radical positivist thesis to ethics as well. Consider these propositions:

(1) Courage is a virtue.
(2) Stealing is wrong.
(3) You ought to help persons in need.

Clearly, none of these assertions can be empirically verified. Therefore, according to Ayer, they must be considered meaningless, tantamount to uttering such nonsense as "The slithy toves did gyre and gimble in the wabe." All moral judgments, the positivist maintains, lack cognitive content and have no more meaning than metaphysical assertions or jabberwocky.

But, then, if moral judgments lack cognitive content, what sort of content *do* they have? Ayer's answer is that they have *emotive* content. Moral statements, he says, "are pure expressions of feeling."[7] But this is not their only function, as Ayer explains:

> It is worth mentioning that ethical terms do not serve only to express feeling. They are calculated also to arouse feeling, and so to stimulate action. . . . In fact, we may define the meaning of the various ethical words in terms both of the different feelings they are ordinarily taken to express and also the different responses which they are calculated to provoke.[8]

So the statement "Courage is a virtue" does not describe reality in any way but is equivalent to something like "Hurrah for courage!" And to say "Stealing is wrong" really means something like "Stealing, yecch!" or perhaps "Please don't steal!" This theory, known as *emotivism*, constitutes a further step away from moral objectivism. Although ethical relativists deny the universal validity of moral statements, they do acknowledge that such judgments have meaning and truth value. Not so for the emotivist.

So what would be the emotivist's take on our case studies? The emotivist certainly cannot offer any reasoned counsel for courses of action

---

[7] A. J. Ayer, *Language, Truth and Logic* (New York: Dover, 1936), 108.
[8] Ibid.

regarding truth-telling, euthanasia, animal torture, or any other moral matter. While she will acknowledge that each of us has feelings about such issues, and often a strong will to influence others' feelings about them, she cannot consistently offer any normative advice for dealing with them. We are left with mere emotion and no possibility for rational engagement with the issues—a situation that is a lot like, well, the *Jerry Springer Show*. As odd as it sounds, perhaps that program is, in an indirect way, one of the unfortunate legacies of logical positivism.

Nihilism and Existentialism

With logical positivism ethics is demoted to the study of emotional outbursts. Since the moral life is central to human meaning, it is no surprise that paralleling the rise of positivism was *nihilism*, the view that life has no meaning. Emotivism and nihilism are probably best understood as effects from a common cause, that being the rejection of God and a theistic worldview in the West (which was, of course, connected with the more general rejection of metaphysics).

Friedrich Nietzsche (1844–1900) was the great prophet of nihilism. Through his character Zarathustra, he proclaimed that "God is dead," meaning by this that as a cultural fact the Western world no longer believes in God. Therefore, Nietzsche maintained, all moral values associated with this belief are without foundation. Just a few years earlier, Dostoyevsky had declared that if there is no God, then "everything is permitted."[9] Nietzsche took this implication seriously; so when he concluded there is no God his immediate concern was to address the specter of nihilism—how does one generate meaning in a meaningless world? How can one create value in life when there are no real values to be found?

Nihilism is the most unstable view among all philosophical perspectives. To reject the notion that one's life has meaning will eventually lead either to self-destruction or to an abandonment of this conviction. One cannot survive for very long—at least not in a healthy psychological condition—believing that life has no meaning. This realization prompted Albert Camus (1913–1960) to write *The Myth of Sisyphus*, in which he says, "There is but one truly serious philosophical problem, and that is suicide."[10] If life is absurd and has no inherent meaning, then why go on?

Nietzsche and Camus, along with philosophers such as Søren Kierkegaard (1813–1855), Martin Heidegger (1889–1976), and Jean Paul Sartre (1905–1980), came to be called *existentialists*. This moniker refers

---

[9] Fyodor Dostoyevsky, *The Brothers Karamazov*, trans. David Magarshack (London: Penguin, 1958), 309.

[10] Albert Camus, *The Myth of Sisyphus*, trans. Justin O'Brien (New York: Random House, 1955), 3.

to the fact that they all shared the conviction that when it comes to human beings *existence precedes essence*. That is, according to existentialism, human beings do not have a fixed nature. Rather, we are radically free, capable of defining ourselves and our destiny with our own choices. In Sartre's words, "[M]an is nothing else but what he makes of himself"; we are "condemned to be free."[11] While some existentialists, such as Kierkegaard, Gabriel Marcel (1889–1973) and Martin Buber (1878–1965), were theists, the leaders of the movement were atheists. And their characteristic themes of radical freedom, alienation, and despair were grounded in the conviction that humans were not created but are the product of natural causes in an indifferent universe. Our only recourse for finding purpose, then, is what we can conjure for ourselves.

The atheistic existentialists all essentially took the same route in answering the pressing question of nihilism. They advocated creating meaning and values for ourselves. For Camus and Sartre this meant living authentically, facing the absurdity of life honestly and carrying on life's projects in spite of it. For Nietzsche, this meant making a "transvaluation of all values"—to reject traditional Christian values in favor of values such as pride and self-reliance. Theistic existentialists emphasized the need to approach God through radical faith, contradicting even reason itself. While acknowledging the basic forlornness of the human condition, they saw this as a symptom of our rebellion and estrangement from God. Sin and despair are, in Kierkegaard's words, a "sickness unto death," from which we can only be rescued through union with God.

Many have argued that nihilism is the inevitable consequence of relativism. Once belief in moral absolutes is abandoned, there remains no more foundation for making sense of life's ultimate meaning. But it is one thing to say that a universally true moral standard is necessary for life to be meaningful, and it is another thing to define such a standard. In the next two sections we will consider a variety of theories which aim to do just this.

Questions for Reflection

1. The fact that there are universally true moral values is compatible with the relativity of other values. Identify some values that are, in fact, culturally relative or personally subjective.
2. The plurality argument appears to be the strongest argument for cultural relativism. Can you think of other reasons a person might have for affirming this view?

[11] Jean-Paul Sartre, *Existentialism*, trans. Bernard Frechtman (New York: Philosophical Library, 1947), 18, 27.

3. The fact that a cultural relativist cannot condemn cultural practices such as female circumcision shows that the view is untenable. Can you think of some other practices or values widely affirmed in some cultures that are also obviously wrong?
4. What are the similarities between moral subjectivism and emotivism? How are the two views different?
5. Do you agree with Dostoyevsky that in the absence of God "everything is permitted"? Why or why not?
6. The version of nihilism discussed here is more precisely known as moral nihilism. A more radical view, known as metaphysical nihilism, says that nothing is real. Is such a view even coherent? Why or why not?
7. Do you see any problem inherent in the notion that one could be a Christian existentialist?

§ 7.3 Moral Objectivism: Naturalistic Theories

We have discussed several forms of moral skepticism, including two varieties of ethical relativism, emotivism, and nihilism. Each of these views constitutes a rejection of moral objectivism, the view that there is a universally true moral standard. The essential claims of objectivism are as follows. First, moral statements have a truth value that is independent of cultural practices, individual preferences, and human emotions. Second, when a person declares, for example, that "Stealing is wrong" or "Giving to charity is good," these judgments describe the acts in question, not cultural or personal attitudes toward them. (For a summary analysis of the theories considered thus far, see Table 7.1.)

Table 7.1

Moral Theory	Moral Judgment	What This Judgment Really Means
Cultural relativism:	X is good	= X accords with this culture's standards
Moral subjectivism:	X is good	= I like X
Emotivism:	X is good	= Hurrah for X!
Moral objectivism:	X is good	= X accords with the universal moral standard

Moral objectivism is far and away the dominant view among philosophers today, as it has been throughout history. This is because objectivism avoids all of the serious problems that plague the other views. To summarize, moral objectivism can account for these common-sense facts, whereas cultural relativism cannot:

- Cultural practices can sometimes be morally wrong.
- Cultures can progress or regress morally.
- Moral reformers may be good even if they go against the cultural grain.

And objectivism accounts for these facts, too, whereas subjectivism and emotivism cannot:

- People sometimes morally disagree.
- People sometimes are mistaken in their moral judgments.
- One's attitude or feelings about a person or behavior might not reflect its actual moral quality.

All objectivists agree that there is an absolute ethical standard, a moral code that applies to every person. This is the key factor in accounting for so many of our common-sense intuitions about ethics. But the question looms: What *is* the universal standard? Here there is much disagreement. Next we will look at the leading theories as to the nature of the moral standard. Some of these theories claim that the moral standard is reducible to natural facts, such as human self-interest, pleasure, or rationality. Such views are sometimes described as *naturalistic* ethical theories. Those which claim that the moral standard transcends the natural world are called *nonnaturalistic* theories. We will examine the varieties of naturalistic ethical systems first.

7.3.1 Ethical Egoism

It is often said that people are naturally selfish. What is much less common is the claim that it is *right* to be selfish. Yet one important moral theory, *ethical egoism*, makes this very claim, or at least something much like it. The actual thesis of ethical egoism is that it is one's basic moral duty to always act in one's self-interest. That is, whatever else might be the case, your actions should contribute to your own long-term good. This is the essence of morality, according to the ethical egoist, and it applies to everyone everywhere.

Rand's Ethical Egoism

The leading modern proponent of ethical egoism is the fiction writer Ayn Rand (1908–1982). Rand claims that humans are ends in themselves, that human life is the sole standard for value, and, therefore, whatever best enables human beings to survive in this world must be our ultimate guide in ethics. And Rand proposes that nothing improves humanity more than competition among individuals, each doing their best to achieve their own ends. As this happens, human society benefits.

Rand denounces altruism, maintaining that "human good does not require human sacrifices and cannot be achieved by the sacrifice of anyone to anyone." This is because, as she says, "the rational self-interests of men do not clash."[12] Anyway, she claims, altruism is counterproductive. Through the main character in her book, *Atlas Shrugged*, Rand argues that altruistic actions damage self-esteem. When we make sacrifices to help someone, we encourage that person to see herself as a victim and parasite. This kills personal initiative and moral motivation, and it encourages the person to approach others from the position of a beggar. Thus, claims Rand, altruism actually does more harm than good. So a morally decent person would not act altruistically.

There are many advantages to the ethical egoist approach. First, as a theory it is simple and easy to understand. Second, acting in one's own self-interest comes naturally. Some would even say that, as a psychological fact, human beings always pursue their own self-interest. This thesis is known as *psychological egoism*. While this may or may not be true, Rand would clarify that our duty is not just to *pursue* our own self-interest but to actually *achieve* it. Third, ethical egoism coheres with insights from biology and economics. As the fittest organisms successfully compete for survival, the entire species benefits. And as businesses compete for profits, consumers and society as a whole flourish. Rand's egoist moral theory can be seen as a direct adaptation of Darwinian and capitalist ideas to the realm of ethics.

It should also be noted that acting to promote one's own self-interest is not inconsistent with the promotion of the good of others or even one's society. Ethical egoists such as Rand do not endorse a "zero sum" concept of egoistic pursuits, such that one person's gain is necessarily another person's loss. In claiming that "the rational self-interests of men do not clash," Rand believes that as each person seeks her own self-interest all of society will flourish. But this benefit to the whole is more a happy consequence than the primary motivation, in Rand's view. Our focus must never be to improve society as a collective, which would only tempt us to deadly altruism and self-sacrifice. Instead, our focus should always be the advancement of our own interests.

So how would the ethical egoist approach our case studies? In each instance, the decisive question would obviously be "What course of ac-

---

[12] Ayn Rand, *The Virtue of Selfishness* (New York: New American Library, 1964), 28

tion will advance my own interests?" Therefore, because of the many factors involved in any concrete situation, we cannot prejudge the egoist's likely choice in most of these cases without knowing specific details about the circumstances. She might see either lying or telling the truth to the Nazis as personally advantageous. Likewise, an ethical egoist might advocate or oppose physician-assisted suicide or animal torture, depending on various factors. An ethical egoist would be open to any of these things, so long as she could be confident that a given course of action would serve her long-term interests.

Criticisms of Ethical Egoism

Ethical egoism has many insights. It rightly recognizes the importance of self-interest as an object of concern and as a motivation for action. And, in particular, Ayn Rand is correct in affirming the great value of human life. However, egoism is problematic for several reasons. First, although Rand claims otherwise, peoples' rational self-interests do sometimes clash. In fact, the field of economics is premised on the observation that there are unlimited wants and limited resources, which leads to competing interests. The sundry economic theories are just so many ways of dealing with this problem. But to illustrate the point in a concrete way, consider two people, Bill and Sue, who have applied for the same job. Both of them need the job desperately, but only one of them can be hired. It is in the interest of each of them to get the job, and one's success implies the other's failure. Their competition involves a clash of interests. Cases like this are quite common, and Rand's theory fails to account for this.

Another problem with ethical egoism, highlighted by James Rachels, is that the theory is fundamentally unjust.[13] Most of us recognize that it is wrong to arbitrarily discriminate against people. We should not maintain biases in moral decision-making on the basis of such things as skin color, ethnicity, gender, or age. Slavery is a notorious example of this, as black Americans were regarded as property for white Americans for generations, and even long after the abolition of slavery black Americans were treated as second-class citizens. The problem boils down to a simple matter of justice. It is an arbitrary, and therefore unjustifiable, preference of one group over another. In much the same way, ethical egoism tells us to prefer one party (oneself) over another (everyone else). Egoism gives us no morally relevant reason for biasing all of our decisions in our own favor, and for this reason it is inherently unjust.

A third problem with egoism is the fact that it denies a common-sense intuition (at least for most people) that altruism and self-sacrifice

---

[13] Rachels, *The Elements of Moral Philosophy*, 88–89.

are good, even noble things. But ethical egoism cannot account for this. Consider the case of Arland D. Williams Jr. He was aboard Air Florida flight 90, which crashed into the Potomac River on January 13, 1982. Most of the passengers perished immediately, but several made their way out of the plane and swam to the surface of the icy Potomac. Within minutes a helicopter was on the scene, and a line was lowered to the survivors who were clinging to debris and already suffering severe hypothermia. Williams grabbed the line and wrapped it around one of the other survivors, who was hauled to safety. Williams did this for several other survivors, but when the helicopter returned for him he had already succumbed to the frigid waters. How are we to assess Williams' self-sacrifice? Most of us would say he was a hero, giving his life to save others. But ethical egoism would tell us that what he did was morally wrong, since he did not pursue his own self-interest.

A final objection to ethical egoism regards an epistemological difficulty facing the egoist as he applies the theory. How is one to ascertain just what courses of action will contribute to one's long-term self-interest? The theory assumes that each person knows what is in her best interest generally and that we can, in any particular case, identify which course of action will serve that interest. But this is questionable at best. At worst, it leads to moral chaos, as it is possible to conceive of many cruel and inhumane behaviors that a person could claim to be in her self-interest in one way or another. Indeed, if psychological egoism is true, then even the most wicked people in history, from Ivan the Terrible to Adolf Hitler, were motivated by self-interest. True moral living must be motivated by something more than this.

7.3.2 Utilitarianism

Perhaps the most widely acknowledged motivation for behavior is pleasure. We all choose careers, friends, spouses, recreational activities, and so forth at least in part because they bring us pleasure. Because the pursuit of pleasure and the avoidance of pain are so basic to human experience, it is no surprise that some philosophers have proposed to make these the foundation of ethics. The moral tradition that focuses on pleasure as the ultimate human end is known as *hedonism*, and its historical roots go back to the ancient philosopher Epicurus (341–270 BC) after whom Epicureanism is named.

As with egoism, both descriptive and prescriptive theses are associated with hedonism. *Psychological hedonism* is the claim that as a matter of fact all human beings seek pleasure. Epicurus affirmed this, saying, "It is to obtain this end that we always act, namely to avoid pain and fear."[14] His main concern was to promote *ethical hedonism*, the thesis that pleasure is the highest human good. But to his mind the two claims were crucially related, the former serving as the foundation for the latter: "pleasure [is] the beginning and end of the blessed life. For we recognize pleasure as the first good innate in us, and from pleasure we begin every act of choice and avoidance, and to pleasure we return again, using the feeling as the standard by which we judge every good."[15]

Classical Utilitarianism: Bentham and Mill

Hedonism was influential in the ancient world and remained so all the way through the Middle Ages. In the modern period, after the scientific revolution, the theory was given a distinctly empirical twist by the British philosopher Jeremy Bentham (1748–1832). Like Epicurus, Bentham believed that the hedonist impulse is innate and that our moral standard is properly built upon this: "Nature has placed mankind under the governance of two sovereign masters, pain and pleasure. It is for them alone to point out what we ought to do, as well as to determine what we shall do. On the one hand the standard of right and wrong, on the other the chain of causes and effects, are fastened to their throne."[16]

Bentham maintained that the universal desire for pleasure implies a standard which he called the *principle of utility*. The principle of utility, explains Bentham, is "that principle which approves or disapproves of every action whatsoever, according to the tendency which it appears to have to augment or diminish the happiness of the party whose interest is in question."[17] In other words, actions should be assessed in terms of their consequences, whether pleasurable or painful, pertaining to all persons involved. The more pleasure, the better the act. The more pain, the worse the act. So far this is no improvement on Epicurus. But Bentham did not leave things so vague. He proposed specific criteria by which pleasure and pain may be evaluated:

- *Intensity*—how strong the pleasure or pain is
- *Duration*—how long the pleasure or pain lasts
- *Certainty or uncertainty*—the likelihood of pleasure or pain occurring as a result of the act
- *Propinquity or remoteness*—how soon the pleasure or pain will occur

---

[14] Epicurus, "Epicurus to Menoeceus"" in *The Extant Remains*, trans. Cyril Bailey (Oxford: Oxford University Press, 1926), 87.

[15] Ibid.

[16] Jeremy Bentham, *The Principles of Morals and Legislation* (New York: Hafner, 1948), 1.

[17] Ibid., 2.

- *Fecundity*—the tendency of a pleasure or pain to be followed by other similar sensations
- *Purity*—the tendency of a pleasure or pain *not* to be followed by the *opposite* sensation
- *Extent*—the number of people who will experience pain or pleasure as a result of the act

Using these seven criteria, Bentham proposed that we perform a *pleasure-pain calculus* to assess the rightness or wrongness of particular acts. With each criterion, numerical values may be assigned to represent both the pleasurable and painful sensations. After totaling both the pleasure values and the pain values, the sums may be compared. A greater total pleasure value indicates the act is good overall. But if the pain value is greater, then it is a bad act. And the greater the difference between the figures, the more good or evil the act is.

Bentham emphasizes that the pleasure-pain calculus be applied equally to all. No individual's pleasure is more or less significant than anyone else's. In fact, Bentham appears to be one of the first Western philosophers to extend the domain of moral consideration to animals, based on the fact that many animals are capable of experiencing pleasure and pain. Bentham argues that the decisive factor regarding whether a being is due moral consideration is not its capacity to reason or communicate, but rather its capacity to suffer. Thus, he says, "The day *may* come, when the rest of the animal creation may acquire those rights which never could have been withholden from them but by the hand of tyranny."[18] These words appear almost prophetic in light of the contemporary animal rights movement.

Jeremy Bentham had a good friend and fellow utilitarian named James Mill. So committed was Mill to his utilitarian convictions that, with Bentham's guidance, he educated his son, John Stuart Mill, in rigorous accord with utilitarian moral precepts. The boy was learning Greek by age three. He had read many classic works of literature by age eight. And by age twelve he was studying Plato and Aristotle in the original language. John Stuart Mill (1806–1873) matured into a world-renowned scholar and became a member of Parliament. He also became a stalwart defender of utilitarian moral theory, which had been the object of much criticism by both philosophers and theologians. One popular complaint was that in supposing that pleasure is the highest human good, utilitarianism is "a doctrine worthy of swine." For, after all, even a pig can feel great pleasure eating slop and basking in mud. In response to this objection, Mill proposed that pleasures should be

[18] Ibid., 311. Author's emphasis.

distinguished according to their quality. Some satisfying sensations, such as intellectual and emotional pleasures, are intrinsically superior to brute physical sensations, however satisfying the latter may be. And even when a person is not enjoying pleasurable sensations, his or her condition is still inherently preferable if only because she is capable of rational thought. Thus, Mill famously concludes, "it is better to be a human being dissatisfied than a pig satisfied; better to be Socrates dissatisfied than a fool satisfied."[19]

Because of his distinction between higher and lower pleasures based on their inherent quality, Mill's version of utilitarianism is sometimes called *qualitative hedonism,* whereas Bentham's is dubbed *quantitative hedonism.* But the question arises, how are we to know which among several pleasures is superior? Mill offers the following "qualitative test" for deciding: "Of two pleasures, if there be one to which all or almost all who have experience of both give a decided preference, irrespective of any feeling of moral obligation to prefer it, that is the more desirable pleasure."[20] So if we were to ask those who had experienced back rubs and played chess, they would prefer the latter. Similarly, watching a good play would be preferable to taking a bubble bath. Or at least this is what Mill would predict. For those who demur, he has an answer. The preference for merely physical pleasures demonstrates an "infirmity of character."

Mill defines happiness as a life of pleasure with as little pain as possible. And as it goes for the individual, so it goes for society. Therefore, each citizen has a duty to help maximize pleasure and minimize pain in society as a whole. When deciding how to behave, each person ought to judge her own actions and their ramifications with strict impartiality. Here is where utilitarianism is most challenging, as it sometimes calls for individual self-sacrifice for the sake of the collective. This is also the locus of attack for many critics of utilitarian doctrine. Requiring that individuals set aside their own satisfaction in order to promote the general good of society seems too demanding. In response, Mill distinguishes the *rule* for action from the *motive* for it. In order to be moral it is not necessary that one always will the good of all society. It is enough that one's actions simply conform to the moral law by bringing about pleasurable consequences for all affected by one's acts.

Let us now consider how a utilitarian would approach our case studies. In each instance, of course, the bottom line would be which course of action produces the most pleasure and the least pain. Regarding the first case, the utilitarian would say that lying is advisable. For by telling the

---

[19] John Stuart Mill, *Utilitarianism and Selected Writings* (New York: New American Library, 1962), 260.
[20] Ibid., 259.

truth, the whole family of Jews will likely die, and it is possible that you would be punished as well, perhaps even executed, for harboring Jews. Therefore, there's a good chance that there are really only two possible outcomes: everyone in the house dying or everyone remaining alive. So the best bet, from the standpoint of utility, seems to be lying to the Nazis, for this is the only scenario offering a chance at the first outcome. Lying to the Nazis maximizes the chances for survival and avoidance of pain.

As for physician-assisted suicide, the utilitarian's approach would depend on the degree of physical pain and emotional distress the patient is suffering. In cases where the patient is suffering severely, the utilitarian would favor euthanasia, given that the patient earnestly desires to die and there are no strenuous objections from loved ones. But if some family members or friends would be distraught at the loss of the patient, this would weaken the pro-euthanasia argument. And it would be further weakened if this decision were likely to have a negative impact on society at large, such as by undermining people's trust in the health care system or causing anxiety about their own future, if they were some day to face a debilitating disease. Now what about a case in which a newly diagnosed Alzheimer's victim, such as Janet Adkins, desires to be euthanized in spite of the fact that she is not yet suffering physically? Here the case for physician-assisted suicide is much weaker from a utilitarian perspective. The person's current physical vitality offers many opportunities for pleasure, whether physical, intellectual, or emotional. The frustrations and sorrows that will come with increasing dementia will surely cause suffering, but this might be compensated by a satisfying sense of a caring community as the patient's family and friends assist her during her final years. So a utilitarian could defend either approach, depending on certain variables.

Finally, consider the cases of dog fighting and bullfighting. Since utilitarians consider all suffering to be significant, they would consider the pain of the animals involved in these activities to be paramount. While it is true that many people derive considerable pleasure from watching such events (or profiting from them), it is doubtful that this pleasure would rise to the level of compensating for the extreme suffering of the animals involved. Thus the utilitarian would probably not sanction these activities.[21]

Criticisms of Classical Utilitarianism

It is easy to see why hedonism has been a popular moral theory for so long. We all desire pleasure in life, and we want to avoid pain. Utilitarianism, in particular, has many attractive points, as it gives equal

---

[21] It is noteworthy that the founder of the modern animal rights movement, Peter Singer, is a thoroughgoing utilitarian. See his *Animal Liberation* (New York: Avon, 1975).

consideration to all, it takes seriously the consequences of actions, and it aims for rigorous analysis of moral situations. But the theory also has many flaws. One traditional criticism of utilitarianism focuses on the fact that it is only forward-looking. As a result, the theory does not provide an adequate account of justice. To illustrate, suppose there is a small community of, say, 30 people (perhaps the size of your philosophy class). Suppose also that everyone in this community has grown weary of doing their own laundry, preparing their own food, and washing their own dishes. The leaders of the community are devout utilitarians, and they are eager to maximize pleasure and minimize pain for everyone. So when someone suggests the idea of designating a person to do all of the community chores, the leaders are interested. Eventually they agree and decide that the criterion for choosing the slave should be shoe size. The person with the biggest feet is then forced to do the laundry, prepare the food, and wash the dishes every day.

Although the person selected, "Big Foot" Bill, as he comes to be called, does not like doing these chores, the rest of the community experiences great relief at no longer being so burdened. The leaders do a pleasure-pain calculus and determine that Bill's discomfort level is fairly high due to all the work, but his basic needs are met and he is treated kindly by the whole community who are very grateful for his services. So the leaders assign a +15 net pain value to his situation. As for the rest of the community, they all experience more freedom and this brings much pleasure. Some of them feel sorry for Bill, but the leaders are careful to make sure that everyone sees how well treated he is, so that the community is not troubled by his fate. The leaders, therefore, figure a net pleasure value of +1 per person, which accrues to a total of +29 for the entire community. They conclude that enslaving Bill in this way is morally justified.

The point of this fanciful thought-experiment is to show that the principle of utility can be used to justify slavery. Most of us recognize that slavery is terribly unjust and therefore should not be permitted in any form. But utilitarianism would allow for some systems of slavery, such as that just described. Here we see how the theory's strength in focusing on consequences is also a severe weakness, as it blinds us to considerations of justice. And, ironically, although utilitarianism is often touted for its equal consideration of persons, it can be used to justify dehumanizing inequalities.

In addition to the problem of justice, utilitarianism suffers a problem of rights. Imagine a voyeur who enjoys sneaking around the neighborhood and peeking into windows to watch people in their private moments. Suppose this "Peeping Tom" experiences a tremendous amount of pleasure in doing this, and he is so stealthy that he can do so without being detected. It seems that the principle of utility would at least allow for such behavior, if not endorse it. After all, the Peeping Tom's pleasure value is very high, while his victims are totally unaffected. Utilitarians often reply to this objection by emphasizing the possibility that the voyeur will be caught and the likely trauma this would cause. But we can easily modify the thought-experiment to overcome this problem, by supposing that the voyeur has the Ring of Gyges, which makes him invisible. This "Peeping Gyges" is safe from detection. The problem here is that he is violating peoples' rights, but the utilitarian has no grounds for condemning his actions.

We have seen that utilitarianism is problematic because it is only forward-looking, focused on consequences without regard to justice or certain personal rights. Another objection to utilitarianism pertains to the fact that looking forward is itself very difficult. Consider the case of Jan Grzebski, a 65 year-old Polish man who was comatose for nineteen years before reviving in 2007. After suffering a severe head trauma in 1988, Grzebski fell into a coma. At the time of the accident Poland was under communist rule, so when Grzebski awoke so many years later he was amazed at how much things had changed—from all the goods in the stores to the prevalence of cell phones. But Grzebski had been diagnosed as being in a permanent vegetative state, from which his physicians said he would never emerge. Still, his wife took care of him in hopes that the impossible would happen. After almost twenty years it did. This is just one example of how difficult it is to predict the future, even in cases where the eventual outcomes seem guaranteed. Had Grzebski been euthanized, as some utilitarians might have advocated, he would not be enjoying his life today, having coffee with his wife and marveling at contemporary life in Poland.

A final objection to utilitarianism concerns what some critics have identified as a problem of unreasonable demands made by the theory. For example, Bernard Williams has shown that a thoroughgoing utilitarian would have to sacrifice moral integrity in some circumstances. He asks us to imagine a chemist named George who because of health problems has found it very difficult to find a job. At last he is offered work at a laboratory that develops chemical and biological warfare technologies. George is strongly opposed to these ends, but this is likely the only job he will be able to find, and he has a family to support. Furthermore, he is informed that if he declines the offer the job will be taken by a person who is a zealous proponent of the lab's purposes and who will likely accelerate the production of chemical and biological weaponry. So what is George to do? The principle of utility would dictate that George take the job, since doing so would give him a rare opportunity to provide for his family *and* this would prevent acceleration of the lab's harmful research. However, doing so would violate some of George's deepest values and thus constitute a significant moral compromise on his part. Williams concludes that in George's case abiding by utilitarianism is "an attack on his integrity."[22]

These are just some of the major criticisms that have been brought against utilitarianism. Together these objections demonstrate that, despite its considerable strengths, utilitarianism is not an adequate moral theory.

7.3.3 Kantian Ethics

The hallmark of utilitarianism is its focus on the consequences of actions in assessing their moral rightness or wrongness. We noted how this feature of the theory is both a strength and a weakness. Enlightenment philosopher Immanuel Kant (1724–1804) took strong exception to the consequentialist approach in ethics. Instead, he preferred to take a *deontological* approach, which places an emphasis on moral duties and sees these as independent of consequences. Kant insisted that the proper locus of moral assessment is the human will. An act may have good or bad consequences, whatever a person's motives or intentions might have been in choosing it. The only thing that is good without qualification is a *good will*. Proper attention to this fact is critical in developing a satisfactory moral theory, claimed Kant.

But what exactly does it mean to say that someone has a good will? To understand Kant's answer we need to spell out his understanding of human rationality and the place of morality in the context of our rationality. This may be summarized as follows. Humans are rational beings, and morality is a part of our rationality. So to be fully rational is to be perfectly moral. Now, as we noted in chapter 1, the ultimate principle of rationality is the law of noncontradiction. This logical principle properly guides us in the pursuit of truth. And to flout this law results in false beliefs. According to Kant, the situation in ethics is exactly parallel. Just as our understanding is properly guided by *theoretical reason*, our will is properly guided by *practical reason*. And as reason mandates logical consistency in what we *believe*, it also demands consistency in what we *choose*. In Kant's view, optimal behavior in both contexts boils down to a proper use of reason. (See Table 7.2.)

---

[22] Bernard Williams, "Against Utilitarianism," in *Utilitarianism: For and Against*, ed. J. J. C. Smart and Bernard Williams (Cambridge: Cambridge University Press, 1973), 97–98, 117.

The Categorical Imperative

If the law of noncontradiction governs our use of theoretical reason, then what principle governs practical reason? This is the supreme moral principle, which Kant calls the *categorical imperative*. It is similar to the law of noncontradiction in that it prohibits contradictions. But because its province is the will, the sorts of contradictions it forbids pertain to choices. According to the categorical imperative, one should never will a course of action that would result in a contradiction within one's own will. And anyone who abides by this principle has a good will.

Table 7.2

Context	Aim	Rational Faculty	Guide
Understanding	True beliefs	Theoretical reason	Law of noncontradiction
The will	Good choices	Practical reason	Categorical imperative

Before applying the categorical imperative, let's unpack the concept a bit more. The term *imperative* suggests a law or command. This in turn implies a certain obligation to obey. The term *categorical* regards the scope of the imperative. It applies to everyone, and it is absolutely necessary that we obey. Kant distinguishes between the categorical imperative and *hypothetical imperatives*, which are contingent upon desire. For instance, if I want to go to the Super Bowl, then it is imperative that I purchase a ticket (or find some generous person who will give me one). Hypothetical imperatives are only as binding as our own aim to achieve some end, which is subject to our own will. The categorical imperative, in contrast, binds us regardless of our specific life interests and aims. We are obliged to abide by it in all situations just because we are rational beings.

Kant says that the categorical imperative (CI) may be expressed in a variety of forms. His first formulation presents the CI as a way of evaluating specific rules for action or *maxims*. Whenever a person makes a choice, this implies some maxim or other. For example, suppose I need to borrow money and I make a false promise to someone that I'll repay them in a few weeks just so I can get the loan. This choice operates on the maxim "Whenever you need money, make a false promise." Or suppose I have a natural talent in some significant area, but I'd rather not go through the effort of cultivating it. This implies the maxim "Whenever developing a talent seems burdensome, then don't do the work to cultivate it."

How do we evaluate the morality of our maxims? This is where the categorical imperative comes in. Kant formulates it as follows: "Act only according to that maxim by which you can at the same time will that it should become a universal law."[23] This means that you should not do something if you could not wish that everyone else did the same thing. So could I will that *everyone* made false promises? Of course not, because this would mean that other people would make false promises to me. In fact, nobody could be trusted, and the whole concept of promising would become meaningless. That's not something that I want. Therefore, I cannot consistently will the maxim behind my false promise, so I should reject it. As for the second example, could I will that everyone let their talents go to waste when they don't want to do the work necessary to cultivate them? Again, no. My way of life depends on the performance of many other people in diverse careers. If every professional abandoned his or her trade as soon as it became a burden, then there would be far fewer experts in their fields. And I could not rely on the competence of my dentist, attorney, mail carrier, auto mechanic, and the like. This is certainly not a situation that I want. Therefore, I cannot consistently will the maxim to ignore my own talents.

These are some of Kant's own examples that he uses to illustrate the first version of the categorical imperative, which essentially asks: *Can you universalize the rule of your action?* If so, then it's okay to do it. If not, then you have a duty to avoid performing the action. Notice, by the way, that if you can will an action to be universalized, this only means it is permissible, not obligatory. So, for example, the maxim to wear plaid on Fridays can be universalized. But this only means that this behavior is morally permissible. You are free either to do it or not do it. For Kant, moral obligations (e.g., truth-telling, diligence, marital fidelity, etc.) exist only when one *cannot* universalize the *opposite* course of action (e.g., lying, laziness, adultery, etc.).

The first version of the categorical imperative focuses on the rationality of willing consistently. Kant says that the same principle can be expressed in another way. He writes,

> Rational nature exists as an end in itself. Man necessarily thinks of his own existence in this way; thus far it is a subjective principle of human actions. Also every other rational being thinks of his existence by means of the same rational ground which holds also for myself; thus it is at the same time an objective

---

[23] Immanuel Kant, *Foundations of the Metaphysics of Morals*, trans. Lewis White Beck (Indianapolis: Bobbs-Merrill, 1959), 39.

principle from which, as a supreme practical ground, it must be possible to derive all laws of the will.[24]

The idea here is that we all have inherent value. We are not mere means to others' ends. Kant believes that this fact serves to ground the supreme moral principle. Thus, his second formulation of the CI is as follows: "Act so that you treat humanity, whether in your own person or in that of another, always as an end and never as a means only."[25] This version of the CI is essentially about respect. All of our actions, to the extent that they affect others, should be respectful of persons.

Consider again Kant's example of the false promise. If I falsely promise to repay your loan to me, then I am not treating you as an end. I am merely using you and have therefore failed to respect you as a rational agent. So this action is condemned by the second version of the categorical imperative. As for the example of refusing to cultivate talents, the same reasoning applies, though the vice is one of omission. By being a slacker I disrespect everyone who might have benefited from my talent as a surgeon, accountant, or pianist. So, again, the second formulation of the CI tells me to cultivate my significant talents, even if this is sometimes a burden to me.

Now let's take a look at how Kant's moral theory applies to our three case studies. Is it right to lie to the Nazis to save the Jewish family? Kant's answer here is a clear and resounding "No." Lying cannot be universalized, as it contradicts our own will to be told the truth. Also, to lie is to disrespect others, treating them as less than rational beings. But, one might ask, what about the lives of the Jews who would be saved by my lying? What about respect for *them* as rational beings? Kant's answer: "A lie is a lie and is in itself intrinsically base whether it be told with good or bad intent. For formally a lie is always evil. . . . There are no lies which may not be the source of evil."[26]

The case of physician-assisted suicide is just as unambiguous from the standpoint of Kantian ethics. Suicide cannot be universalized because this would mean the end of the human race. Nor is it an act that treats oneself or others with respect. So suicide, whether assisted or undertaken alone, is condemned by both versions of the categorical imperative.

When it comes to cruelty to animals, Kant takes a negative view, but for different reasons than someone like Bentham or Mill. Remember that Kant's ethics is solely concerned with rational agents, and he does not consider animals to be rational. Thus, he maintains that whatever

---

[24] Ibid., 47.

[25] Ibid.

[26] Immanuel Kant, *Lectures on Ethics*, trans. Louis Infield (Indianapolis: Hackett, 1963), 229.

duties we have regarding animals are indirectly duties to other human beings. Still, Kant takes a strong stand against mistreatment of animals. He says, we "must practice kindness towards animals, for he who is cruel to animals becomes hard also in his dealings with men."[27] So taking proper care of animals is a way of respecting other people. Therefore, a consistent Kantian would oppose dog fighting, bullfighting, and any other recreational activity involving harm to animals.

Criticisms of Kantian Ethics

Kant's moral theory has many strengths. As we have just seen, it gives clear counsel on difficult moral issues. It also provides a strong emphasis on duty and respect for persons. And proper application of the theory does not make an unrealistic demand on one's ability to anticipate the future. Also, Kant's approach places a strong emphasis on human *autonomy*, which is the right of self-determination in ethics. As an Enlightenment thinker, Kant was keen to show that rational agents could discover moral truth on their own, without the guidance of the church or other external authorities. Since Kant, the principle of autonomy has been exalted in the West in ways that he would never have envisioned, not just in ethics but in the political arena as well.

That Kant *over*emphasized human autonomy is a criticism that is sometimes lodged against his theory. While we are free rational agents, we should not confuse this freedom *to* choose and act with a freedom *from* the claims of all external moral authorities, whether this might be loved ones, church leaders, or civil authorities. Some also object that Kant places too much emphasis on duty, at the expense of a reasonable consideration of consequences. The case of the Nazis shows just how unyielding Kant is on truth-telling. Shouldn't innocent human lives take priority over one's commitment to telling the truth in some circumstances?

Many see Kant's refusal to compromise on this point as a severe flaw in his theory. But is Kant's theory at fault here or is it his own application of it? One might propose that both the first and second formulations of the categorical imperative would actually justify lying to the Nazis. For example, while we may grant that the maxim to lie cannot be universalized, a maxim *to lie to save innocent human lives* could indeed be universalized. So the problem is resolved by simply qualifying the maxim. When it comes to the second version of the CI, one could argue that lying to the Nazis actually is the choice that most respects all of the people involved. It respects the Jewish family by protecting them from the Nazis. And it respects the Nazis by saving them from the guilt of killing more innocent people.

---

[27] Ibid., 240.

While this strategy might salvage Kant's theory from one criticism, it reveals a more fundamental problem with the CI. When evaluating actions, how specific are we to make the maxims? We can't always select the most general maxim, in Kant's view. In punishing criminals, for instance, we must inflict harm on them or take away their freedom (or both). But one cannot universalize the maxim to simply harm or incarcerate other people. To justify this, Kant must consider a more specific maxim, such as "Inflict harm on those who are guilty of crimes." Kant was an advocate of the death penalty, so he was obviously prepared to make some specific qualifications of maxims (e.g., "Do not kill a person, unless she is guilty of a capital crime"). But to concede this opens a Pandora's Box. Could we not universalize this maxim: "Do not make false promises except when you need money desperately to meet some basic needs"? Or this one: "Do not kill yourself, unless your life is a total disaster and you see no way that things could improve." One could imagine any number of immoral acts that one could justify by simply tweaking the maxim behind them.

So, it seems, Kant's theory is flawed in that it is insufficiently clear and even invites abuse. Perhaps a Kantian could insist that the principle of respect for persons could bring clarity and temper abuse of the first version of the CI, but this raises further questions. How are we to determine in each case what it means to treat a person as an "end"? What, precisely, *is* respect for persons? These are questions to which there are no ready and uncontroversial answers. In the end, then, those who apply Kantian principles must resort to their own intuitions when making moral assessments.

A final objection to Kant's theory regards the question of motivation. Other objectivist theories like ethical egoism and utilitarianism offer some inspiration to act morally, such as to advance one's individual interests or one's society. However, the Kantian program is so focused on duty and rationality that it would not sufficiently motivate a person who is not already geared toward satisfying the theory's demands. Kant says that a person who disobeys the categorical imperative is acting irrationally. Suppose a Kantian admonishes someone for making a false promise. One can imagine the person responding, "Who cares? So long as I get the money, I'm happy." Here the immense value of consequentialist reasoning becomes apparent, as such a person would be better motivated by being shown how his actions hurt others and, ultimately, himself.

7.3.4 Rule Utilitarianism

We have seen how Kant's extreme deontology overcomes many problems that plague consequentialism. However, it does so at a price, as it introduces other problems that might be just as severe. Wouldn't it be nice if there were a theory that incorporated the best of both worlds? Well, some maintain that there is, and it is called *rule utilitarianism.* Recall that the utilitarianism of Bentham and Mill instructs us to apply the principle of utility to individual acts. For this reason their view is sometimes called *act utilitarianism* (also known as *classical utilitarianism*). Rule utilitarians agree that we should focus on consequences, but not of individual acts. Rather, they say we should use the principle of utility to evaluate general moral *rules.* So, according to this view, we must ascertain which rules are most likely to bring about the best consequences when followed. Then we can evaluate individual acts based on whether or not they adhere to those rules. In this way, rule utilitarianism preserves the context-sensitiveness of act utilitarianism while also incorporating the sense of moral duty provided in a deontological theory like Kant's.

But which rules ought we to follow? This is the sticky question for rule utilitarianism, and advocates of the theory are often reluctant to specify.[28] One might presume that such rules as "fulfill your promises," "do not lie," "respect the freedom of others," and "do not harm innocent people" would be good candidates. But although we might recognize these as sound general rules, problems emerge as we inquire whether exceptions are ever appropriate. For example, suppose we affirm truth-telling as a good general rule. Most would make an exception in the case of the Nazis in order to promote the welfare of the Jewish family. But if we can make an exception in that case, then what of other cases? Shall I not break a promise to give a gun back to a friend if she demands it back while in a fit of rage? And are there not many instances in which it is proper to restrict a person's freedom? However, once we start making exceptions to general rules, there seems to be no end. And, most significantly, such exceptions will usually be made based on specific cases where observing the rule leads to unpleasant consequences. For this reason, some have argued that rule utilitarianism collapses into act utilitarianism.[29]

A further problem with this approach is that it faces the same problem of knowledge facing act utilitarianism, though on a different level. Just as the principle of utility does not always give us clear guidance when it comes to choosing a particular course of action, neither can we decide with confidence which rules, when followed, will produce the most pleasurable result. And, as a final objection, even if we could

---

[28] A prominent, well-developed version of the theory was set forth by Harvard philosopher John Rawls (1921–2002). Since his proposal was primarily devised as a political philosophy, we will discuss Rawls' theory in the next chapter.

[29] David Lyons presents this criticism in his *Forms and Limits of Utilitarianism* (Oxford: Oxford University Press, 1965).

decide on a clear set of rules, the problem remains as to how we are to resolve conflicts between these rules when we encounter moral dilemmas. So in the case of physician-assisted suicide we may be torn between respecting the autonomy of the patient and respecting the sanctity of life. Which rule takes precedence? Or, regarding bullfighting, we may be torn between respecting cultural traditions and promoting welfare to animals. Again, which rule trumps the other? Here rule utilitarianism provides no advance over act utilitarianism or Kantian ethics. Perhaps it is even a step backward.

7.3.5 Virtue Ethics

The objectivist theories examined so far are all principle-oriented. Each proceeds on the assumption that the key in approaching ethics is to use moral principles to assess actions. But this method has not always been dominant. In fact, it was not until the modern period that principle-based theories became the standard approach in the West. Prior to that time ethics was more commonly viewed in terms of personal character. Instead of asking which actions conform to which rules, philosophers were more inclined to ask which *qualities* would be possessed by a good *person*. Since the 1980s this approach, known as *virtue ethics*, has made a strong comeback, as ethicists have rediscovered the importance of personal character in ethics.

Aristotelian Virtue Ethics

Virtue ethics dates all the way back to the ancient Greeks. Many of Plato's dialogues were devoted to the exploration of particular virtues. And how to be a virtuous person was the overriding concern of the father of Western philosophy, Socrates. But the true founder of virtue ethics as we know it today was Aristotle (384–322 BC). Like his philosophical forebears, Aristotle believed that everything has a *telos*, a function or purpose. Cups are designed to hold liquid, clocks function to tell time, and boats are made to carry people and things on water. And anything that fulfills its function achieves a certain excellence for its kind. *Virtue* is the term for such excellence.

This applies to human beings too, as determined by the various roles we play in society. Each person is a family member, and one may have multiple roles as, say, a son, brother, husband, and father. Most people also have some sort of career as, say, a physician, teacher, retailer, or homemaker. Most people also have recreational interests, hobbies, or interests in the arts. Each of these contexts demands certain virtues from a person in order to succeed in them. And the more of these traits one has, the better moral specimen a person is.

Aristotle distinguishes between *intellectual virtues* and *moral virtues*. Intellectual virtues can be taught,[30] but moral virtues can only be developed through practice. So, for example, a person becomes more generous by giving to those in need. A person becomes more courageous by standing strong in dangerous situations. And so on. Becoming a good person takes hard work. We develop a virtuous character by doing virtuous things repeatedly over time.

The virtues, as Aristotle catalogues them, include such traits as courage, temperance, generosity, wittiness, and modesty. Each trait enables a person to be a functional part of society in some context or other. To help us identify the virtue in any particular case, Aristotle notes that it usually lies midway between two vices. So, for example, courage is a midpoint between the vices of cowardice and foolhardiness. And temperance is the moral peak between the immoral valleys of insensibility and profligacy. (See Table 7.3 for a more complete list of Aristotelian virtues and their corresponding vices.) Thus, Aristotle notes, "moral virtue is a mean . . . between two vices, the one involving excess, the other deficiency, and . . . its character is to aim at what is intermediate in passions and in actions."[31]

Table 7.3

Subject	Deficiency	Mean	Excess
Danger	Cowardice	Courage	Foolhardiness
Pleasure	Insensibility	Temperance	Profligacy
Possessions	Stinginess	Generosity	Prodigality
Public opinion	Pettiness	Pride	Vanity
Amusement	Boorishness	Wittiness	Buffoonery
Feelings	Shamelessness	Modesty	Prudishness
Anger	Lack of spirit	Good temper	Irascibility
Money	Meanness	Magnificence	Vulgarity
Pleasantness	Churlishness	Friendliness	Obsequiousness
Honor	Pusillanimity	Magnanimity	Vanity
Indignation	Spitefulness	Righteous indignation	Envy

[30] For a discussion of intellectual virtues, see chapter 2.

[31] Aristotle, *Nicomachean Ethics*, trans. W. D. Ross, in *The Basic Works of Aristotle*, ed. Richard McKeon (New York: Random House, 1941), 963.

Aristotle's list of virtues is far from canonical. Other virtue ethicists have identified dozens of other virtues, such as loyalty, patience, humility, justice, courtesy, sincerity, discretion, gentleness, frugality, diligence, compassion, perseverance, and self-control. Christian virtue ethicists typically include other traits, such as joy, mercy, faith, hope, and love. But the shared conviction of all virtue ethicists is that being moral is about more than abiding by principles. It is about being a certain kind of person.

Strengths and Weaknesses of Virtue Ethics

One of the great strengths of virtue ethics is its context sensitivity, which provides for a realism about personal biases. According to utilitarianism and Kantian ethics, the moral ideal is impartiality. As one applies the principle of utility or the categorical imperative, one must go about this in an unbiased way, without giving preference to anyone involved in a given moral situation. This creates problems as one considers certain cases. Imagine, for example, that you are on a boat with your mother and an oncologist who knows the cure for cancer. The three of you are lost in conversation as you float down the river when suddenly you notice that you are about to go over a waterfall. In your panic the three of you jump out of the boat, but neither your mother nor the oncologist can swim very well and they are both just a few feet from going over the falls. You only have time to rescue one of them. So whom do you save? The utilitarian would clearly advise saving the oncologist. Yes, this means Mom plummets to her death, but think of all the people whose lives will be saved by the oncologist. The Kantian might also favor saving the oncologist, because one cannot universalize a maxim which says, "When saving lives, always favor those who benefit society the least." But then again, perhaps a Kantian would opt for a more specific maxim in order to allow for exceptions to this general rule. (This is yet another example of the problematic ambiguity of the first version of the CI.) At any rate, neither utilitarianism nor Kantian ethics would clearly sanction saving Mom instead of the oncologist. Even an ethical egoist could argue in either direction, since one never knows when one will be stricken with cancer.

In contrast to these theories, the virtue ethicist may unabashedly endorse saving your mother instead of the oncologist. This is because your personal character is most directly informed by your life roles, and your relationship to your mother is one of the most vital of these. Simply put, your devotion to her trumps your devotion to the oncologist and, by extension, all of her patients. Of course, for most people saving Mom would be a natural reflex anyway. While the utilitarian and Kant might have us feel ashamed about that, the virtue ethicist would say our instincts in this case are perfectly in line with moral truth.

Another virtue of virtue ethics is the fact that it provides personal motivation for being moral. Principle-oriented theories tell us to behave in certain ways because it is our duty or because it will maximize happiness in society. This is not as inspiring as the virtue ethics emphasis on personal character traits. To focus on the fact that certain behaviors improve one's character and foster strong relationships is better motivation for moral living than devotion to abstract principles.

For all its strengths, however, virtue ethics suffers some fairly serious shortcomings as a moral theory. One problem pertains to the fact that virtue ethics does not give us clear direction when it comes to particular actions. Consider our three case studies. What is the right thing to do in each instance? While we can point to particular virtues that are relevant to each of these situations (e.g., truth-telling, loyalty, courage, compassion, faithfulness, justice, etc.), the applicability of such traits to the specific contexts does not tell us which course of action is the *right* one. Some virtue ethicists have attempted to solve this problem by defining rightness in terms of the virtues. Thus, for example, Rosalind Hursthouse says, "An action is right if and only if it is what a virtuous agent would characteristically (i.e. acting in character) do in the circumstances."[32]

While this approach might sound promising, it only begs the question: What *would* a virtuous person do? How can we know what she would do without an account of moral rightness that applies to specific situations? If we understand a virtuous person as someone who does the right thing in certain circumstances, then rightness is logically prior to virtue. For this reason, it appears that the concept of virtue is not sufficient to provide an account of what is morally right.

This failure to provide a clear concept of moral rightness is probably one of the reasons that principle-oriented moral theories arose in the first place. In the history of philosophy, new ideas and theories usually emerge for a reason. While having a good character is a crucial, perhaps central, part of the moral life, knowing and choosing the right courses of action in life are also critical. Principle-oriented theories offer a solution to this problem and thus address a serious shortcoming in a virtue ethics approach.

---

[32] Rosalind Hursthouse, *On Virtue Ethics* (Oxford: Oxford University Press, 1999), 28.

Questions for Reflection

1. Is psychological egoism true? What reasons might be given for and against this view?
2. Utilitarianism demands that when applying the principle of utility one must weigh the pleasures and pains of all people equally. Is this possible?
3. Kant maintains that the different versions of the Categorical Imperative lead to the same conclusions when applied to moral questions. Can you think of a case in which the two versions of the CI discussed here might lead one in different directions morally?
4. According to Aristotle, moral virtues are developed through practice. Is this true? What might be some other ways in which moral virtues are developed?
5. If you were a rule utilitarian, what general rules would you identify as those which, when followed, tend to bring about the most happiness? How would you rank order these rules?
6. Which of the naturalistic moral theories discussed in this section seems most plausible overall? Explain why.

§ 7.4 Moral Objectivism: Nonnaturalistic Theories

Having discussed the major naturalistic ethical theories, we will now examine the major forms of ethical nonnaturalism. These include natural law ethics and divine command theory.

7.4.1 Natural Law Ethics

Virtue ethics is sometimes called a *teleological* ethical theory, because it defines human good in terms of our ultimate purpose or *telos*. Another moral tradition that falls into this category, and is in fact historically related to virtue ethics, is natural law ethics. Proponents of this view, such as St. Augustine (354–430) and Thomas Aquinas (1225–1274), agreed with the ancient Greeks that all things have a *telos*, but they understood this explicitly in terms of God's creative design. God made all things for a purpose, and the purposes for things define their specific goods. This includes human beings, who were made in God's image and share in God's rationality. As Aquinas puts it, "The rational creature is subject to Divine providence in the most excellent way, in so far as it partakes of a share of providence. . . . Wherefore, it has a share of the Eternal reason."[33]

---

[33] Thomas Aquinas, *Summa Theologica*, trans. English Dominican Fathers (New York: Benziger Brothers, 1947), 1:997.

Since the entire created order is rational, human beings are capable of discerning the Creator's decrees which are evident in nature. As we examine the world, we observe a system of natural regularities and norms that are law-like. In other words, we can discern *natural laws* in the world. Some of these laws are *descriptive*, pertaining to physical regularities that we now call the laws of nature, such as the law of gravity, Boyle's law, the laws of thermodynamics, and so forth. But other laws are *prescriptive* and constitute moral norms. These are the precepts of natural moral law, and the most fundamental of these is the principle that good is to be pursued, while evil is to be avoided. Aquinas calls this the "first principle of practical reason," and he regards it as the moral analogue to the law of noncontradiction. Other precepts of natural law, according to Aquinas, include the duties to preserve one's life, to procreate and educate offspring, to gain understanding, to live in society, and to avoid offending others. All of these are both morally right and natural inclinations of rational beings.

An influential moral norm inspired by the natural law tradition is the principle of the *sanctity of life*. This is the notion that all human life is sacred and worthy of being preserved in all circumstances. It is grounded both in the natural law precept of self-preservation and the biblical doctrine of the *imago Dei*, that human beings are made in God's image (cp. Gen 1:27; 5:1). Because God created us and made us like Himself in crucial ways, most notably in our rationality and freedom, the value of human life is inestimable and not diminished by the quality of one's life.

The principle of the sanctity of life is easily applied in most moral situations. This naturally gives rise to moral dilemmas in which respecting one person's life necessarily results in harm to someone else. In such cases, a single act may have a "double effect" of both good and evil consequences. For example, consider the case of a drawbridge operator whose child is caught in the gears of the bridge. A train carrying hundreds of passengers is rushing toward the bridge, and the operator has no time to free his child. Should he lift the bridge to prevent dozens or perhaps hundreds of deaths, though he knows this will kill his child? Or should he save his child and allow the train passengers to die? This is an excruciating moral dilemma.[34] In light of such situations, Aquinas introduced the *principle of double effect*, which offers criteria for determining the permissibility of such an act. According to this principle, an act that has both good and evil consequences may be performed only if:

---

[34] For an excellent dramatic depiction of this dilemma, see the short film *Most* (Eastwind Films, 2003; 32 mins.; PG), directed by Bobby Garabedian.

(1) The evil consequence is not directly intended.
(2) The evil consequence is not the means of producing the good effect.
(3) There is proportionate reason for performing the action in spite of its evil consequences.

In the case of the drawbridge operator, each of these conditions obtains. The operator intends to save lives, not to kill his child. Second, the death of his child is not the means of saving the passengers' lives but rather an unfortunate consequence of the means (i.e., lifting the drawbridge). Third, there is proportionate reason for performing the action, as many lives will be saved, while only one life will be lost. Therefore, raising the drawbridge would be the right thing to do. It satisfies the principle of double effect. This choice would also show a greater respect for the sanctity of life than the choice not to raise the drawbridge.

So how would natural law ethics guide us with regard to our case studies? Regarding the first case, there would be a presumption against lying to the Nazis. Lying violates an aspect of the human *telos*, specifically our rationality and thus our natural good of truth-telling. Therefore, lying is evil, but so is doing something that will lead to the death of innocent people. So we must apply the principle of double effect to the option of lying to the Nazis. While the third criterion is satisfied, the other two are not. In lying to the Nazis the lie is certainly intended and it is also the means of producing the good effect of saving innocent lives. So it would appear that we must tell the Nazis the truth about the Jewish stowaways.

As for physician-assisted suicide, a natural law ethic would not approve of this, as it violates the natural law of the preservation of life. However much the patient might suffer, it is never right to terminate her life. Instead, a natural law ethicist would advocate using strong pain killers and/or drugs to alleviate psychological stress. In some instances a strong pain killer, such as morphine, might accelerate a patient's demise. But this would be permissible, given the principle of double effect, so long as the goal is to kill the pain not the person.

Finally, what would a natural law ethic say to the practice of dog fighting or bullfighting? Some have argued that the concept of the natural law to preserve life can be extended to animals without denying the special place of human beings in creation. One of Aquinas' doctrines, inherited from St. Augustine, was the "hierarchy of being," that is, the notion that every creature differs in its degree of perfection, from high angelic beings all the way down to inanimate matter. For these philosophers this hierarchy implies a hierarchy of value as well, such that each being should be respected according to its degree of perfection. Accordingly, living creatures deserve respect just because they are alive, and mammals, such as dogs and bulls, deserve more respect than most living things because of their greater mental capacities. These considerations would seem to dictate that both dog fighting and bullfighting for sheer human entertainment are morally wrong.

As far as criticisms of natural law ethics go, a problem with the theory is the fact that it cannot provide clear direction on many moral issues. For all its usefulness, the concept of *telos* provides little help for such issues as affirmative action, the ethics of war, and issues arising in the context of various technologies, such as in business and computer ethics.

Another shortcoming of the natural law approach is its failure to provide for a strong concept of duty. Just because engaging in a particular behavior contradicts one's *telos*, it does not follow from this that one ought not to do it. For example, it might be unnatural for someone to marry multiple people, but how does it follow from this that I have an obligation not to do so? Moreover, just because it does fulfill my *telos* as a rational being to give my children a decent education, this does not by itself generate a duty to do so.

Finally, many critics find the Aristotelian concept of *telos* to be suspect. This concept entails a belief in essences or natural kinds, a view which is itself controversial and requires defense, as we saw in a previous chapter.

7.4.2 Divine Command Theory

The failure of natural law ethics to provide sufficiently clear moral direction and an adequate sense of duty has led some theistic ethicists to endorse *divine command theory*. This is the view that the moral standard is determined by God's commands. Most versions of divine command theory (DCT) would say that moral terms such as *good, bad, right*, and *wrong* are properly defined in terms of divine commands. So to say "It is right to do X" *means* "X coheres with God's commands" and to say "It is wrong to do X" *means* "X contradicts God's commands."[35]

One of the major advantages of DCT is the fact that the hundreds of commands in Scripture speak to so many specific life situations. In fact, the Pentateuch features dozens of case studies in which various hypothetical moral situations are considered and directives are

---

[35] Two contemporary proponents of DCT are Robert Adams and Phillip Quinn. See Adams' "A Modified Divine Command Theory of Ethical Wrongness," in *Divine Commands and Morality*, ed. Paul Helm (Oxford: Oxford University Press, 1981) and Quinn's *Divine Commands and Moral Requirements* (Oxford: Clarendon, 1978).

provided.[36] Even where a specific moral dilemma is not addressed in Scripture because of, say, advances in technology, the spirit of various biblical directives can be usefully adapted to novel cases. For example, the case study in Exodus 21:22–25 deals with how to handle a situation in which two fighting men inadvertently cause a woman to have a miscarriage. Although the case does not address the subject of abortion *per se*, the implication of the judgment (that any further injury should be dealt with retributively—"eye for eye, tooth for tooth") seems to be that the life of an unborn child is as valuable as that of any adult. Accordingly, an implicit divine command about the morality of abortion may be inferred from this text.[37]

The Nature of Divine Commands

Biblical commands take many forms. Some, such as the Ten Commandments and many of Jesus' directives, come in the form of literal commands. Others are more subtle, presented in allegories, parables, metaphors, predictive prophecies, and even historical events interpreted as divine instruction. And divine judgments on human actions, governmental policies, or cultural trends, whether positive or negative, imply moral norms.

Biblical commands also vary in scope. Some pertain to specific situations, such as the Old Testament case laws and instructions for local churches in the Pauline epistles. The Ten Commandments, however, are much more general decrees, each mandating behavior of a certain kind, such as respect for life, marital fidelity, and honor toward one's parents. Others are more general still, such as Jesus' summation of the moral law in the form of the principles of love for God and love for one's neighbor in Matthew 22:37–39,[38] the latter sometimes expressed as the Golden Rule (discussed below).

Why do divine commands impose obligations? This might seem like a silly or irreverent question to some, but it deserves an answer. Richard Swinburne notes two reasons why we are bound by God's commands. First, God created and sustains the universe, so He is the owner of all that is, including every human being. Our lives here are ours on loan from Him. Thus, God has the right to tell us what sorts of things we may or may not do with our lives. Second, those who benefit from the actions of another are generally obliged to their benefactors. God has, to say the least, benefited each of us in myriad ways, so we are natu-

---

[36] See especially Exodus chaps. 21–22 and Leviticus chaps. 11–22.

[37] Other biblical texts that appear to imply a pro-life position on abortion include Ps 139:13–16; Jer 1:5; Gen 25:22–23; Judg 13:2–7; Isa 49:1; Luke 1:41, 44; and Gal 1:15.

[38] In this passage Jesus actually quotes Deut 6:5 and Lev 19:18.

rally obligated to Him. And this general obligation implies a duty to do whatever He commands.[39]

A further benefit of DCT has to do with moral motivation. We noted earlier how the moral visions of other objectivist theories are limited in their capacity to inspire us ethically. Divine commands, however, are backed by maximum authority and power. They are accompanied by a promise of eventual divine judgment to be carried out by a holy and omnipotent God. Scripture makes clear that there will be rewards for the righteous and punishments for the wicked.[40] So the psychological force of divine commands could not be greater for those who recognize this authority.

Now let's consider how DCT would handle our three case studies. Divine command theorists would disagree over whether to lie to the Nazis, as it is not clear whether the command not to lie might have exceptions. Some appeal to such apparent precedents for morally appropriate lying as the case of the Hebrew midwives (Exod 1:15–20) and Rahab and the spies (Josh 2:1–7), but some biblical scholars claim that these are not true instances of lying.

As for physician-assisted suicide, divine command theorists would say that this is always wrong. God has explicitly prohibited killing innocent people (Exod 20:13), and this is irrespective of their desires or quality of life. Still, there is some tension in this perspective of DCT. Scripture also counsels compassion for those who suffer (Zech 7:9; Mt. 14:14; Col. 3:12). But few divine command theorists would acknowledge that the duty of compassion could ever trump the duty to respect life. Rather, DCT would see the biblical duty of compassion as recommending the use of strong pain killers to alleviate suffering.

Dog fighting and bullfighting are problematic, at the least, according to DCT, since the Bible teaches stewardship of creation. Also, a proverb says, "A righteous man cares about his animal's health" (Prov 12:10). A psalmist specifically emphasizes that God owns all of the animals (Ps 50:10–11), and one's treatment of an owner's property constitutes respect or disrespect toward the owner himself. And there are many other passages that either give directives regarding caring for animals (e.g., Exod 23:12 and Deut 25:4) or emphasize God's care for them (e.g., Ps 104:10–23). Cruel treatment of animals for the purpose of amusement contradicts such biblical concern for animal welfare, so dog fighting and bullfighting would appear to be morally wrong, according to DCT.

---

[39] Richard Swinburne, *The Coherence of Theism*, revised ed. (Oxford: Oxford University Press, 1993), 212–14.

[40] See, for example, Eccl. 12:13–14 and 1 Cor 5:10.

Criticisms of Divine Command Theory

The most significant objection to DCT is also the oldest, originating with Socrates. In one of Plato's dialogues, the *Euthyphro*, Socrates proposes a dilemma facing anyone who defines moral goodness in terms of divine approval. Although Socrates poses the dilemma in polytheistic terms, it can be easily modified as an objection to a theistic DCT, as follows: *Does God command X because it is right, or is X right because He commands it?* Suppose we take the first option and say that God commands X because it is right. This implies that something besides God's command makes X right, and this contradicts the basic claim of DCT. But, then, suppose we go with the second alternative and grant that an action is right just because God commands it. This answer leads us to the conclusion that God could have made any form of conduct morally right. Though He did command us to be kind, tell the truth, and be faithful to our spouses, God could just as easily have commanded us to be cruel, tell lies, and commit adultery. This seems to imply that moral goodness is arbitrary. So the divine command theorist appears to be stuck between giving up her thesis or admitting that the moral law is the result of divine whim. Neither route is very attractive.

Most ethicists today believe Socrates' dilemma of goodness is devastating to DCT. But this objection overlooks a basic point that actually makes for an easy solution. As was discussed in the previous chapter, God has an immutable nature, and among His attributes is moral perfection. But when we say that God is morally perfect we do not mean that there exists some standard for perfection external to God. Rather, it means that God *is* the moral standard. Just as He is the ground of all being and knowledge, so is He the source of all value. (As we noted in the introduction, all three branches of philosophy—ontology, epistemology, and axiology—are grounded in God. He is the source of all truth and, indeed, *is* truth.) Thus, to respond to the dilemma directly, we should go with the first option—that God commands X because it is right—but then clarify this. *What makes X right is the fact that it coheres with the nature of God.* Kind behavior is right because God is kind. Truth-telling is right because God is truth. Faithfulness is right because God is faithful. And so on.

By this analysis, we see that the moral standard is the nature of God. All divine commands essentially tell us to be *like* God, morally speaking. So divine commands do not *make* moral truth so much as they *communicate* it, which confirms our obligation to abide by it. This helps to make sense of the common-sense intuitions that moral truth is eternal and unchanging and that right actions would have been right even if God had never commanded us to do them. Kindness, truthfulness, faithfulness, and every other moral virtue have been good all along because they reflect the nature of the immutable God.

So, to summarize and conclude, it appears that the DCT is mistaken in its essential claim that "It is right to do X" *means* "X coheres with God's commands." God's commands are not the metaphysical foundation of our moral standard. Rather, God's *nature* is the foundation. Divine commands serve the critical *epistemological* functions of making that standard known to us and confirming our duty to obey it. In other words, divine commands do not *make* things right or wrong, but they are at least one way that we *know* what things are right and wrong.

The Golden Rule

The biblical injunction to "do to others what you would have them do to you" (Mt. 7:12 [NIV]; see also Luke 6:31), popularly known as the *Golden Rule*, originated in the Old Testament levitical law (Lev 19:18) and was emphasized by Jesus in the Gospel narratives. It deserves primacy of place in a Christian ethic, as is apparent in Jesus' declaration that it "sums up the law and the prophets."

What does it mean to "do to others what you would have them do to you"? Consider this concrete situation. Al asks his coworker Bob to cover for him at the office so that he can take care of a family crisis at home. Al's teenage son has been misbehaving, and his infant girl is sick, needing constant attention. Bob, however, is busy making final preparations for a conference presentation that he must deliver in Chicago the next week and is concerned that he will not be adequately prepared to do so if he doesn't use the afternoon to work on the project. So what does he do? As a morally circumspect person, Bob decides to apply the Golden Rule to the situation. He asks himself, "How would I want to be treated if I were in Al's shoes?" Surely he would want to be shown sensitivity and sympathy. He would also want his request to be granted or at least seriously considered. So Bob offers a sympathetic ear and then consents to covering for his friend.

The first thing to notice about the Golden Rule is that it appeals to the concept of reciprocity. One's treatment *of* others ought to be guided by how one would prefer to be treated *by* others. When considering how to behave toward someone, one should consider what it would be like to be on the receiving end of that behavior. This suggests that a basic precondition for application of the Golden Rule is *knowledge*. One cannot treat others as one would be treated if one does not *know* how others would prefer to *be* treated. In our example, Bob must know the basic facts of Al's situation and something of his perspective. This might seem to be trivial or a matter of simple reflection, until one considers how one's own actual desires or preferences would be changed by one's being placed in the other's situation. This demands understanding what one's preferences *would be* within a certain specified context, a context that includes a range of specific circumstances, such as emotional states, cognitive states, personal relationships, physical conditions, economic factors, and so on.

The Golden Rule does not demand omniscience on these matters, of course, but it does require a basic understanding of such conditions, if only at the level of common sense. Objective awareness of the basic circumstantial facts is not enough. As we saw, Bob must somehow imagine what it is like to *be* Al, and not just in a general sense but *in his particular circumstance.* Here application of the Golden Rule proves especially challenging. But it is worth noting that this is the challenge of moral commitment in a general sense. As R. M. Hare notes, in any moral situation involving persons A and B, person B

> must be prepared to give weight to *A*'s inclinations and interests as if they were his own. This is what turns selfish prudential reasoning into moral reasoning. It is much easier, psychologically, for *B* to do this if he is actually placed in a situation like *A*'s *vis-à-vis* somebody else; but this is not necessary, provided that he has sufficient imagination to envisage what it is like to be *A*.[41]

If Hare is correct, then this explains why versions of the Golden Rule are found in most world religions. All religions are fundamentally concerned with moral living, and the imaginative leap into the subjective viewpoint of others, as advocated in the Golden Rule, is foundational to moral assessment. This means that much of what we have to say here can be extended not only to most religions but to all objectivist moral theories. Whether one aims to apply Kant's Categorical Imperative, the principle of utility, an Aristotelian virtue ethic, or any other moral guideline, consideration of other points of view is essential.

What demands the work of imagination when applying the Golden Rule is the fact that it is presented as a counterfactual: "Do to others as you *would* have them do to you." Otherwise put, "Treat others in ways that you would want to be treated if you were they." Of course, when I consider this principle, I realize that I *am not* nor will I ever *be* another person. So when applying this principle I necessarily entertain a scenario that is contrary to actual fact. But how does one go about considering such a thing? Obviously, as Hare suggests, the key is imagination. The only way I can apply the Golden Rule is if I have, in his words, "suf-

---

[41] R. M. Hare, *Freedom and Reason* (Oxford: Oxford University Press, 1963), 94.

ficient imagination to envisage what it is like to be" someone else. If this is correct, then imagination is actually crucial to the Christian moral life, since the Golden Rule is central to a Christian ethic. This will be an important point to keep in mind for the final chapter when we discuss aesthetics.

There are some important qualifiers to the Golden Rule that deserve notice. First, the principle assumes the basic *psychological health* of the person applying it. In the hands of a sadomasochist the Golden Rule may be used to justify all sorts of abhorrent behavior. Such a person takes pleasure in being hurt and treated cruelly, so this principle would seem to counsel cruel behavior. But it is safe to assume that Jesus and other advocates of the Golden Rule would not condone cruelty, much less its justification via moral principle. Presumably, they would view sadomasochism as a psychological disorder. The peculiar applications of a person so disposed do not impugn the Golden Rule. This is one instance of a general point regarding moral principles. Unreasonable use of a principle does not undermine its reasonableness.

The need for another important qualifier becomes apparent when we consider an objection raised by Henry Sidgwick.[42] What are we to say of a situation in which a person wielding the Golden Rule is quite willing to act immorally, as many people in fact are? If I would like you to sin with me in some way, then by the Golden Rule, I should invite you to do so. After all, that is how I would prefer you to behave toward me. But surely we cannot sanction a moral principle that would advocate sinning and tempting others to do the same.

This problem shows that the Golden Rule assumes that those who use it are *morally serious*, genuinely committed to doing what is right. It also suggests that the Golden Rule is not by itself an adequate moral guideline. That is, while it is a serviceable guide for testing our moral convictions, this principle is not the sole criterion for good conduct. What, then, is the use of the Golden Rule? In what sense can it be valuable if it does not give complete guidance? The answer lies in the distinction between necessary and sufficient conditions for proper moral guidance. Observance of the Golden Rule is not a sufficient condition but it is a *necessary* condition for discovering how to behave morally. Its practicality lies not in its sovereignty as a moral principle, but in its usefulness for testing the consistency of our moral convictions, however those convictions might originate.

---

[42] Henry Sidgwick, *Methods of Ethics* (Indianapolis: Hackett Press, 1981), 380.

7.4.3 Toward a Complete Ethical Theory

Our review of the major moral theories has generated some good news and bad news. The bad news is that none of the views we have examined are satisfactory as a moral theory. Each has significant flaws of one kind or another. The good news is that each theory has significant insights that we may affirm even if we do not accept the theory as a whole. While some would prefer to stake their claim with just one of these moral theories, we believe that the best route is to take an eclectic approach and incorporate elements of each within a broader Christian moral perspective.

What we are looking for is a truly complete moral theory. In any field, including ethics, a theoretical position must be evaluated for its ability to explain the relevant data within that field. As was shown above, we must affirm some version of moral objectivism, because of a variety of facts that we cannot otherwise account for. These include the following:

- While many practices are a matter of cultural or personal preference, there are some practices that are universally right or wrong.
- It is appropriate in some instances to criticize foreign cultures, such as those that practice cruelties like female circumcision or injustices like slavery.
- While moral convictions often are linked to emotions and personal preferences, (a) our moral judgments have truth value, (b) our moral beliefs can be mistaken, and (c) moral debate is meaningful.

Notice that to affirm moral objectivism is not to deny every element of cultural relativism, subjectivism, and emotivism. Admitting the reality of cultural and personal preferences need not lead us to deny universal moral truth.

Granting the truth of moral objectivism, we may also acknowledge the importance of each of the following:

- Consequences of actions do matter when making moral assessments.
- Our moral obligations are vitally connected to the fact that we are rational beings, and immoral actions cannot be consistently universalized.
- Human beings are ends in themselves and should not be treated as mere means.
- Personal character is a crucial aspect of the moral life.

In view of these factors, we would grant that consequences, duty, and virtue are all vital moral categories. Thus, utilitarianism, Kantian ethics, and Aristotelian virtue ethics each capture some vital aspect of a complete moral theory. Specifically, the principle of utility, the Categorical Imperative, and the notion of virtue as a mean between two vicious extremes are all valuable tools for ethical analysis. We may even grant the insight of ethical egoism, namely that acting morally is in one's self-interest, though we would deny the egoist's claim that this is a proper moral focus.

Finally, we would emphasize the central place that theistic metaphysics plays in a complete moral theory, affirming that:

- God communicates morally through creation and the *telos* of various aspects in nature, including human beings.
- All living things are precious to God, but human life is especially sacred.
- God has issued many commands in Scripture, varying in form, scope, and degree of importance. These commands generate moral obligations.

To embrace these insights is to affirm key elements of a natural law ethic and divine command theory.

We believe that a full-orbed Christian ethic would indeed affirm all of these key factors in the moral life. And, although space does not allow us to demonstrate this, Scripture itself confirms each of these points. So to say that we endorse an "eclectic" moral theory is actually misleading. Closer to the truth is the notion that each of the objectivist theories seizes upon some significant moral truth and then presents it as the whole truth. In this sense, each moral objectivist theory is essentially a truncated Christian ethic. The theoretical approach we are advocating would invite application of a variety of moral principles but would affirm the priority of those that are explicit or implicit in Scripture. And, in all things, whether dealing with perennial moral issues or a personal situation, we should apply the Golden Rule.

This question remains: Why be moral? Why bother to live rightly? Any decent moral theory must provide a good answer to this pressing matter of moral motivation. Each of the major objectivist theories we discussed offers some incentive to be morally serious. The ethical egoist appeals to self-interest. The Utilitarian appeals to our desire to live in a happy society. Kantian ethics relies on our nature as rational beings. And virtue ethics appeals to our desire to maximize our excellence as human beings. While each of these incentives is effective motivation for many people, it is easy to see how some would ignore such concerns.

This underscores, again, the importance of a theistic foundation for ethics. The authority of an all-powerful, holy God is absolute, and His promises of rewards and warnings of punishment for the righteous and wicked, respectively, provide maximum incentive for moral living. Here is another profound advantage of a Christian ethical perspective.

Conclusion

In this chapter we have surveyed numerous perspectives on the good life and what it means to say that an action is right or wrong. We have seen how ethical relativism fails to account for some basic facts about human experience. And we have also seen how the major objectivist theories have significant insights about how the principles they propose should guide our conduct. Our application of these principles to the case studies revealed that it is no trivial matter which principle(s) one affirms, as each may lead one to a different conclusion regarding what is best in each situation.

It can be overwhelming to see the variety among moral perspectives and the different directions they might lead us when it comes to practical moral issues. But, again, it is important to remember that most life situations are not so vague or excruciating as the moral dilemmas discussed in this chapter. Most of life, thankfully, features straightforward moral choices, such as whether to be kind to a stranger, whether to be faithful to one's spouse, whether to be diligent in one's job, or whether to tell the truth (in situations where doing so won't cost a person's life!). At the end of the day, most of our moral decisions are not as challenging epistemologically as they are difficult to practice consistently. Where we fail, in most cases, is not due to our ignorance so much as our weakness of will.

The Bible says that God "has given us everything we need for life and godliness."[43] This is an encouraging reminder that although there is much that we do not understand in this life, we do have enough ethical information to live righteously. So let us study diligently to understand what is right and, just as importantly, work diligently to live accordingly.

Questions for Reflection

1. Is the principle of double-effect a sound moral guideline for deciding when it is permissible to perform an act that has partly evil

---

[43] 2 Peter 1:3.

consequences? Are the criteria it proposes necessary? Are they sufficient?

2. Some Christians believe that the Bible is free of all error, while others believe that it contains some mistakes, if only on trivial matters. Does one's position on this issue make divine command theory more or less plausible? Explain why or why not.

3. The Golden Rule is sometimes compared to Kant's Categorical Imperative. How are the two principles similar and how are they different?

4. What do you think of the authors' eclectic approach to moral theory? Is it correct? Why or why not?

For Further Reading

On Ethics in General

Pojman, Louis P., and Lewis Vaughn. *The Moral Life: An Introductory Reader in Ethics and Literature*. 3rd ed. New York: Oxford University Press, 2007.

Rachels, James, and Stuart Rachels. *The Elements of Moral Philosophy*. 5th ed. Boston: McGraw Hill, 2007.

White, James E. *Contemporary Moral Problems*. 9th ed. Belmont, CA: Wadsworth, 2008.

On Ethical Relativism

Beckwith, Francis J., and Gregory Koukl. *Relativism: Feet Planted Firmly in Mid-Air*. Grand Rapids: Baker, 1998.

Kreeft, Peter. *A Refutation of Moral Relativism: Interviews with an Absolutist*. San Francisco: Ignatius, 1999.

Moser, Paul K., and Thomas L. Carson. *Moral Relativism: A Reader*. New York: Oxford University Press, 2000.

On Objectivist Theories

Boyd, Craig A. *A Shared Morality: A Narrative Defense of Natural Law Ethics*. Ada, MI: Brazos, 2007

Comte-Sponville, Andre. *A Small Treatise on the Great Virtues*, trans. Catherine Temerson. New York: Metropolitan, 2001.

Hare, John E. *The Moral Gap: Kantian Ethics, Human Limits, and God's Assistance*. Oxford: Oxford University Press, 1997

MacIntyre, Alasdair. *After Virtue*. Notre Dame: University of Notre Dame Press, 1981.

Quinn, Phillip L. *Divine Commands and Moral Requirements*. New York: Oxford University Press,1978.

West, Henry R. *Mill's Utilitarianism: A Reader's Guide*. New York: Continuum, 2007.

Wood, Allen F. *Kantian Ethics*. Cambridge: Cambridge University Press, 2007.

On Christian Ethics

Geisler, Norman L. *Christian Ethics: Options and Issues*. Grand Rapids: Baker, 1989.

Holmes, Arthur F. *Ethics: Approaching Moral Decisions*. 2nd ed. Downers Grove, IL: InterVarsity, 2008.

Rae, Scott B. *Moral Choices: An Introduction to Christian Ethics*. 2nd ed. Grand Rapids: Zondervan, 2000.

Chapter 8

POLITICAL PHILOSOPHY: WHAT IS A JUST SOCIETY?

*"Freedom exists only where people
take care of the government."*

—Woodrow Wilson

8.1 Justice, Rights, and Laws

8.1.1 Justice

8.1.2 Rights

8.1.3 Laws

8.2 Theories of the State

8.2.1 Anarchy and the Need for Government

8.2.2 Monarchy

8.2.3 Social Contract Theory

8.3 Distributive Justice

8.3.1 Libertarianism

8.3.2 Socialism

8.3.3 Welfare Liberalism

8.3.4 Applications to Contemporary Issues

8.4 Theological Reflections on the State

8.4.1 Biblical Perspectives on Distributive Justice

8.4.2 Religion in the Public Square

8.4.3 Civil Disobedience

Glossary Terms

Anarchy	*Libertarianism (political)*
Commercial justice	*Monarchy*
Communitarianism	*Natural law*
Difference principle	*Negative right*
Distributive justice	*Positive right*
Divine law	*Remedial justice*
Eternal law	*Right*
Human law	*Social contract*
Justice	*Socialism*
Law	*Welfare liberalism*
Legal positivism	

When, in the course of human events, it becomes necessary for one people to dissolve the political bands which have connected them with another, and to assume among the powers of the earth, the separate and equal station to which the laws of nature and of nature's God entitle them, a decent respect to the opinions of mankind requires that they should declare the causes which impel them to the separation.

We hold these truths to be self-evident, that all men are created equal, that they are endowed by their Creator with certain unalienable rights, that among these are life, liberty and the pursuit of happiness. That to secure these rights, governments are instituted among men, deriving their just powers from the consent of the governed.

These are the opening lines to the United States Declaration of Independence, penned by Thomas Jefferson in 1776. Because these words are so familiar, it is easy to overlook the fact that they call upon some very weighty philosophical concepts. These two short paragraphs make profound metaphysical, epistemological, and moral assumptions. There are also references here to such notions as "rights," "law," "liberty," "equality," and "justice." What do these terms *mean*? And what philosophical justification did Jefferson have for using them?

Among the philosophers who influenced Jefferson and the other founding fathers was Aristotle. He famously declared that human beings are "social animals." It is our nature to dwell together in groups of all kinds, beginning with the family. Thus, in his view, moral inquiry cannot be limited to the personal sphere. Goodness and virtue, and their contraries, must also apply at the level of human collectives—our social arrangements and institutions, including government. When we do value theory at this level, we have political philosophy.

This chapter will address the central issues in political philosophy: What is the best state or civil society? How, if at all, should we be governed? Where does governmental authority come from and what are its proper limits? What are "rights" and what is their source? Are laws discovered or are they just made up? And what influence, if any, should government have regarding how goods and services in society are distributed among the citizens?

The final question in the previous paragraph pertains to economics. Just as ethics fades into political philosophy, it is also difficult to draw a clear line between political philosophy and economics or, for that matter, social thought. Indeed, they are all interconnected. For this reason, in this chapter our discussion will delve into all of these areas. But we will do so always in order to get a better fix on the central concern of political philosophy—specifically, to figure out what a just society looks like.

In the previous chapter we discussed some practical moral issues in order to help clarify the implications of the various ethical theories we considered. Since political philosophy deals with many practical issues, it will be helpful to use some case studies in this chapter as well. It should be noted that each of the following three cases is a moral as well as a political issue. In the present context, however, we will be mainly concerned with the political dimensions of these cases.

1. Abortion. Since the Supreme Court's landmark decision *Roe v. Wade* (1973), abortion has been legal in the United States. Since that time over 50 million abortions have been performed in this country. Yet, while every year hundreds of thousands of unborn babies are killed legally, most states have "fetal homicide" laws, many of them making it a crime to kill a fetus even during the early stages of gestation. Many claim that this demonstrates an incoherence in the American legal system. But others argue that this combination of laws is reasonable, since the decisive factor is whether the mother *chooses* to terminate her pregnancy. Which side is correct? Should all or most abortions be illegal? When, if ever, does a woman have a right to choose to terminate her pregnancy?

Should this be considered a private choice or a matter for government regulation?

2. Capital Punishment. One of those who was recently convicted under California's fetal homicide law was Scott Peterson. He was also convicted of first-degree murder of his pregnant wife, Laci Peterson. For his crime he was sentenced to death in May 2005 and is awaiting his execution by lethal injection at San Quentin State Prison. Apparently Peterson strangled her at their home, dismembered her body, and dumped her in the San Francisco Bay. Portions of Laci Peterson's body and their unborn child, Connor, later washed up on the shore. Does Peterson deserve to die for his horrific act? Does the government have the right to put any of its citizens to death?

3. Censorship. Every year the Southeastern Center for Contemporary Arts presents awards to artists for achievements in numerous categories. The center is funded by the National Endowment for the Arts, a government agency that supports the arts in the United States. In 1989 the winner in the visual arts category was a photograph titled "Piss Christ" by Andres Serrano. The photograph depicts a plastic crucifix submerged in a glass of Serrano's urine. The award caused public furor, as critics called the artwork sacrilegious and profane. Others defended the work on the basis of free speech and freedom of artistic expression. Is it the government's place to provide funding for the arts? Should certain works of art be refused funding or even legally banned because of offensive content?

§ 8.1 Justice, Rights, and Laws

Before diving into the substantive questions of any field, it is crucial that key terms be defined. One of the challenges of political philosophy is that many of its substantive questions are *about* its key terms and how they should be defined. Among the most important of these are the concepts of justice, rights and laws.

8.1.1 Justice

The central concern of political philosophy is the just state. But what is *justice*? The term is heard frequently in various contexts of public discourse. However, it is one thing to use a term and quite another to understand it well enough to be able to define it. As with so many philosophical issues, the subject of justice takes us back to Plato. His dialogue, the *Republic*, was devoted to understanding this one concept.

This fact is a tribute both to Plato's analytical rigor and the difficulty of understanding what justice is. As was typical with Plato, in the *Republic* he takes time not only to defend his own views but to roundly critique those of his opponents. One of the theories of justice he dismisses is proposed by Thrasymachus, an older contemporary of Plato's (belonging to the Sophist camp). According to Thrasymachus, justice is what is in the interest of the stronger party.[1] This is the earliest known articulation of what has become known as the "might makes right" theory of justice, a view which found later advocates in Machiavelli and Nietzsche. On this view, rulers are free to frame whatever laws they want, so long as the laws serve their own interests.

Plato, through his mouthpiece Socrates, challenges Thrasymachus by noting that every art seeks an end. For example, medicine and seamanship are arts, and they seek the ends, respectively, of bodily health and safe sailing. Practitioners of these arts serve their subjects' interests. Ruling or "statecraft" is an art as well, and its end is the flourishing of the state. Like a physician or sailor, a ruler is a servant, seeking the interests of those whom he serves, namely the citizens of the state. A ruler's proper role, then, is not to seek his own interests but to govern the state in such a way that it flourishes.

Plato eventually gives a full articulation and defense of his own view of justice. (He spends several hundred pages doing so!) His general perspective is that justice always pertains to situations where there are multiple parties involved, and justice occurs when each party fulfills its proper role.[2] Plato's view might be the original version of the common conception of justice as "each doing its part" or "giving to each its due." Plato regarded a civil society as consisting of three basic components: workers, soldiers, and ruler. When functioning properly, workers produce goods, soldiers defend the state, and the ruler makes wise decisions in governance. Thus, when each does its job, the society is just and therefore flourishes. Such harmony of tasks constitutes justice. However, when a part of the state malfunctions, either by failing to fulfill its role or by usurping the role of another part, then the state is unjust and suffers as a whole. While Plato's particular vision for the state has few proponents among contemporary philosophers, his general concept of justice has stuck. Justice involves proportionality—each doing its part.

Note that this simple conception of justice, as a kind of proportionality, illuminates each of the issues addressed in our case studies. Are all key parties given their proper due in situations involving abortion? Is

---

[1] Plato, *The Republic*, 338c.
[2] See especially *Republic*, books 2–4.

the death penalty proportionate to the crime for which it is commonly applied in our country, such as murder or high treason? And is government censorship a proportionate response to certain forms of offensive art? Each of these queries essentially asks a question about the justice of the act, policy, or law at issue.

Plato's prize student, Aristotle, recognized the reasonableness of his mentor's basic approach. He distinguished between what is merely *lawful* from what is *fair* and emphasized that justice regards proper proportion. Aristotle also extended the concept to several particular subject areas, making a three-fold division between remedial, commercial, and distributive justice.[3] *Remedial* justice pertains to situations in which one person has harmed another, whether through voluntary transactions (e.g., selling, lending, contracts, etc.) or through involuntary transactions (e.g., fraud, force, etc.). Aristotle says that such situations must be rectified by taking from the perpetrator and giving to the victim. This reestablishes proportion between the parties and thus is just. *Commercial* justice is proportion in exchange of goods or services. This kind of justice occurs when, for example, a worker is paid appropriate wages or when goods are sold at a fair price, taking into account such factors as supply and demand.

Lastly, *distributive* justice pertains to the distribution of honor and wealth in a society. According to Aristotle, due proportion in this context requires that goods be divided in a ratio that matches the merit of the individuals. Each person's share should match what they actually deserve. But, then, what do people deserve? Here Aristotle acknowledges divergence of opinion based on different theories of the state. In some societies, equality is prioritized such that all citizens are regarded as deserving an equal share. Elsewhere, nobility is valued most highly, so they will be deemed as meriting more wealth. And in other societies virtue is regarded as the proper criterion for distributing wealth. Thus, Aristotle rightly observes that one's sense of distributive justice hinges on the criteria one employs. Such criteria call for philosophical appraisal, and the history of political and economic thought has seen a rich dialogue on the matter. Later in this chapter we will discuss the major approaches and their proponents.

From a Christian perspective, it is noteworthy that the concept of justice is not explicitly defined in Scripture. This has given rise to widespread debate about what is a "Christian" view of justice. In most biblical passages where the term is used, the reader is presumed to have a basic understanding of the concept, and the notion that justice is a kind of fairness or due proportion makes sense in each case. However,

---

[3] Aristotle, *Nicomachean Ethics*, book V.

depending on the context, justice may be understood as implying: (1) remediation or retribution (Isa 61:8; Jer 30:11), (2) procedural fairness (Exod 23:2; Lev 19:15; Ps 112:5), (3) help for the needy (Ps 140:12; Zech 7:9), or (4) mercy for the oppressed (Isa 1:17; Jer 21:12). So the disagreement, or difference of emphases, among political theologians is understandable. Perhaps all of these elements should be understood as contained in a Christian view of justice. In this case, one might embrace an eclectic view of justice much like what we proposed about a Christian moral theory in the previous chapter. (More will be said about this later in this chapter.)

8.1.2 Rights

Another concept that plays a significant role in political thought is *rights*. In public discourse we hear of minority rights, women's rights, gay rights, children's rights, animal rights, and rights of the unborn. Rights are generally understood as claims or entitlements, and they take negative and positive forms. A *negative right* is a freedom from interference with regard to some activity or pursuit. Thus, the right of free speech is an entitlement to noninterference when it comes to oral or written expression. And a right to worship entitles one to noninterference in the practice of one's religion. A *positive right*, on the other hand, is a claim *to* some good or service. Rights to education or health care, for example, are entitlements to be provided with educational services or medical treatment when needed.

Rights are sometimes distinguished as moral or legal. A *legal right*, such as the right to an attorney or to bear arms, is stipulated in a civil legal code, whereas a *moral right*, such as the right to life or the right to autonomy, is often regarded as transcending local legal codes, either because of our inherent standing as human beings or because of our having been so endowed by God. Thus, when Thomas Jefferson writes in the U. S. Declaration of Independence that all men are "endowed by their Creator with certain unalienable rights," the rights of which he speaks are moral rather than legal in nature. That they are "unalienable" is meant to suggest that no political or legal system can deny them. In fact, such rights are supposed to form the basis of a just political system and to serve as a standard for evaluating the justice of any such system. Moral skeptics, however, challenge the distinction between moral and legal rights, insisting that all rights are legal—stipulated by human agreement rather than being inherent in our nature or endowed by God.

Rights appear always to correlate with duties. To have a right to life, free speech, or free worship implies that others have duties to respect these freedoms. And, with regard to positive rights, my right to education, health care, or social welfare implies that someone—that is, the government—has a duty to provide these things for me. It is here, some object, that such positive rights prove to be problematic, as they claim that the government has no duty to provide these services to citizens. And if the government, and no one else, has a duty to provide these things, then no one has a right to them.

With this basic understanding of rights, the dilemmas in our three case studies may be better understood. The abortion debate features a conflict between a mother's right of autonomy and the unborn child's right to life. Those on the pro-choice side insist that it is a mother's right to choose what she will do with her own body, while pro-lifers point out that it is not just her own body that is at stake. Since most people would agree that the right to life trumps the right of autonomy, the debate really boils down to the question of the ontological status of the fetus. Is it fully human or not? If not, then the mother's right to choose might trump whatever value the fetus has, and the rest of us have a duty to allow her to terminate the pregnancy if she so desires. And it is the proper role of government to protect this right, as was found in the *Roe v. Wade* decision. However, if the fetus is fully human, then its right to life trumps all rights of autonomy. The rest of us, including the mother, have a duty not to take the unborn child's life (unless the *mother's* right to life can be respected only by terminating the pregnancy). And it is the proper role of government to protect unborn children and to prosecute those who harm them, as was the case with Scott Peterson.

The issue of capital punishment also crucially involves the right to life, though in a very different way. A murderer has a right to life like anyone else. But proponents of the death penalty insist that a murderer forfeits this right when he takes the life of an innocent person. Moreover, they claim, it is out of respect for the right to life that murderers must pay with their own lives. And since government is an agent of the people, it is the government's role to execute the murderer. Opponents of the death penalty claim, however, that the right to life is inviolable, and even the act of murder does not revoke it. That a person has killed someone does not annul anyone's duty to respect his life, and this includes the government.

Finally, the issue of censorship pits the right to free speech against the autonomy of citizens to make decisions about what counts as profane or indecent. Those who oppose censorship insist that art should not be so regulated, since citizens are not forced to view questionable artworks, such as Andres Serrano's "Piss Christ." Supporters of censorship, however, claim that although an artist should indeed be allowed to make whatever art he desires, government funding of such art is a different matter. The National Endowment for the Arts should not fund a work such as Serrano's "Piss Christ," since it offends the religious sensibilities of so many citizens—people whose taxes are used to fund the NEA.

Another critical issue regarding rights concerns how they are grounded. Where do our rights come from? There are two basic approaches to the justification of rights, consequentialist and deontological. A consequentialist, as one might guess, grounds the concept of rights in the consequences of actions. Classical utilitarians, for example, argue that we have a duty to act for the greatest pleasure and the least pain for all involved, while rule utilitarians argue that we have a duty to abide by those rules that, if followed, would result in the welfare of society. This duty implies the correlative right of the citizenry to live in a society whose happiness (overall pleasure) is maximized. Deontologists take a different approach to the justification of rights, arguing that consequences are irrelevant to the grounding of rights. A Kantian, for instance, would say that rights are inherent to our nature as rational beings. A natural law approach would justify rights by appealing to various aspects of the *telos* of human beings and human community. And a divine command theorist would appeal to God's directives in Scripture. Thus, for the deontologist, our rights are known directly rather than via an inference on the basis of duties which are known, in turn, on the basis of consequences.

8.1.3 Laws

The concept of law is also central to political philosophy. What are the ultimate source and justification for the legal standards established in a civil society? There are two general perspectives on this question, distinguished by their view on the relationship between law and morality. *Natural law theorists* affirm an overlap between the two realms, in the sense that at least some legal standards are ultimately grounded in moral truths. *Legal positivists* reject the "overlap thesis," as it is sometimes called, insisting that laws are mere human conventions grounded in social facts.

Natural Law Theory

According to the natural law tradition, some moral laws are universally binding and serve as the foundation for some legal standards that must be upheld in any civil society. The most ancient advocates of this approach were the Stoics, including Seneca (c. 4 BC–AD 65), Epictetus (c. AD 55–135), and Marcus Aurelius (AD 121–180). The Stoics maintained that all human beings are united by our common share in universal reason or, as some put it, the divine *logos*. This rational principle, they claimed, grounds not only law but civil society itself. Aurelius explains:

> If the power of thought is universal among mankind, so likewise is the possession of reason, making us rational creatures. It follows, therefore, that this reason speaks no less universally to us all with its 'thou shalt' or 'thou shalt not.' So then there is a world-law; which in turn means that we are all fellow-citizens and share a common citizenship, and that the world is a single city.[4]

On this view, then, we are not free to make up just any laws we wish. Reason itself dictates standards that we should abide by in the public sphere no less than in our private lives.

Christian political thinkers, such as St. Augustine (354–430) and Thomas Aquinas (1225–1274), conceived of natural law as grounded not in a rational principle but in a personal God. Aquinas defined law generally as "an ordinance of reason for the common good, promulgated by him who has the care of a community."[5] And he distinguished between several different kinds of laws. *Eternal law* refers to the sum of God's decrees governing the universe, while *natural law* is that part of eternal law that humans can discover using reason. As we strive to apply natural law to our specific civil circumstances, the result is *human law*. There is also *divine law,* which refers to special ordinances God has laid down in Scripture.

Legal Positivism

Legal positivists maintain that there is nothing natural or universal about law. Some ancient Sophists were early proponents of this view. For example, Protagoras (490–420 BC) famously proclaimed that "man is the measure of all things," a claim which when applied to law well-articulates the positivist thesis. All norms, including those of a legal nature, merely reflect our practical sense about human life.

Contemporary legal positivists make three interconnected claims. First, they defend the *pedigree thesis* that all legal standards are completely grounded in social facts, especially customs and practical concerns. Second, legal positivists embrace the *conventionality thesis,* which says that legal standards are purely human conventions. They do not have any intrinsic necessity or universal truth. Third, legal positivists' *separation thesis* pertains to the notion that there is no overlap between law

---

[4] Marcus Aurelius, *Meditations,* trans. Maxwell Staniforth (Harmondsworth: Penguin, 1964), 65.

[5] Thomas Aquinas, *Summa Theologica,* trans. English Dominican Fathers (New York: Benziger Brothers, 1947), 1:995.

and morality. A positivist may affirm the existence of universal moral truths, but he claims that if they exist, legal standards are separate and unaffected by them.

The leading legal positivist of the twentieth century was H. L. A. Hart (1907–1992). By Hart's account, laws originate in customs that have gained widespread approval within a society, such as prohibitions against violence or theft. Hart calls these *primary rules*. They are reinforced and formalized by various *secondary rules*, including a "rule of recognition," by which the primary rules are formally affirmed as authoritative, and a "rule of change," which "empowers an individual or body of persons to introduce new primary rules for the conduct of the life of the group, or of some class within it, and to eliminate old rules."[6] Notice that Hart's approach to legal standards parallels that taken by Benedict and Sumner with regard to ethics. Legal positivism is a form of value relativism.

Critical Reflections

Both natural law and legal positivist approaches to law have their problems. In claiming that some legal standards are founded on moral laws, natural law theorists obviously face the daunting task of demonstrating (1) that there is a moral law and (2) what that moral law stipulates. This requires careful philosophical and, often, theological analysis. Also, in a pluralistic society, such as the United States, specific claims about the moral law are naturally controversial, which in part explains why there seems to be such a strong presumption in favor of legal positivism in American culture today.

Legal positivism, however, is even more problematic. First, this view cannot explain why it is *right* to obey civil laws. While a given law (or "primary rule") may represent a shared conviction within society and may be reinforced with the threat of punishment for those who disobey, these facts by themselves cannot account for why we laud those who are consistently obedient. Only a "higher" (i.e., moral) law can enable one to make such a meta-judgment about obeying civil laws. Secondly, legal positivism cannot account for the rightness of civil disobedience in some cases, such as resistance to Jim Crow laws during the civil rights movement. Nor can positivism make sense of the concept of unjust laws. For example, the 1896 U. S. Supreme Court decision *Plessy v. Ferguson* upheld a Louisiana law requiring black people to ride in separate railroad cars from white people, thus launching the Jim Crow era of "separate but equal." Although this legal tradition represented the predominant

---

[6] H. L. A. Hart, *The Concept of Law* (Oxford: Oxford University Press, 1961), 93.

social customs of the time, common sense tells us that they were unjust (or not) all along. Yet legal positivism cannot account for this.

It is no wonder that the American civil rights movement that challenged and ultimately overturned this tradition of discrimination was inspired by natural law and led by a strong proponent of natural law in Martin Luther King. His enormously influential "Letter from Birmingham Jail" appeals to natural law concepts from Augustine and Aquinas. King's defense of his approach is a definitive statement of natural law theory: "How does one determine whether a law is just or unjust? A just law is a man-made code that squares with the moral law or the law of God. An unjust law is a code that is out of harmony with the moral law."[7] Such words are antithetical to the legal positivist view. If the ideas of a Protagoras or H. L. A. Hart had been accepted by King and other black leaders of his day, it is fair to say that the civil rights movement would never have happened.

Questions for Reflection

1. Is Aristotle's three-fold distinction between remedial, commercial, and distributive justice complete or are there some other kinds of justice? If so, what are they?
2. Do human beings have rights? If so, where do they come from? Are all rights correlated with duties?
3. How might one go about determining which rights and duties are most fundamental?
4. With which perspective are you most sympathetic, natural law theory or legal positivism? Why so?

§ 8.2 Theories of the State

Having clarified the concepts of justice, rights, and laws, we can now turn to the area of political philosophy in which they figure most prominently: the matter of civil government. Which form of government is best? And what system of rights and laws for ordering society is most just? In this section we will discuss some of the major theories of the state.

8.2.1 Anarchy and the Need for Government

Lest we presume too much, let us first consider the question of whether human beings should be governed at all. Those who answer this

---

[7] Martin Luther King, "Letter from Birmingham Jail," in *Why We Can't Wait* (New York: Penguin, 1963), 82.

question negatively endorse *anarchy*. Anarchists reject all forms of government or civil authority and hierarchy. However, they differ over the appropriateness of social ordering and economic arrangements. Thus, one might reject all forms of authority and formal legal codes, while affirming the social goal of shared goods or equal distribution of goods. This is *anarcho-socialism*. In contrast, *anarcho-capitalists* would favor private property and a free-market economic system. In either case, the question arises as to how such social goals can be attained without some sort of enforcement of rules. In response, anarchists insist that voluntarism—reliance on people's voluntary actions—would suffice to achieve these goals. A major problem with this approach, however, is motivation. When left to their own devices, many people are not sufficiently inspired to act toward a shared end. Furthermore, some anarchists fear that stated economic goals can quickly become authoritarian rules. For this reason *absolute anarchists* reject even economic guidelines to achieve social ends. However, this more extreme version of the theory faces an even more severe problem of motivation.

More basic than the problem of motivation for anarchists is the problem of human nature. Many early modern political philosophers (to be discussed below) considered what life would be like in a "state of nature" where there were no government, laws, or rules of any kind—essentially an anarchist situation. Most of them concluded that it would be a miserable affair. Thomas Hobbes, for example, noted that in a state of nature there would be constant competition for scarce resources. Without laws or governmental authorities, people would resort to violence without concerns about punishment. Consequently, there would be a continual condition of war, "every man against every man," where life is "solitary, poor, nasty, brutish, and short."[8] Hobbes' bleak picture of human nature is often mocked but has never been refuted. In fact, every day of human history brings countless more confirmations of Hobbes' view. Indeed, as philosophical claims go, it is hard to imagine a thesis more highly confirmed than that human nature is corrupt. From a Christian perspective Hobbes' moral anthropology should be affirmed as well. Scripture is replete with judgments about human nature that are many times more damning than those of Hobbes, declaring not only that "all have sinned and fall short of the glory of God" (Rom 3:23), but that we are sinful from birth (Pss 51:5; 58:3) and that we have continuously evil inclinations even from childhood (Gen 6:5; 8:21).

When it comes to anarchy, then, it is no surprise that very few scholars endorse this view. It simply fails to come to grips with the fact that humans are morally corrupt and that our evil tendencies must be curbed

---

[8] Thomas Hobbes, *Leviathan* (New York: Macmillan, 1958), 107.

somehow. We need to be motivated in our laziness, discouraged in our greed and selfishness, and our violent impulses must be tempered. We cannot rely on sheer voluntarism to bring about an ordered and just society. A system of laws is needed to achieve this end. And government is necessary to create and execute the laws.

So what form of government is best? Next we will consider a variety of answers to this question. But every political philosophy can be placed into one of two categories when it comes to how it conceives the relationship between the ruling power and the laws of the land. The dominant view for centuries in the West was that the ruler is supreme, sovereign over all laws. This perspective is sometimes called *rex lex* ("king is law"). However, in the early modern period a dramatic shift occurred, in which the opposite view ascended to dominance: *lex rex* ("law is king"). According to this perspective, no human being can have absolute power. Even rulers are subject to law.

8.2.2 Monarchy

The *rex lex* perspective is most typically associated with *monarchy*. This is the view that the state should be led by a single ruler. (To be precise and complete, there is also *aristocracy*, which is rule by a few. But for simplicity's sake, we will collapse this view under what we have labeled "monarchy.") Monarchical systems may be absolute or limited. In this section we will discuss these two versions of monarchy.

Absolute Monarchy: Machiavelli

One of the more controversial political thinkers in the early sixteenth century was Niccolo Machiavelli (1469–1527). His book, *The Prince*, was essentially a manual in how a ruler can acquire, retain, and expand power. Machiavelli lived in Italy during a tumultuous period, when there was much conflict in Europe and his own country was often under siege. The instability and danger probably affected his assessment of human nature, which like that of Hobbes regarded human beings as inherently wicked and depraved. This in turn impacted Machiavelli's political philosophy, resulting in the severe pragmatism of *The Prince*.

For Machiavelli, power is an end in itself—a view that hearkens back to Thrasymachus' view of justice. As the strongest party, whatever serves the ruler's interest is right. In pursuing political power, says Machiavelli, "the end justifies the means. Let a prince therefore aim at conquering and maintaining the state, and the means will always be judged honourable."[9] To succeed in gaining and keeping power, the

[9] Niccolo Machiavelli, *The Prince*, trans. Luigi Ricci, in *The Prince and the Discourses* (New York: Random House, 1950), 66.

ruler must be like both a fox and a lion—crafty and powerful: "the lion cannot protect himself from traps, and the fox cannot defend himself from wolves. One must therefore be a fox to recognize traps and a lion to frighten wolves."[10]

According to Machiavelli, the state is an autonomous system of values. The values of the state are not based in anything beyond itself. The only good for the state is efficiency. And when it comes to efficiency in preserving the state, sometimes the price is virtue. As Machiavelli puts it, the ruler "must not mind incurring the scandal of those vices, without which it would be difficult to save the state, for if one considers well, it will be found that some things which seem virtues would, if followed, lead to one's ruin, and some others which appear vices result in one's greater security and well-being."[11] Such disregard for any values higher than those found in the state reveals Machiavelli to be a strong legal positivist.

Some scholars express uncertainty as to whether Machiavelli intends to endorse the ideas in *The Prince*. That is, is the book truly prescriptive or is it merely descriptive of how political systems—or monarchies in particular—actually work? We will not quibble here about this interpretive issue. Whether or not Machiavelli intends to endorse absolute monarchy, the more important point is that the principles in his work have in fact been embraced and put into action by many heads of state—in contemporary times no less than in centuries past. Recent examples include the tyrannical regimes of Stalin, Hitler, Saddam Hussein, Fidel Castro, and Kim Jong Il.

Limited Monarchy: Plato and Aquinas

Most proponents of monarchy recognize the need for proper limits to the ruler's power. But what form should those limits take? Some, such as Plato, have appealed to the moral law as the best bulwark against abuse of power. Plato recognized the dangers of placing so much power in the hands of one individual, but he apparently felt that the benefits of having a truly wise ruler justified the risk. Besides, according to Plato, a monarchical system most naturally reflects human nature. We noted above how Plato saw civil society as consisting of three basic elements: workers, soldiers, and ruler. The human soul is similarly tripartheid, Plato argued, consisting of appetite, spirit, and reason. Just as reason must guide the other aspects of the soul, so must the ruler guide the state. Both demand wisdom in guiding the other two components, and when this is achieved, there is harmony and the virtue of justice.

[10] Ibid., 64.
[11] Ibid., 57.

Since a wise person is required to govern the state properly, it follows that the king must be a philosopher. After all, philosophy is the love of wisdom. Thus, Plato concludes,

> Unless . . . either philosophers become kings in our states or those whom we now call our kings and rulers take to the pursuit of philosophy seriously and adequately, and there is a conjunction of these two things, political power and philosophical intelligence, . . . there can be no cessation of troubles . . . for our states, nor, I fancy, for the human race.[12]

As for the specific qualifications of the philosopher-king, Plato says that he will need to be courageous, generous, magnificent, gracious, friendly, just, sober-minded, and have an excellent memory. Most importantly, he will need to have a special capacity for apprehending eternal and immutable truths. Such insight is essential, says Plato, because rulers are like shipmasters. In navigating the ship through high seas and tempests, a sailor cannot rely on his immediate surroundings for guidance but rather must consult the stars, which are fixed and reliable. Similarly, a wise ruler must not focus exclusively on the particulars of his state's current situation but must consult eternal truths—the "forms," as discussed in chapter 4—in order to navigate the state properly.

Here is where the limits of the monarchy lie—in the eternal forms of justice and other virtues. In a just state, the ruler makes laws that conform to these immutable values; the good ruler also judges and executes the laws accordingly. Thus, Plato's vision for the ideal state is essentially a natural law approach, for he recognizes a moral law above local legal codes—a higher law according to which any nation's laws, and those who create and enforce them, must be evaluated.

Thomas Aquinas agreed with both Plato's endorsement of monarchy and the concept of a higher moral law constraining the king. But Aquinas recognized the legitimacy of further, more tangible, limits to the king's authority:

> the best form of government is in a state or kingdom, wherein one is given the power to preside over all; while under him are others having governing powers: and yet a government of this kind is shared by all, both because all are eligible to govern, and because the rules are chosen by all.[13]

---

[12] Plato, *Republic*, trans. Paul Shorey, in *The Collected Dialogues of Plato*, ed. Edith Hamilton and Huntington Cairns (Princeton: Princeton University Press, 1961), 712–13.

[13] Thomas Aquinas, *Summa Theologica*, 1:1092.

So the power of government, and of the ruler in particular, should be subject to the will of the people. This is a decided move in the direction of democracy.

According to Aquinas, the government's function has both negative and positive aspects. Its negative function is disciplinary: to punish those who disobey. The positive role of government is to produce virtuous, educated citizens. Government achieves these ends through its creation and enforcement of human law. This is essentially a secular matter, but the church may advise on such ordinances where divine law is directly relevant. Aquinas also recognizes ecclesial authority to censure secular rulers, suggesting that the church has "the power of curbing earthly princes."[14] The lines between church and state are further blurred by Aquinas as he affirms laws against public renunciation of one's faith, and he regards the public teaching of theological heresy as a capital offense. Thus, for Aquinas, the church represents another limitation on the ruler's authority.

In Aquinas' political theory perhaps the most significant limitation on the ruler's authority, and the power of the state generally, is the people's right of rebellion. When functioning properly, the government frames civil laws that conduce to the good of the community, and citizens have a duty to comply with all such laws. But if a government makes laws that require citizens to sin, then these laws have no moral authority and the citizen has a moral obligation to disobey them. As Aquinas notes, "if . . . a thing is, of itself, contrary to natural right, the human will cannot make it just."[15] Here we see a key development in the history of political philosophy: emergence of the rule of law. Even though monarchy would continue to be the rule after Aquinas until the modern era, he had worked out a framework for the paradigm shift that was to come in political philosophy: from *rex lex* to *lex rex*.

Criticisms of Monarchy

General difficulties are encountered by any monarchical system. First, there is the problem of finding a worthy ruler. Plato's list of requisite skills for ruling is formidable, and one wonders whether anyone could adequately answer to such a description of a fit ruler. And even if someone were so wise as to qualify, for just this reason they might be unwilling to take the job! Socrates was apparently tempted to a political career, but he shunned it in favor of a life in pursuit of wisdom. Perhaps he was wary of what political power might do to him.

---

[14] Ibid., 2:1230.
[15] Ibid., 2:1432.

This leads us to the second problem with monarchy, captured in Lord Acton's famous phrase that "power tends to corrupt, and absolute power corrupts absolutely."[16] Aristotle observed that the corrupting temptations of power should be taken into account when selecting a political philosophy. One must consider what it takes to reform a government once it has gone bad, for some are worse than others. Aristotle argued that since a corrupt monarchy—tyranny—is the most pernicious of all corrupted forms of government, this form must be avoided. Monarchy might be the best in an ideal world—such as that imagined by Plato in the *Republic*. But, alas, ours is far from an ideal world.

Another criticism of monarchy discussed by Aristotle is the problem of succession. What criteria should be used to select the next king? While the hereditary criterion works well when the ruler has a proper descendent to assume the throne, the lack of a descendent—or of one sufficiently qualified for the post—can cause enormous conflict. Indeed, many civil wars have erupted as a result. In the eighteenth century alone there were wars over succession in Spain (1701–1714), Poland (1733–1738), and Austria (1740–1748).

8.2.3 Social Contract Theory

During the modern period the shift from *rex lex* to *lex rex* was relatively sudden, at least as historical trends go. But as we have seen, the concept of rule by law has ancient roots, and there were some philosophers along the way who catalyzed the emergence of this paradigm by using natural law to defend kingship. Thomas Hobbes (1588–1679) is a pivotal case in point. Hobbes's paradoxical approach was to appeal to natural law to justify absolute monarchical sovereignty. And he was the first modern thinker to employ the concept of a *social contract* by which members of society agree to establish government. Hobbes' younger contemporary, John Locke (1632–1704), and Jean Jacques Rousseau (1712–1778) used this same concept to argue for a more democratic form of government. In this section we will discuss these versions of modern social contract theory.

Social Contract Absolutism: Hobbes

The historical context in which Thomas Hobbes wrote was one of political upheaval in his native England. On one side were the Royalists, who favored the monarchical system, and on the other were the Parliamentarians who wanted more power for the representatives of British constituents. Hobbes' magnum opus *Leviathan* presented a compromise of sorts, affirming the sovereignty of the throne while grounding this in

---

[16] John Acton, *Essays on Freedom and Power* (Glencoe, IL: The Free Press, 1949), 364.

natural law and the will of the people. This was radical enough in itself, but the fact that his was a purely secular defense of monarchy made his theory that much more controversial.

As noted above, Hobbes appealed to a hypothetical "state of nature" to demonstrate the need for government and, more specifically, to give a rationale for a political covenant among the people. This covenant or social contract would rescue them from the "condition of war" that would characterize life in a world without laws. The underlying cause of the inevitable strife is equality among people.

According to Hobbes, in a state of nature people would lay claim to the same things. Competition for limited goods would result in enmity and fighting. And even where no actual fighting occurred, there would be constant fear and anxiety. It is to rescue us from this condition of war that a social contract is necessary, claims Hobbes. However, this contract is not merely pragmatic but is rooted in natural law that is "found out by reason." First, there is a fundamental *right of nature*, says Hobbes, specifically "the liberty each man has to use his own power . . . for the preservation of his own nature—that is to say, his own life."[17] Along with this basic right to life there is a corresponding *law of nature*, which is "a precept or general rule . . . by which a man is forbidden to do that which is destructive of his life or takes away the means of preserving the same and to omit that by which he thinks it may be best preserved."[18]

Now the right of self-preservation and the duty to preserve life are universally binding, and together they call us out of the state of nature and to a condition of peace. But, as the old saying goes, there's no such thing as a free lunch. We must be willing to lay down certain rights to obtain security, and this is how government is born. Free and rational people must mutually transfer their rights to another in exchange for social order and personal safety. As the people contract together they create a commonwealth, led by a sovereign whose power is absolute. The sovereign is given all legislative, judicial, and executive powers. The sovereign will then control what all subjects will be taught, declare all wars, and decide on all punishments. And once the sovereign's authority has been established, any change in the government by the subjects is unjust. To rebel against the sovereign or to propose a new social contract is inherently unjust. And "if he that attempts to depose his sovereign be killed or punished by him for such attempts, he is author of his own punishment."[19]

---

[17] Thomas Hobbes, *Leviathan* (New York: Macmillan, 1958), 109.
[18] Ibid.
[19] Ibid.

Modern Liberalism: Locke and Rousseau

Hobbes' political philosophy was controversial in his day, and it is easy to see why. For one thing, even though it is purported as a compromise between monarchical and representative forms of government, it is really a wholesale concession to *rex lex*. Once the sovereign is in power, his rule is absolute and irrevocable. This invites the obvious objection that such a system is prone to degenerate into tyranny. Lord Acton's dictum that power corrupts applies here. Hobbes' theory places an unrealistic expectation that the people can reliably choose someone who can resist the temptations of power. Moreover, Hobbes' system offers no cure for situations when the sovereign's power is abused. By stipulating that all revolts are unjust by definition, he provides no recourse for deposing a despotic ruler.

Later philosophers presented versions of social contract theory that made accommodations for these problems in a Hobbesian approach. Among these were the theories of Locke and Rousseau, whose approach is often called liberal, because they were concerned to restrain the power of government. Liberalism is always about curbing power, while conservatism is about maintaining order. While Hobbes' theory emphasized the latter, the theories of Locke and Rousseau emphasized the former.

The most influential social contract theory in the English-speaking world has been John Locke's theory, as set forth in his *Second Treatise of Civil Government*. The theoretical foundations of Locke's theory of government are essentially the same as Hobbes'. Locke begins with a state of nature, where there is a recognized law of nature to preserve one's life and "every one has the executive power of the law of nature."[20] In such a lawless condition, all people are equal and the result is "enmity and destruction." Unlike Hobbes, however, Locke does not take this to be a mere hypothetical fiction. Rather, he maintains, "it is plain the world never was, nor ever will be, without numbers of men in that state."[21]

Another distinguishing feature of Locke's contractarian theory is his concern for individual rights. And it is not just the rights of life and liberty that he is interested in preserving through the social contract, but it includes the right to own property as well. Locke also improves upon Hobbes by establishing a clear selection criterion when it comes to formation of the social contract: majority rule. He writes, "the act of the majority passes for the act of the whole, and of course determines, as having, by the law of nature and reason, the power of the whole."[22]

---

[20] John Locke, *Second Treatise of Civil Government* (Indianapolis: Hackett, 1980), 12.
[21] Ibid., 13.
[22] Ibid., 52.

Locke's most significant contribution, however, is his concept of rule by consent of the governed. Whereas the subjects in Hobbes's system abdicate all of their power to the sovereign in return for protection, Locke maintained that the rulers appointed by the people remain accountable to them as they frame, execute, and judge upon laws. And if the government fails to represent those whom they serve, then the citizens reserve the right to depose them. Locke even grants that the people have a right to dissolve the government and its contract if those in power are so abusive as to take away the property or other basic rights of the people. Such actions by the government effectively return the people to a state of nature and a condition of war. Thus,

> By this breach of trust they forfeit the power the people had put into their hands for quite contrary ends, and it devolves to the people, who have a right to resume their original liberty, and, by the establishment of a new legislative . . . provide for their own safety and security.[23]

Civil government, then, on Locke's view, is always beholden to the people. The rulers' power is not absolute but invested and conditional.

The Lockean political philosophy had a profound effect on the American founding fathers, and our Declaration of Independence is essentially a distillation of Locke's ideas. More than any other modern political theory, Locke's *Second Treatise* represents the final triumph of *lex rex* over *rex lex* in Western political thought, just as the American revolution it inspired constitutes the moment of triumph of *lex rex* in Western political practice.

As Locke's ideas were percolating in Great Britain, Jean Jacques Rousseau was setting forth his own variation of social contract theory in France. Rousseau famously declared, "Man is born free, and everywhere he is in chains."[24] That is, human beings are not naturally in a condition of war as Hobbes and Locke had maintained. Rather, to Rousseau, humans are basically decent, noble savages. Enmity and strife are the result of inequalities created by private property. As people begin to gather goods for themselves, they compare their possessions to those of others, and envy, resentment, pride, greed, and vanity emerge. These negative emotions give rise to more conflict, as people compete for more goods. Thus, anything like a "condition of war" is the result of unnatural, artificial conditions in society. And Rousseau's social contract is intended to rectify this problem.

---

[23] Ibid., 111.

[24] Jean Jacques Rousseau, *The Social Contract and Discourses*, trans. G. D. H. Cole (London: J. M. Dent and Sons, 1947), 5.

Unlike his predecessors, Rousseau rejects the concept of natural law, insisting that "conventions form the basis of all legitimate authority among men."[25] Whatever political rights or laws are to be recognized in the state are completely contrived by the people. This occurs, says Rousseau, as individuals voluntarily assemble to form a collective and establish a common identity. This collective identity is established through a social contract whereby each person gives himself to the whole. The result is the state, and its purpose is always the common good. The state is directed to the achieving of the common good through the general will of the people. By "general will" Rousseau does not mean unanimous will or the will of all as regards particular interests. Rather it pertains to the shared interests and common good of the people. The general will constitutes what Rousseau calls the "Sovereign." Because the power of the Sovereign resides in the will of the people themselves, it is indivisible and inalienable. In expressing the general will, the Sovereign "is always in the right" and "the social compact gives the body politic absolute power over all its members."[26]

Criticisms of Social Contract Theory

Just as Locke's theory helped to inspire many of the founding fathers in the American Revolution, Rousseau's ideas inspired key figures involved in the French Revolution—a far bloodier affair than its American counterpart. Many in France, including Maximillien Robespierre, thought that the general will of the people demanded a change in government, as French leaders ignored the plight of the poor. Robespierre and his fellow architects of the "reign of terror" conceived of their deeds as a means of achieving the common good. This application of Rousseau's theory demonstrates how even liberal social contract theories may be abused.

We have already noted some problems with the Hobbesian approach. Social contract theory in general is also subject to criticism. Some object that it places too much power into the hands of political ignoramuses—those who know little or nothing about public policy or how government works. If we insist that only experts in their particular fields should be dentists, attorneys, or auto mechanics, then shouldn't the same be true of those who have a hand in government? Therefore, the objection goes, the social contract approach is foolish because it allows amateurs to do some of the most important work of government.

A potent criticism of liberal versions of social contract theory was pronounced by Alexis de Tocqueville (1805–1859) in his *Democracy in*

[25] Ibid., 9.
[26] Ibid., 27.

America. Tocqueville carefully studied the great American experiment in Lockean social contract theory, and he concluded that our system is not a sure bulwark against tyranny. On the contrary, Americans suffer under a "tyranny of the majority." Majority opinion is so revered in our system that genuine freedom of opinion is even less likely than in a monarchy. Tocqueville writes,

> The authority of the king is purely physical, and it controls the actions of the subject without subduing his private will; but the majority possesses a power which is physical and moral at the same time; it acts upon the will as well as upon the actions of men, and it represses not only all contest, but all controversy.[27]

To this, Tocqueville adds this stinging indictment: "I know no country in which there is so little true independence of mind and freedom of discussion as in America."[28] One wonders if Tocqueville would say the same thing about the United States today. Whether or not he would, his objection still stands. Even where governmental power is subject to popular opinion the threat of oppression still looms. And the danger just might be greater because it is so insidious.

Questions for Reflection

1. Which is the better approach, *rex lex* or *lex rex*? Or is neither to be preferred over the other?
2. The concept of *lex rex*—the rule of law—is basic to Western political thought, but it has not taken root in the East. Why might this be so?
3. Do you believe in a "right of revolution"? If so, what are some examples of just revolutions? Was the American revolution just? Why or why not?
4. Does Tocqueville's criticism of the U. S. governmental system still apply today? Has the problem he cites gotten better or worse?
5. Which form(s) of government can be found in Old Testament Israel? Does Scripture appear to show a divine preference for a particular theory of the state? If so, which one?

[27] Alexis de Tocqueville, *Democracy in America*, trans. Henry Reeve (New York: Oxford University Press, 1946), 164.
[28] Ibid.

§ 8.3 Distributive Justice

Political philosophy is vitally related to economic issues. Any society's well-being crucially involves the just distribution of goods. And it is the role of government to decide how, if at all, such distributive justice will be ensured. When it comes to this issue, however, two political values must be balanced: freedom and equality. In this section we will consider three different perspectives: libertarianism, socialism, and welfare liberalism. As we will see, libertarians emphasize liberty over equality, socialists emphasize equality over liberty, and welfare liberals aim for a compromise between the two.

Arguably, the field of economics began—as did so many fields of study—with Aristotle. In his *Politics* he discusses issues pertaining to the acquisition of wealth, and he gives a classic defense of private property.[29] He notes that private property is good because it is pleasurable. It brings great satisfaction and joy to earn one's keep. Second, private property is a powerful incentive. When people can work for their own goods, they are likely to be more efficient than they would be otherwise. Private property also provides opportunities for virtue, since people who own their own goods can therefore be more generous in giving. Finally, private property diminishes dissension, since people are less likely to complain about their share of goods when the amount they have is linked to how much work they have done.

8.3.1 Libertarianism

Most people take it for granted that private property is a reasonable thing, even if they have never heard Aristotle's arguments in defense of it. But now, supposing Aristotle is correct, what limits, if any, should be placed on private property? Those who would favor minimal limits on private property are called *libertarians*. Libertarianism is the view that government should be small and should not intrude on the personal lives of citizens.[30] Perhaps the most significant modern proponent of this perspective is John Stuart Mill (1806–1873), whose *On Liberty* has proven to be even more influential than his writings on utilitarian moral theory. There Mill sums up the libertarian thesis as follows:

> The sole end for which mankind are warranted, individually or
> collectively, in interfering with the liberty of action of any of

---

[29] Aristotle, *Politics*, book II.

[30] Note the ambiguity of the term *libertarian*, as it is also used to refer to a particular theory regarding the metaphysics of human freedom. In that context, libertarianism is the view that human freedom can only exist in the absence of causal determination of the will. See chapter 5, section 5.3.1.

their number is self-protection. . . . the only purpose for which power can be rightfully exercised over any member of a civilized community, against his will, is to prevent harm to others. His own good, either physical or moral, is not a sufficient warrant.[31]

In other words, as it is sometimes expressed, my right to swing my arms stops at the end of your nose. I am free to act however I want whenever I want, so long as it doesn't harm or risk harm to anyone else.

When the libertarian thesis is applied to economic matters, a strong doctrine of free-market capitalism results. Government should have no part in redistributing wealth among people, from the wealthy to the poor. The founder of libertarian economics in the modern period was Adam Smith (1723–1790). In his *Wealth of Nations* Smith argued that market forces ought to be allowed to operate freely, a view that has become known as laissez-faire economics. Smith vigorously critiqued all forms of government interference with the market, including taxation. While some would object that lack of government involvement would lead to intolerable inequities, Smith insisted that a free market is led by an "invisible hand" which ensures that individuals acting in their own self-interest will bring about benefits to society as a whole. Thus Smith says of the typical buyer or seller, "By pursuing his own interest he frequently promotes that of society more effectually than when he really intends to promote it."[32]

More recently, the libertarian thesis has been defended by Harvard political philosopher Robert Nozick (1938–2002) in *Anarchy, State, and Utopia*.[33] His argument hinges on the concept of consent—that in a free society the choices of individuals must be respected. And if such freedom is allowed, then we must accept the consequences of their free exchanges as just even when there are significant inequities in what people are able to acquire. Nozick illustrates his point with the example of a famous basketball player. (We will update the example with a more current player and different monetary figures.) Suppose that LeBron James signs a contract with his basketball team such that he is to be paid $25.00 per ticket sold. And suppose that in one season a million fans come to watch him play, each by their own free choice. Thus, at the end of the season James has made $25,000,000—a figure many times greater than the yearly salary of any other player in the league and most people in the world for that matter. Is this unjust? Nozick asks, how could it be? Those who paid him did so with full consent. They were entitled to dispose of their resources the way they did, so LeBron James is entitled to

---

[31] John Stuart Mill, *On Liberty* (Indianapolis: Bobbs-Merrill, 1956), 13.
[32] Adam Smith, *Wealth of Nations* (New York: Random House, 1937), 423.
[33] Robert Nozick, *Anarchy, State, and Utopia* (New York: Basic Books, 1974).

the outcome. Any governmental redistribution of those resources would interfere with just holdings and would therefore be unjust.

One of the most attractive features of libertarianism is its simplicity. It gives us a clear criterion for justice, and it is easy to apply to most situations, since it is usually fairly easy to tell whether an action is potentially harmful to others. Libertarianism also appeals to our natural desire for liberty. We value freedom so much, in fact, that it is tempting at times to use this as our only lens when thinking about distributive justice. Indeed, according to many critics of libertarianism, this is one of the main problems with the doctrine. Libertarianism puts an imbalanced emphasis on the value of personal autonomy as a criterion for justice. Why should this be the decisive factor when considering distributive justice? What argument can be given in support of this approach? Are there not other social values that are arguably at least as important as freedom, such as compassion and social utility? Certainly from a Christian perspective these other factors should play a part in considerations of distributive justice, as we will see below.

Secondly, libertarianism arbitrarily restricts considerations of justice to the context of resource *transfers* while it ignores the context of resource *holdings*. In the modified thought experiment from Nozick, consider LeBron James' wealth resulting from his basketball talent. While it is true that James' wealth was fairly garnered from the consensual ticket purchases of his fans, we must remember that James did nothing to earn his *talents*. He was providentially blessed with his athletic ability as well as other factors—genetic and environmental—which culminated in his work ethic to make good use of his physical abilities. So the original natural resources that enabled James to become wealthy via basketball were not earned by him. Why, then, should we stipulate that government treat him as if they were?

This leads us to a final criticism that aims to reduce libertarianism to absurdity. If followed consistently, libertarianism would result in extreme disparities between the wealthy and the poor. If government programs did not provide a "safety net" for the indigent and destitute who have no family or friends to care for them, then many would die or suffer severely as a result. While we can assume that individual and corporate charity would help many such people, it is likely that these efforts would be insufficient to help everyone in need. While some thinkers, such as the nineteenth-century political theorist Herbert Spencer (1820–1903), have explicitly discouraged charity to the poor, in order to strengthen society, most recognize that this is callous, not to mention unbiblical. Thus, most see the necessity for government to mandate some wealth distribution, if only to meet the most basic needs of the poor.

8.3.2 Socialism

In the spectrum of views on distributive justice, lying at the opposite pole from libertarianism is *socialism*. Prioritizing equality over all other political values, socialists maintain that there should be no private property and that all resources in society should be held in common. One of the earliest exponents of this approach, albeit in a limited form, was Plato. Recall that in his *Republic* Plato distinguished three main sectors of the state—workers, soldiers, and ruler. In the soldier class, Plato maintained, no one should own goods for themselves, but all resources should be shared. Among the benefits he lists on behalf of this approach is reduced conflict. Given a socialized soldier class, he asks, "will not lawsuits and accusations against one another vanish, one may say, from among them, because they have nothing in private possession but their bodies, but all else in common?"[34] And elsewhere Plato waxes even more sanguine about his socialist vision for the soldier class:

> I hesitate, so unseemly are they, even to mention the pettiest troubles of which they would be rid, the flatterings of the rich, the embarrassments and pains of the poor in the bringing up of their children and the procuring of money for the necessities of life for their households, the borrowings, the repudiations, all the devices with which they acquire what they deposit with wives and servitors to husband, and all the indignities that they endure in such matters, which are obvious and ignoble and not deserving of mention . . . from all these . . . they will finally be free, and they will live a happier life than that men count most happy, the life of the victors at Olympia.[35]

Plato's utopian vision for the soldier class in the *Republic* was extended to all of society by later socialists, most notably Karl Marx (1818–1885). Marx developed an elaborate argument for socialism based on (1) a critique of capitalist economics and (2) a thesis about human dignity and self-fulfillment. The problem with a laissez-faire approach to the market, according to Marx, is that it is oppressive and alienating. He claimed that, historically, the ruling "bourgeoisie" class has been a minority of wealthy folks who exploit the majority "proletariat" underclass. As the bourgeoisie oppress the workers, the latter become alienated from their own labor so that they can't realize their potential as human beings.

A capitalistic system produces such oppression by encouraging the creation of false needs—artificially induced desires for luxuries—for the sake of profit. This in turn is the result of private ownership of the means

[34] Plato, *The Republic*, trans. Paul Shorey, in *The Collected Dialogues of Plato*, 703.
[35] Ibid.

of production. As companies make more profits, they grow more powerful and can oppress employees even more. Thus, the consolidation of power leads to further alienation of the proletariat. In a truly just society, Marx argues, only real needs would be addressed in the marketplace. Just those goods that are necessary for survival and a decent life would be produced. This would enrich the workers by giving them a greater sense of purpose in their work, and it would benefit consumers by having goods that they actually needed. The way to achieve this, claimed Marx, is through social ownership of the means of production and the elimination of private property.

Marx was critical of the hyperspecialization spawned by capitalism. He insisted the workers must be free to act on their true creative impulses rather than being constrained to the same tedium of forced labor day after day. Thus he says,

> in communist society, where nobody has one exclusive sphere of activity but each can become accomplished in any branch he wishes, society regulates the general production and thus makes it possible for me to do one thing today and another tomorrow, to hunt in the morning, fish in the afternoon, rear cattle in the evening, criticize after dinner, just as I have a mind, without ever becoming hunter, fisherman, shepherd or critic.[36]

In such a system individual creativity is realized and true human freedom is respected. Wealth is thus redistributed, "from each according to his ability to each according to his need."[37]

Socialism is remarkably optimistic. It envisions a utopian society that is naturally attractive to all of us. Who wouldn't want to live in a world where people freely produced everything necessary for life, without ornery bosses, paltry wages, market competition, corporate seminars, and labor unions? But the optimism of the socialist vision is also its downfall, because it is simply not realistic about human nature. Socialists such as Marx mistakenly assume that people will always work hard even when lazy people receive the same ultimate benefits from the work force. The truth is that when someone sees another person slacking on the job this creates resentment and undermines motivation. Marx provides no remedy for this universal fact of human nature. People need a personal incentive such as is provided by private property. And here is the ingenious insight of capitalism, which parleys self-interest into benefits for the whole society. While it is true that capitalism often leads

[36] Karl Marx, *German Ideology*, in *Marx's Concept of Man*, ed. Erich Fromm, trans. T. B. Bottomore (New York: Frederick Ungar, 1969), 42.

[37] Karl Marx and Frederick Engels, *Marx and Engels on Religion* (Amsterdam: Fredonia Books, 2002), 203.

to exploitation and oppression, these tendencies can be curbed without abandoning the entire system, as we will discuss below.

Second, socialism is prone to degenerate into totalitarianism. As Aristotle once said, what is everybody's business is nobody's business. When Marx says the means of production must be "socially controlled," this begs the question: Who is to control the means of production on behalf of society? Everyone cannot do it together, because this would be chaos. A select few must take control, which presents us again with Lord Acton's problem of corruption by power. Those in control are likely to be even more oppressive than the most brutal capitalist systems. In fact, this is how it almost always happens in Marxist systems, from Stalinist Russia to Castro's Cuba. And even non-Marxist forms of socialism tend to oppress and lead to despotism. If the twentieth century did not teach us that socialism is fundamentally flawed, nothing will. Between Marxist systems in Russia and China and the Nazis (National Socialist Party), at least 70 million innocent people were slaughtered. This is perhaps the closest thing possible to an empirical refutation of a philosophical thesis.

8.3.3 Welfare Liberalism

In examining libertarianism and socialism we have seen that the two views are polar opposites in key respects, most importantly as regards their priorities when it comes to the political ideals of freedom and equality. Libertarians promote individual liberty and sacrifice equality as a result, while socialists prioritize equality at the expense of personal liberty. Is some sort of compromise possible that incorporates some of the best of both approaches? *Welfare liberalism* is the name of a cluster of views that advocate precisely this approach to the problem of distributive justice. We say "cluster" of views, because there is a range of positions that may qualify as examples, though all of them would affirm, to some degree, the justice of wealth distribution in society.

Before unpacking this view, let us make a clarification in terminology. Why do we speak of "welfare *liberalism*" with regard to a view that would limit human freedom, when the liberals of early modernism, such as Locke and Rousseau, were great champions of freedom? To understand why, we must recall that liberalism, generally speaking, is about curbing power. Up to the modern era government wielded the most power among human institutions. So the liberals in those days included thinkers like Locke and Rousseau, whose social contract theories imposed strong limits on the powers of the state. But since the industrial revolution the greatest sources of power have become economic in nature. So today's liberals opt to *use* government to curb economic power.

Thus, socialists like Marx, who aim to completely harness economic powers, are considered ultraliberal.

Welfare liberals are much more balanced than thoroughgoing socialists, as they allow for economic inequities up to a point. A good example of a contemporary welfare liberal is John Rawls (1921–2002), a political philosopher who happened to be a colleague of Robert Nozick's at Harvard. In *A Theory of Justice* Rawls crafted a social contract theory aimed at guaranteeing equality among citizens while also preserving a significant amount of freedom. To achieve this, Rawls proposes that society must be guided by principles that are most just. And which principles are most just? Those, according to Rawls, that people would choose in a perfectly fair situation. Rawls provides such a situation by asking us to imagine what principles we would select if we had to do so behind a hypothetical "veil of ignorance" about one's life circumstances, where one knows nothing about one's own socio-economic status and natural assets (e.g., money, talents, physical features, etc.) and where one is also ignorant about the social and political circumstances of his own society. If you were ignorant about all of these facts, what principles would you want to guide the society in which you were placed? That is, which principles would be most fair to everyone, regardless of where they fell on the socio-economic ladder?

Rawls proposes that the two principles chosen would be these: (1) *equal liberty*—"each person is to have an equal right to the most extensive basic liberty compatible with a similar liberty for others" and (2) *the difference principle*—"social and economic inequalities are to be arranged so that they are both (a) reasonably expected to be to everyone's advantage and (b) attached to positions and offices open to all."[38] The principle of equal liberty strongly affirms the value of freedom, so long as no person's freedom interferes with the freedom of others. And the difference principle allows for some socio-economic inequalities so long as they serve the larger interests of society. Thus, for example, consider stock trading. Absolute liberty here would be social chaos. I may buy and sell stocks only within certain boundaries, namely according to certain financial laws that protect people in the market from being harmed. Notice that this is essentially a libertarian value. However, for Rawls, the difference principle prescribes further limits and grounds for adjusting financial holdings in some circumstances, even when laws have been strictly obeyed. Thus, it seems that Rawls would allow for redistributing some of the wealth of the rich in order to correct for the fact that certain modes of money-making are not available to the poor. Moreover, a Rawlsian would likely say that some holdings are so exorbitant—such as

[38] John Rawls, *A Theory of Justice* (Cambridge, MA: Harvard University Press, 1971), 60.

those of Bill Gates (a billionaire more than a hundred times over)—that it is just for the government to take some of his wealth, via taxation, and redistribute this to those in the lower economic strata. At the same time, the difference principle may also be used in defense of the exceedingly wealthy since they often use their resources for private enterprise and the creation of jobs, which in turn help people on the lower rungs of the economic ladder.

In fact, the United States practices a form of welfare liberalism, as a certain bare minimum is guaranteed to the poorest in our society. Programs such as Medicaid enable even the poorest among us to obtain basic medical care, and food stamps and other tools in the U.S. welfare program ensure that everyone can eat. Note also that we have a somewhat graduated income tax system in which the rates that people pay are proportional to their yearly income. For example, in 2008 a person making $50,000 per year paid 14 percent in income tax, while a person making $100,000 yearly paid at a rate of 27 percent All of these means of adjusting for economic inequities are essentially ways of applying Rawls' difference principle, and they are policies that demonstrate that our system is indeed a form of welfare liberalism.

Naturally the question arises, to what degree should inequities be adjusted? This is the practical issue over which welfare liberals endlessly argue. And it is here that interpretations of Rawls' specific version of the theory wildly diverge. Some critics claim that his principles justify a fairly conservative form of welfare liberalism, while others insist that they actually imply something close to socialism. Indeed, this divergence of interpretation of Rawls suggests one of the major problems with his theory—vagueness. For Rawls' part, he seemed to consider his theory's vagueness (or, perhaps in his view, "malleability") to be a strength. However, it seems appropriate to question the ultimate usefulness of any socio-economic theory that may be interpreted as justifying very liberal or conservative policies.

Other criticisms commonly lodged against Rawls' theory concern his argument in support of his two principles of justice. First, what guarantee have we that behind the "veil of ignorance" we would select just those principles Rawls says we would? In proposing that the rational person would choose the principle of equal liberty and the difference principle, Rawls seems to assume that he prefers to minimize risk rather than offer the best opportunity to maximize personal gain. But why assume this? Surprisingly Rawls admits that his theory appeals to intuition at this stage, but what if we don't share his intuitions? And, in any case, don't we deserve something in the way of an argument when it comes to whether we should embrace such foundational principles?

Secondly, how does the fairness of the initial situation—using the "veil of ignorance" thought experiment—guarantee the fairness of the principles chosen? That is, even if we did all share Rawls' intuition that we would choose the principles he proposes, it does not follow that these principles are themselves *just*. There is a significant logical gap here. Fairness of the *procedure* in choosing principles does not imply fairness of the *content* of those principles. Consider the analogy of a game of Monopoly in which the players decide to create a new rule regarding the distribution of properties. Suppose all of the players have a particular dislike for the number "2." So they agree to adopt a rule stipulating that the first person to roll a "2" must surrender one property per turn for the rest of the game (but after the first "2" is rolled, there is no such consequence for other players who later roll that number). Now since all of the players agreed on this rule, the procedure for choosing it was fair. Yet the rule itself is quite unfair, since the first player to roll a "2" is essentially guaranteed to lose the game. This shows that a fair procedure for selecting a rule is far from reliable in guaranteeing that the rule will be just. So a crucial assumption in Rawls' theory (that a fair procedure for rule selection guarantees that fair rules will be chosen) turns out to be false.

8.3.4 Applications to Contemporary Issues

We have looked at three major positions on distributive justice. Let us now consider what implications these views would have on how we should approach our three case studies. Regarding abortion one's particular position on the issue will hinge on his view of the status of the fetus. And this seems to transcend the issue of distributive justice. If one views the fetus as a full-fledged human being, then laws proscribing abortion are just as legitimate as any other laws prohibiting murder. However, if one regards the fetus as somehow less than human, then a woman's right to terminate her pregnancy would likely take priority. Thus, given that one has a decided view on the status of the fetus, one will be steered clearly in one direction or the other when it comes to abortion. However, for socialists and welfare liberals who believe in abortion rights (not that all in fact do), many would be inclined to provide government funding for abortions for the poor. Libertarians, on the other hand, would insist that it is not the government's place to provide such support.

As for capital punishment, libertarians are divided here as well. Some favor the death penalty as a just punishment for a crime such as murder or high treason. Others support the death penalty as a way of deterring capital crimes and thus protecting citizens. Libertarians who oppose capital punishment typically do so because they see it as too extreme a penalty for any crime, though other kinds of punishment would be appropriate. Government, many would argue, should not be in the business of making decisions about life and death, even in the case of a murder as heinous as Scott Peterson's. Socialists tend to oppose capital punishment because it is unequally applied in favor of whites and the rich. That is, there is a disproportionately high number of minorities and poor people who receive the death penalty. So until these inequities can be corrected, it is best not to use this form of punishment. Welfare liberals would disagree among themselves about the propriety of the death penalty, but the stronger their sympathies with socialism, the less likely they would be to favor it.

Finally, when it comes to censorship, a libertarian would strongly oppose this. Government should allow freedom of discourse in all media— print, radio, television, and Internet. And when it comes to the arts, total freedom of expression must be the rule. The only exception would be if certain art works or forms of communication could be proven to harm people, either directly or indirectly. Short of this, the libertarian would say that censorship must be avoided. (But, it should be noted, many libertarians would oppose the whole idea of government funding of the arts, which would further complicate our specific example.) Socialists tend to oppose censorship as well, though for different reasons. They emphasize the fact that art enriches society and exalts the human spirit, so artists should be completely free to express themselves. As offensive as Serrano's "Piss Christ" is to many people, this does not justify censoring it. However, artworks that strongly undermine the socialist value of equality might be censorable for the socialist. (Indeed, both Plato and Marx advocated various forms of censorship.) Also, socialists tend strongly to support government funding of the arts. Welfare liberals would, again, disagree among themselves on the appropriateness of censorship, depending upon which government-constraining principles they would embrace.

Questions for Reflection

1. Are freedom and equality objectively valuable things? If so, why? In what are these values grounded?

2. Consider your most cherished resources, from natural talents to physical possessions. Do you deserve them in any sense? If so, how?

3. Where along the spectrum from libertarianism to socialism do you fall and why? When it comes to balancing the ideals of freedom and equality, to which do you give preference and why?

4. Besides those discussed above, what are some other contemporary moral-political issues which feature a tension between freedom and equality? Explain your stance on these issues in light of these values.
5. Does the government have the right to tax you to give money to those less fortunate than you? Why or why not?

§ 8.4 Theological Reflections on the State

So far in this chapter we have discussed several political philosophical issues. In this section we will look at a few subjects of special interest to Christians, namely the issues of civil disobedience and the role of religion in politics. We will also do some theological reflection on the issue of distributive justice. To this latter issue we turn first.

8.4.1 Biblical Perspectives on Distributive Justice

In our preceding discussion of libertarianism, socialism, and welfare liberalism, we looked solely at philosophical arguments for and against each view. However, there are also many scriptural passages that speak to the issue of distributive justice. For example, many passages emphasize the importance of taking care of the poor and needy. In the Old Testament we are told that "the one who oppresses the poor insults their Maker" (Prov 14:31) and that those are blessed who share with the poor (Prov 22:9). And the ancient Israelites are given this special command: "When you reap the harvest of your land, you are not to reap all the way to the edge of your field or gather the gleanings of your harvest. Leave them for the poor and the foreign resident" (Lev 23:22; cp. 19:9–10). This was to ensure that the needy always had access to basic food resources. God's stated objective was that "there will be no poor among you" (Deut 15:4).

In the New Testament we find that Jesus had a special ministry to the poor (Luke 4:18), and all of the apostles were agreed that ministry to the poor was paramount (Gal 2:10). Paul notes that churches in Macedonia and Achaia made a special "contribution to the poor among the saints in Jerusalem" (Rom 15:26). And the early church was characterized by a remarkable redistribution of resources. Luke observes that "all the believers were together and had everything in common. So they sold their possessions and property and distributed the proceeds to all, as anyone had a need" (Acts 2:44–45). And a little later he notes:

Now the multitude of those who believed were of one heart and soul, and no one said that any of his possessions was his own, but instead they held everything in common. . . . For there was not a needy person among them, because all those who owned lands or houses sold them, brought the proceeds of the things that were sold, and laid them at the apostles' feet. This was then distributed to each person as anyone had a need (Acts 4:32, 34–35).

Complementing this emphasis on generosity to the poor and wealth redistribution are biblical passages that teach personal responsibility for meeting one's own needs. The Bible says that lazy hands make a man poor (Prov 10:4) and that the sluggard will be overcome with poverty (Prov 6:9–11). It also strikes a realist chord regarding poverty, declaring that "there will never cease to be poor people in the land" (Deut 15:11), a judgment echoed by Jesus (Matt 26:11).

In the New Testament we also find some particularly striking exhortations from Paul regarding the importance of earning one's keep. He writes, "We encourage you . . . to seek to lead a quiet life, to mind your own business, and to work with your own hands, as we commanded you, so that you may walk properly in the presence of outsiders and not be dependent on anyone" (1 Thess 4:10–12). In his follow-up letter to this same church Paul revisits this same theme using even stronger language:

we command you, brothers, in the name of our Lord Jesus Christ, to keep away from every brother who walks irresponsibly and not according to the tradition received from us. For you yourselves know how you must imitate us: we were not irresponsible among you; we did not eat anyone's bread free of charge; instead, we labored and toiled, working night and day, so that we would not be a burden to any of you. It is not that we don't have the right [to support], but we did it to make ourselves an example to you so that you would imitate us. In fact, when we were with you, this is what we commanded you: "If anyone isn't willing to work, he should not eat" (2 Thess 3:6–10).

How do we reconcile these seemingly conflicting messages from Scripture regarding compassion toward the poor, on the one hand, and the biblical command to work for a living? Apparently, there is a biblical mandate to help the poor *and* a mandate to meet one's own needs. But if, as Paul says, failure to work means that one "shall not eat," whence comes any mandate to take care of the needy? Precisely from the fact that not everyone is *able* to work, such as the physically disabled, the mentally handicapped, and the elderly. Such people must be cared for by others.

But whose responsibility is it to care for these people? Friends and families? Private institutions such as the church? Or civil government? It appears that in Scripture we find some precedent for each. God's command to ancient Israel was for every landowner to make sacrifices for the poor, which was effectively a sort of government-mandated wealth redistribution. And in the New Testament we find local churches and individual Christians giving to other believers in need. But it is noteworthy that in these latter examples the giving is voluntary rather than state-sponsored. To many this suggests a sort of *communitarian* approach. Communitarians affirm the socialist ideal of equality and resource redistribution, but they reject the socialist reliance on government as the tool for realizing this end. Otherwise put, they prefer a voluntary *decentralized* system of wealth redistribution.

Even granting some form of communitarianism for local communities, Christian and otherwise, this question remains: In light of the biblical norms surveyed above, what role, if any, should government play in wealth redistribution? This is a difficult and complex question that we cannot settle here, but a Christian's answer to this question will reflect his sympathies with one of the three general views discussed above. Christian libertarians insist that government should not be in the business of redistributing any wealth. This, they say, is properly the exclusive work of the church and other private institutions. All resource sharing should be communitarian in nature: voluntary and non-state-sponsored. Christian socialists, by contrast, insist that it is the proper business of government to work toward the social ideals of the early church. Communitarianism is laudable, but not sufficient to realize this ideal. Centralized state-sponsored wealth redistribution is the only way to achieve this. Finally, Christian welfare liberals would recognize the need for some wealth redistribution, such as to make sure that everyone has food, decent housing, and basic medical care. But beyond this they would disagree as to what resources government should ensure for all citizens.

8.4.2 Religion in the Public Square

In the previous section we noted several biblical arguments for various politico-economic perspectives. This whole discussion takes for granted something that many people call into question, namely the notion that it is appropriate to consider religious arguments when making decisions about public policy. The First Amendment of the U.S. Constitution stipulates that "Congress shall make no law respecting an establishment of religion." Some interpret this clause as prohibiting not only formal church institutional intrusion into state affairs but also as implying that not even religious doctrine should be allowed to impact laws. Such a far-reaching interpretation of the Establishment Clause, as it has come to be called, is problematic, but we need not be detained with this debate in constitutional law. Let us, rather, consider the more fundamental philosophical issue at stake here (which, of course, impacts the thinking of legal scholars as they debate the constitutionality of the use of religious arguments in the political process). Is it appropriate to allow religious perspectives to impact public policy?

Our three case studies provide good examples of issues in which religious arguments are often used to justify one position or another. With regard to abortion, arguments from Scripture for the pro-life view are commonly made, such as those which appeal to Psalm 139:13 ("it was You who created my inward parts; You knit me together in my mother's womb") and Jeremiah 1:5 ("I chose you before I formed you in the womb; I set you apart before you were born"). When it comes to capital punishment, both proponents and opponents of the practice make biblical arguments, appealing to Old Testament civil law mandates for the death penalty on the pro-side and appealing to biblical ideals of mercy and compassion on the other. And as for censorship, those who defend stricter decency standards in broadcasting or in public funding of the arts frequently do so from the standpoint of Christian conviction. Many of the most outspoken groups on the issues, such as the Christian Coalition of America and Focus on the Family, are Christian organizations.

Another major issue where the propriety of religious arguments comes into play concerns teaching on biological origins in public schools. Critics of the evolution-only approach in public education often argue from Scripture in defense of teaching creationism as well. While advocates of Intelligent Design theory do not lead with theological arguments in this way—preferring rather to appeal to the scientific method and philosophical arguments—many special creationists do prefer this approach, thus bringing to the fore the issue of the use of religious arguments in making public policy.

What philosophical reasons are given by those who oppose use of such reasoning? One popular tack is to appeal to the concept of pluralism. Many reason that religious arguments are not accepted by everyone, especially atheists and agnostics, so it is against the spirit of democracy to create public policy on religious grounds. While people of faith should have the liberty to practice their religion as they want, basing public laws and policies on religious beliefs would create an imposition on those who don't share these convictions.

Two points can be made in response to this argument. First, this same complaint can be made just as readily against secular arguments in public discourse. No matter what one's position may be regarding any issue, from immigration to speed limits, there are plenty of people out there who disagree. And whatever arguments one gives for one's · view, there are many who will not accept them. But is this fact grounds for disqualifying the use of such arguments in deciding public policy? Of course not. Secondly, allowing religious arguments does not violate the spirit of democracy or our respect for one another in a pluralistic society. On the contrary, it is the *censoring* of religious arguments that contradicts pluralism. The guiding idea behind democratic systems is the notion that all views should be heard, not just those which fit a favored worldview. The refusal to consider religious arguments violates this value and thus is essentially antidemocratic.

Another line of reasoning against public use of religious arguments appeals to the notion that the state, at least in the West, is a secular institution. In the United States in particular, we conceive of government as borne out of human reason, not divine fiat. This was why our founding fathers made a point of establishing the powers of the state independently of the church. Therefore, religious convictions have no proper bearing on how the state is run. Religious people are free to make arguments in defense of their convictions about public policy so long as these arguments appeal to secular beliefs and values. And they are free to maintain their theological convictions, but they may not introduce them into public discourse about political issues.

This is a very subtle argument, and if one is not careful it is easy to miss its flaws. First, from an historical standpoint, the argument is factually mistaken. While the U. S. government never was, nor was ever meant to be, founded upon ecclesial authority, the framers of the Constitution were deeply influenced by religion. And as we saw earlier, our Declaration of Independence affirms that our most cherished rights—which are foundational to our system of government—are themselves divinely endowed. Second, even if it were the case that our Constitution was entirely devoid of religious influence, it would not follow that religious arguments should never be used in the political process. In other words, the argument above is simply invalid—the nature of the origins of the state do not have any implications for the place of religious arguments in public discourse.

The truth is that all government is put in place by God. As Paul writes, "Everyone must submit to the governing authorities, for there is no authority except from God, and those that exist are instituted by God" (Rom 13:1; see also 1 Pet 2:13–14). So the notion that the state is essentially secular is mistaken, at least in this ultimate sense. However natural the origins of a particular government might appear to have been, its only authority, in the final analysis, derives from God Himself. Of course, this doesn't imply that the church as an institution should be involved in political affairs. Nor does it mean that Christians or other religious folks should wield their religious convictions heedlessly when engaging in public discourse regarding policy issues. Some political contexts are more congenial than others—both within and outside the United States—and great care must always be taken when appealing to religious beliefs and values when defending a political stance.

A third argument against allowing religion to impact politics is more pragmatic in nature. Some scholars, many Christians among them, make the point that religious arguments are not necessary to justify our most precious social values, such as liberty and equality. While ours is a pluralistic society, it is always best to reason from beliefs and assumptions that nearly everyone shares. A democratic system such as ours thrives on consensus. Religious arguments only divide and cause rancor. So it is best to proceed politically without any appeal to religion, even for those of us who happen to be religious.

This argument, too, has a couple of problems. First, it falsely assumes that the so-called "secular" values of liberty and equality can be adequately grounded in a naturalistic worldview. However, arguably, only theism—a religious worldview—can justify these values. Only a conception of natural law can make sense of liberty and equality as ideals that transcend local legal standards. Without a higher moral law, there are only conventions that cannot be judged right or wrong in an absolute sense. Civil laws can only be regarded as practical or not, and who is to say what counts as practical? Second, even if it is most "practical" to appeal to universally shared values when doing politics in a democratic system, it doesn't follow that this is normative. Besides, in some instances political policies can only be justified using religious arguments, as might be the case with laws banning same-sex marriage, sacrilegious art, and abortion. So to insist that religious arguments never be used would potentially bar society from access to some very important moral-social truths.

There is a final point we would like to make regarding all of the above arguments and the general claim that religion should not play a role in politics. This view insists upon an unreasonable concession to a procedural guideline that by now is quite familiar. It asks us to assume *methodological naturalism* as applied to political philosophy. Earlier, in chapters 3 and 5, we saw the irrationality and insidiousness of methodological naturalism as it comes into play in the contexts of biological

origins and consciousness studies. This perspective is just as unjustified and pernicious here. Though disguised as a procedural guideline,
methodological naturalism turns out to be a substantive claim about
the nature of political truth and, more broadly, reality. Who says that
government is or should be approached as an inherently natural or secular thing? One may, of course, draw this conclusion after first *assuming*
naturalism. But we cannot simply assume this. An argument for naturalism is necessary. This reveals that methodological naturalism in politics
depends upon a deeper *metaphysical* naturalism (paralleling the situation
in science and consciousness studies, as we saw earlier). And if metaphysical naturalism cannot be proven, then methodological naturalism
should be rejected.

8.4.3 Civil Disobedience

If Christians have struggled with having their views heard in the
public square, they have also struggled when public policies have contradicted their beliefs and values. When, if ever, is it appropriate to break
laws that violate moral values, whether these values are theologically
grounded or not? This is the traditional problem of civil disobedience,
the origin of which goes all the way back to ancient Greece. When Socrates was awaiting execution for his alleged impiety, one of his disciples,
Crito, arranged for his escape by bribing one of the jailers. Socrates and
his family would be secretly taken to another town where he could live
out the rest of his days. However, when told of this plot, Socrates de-
murred, insisting that it would be wrong to disobey the laws of the state
in this way. A city would be "turned upside down," he declared, "if the
legal judgments which are pronounced in it have no force but are nulli-
fied and destroyed by private persons."[39] However unjust his conviction
might have been, according to Socrates it would never be right to break
the law in response.

An apparent critic of the Socratic position on this issue is the modern champion of civil disobedience, Henry David Thoreau. A strong
opponent of slavery and the Mexican-American War, Thoreau refused
to pay his taxes, an offense for which he eventually served jail time. In
support of his position Thoreau subsequently penned his classic essay
"Civil Disobedience," in which he declares that if the "machine of government . . . is of such a nature that it requires you to be the agent of
injustice to another, then, I say, break the law. Let your life be a counter
friction to stop the machine."[40] It is noteworthy that both Socrates and

---

[39] Plato, *Crito*, trans. Hugh Tredennick, in *The Collected Dialogues of Plato*, 35.
[40] Henry David Thoreau, *Walden and Civil Disobedience* (New York: New American Library, 1960), 229.

God ordains gov't But not every laws

Find verses for support

Thoreau believed that there are moral values that transcend civil legal codes. The difference between them concerns when, if ever, this higher standard justifies breaking civil law.

Civil disobedience is generally defined as conscientious, public, and nonviolent resistance to unjust public laws or policies. To clarify our thinking about civil disobedience it is critical to make some distinctions, both in terms of the nature of unjust laws and the mode of disobedience to them. First, some legal systems are unjust because they *require evil*. A law requiring citizens to worship the king, such as in ancient Babylon or Rome, would be an example. And some would argue that legal systems which apply the death penalty or laws requiring the exclusive teaching of Darwinism in public schools would fall into this category. Second, legal systems may be unjust because they *promote evil*. Thus, many would argue that public funding of obscene or sacrilegious artworks falls into this category, and some pacifists would argue that military recruitment is an example of this as well. Third, a legal system may be unjust because it *permits evil*. The U.S. government's allowance of slavery, to which Thoreau and his fellow abolitionists objected, would be an example. And today many would argue that allowances of abortion, pornography, and extreme poverty, would also fall into this category. Finally, a legal system may be unjust because it *prohibits good acts*. Oppressive regimes that outlaw Bibles and prohibitions of prayer in public schools would be examples, as would a recent California court ruling prohibiting home schooling without a teaching license.

So in which cases, if any, is civil disobedience justified? Here people disagree. As for Christians, only one category is noncontroversial: disobeying laws of the first variety where evil actions are mandated. But notice that in this case civil disobedience is passive. This suggests another distinction, namely that between *passive* and *active* civil disobedience. Passive civil disobedience involves a refusal to do what the law requires, while active civil disobedience involves doing what the law prohibits. This distinction applies to the cases of Socrates and Thoreau, as the latter's refusal to pay taxes was an instance of passive civil disobedience, while Socrates was tempted to engage in active disobedience by escaping. In all probability, Socrates would actually endorse passive civil disobedience in some cases, as he believed it was always right to be virtuous. Socrates would likely have refused to obey any law that required severe injustice or taking an innocent life, so he would not really be thoroughgoing in his rejection of civil disobedience (as few people would be).

A final category of distinctions needs to be made between the *degrees of evil* that an unjust law endorses or allows. A legal system that requires, promotes, or permits the shedding of innocent blood is much more justifiably resisted than one that requires, promotes, or permits unjust inequalities or the teaching of blatant falsehoods. Similarly, laws that prohibit good acts will differ in degree of evil depending upon how fundamental those good acts are to human flourishing. For instance, a law that prohibits private possession of Bibles is much more unjust and worthy of resisting than a law that prohibits prayer in public.

Depending upon the degree of evil endorsed or allowed by a government, it is easy to imagine cases of justifiable passive civil disobedience regarding laws that compel citizens to sin. Clearly, refusal to obey such laws is not only permissible but morally obligatory. As for active civil disobedience, peaceful forms may be justifiable in some instances, such as refusal to abide by discriminatory ordinances during the Jim Crow era. Other examples may include nonviolent but illegal public demonstrations against immoral laws or the choice to teach the creationist view of origins in a public school as an alternative to Darwinism.

But what of violent opposition to unjust laws or regimes? In July 1944 an anti-Nazi group, including Christian theologian Dietrich Bonhoeffer, plotted to assassinate Adolf Hitler. They arranged to have a bomb carried into a conference attended by the Führer. The plan was to kill Hitler and seize key government buildings and communication centers, thus ending the Nazi regime. A suitcase containing the bomb was carried into the conference by Claus von Stauffenberg, shortly after which he left, pretending to take a phone call. The bomb exploded as planned, and several people were killed, but Hitler only sustained an injury to his right arm. Thus, the plot failed and Stauffenberg, Bonhoeffer, and several others were executed for their involvement in the plan.

Were Bonhoeffer and his fellow conspirators justified in attempting the assassination? Defenders of their actions typically offer a utilitarian argument, maintaining that killing Hitler would have saved many innocent lives. But as we saw in the previous chapter, such "future looking" reasoning is always suspect, and too often it overlooks contingencies that don't become apparent until the action in question is taken. In the case of the plot to kill Hitler, it is likely that the near miss (and injury to Hitler) only aggravated the Nazi leaders, perhaps inspiring even more intense and extensive cruelty and murder. Thus, even in what seems to be a paradigm case, if ever there was one, for violent opposition to an evil government, the argument in favor of such action is tenuous.

Such utilitarian reasoning has been used in the United States by advocates of violent opposition to the abortion industry. Some have bombed abortion clinics, and in at least one instance a pro-lifer shot to death a physician who performed abortions. Proponents of this approach argue that they are saving lives by their actions. But are they? It appears more likely that such actions have cost lives in the long run, as laws have consequently been passed in many states that make it much more difficult for protestors to interfere nonviolently with abortion clinics. Moreover, popular media have exploited the violent actions of a few pro-lifers to marginalize the movement and make it less effective overall.

In any case, the use of violence to oppose unjust political regimes or immoral laws is not *civil* disobedience. Such tactics, at least when used by private citizens, usually go by a different name: terrorism.

Conclusion

In this chapter we have discussed some of the central issues in political philosophy, and we have seen how each one presents special challenges. Like all of the topics explored in this book, these issues are unavoidable if we are to be responsible people. None of us has the luxury (or curse?) of living in a state of nature. We all find ourselves living in a civil society, governed by leaders, and participating in an economic system of some kind. So it behooves us to reflect on these realities all around us and even to consider what we can do to improve things.

Because we live in a fallen world and sin plays havoc in all political institutions, it is tempting to become cynical and apathetic about civic life. And recurring scandals in the news involving political leaders only make it more difficult to resist cynicism. But to give up hope and ignore our civic duties is an irresponsible and un-Christian response. As followers of Christ we are called to be redemptive agents in all facets of life, whether private or public. Anyway, as students of Scripture we, of all people, should not be surprised by the ubiquity of sin in the political arena. In a fallen world, the wickedness and injustice we see in government is really a likely story, and there is a sense in which we are only getting what we deserve when we suffer under vile leaders. Martin Luther made a realistic assessment of the situation when he said, "The world is too wicked and does not deserve to have many wise and upright princes. Frogs must have their storks."[41]

So as we strive to deal with political issues, both theoretical and practical, we need to be hopeful realists. The conclusions we draw about what constitutes a just society really can make a difference, but we must always keep in mind that complete, lasting justice will not be achieved until the reign of Christ.

---

[41] Martin Luther, "Temporal Authority: To What Extent It Should Be Obeyed," trans. J. J. Schindel, in *Luther: Selected Political Writings* (Philadelphia: Fortress, 1974), 63.

Questions for Reflection

1. When it comes to the issue of distributive justice, how, if at all, should Old Testament civil laws guide us today? How, if at all, should the practice of the early church impact our thinking about the issue?
2. There is an old dictum that says you should never discuss religion or politics at a social gathering. Why is this advice commonly accepted? Do you agree with it?
3. Some believe there to be increasing public hostility to religious viewpoints in American politics. If this is so, then why is it the case? If it is not true, then why do many people share this perception?
4. Read Judges 3:12–30. Was Ehud's assassination of Eglon a just act? Why or why not?

For Further Reading

On Political Philosophy in General

Miller, David. *Political Philosophy: A Very Short Introduction*. New York: Oxford University Press, 2003.

Strauss, Leo, and Joseph Cropsey, eds. *History of Political Philosophy*. 3rd ed. Chicago: University of Chicago Press, 1987.

Tinder, Glenn. *Political Thinking: The Perennial Questions*. 6th ed. Upper Saddle River, N.J.: Longman, 2003.

Wolff, Jonathan. *An Introduction to Political Philosophy*. Rev. ed. New York: Oxford University Press, 2006.

On Rights and Law

Budziszewski, J. *Written on the Heart: The Case for Natural Law*. Downers Grove: InterVarsity, 1997.

Finnis, John. *Natural Law and Natural Rights*. New York: Oxford University Press, 1980.

Hart, H. L. A. *The Concept of Law*. 2nd ed. New York: Oxford University Press, 1997.

Murphy, Mark C. *Natural Law and Practical Rationality*. Cambridge: Cambridge University Press, 2007.

On Distributive Justice

Nash, Ronald H. *Social Justice and the Christian Church*. Lima, OH: Academic Renewal Press, 2002.

Roemer, John E. *Theories of Distributive Justice*. Cambridge, MA: Harvard University Press, 1998.

Sider, Ronald J. *Just Generosity: A New Vision for Overcoming Poverty in America*. Grand Rapids: Baker, 2007.

On Politics and Religion

Neuhaus, Richard John. *The Naked Public Square: Religion and Democracy in America*. 2nd ed. Grand Rapids: Eerdmans, 1986.

Sweetman, Brendan. *Why Politics Needs Religion: The Place of Religious Arguments in the Public Square*. Downers Grove: InterVarsity, 2006.

Tinder, Glenn. *The Political Meaning of Christianity: An Interpretation*. Eugene, Oregon: Wipf & Stock, 2000.

Yoder, John Howard. *The Politics of Jesus*. Grand Rapids: Eerdmans, 1994.

Chapter 9

AESTHETICS: WHAT IS BEAUTY?

*"Beauty is truth, truth beauty—that is all ye
know on earth, and all ye need to know."*

—John Keats

9.1 What Is Art?

    9.1.1 The Definition of Art

    9.1.2 The Function of Art

9.2 Are There Standards for Art?

    9.2.1 The Truth of Aesthetic Objectivism

    9.2.2 What Are the Objective Standards?

9.3 Art and Ethics

    9.3.1 Three Perspectives on Art and Ethics

    9.3.2 A Christian View of Aesthetic Value

    9.3.3 Some Helpful Distinctions

Glossary Terms

Aesthetic objectivism	*Expressionism*
Aesthetic subjectivism	*Formalism*
Aesthetic virtues	*Institutional theory of art*
Aestheticism	*Mimesis*
Ethicism	*Moralism*

A n old song by Ray Stevens has this refrain:

> Everything is beautiful in its own way
> Like a starry summer night
> Or a snow covered winter's day.
> And everybody's beautiful in their own way.
> And under God's heaven
> The world's gonna find a way.[1]

It's natural to think that in this song Stevens is saying that beauty is a real quality of everything and everyone, but in one of the verses he sings, "It's time to realize that beauty lies in the eyes of the beholder." So which is it, Ray? Is beauty a real quality of things or just a matter of personal opinion? This is actually one of the central questions in the philosophy of art.

The previous two chapters concerned issues in the study of value. This concluding chapter takes up the third major subject in value theory, which is aesthetics. We have seen how moral and political questions are difficult and unavoidable. Yet, as commonplace as moral and political judgments are, they might not be as popular as aesthetic judgments. Every time a person says, "You are beautiful," "What a lovely dress," or "That is a pretty sunset," she makes an aesthetic judgment. And, of course, hundreds of popular songs, books, and films are concerned with beauty.

Human beings are not merely interested in experiencing and talking about beauty. We also have an insatiable desire to *make* beautiful things. The ubiquity of art across cultures and time is a testament to this fact. And it is human creativity that typically is the focus of most philosophical discussions of beauty. What is a work of art? What is the purpose or function of art? What does it mean to say a work of art is "good" or "bad"? Are there objective standards for aesthetic interpretation and criticism? And what is the proper relationship between art and ethics? Can we make moral assessments of works of art? Such are some fundamental questions in the philosophy of art that we will explore in this chapter.

§ 9.1 What Is Art?

Let's begin with the basic question "What is art?" As we've seen in many contexts already, such a simple query can be more challenging than one might think. The subject of art is no exception. In this section

---

[1] Ray Stevens, "Everything Is Beautiful" (1970) by Ahab Music Co.

we will address this question by considering a variety of attempts to define art as well as several popular theories about the purpose of art.

9.1.1 The Definition of Art

One approach defines art as *any human-made object*. Art, on this view, is whatever results from human creative activity. One thing that songs, paintings, ballets, films, plays, and fine wines have in common is that they are all the product of intentional human action. So might not art be defined accordingly? The strength of such an approach is its recognition that art is the result of purposeful activity, which most of us would grant. But this definition is too broad, as it implies that such things as pollution and the blowing of one's nose are works of art. Surely no definition of art should include these things, so the definition of art as human-made objects is too broad.

A second definition seeks to improve upon this approach by narrowing art down to *whatever is presented as art*. What is known as the "institutional theory" of art says that any object that is displayed for aesthetic appreciation, such as in a museum or on a living room wall, is art. In the words of George Dickie, a proponent of this view, "Works of art are art as the result of the position they occupy within an institutional framework or context."[2] So it is the *presentation* of a work, such as its hanging on a museum wall or appearing upon a theater stage that clinches its status as a work of art. Marcel Duchamp's *Fountain* is perhaps the most notorious example of a work that is premised on the institutional view. Duchamp took an ordinary urinal, rotated it 90 degrees from its normal position, and presented it as a sculpture, entitled "R. Mutt 1917." This move not only created much controversy in the art world but helped to galvanize the "ready mades" movement in twentieth-century art. However, to many audiences, Duchamp's *Fountain* and other "ready mades" effectively served to refute the institutional theory. A theory that implies any object can be art, so long as it is designated as such by an artist or museum curator, seems too arbitrary to be acceptable.

Yet another approach to defining art appeals to the artistic process as the key consideration. A work of art, on this view, is *the product of the artistic process*. Thus, Michelangelo's *David*, Homer's *The Iliad*, and Bach's Brandenburg Concertos are properly considered art, because they are the result of a painstaking artistic process. This definition has the merit of providing a criterion for ruling out such objects as Duchamp's urinal as genuine artworks. However, this definition is nonetheless problematic. Just how are we to understand "artistic process" if not in terms

[2] George Dickie, "The New Institutional Theory of Art," in *The Philosophy of Art*, ed. Alex Neill and Aaron Ridley (Boston: McGraw Hill, 1995), 213.

of the art *object* in which this process culminates? But the art object is precisely what we are trying to define. So this definition actually begs the question.

A further definition avoids this problem by appealing to the audience response to a work of art. Art, on this view, is *whatever brings (or tends to bring) aesthetic pleasure to those who experience the object.* There is a certain qualitative feature to the experience one has when reading Shakespeare, listening to Beethoven, or watching a Woody Allen film, as opposed to when one is reading a car owner's manual, listening to a dentist's drill, or watching a plumber work. One might find the latter experiences to be intensely pleasurable, but that pleasure is not essentially aesthetic in nature. So might not works of art be identified in terms of their capacity to produce such aesthetic pleasure in their audiences? While promising in some respects, this approach introduces a whole nest of problems. For example, just what *is* aesthetic pleasure? While we can give clear instances of works that produce such experiences, arriving at a clear definition of this term seems hopelessly difficult. And even granting a clear conception of aesthetic pleasure, to *whom* exactly must an object effectively bring pleasure in order to be considered successful in this regard? Just anyone or only well-trained art critics?

It appears that arriving at a satisfactory definition of art is not a very easy task. Because of this difficulty, many prefer to take an approach that works from the bottom up, so to speak. Suppose we begin with clear cases of art and use these as standards. That is, we may consider some art works "paradigm cases" and thus use these to establish criteria for identifying art generally. For instance, Vivaldi's *Four Seasons*, Milton's *Paradise Lost*, Michaelangelo's *David*, Da Vinci's *Last Supper* and Orson Wells' *Citizen Kane* are works of art, if *anything* is a work of art. They are also undeniably excellent works of art. So what general characteristics do they tend to share? The answer to this question may lead us to the criteria we are seeking in order to find a workable definition for art.

The *paradigm case approach* has many advantages. For one thing, it ensures that our definition of art will not be too abstract or esoteric, as it will be grounded in concrete cases. It also has the merit of being historically informed and thus immune to influence by passing trends, such as we saw with the institutional theory of art. But the paradigm case approach also has its problems. It tells us just where to look to find criteria for defining art, namely the shared characteristics of paradigm instances of art. But it is just not clear what those shared characteristics are. What do *The Last Supper* and *Paradise Lost* have in common? What common characteristics are there in the *Four Seasons* and *Citizen Kane*? These questions are far from easy to answer. Some general features can be readily identified, such as their having been made by humans for the purpose of being enjoyed. But since many non-artworks, from bubble gum to back-scratchers, also meet this description, these criteria appear too vague to be useful.

Perhaps we could narrow the definition a bit more and add a criterion of beauty, as many dictionary definitions do. After all, if any artworks are beautiful, the above mentioned ones are. Thus, we might propose that artworks are *human-made objects created to be enjoyed for their beauty.* This definition might succeed in excluding bubble gum and back-scratchers, but it problematically implies that the identification of an object as an artwork depends on the intention of its creator. Suppose I decide to stick a pencil into a mound of dirt, thinking someone will enjoy it for its beauty. Shall we then call this art? Surely not. So this definition does not identify sufficient conditions for art. Something more is required. Nor does it even provide necessary conditions for art, since we can imagine artworks that were not made to be enjoyed for their beauty. Suppose a painter is commissioned to do a portrait to honor someone and the painter does it solely for the profit. The resulting work would not have been created to be enjoyed for its beauty, and yet it might turn out to be an aesthetically excellent work and worthy of recognition as art. So the artist's intentions should not be a determining factor in deciding what counts as art.

We may narrow our definition even further, still guided by the paradigm cases mentioned earlier, to eliminate this problem of intention. Art works, we might say, are *human-made objects that are enjoyable for their beauty.* This succeeds in ruling out bubble gum, back-scratchers, and my pencil-in-mud creation as works of art. It also allows for the commissioned portrait to be considered a work of art. But notice that this definition introduces yet more problems. It fails to allow a distinction between beautiful and ugly works of art. I might draw a painting that is so bad no reasonable person could enjoy it, but surely we don't want to say that its not art just because it's so ugly. A reasonable definition of art must include even ugly works of art. To this one might reply that surely there is some aesthetic dimwit out there who could enjoy my repugnant painting. This leads us to another problem with this definition: For *whom* must an object be enjoyable in order to qualify as art? The person who made it? Any person on the street? Art critics only?

Because of the difficulty of defining art, some prefer to scuttle the endeavor altogether. One alternative is to give up on finding criteria to *define* art and to settle for criteria that merely *identify* art. The point of pursuing a definition of art in the first place was to enable us to identify works of art. So if we can find an alternative means of doing the latter, then we need not even bother with the former. A natural way to go about this is to rely on those who have a demonstrated expertise in art and aesthetics. In other fields, such as business, law, and medicine, we consult experts for information that lay people cannot discover for themselves, so why not here? Thus, we may ask, which works are generally regarded as art by the community of artists and art critics? Surely the consensus of experts is a reliable guide for ascertaining which works are genuinely art. Another version of this general approach is the historical approach, as expressed in the popular slogan, "Great art works stand the test of time." Such are two ways of identifying art works without defining them, but is this an adequate approach?

The great strength of the "identification criteria" alternative to defining art is its practicality. To know what counts as art we need not bog down in heady and tedious definitions; we need only ask a conductor, literature professor, or museum curator. But there are some serious limitations to this approach as well. First, as in the fields of business, law, and medicine, the experts in the art world do not always agree. While there is a general consensus on the paradigm cases in each of these fields, there is also much debate on a great many issues. Visual art experts in particular have disagreed as to whether Andy Warhol's Campbell's Soup can paintings are bona fide artworks. And musicologists have disagreed as to whether many of John Cage's sonic works are properly considered art. Without appealing to a definition of art, where can we turn to settle such disputes? Moreover, the "identification criteria" approach fails to give adequate guidance when it comes to new and original works about which experts have yet to comment and which have not had the time to pass the historical test.

The fundamental challenge in defining a concept is finding criteria that are neither too narrow nor too broad. The preceding discussion demonstrates just how difficult it is to arrive at a definition of art that achieves this balance. Perhaps no hard and fast definition is possible and in the end we must appeal to our intuitions. But there seems to be a pressing need for at least a rough definition of art in order properly to identify objects as works of art.

9.1.2 The Function of Art

Just as there have been many perspectives on what an art object is, there are many opinions about the purpose of art. What, if anything, is artistic creativity supposed to accomplish?

Mimesis—Art as Imitation

As with so many philosophical questions, a good place to start here is with the ancient Greeks. They agreed that the purpose of art is *mimesis* or imitation. That is, a painting, a poem, or a piece of music properly reflects something in nature or human experience, such as a beautiful woman, a triumph in battle, or a birdsong. However, the Greek philosophers were divided about the implications of this view. As discussed in chapter 4, Plato made a strong distinction between the world of appearances (physical reality) and the world of reality (eternal Forms). Sensible objects are mere copies or representations of their changeless, universal essences. And genuine knowledge involves moving beyond one's sensory awareness and grasping those essences. Now art, being imitative, copies the appearances of physical objects that are themselves copies of universal essences. So a painting, for example, is the copy of an appearance of an object that is itself an imitation of the real thing. For Plato, then, art works are three times removed from reality. We should therefore be wary of art and its potential to distort truth. For this reason, Plato advocated strong censorship of art in the *Republic*, where he outlines his ideal society.

Aristotle did not take such a negative view of art. In his *Poetics* he affirmed that artistic imitation is not only a natural and pleasurable human activity but also a source of genuine understanding. Good poetry provides insight into truth, but not the same way that, say, history does. Historians describe what *has* happened, while the poet attends to what *must* happen or what *might* happen. For this reason, Aristotle claimed that "poetry is something more philosophical and more highly serious than history, for poetry tends to express universals, history particulars."[3] In addition to being a source of truth, art also has emotional benefits, according to Aristotle. Both comedy and tragedy serve the purpose of *catharsis* or the purging of emotion. Comedies do so by inspiring laughter through the representation of ridiculous action. Tragedies bring catharsis by arousing feelings of fear and pity in the audience through the dramatic imitation of the fall of a good person.

Despite their differences, Plato and Aristotle agreed that artworks are essentially imitative. This view has an intuitive appeal when it comes to certain art forms, such as drama, film, photography, sculpture, and some kinds of music, painting, and architecture. But in what sense can abstract art—such as many works by Kandinsky and Picasso—be said to be imitative? What about jazz music? What does the music of Duke Ellington and Miles Davis imitate? Even some films, such as *Fantasia*,

---

[3] Aristotle, *Poetics*, trans. Philip Wheelwright, in *Aristotle* (Indianapolis: Bobbs-Merrill, 1951), 302.

seem to defy this approach. So by excluding what seem to be clear cases of art, the mimetic theory is seriously flawed. At best, it might identify just one function of art.

Expressionism—Art as Expression of Emotion

Aristotle recognized that drama has significant emotive benefits. Some aestheticians have made this observation about art generally and suggested that the emotional power of art constitutes its essence. William Wordsworth articulated this *expressionist* theory when he declared that "poetry is the spontaneous overflow of powerful feelings; it takes its origin from emotion recollected in tranquility."[4] In making this assertion, Wordsworth was speaking only of his own art form, but other aestheticians have extended this to art generally. R. G. Collingwood, perhaps the strongest proponent of expressionism, maintained that the artistic process is all about exploring one's emotions and expressing them intelligibly—to *oneself*. "The characteristic mark of expression proper is lucidity or intelligibility; a person who expresses something thereby becomes conscious of what it is that he is expressing, and enables others to become conscious of it in himself and in them."[5] So while communication to an audience is not the main goal in art, it is a natural consequence of good art.

Collingwood distinguishes between craft and true art. A work of craft, such as the construction of bookshelves, is characterized by a clear distinction between planning and execution. The craftsman knows precisely what he wants to make before work begins. Not so with art. While the painter, poet, or composer has a subject matter or general intention for his work, his candid and somewhat spontaneous expression of emotion may lead in any of a number of creative directions, any number of which may be considered successful. Collingwood would therefore reject Warhol's Campbell's Soup can paintings as mere fabrication. He would likely say that while such work by Warhol might qualify as skilled craftsmanship, it is not genuine art.

One of the strengths of the expressionist theory is that it makes sense of the way most people talk about art, such as when they praise a film because "it moved me" or when they criticize a poem or a song because it "lacks feeling." In many, if not most, art works we demand that they touch us emotionally or that they evoke certain feelings, whether positive or negative. The song "Over the Rainbow" and the play *Romeo and*

---

[4] William Wordsworth, Preface to *Lyrical Ballads*, in *Lyrical Ballads and Other Poems, 1797–1800*, ed. James Butler and Karen Green (Ithaca: Cornell University Press, 1992), 756.

[5] Robin G. Collingwood, *The Principles of Art* (New York: Oxford University Press, 1958), 122.

Juliet express deep emotions with which we all can identify. This seems to constitute much of their greatness. But is such emotional content true of all art, even all *great* art? Some highly regarded minimalist paintings seem altogether void of emotion. The expressionist theory also has difficulty in accounting for architecture and the culinary arts. Isn't it pushing things too far to insist that every building or every meal expresses the emotions of the designer or cook?

Formalism—Art as Significant Form

While proponents of the expressionist theory of art talk much about the emotional dimensions of art and the creative process, they often neglect to explain just what it is about certain works of art that makes them so emotionally powerful. Why do some poems, songs, and paintings evoke sadness or joy while others do not move us at all? Are our responses to artworks merely a matter of subjective fancy? Clive Bell proposed that there are indeed objective, formal qualities shared by all art works that affect us in this way, at least when it comes to the visual arts. That quality, claimed Bell, is "Significant Form." As applied specifically to painting, Significant Form refers to "these relations and combinations of lines and colours, these aesthetically moving forms."[6] To appreciate and be moved by a painting one need only have a decent sense of shape, color, and three-dimensional space.

Consider Picasso's painting *Guernica*, for example. The work, named for the Spanish town mercilessly bombed by the Nazis in the 1930s, depicts the horrors of war. Picasso was appalled by such unprovoked mass destruction and infliction of suffering on innocent people, and this is reflected in his painting. However, formalists such as Bell insist that the essence of the emotive power of the painting is not contingent upon the viewer having such background information about the painting. No knowledge about the work's meaning, the artist's intentions, or the work's historical context is necessary. The formal qualities of *Guernica* alone are sufficient to prompt the aesthetic emotion.

Many critics find this claim to be counterintuitive, insisting that a work's content and meaning in many cases are vital to the emotional experience of an artwork. If attention to a work's content and meaning is critical for the visual arts, it seems all the more necessary when it comes to other genres of art, especially literary forms such as novels, poems, and plays. How can we conceive of the significant form of, say, Harper Lee's *To Kill a Mockingbird* or Rogers and Hammerstein's *South Pacific* without thinking about the plots, characters, and even the dialogue

---

[6] Clive Bell, *Art* (New York: G. P. Putnam's Sons, 1958), 17–18.

within these works? Thus, the formalist theory appears to be limited in its application.

Marxism—Art as Ideology and Political Power

Some would claim that a major flaw in the preceding views is that they ignore the social and political conditions that give rise to art. Marxist aestheticians focus on such conditions and emphasize that, like anything else that human beings produce, art is both the product and the tool of ideology. That is, the art we make has been influenced by a system of social values and practices, and, in turn, it has the potential to persuade audiences to embrace this system. In this way, art is a potentially powerful agent of political influence. Marx himself seemed conflicted about this point, as he nonetheless regarded artistic creativity as fundamental to human nature and definitive of one's individuality. To be fully human, according to Marx, is to be aesthetically concerned and to live "in accordance with the laws of beauty."[7]

Marxist aestheticians not only recognize the social-cultural impact of artworks but also tend to approve of those works of art that contribute to realizing Marx's vision of a classless society. And they are critical of artworks that reinforce economic class divisions. In terms of American culture, of course, this means that artworks that endorse capitalism in any sense are corrupt. Marxist scholar Theodor Adorno, for example, critiques American popular music because it militates against two principal Marxist ideals: human individuality and the classless society. Popular music, he says, is not just overly simplistic but enslaved to *standardization*, the practice of strict adherence to a formula that is simplistic and predictable. Listen to any song by a pop artist from Elvis Presley to Shania Twain, and the form and content of the song will be easily memorized, even after just a few listenings. Pop music also suffers from *commodification*—items to be bought and sold within a capitalistic system that is oppressive and dehumanizing. Truly good art, from a Marxist standpoint, is revolutionary in the sense that it both resists standard formulas and challenges our culture's class system. Of course, to do this successfully in today's American music market, artists must participate in the very system they are revolting against. Some socialist rock bands, such as The Clash, have noted this irony, lamenting that they must act like capitalists in order to challenge capitalism.

Perhaps the most important insight of Marxist aesthetics is that art is politically significant and a potentially powerful social force. This is why art is so commonly used as a propaganda device. However, the Marxist

[7] Karl Marx, "Alienated Labor," in *Marx's Concept of Man*, ed. Erich Fromm and T. B. Bottomore (New York: Continuum, 2005), 102.

analysis of art is too narrow in this regard. While having an ideological dimension, art objects are also much more than this and should be appreciated in other respects as well. As for the Marxist critique of popular art, those of us who are capitalists should take careful note. Commodification of music and film is especially problematic in our culture and ought to be resisted both for social and aesthetic reasons. But one need not be a committed Marxist to sustain these critiques, nor to find good reasons to prize artistic excellence.

Because of the atheism inherent to their worldview, Marxists might actually lack sufficient resources to warrant appreciation of beauty for its own sake. For theists, the entire cosmos is properly seen as a work of divine art the beauty of which extends far beyond its practical usefulness. Such an aesthetic perspective, when applied to human-made artworks, fosters a readiness to appreciate nonpractical beauty. Atheistic worldviews such as Marxism, however, cannot see the cosmos as an artwork. This necessarily results in a truncated aesthetic perspective, including the way they see value in human-made artworks. Marxists' preoccupation with the ideological utility of art is perhaps symptomatic of this fact.

Christian Aesthetics—The Imago Dei and World Projection

Among Christian scholars there is no consensus about the function of art. In fact, while most agree that art may serve to glorify God, there is not even complete agreement about whether art should be viewed positively. Great Christian thinkers, from Kierkegaard to Tolstoy, have been conflicted about art because of its power either to undermine or bolster the life of faith. Still, most Christian aestheticians agree that artistic talent is a divine gift and that all beauty derives ultimately from the being of God. More than this, human beings bear the image of God, and all of our creative efforts reflect this fact. As God's creation of the world is a self-expression, so are human artistic works.

Nicholas Wolterstorff has developed this theme in terms of "world-projection." With the exception of purely instrumental music and highly abstract artworks, the artistic process involves presentation of an alternative world for consideration by an audience. In most cases, such as Dickens' *A Tale of Two Cities* or Vermeer's *Woman with a Balance*, the artwork presents a possible world, in the sense that the story or scene depicted could occur. But in other instances, such as Pirandello's "Six Characters in Search of an Author" or Escher prints like *Waterfall* and *Relativity*, the fictional world is not possible. In every case of world projection, however, the artist mimics God's original creative act, by fashioning a world for public appreciation.

Artistic world projection, says Wolterstorff, serves numerous functions. At the most basic level, world projection in art serves the function of *communication* between an artist and her audience. When I read a poem or watch a film, I learn what the artist thinks. Projected worlds also serve to *evoke emotion*, whether positive or negative, in the audience. Third, worlds in artworks serve a *confirmatory* function. While fictional realms are not literal presentations of actual events, they do properly convey truths about the real world. In Wolterstorff's words, "the artist is not merely projecting a world which has caught his private fancy, but a world true in significant respects to what his community believes to be real and important."[8] Moreover, fourth, artworks not only confirm but *illuminate* the world in which we live. Artists grant us new insights and clarify our thinking, showing us things about the world we have overlooked or ignored. Fifth, a projected world in a work of art may even persuade us to change our minds about an issue or show us how the world could be improved in some way. Artworks often do this by *modeling*. That is, they provide instructive examples regarding behavior. Such modeling may be good or bad, of course, depending upon the nature of the behavior exemplified. Finally, a projected world may provide *consolation* by training our minds upon some hopeful aspect of the human condition.

Notice that these diverse functions of world projection incorporate many, if not all, of the central elements of the above theories. The mimetic function appears in the artist's imitation of God's original creative act. The Marxist emphasis on ideology and social change is affirmed in the concept of modeling and the recognition of art's power of persuasion. And Wolterstorff explicitly notes the expressive function of art emphasized by Collingwood and Bell. Perhaps the lesson here is that there is wisdom in affirming an eclectic Christian view of the function of art. That is, to some degree each of the above theories is correct. But their insights can be brought together in a unified way only within the context of a Christian theology of divine artistry.

Questions for Reflection

1. Which of the definitions of art discussed above is most plausible and why? Is there some alternative way of defining art that seems more reasonable? Or is "art" a concept that is even susceptible to a clear definition? If not, then why not?

---

[8] Nicholas Wolterstorff, *Art in Action: Toward a Christian Aesthetic* (Grand Rapids: Eerdmans, 1980), 144.

2. Which view of the function of art discussed in this chapter seems most plausible to you and why? The authors suggest that each of these major views has significant insights, so they recommend an "eclectic" theory that incorporates all of these. Is this an appropriate approach to the issue?

3. Can a work of art be aesthetically good, yet contain ugliness? And must we always equate "aesthetically good" with "beautiful"? Why or why not?

4. Think of two or three artworks (e.g., poems, paintings, songs, films, etc.) that you find particularly striking and describe them in terms of the various possible functions of art discussed in this section. How does each work exhibit mimesis or express emotion? How might the work serve some ideology or project a world?

§ 9.2 Are There Standards for Art?

Recall Ray Stevens' "Everything is Beautiful," quoted at the beginning of this chapter. In that song he incorporates a popular slogan in our culture—the notion that beauty is "in the eye of the beholder."[9] This expression reflects a familiar perspective on art and beauty today. According to this view, an artwork (such as a song or a painting) or a part of nature (such as a flower, a sunset, or a human face) is not beautiful in itself but is only subjectively pleasing. Aesthetic judgments (like "This song is lovely" or "That painting is ugly") do not state facts about the world, but merely reflect an observer's *response* to some aspect of the world. This view is known as *aesthetic subjectivism*.

It is important to note that aesthetic subjectivism parallels a similar view in ethics (discussed in chapter 7) known as *moral subjectivism*, which says that right and wrong are merely matters of individual preference. Both forms of subjectivism see value judgments, whether regarding goodness or beauty, as relative to the individual. Together these value relativisms rose to prominence in the twentieth century, reflecting a general skepticism in Western civilization towards the objectivity of values.

In recent decades many moral philosophers have labored to defend moral objectivism, citing overwhelming reasons for believing that there are moral absolutes and that ethical relativism (whether individual or

[9] This phrase originated with Margaret Wolfe Hungerford, in her 1878 novel *Molly Brown* (New York: A. L. Burt, n.d.). The idea behind it predates this statement by many centuries, however. In *Love's Labours Lost*, Shakespeare wrote, "Beauty is bought by judgment of the eye" (Act II, Scene I). And David Hume asserted, "Beauty is no quality in things themselves: It exists merely in the mind which contemplates them" (from "Of the Standard of Taste," in *Essays, Moral, Political and Literary*, ed. Eugene F. Miller [Indianapolis: Liberty Classics, 1985], 230).

cultural) is untenable.[10] But are there *aesthetic* absolutes? Do we have good reasons to believe that beauty is not merely "in the eye of the beholder"? And if beauty is objective, then what are the standards for making aesthetic judgments? These are the questions we will consider in this section.

9.2.1 The Truth of Aesthetic Objectivism

The claim that judgments of beauty are relative to an individual or culture has a generous ring about it, but the absurdity of this view becomes apparent upon close inspection. First, consider the implications of aesthetic subjectivism when it comes to comparing works of art. In my office I have a finger-painting made by my son, Bailey. It is basically a scramble of pastels on black construction paper. Now, we might ask, how does it compare, in terms of aesthetic quality, to Leonardo Da Vinci's *Mona Lisa*? Is one of these works better (i.e., more objectively beautiful) than the other? Not according to aesthetic subjectivism. Remember, on this view, no work of art can be objectively superior to another, because the subjectivist maintains that beauty is entirely relative to an individual's preference. So if I happen to prefer Bailey's finger-painting to Da Vinci's *Mona Lisa*, then the former is superior to the latter *for me*. You might consider the latter more beautiful, in which case the *Mona Lisa* is more beautiful *to you*. Objectively speaking, neither is aesthetically superior to the other. All responses to works of art are merely subjective.

But such a view of things clearly contradicts common sense. Obviously the *Mona Lisa* is superior to Bailey's finger painting, regardless of how fond I might be of my son's artistic efforts. But the only way this judgment can be justified is if beauty is an objective matter, not merely in the eye of the beholder. Only an *objectivist* view can account for the common-sense distinction we ordinarily make between personal tastes and real excellence in works of art. So if we are to maintain (as we should) that the *Mona Lisa* is better than my son's finger painting, we must admit that aesthetic qualities (whether good or bad) are public facts about the world, not merely private preferences.

Also, if aesthetic subjectivism is true, then we cannot account for the universal, time-tested appreciation of many works of art. All educated people will agree, as they have for centuries, that Milton's *Paradise Lost* is a great poem, that Vivaldi's *Four Seasons* is an excellent piece of music, and that Michelangelo's *David* is a superb sculpture. How do we explain

---

[10] See Peter Kreeft, *A Refutation of Relativism* (San Francisico: Ignatius, 1999) and Francis J. Beckwith and Gregory Koukl, *Relativism: Feet Firmly Planted in Mid-Air* (Grand Rapids: Baker, 1998).

such continuing consensus of opinion among intelligent connoisseurs of art except by acknowledging that the tremendous aesthetic qualities of these works are public facts? If aesthetic subjectivism is true, then the convergence of opinion by hosts of art critics is mere coincidence. They all just happen to have similarly positive responses to these artworks. But, of course, this is absurd. So aesthetic objectivism must be true.

Furthermore, consider the fact that we often debate the quality of artworks and we sometimes change our opinions about whether a film, book, or song is good or not. We might find ourselves defending the merit of a novel we have read or saying something like "I was wrong about that movie. I think it is good after all." These are everyday occurrences in discussions of art, and they confirm the basic intuition that aesthetic judgments are objective, whether correct or incorrect. Aesthetic qualities must be public facts and not simply subjective responses. Otherwise, we could not meaningfully argue about them or improve our views on works of art. To debate an issue is to try to convince someone of the truth of a view. And to admit one was wrong in a judgment about an artwork is to acknowledge that aesthetic truth is independent of one's preferences. Only aesthetic objectivism can make sense of these things.

Finally, that aesthetic qualities are public facts is also confirmed by our shared use of aesthetic concepts and terms such as *beautiful, sublime, gaudy, refined, delicate, elegant, dramatic,* and *powerful*. We would have no shared idea of what these terms mean if they were merely subjective and not based in anything public and objective. Our shared understanding of the meanings of such aesthetic terms shows that they are grounded in something beyond subjective responses. Beauty and related aesthetic attributes, therefore, are not merely in the eye of the beholder. They are objectively real facts about the world.[11]

9.2.2 What Are the Objective Standards?

If aesthetic subjectivism is so problematic, then why does it remain so popular? There are two primary reasons for this. One has to do with the fact that there are conflicting aesthetic judgments among people, and the other reason is the widespread assumption that there are no standards for good art. As for the first point, the fact that people's aesthetic judgments sometimes conflict does not imply that there is no objective aesthetic truth anymore than disagreement about the age of the universe or the morality of abortion implies that there is no truth about those matters. We all recognize that the earth is some age and that

[11] For an excellent defense of aesthetic objectivism, including an elaboration on some of the arguments that we employ here, see Eddy M. Zemach, *Real Beauty* (University Park, PA: Pennsylvania State University Press, 1997).

abortion is either right or wrong, even though different parties dispute these things. A plurality of views on an issue does not imply that truth in that context is entirely relative. Similarly, people may dispute the aesthetic quality of a Monet painting or a Spielberg film, but it does not follow that there is no objective truth to be found there. Sometimes it is just hard to find the truth.

But here some object that while we have shared criteria for assessing truth claims in science and ethics, this is not so in aesthetics. Objective truth and knowledge presuppose objective standards, and there are no such standards for aesthetic judgments. But is this so? This brings us to the main point of this discussion. On the contrary, there are numerous objective guidelines that are, and should be, used to evaluate both works of art and artists.

Standards for Works of Art

Some aesthetic standards are *genre specific*, that is, they pertain to particular rules within a major art form. Most significantly, there are guidelines for proper technique in each art form that one must master in order to become proficient in that kind of artistry.

These techniques, in turn, define the standards for excellence in that genre. For example, to be a good potter, one must learn how to drive and regulate the speed of the pottery wheel, how to maintain optimum clay moisture, and how to use dexterity to finesse the clay in various ways. To be a good photographer, one must learn how to frame a subject, how to achieve ideal lighting, and how to determine appropriate shutter speeds for various contexts. And to be a good poet, one must know how to exploit rules of syntax, how to create rhythm and images with words, and how to work with simile, metaphor, hyperbole, and paradox to achieve different effects. So it goes for every art genre. One must master basic rules of proper technique if one is to achieve artistic excellence.

There are also standards that are *non-genre-specific*. These are general principles of beauty that we can apply across the spectrum of genres to art forms as diverse as painting, music, and theater. These include such features as complexity, unity, intensity, originality, and expressiveness.[12] But each of these attributes must be balanced against the others. A painting or song that is complex without being unified by some image or central theme is likely to be confused or overly busy. On the other hand, a lack of variety of shades, colors, textures, and images will tend to

---

[12] For an excellent discussion of aesthetic standards from a Christian perspective, see Nicholas Wolterstorff's *Art in Action*, 156–174. See also Leland Ryken, *The Liberated Imagination: Thinking Christianly About the Arts* (Wheaton, IL: Harold Shaw, 1989) and Frank Burch Brown, *Good Taste, Bad Taste, and Christian Taste: Aesthetics in Religious Life* (Oxford: Oxford University Press, 2000).

make a painting bland, just as a lack of melodic or rhythmic variety will make a song boring. And a work that is both unified and complex may be nonetheless fatally bland if it is not sufficiently intense or lively.

All excellent artworks are original in some way as well. They provide new and interesting ways of viewing, feeling, or thinking about something. Or they recombine familiar elements in creative and compelling ways. But in its originality a good work of art does not totally break from standard forms; otherwise the audience will have no reference points for meaningfully experiencing it and will be disoriented as a result. Excellent artworks establish familiar contact points for the audience and use these to lead them into new and unfamiliar territory, whether regarding subject matter, emotions, or truth claims. This explains why art is inherently risky. To be aesthetically excellent, an art object must explore new terrain, but to do this effectively the artist faces the hazard of going too far in one direction or another, such as by frightening, irritating, or offending the audience in some way.

Also, as observed by several aestheticians discussed earlier, great works of art tend to be powerfully expressive. They transmit ideas and emotions in significant and lasting ways. Every art form is, in an essential respect, a mode of communication, a means by which personal connections are established or deepened. These connections may pertain to everything from specific feelings to whole worldviews. This explains the significant social and moral impact—for better or worse—that great artworks have. Consider the impact of two films in these respects. In the late 1960s the film *Easy Rider* portrayed the hippie generation's rambling "free love" hedonism and their frustrating conflict with "establishment" authorities. The film drew from and extended the social sensibilities of that subculture and, consequently, deepened its impact on American culture for many years following. A little over a decade later, *Chariots of Fire* helped millions of viewers better understand the anguish of maintaining one's moral-spiritual integrity when faith commitment is challenged by social pressure and even one's own desire for success. This film inspired many to take divine authority and personal faith more seriously. While antithetical in their ultimate messages as well as their long-term moral and social impact, *Easy Rider* and *Chariots of Fire* are quite similar in so far as they creatively portray conflict with authority and compellingly depict human anguish in the midst of that struggle.

So great works of art tend to be complex, unified, intense, original, and expressive. But on top of this, as aesthetician Richard Eldridge observes, there is an appropriate "fit" between form and content in great works of art.[13] That is, there must be a proper match between the formal features of a work, such as its style, mood, or manner, and its subjects and themes. A good example of such appropriate fit is The Beatles' song "Eleanor Rigby," which draws terse portraits of lost and lonely individuals, including the song's namesake who "lives in a dream . . . wearing a face that she keeps in a jar by the door" and one Father Mackenzie "writing a sermon that no one will hear . . . darning his socks in the night when there's nobody there." The song concludes with the death of the former and the latter "wiping the dirt from his hands as he walks from the grave," followed by the song's mournful refrain: "Ah, look at all the lonely people."[14] Matched to these lyrics is an exquisite string-quartet score in a minor key. The vocal and string melodies themselves seem to weep and the whole arrangement echoes the theme of loneliness. Here we have an appropriate fit of form to content, a crucial feature of any excellent art work.

Standards for Artistry

In addition to standards for artworks, there are standards that apply to *artists* themselves as they do their aesthetic work. Such traits might be called "aesthetic virtues," as they are marks of excellence, enabling an artist to fulfill her creative function in a particular domain. Most such qualities are simple applications of standard moral virtues applied in the aesthetic realm. (Recall our discussion of virtue in chapter 7.) For example, *diligence* is a vital characteristic of any artist, just as it is in any human relationship or meaningful practice. But work in the arts is especially challenging, because tangible rewards for aesthetic excellence do not come as readily as they do for other more "practical" tasks that occupy us. Often, perhaps typically, great artists must make significant sacrifices even to finish a project, much less do it well.

Artists must also display *veracity* in their work. They must be aesthetically sincere in their personal expressions and truthful in presenting their beliefs about the world. Art is an emotionally rich mode of expression. As discussed earlier, some aestheticians have claimed that expression of feelings is the primary purpose of art. In order to express a feeling artistically, of course, one must have actually experienced it. This is why young writers are often advised to "write what you know best." Doing so maximizes one's ability to tap and express real emotions rather than to

---

[13] Richard Eldridge, "Form and Content: An Aesthetic Theory of Art," *The British Journal of Aesthetics* 25:4 (1985): 303–16. Eldridge, in fact, believes this quality is definitive of art. He says, "The aesthetic quality possession of which is necessary and sufficient for a thing's being art is the satisfying appropriateness to one another of a thing's form and content" (p. 308).

[14] The Beatles, *Revolver*, Capital Records, 1966.

be a sham. A poet or painter cannot express feelings she has never had, and audiences are always quick to spot a lack of authenticity.

Of course, it is not enough just to be personally authentic in one's artwork. Aesthetic veracity in the fullest sense implies telling the *truth* in one's art, both in terms of reporting how one sees or understands the world and in terms of matching that interpretation to the way things really are. Excellent artists are excellent perceivers. They have an eye for truths about God, the world, and human nature that most people lack, and they possess a special ability to communicate these insights through their art. In poetry and prose, such truthfulness is what distinguishes the truly great writers from merely great stylists. Whether it is Wordsworth lamenting "the world is too much with us"[15] or Camus warning that "there can be no peace without hope,"[16] the great writer unveils for us something about how things really are.

An artist should also exhibit *boldness* or what might be called aesthetic courage. This is a willingness to take risks, to explore new ground or to challenge conventional ways of thinking about a subject. At the same time, an artist must exhibit discretion, resisting the temptation to sensationalize or go too far in challenging accepted practices and points of view. Clear moral boundaries must be respected in all art forms. Art, like all human projects, is an inherently moral activity. No artist can escape this fact, however much she might claim otherwise. And every art object has moral implications, however neutral it might appear to be. It was for this reason that Tolstoy claimed that a major function of art is to reinforce the prevailing moral and religious perceptions of a society.

This is just a sampling of the virtues that characterize good artistry.[17] Many others, such as humility, generosity, compassion, and wit, could be discussed in this context. It is not just art objects that are objectively good, bad, or mediocre. Artists themselves may be so described from an objective aesthetic standpoint. Now it is important to note that the Christian brings a unique perspective to the whole issue of standards in aesthetic assessment. We have intentionally avoided discussing norms of aesthetic judgment in exclusively Christian terms. But we have only refrained from doing so to demonstrate that aesthetic objectivism is reasonable in the most general sense. That is, one need not be a Christian to embrace this perspective on aesthetic values. Christian apologists often first show that there are absolute moral values and on this basis make a

---

[15] William Wordsworth, "The World Is Too Much with Us," in *The Complete Poetical Works of William Wordsworth* (London: Macmillan and Co., 1926).

[16] Albert Camus, *The Plague*, trans. Stuart Gilbert (New York: Vintage, 1972), 271.

[17] For a further discussion of this topic in the context of Christian worship, see James S. Spiegel, "Aesthetics and Worship," *The Southern Baptist Journal of Theology* 2:4 (Winter 1998): 40–56.

reasonable case for the existence of God to account for them. Similarly, one may argue for absolute *aesthetic* values (as we have done here) and then proceed to argue for theism on this basis. Indeed, Christian thinkers, from Augustine to contemporary times, have sometimes reasoned this way. But such aesthetic theistic proofs are much less common than their moral counterparts. This is something that might change in time, but the success of such a project will depend on whether one can first successfully dispel aesthetic relativism and the myth that "beauty is in the eye of the beholder."

Questions for Reflection

1. The authors argue for the objectivity of aesthetic values, using the same sorts of arguments used in chapter 7 to defend moral objectivism. Do you think this approach is reasonable, or is there something unique about aesthetics that allows for value relativity?
2. Read Exodus 35:30–36:2 and Philippians 4:8. What, if anything, do these texts have to say about the nature of art and the question of aesthetic values?
3. Consider the same artworks you brought to mind in the last section (Questions for Reflection 9.1 #4), and evaluate them using the criteria outlined in the present section. Are they good works of art? Why or why not?
4. What implications does the truth of aesthetic objectivism have for the way Christians view and produce art? How should it affect our use of art in public worship?

§ 9.3 Art and Ethics

Those who are both morally and aesthetically serious face some difficulties arising at the interface of art and ethics. How are we properly to assess or otherwise deal with artifacts in which beauty and immorality collide? Do either moral or aesthetic values ever deserve priority when making overall assessments? If so, then when and why?

9.3.1 Three Perspectives on Art and Ethics

The first matter we must address is the relationship between ethics and art. One perspective is known as *aestheticism*, the notion that art and the artist are insusceptible to moral judgment. Art and ethics never conflict, on this view, because the creative artist is above morality. Oscar Wilde, a strong advocate of aestheticism, proclaimed that "there is no such thing as a moral or an immoral book. Books are well written or badly written. That is all."[18] And Benedetto Croce represents this perspective when he says, "The artist is always morally blameless and philosophically irreproachable, even though his art may have for subject matter a low morality and philosophy: insofar as he is an artist, he does not act and does not reason, but composes poetry, paints, sings, and in short, expresses himself."[19] Another proponent of aestheticism, John Dewey, affirms that art is indifferent to ideas of praise and blame. Dewey notes that "this indifference to praise and blame because of preoccupation with imaginative experience constitutes the heart of the moral potency of art. From it proceeds the liberating and uniting power of art."[20] Thus, Dewey goes even farther than Croce, suggesting that morality is actually subject to art.

The *moralist* takes precisely the opposite stance, maintaining that art is wholly subservient to ethics. A well-known spokesman for this view is Leo Tolstoy, who penned his aesthetic treatise *What Is Art?* many years after his conversion to Christianity. His brand of moralism is a specifically Christian one. Tolstoy writes, "The estimation of the value of art . . . depends on men's perception of the meaning of life, depends on what they consider to be the good and the evil of life. And what is good and what is evil is defined by what are termed religious."[21] And, he continues,

> if a religious perception exists among us, then our art should be appraised on the basis of that religious perception; and, as has always and everywhere been the case, art transmitting feelings flowing from the religious perception of our time should be chosen from all the indifferent art, should be acknowledged, highly esteemed, and encouraged, while art running counter to that perception should be condemned and despised, and all the remaining indifferent art should neither be distinguished nor encouraged.[22]

Thus, for Tolstoy, moral-spiritual value is the sole criterion for assessing art. The only relevant judgments of art are ethical in nature. As narrow and counterintuitive as this perspective is, he was prepared to follow it to

---

[18] Oscar Wilde, Preface to *The Picture of Dorian Gray*, in *The Portable Oscar Wilde*, ed. R. Aldington (New York: Viking, 1946), 138.

[19] Benedetto Croce, *Nuovi saggi di estetica*, 3rd ed., 1948.

[20] John Dewey, "Art and Civilization," in *The Philosophy of Art: Readings Ancient and Modern*, ed. A. Neill and A. Ridley (Boston: McGraw Hill, 1995), 525.

[21] Leo Tolstoy, *What Is Art?*, trans. Almyer Maude (Indianapolis: Bobbs-Merrill, 1960), 54.

[22] Ibid., 145.

its absurd conclusions. While affirming many classics for their religious content, including Hugo's *Les Miserables*, Dickens' *A Tale of Two Cities*, Eliot's *Adam Bede* and Dostoyevsky's novels, Tolstoy rejected Dickens' *David Copperfield* and *The Pickwick Papers*, Moliere's comedies, and *Don Quixote*. He also rejected most chamber music and opera of his time, including Beethoven, Schumman, Liszt, and Wagner. Tolstoy's judgment was not that these are immoral works of art but that, because of their failure to endorse society's moral-spiritual values, *they are not truly art.*

The third perspective on the relationship between art and ethics, known as *ethicism*, falls between the aestheticist and moralist extremes. According to this view, moral attributes of an artwork are relevant to, but not wholly determinative of, its aesthetic merit. Negative moral qualities may detract from a work's aesthetic quality, and positive moral qualities may enhance its aesthetic quality. Many advocates of this view, such as Berys Gaut, would put it like this: positive moral qualities are neither necessary nor sufficient conditions for aesthetic excellence. A Monet painting of a hay bail may be aesthetically excellent, though it is morally neutral. And a Cecil B. DeMille film may be aesthetically poor in spite of its morally admirable message. But the positive moral qualities of the latter do add to its aesthetic merit, just as the moral lessons in Shakespeare's *King Lear* or an episode of *The Andy Griffith Show* add to the overall aesthetic quality of these works. Similarly, on the negative side, poor moral qualities are neither necessary nor sufficient conditions for an overall negative aesthetic judgment of an artwork.

Thus, ethicism maintains that moral values are among the many considerations that should be taken into account when doing aesthetic evaluations—along with the usual nonmoral considerations such as expressiveness, unity, originality, elegance, poignancy, and so forth. The reason that artworks may be treated similarly to moral agents in this way is that they have the potential to impact moral agents for good or ill. Anne Eaton suggests, for example, that Titian's painting *Rape of Europa* could have "a morally corrupting effect by encouraging its audience to have erotic feelings toward rape, even inciting some to go so far as to commit acts of non-consensual sexual violence."[23] And Mary Devereaux notes how the Leni Riefenstahl documentary *Triumph of the Will*, a work of Nazi propaganda, is "morally repugnant" just because "it presents as beautiful a vision of Hitler and the New Germany" and thereby inspires sympathy with the anti-Semitism of the Nazis.[24]

---

[23] Anne Eaton, "Painting and Ethics," *Aesthetics: A Reader in Philosophy of the Arts,* 2nd ed., ed. David Goldblatt and Lee B. Brown (Upper Saddle River, NJ: Prentice Hall, 2005), 64.

[24] Mary Devereaux, "Beauty and Evil: The Case of Leni Riefenstahl," *Aesthetics and Ethics: Essays at the Intersection,* ed. Jerrold Levinson (Cambridge: Cambridge University Press, 1998),

Ethicism is a balanced position that recognizes both some autonomy and some interaction and mutual accountability between the moral and aesthetic spheres. Art and aesthetic experience are not morally indifferent, but neither are all judgments about art reducible to moral assessments. Rather, art may be evaluated both morally and aesthetically, and our moral judgments about art objects should inform our overall aesthetic judgments about them. Of course, there are no hard and fast principles for making such assessments; rather, there is a complex interplay of moral and aesthetic qualities in works of art. However, there are some important points to keep in mind when going about the difficult task of making overall assessments, as will be discussed in section 9.3.3 below. But first we must address a critical question raised by our discussion thus far: From a Christian perspective, what value does aesthetic evaluation have by itself?

9.3.2 A Christian View of Aesthetic Value

Thus far, we have taken for granted that aesthetic values are significant in their own right. But apart from moral matters, why should the Christian even be concerned with an artwork's aesthetic merit? The first thing to note in answering this question is divine example. God Himself has demonstrated His own emphatic concern for aesthetics. In the Genesis creation account the writer notes how "God saw all that He had made, and it was very good" (Gen 1:31). Seven such divine expressions of praise appear in this chapter, each using the Hebrew term *tov*, which denotes something pleasant or delightful. Other uses of the term in the Old Testament confirm that in this context it describes that which is *good or excellent of its kind.*

When it comes to evaluative judgments, the basic categories are moral, legal, political, prudential, and aesthetic. That is, when we declare something to be "good," we use the term in one of these senses. So in what sense is *tov* used in Genesis 1? Obviously, it is not used in a moral, legal, or political sense, since the judgment is repeatedly made prior to the creation of human beings (to whom alone among earthly creatures do moral, legal, and political concepts apply). Nor could *tov* be used here in a merely prudential sense, as there is much in creation that has no practical use. This oft-repeated evaluative judgment in Genesis, then, must be aesthetic in nature. When God declares that the various aspects of His creation are "good," He is saying that they are aesthetically excellent or beautiful.

227.

Divine concern for aesthetics is evident elsewhere in Scripture. God specially gifted Bezalel and Oholiab with artistic skill and called them to recruit and train other similarly talented persons to do "artistic crafts" for the tabernacle (see Exod 35:30–35). God also commands the use of a variety of art forms in praising and teaching about Him, including drama (Ezek 4:1–3), dance (Ps 149:2–3), and songs (Pss 33:1; 98:1), which are to be played "skillfully" (Ps 33:3). Also, the form of God's revelation itself speaks to the importance of the arts and aesthetics. The Bible is composed of a wide range of literary forms, including epic narratives, poetry, hymns, and oratory, and it employs a variety of literary conventions, including metaphor, simile, allegory, hyperbole, symbolism, irony, and satire. All of these aspects of Scripture are, of course, not just effective for the communication of God's truth but are also aesthetically excellent in themselves.

That the Creator is aesthetically concerned should motivate us to be so as well. But there is an even more fundamental motive for the Christian to take aesthetics seriously—a fact which, we might say, even motivates the divine aesthetic concern—and that is *God's nature as a beautiful being.* The attribute of divine beauty has been recognized by the greatest of Christian theologians, such as Augustine, who writes,

> I have learnt to love you late, Beauty at once so ancient and so new! I have learnt to love you late! You were within me, and I was in the world outside myself and, disfigured as I was, I fell upon the lovely things of your creation. You were with me, but I was not with you. The beautiful things of this world kept me far from you and yet, if they had not been in you, they would have had no being at all.[25]

Aquinas, too, notes that God is the source of all beauty in the cosmos, as He "gives beauty to all created beings, according to the properties of each."[26] God is the ontological spring of all beauty, says Aquinas, because God is Himself "super-beautiful." And Jonathan Edwards strikes the same theme when he declares God to be "infinitely the most beautiful and excellent: and all beauty to be found throughout the whole creation is but the reflection of the diffused beams of that being, who hath an infinite fullness of brightness and glory."[27] Today Christian theologians

---

[25] Augustine, *Confessions* (New York: Viking Penguin, 1961), 231–32.

[26] Quoted in Michael A. G. Haykin, "Beauty as a Divine Attribute: Sources and Issues," *Churchman* 116 (2002): 131.

[27] Jonathan Edwards, "The Nature of True Virtue," in *The Works of Jonathan Edwards* (Edinburgh: The Banner of Truth Trust, 1974), 1:125.

continue to be interested in the divine attribute of beauty, as recent works in theological aesthetics demonstrate.[28]

So the subject of aesthetics is not properly of tangential or trivial concern for the Christian. On the contrary, we have good biblical and theological reasons to take aesthetic values and judgments very seriously.[29]

9.3.3 Some Helpful Distinctions

Having concluded that aesthetic values are important from a Christian perspective and that ethicism is the proper approach to art and ethics, we have only settled the most general theoretical questions regarding the subject. We must now confront the much thornier matter of working out this perspective in practice—something that writers on this issue typically neglect to do. If ethical considerations properly impact aesthetic assessment of art objects, then what does this look like when it comes to evaluating actual works of art? Are there any conceptual guidelines to assist us in this process, or are we merely left to our naked intuitions? Happily, there *are* some practical guidelines for making such assessments.

1. Depiction of Evil versus Endorsement of Evil

Evil, both in the form of human sin and suffering, is a fundamental aspect of the human condition in this world. And, like the study of history, analysis of most art forms necessarily brings us face to face with the full panorama of evil. And yet some art works are more like history texts in so far as they describe or depict sin and suffering without endorsing or approving of it. Those that endorse evil to this extent rightly deserve our moral condemnation, while those that merely depict evil may or may not be morally justified in doing so. Myriad popular songs, especially in the blues category, refer to sexual promiscuity. Some of these, such as "You Are My Sunshine," simply describe the sin, while others, such as Dion's "Runaround Sue," condemn it. But others actually celebrate promiscuity, such as, ironically, another Dion hit, "The Wanderer" (which, given his previous hit single, also demonstrated an immoral double-standard regarding sexual faithfulness and thus the vice of sexism). Still others actually celebrate rape and other forms of sexual violence, such as Nine Inch Nails' "Closer" and numerous songs in the rap category.

---

[28] See, for example, Edward Farley, *Faith and Beauty: A Theological Aesthetic* (Burlington, VT: Ashgate, 2001); David Bentley Hart, *The Beauty of the Infinite: The Aesthetics of Christian Truth* (Grand Rapids, MI: Eerdmans, 2003); Patrick Sherry, *Spirit and Beauty: An Introduction to Theological Aesthetics* (Oxford: Clarendon, 1992).

[29] For more detailed expositions on these points, see James S. Spiegel, "Aesthetics and Worship," and *idem*, "Towards a New Aesthetic Vision for the Christian Liberal Arts College," *Christian Scholar's Review* 28:3 (Spring 1999): 466–75.

Steven Spielberg's *Saving Private Ryan* and Mel Gibson's *The Passion of the Christ* are films that depict a tremendous amount of evil (overwhelmingly so to some viewers). These directors strove to realistically depict the relentless brutality of war and the suffering of Christ, respectively, but such violence is in no sense endorsed by either film. Similarly, Kubrick's *A Clockwork Orange*, Kaplan's *The Accused*, and Robbins' *Dead Man Walking* each graphically depict sexual violence, but these are anything but endorsements of such acts. On the contrary, these films effectively communicate the cruelty and heinousness of rape and its devastating psychological and legal consequences for the perpetrator. On the other hand, films such as Hallstrom's *Cider House Rules*, Eastwood's *Million Dollar Baby*, and Cameron's *Titanic* are much more conservative in their depiction of evil, but the stories in each case are calculated to condone or endorse immoral acts: abortion, euthanasia, and fornication, respectively. For this reason, these films *as art works* are morally problematic. And, given ethicism, to this extent they are also aesthetically flawed.

2. Necessary Depiction versus Gratuitous Depiction of Evil

Within the category of depiction of evil another important distinction must be made, namely that between those that are necessary and those that are gratuitous. Truman Capote's historical novel *In Cold Blood* and Christopher Marlowe's *Faust* both depict terrible evils—gruesome murders and blasphemies, respectively—but these depictions are necessary given the themes of these works. On the other hand, a book such as Michael Slade's *Ripper*, which concerns a serial murderer, provides far more graphic detail in the murder accounts than is necessary either to sustain the book's predictable plotline or develop its shallow theme.

Films such as Cimino's *The Deerhunter*, Meirelles' *City of God*, and Friedkin's *The Exorcist* feature scenes so disturbing that they are unforgettable for many viewers. It is clear in each instance, however, that even these depictions of horrifying evil are justified because they are both crucial for the plotline and for the development of a significant theme within the film. By contrast, much of the violence in the film *Natural Born Killers* is wanton and likely superfluous to the film's theme (whatever it is). And popular horror films in the seemingly endless *Friday the 13th* and *Nightmare on Elm Street* series feature numerous grisly slayings. Of course, this category of horror itself is essentially premised upon the gratuity of the violence. Just as depictions of sex acts in pornography are by definition gratuitous, so is the violence in teen horror films. In both cases, there are no genuine themes for the scenes to serve, so there can be no sense according to which the depictions of violence or sex can be necessary.

3. Depiction in Service of a Noble Theme versus Depiction in Service of a Trivial Theme

The concept of depicting evil for the sake of a theme must be further analyzed, as the question arises: *which themes are worthy?* Presumably, an artist must have good reasons for depicting immoral actions, reasons that pertain to some significant theme within the work. Accordingly, the depiction of evil within an artwork may serve a theme that is relatively noble or trivial, and this will determine just to what extent this depiction is morally and aesthetically justified.

Many popular songs make reference to immoral actions for comedic effect. Some of these are morally justified because their themes are inherently important. Johnny Cash's "Boy Named Sue" and Billy Kirchen's "Hot Rod Lincoln" fall into this category, as their humor is both clever and serves a deeper theme regarding the father-son relationship. ACDC's "Dirty Deeds Done Dirt Cheap" and the Rolling Stones' "Some Girls" are vulgar (and the latter racist) without being either especially creative or interested in meaningful relational issues. Other songs depict evil in order to call attention to social injustice. Many Bob Dylan songs do this, such as "The Ballad of Hollis Brown" (murder-suicide) and "The Hurricane" (murder and racism).

Two films that depict evil in the interest of a noble theme are Elia Kazan's classic *On the Waterfront* and Zlotoff's *The Spitfire Grill*. The former features several murders by mafia members who are finally opposed by the local parish priest who in turn challenges others to stand up for what's right, regardless of the danger. The priest, it is worth noting, is perhaps the most compelling Christian character in the history of film—an ironic fact, given that the film was directed and produced by Jews (Kazan and Sam Spiegel, respectively). *The Spitfire Grill* features a tragic death that crucially serves a powerful theme of redemption in the film. By contrast, Frank Miller's *Sin City* not only depicts an exorbitant amount of violence and debauchery but it does so in the service of a trivial end, namely to take a comic book story (a simple tale of revenge) and adapt it to the screen in a stylized fashion matching that of the comic genre. (*Requiem for a Dream* is another disturbing example of a film whose depictions of evil are excessive relative to its theme—simply to display the hopeless spiral of drug addiction.)

4. Provision of Insight into Truth vs. Obscuring of Truth

Because knowledge is inherently valuable, this must be recognized in any complete moral analysis of art. Moreover, art objects—especially in literature, theater, and film—often aim to impact the beliefs of the reader or viewer. Such a work may do so in a way that provides genuine insight into the subject depicted, or it may fail to do so and actually obscure the truth or distort one's understanding of the subject.

The Beatles' "With a Little Help from My Friends" and "Hey Jude" provide insights into the importance of friendship during hard times, and their song "Revolution" wisely tempers the fashionable late-sixties anarchists' fervor to see the U.S. government overthrown. Swanbeck's film *The Big Kahuna* portrays a young and idealistic evangelical Christian's interactions with two jaded salesmen. The sometimes coarse language is more than compensated for by the profound insight afforded by the film's plot, specifically regarding the conservative Christian tendency to model evangelism after corporate sales techniques. And *Les Misérables*, in each of its three genres—Hugo's original book, August's film, and the Broadway stage production—uses authentic depictions of evil to powerfully communicate the Christian doctrine of grace.

Artworks that obscure or distort truth are morally suspect and, because of this fact, aesthetically diminished as well. The Beatles' "Within You and Without You," though unique and creative, is vaguely pantheistic and offers a false optimism inspired by the use of hallucinogenic drugs. Led Zepellin's "Stairway to Heaven" diminishes the urgency of moral-spiritual seriousness and presents a similarly pantheistic message, declaring, "all are one and one is all." Whereas these songs distort metaphysical truth, films such as Hallstrom's self-consciously chic *Chocolat* undermines the legitimacy of moral rules and traditional authorities, celebrating and exalting passion instead. And Oliver Stone's *JFK* presents an amalgam of conspiracy theories of the Kennedy assassination as if it were a straightforward historical account. Consequently, viewers are neither historically enlightened nor aesthetically edified.

5. Final Justice and Personal Redemption versus Moral Lawlessness and Personal Hopelessness

The subject of moral truth deserves special consideration when making moral assessments of art. Every artistic narrative has what might be called a "moral trajectory." Some important themes to keep in mind in this connection are final justice, as opposed to moral lawlessness, and personal redemption, as opposed to personal hopelessness. Two books that appear to fail in this category—while succeeding in most others, it should be emphasized—are Sylvia Plath's *The Bell Jar* and Albert Camus'

The Plague. Both of these excruciating novels depict the human condition as ultimately hopeless. The former accurately captures something of the internal phenomenology of manic depression, and the latter authentically renders an atheistic existentialist account of human suffering. But neither work transcends the human squalor it so painfully depicts. Jonathan Demme's film *The Silence of the Lambs* is even more egregious, warping fundamental concepts of morality. Letting alone the fact that this film mainstreamed the erstwhile underground slasher genre, Demme managed to make the sadistic and cannibalistic main character, Hannibal Lecter, genuinely charming and appealing. A sure sign that the moral universe has been inverted is that the audience is perversely satisfied when Lecter cleverly escapes at the end, no doubt to maim, torture, and kill again. Rarely, if ever, has the history of art seen such a fundamental distortion of moral values so widely embraced by popular audiences.

At the other end of the moral spectrum are T. S. Eliot's play *Murder in the Cathedral* and Dostoyevsky's novel *Crime and Punishment.* Both works feature murders, but these are only the occasions for agonizing soul-searching on the part of the main characters, Thomas Beckett and Raskolnikov. In the Eliot play, it is the murder victim whose inner life we are privy to and which reveals to us the many layers of pride and selfishness that must be peeled back in order to achieve true righteousness. In Dostoyevsky's novel we enter the mind of the murderer and study the shame and paranoia that follow upon his ghastly deed. Not only are both works valuable for their insightful (Christian) moral psychology, they culminate hopefully, as both main characters find redemption—Becket in dying well and Raskolnikov in personal repentance *and* imprisonment in Siberia. Both works illustrate the redemptive power of suffering, a deeply Christian theme.

6. Objective Content of the Artwork versus Subjective Response of the Audience

Even taking all of the above considerations into account, it is still to be expected that well-meaning Christians will disagree in their assessments of artworks on the basis of the depiction of immoral actions. This is because there will always remain an irreducibly subjective component to the experience of art. This does not mean that aesthetics is entirely subjective. On the contrary, there is objective truth in aesthetics just as there is in any domain of inquiry. However, a degree of subjectivity in aesthetics cannot be denied. Accordingly, a final distinction should be made between an artwork's objective content and an audience's subjective response to that work. Because we are all wired differently, each person has a different level of tolerance for such things as violence, profanity, and sexual content in a book, song, or film. One person may be appalled by the amount of profanity in *Catcher in the Rye* or *Good Will Hunting* while another person is unfazed, despite their shared conviction that the language is morally inappropriate. Similarly, we know some Christians who were so disturbed by the sexual content and violence of *American Beauty* and *Pulp Fiction*, respectively, that they walked out on these films. Other Christians regard these same films as not only worth viewing in their entirety but as aesthetically excellent works overall and even as illustrating profound theological doctrines (divine providence in *American Beauty* and divine grace in *Pulp Fiction*). In such cases not all divergences of opinion can be explained in objective terms, appealing to poor moral or aesthetic judgment on one side or the other. Surely we must allow for subjective responses in some cases like these, realizing that some people are simply more sensitive than others to certain kinds of immoral content. In these cases, the wise approach seems to be simply to allow for our personal differences. Just as we sometimes agree to disagree, so may we also agree to respond differently to an artwork.

Again, this is not to advocate a wholesale moral or aesthetic subjectivism. There is a reason that we saved this distinction until the end, namely to indicate that it is a final conceptual court of appeal when it comes to the moral analysis of art. Also, there are commonly instances in which our subjective responses can be *corrected* by due attention to objective facts. Consider the songs "From a Distance" by Bette Midler and "You Light up My Life" by Debbie Boone. Some well-intended Christians might very well appreciate these songs and readily regard them as aesthetically good or at least as morally unproblematic. It often comes as a surprise to people when they are told that both of these songs are morally problematic (and therefore aesthetically flawed) because they advocate some significant theological and moral lies. Midler's song advocates a version of deism when she says "God is watching us from a distance," and the Boone song affirms moral subjectivism when she sings, "it can't be wrong when it feels so right." A Christian may be neither aware of nor bothered by these falsehoods. Nonetheless, one *ought* to be both aware of and bothered by them.

Another example pertains to scenes from two films: Spielberg's *Raiders of the Lost Ark* and Tarantino's *Pulp Fiction*. In the former there is a scene in which Indiana Jones encounters an Arab wielding a long sword. The crowd parts in expectation of their battle. Exasperated, Jones pulls out a pistol and casually shoots the Arab dead. At this point, the audience viewing the film typically erupts in laughter. Consider now a scene in *Pulp Fiction* featuring John Travolta, who of course is every bit as charming as Harrison Ford. Travolta's character, Vincent Vega, is conversing with a fellow hit man and their young hostage, carelessly wagging his gun in the young man's face. Suddenly the gun goes off in the man's face and he is killed. Vega's response and the ensuing situation are somewhat comical and at this point the film audience again erupts in laughter. But here is where the Christian catches himself and thinks, "I shouldn't be laughing at this." It is also here that we have known some Christians to walk out on the film. But what usually goes unnoticed is that this scene is actually more redemptive than the scene from *Raiders* precisely because the former elicits a self-rebuke for laughing at the death of a human being. So here we have a case in which the response of many (most?) Christians is superficial and overly subjective and fails to take adequate account of the objective features of an art work.

These cases are intended to illustrate that there is some degree of normativity even when it comes to our subjective feelings regarding art (or anything else, for that matter) and this should be borne in mind when working through our conflicting responses to particular works. Just to what degree certain feelings are normative in a particular case is a difficult matter to assess, and there are not hard and fast criteria for making this evaluation. The best we can do is to apply the distinctions above to concrete cases and adjust our intuitions accordingly.

Conclusion

In this chapter we have explored some fundamental issues in aesthetics, specifically concerning the definition of art, the purpose of art, the objectivity of aesthetic values, and the relationship between art and ethics. We have discussed the latter issue at some length both to illustrate the difficulty of dealing with the interplay of art and ethics and to offer some conceptual guidelines for discernment in this area. Curiously, while many people wrestle with moral issues pertaining to art, little of substance has been offered in the way of practical counsel for working through them. This is likely due to the fact that providing such counsel requires integrative philosophy—careful thinking regarding both ethics and aesthetics. As we have seen, treating ethical or aesthetic issues alone is difficult enough. To do both simultaneously might be one of the biggest challenges in philosophy.

Questions for Reflection

1. The authors discuss six distinctions in order to provide guidance when dealing with issues regarding art and ethics. Which of these distinctions are most helpful and which are least helpful? What other considerations, not discussed by the authors, might be helpful when approaching moral issues related to art?

2. When you hear the phrase "Christian values," the first thing that comes to mind is probably not aesthetic values. Why is this so? From a biblical standpoint, how important are aesthetic values? And which deserves greater weight, moral or aesthetic values? Why?

3. Do you agree with the moral and aesthetic assessments of the artworks discussed in this section? Why or why not?

4. Consider again the art works that you evaluated in the last two sections and apply to them the distinctions discussed in this section. What is your moral evaluation of these artworks and how does that evaluation affect their aesthetic value? Why do you think so?

For Further Reading

On Aesthetics Generally

Collingwood, Robin G. *The Principles of Art.* Oxford: Clarendon, 1958.

Dickie, George. *Art and the Aesthetic.* Ithaca: Cornell University Press, 1974.

Eaton, Marcia Muelder. *Basic Issues in Aesthetics.* Belmont, CA: Wadsworth, 1988.

Goodman, Nelson. *Languages of Art.* Indianapolis: Hackett, 1976.

Neill, Alex, and Aaron Ridley. *Arguing about Art: Contemporary Philosophical Debates.* New York: McGraw Hill, 1995.

Zemach, Eddy M. *Real Beauty.* University Park, PA: Pennsylvania State University Press, 1997.

On Christian Aesthetics

Brown, Frank Burch. *Good Taste, Bad Taste, and Christian Taste: Aesthetics in Religious Life.* Oxford: Oxford University Press, 2000.

L'Engle, Madeleine. *Walking on Water: Reflections on Faith and Art.* Wheaton, IL: Harold Shaw, 1980.

Rookmaaker, Hans. *Modern Art and the Death of a Culture.* Downers Grove, IL: InterVarsity Press, 1970.

Ryken, Leland. *The Liberated Imagination.* Wheaton, IL: Harold Shaw, 1989.

Sayers, Dorothy. "Toward a Christian Aesthetic." In *The Whimsical Christian.* New York: MacMillan, 1969.

Schaeffer, Francis. *Art and the Bible.* Downers Grove, IL: InterVarsity, 1973.

Seerveld, Calvin. *Rainbows for a Fallen World.* Toronto: Toronto Tuppence, 1980.

Tolstoy, Leo. *What Is Art?* Indianapolis: Bobbs-Merrill, 1960.

Wolterstorff, Nicholas. *Art in Action: Toward a Christian Aesthetic.* Grand Rapids: Eerdmans, 1980.

GLOSSARY

a posteriori **knowledge.** Knowledge that is acquired on the basis of sense experience.

a priori **knowledge.** Knowledge that is acquired immediately or intuitively independent of sense of experience.

act utilitarianism. A version of consequentialism that requires that one apply the *principle of utility* to individual acts to determine their rightness or wrongness. According to act utilitarianism, an action is right if and only if it brings about the greatest pleasure for the greatest number of people.

actual infinite. In set theory, a set that contains an infinite number of members.

aesthetic objectivism. The view that there are aesthetic values that are independent of an observer's preferences and that aesthetic judgments make claims about the world.

aesthetic subjectivism. The view that aesthetic judgments do not make claims about the world, but merely reflect an observer's aesthetic preferences.

aesthetic virtues. Standards for good artistry that apply to the artists themselves. They are marks of excellence that enable the artist to fulfill his or her creative function in a particular domain. Examples include diligence, veracity, and boldness.

aestheticism. A perspective on the relationship between art and ethics which holds that art is immune to moral evaluation because the creative artist is above morality.

agent causation. A theory held by many libertarians which holds that personal agents are the direct, uncaused causes of their actions.

anarchy. The view that human beings should not be governed by any civil authority.

argument. A set of propositions or statements that purports to prove something. An argument has two parts: premises and a conclusion. The conclusion of the argument is that proposition which one is trying to prove, and the premises of the argument are those propositions which provide reasons for accepting the conclusion.

atemporalism. The view that God transcends time and is not bound or limited by it; time is not co-eternal with God but is created.

basic belief. A belief that is not based on or justified by another belief but is held independently of other beliefs. If a basic belief is warranted, it is called a *properly* basic belief.

behaviorism (philosophical). A physicalist theory of mind that analyzes mental phenomena entirely in terms of behavior and dispositions to behave. For example, a desire to eat is simply the activity of going to the kitchen to get food; a belief that God exists is the tendency to pray or attend church.

belief. A mental state consisting in affirming, or being disposed to affirm, a proposition.

bundle theory. The view that particulars are collections of properties and that there is nothing more to a particular than the sum of the properties it exemplifies.

categorical imperative. Proposed by Immanuel Kant, the categorical imperative is the supreme, universal moral principle from which all ethical duties may be deduced. In its most familiar formulation, it stipulates that one must be able to universalize one's rule of action for it to be considered moral.

coherence theory of truth. A view of the nature of truth that holds that a proposition is true if and only if it coheres with the set of beliefs that a person holds.

coherentism. A theory of epistemic justification that holds that beliefs are justified by their coherence with a person's whole system of beliefs. This view rejects the idea of basic beliefs, holding that all beliefs are nonbasic.

commercial justice. An aspect of justice involving fairness in the exchange of goods and services.

communitarianism. The view that economic equality is a desired goal of society, but that the achievement of this goal is not the responsibility of government but should be accomplished within local communities with citizens acting voluntarily to redistribute their wealth.

compatibilism. The view that freedom and determinism are logically compatible.

conceptualism. A view that attempts to steer a middle course between Platonism and nominalism by claiming that properties and other universals are mental concepts that we use to think about things.

consequentialism. Along with deontology and virtue theory, one of the three types of normative ethical theory. Consequentialism takes the most basic moral duty to be the achievement of some specified end (e.g., happiness), and an action is considered right if and only if it contributes to bringing about that end.

contextualism. A theory of epistemic justification which holds that beliefs are justified relative to a specific context. A prominent version of contextualism is the *relevant alternatives view* according to which a person is justified in believing a particular proposition just in case she can rule out all relevant alternatives to the belief.

correspondence theory of truth. A view of the nature of truth which holds that a proposition is true if and only if it corresponds to the way things actually are.

cosmological argument. A theistic argument that attempts to prove the existence of God from the existence of some dependent, finite being(s) in the world.

cultural relativism. The view that all moral values are merely the products of the customs, tastes, and standards of a culture and therefore are neither objectively true nor universally binding.

deduction. A type of reasoning by which one aims to draw conclusions that are guaranteed by a set of premises. Thus, the conclusion of a *valid* deductive argument follows from the premises with absolute certainty.

deontology. Along with consequentialism and virtue theory, one of the three types of normative ethical theory. In deontology, an action is right if and only if it accords with the relevant moral rules, regardless of its consequences.

difference principle. A principle in Rawls's theory of distributive justice which states that the only economic inequalities that are permissible are those that (1) are reasonably expected to be to the advantage of all and (2) are attached to positions and offices open to all.

distributive justice. An aspect of justice involving fairness in the distribution of wealth in society.

divine command theory. A deontological moral theory which maintains that all moral standards are derived from God's commands. On the divine command theory, what makes an action right or wrong depends upon whether or not it is consistent with God's commands.

divine law. An aspect of Thomas Aquinas's natural law theory. Divine law refers to the special ordinances laid down by God in Scripture.

doxastic voluntarism. The view that the acquisition of beliefs is under a person's voluntary control.

dualism. One of the three broad approaches to the nature of the world, dualism is the view that there are two fundamental types of things, the physical or material and the immaterial or spiritual.

eliminative materialism (eliminativism). A physicalist theory of mind that seeks to eliminate the concepts of traditional folk psychology (which refers to mental entities such as beliefs and desires) and replace them with references to behavior or some other physical facts.

emotivism. The view that moral judgments have no truth value but are merely expressions of emotion. On the emotivist view, the moral judgment "Torturing animals is evil" means something like "Torturing animals—yecch!"

empiricism. In epistemology, the view that all knowledge arises from sense experience.

epistemology. The branch of philosophy that is concerned with the nature and scope of knowledge and the justification of belief.

eternal law. An aspect of Thomas Aquinas's natural law theory. Eternal law is the sum of God's decrees that govern the universe.

ethical egoism. A version of consequentialism which holds that one's most basic moral duty is to do what is in one's own best interest.

ethical hedonism. The ethical theory that one's most basic moral duty is to do that which results in the most pleasure.

ethical naturalism. The view that moral standards are grounded in, or reducible to, facts about the natural world.

ethical nonnaturalism. The view that moral standards are not grounded in or reducible to natural facts but rather transcend the natural world.

ethical relativism. The view that there are no objective, universally true moral values; all moral standards are a matter of cultural or personal preference.

ethicism. A perspective on the relationship between art and ethics that falls between the aestheticist and moralist extremes. According to ethicism, the moral qualities of an artwork are relevant to, but do not entirely determine, its aesthetic merit.

evidentialism. The view that it is wrong or irrational to hold a belief without sufficient evidence to do so.

existentialism. A school of philosophy that rose to prominence in the mid-twentieth century, which denies that there is a fixed human nature. This implies that humans are radically free and must define life's meaning in light of their own goals and desires.

expressionism. An aesthetic theory which claims that the function of art is to express emotion.

externalism. The view that the justifying grounds of belief are external to the mind. Thus, a person does not have to have cognitive access to the grounds of his belief. Rather, what matters for knowledge is that the belief be formed in an appropriate way, regardless of whether the person is aware of this.

fallacy. A mistake in reasoning that involves drawing a conclusion without adequate reasons to support the conclusion. There are *formal* fallacies that relate to the form or structure of an argument and *informal* fallacies that relate to the argument's content.

falsificationism. In the philosophy of science, the view that in order for any theory to be legitimately scientific it must be capable of being disproved by empirical observations.

formalism. An aesthetic theory which holds that the defining characteristics of artworks are objective, formal qualities (e.g., shapes, colors, rhythms, tones, etc.).

foundationalism. A theory of epistemic justification which holds that beliefs are justified only if they are properly basic or are inferred from properly basic beliefs. Different versions of foundationalism are distinguished by how they define a properly basic belief.

functional integrity. A concept cited by some theists in support of methodological naturalism. It is the idea that the physical world was initially equipped by its Creator with the capacities necessary to develop on its own, without need for supernatural intervention.

functionalism. A physicalist theory of mind which claims that mental states are reducible to the functional operations of the brain and the causal roles these play in the larger human system, such as their relations to the body's behavior and environment.

hard determinism. A version of incompatibilism that affirms determinism and denies that humans are free or morally responsible.

human law. An aspect of Thomas Aquinas's natural law theory. Human law is the set of laws promulgated by human authorities as they apply natural law.

hypothetical imperative. Contrasted with the categorical imperative, a hypothetical imperative is a command that is binding on a person only if she meets a specified condition. For example, "If you desire *x*, then do *y*."

idealism. One of the three broad approaches to the nature of the world, idealism is the view that reality is mental or ideal. The idealist denies the existence of mind-independent matter.

incompatibilism. The view that human freedom and moral responsibility are incompatible with determinism.

induction. A type of reasoning in which one draws a conclusion that is likely, but not guaranteed, given the premises. The premises imply that the conclusion is probable, though not certain.

inductivism. A view that characterizes science as the objective formation and confirmation of scientific theories through the process of (1) making theory-neutral observations that lead to inductive generalizations, (2) forming hypotheses to explain the observations, and (3) testing the hypotheses by experimentation until they are falsified or satisfactorily confirmed.

institutional theory of art. An aesthetic theory that defines art as any object presented or displayed for aesthetic appreciation, especially within a recognized art institution (e.g., a museum or theater).

instrumentalism. A nonrealist view of science that sees scientific theories as tools for predicting and explaining observable phenomena, rather than producing accurate descriptions of the world.

intelligent design theory. The theory that some physical systems (e.g., biological or astrophysical) exhibit features regarding which scientists may reasonably conclude that they were the product of design by an intelligent being.

interactionism. A version of mind-body dualism which claims that mind and body are causally interactive, mental operations being caused by the body (brain) and bodily movements being caused by mental operations.

internalism. The view that the grounds or basis for a person's justification for a belief must be internal to his mind. Thus, internalism requires that a person have cognitive access to the justifying grounds for his belief.

justice. A condition in which a person gets what he or she is due. Depending on the context, justice may refer to such things as a fair exchange of goods, the fair distribution of wealth, or the fair meting out of reward or punishment.

justification. In epistemology, the reasons or grounds that a person has to hold a certain belief.

knowledge. In epistemology the concern is primarily with "propositional knowledge" that has to do with a person's knowledge that particular propositions are true. Traditionally, propositional knowledge is defined as justified true belief.

law of excluded middle. One of the three laws of thought, this states that every proposition must be either true or false, thus excluding a third alternative.

law of identity. One of the three laws of thought, this states that every proposition is identical to itself. If a proposition is true, then it is true.

law of noncontradiction. One of the three laws of thought, this states that no proposition can be both true and false at the same time and in the same sense.

legal positivism. In political theory, the view that legal standards are merely social conventions and do not reflect a universal moral law.

libertarianism. (1) In metaphysics, a version of incompatibilism that rejects determinism, holding that (at least sometimes) humans have the power of contrary choice and that having this power is necessary for freedom and morally responsibility. (2) In political theory, the view that government should be small and that its primary responsibility is the protection of individual liberties. Libertarians strongly oppose the redistribution of wealth by government.

logic. The science of reasoning, which sets forth the basic principles for correct thinking.

logical positivism. An early twentieth-century philosophical movement that sought to elevate science as a privileged way of knowing and to eradicate speculative metaphysics. To accomplish this goal the Positivists developed the *verification principle* of meaning.

materialism. One of the three broad approaches to the nature of the world, materialism is the view that all that exists is matter and the physical laws that govern its behavior. In this view, no immaterial substances (e.g., God, angels, souls) exist.

memory view of personal identity. The view that a person is the numerically same person from one moment to the next as long as he or she maintains a continuity of memory.

mereological essentialism. The idea that every attribute or part of a particular is essential to it.

metaethics. A branch of ethics that seeks to ascertain the meaning of ethical concepts such as "good," "bad," "right," "wrong," etc. and to discover whether these concepts refer to objective truths or mere conventions.

metaphysical naturalism. See *naturalism.*

metaphysics. The branch of philosophy concerned with the nature of reality. It seeks to answer the question: What is real? Metaphysics may be divided into *ontology*, which investigates the most fundamental features of reality, and *special metaphysics,* which addresses specific topics like the existence of God, free will, the nature of the mind, time, and causality.

methodological naturalism. A view of the scientific method which insists that science must explain natural phenomena in terms of other natural phenomena, thus ruling out as unscientific any supernatural explanations.

middle knowledge. God's knowledge of the truth-values of counterfactuals of freedom (conditional propositions concerning what someone with libertarian freedom would do in a hypothetical situation).

mimesis. A view of the function of art that artworks properly imitate something in nature or human experience.

mind-body dualism (substance dualism). The view that mind and body are two distinct entities or substances.

miracle. An event occurring in the context of legitimate religious expectation that is so contrary to the ordinary course of nature that the causal activity of God is the best explanation for its occurrence.

molinism. First formulated by the 16th-century philosopher Luis de Molina, this is a libertarian solution to the puzzle concerning divine foreknowledge and human freedom based on God's alleged *middle knowledge.* With middle knowledge God's knowledge of the future is not direct, but indirect in that God knows all of the courses of action that agents would freely take in any given circumstance. And God chose to create the world in which human choices would bring about the best possible outcomes.

monarchy. A form of government in which the state is led by a single ruler.

moral objectivism. The view that there are universally binding moral standards which are independent of cultural norms and individual preferences.

moral subjectivism. The view that moral values are relative to each person's subjective preferences.

moralism. A perspective on the relationship between art and ethics which states that art is wholly subservient to ethics. The only relevant judgments of art are moral in nature.

natural law theory. (1) In ethics, a normative ethical theory which holds that objective moral standards may be derived from reason and the observation of human nature. The Christian version of natural law ethics holds that God created human beings for a specific purpose and that basic ethical principles may be discerned by critical reflection on that purpose. Such natural laws reflect God's eternal law and form the proper basis for human law. (2) In political theory, the view that legal standards can and should be based on objective moral principles. Usually such moral principles are derived in accordance with natural law ethics.

natural theology. A discipline that seeks to discover what can be known about God through human experience and reason without the aid of special revelation. Natural theology often involves the construction of theistic arguments (i.e., arguments for God's existence).

naturalism. The worldview which holds that all that exists is the physical world.

near-death experience. An experience had by a person who meets the criteria for clinical death in which he experiences phenomena that seem to be, or are taken to be, of a disembodied existence and/or other aspects of an afterlife.

necessitarian theory of natural laws. The view that the laws of nature are necessary features of the universe, thus implying that the natural processes we observe could not be otherwise.

negative right. A right that one has to freedom from interference by others in regard to some pursuit or activity.

nihilism. The view that life has no objective meaning.

nominalism. The view that there are no universals (e.g., properties, propositions, and relations). The nominalist only admits the existence of particulars and claims that universal terms are simply names that we adopt by convention for things that appear similar to us. *Extreme nominalism* denies the existence of universals altogether. Moderate nominalism or *trope theory* admits the existence of properties but claims that they are abstract particulars.

nonbasic belief. A belief that is based on and justified by other beliefs.

normative ethics. The branch of ethics that seeks to ascertain how we should live by evaluating our actions, motives, and characters in light of metaethical commitments.

noumena. In Kantian epistemology, those entities beyond our experience and knowledge that supposedly provide the data for our experience.

objectivism (about truth). The view that there are absolute truths. Truth is independent of any person's or group's beliefs and preferences.

occasionalism. A version of mind-body dualism which claims that the mind and body are causally independent, mental operations being the activity of soul alone, though they are (typically) associated with brain and other bodily activity.

Ockhamism. First formulated by the medieval philosopher William of Ockham, this position is a libertarian solution to the puzzle concerning divine foreknowledge and human freedom which holds that God's beliefs about the future are caused by the events of the future and not vice versa, thus leaving the future actions of human beings unconstrained. God foresees what happens in the future, including the free actions of human beings, and thus acquires true beliefs about those actions and events.

omnipotence. An attribute of God by which He is able to do anything that is logically possible and consistent with His nature.

omniscience. An attribute of God by which He knows all truths.

omnitemporalism. The view, proposed by William L. Craig, that God is atemporal without creation but temporal with creation.

ontological argument. A theistic argument first developed by Anselm of Canterbury which argues that the very idea of God implies His actual existence.

ontology. A subdivision of metaphysics that studies the most fundamental features of reality. It may be characterized as the study of "being as being," asking the basic question "What is there?"

open theism. Also referred to as free will theism, open theism is (among other things) the view that God does not have foreknowledge of all future human actions. As such, open theism offers a libertarian solution to the puzzle concerning divine foreknowledge and human freedom by denying a crucial aspect of the divine-foreknowledge half of the problem.

pantheism. The worldview which holds that all of reality is divine.

paradigm. In philosophy of science, the set of assumptions, concepts, and theories that form a large-scale framework within which science is conducted by a particular community at a particular time, and which largely determines what questions are deemed scientifically significant and how they are to be answered. Examples of scientific paradigms would include geocentrism, Newtonian physics, and Big Bang cosmology.

passibilism (and impassibilism). *Passibilism* is the view that God experiences feelings and emotions. *Impassibilism* is the view that God does not experience feelings and emotions.

personal identity. The features or characteristics which a person has that, despite qualitative changes, make him or her numerically the same person across time.

phenomena. In Kantian epistemology, those entities that are the objects of our experience; the things experienced through the senses.

physical view of personal identity. The view that what makes a person numerically the same person from one moment to the next is that she maintains certain relevant physical characteristics.

physicalism. The view that everything, including human beings, is fully explainable in terms of natural processes.

Platonism. The view that universals exist independently of particulars.

positive right. A right to have others provide some good or service.

potential infinite. In set theory, a series that can potentially increase without end, but that at any given point is actually finite.

pragmatic theory of truth. A view of truth which holds that a proposition is true if and only if it is useful for achieving desirable results.

principle of sufficient reason. The principle which states that there is an explanation for every contingent fact.

principle of utility. The utilitarian ethical standard that judges every action as good or bad according to its tendency to promote or diminish happiness (usually defined in terms of pleasure).

problem of evil. The problem of the apparent incompatibility between the existence of God and the existence of evil. The *logical problem of evil* argues that the existence of any evil is inconsistent with the existence of God, while the *evidential problem of evil* argues that God's existence is inconsistent with pointless or gratuitous evil.

problem of induction. The problem of justifying inferences from observed phenomena to unobserved phenomena, especially those inferences involving future events. The problem is that attempts to justify such inferences will have to assume the uniformity of nature, arguing that natural processes will continue as they have in the past. But this line of reasoning appears circular since it presupposes the very uniformity of natural processes that it seeks to prove.

properties. A type of universal, specifically a characteristic or quality of a thing such as *being brown*, *being a dog*, or *being a philosopher*.

property dualism. The physicalist theory of mind which claims that mental states are aspects of bodily (brain) states.

propositions. A type of universal, specifically the content or meaning of a statement. Propositions are those abstract entities that can be true or false such as *Rover saved my life, George Washington was the first U. S. president, New York is east of California*, etc.

psychological egoism. The view that people always naturally strive to do what is in their own best interest. This view is distinct from ethical egoism which is a normative view about how people *ought* to behave. In contrast, psychological egoism is a descriptive view about how people actually *do* behave.

psychological hedonism. The view that the ultimate motivation behind every person's actions is the desire for pleasure and that every action is aimed at achieving this end.

qualitative hedonism. A version of utilitarianism that takes into account the quality of pleasures.

quantitative hedonism. A version of utilitarianism that focuses entirely on the amount of pleasure produced by acts, irrespective of the quality of pleasure involved.

rationalism. In epistemology, the view that all knowledge comes through human reason. Rationalists typically distrust the senses and believe that gaining knowledge is a matter of logically deducing true propositions from absolutely certain starting axioms.

regularity theory of natural laws. The view that the laws of nature are simply descriptions of how the natural world has behaved in the past and, presumably, will continue to behave in the future.

reincarnation. The view that when a person dies his soul or karmic energy transmigrates to another newborn human being. Reincarnationists generally believe that human persons have experienced hundreds, perhaps thousands, of such incarnations.

relations. A type of universal that links multiple particulars together in various ways. Relations mark how one thing stands in relation to others such as *taller than, older than, to the left of,* etc.

relativism (about truth). The view that there is no absolute truth. What counts as true is simply a matter of personal or cultural preference. The view that truth is a matter of personal preferences is called *subjectivism*; the view that it is a matter of cultural preference is called *conventionalism*.

reliabilism. The view that in order for a person to know p, his true belief p must be produced by a reliable belief-forming process. By a "reliable process" the reliabilist usually means a process that generally (or mostly) produces true beliefs.

religious exclusivism. The view that only one religion can be true and adequate to lead its followers to salvation.

religious pluralism. The view that many different religions are true and adequate to lead their followers to salvation.

remedial justice. An aspect of justice involving fairness in the rectifying of harms done by one person to another.

right. A justified claim or demand of one person upon another.

rule utilitarianism. A version of utilitarianism that, in contrast to act utilitarianism, focuses on the utility of following rules rather than particular acts in producing happiness. The rule utilitarian claims that a rule should be followed only if following it generally brings about the most happiness for the most people.

scientific nonrealism. The view that scientific theories do not aim to provide a true description of the physical world but rather aim to provide interpretive schemes that allow the scientist to organize data, make predictions, control phenomena, etc.

scientific realism. The view that scientific theories properly aim to provide a true description of the physical world.

scientism. The view that only what can be scientifically verified can be known.

sempiternalism. The view that God is inherently temporal; He exists in time, which is co-eternal with Him.

skepticism. The view that we have no knowledge or that our knowledge is extremely limited.

social contract. In political theory, the actual or implied agreement between members of a society to the establishment of a government.

socialism. The view that distributive justice requires the prohibition of private property and that all resources should be held in common by members of society.

solipsism. The view that only I and my thoughts exist.

soul view of personal identity. The view that what makes a person numerically the same person from one moment to the next is that she has the same immaterial soul throughout any physical changes.

soundness. The property of a deductive argument that is both valid and has true premises.

strict-identity theory (reductive materialism). A version of physicalism that identifies mental states with brain states. Sensations, beliefs, and general awareness are nothing more than processes in the brain so that to say "I have a pain in my elbow" is just another way of saying something like "Nerve bundle CL-468 is firing."

substance view. The view that particulars themselves should be taken as the most fundamental entities and that they cannot be reduced to more basic entities. Particulars so understood are called "substances."

substratum view. The view that, in addition to its properties, a particular has a distinct component called the "substratum" that underlies and is the bearer of the particular's properties but considered in itself is "bare" or propertyless.

syllogism. An argument form that contains exactly three propositions (two premises and a conclusion). There are three main types of syllogisms: categorical, hypothetical, and disjunctive.

teleological argument ("design argument"). A theistic argument that attempts to prove God's existence from the evidence of design in the world.

theism. The worldview that affirms the existence of a personal God who is the transcendent Creator of everything distinct from Himself.

theistic science. The view that theists who are scientists should take all of their knowledge into account when developing explanatory hypotheses, including their theological knowledge. Theistic science, then, allows for supernatural explanations in science, in contrast to methodological naturalism, which only allows one to appeal to natural explanations.

truth. A property of propositions or statements that is an essential component of knowledge. Major theories of truth include the correspondence theory, the coherence theory, and the pragmatic theory.

uniformity of nature. The idea that the laws of nature will remain constant, thereby assuring that natural processes in the future will resemble those of the past.

universals. Abstract entities (i.e., not existing in space and time) that can be exemplified by more than one particular thing at the same time (e.g., *being brown* is had by the dog Fido and the Cleveland Browns' jerseys). They include properties, propositions, and relations. Universals purport to explain the resemblances between things and how we are able to predicate.

validity. The property of a deductive argument that has a structure such that true premises would guarantee the truth of the conclusion.

verification principle. The principle employed by logical positivists which stipulates that a proposition is meaningful if and only if it is either true by definition or empirically verifiable in principle.

virtue. A stable character trait or habit that provides a person with a disposition to act in certain excellent ways. Virtues can be *moral* or *intellectual*. A moral virtue disposes a person to act morally, while an intellectual virtue disposes a person to acquire true beliefs and avoid acquiring false beliefs.

virtue epistemology. A view of either epistemic justification or knowledge which holds that knowledge or the justification of beliefs arises from intellectual virtue.

welfare liberalism. A view of distributive justice that attempts a middle course between libertarianism and socialism, seeking to uphold personal liberties while limiting socio-economic inequalities.

Name Index

Subject Index

Scripture Index